The Psychology of Happiness in the Modern World

James B. Allen, PhD, is associate professor in the Department of Psychology at SUNY Geneseo, where he has taught for the past 23 years. He regularly teaches courses on the psychology of happiness, social psychology, environmental psychology, and advanced research in psychology. Dr. Allen regularly attends and presents at the annual conventions of the Association for Psychological Science and the Eastern Psychological Association. He has published articles in the *Journal of Personality and Social Psychology, Basic and Applied Social Psychology, Sex Roles*, and *Environment and Behavior.* He earned his PhD and master's degrees in social psychology from Arizona State University and a bachelor's degree in psychology from Auburn University.

The Psychology of Happiness in the Modern World

A Social Psychological Approach

James B. Allen, PhD

SPRINGER PUBLISHING COMPANY
NEW YORK

Springer Publishing Company, LLC
11 West 42nd Street
New York, NY 10036
www.springerpub.com

Acquisitions Editor: Debra Riegert
Compositor: Westchester Publishing Services

ISBN: 9780826132826
Ebook ISBN: 9780826132833

Instructor's Materials: Qualified instructors may request supplements by emailing textbook@springerpub.com
Instructor's Manual ISBN: 9780826133281
Instructor's PowerPoints ISBN: 9780826133298

17 18 19 20 21 / 5 4 3 2 1

The author and the publisher of this Work have made every effort to use sources believed to be reliable to provide information that is accurate and compatible with the standards generally accepted at the time of publication. The author and publisher shall not be liable for any special, consequential, or exemplary damages resulting, in whole or in part, from the readers' use of, or reliance on, the information contained in this book. The publisher has no responsibility for the persistence or accuracy of URLs for external or third-party Internet websites referred to in this publication and does not guarantee that any content on such websites is, or will remain, accurate or appropriate.

Library of Congress Cataloging-in-Publication Data

Names: Allen, James B. (Psychologist), author.
Title: The psychology of happiness in the modern world : a social psychological approach / James B. Allen, PhD.
Description: 1 Edition. | New York : Springer Publishing Company, LLC, [2017] | Includes index.
Identifiers: LCCN 2017006316 | ISBN 9780826132826 (hardcopy : alk. paper) | ISBN 9780826132833 (ebook)
Subjects: LCSH: Happiness. | Social psychology.
Classification: LCC BF575.H27 A444 2017 | DDC 152.4/2—dc23
LC record available at https://lccn.loc.gov/2017006316

Contact us to receive discount rates on bulk purchases.
We can also customize our books to meet your needs.
For more information please contact: sales@springerpub.com

Printed in the United States of America by McNaughton & Gunn.

This book is dedicated to my wife, Deb Howe-Allen, and to the memory of my mother, Cynthia Barden Allen.

CONTENTS

PREFACE

This book tells the story of the scientific study of what makes us feel happy, content, joyous, and satisfied with our lives. It is an inherently engaging and captivating story of how the social environment, our personal choices, and our shared human evolutionary heritage shape our happiness. By social environment I mean not only the friends, family, acquaintances, and coworkers who surround us, but also the cultural and economic forces that help shape our lives. These forces are a major focus of the book. By personal choices I mean positive psychology's important focus on "character strengths" and the ways in which we interpret the events around us.

The book considers how economic factors such as unemployment, income inequality, economic growth, and social welfare policies impact happiness. Relatedly, it explores how economic systems are associated with distinct cultural values that importantly affect happiness. Taking a close look at the capitalistic economic system and its accompanying values of individualism, competition, and material wealth, we discover that these values, coupled with widespread advertising of consumer products, have important implications for happiness.

Social and cultural environments are related to happiness in other ways as well. For instance, culture affects how happiness and physical health are related. Furthermore, the relationship between religious faith and happiness is strongly influenced by cultural attitudes toward religion, as well as by societal levels of material wealth. Our work environment also affects our happiness; hence, cultural values regarding the importance of work matter. In addition, work stress can interfere with family life, and this has important implications for happiness. Thus, the book examines how workplace and governmental policies interact with work-to-family interference to raise or lower happiness. We discover the importance of more immediate social environments by examining marriage, parenthood, and friendships.

Along the way we grapple with important questions. Some of these connect directly with economics. Will I be happier if I make more money? How does advertising affect children's well-being? Does the presence of a social safety net such as unemployment insurance affect the happiness of everyone, including those with jobs? Others concern our personal social relationships. Will I be happier if I get married? How will parenthood affect my happiness? How important is it to have friends at work?

It is fascinating to learn that a large part of our happiness is within our own control. Sure, our inborn personalities matter, and humans' ability to find happiness seems to have been partially shaped by evolution. But these effects are not the end of the story. To a large extent, *happiness is all in our heads*, because the way we interpret the events in our lives has a tremendous impact on our happiness. For instance, avoiding social comparisons, seeking out positive experiences and emotions, and feeling gratitude and optimism can enhance our happiness and feeling of satisfaction with our lives. All of these are largely within our own control.

The book examines other fundamental questions that flow from this insight. For instance, psychologists have long thought that happiness was resistant to change—that the happiness we have now is likely the happiness we will have in the future. This is not completely true. Happiness can change, for better or worse. This prompts the question, "How can we go about improving our own personal happiness?"

The insight that happiness can change leads to other questions. Can we predict what is going to make us happier? Do people know what actions to pursue to increase their happiness? Or do the actions that seem right lead to dead ends of unhappiness? And perhaps most importantly, can happiness be directly sought and vigorously pursued? Can we find happiness by actively seeking it out? Or is it true, as many have argued, that any direct pursuit of happiness is doomed to fail—that happiness slips away from us if we self-consciously try to obtain it? That instead of actively seeking "happiness" we should seek out various "virtues" that will indirectly make us happier? This book provides some answers to these questions.

The book also tells a story of scientific progress. It is thoroughly grounded in the scientific literature, providing empirically verified answers to some of the preceding questions, as well as answers to questions about how happiness can be increased. Readers get a sense not only of the facts of the field, but also of the scientific processes by which these facts were obtained and some understanding of the boundaries between what we do and do not currently know about happiness.

INTENDED AUDIENCE

This book is intended as a primary text for students in undergraduate courses in happiness or positive psychology with minimal background in psychology, statistics, and research methods. Technical terms are defined and research methodologies and statistical results are described using straightforward, nontechnical language. Students with a basic grasp of introductory psychology should find the book accessible and understandable.

The book can also be used as a supplementary text for courses in social, introductory, or health psychology or psychology of adjustment. It delves deeply enough into the theory, methods, and implications of the results to provide more advanced students with a springboard for understanding the empirical literature. I invite these students to read the book to get an understanding of the important issues, and then broaden and deepen their understanding through further reading of the studies cited in each chapter.

UNIQUE FEATURES

Coverage of Socio-Structural Issues

An important and unique feature is the book's emphasis on what we know about the *conditions* that affect our happiness and well-being. For example, the book delves deeply into areas such as consumer culture, unemployment, income inequality, social welfare systems, cultural understandings of work, and work interference with family and national and corporate policy, exploring how these relate to happiness. This gives students a stronger sense of what they can do directly to increase their own happiness. No other text covers these socio-structural topics in any depth, and many seem to completely ignore them. However, any full discussion of the psychology of human happiness should include these factors.

Humans are social creatures, and the "social" extends beyond the immediate circle of people with whom we directly interact. Therefore, students are shortchanged if they do not have the chance to learn about the connections between economics, culture, and happiness. They are shortchanged not only on an intellectual level, but also in terms of their ability to be fully informed and aware citizens, because citizens need to know the relationship between economic growth and happiness, and all the complications that come with it. They also need to know something about whether unemployment "scars" individuals such that their happiness does not fully recover even when they are reemployed at a similar level of pay. This book addresses these questions and others like them.

Comprehensive Coverage of the Field

The book balances coverage of both socio-structural issues and the more individualistic concerns of positive psychology. There is a chapter on personality, and other chapters address individual differences and happiness. The book examines how positive emotions can build happiness, and the importance of how we construe or interpret events. There is also extensive coverage of positive psychology interventions that can improve individuals' happiness.

Evolution has gained a prominent position among psychological theories, offering important insights about happiness. It suggests not only that there are limits to human happiness, but also that happiness can be enhanced by pursuing behaviors associated with our ancestors' survival and reproductive success. The suggestions offered by evolution are sometimes quite different from those offered by other perspectives, and students need to grapple with this evolutionary perspective to gain a full understanding of the field. For these reasons, the book includes a chapter exploring evolution and happiness.

More direct emphasis is placed on the ways we can increase happiness than in other texts. In addition to empirically verified positive psychology interventions, the book explores possible systemic changes that might increase happiness for society as a whole. These changes, such as reconsidering tax and social welfare policies, are also strongly empirically based. The book also acknowledges and discusses some of the political ramifications involved.

The Science of the Psychology of Happiness

The book emphasizes the science of the psychology of happiness. I have tried to weave into the text a story that includes not just the facts, but also how those facts are obtained and how to make theoretical sense out of them, which are two critically important components of any science. I think this makes the story more interesting and helps further student learning. There is nothing less intellectually fulfilling than simply reading a litany of facts. Facts are only minimally helpful unless we also know why they are important, how they relate to other things we know, and how sure we are that they are true.

I think the fact of money's relationship to happiness becomes more interesting, easier to remember, and more useful when we know that much of the research is necessarily correlational, and therefore that causality must be carefully considered. Knowing how causality is evaluated helps us understand why some results are more important than others. Having more detailed information about what a "small" relationship means is also helpful. And understanding some detail about the argument that money does not matter much once a minimum wealth threshold is passed is also essential. This book investigates these matters.

This necessitates giving more detail about specific studies than is typical for undergraduate texts. I describe research methodologies and discuss whether causal attributions are appropriate; discuss the results of many of the studies; and invite students to interpret tables and graphs from primary source articles. Mediated and moderated relationships are also discussed. I guide students through the results by pointing toward important findings and explaining how they should be interpreted.

Accessible Science for Introductory Students

Although the science of the field is emphasized, the book is accessible to introductory students. It assumes students have only basic knowledge of introductory psychology, and no knowledge of research methods or statistics beyond what they learned in their introductory course. When technical issues arise, such as when describing mediated relationships, I discuss them on a broad conceptual level without descending into technical specifics. Concepts are clearly defined when first introduced.

The very material of the book sparks intrinsic interest and makes the book accessible. Topics such as the nature of happiness, the importance of joy, the role of money in producing happiness, marriage and children and happiness, whether happy people are successful, whether career success leads to happiness, whether and how happiness can change, whether it can be directly pursued, and so on, naturally invite students into the book.

LEARNING TOOLS AND INSTRUCTOR RESOURCES

The use of a conversational style in this book is deliberate, to aid student learning. I wrote as if a student were sitting in my office with me, and I were simply and informally (but accurately) telling the story of what we know about the science of happiness. Introductory and summary paragraphs bracket not just the opening and close of each chapter, but also main topics within it. Gentle repetition facilitates learning, and summarizing important points by recapping major sections helps keep track of larger themes while moving through the chapter. This aids thematic thinking, helping to place important details in context so they are easier to remember and understand.

Nearly everything about the subject matter relates to students' own lives and concerns, and these connections are made clear. The central questions of the book, relating to money, marriage, career success, religious faith, and positive experiences, are posed in practical terms with which students can identify. This sparking of intrinsic interest is perhaps the most powerful learning tool of all.

Instructor's resources are available to qualified adopters. These materials include sample syllabi and information about potential ways to organize the course; lecture-building tips, including potential lecture topics and outlines; and suggestions for out-of-class writing assignments. Discussion questions provided for each chapter can be used to spark students' thinking and conversations about the material, serve as starters for classroom discussions and homework assignments, or build potential test questions.

Readings, videos, websites, and real-world examples of topics supplement each chapter. All are designed to help students become more involved with the material and think actively about what they read, since active thinking, rather than passive listening or reading, is the key to learning. Suggestions for small group, in-class activities include a mix of short lecture ideas, short videos, small group activities and discussions, and whole class discussions. PowerPoint slides are provided for each chapter.

I hope that the suggestions in the manual will be a launching pad that inspires instructors to build on these ideas. I am confident that instructors will find that teaching a course on happiness is a gratifying and rewarding experience. **For more information on the instructor resources, qualified adopters should contact textbook@springerpub.com.**

James B. Allen, PhD

ACKNOWLEDGMENTS

I would like to thank numerous people for their help while I was writing this book. Certainly the team at Springer Publishing Company, particularly Mindy Chen and Debra Riegert, deserve medals for their patience with me. My students at SUNY Geneseo, including those in my Psychology of Happiness class and the members of my research team, were tremendously helpful as I was writing.

I also want to thank the two people who taught me the most about how to think clearly: my father, Zeke Allen, and my graduate school advisor, Doug Kenrick. And I thank my brothers, Andy and Pat, for teaching me the most about how to laugh. No one is as much fun as the two of them. Finally, I thank my wife, Deb, and my two children, Paul and Claire, for their unwavering support and love. They bring me the most happiness.

CHAPTER 1

Studying Happiness

When I was in grade school, they told me to write down what
I wanted to be when I grew up.
I wrote down happy. They told me I didn't understand the assignment,
I told them they didn't understand life.

—Anonymous

Welcome to the psychology of happiness! What make us happy and satisfied with our lives? Are we just born that way? Or is this something that is reinforced in us from childhood on? Is happiness tied to internal factors, or to outside influences, or both?

We have probably all known people who just seemed naturally happy and optimistic. I remember a fellow student in my high school who was neither well-to-do nor highly ranked in the teen-aged social hierarchy. We were both seniors, and although neither of us was very athletic, we had been enrolled in the "jock" Phys Ed class that was normally reserved for varsity athletes. We were both out of place, scorned by the coaches and other students.

I felt miserable, although I knew that my life was going to get better after I got through this awful Phys Ed class. After all, I was going to college next year, and anticipating the coming opportunities and responsibilities with a mixture of anxiety and hope. But the other student, who was just as out of place as I was, and with fewer prospects ahead at the end of high school, wore a smile much of the time. He was happy to greet each moment and looked at the world with joy.

So is happiness largely a matter of personality? And if so, can our happiness change, or is it a fixed and unchangeable individual difference, in the same way some people never tire of anchovies on pizza, while others are sure they could never develop a taste for fishy pizza? Some answers to these questions are explored in Chapter 3. Can we intentionally pursue happiness? And if so, what is the best way of doing so? Chapter 4 explores these questions, looking as well at how we often are mistaken about the factors that will really make us happy or unhappy.

Is there something about being human that limits our ability to feel happiness and satisfaction? Humans are set apart from other animals by our ability to form culture, but we still evolved under the same natural selection pressures as did other animals. When were joy, contentment, and satisfaction useful to our prehistoric ancestors? Under what circumstances did these positive emotions help them survive and reproduce more successfully? Is it possible that positive emotions might not always have aided our survival and reproductive successes? Would individuals who too readily felt contentment and satisfaction have lacked the necessary motivation to keep striving, and would this have hindered their evolutionary success? These and similar questions about evolution are discussed in Chapter 2.

Did evolution prepare us to need social contacts in order to be happy? If so, is it enough to merely be affiliated with other people, or must we form deep emotional bonds with others? Is there an optimal number of these bonds, or is more always better? What about marriage and parenthood: Do they make us happy? Or is it merely that happier people are more likely to get married and become parents? Chapter 5 provides some answers.

How is happiness correlated with money and materialism? In Chapters 6 and 7, we examine important and politically relevant issues such as how unemployment, income inequality, and economic growth relate to happiness. You may be surprised by some of the conclusions researchers have reached.

Chapter 8 raises fascinating questions about work and happiness. Are we happier if we have a successful career? And, on the flip side, are happy people successful, or do they become complacent, "blissfully ignorant," and generally oblivious? Other questions abound. Is it possible to love our work so much that it reduces our happiness? What features of work affect our happiness, and how does the intersection between work and family life affect us?

Chapter 9 discusses a topic that has consumed philosophers, theologians, and scholars for thousands of years: how happiness relates to the meaning of life. It also explores researchers' efforts to understand why religion often improves happiness.

What is the connection between happiness and health? Does happiness cause health, and does health cause happiness, or are the two merely correlated? Chapter 10 examines these questions closely. It also explores the science behind these questions and answers, examining how scientists have addressed these questions and how certain we are of their answers.

Lastly, what specific interventions can improve individual happiness? And how might happiness on a societal level be improved by addressing socio-structural factors? The final chapter pulls together research and theory from the entire book to make suggestions about how we could all live happier lives.

THE PSYCHOLOGY OF HAPPINESS

This book tells the story of the scientific study of what makes us feel happy, content, joyous, and satisfied with our lives. I have tried to weave into this story not just the facts of the psychology of happiness, but also how those facts are obtained: the *science* of the psychology of happiness. I think this approach makes the story more interesting. It is also important that word about the science of the psychology of happiness gets out, to counter the misinformation, opinion, and trendy psychobabble that pervades this topic in the popular press.

I hope you find the prospect of studying happiness exciting and interesting. It is certainly a topic that connects easily to our everyday lives and experiences. In the chapters that follow, we also investigate issues related to whether and how our happiness can change over time.

Although this book explores factors that affect our happiness, it is not a self-help book to be used as a manual with specific suggestions to increase individual happiness. Nonetheless, general themes and insights emerge from the study of the psychology of happiness that can be useful, and I hope these add to your interest and enjoyment of the book. For instance, exploring the relationship between money and happiness, or material goods and happiness, is important in a consumeristic culture such as ours. I hope these discussions give you some things to consider, in terms of both your own individual happiness and how we might increase the happiness and well-being of our society as a whole.

Situational and Socio-Structural Factors

The book also emphasizes what we know about the *conditions* that affect our happiness and well-being. Chapter 3 is focused on personality, and questions about individual differences and happiness are also addressed in the other chapters. However, as you can see from the chapter titles, the topics we cover place more emphasis on important social factors that influence our happiness than on individual differences in personality.

For instance, in Chapter 6, we examine how the structure of our society and economy can influence our happiness, and we learn more about these socio-structural factors in Chapter 7, as we examine the influence on happiness of advertising and the cultural values promoted by economic systems. We investigate how culture and social norms influence happiness in social relationships such as marriage (Chapter 5), in combination with religious faith (Chapter 9), and with respect to physical health (Chapter 10). These are just a few examples, but they give an idea of the book's approach.

Positive Psychology: An Introduction

Some readers may wonder why I have not used the phrase *positive psychology* in the title of this book. Positive psychology is a widely recognized phrase that returns over nine and a half million hits on Google and calls up close to 12,000 academic publications as a subject term on PsycINFO, the electronic database of social science research sponsored by the American Psychological Association (APA). In many ways, positive psychology is the face of modern scientific efforts to understand human happiness.

Positive psychology is largely associated with the study of human virtues or strengths. For instance, positive psychologists have found that strengths such as love, gratitude, control, and hope help individuals effectively deal with challenges in their lives (Ingram & Snyder, 2006; Gallagher & Lopez, 2009; Snyder & McCullough, 2000). Positive psychology also emphasizes intrinsic, or self-motivational, forces as an important pathway to happiness (Kasser, 2004; Ryan & Deci, 2000; Sheldon & Kasser, 2001). This valuable and important approach has pushed psychology away from a sole focus on what is wrong with individuals to a stronger focus on what is *right* with them. This study of individual strengths and intrinsic motivations, and the change in focus they have produced in psychology, have led to important new understandings of how individuals can be happier and live more fulfilling lives. Chapters 3 (on personality) and 4 (on joy and positive emotions) review much of this research.

Nonetheless, positive psychology tends to have an individualistic focus. The research often begins by identifying individuals in a given environment who seem to thrive, and then proceeds to cataloging the features of their personality that are associated with their success. Other researchers approach the issue from the opposite direction, beginning with positive characteristics that seem likely to help an individual thrive and be happy, and then testing whether they are actually associated with happiness and well-being. In either case, the emphasis is placed on positive characteristics of the individual that promote well-being and happiness.

This individualistic approach is readily apparent in the writings and work of Martin Seligman, who is often credited as the founder of positive psychology. Seligman's books for popular audiences reflect positive psychology's individualistic approach by emphasizing individual "character strengths" that predict well-being. These character strengths include gratitude, optimism, originality, judgment, and wisdom, among others. His three most recent books for this audience emphasize individual character strengths that people can develop to increase their happiness (Seligman, 2002, 2006, 2011).

Seligman is also coauthor of a book about character strengths for professional audiences (Peterson & Seligman, 2004), *Character Strengths and Virtues: A Handbook and Classification*. This text seeks to classify positive character strengths in much the same way the American Psychiatric Association's *Diagnostic and Statistical Manual of Mental Disorders* (*DSM*) classifies mental disorders. Furthermore, he founded and directs the Positive Psychology Center at the University of Pennsylvania, where he works. The center has a website whose stated purpose is to provide free resources to those who want to learn more about positive psychology. A recent check of the website shows it promoting a new book by Duckworth (2016) titled, *Grit: The Power of Passion and Perseverance*, which it describes as teaching how passion and persistence can lead to success. This is another example of the emphasis on individual characteristics as opposed to environmental and social factors.

Seligman does mention the importance of environmental and situational influences (i.e., not individualistic aspects of an individual's character) in his writings (e.g., Seligman, 2006). However, his main interest in individual character strengths is apparent in both his books and in his opening statement about positive psychology when the field was in its infancy. In 2000, he coedited a special issue of the journal *American Psychologist* (with Mihaly Csikszentmihalyi) on the then-emerging field of positive psychology. Seligman argued that psychology had overemphasized situational forces to the point of creating a "victimology" in which individuals were viewed as excessively "passive" responders to their environment (Seligman & Csikszentmihalyi, 2000, p. 6). Seligman clearly wanted positive psychology to move away from this environmental focus.

Seligman's work is very valuable. In fact, he has been one of the most heavily cited and influential psychological scientists from the latter part of the 20th century into the beginning of the new millennium. I respect his work very much. But, as I explain in the next sections, my interests in writing this book differed in some respects from those of the leaders in positive psychology. Thus, throughout the book, we explore a world of research about happiness and well-being that takes a somewhat different approach.

A Critique of Positive Psychology

Some thinkers have questioned the individualistic aspects of positive psychology. For instance, Barbara Ehrenreich (2009), a prominent social critic, suggests that positive psychology, with its emphasis on individualism and positive thinking, gives too much aid and comfort to a racket of hucksters who sell "life coaching" services to individuals. Isolated individuals, set apart from the larger culture, are overpromised that they have the power to transform their lives by merely thinking more positively.

Similarly, she points out that there is a big business selling "positive thinking" and happiness-increasing courses to the corporate world and that positive psychology might unwittingly encourage some of these dubious practices. Ehrenreich (2009) is not accusing positive psychologists of being dishonest. Instead, she is concerned that the field's (over-?) promotion of positive thinking encourages some of the unsavory cultural tendencies already at work in the United States.

Ehrenreich (2009) is also concerned that positive psychology might blunt calls for social reforms. She speculates that its focus places too much of the responsibility for increasing happiness on the shoulders of individuals and suggests that positive psychology is more likely to advise individuals to change themselves than to advocate for changing social institutions. For instance, anyone seeking greater happiness should change his or her own outlook on the world, perhaps by practicing optimism, rather than, say, by demanding better unemployment insurance from the government.

Other critics, such as William Davies (2016), author of the book *The Happiness Industry: How the Government and Big Business Sold Us Well-Being*, have voiced similar concerns about how positive psychology might be used to squelch social reforms. Davies discusses social reform in general, but he also points out that American workers are increasingly alienated, stressed, and unhappy for various cultural and economic reasons. He makes an explicit argument that government and business would prefer to solve the productivity problem by "fixing" workers rather than by modifying the environment that harms them.

And some psychologists even have concerns about how the study of happiness has progressed. For instance, the field has been criticized (e.g., by Hart & Sasso, 2011) as catering to, and merely offering platitudes to, an elite population of relatively wealthy, pampered, and privileged First-Worlders. These authors have argued that the field should more strongly address the problems in well-being of really needy individuals in the developing world.

Other psychologists share Ehrenreich's (2009) and Davies's (2016) concerns even more closely. For instance, Held (2002, 2005) is also concerned about positive psychology's emphasis on positivity and on individualism. Neither Ehrenreich (2009) nor Held is against "being positive," but they worry that it is overemphasized. Both authors point out numerous examples in which "positivity" is unlikely to be of much help. For example, many medical problems do not respond to "positive thinking," although a significant part of our culture, including those making a living selling positivity, want us to think so.

And similarly to Ehrenreich (2009) and Davies (2016), Held (2002) worries positive psychology's individualism might lead to a form of blaming the victim. She cites the comedian George Carlin saying that he did not like it when people told him to have a good day, because this put all the burden on him. Held (2002, p. 987, emphasis in the original) sees this as a form of cultural tyranny, and responds, ". . . if in America you just can't have a nice day, no matter how hard you try, it is your own personal failing. It is your own personal *moral* failing."

The Psychology of Happiness: A Social Psychological Approach

I do not want to overstate positive psychology's emphasis on the individual. The field does examine which environments enhance human strengths and virtues, and it also considers how environments can be enhanced to better nurture these strengths. For instance, Ingram and Snyder (2006) argued that psychological therapists should consider how character strengths interact with stressful environments to produce psychological dysfunction. Thus, positive psychologists do not focus *solely* on individualistic concerns such as character strengths, but also consider how these affect and are affected by the environments in which individuals live.

Still, the major emphasis is on individual character strengths and how to nurture them. You can see this emphasis in a very fine textbook, aptly named *Positive Psychology: The Scientific and Practical Explorations of Human Strengths*, by Lopez, Pedrotti, and Snyder (2015). Many of the chapter titles include references to individualistic concepts such as optimism, self-efficacy, wisdom, empathy, and coping. While one chapter examines both school and work, this book does not include an entire chapter devoted to work. Nor does it devote chapters to socio-structural concepts such as money, materialism, and religion or include extensive discussions of the institution of marriage and the alternative of cohabitation, which are also socio-structural variables. While the Lopez et al. (2015) text is very good, it is limited by being rooted firmly in the tradition of positive psychology.

I chose the title *The Psychology of Happiness in the Modern World*, and included a reference to social psychology in the subtitle of this book, to reflect a different emphasis. Although the chapters that follow review much of the work on human character strengths that forms the basis of positive psychology, I wanted to emphasize such socio-structural concepts as money, unemployment, marriage, and work, among others, that also have important implications for happiness. I wanted this book to have an extensive discussion of ways that societies might improve their citizens' happiness. This, I think, necessarily includes a discussion of changes in at least some socio-structural elements of our societies. Thus, the subtitle *A Social Psychological Approach* reflects a way of studying human happiness and well-being that is different from, although complementary to, positive psychology.

THE POLITICS OF HAPPINESS

The points we have discussed in the last two sections, about criticisms of positive psychology and about why I chose to title this book in the way I did, teeter on the edge of politics, a subject that most psychologists would rather avoid. We see our science as objective and value-free, and while we would like the public and policy makers to consider our findings when making decisions, we would mostly like to stay out of that discussion ourselves. I think this is a healthy approach, but I also think that teachers have an obligation to point out the political implications of their subjects.

The psychology of happiness, perhaps even more than other areas of psychology, has important political implications. Some of these are probably obvious to you by now. If positive psychology does have an (over?) emphasis on the "power of positivity" and the ability of each of us as individuals to make our own happiness, this belief in personal empowerment suggests that the need for social reforms is less urgent. We will see several more specific political implications as well as we go through the book. For instance, data indicate that income and wealth inequality are associated with lower happiness. Furthermore, data also show that some of the values associated with capitalism, the system that forms the basis of our economy, predict lower levels of well-being. We will also see findings throughout the book, particularly in Chapters 5, 8, 9, and 11, that have political implications.

My role is simply to point out these implications. It would be wrong to suggest what you should do about them. This reminds me of a story a fellow graduate student who was studying clinical psychology told me. She had picked up the expression "Don't 'should' on me" as a useful message for her clients. They sometimes needed to learn that they were in charge of their own lives and that they could make their own decisions without someone telling them what they "should" or "ought to" do.

That lesson applies very strongly here. For instance, the relationship between income inequality and well-being is fact, and that relationship is probably causal in that inequality is one cause of (lower) well-being.

You could recognize the fact that income inequality and happiness have a negative relationship but believe that income inequality serves the larger purpose of sorting the productive from the nonproductive and is therefore an essential element of our society. You might also decide that there are more important goals than happiness that income inequality serves. This may lead you to respond to the income inequality–happiness relationship differently from someone else. And that is fine. Do not let other people "should" on you.

A big part of my role as a teacher is to help you learn facts and, even more importantly, to help you distinguish between facts and fiction. And I need to point out the political implications of these facts. But what you decide to do with those facts is up to you. I do not want to "should" on you.

Is the Study of Happiness Frivolous or Harmful?

When I started teaching a course about the psychology of happiness, and particularly when I began to write this book, several cynics asked me questions that essentially amounted to whether happiness is "good" for people. One line of questioning asked whether the pursuit of happiness was productive. "Can you find happiness by actively pursuing it?" "Isn't happiness something that happens when you're doing something else that is worthwhile?" "Will your book send people on a fool's errand by making them think that they can go out looking for happiness?"

Another line of questions asked whether happiness is morally healthy. Even some psychologists, including Pérez-Álvarez (2016), have asked whether there are more important goals than happiness. Is living a "meaningful" life more important than living a happy one? "Aren't happy people kind of selfish? They seem so wrapped up in their own enjoyment that they're not very concerned about other people." "Do happy people get kind of lazy? If you're really happy, do you lose motivation to work hard and be creative?"

These are great questions, and I have tried to address them in this book. Chapter 4, in particular, investigates whether we can find happiness through direct pursuit. We also address the related question of whether it is possible to change our happiness in Chapter 3. The questions about the productivity of happy people are largely addressed in Chapter 8. Throughout the book, the happy life versus meaningful life question is addressed. Decide for yourself whether happiness and meaningfulness are contradictory as you read through the book. For now it is enough to be aware of these questions and to keep them in the back of your mind.

THE SCIENCE OF HAPPINESS

Finally, this book is about the *science* of happiness. The most important thing this means is that the conclusions reached here are empirically based (i.e., based on research data). In other words, these conclusions are "reality based" and are not mere opinions or folk tales. It is exciting to know that there is a consistent reality to human happiness, and I hope you will enjoy learning about it.

Another important aspect about the science of happiness is that, as with all sciences, our knowledge is limited. We will come across several topics for which the answers are just not clear yet. We do not yet have appropriate data to answer these questions. I hope you will not be frustrated by these instances, but instead see these cases as exciting opportunities for hypothesizing and further data collection.

I have made special efforts to clarify the process of scientific discovery. Rather than just report the facts and move on, I try to help you understand how the data were collected and how the researchers reached their conclusions. I also discuss some important technical details such as results that are "moderated" and "mediated." The discussion assumes that the reader has little or no background in research methods and statistics. My thinking is that it is both boring and exceptionally unhelpful just to read a list of facts. To really understand a topic and learn much about it, you must understand why researchers ask the questions they do and how they go about answering them.

IS THE PSYCHOLOGY OF HAPPINESS A NEW FIELD?

Building Positive Psychology

The scientific study of the psychology of happiness is not really new. However, the field can seem new because of a dramatic change in focus prompted by Martin Seligman when he became president of the APA in 1998. In the President's Report (Fowler, Seligman, & Koocher, 1999, p. 559), Seligman urged psychology to reorient itself toward a science of, ". . . 'positive psychology,'. . . that emphasizes the understanding and building of the most positive qualities of an individual: optimism, courage, work ethic, future-mindedness, interpersonal skill, the capacity for pleasure and insight, and social responsibility."

Seligman (Fowler et al., 1999) argued (and others agreed, e.g., Gable & Haidt, 2005; Maddux, 2002; Simonton & Baumeister, 2005; Snyder & McCullough, 2000) that psychology was too focused on curing mental illness and not focused enough on what makes individuals happy. This criticism was largely due to the post–World War II establishment of the Department of Veterans Affairs and the National Institute of Mental Health. Both these organizations were dedicated to treating mental illnesses, and psychologists found that employment and grant money were available to those who studied and tried to treat psychopathology. As a result, psychology moved away from its original mission of helping people live more fulfilling and productive lives. The critics believed that a new focus on positive psychology could help restore a proper balance in the field between treating mental illness and helping "normal" individuals become happier and more fulfilled (Fowler et al., 1999; Seligman & Csikszentmihalyi, 2000).

As president of the APA, Seligman did much more that merely advocate for a new direction for psychology. He was also instrumental in building the structural frameworks to support this new orientation. For instance, during Seligman's tenure as president, the APA established outside funding for an annual "Positive Psychology Prize" that was the largest monetary award given in psychology up to that time. He also helped to establish networks of psychological scientists interested in studying positive psychology (Fowler et al., 1999; Linley, Joseph, Harrington, & Wood, 2006). Seligman's efforts were hugely successful. The new subdiscipline of positive psychology quickly established journals and built connections with funding sources (Linley et al., 2006). Positive psychology has seen rapid growth during the short time since Seligman's 1999 presidential address (Fowler et al., 1999), and it is now a thriving scientific discipline (Rusk & Waters, 2013).

In addition, what began as positive psychology has expanded beyond the original emphasis on character strengths to include a more general study of human happiness. Researchers from multiple disciplines outside of psychology, including sociology, political science, and economics, have been inspired by positive psychology to begin to study human happiness. In addition, scholars of "well-being," who once thought of themselves as working in different areas, now see themselves as linked by the study of human happiness because of the inspiration of positive psychology (Rusk & Waters, 2013).

Historical Roots

Positive psychology's emphasis on human strengths and the factors that create happiness is not a recent focus. Although positive psychology did bring these emphases more to the forefront of psychology, they have always been there. For instance, William James, who is perhaps the founder of American academic psychology, can be considered the first positive psychologist because of his work on promoting what we would recognize today as "character strengths" among teachers and students in order to better facilitate learning (Taylor, 2001).

James did other work that we would recognize today as positive psychology. In his own address as president of the APA in 1906, he theorized about why some individuals seem able to meet their fullest potential while others do not. He also asked how we might learn to help all individuals optimize their potential (Froh, 2004). This again clearly connects modern positive psychology's interest in character strengths. The fact that James did his most important work as a psychologist at the turn of the 20th century shows that positive psychology has its beginnings much before Seligman's term as APA president.

But positive psychology's clearest roots come from humanistic psychology. Led by Abraham Maslow, Carl Rogers, and others, humanistic psychology had been brewing during much of the 20th century, but reached its peak in popularity and prestige in the 1960s and 1970s. It was largely a response against behaviorism, which it criticized for not recognizing the full extent of human potential, and of Freudian psychoanalysis, which it criticized as overly concerned with mental illness (DeCarvalho, 1990; Hergenhahn, 1997; Schultz & Schultz, 1996, and see also Aanstoos, Serlin, & Greening, 2000; Bugental, 1963).

For example, humanistic psychologists urged their colleagues to study positive characteristics of the human experience such as joy, contentment, and gratitude (Schultz & Schultz, 1996). They also advocated the study of factors that would enrich the human experience and help make life better for all of us (Hergenhahn, 1997). Thus, humanistic psychology championed the study of mentally healthy individuals and focused on the positives of human nature long before Seligman's presidential address to the APA. Interestingly, Seligman and Csikszentmihalyi (2000) acknowledged that positive psychology had some debt to humanistic psychology but argued that it was minimal because humanistic psychology never produced strong empirical findings. This prompted an indignant response from many humanistic psychologists (see Froh, 2004; Taylor, 2001, for reviews).

Finally, a close examination of some of the publication dates of articles cited in this book shows that researchers outside of humanistic psychology were already beginning to examine happiness before Seligman's 1999 APA address (Fowler et al., 1999). For instance, Ed Diener, a leading researcher in the field, was involved in developing a "Satisfaction With Life Scale" as early as 1985 (see Diener, Emmons, Larsen, & Griffin, 1985).

Of course, none of these citations of earlier research are meant to deny the important impact that Seligman had on the field. He was able to reorient psychology more firmly toward the psychology of happiness, and he also helped bring important institutional resources to the field. Still, it is interesting and important to understand something about the historical roots of the psychology of happiness.

WHAT DO RESEARCHERS MEAN BY HAPPINESS?

I use the term *happiness* in the title of this book because it is easily recognizable and understood by those who are unfamiliar with the field. However, instead of happiness, researchers often use the phrase *well-being* as a label for what we often think of as happiness: the extent to which an individual feels content, is satisfied, is emotionally and physically healthy and engaged with life, believes his or her life is meaningful, and so on (Dodge, Daly, Huyton, & Sanders, 2012; Gillett-Swan & Sargeant, 2015). I use the terms *well-being* and *happiness* interchangeably throughout the book.

Still, there is no clear consensus on how happiness, or well-being, should be defined. Researchers do agree, however, that the definition should give an overall or global sense of an individual's quality of life. Thus, the definition should encompass emotions, cognitions, motivations, and social interactions and life circumstances, among other characteristics of individuals living high-quality lives (Dodge et al., 2012; Gillett-Swan & Sargeant, 2015). Finding a single conception of happiness that covers all these dimensions is obviously a very tall order, and is one of the main reasons why there is no consensus on how to define well-being.

Hedonic and Eudaimonic Conceptualizations of Well-Being

Hedonic Well-Being

Although there is no consensus on how to define happiness or well-being, there are well-established schools of thought that most researchers choose between. The two most prominent of these are the hedonic and the eudaimonic traditions. The hedonic view is that well-being is best measured in terms of an individual's own subjective evaluation of his or her current state. By "subjective" we mean that researchers rely on individuals' self-reports of their internal states of happiness (Deci & Ryan, 2008; Ryan & Deci, 2001).

As we will see, the hedonic approach has the advantage of more directly assessing how individuals perceive their own well-being. This differs from the eudaimonic approach, which probes for the extent to which the person is living a fully self-directed and engaged life and uses this information to infer his or her level of well-being. This is an important distinction that we will discuss at length.

Hedonic well-being is often referred to as *subjective well-being*. This subjective evaluation is not limited to physical pleasure or fleeting feelings of positive mood. Instead, it includes the individual's cognitive assessment of his or her overall satisfaction with life as a whole, and current feelings of positive and negative emotions (Deci & Ryan, 2008; Ryan & Deci, 2001). These are assessed by measures of *life satisfaction*, and positive and negative *affect*, which is psychological terminology for emotion.

The hedonic tradition is widely associated with the study of happiness, rather than with more global measures of well-being that assess the extent to which a person is "fully functioning" and has reached his or her full potential. The eudaimonic tradition places more emphasis on these global measures. The hedonic approach is more associated with "happiness" because it emphasizes subjective reports of cognitive satisfaction with life and emotional states (Deci & Ryan, 2008).

Much of the research described in this book follows the hedonic tradition. We will see many studies that use measures of life satisfaction, in particular, as the primary outcome variable. In fact, the hedonic tradition has been the dominant model within the field (Deci & Ryan, 2008; Ryan & Deci, 2001). However, the eudaimonic approach may be becoming more prevalent, so it is worth reviewing at some length.

Eudaimonic Well-Being

The eudaimonic view is that subjective reports of "happiness" or satisfaction do not necessarily indicate psychological health. Instead, real psychological health means working toward one's full potential. Thus, well-being is a process, and not an end state. The individual with high well-being strives to reach, and is making good progress toward, his or her full potential and is "living as [he or she] was inherently intended to live" (Deci & Ryan, 2008, p. 2). Implicit in this perspective is that an individual can feel content or even "happy," but not necessarily have high levels of well-being without also making progress toward his or her full potential.

Ryff's model   An example from the eudaimonic tradition is Ryff's (1989, Ryff & Singer, 2006, 2008) multidimensional model of psychological well-being (Deci & Ryan, 2008). This model was developed by a careful reading of what various philosophers, particularly Aristotle, wrote about psychological health and reaching one's true potential as a human being. This study led to the identification of six dimensions of eudaimonic well-being: self-acceptance, purpose in life, autonomy, personal growth, positive relationships, and environmental mastery. Research then validated these dimensions by showing that they predicted established measures of well-being such as life satisfaction and self-esteem, and by also demonstrating that they were correlated with changes in life situations that likely affect happiness and well-being (Ryff & Singer, 2008).

Self-Determination Theory   Another prominent example of the eudaimonic tradition is derived from Ryan and Deci's (2000) Self-Determination Theory (SDT). SDT hypothesizes that humans have basic psychological needs for autonomy (i.e., to feel in control of their own lives), competence, and relatedness (i.e., feeling emotionally connected to others). We are motivated to satisfy these needs, and, as predicted by other eudaimonic theories of well-being, we cannot reach our full potential and become fully functioning human beings unless these needs are met. Thus, merely feeling satisfied with our lives is not enough to warrant complete well-being if we do not also meet these basic needs (Ryan & Deci, 2001). The SDT approach to well-being is particularly important to our discussion of materialism in Chapter 7.

The SDT approach differs somewhat from Ryff and Singer's (2008) approach. One of these differences is that SDT recognizes measures of subjective well-being (i.e., life satisfaction and positive and negative emotion) as valid, although incomplete, measures of global well-being. Another difference is that the basic needs for autonomy, competence, and relatedness are seen as essential causes of well-being, but not measures of well-being in and of themselves. Instead, SDT largely relies on measures of vitality (i.e., feeling energetic and self-directed), self-actualization (i.e., feeling that our full potential has been reached), and positive mental health as indicators of well-being (Ryan & Deci, 2001).

Flourishing   Several groups of authors, including Keyes (2002), Huppert and So (2013), Diener et al. (2010), and Seligman (2011) have used the term *flourishing* to indicate high well-being. Although these efforts have tended to lean toward the eudaimonic side of the well-being spectrum, they contain elements of the hedonic tradition as well (Hone, Jarden, Duncan, & Schofield, 2015). I discuss only Seligman's (2011) model here for the sake of brevity and because he has some particularly interesting things to say about how well-being should be defined.

Seligman (2011) proposed the term *flourishing* as the best definition of well-being because it suggests a more global and overall state of well-being than do concepts like "happiness" or life satisfaction. This model of flourishing has five elements: positive emotion, engagement, relationships, meaning, and accomplishment, which are identified by the handy acronym PERMA.

Some of these elements probably need a bit of explanation. By engagement, Seligman (2011) means that we have activities that fully capture our attention, and with which we feel fully involved. Seligman is drawing upon the concept of flow (Csikszentmihalyi, 1990) here, which we discuss at length in Chapter 4. Meaning refers to the sense that our life has meaning and purpose. To have meaning, one needs to feel involved in a task or a cause that is bigger than oneself. Finally, and similar to the autonomy principle from SDT, self-direction and intrinsic motivation are an important component of the model. In order to have high well-being, the person must pursue each element, particularly accomplishment, for its own sake, rather than for an external reward.

Seligman (2011) chose these elements based on a careful reading of the scientific literature on well-being. He decided that these are the factors that most importantly accompany high well-being and living the "good life." As a result, the model is largely theoretical rather than completely empirical. For instance, we do not have good data about whether these five elements make up the complete set of factors that are important for well-being.

Regardless, in order to flourish, and to therefore achieve the highest levels of well-being, an individual must find high levels of each of these elements. Simply being "happy" or having high life satisfaction is not enough (Seligman, 2011). This requirement makes the model tilt heavily toward the eudaimonic side of the well-being spectrum.

In fact, Seligman (2011) rejects the term *happiness*, and he also criticizes what he sees as an overreliance on life satisfaction measures among researchers studying well-being. He argues that the term *happiness* is not useful because it is too vague and incompletely captures the full nature of flourishing. Instead, happiness seems merely to suggest merriment and joy, and so on, and not a fully flourishing person.

Seligman (2011) levels a similar criticism against life satisfaction measures. A person could be satisfied with his or her life, and still not flourish. Seligman (2011) is also dissatisfied with the heavy use of life satisfaction measures because they seem to be strongly affected by current mood. According to Seligman, true well-being has to be more than merely being in a good mood. These are important criticisms of life satisfaction measures. We discuss these in more detail in the next section about how researchers measure well-being.

Seligman's (2011) model is a significant example of the eudaimonic approach. It is important to recognize, however, that it is not a completely "pure" example because, like SDT, it gives some weight to current emotions (the "P" in PERMA). It also gives a good contrast of the conceptual differences between the hedonic and eudaimonic approaches to defining well-being. Note again that in Seligman's (2011) approach, a person might feel "happy" in terms of expressing positive mood and a positive evaluation of his or her life but be considered relatively low in well-being if he or she was not also engaged in finding meaning, and so on. This would not be the case with the hedonic approach.

Are Hedonic and Eudaimonic Approaches Really Different?

First, notice the conceptual differences between these two examples of eudaimonic conceptions of well-being and hedonic conceptions. Neither Ryff's model nor the SDT model of eudaimonic well-being relies heavily on individuals' assessments of their own internal emotional states or "happiness." Neither do they rely on individuals' cognitive evaluations of how well their lives are going. Instead, both these eudaimonic models assess individuals' sense of the extent to which they are in control of their own lives and are striving toward their own destiny and purpose. These responses are then interpreted as well-being.

However, some researchers have questioned whether there is a meaningful empirical difference between these two approaches to well-being. Disabato, Goodman, Kashdan, Short, and Jarden (2016; see also Kashdan, Biswas-Diener, & King, 2008) examined responses from 7,617 participants representing 109 countries from around the world to address this question. Their results largely suggested that hedonic and eudaimonic well-being are similar rather than distinct constructs. For instance, measures of hedonic and eudaimonic well-being were highly correlated with each other. Even more importantly, these two conceptions of well-being tended to make similar predictions of important outcome variables such as loneliness, raising the reasonable question of whether the distinction between them is important (see Raibley, 2012, for a dissenting opinion).

SOCIAL INDICATORS

Researchers also use social indicators such as rates of suicide, child mortality, teen pregnancies, high school graduation, and obesity and crime statistics to define well-being. The logic here is that individuals who live in a community with high crime and/or suicide rates must necessarily have lower well-being. These social indicators are often used as outcome variables to test the possible effects of social and economic factors on well-being (Diener, Lucas, Schimmack, & Helliwell, 2009).

We see several examples of this kind of measure in Chapter 6. For instance, research links income inequality to several social indicators (Pickett & Wilkinson, 2007). Other research shows a relationship between unemployment and suicide rates (Stuckler, Basu, Suhrcke, Coutts, & McKee, 2009).

The use of social indicators offers some advantages. Social indicators are "objective" measures that do not depend on individuals' self-reports of their subjective states. They also reflect the behaviors of "real" people living in naturalistic environments, rather than biased samples such as college sophomores taking a psychology course. Finally, a strong argument can be made that they reflect important components of well-being.

But there are also problems with using social indicators. One is that it is often unclear which indicators should be used. For instance, a researcher interested in the possible relationship between unemployment rates and well-being would have to choose among a number of possible social indicators. Perhaps there is a theoretical reason to expect the unemployment rate to affect suicide rates. But is there a reason to expect unemployment to affect obesity? What about child mortality? Not knowing which social indicator to pick can lead to inaccurate or incomplete results (Diener et al., 2009).

Another potential problem concerns the measurement quality of the social indicators. Social indicator data are usually accessed in government or social services archives. Therefore, the researcher was not involved in the data collection and collation process. Social indicators look impressive but can sometimes be misleading or hard to interpret (Diener et al., 2009).

For example, there can be some uncertainty regarding whether a death should be classified as a suicide. Do the collectors of these statistics err away or toward classifying a death under ambiguous circumstances as a suicide? Does this tendency change over time, or across political boundaries? For instance, does the definition of a suicide change depending on who heads the statistical recordkeeping department and from one state to another? The researcher often has limited knowledge and usually no control over these kinds of factors because he or she was not involved in the data collection (Diener et al., 2009). In conclusion, although social indicator data can be an effective way to define and measure well-being, the potential problems with this approach must be kept in mind.

ECONOMIC APPROACHES TO WELL-BEING

Economists have long relied on economic data to define well-being. This use of economic data is based on the assumption that people are rational actors who use money to thoughtfully acquire the things that increase their well-being. For instance, if I have money, I can then buy leisure time, recreational opportunities, and goods and services that increase my well-being. Therefore, the more money I have, the higher my well-being. Although economists are not this simplistic in practice, this reasoning describes the basic outlines of their approach (Diener et al., 2009).

The most important among these economic measures is probably gross domestic product (GDP), which is the total sum of the cost of all goods and services sold in a country in a given period of time. A closely related measure is gross national product (GNP), which for our purposes measures essentially the same thing as GDP. Therefore, economists have long looked upon GDP (or GNP) as an indicator of the general well-being within a country. Again, I am oversimplifying a bit, but the logic is straightforward. If a country's wealth increases (as indicated by a rise in GDP), then we can assume that citizens have more money to spend on the things that increase their well-being (Diener et al., 2009).

We discuss the merits of these economic definitions of well-being in detail in several chapters, especially Chapters 6, 7, and 11. However, to foreshadow just a bit it is worth noting that years of psychological research call into question the chief economic assumption that people are rational economic actors, at least under many circumstances. Furthermore, the strict economic approach is unsatisfying to psychologists because it does not give clear access to a person's subjective feelings or goals (Diener et al., 2009).

HOW IS HAPPINESS MEASURED?

Simple Self-Report Questionnaire Measures

In the previous section we discussed how social science researchers define happiness and well-being. Now we explore general techniques of how happiness is measured without going into great detail about any particular happiness scale. We also discuss the merits of these techniques.

The most common and straightforward approach to measuring happiness is simply to ask people to self-report their level of well-being. This is done in a variety of ways, including asking individuals to rate their well-being on a simple scale. For instance, the frequently used Satisfaction With Life Scale (Diener et al., 1985, p. 72) poses questions such as "In most ways my life is close to ideal," and then asks for responses on a one to seven scale with anchors of 1 = strongly disagree through 7 = strongly agree.

Other scales try to help respondents with visual or mnemonic aids. For instance, one scale (see Myers & Diener, 1996) gives a series of seven "faces" (actually yellow circles of smiley/frowny faces) that provide a mnemonic aid to guide responses. The faces are arranged in order from the deepest frown to the happiest smile, and respondents are asked to circle the one that best represents the way they feel about their life as a whole. The Cantril "Ladder" scale is another example of a measure that provides a visual aid. Respondents see a picture of a nine-step ladder. The top of the ladder is labeled "Best possible life for you," while the bottom of the ladder is labeled "Worst possible life for you" (Larsen, Diener, & Emmons, 1985, p. 3). Respondents are then asked, "Where on the ladder do you stand at the present time?"

Are These Good Measures?

The bottom line   I am going to restrict our discussion mostly to measures of life satisfaction here because so much has been written about these measures. The short answer is that questionnaire measures of life satisfaction are "good" measures. More specifically, they are reliable and valid in that they are accurate enough to be of use to researchers, therapists, and even public policy makers (Diener et al., 2009). Following is a summary of the reasons why we have confidence in the validity of these measures.

Specifically, life satisfaction measures are reasonably stable across time. This is important because, if valid, these measures should change only when major changes (that are relatively rare) occur in individuals' lives. Furthermore, and as expected if life satisfaction measures are valid, these measures are not affected by trivial events such as temporary mood states or day-to-day changes in the weather. In addition, evidence also indicates that individuals think about theoretically relevant subjects, such as family, career, and romance, that are expected to influence life satisfaction ratings when they complete these measures (Diener et al., 2009).

There is also some objective verification of the validity of life satisfaction measures. Brain imaging technology has made it possible to identify areas of the brain associated with happiness. Research shows that responses to life satisfaction questionnaires are correlated with activity in these areas of the brain. Also, individuals' responses to questionnaire measures of happiness are associated with peers' opinions of an individual's happiness. These outside verifications of questionnaire responses help researchers feel more confident about the validity of these measures (Diener et al., 2009).

Finally, as expected, major life events, such as becoming disabled or unemployed, affect life satisfaction measures. All of these findings support the notion that life satisfaction measures are valid assessments of how individuals assess their global life quality (Diener et al., 2009).

Temporary mood states and life satisfaction   One concern about the validity of life satisfaction measures is that self-reports may reflect a person's temporary mood state more than they do true global evaluation of their life. Obviously, life satisfaction measures will not be valid if our responses to them change wildly depending on our present mood. (Ask me how satisfied I am with my life after I have just finished an ice cream cone, and I respond that it's great! But ask me after I've just finished a dish of tofu—not my favorite— and my response might be much more muted.) Recall that this concern was one basis for Seligman (2011) to minimize the role of life satisfaction in his Flourishing Model.

It is true that mood has some influence on life satisfaction judgments. Individuals do not typically take the time and effort to carefully examine all parts of their lives when asked to respond to global life satisfaction measures. Instead, they take mental shortcuts, including basing their judgments at least in part on their mood (Diener, Napa Scollon, & Lucas, 2003).

But fortunately for the life satisfaction measures, research shows that temporary mood states have only moderate effects on judgments of global life satisfaction. Individuals also use other information, including life circumstances, to form their judgments of life satisfaction (Diener et al., 2003; Schimmack & Oishi, 2005). For instance, we see in Chapter 3 that major life events, such as becoming disabled or unemployed, impact life satisfaction judgments (e.g., Lucas, 2007). Furthermore, these judgments are fairly stable over time in the absence of major life events (Diener et al., 2003; Krueger & Schkade, 2008; Schimmack & Oishi, 2005).

The fact that major life events affect life satisfaction, and that life satisfaction is reasonably stable in the absence of such events, speaks against the mood interpretation. Our mood fluctuates fairly dramatically from day to day, so we would expect that our life satisfaction would too, *if it were strongly affected by mood*. However, that is not the case.

Differing results from experimental and nonexperimental studies may have caused some confusion in the literature about the cross-time stability of life satisfaction judgments. Most of the research that appears to show that mood affects life satisfaction comes from experimental studies. Participants in these studies were exposed to some stimuli that temporarily raised or lowered their mood in an artificial laboratory environment.

However, Eid and Diener (2004) found that the relationship between mood and life satisfaction was much weaker when assessed in naturalistic environments in which mood was not artificially manipulated. In other words, participants' natural fluctuations in mood were not strongly related to their life satisfaction ratings. The evidence points to the conclusion that temporary mood states do not have a strong effect on life satisfaction.

Weather and life satisfaction A related concern is that other trivial factors, such as the weather, may affect life satisfaction ratings. Although researchers expect life satisfaction ratings to respond to *major life events*, these satisfaction ratings would not mean much if they were strongly bounced around by such trivial events as changes in the weather. Lucas and Lawless (2013) tested for this possibility with a nationally representative sample of more than one million participants from all 50 states from the United States. The data were collected over 5 years, and life satisfaction scores were compared to weather changes as reported by governmental and commercial weather sources.

Results showed that day-by-day weather changes had only very minimal effects on life satisfaction. Changes in temperature, barometric pressure, wind speed, cloud cover, and humidity were not associated with life satisfaction differences. These results held even after controlling for the area of the country, season of the year, regional weather patterns, and other variables. The implication is that life satisfaction is a stable construct that meaningfully reflects respondents' actual feelings and evaluations of their lives (Lucas & Lawless, 2013).

Respondents' thoughts Are people really thinking about their lives in any global sense when they complete life satisfaction measures? Or are they thinking about other trivial factors such as what they had for lunch that day? Obviously, life satisfaction measures will be valid only if respondents are thinking about the quality of their overall life when they make the ratings.

Luhmann, Hawkley, and Cacioppo (2014) examined this question by asking participants to complete a life satisfaction measure and then list what they had been thinking about while completing the measure. Across two separate studies, results showed that more than 80% of these thoughts were related to important life circumstances such as career, family, and romance. These are just the factors that researchers expect to influence respondents' life satisfaction. These findings led Luhmann et al. (2014, p. 777) to conclude that, "When people think about how satisfied they are with their lives, they think about things and events that actually matter for their life satisfaction."

Brain scans and peer reports Research shows that responses to measures of subjective well-being correlate with outside or "objective" measures of an individuals' happiness. For example, Sato et al. (2015) used structural MRI scans and found that responses on a subjective happiness (life satisfaction) scale were correlated with gray matter volume in the right precuneus region of the brain. This and other studies (e.g., Davidson, Ekman, Saron, Senulis, & Friesen, 1990; George, Ketter, Parekh, Herscovitch, & Post, 1996; Habel, Klein, Kellermann, Shah, & Schneider, 2005) show that reports of subjective well-being can be objectively verified, and increase our confidence in their validity.

Other studies show that responses to subjective well-being measures correlate with the impressions that acquaintances have about the respondent. For instance, Nave, Sherman, and Funder (2008) found that college students' responses to subjective well-being measures correlated with ratings made by professional clinicians who interviewed them. The students' responses also correlated with those made by two acquaintances who knew them well. These results also lend some objective verification to these subjective well-being measures and increase our confidence in them.

Reply to Skeptics of Self-Report Measures

Skeptics may still question the validity of self-report measures. Can we trust what people say about their happiness? Do they take the questionnaire seriously, or do they simply rush through it to get it done as quickly and thoughtlessly as possible? If they do take the questionnaire seriously, will they answer the questions about happiness truthfully? Or will they try to "self-present" as being happier or unhappier than they really are?

And finally and perhaps most importantly, do people even know whether they are happy? Do they understand what happiness is? These are all great questions.

Response biases   Participants are sometimes biased in the way they respond to questionnaires. For instance, they can rush through the questionnaire without taking it seriously. However, there are ways for the researcher to control the environment that make this less likely. Specifically, research environments that are friendly but professional and that help communicate the importance of the study seem to minimize this problem.

There are also ways of detecting this problem if it does occur so that the totality of the data is not "infected" by the meaningless responses of some of the participants. Random or rushed responses to a questionnaire often produce outlying patterns of data that are readily apparent. Researchers can also pick up clues about this problem by noting whether responses replicate well-established findings from previous research.

Another potential response bias is that participants may try to self-present or "fake" being happier (or less happy) than they actually are. If this occurs, it would not be a problem for most social science research as long as it is a general human tendency that almost everyone is motivated toward. This is because social scientists are rarely interested in estimating absolute levels of happiness. For example, we do not care much whether a population average well-being score is a 2.6 versus a 2.5 on a 5-point scale. Instead, we want to investigate relationships between well-being and other variables, and we also want to see whether well-being changes over time. Self-presentation effects would not influence these calculations as long as they affected all participants more or less equally.

More of a problem occurs if some participants are more motivated toward self-presentation than are others. Unfortunately, research indicates that this is the case (Wojcik & Ditto, 2014). There is some controversy concerning what to do about this problem. One potential solution is to administer an additional scale that measures individuals' tendency for socially desirable responses (the tendency to make oneself "look good") and then statistically control for this motivation.

However, Diener, Sandvik, Pavot, and Gallagher (1991) argue that this solution is inappropriate because motivations to self-enhance are an authentic component of high well-being. Thus, by statistically removing this tendency, researchers are removing a genuine part of respondents' well-being scores. Other authors, such as Wojcik and Ditto (2014), disagree.

My own feeling is that this is an important, but nonfatal problem. Having people with differing levels of motivation to self-enhance in a study throws an additional source of variability into a data set. Ordinarily, this would make it more difficult to find an effect that really does exist, rather than making a relation appear to exist that really does not. Furthermore, researchers can run analyses both controlling and not controlling for self-enhancing (social desirability) effects and see whether the outcomes differ. If they do, researchers can then make careful judgments about how to interpret the data.

Do people know when they are happy?   Is it possible that people can think they are happy when they are really not? If so, then simply asking for self-reports of happiness is an obviously flawed procedure. Gilbert (2006) addresses this question using Lori and Reba Schappell as a case study. These two sisters are conjoined twins, permanently attached at the forehead since birth, and, by the standards of us singletons, unable to have a minute's privacy or independence, and completely unable to live a "normal" life.

Imagine trying to go to the bathroom, much less on a date, with your sibling attached to your forehead. What do the siblings do if one wants to go to sleep earlier than the other? Can you imagine being attached at the forehead with your sibling when he or she has a cough or a runny nose? They each want to pursue different careers, and one wants to eventually have children one day. How could they manage this? Their lives seem frustrating and difficult (to us), and, if we are being honest with ourselves, we have to wonder how they could ever be happy.

But surprisingly, Gilbert (2006) describes Reba and Lori as abundantly happy. And he is right. You can look them up on the Internet and find several videos about them and see for yourself. They do seem happy. And they certainly say they are.

Can this be true? Or do they somehow misunderstand what it means to be happy? Perhaps they do not know how unhappy they really are because they have never known any different life? If they knew what we know about what it is like to live as a singleton, then they would understand what it is like to really be happy. Obviously, their background is emotionally impoverished.

Gilbert (2006) will have none of this, and rejects all the arguments in the previous paragraph. Instead, he argues that we should take Lori and Reba at their word.

Gilbert's argument for self-reports   Gilbert's (2006) argument comes in two parts. First, he reminds us that we are not very good at interpreting our own experiences, so we should be cautious about trying to interpret someone else's for them. If you have not already seen the video "Gorilla in the Midst," Google it before you start reading the next paragraph.

The video shows several people wearing different color shirts standing in a circle passing a basketball around. Viewers are told to count how many times the ball is passed by the people in the white shirts. Toward the middle of the video a person in a gorilla suit walks through the middle of the circle, stops to beat his chest, and then walks off screen. At the end of the video, viewers are asked whether they saw the gorilla. A surprising number of naive viewers do not notice the gorilla! Again, if we are so clueless about our own experiences, we should be careful telling other people (like Lori and Reba) that they do not understand their own (Gilbert, 2006).

The next part of Gilbert's argument deals with Lori and Reba's alleged "impoverished emotional experience." But this argument does not show that Lori and Reba do not understand what happiness really is. Perhaps it is we who live impoverished emotional lives and not Lori and Reba. After all, we have never known the comfort of having the emotional security of a trusted partner always nearby.

The impoverished emotional experience argument also falls apart because it could be used against almost anyone (Gilbert, 2006). For example, if I, as an adult over age 50, have never heard the popular singer Beyoncé perform, does that mean that I am living an impoverished emotional life, and that I do not know what it means to be truly happy?

If you are tempted to say "yes," let me ask you whether you have ever heard the Grateful Dead, who toured from the 1960s through the mid-1990s, perform live, as I have? If you have not, it would be silly for me to say that you are unhappy even though you do not realize it because of your impoverished emotional experience. My only available valid conclusion: If you insist you are happy even though you have never been to a Dead show, then I should take your word for it. If a respondent to a life satisfaction questionnaire does not share an experience that the researcher associates with happiness, one cannot automatically conclude that the respondent is emotionally impoverished.

And that is Gilbert's main point. Self-reports are really the only game in town when it comes to measuring happiness. Happiness is a fully subjective experience, and the best, and even the only, way to assess it is to ask people how they feel. Sure, you can scan my brain to peek at the neurological substrates of my feelings, or you can ask my closest friends how happy I am. You could also hire a shrink to assess my happiness. But for Gilbert (2006), all those "objective" measures of my happiness are not as valid as what I tell you about my happiness. And this is the position taken by most happiness scholars.

Some Other Ways of Measuring Happiness

So far we have discussed only global reports of subjective well-being in which participants are asked to make overall assessments of recurrent and ongoing happiness over long periods of time. In contrast, two other techniques, referred to as *momentary methods*, ask participants to assess their well-being during specific and relative short time spans (Tay, Chan, & Diener, 2014).

The Daily Reconstruction Method (DRM) is one of the two momentary methods. With this technique, participants are instructed at the end of the day to segment their day into specific time periods and report what they were doing and how happy they were during these times. The other momentary method is called the Ecological Momentary Assessment (EMA). Here participants periodically report what they are doing and their happiness in real time as they go through the normal course of their day (Tay et al., 2014).

We see an interesting example of the EMA technique at work in Chapter 5. Mehl, Vazire, Holleran, and Clark (2010) monitored participants' real-time happiness and social interactions. Their results showed that participants who spent the most time in meaningful social interactions reported the most happiness.

There is no clear agreement concerning which method is best, although some researchers advocate for momentary methods because they may be less susceptible to recall biases (Tay et al., 2014). Diener and Tay (2014) argue that while the global technique has been thoroughly validated, there is less information about the validity of the momentary methods. These momentary methods seem to be gaining in popularity however, and research may benefit from using them more often in the future in combination with the global assessments (Tay et al., 2014).

SUMMARY

So now you know about the plan for the book and something about the topics we cover, and the history of the scientific study of happiness. You also know more about how happiness is defined and measured. Although in the chapters that follow we examine some relatively objective measures of happiness, such as suicide and crime rates, most of the data we discuss come from self-reports. We want to know what individuals think and feel about their own happiness.

I am confident that you will find the topics we discuss inherently interesting. They touch on important social issues with vital political implications. But they also relate to things we all experience in our everyday lives. For instance, will you be happier if or when you get married? What is it about being religious that makes someone happier? Do you need money to be happy? Will you be healthier if you are happy?

What could be more fun than addressing these kinds of questions? In examining these issues, we take into consideration personal characteristics of the individual. But we also take a close look at social and cultural factors that influence happiness. The book concludes with a detailed discussion of things that we, as individuals and as a society, working together, might do to increase happiness within ourselves and in those around us. I hope that this book, and the final chapter, in particular, provoke discussion and generate ideas among you and your classmates.

REFERENCES

Aanstoos, C., Serlin, I., & Greening, T. (2000). History of Division 32 (humanistic psychology) of the American Psychological Association. In D. Dewsbury (Ed.), *Unification through division: Histories of the divisions of the American Psychological Association* (Vol. 5, pp. 85–112). Washington, DC: American Psychological Association.

Bugental, J. F. T. (1963). Humanistic psychology: A new breakthrough. *American Psychologist, 18*(9), 563–567.

Csikszentmihalyi, M. (1990). The domain of creativity. In M. A. Runco & R. S. Albert (Eds.), *Theories of creativity* (pp. 190–212). Thousand Oaks, CA: Sage.

Davidson, R. J., Ekman, P., Saron, C. D., Senulis, J. A., & Friesen, W. V. (1990). Approach-withdrawal and cerebral asymmetry: Emotional expression and brain physiology I. *Journal of Personality and Social Psychology, 58*(2), 330–341.

Davies, W. (2016). *The happiness industry: How the government and big business sold us well-being.* London, UK: Verso.

DeCarvalho, R. J. (1990). A history of the "third force" in psychology. *Journal of Humanistic Psychology*, *30*(4), 22–44.

Deci, E. L., & Ryan, R. M. (2008). Hedonia, eudaimonia, and well-being: An introduction. *Journal of Happiness Studies*, *9*(1), 1–11.

Diener, E., Emmons, R. A., Larsen, R. J., & Griffin, S. (1985). The Satisfaction With Life Scale. *Journal of Personality Assessment*, *49*(1), 71–75.

Diener, E., Lucas, R., Schimmack, U., & Helliwell, J. (2009). *Well-being for public policy.* New York, NY: Oxford University Press.

Diener, E., Napa Scollon, C., & Lucas, R. E. (2003). The evolving concept of subjective well-being: The multifaceted nature of happiness. *Advances in Cell Aging and Gerontology*, *15*, 187–219.

Diener, E., Sandvik, E., Pavot, W., & Gallagher, D. (1991). Response artifacts in the measurement of subjective well-being. *Social Indicators Research*, *24*(1), 35–56.

Diener, E., & Tay, L. (2014). Review of the Day Reconstruction Method (DRM). *Social Indicators Research*, *116*(1), 255–267.

Diener, E., Wirtz, D., Tov, W., Kim-Prieto, C., Choi, D., Oishi, S., & Biswas-Diener, R. (2010). New well-being measures: Short scales to assess flourishing and positive and negative feelings. *Social Indicators Research*, *97*(2), 143–156.

Disabato, D. J., Goodman, F. R., Kashdan, T. B., Short, J. L., & Jarden, A. (2016). Different types of well-being? A cross-cultural examination of hedonic and eudaimonic well-being. *Psychological Assessment*, *28*(5), 471–482.

Dodge, R., Daly, A., Huyton, J., & Sanders, L. (2012). The challenge of defining wellbeing. *International Journal of Wellbeing*, *2*(3), 222–235.

Duckworth, A. (2016). *Grit: The power of passion and perseverance.* New York, NY: Scribner.

Ehrenreich, B. (2009). *Bright-sided: How the relentless promotion of positive thinking has undermined America.* New York, NY: Metropolitan Books.

Eid, M., & Diener, E. (2004). Global judgments of subjective well-being: Situational variability and long-term stability. *Social Indicators Research*, *65*(3), 245–277.

Fowler, R. D., Seligman, M. E. P., & Koocher, G. P. (1999). The APA 1998 annual report. *American Psychologist*, *54*(8), 537–568.

Froh, J. J. (2004). The history of positive psychology: Truth be told. *NYS Psychologist*, *16*(3), 18–20.

Gable, S. L., & Haidt, J. (2005). What (and why) is positive psychology? *Review of General Psychology*, *9*(2), 103–110.

Gallagher, M. W., & Lopez, S. J. (2009). Positive expectancies and mental health: Identifying the unique contributions of hope and optimism. *The Journal of Positive Psychology*, *4*(6), 548–556.

George, M. S., Ketter, T. A., Parekh, P. I., Herscovitch, P., & Post, R. M. (1996). Gender differences in regional cerebral blood flow during transient self-induced sadness or happiness. *Biological Psychiatry*, *40*(9), 859–871.

Gilbert, D. T. (2006). *Stumbling on happiness.* New York, NY: A. A. Knopf.

Gillett-Swan, J., & Sargeant, J. (2015). Wellbeing as a process of accrual: Beyond subjectivity and beyond the moment. *Social Indicators Research*, *121*(1), 135–148.

Habel, U., Klein, M., Kellermann, T., Shah, N. J., & Schneider, F. (2005). Same or different? Neural correlates of happy and sad mood in healthy males. *NeuroImage, 26*(1), 206–214.

Hart, K. E., & Sasso, T. (2011). Mapping the contours of contemporary positive psychology. *Canadian Psychology/Psychologie Canadienne, 52*(2), 82–92.

Held, B. S. (2002). The tyranny of the positive attitude in America: Observation and speculation. *Journal of Clinical Psychology, 58*(9), 965–992.

Held, B. S. (2005). The "virtues" of positive psychology. *Journal of Theoretical and Philosophical Psychology, 25*(1), 1–34.

Hergenhahn, B. R. (1997). *An introduction to the history of psychology.* Belmont, CA: Thomson Brooks/Cole.

Hone, L. C., Jarden, A., Duncan, S., & Schofield, G. M. (2015). Flourishing in New Zealand workers: Associations with lifestyle behaviors, physical health, psychosocial, and work-related indicators. *Journal of Occupational and Environmental Medicine, 57*(9), 973–983.

Huppert, F. A., & So, T. T. C. (2013). "Flourishing across Europe: Application of a new conceptual framework for defining well-being": Erratum. *Social Indicators Research, 110*(3), 1245–1246.

Ingram, R. E., & Snyder, C. R. (2006). Blending the good with the bad: Integrating positive psychology and cognitive psychotherapy. *Journal of Cognitive Psychotherapy, 20*(2), 117–122.

Kashdan, T. B., Biswas-Diener, R., & King, L. A. (2008). Reconsidering happiness: The costs of distinguishing between hedonics and eudaimonia. *The Journal of Positive Psychology, 3*(4), 219–233.

Kasser, T. (2004). The good life or the goods life? Positive psychology and personal well-being in the culture of consumption. In P. A. Linley & S. Joseph (Eds.), *Positive psychology in practice* (pp. 55–67). Hoboken, NJ: John Wiley.

Keyes, C. L. M. (2002). The mental health continuum: From languishing to flourishing in life. *Journal of Health and Social Behavior, 43*(2), 207–222.

Krueger, A. B., & Schkade, D. (2008). Sorting in the labor market: Do gregarious workers flock to interactive jobs? *Journal of Human Resources, 43*(4), 859–883.

Larsen, R. J., Diener, E., & Emmons, R. A. (1985). An evaluation of subjective well-being measures. *Social Indicators Research, 17*(1), 1–17.

Linley, P. A., Joseph, S., Harrington, S., & Wood, A. M. (2006). Positive psychology: Past, present, and (possible) future. *The Journal of Positive Psychology, 1*(1), 3–16.

Lopez, S. J., Pedrotti, J. T., & Snyder, C. R. (2015). *Positive psychology: The scientific and practical explorations of human strengths* (3rd ed.). Thousand Oaks, CA: Sage.

Lucas, R. E. (2007). Long-term disability is associated with lasting changes in subjective well-being: Evidence from two nationally representative longitudinal studies. *Journal of Personality and Social Psychology, 92*(4), 717–730.

Lucas, R. E., & Lawless, N. M. (2013). Does life seem better on a sunny day? Examining the association between daily weather conditions and life satisfaction judgments. *Journal of Personality and Social Psychology, 104*(5), 872–884.

Luhmann, M., Hawkley, L. C., & Cacioppo, J. T. (2014). Thinking about one's subjective well-being: Average trends and individual differences. *Journal of Happiness Studies, 15*(4), 757–781.

Maddux, J. E. (2002). Stopping the "madness": Positive psychology and the deconstruction of the illness ideology and the *DSM*. In C. R. Snyder & S. J. Lopez (Eds.), *Handbook of positive psychology* (pp. 13–25). New York, NY: Oxford University Press.

Mehl, M. R., Vazire, S., Holleran, S. E., & Clark, C. S. (2010). Eavesdropping on happiness: Well-being is related to having less small talk and more substantive conversations. *Psychological Science, 21*(4), 539–541.

Myers, D. G., & Diener, E. (1996). The pursuit of happiness. *Scientific American, 274*(5), 70–72.

Nave, C. S., Sherman, R. A., & Funder, D. C. (2008). Extending the personality triad to nonhuman samples. *European Journal of Personality, 22*(5), 461–463.

Pérez-Álvarez, M. (2016). The science of happiness: As felicitous as it is fallacious. *Journal of Theoretical and Philosophical Psychology, 36*(1), 1–19.

Peterson, C., & Seligman, M. E. P. (2004). *Character strengths and virtues: A handbook and classification.* New York, NY: Oxford University Press and Washington, DC: American Psychological Association.

Pickett, K. E., & Wilkinson, R. G. (2007). Child wellbeing and income inequality in rich societies: Ecological cross sectional study. *British Medical Journal, 335*(7629), 1080–1085.

Raibley, J. R. (2012). Happiness is not well-being. *Journal of Happiness Studies, 13*(6), 1105–1129.

Rusk, R. D., & Waters, L. E. (2013). Tracing the size, reach, impact, and breadth of positive psychology. *The Journal of Positive Psychology, 8*(3), 207–221.

Ryan, R. M., & Deci, E. L. (2000). Self-determination theory and the facilitation of intrinsic motivation, social development, and well-being. *American Psychologist, 55*(1), 68–78.

Ryan, R. M., & Deci, E. L. (2001). On happiness and human potentials: A review of research on hedonic and eudaimonic well-being. *Annual Review of Psychology, 52,* 141–166.

Ryff, C. D. (1989). Happiness is everything, or is it? Explorations on the meaning of psychological well-being. *Journal of Personality and Social Psychology, 57*(6), 1069–1081.

Ryff, C. D., & Singer, B. H. (2006). Best news yet on the six-factor model of well-being. *Social Science Research, 35*(4), 1103–1119.

Ryff, C. D., & Singer, B. H. (2008). Know thyself and become what you are: A eudaimonic approach to psychological well-being. *Journal of Happiness Studies, 9*(1), 13–39.

Sato, W., Kochiyama, T., Uono, S., Kubota, Y., Sawada, R., Yoshimura, S., & Toichi, M. (2015). The structural neural substrate of subjective happiness. *Scientific Reports, 5.* doi:10.1038/srep16891

Schimmack, U., & Oishi, S. (2005). The influence of chronically and temporarily accessible information on life satisfaction judgments. *Journal of Personality and Social Psychology, 89*(3), 395–406.

Schultz, D. P., & Schultz, S. E. (1996). *A history of modern psychology.* Orlando, FL: Harcourt Brace College.

Seligman, M. E. P. (2002). *Authentic happiness: Using the new positive psychology to realize your potential for lasting fulfillment.* New York, NY: Free Press.

Seligman, M. E. P. (2006). *Learned optimism: How to change your mind and your life.* New York, NY: Vintage Books.

Seligman, M. E. P. (2011). *Flourish: A visionary new understanding of happiness and well-being.* New York, NY: Free Press.

Seligman, M. E. P., & Csikszentmihalyi, M. (2000). Positive psychology: An introduction. *American Psychologist, 55*(1), 5–14.

Sheldon, K. M., & Kasser, T. (2001). Goals, congruence, and positive well-being: New empirical support for humanistic theories. *Journal of Humanistic Psychology, 41*(1), 30–50.

Simonton, D. K., & Baumeister, R. F. (2005). Positive psychology at the summit. *Review of General Psychology, 9*(2), 99–102.

Snyder, C. R., & McCullough, M. E. (2000). A positive psychology field of dreams: "If you build it, they will come. . . ." *Journal of Social and Clinical Psychology, 19*(1), 151–160.

Stuckler, D., Basu, S., Suhrcke, M., Coutts, A., & McKee, M. (2009). The public health effect of economic crises and alternative policy responses in Europe: An empirical analysis. *Lancet, 374*(9686), 315–323.

Tay, L., Chan, D., & Diener, E. (2014). The metrics of societal happiness. *Social Indicators Research, 117*(2), 577–600.

Taylor, E. (2001). Positive psychology and humanistic psychology: A reply to Seligman. *Journal of Humanistic Psychology, 41*(1), 13–29.

Wojcik, S. P., & Ditto, P. H. (2014). Motivated happiness: Self-enhancement inflates self-reported subjective well-being. *Social Psychological and Personality Science, 5*(7), 825–834.

CHAPTER 2

Evolution

Happiness is a common goal toward which people strive, but for many it remains frustratingly out of reach. An evolutionary psychological perspective offers unique insights into some vexing barriers to achieving happiness and consequently into creating conditions for improving the quality of human life.
—Buss (2000, p. 15)

"But people are meant to be happy!" This is a plaintive call that I often hear. The apparent common feeling is that people are inherently destined for happiness, and when the target is missed, it must mean that someone or something has gotten in the way. We would all be happy if we had not strayed from God's path, or except for the corrosive effects of civilization, or perhaps if we had better parents, and so on. But is this true? Are humans truly meant to be happy? Evolutionary psychologists do not think so (Buss, 2000; Hill & Buss, 2008). And their theories about factors that reduce human happiness may surprise you.

Here is the crux of the evolutionary argument. Imagine one of our distant prehistoric ancestors, a hominid that is not fully human, living on the edge of an African jungle that is slowly shrinking because of climate change. For reasons largely unknown, our ancestor and his or her mates decide to cling to the edge of the jungle and emerging savannah rather than retreating into the more familiar thick jungle habitat. Their survival is in doubt. Predators are ever-present, competition for food and shelter is fierce, as is competition for sexual partners. What sort of emotional characteristics would help our ancestor survive and reproduce in that environment?

Would evolution favor individuals with happy-go-lucky dispositions who are easily satisfied? Would unmitigated cheerfulness and optimism be an advantage? Not according to evolutionary psychologists (Buss, 2000). While recognizing that some degree of these positive characteristics could be advantageous, evolutionists argue that individuals who were careful, cautious, not easily contented, and competitive would have survival and reproductive advantages and would therefore be more likely to pass genetically linked emotional patterns on to subsequent generations (Buss, 2000; Hill & Buss, 2008).

For example, caution, even to the point of being overly careful and a bit anxious or neurotic, would help protect our ancestor from predators. And a difficult-to-quench drive always to want more, not to be easily satisfied with the current food supply or sexual partner, would have provided more and better food, and more sexual access to the healthiest and most prolifically breeding mates. Life was so dangerous that there was no way to ever have "enough" food and shelter, so our ancestor always had to look for more and better. And our ancestors were competitive. Although they were also cooperative in many situations, competitiveness was a vitally important characteristic. The successful male ancestor monitored his fellows carefully and felt deeply bothered when they appeared to have more or better of something. He had to because our successful female ancestor was attracted to sexual partners who offered "more" and "better" and because rivals might outmaneuver our male ancestor for access to resources.

So what were these ancestors I asked you to imagine like? According to evolutionists, they were cautious to the point of being a bit neurotic, not at all what we moderns would call "content," and they were competitive with their fellows (Buss, 2000; Hill & Buss, 2008). Not the picture of happiness. But because they were all these things, they managed to survive and reproduce, and, importantly, they passed their genes down to us. Because genetic evolution moves so slowly, we have those genes today. We are much like our ancestors.

EVIDENCE OF EVOLUTIONARY INFLUENCE ON HAPPINESS

Evolutionary Psychology

It is important to understand that evolutionary psychology in general is well supported empirically. A variety of evolutionary hypotheses have been confirmed, including behavioral aspects of immune functioning (Schaller & Park, 2011), human decision making (McDermott, Fowler, & Smirnov, 2008), mating strategies, and mate preferences (Buss, 1989a, 1989b; Gangestad, Garver-Apgar, Simpson, & Cousin, 2007; Kenrick & Keefe, 1992), men's investment in their children (Anderson, Kaplan, & Lancaster, 1999), aggression (Buss, 2004), cooperation (Kenrick, Neuberg, Griskevicius, Becker, & Schaller, 2010; Tooby, Cosmides, & Price, 2006), and morality (Krebs, 2011), to name just a few examples. Therefore, the evolutionary account of human happiness is well within the mainstream of contemporary psychology theory and research. The fact that this hypothesis has been so well supported in other areas lends a certain degree of confidence about hypotheses concerning well-being.

However, it is important to realize from the start that although there is convincing evidence that evolution has influenced human behavior and emotions in many domains, including well-being, no reputable scientist thinks that we are mere robots who blindly follow our genetically encoded instructions. Instead, it is clear that our behavior and emotional responses are the product of both genetic (i.e., evolutionary) *and* social and cultural influences (Kenrick, 1987). The next sections of this chapter are devoted to describing evidence that evolution influences human happiness. My purpose is to highlight this evidence, and I think you will agree that there is a strong case for evolution. However, later we will return to the idea of how genes and environment interact to predict behavior. This interaction is the big picture, and it is important to not lose sight of this point.

Twin Studies and Behavioral Genetics

It is clear that genetics influence well-being. Tellegen et al. (1988) were able to estimate the influence of genetics on personality, including happiness, by comparing identical (monozygotic) and fraternal (dizygotic) twins who were raised in either the same or different families. They found that genetically identical twins had similar personalities, including levels of happiness, regardless of whether they grew up in the same family. In other words, not only were identical twins similar in terms of their personalities (indicating the influence of genetics), the environment in which they were raised had little influence on them. This was not the case for fraternal twins. Although there were fewer fraternal twin pairs, which necessitates some caution interpreting these results, these twins, who shared only 50% of their genetic material, were much less similar to each other.

Subsequent research confirms these findings. For instance, Nes, Røysamb, Tambs, Harris, and Reichborn-Kjennerud (2006) tracked identical and fraternal twins in Norway for 6 years. Consistent with Tellegen et al.'s (1988) findings demonstrating the importance of genetics, results indicated that identical twins were more similar in their happiness levels than fraternal twins both at the beginning and at the end of the 6-year study. Furthermore, identical twins' happiness at the beginning of the study more strongly predicted their co-twin's happiness at the end of the study than was the case for fraternal twins.

Thus, imagine that Ivan and Irving are identical twins, and that Paul and Pete are fraternal twins. Ivan's happiness level at the beginning of the 6-year study was similar to Irving's at the end of the 6 years. However, Paul's happiness level at the beginning of the study was much less similar to Pete's at the end of the study. The influence of our genes is clear. If I am genetically identical to my twin, not only do I have a similar level of happiness with him or her right now, I also have a similar level of happiness even after my twin has experienced 6 years of environmental events and changes that I have not!

Interestingly, environmental influences accounted for about half the variability in happiness levels at the beginning and the end of the Nes et al. (2006) study, which is a meaningful effect and indicates that genetics are not the only important factor. However, environmental influences were short lived: Environmental effects at the beginning of the 6-year study did not influence happiness at the end of the study. Nes et al. note that this finding is consistent with other research indicating that environmental effects are unlikely to be permanent unless they are repeatedly applied. This conclusion has important implications later in this book for our discussion of personality and happiness, and of enhancing happiness.

A final interesting finding from the Nes et al. (2006) study is that the long-term genetic effects were weaker for women than for men. This contradicts results from cross-sectional studies (research examining participants at a single point in time) that generally find consistent patterns of genetic influence for men and women (Keyes, Myers, & Kendler, 2010). However, these cross-sectional studies are not able to detect *changes* in the effects of genetics over time. Nes et al. (2006) note that a similar pattern of gender difference in the effect of genetics over time occurs for personality characteristics such as neuroticism, and suggest that environmental influences such as role changes involving relationships might affect women more strongly over time than they do men. It would be interesting to know whether this pattern exists cross-culturally. Does Western culture have an inordinate effect on women's behavior, or is the tendency for the environment to shape women's behavior more than men's a cultural universal?

More recent research not only demonstrates genetic influences on happiness, but also tells us something about the mechanism of this influence. In another twin study, Franz et al. (2012) found the strength of genetic and environmental influences on happiness depended on the type of happiness assessed (see also Keyes et al., 2010). Specifically, genetic factors were the most important of a collection of items assessing "self-appraisal" and "social comparisons." For instance, identical twins' responses to items such as "I like most aspects of my personality" (self-appraisal) and "In many ways, I feel disappointed about my achievements in life" (social comparison) were quite similar. However, identical twins' responses were significantly related, but more weakly so, on items assessing "global satisfaction." Specifically, identical twins did not respond as similarly to items such as, ". . . feeling that the quality of one's life on the whole is good" (Franz et al., 2012, p. 587), thus indicating stronger environmental influences on this type of well-being. Note that these findings also match our expectations from the beginning of this chapter. Recall that we expected evolution to select individuals who monitored their status (self-appraisal) and compared themselves to others. Interestingly, measures of depression were associated with both collections of items, indicating both genetic and environmental effects on this measure.

Franz et al. (2012) suggest that while global life satisfaction may be more likely to vary with life circumstances, the apparent genetic influence on "self-appraisal" and "social comparison" may explain the stability of long-term well-being. They also argue that the heritability evidence for happiness is strong enough to suggest that researchers may be able to locate genes that promote well-being. Furthermore, there may be independent genetic structures that regulate different aspects of well-being, as suggested by the multidimensional nature of the well-being–genetics relationship found in their research.

Physiological Evidence

Human well-being is linked to physiological processes (Lindfors, 2013; Steptoe, Dockray, & Wardle, 2009). Because these physiological processes, including brain functioning, were undoubtedly shaped by evolution, it is easy to argue that well-being was also subjected to evolutionary processes. For example, Steptoe et al. (2009) reviewed the literature and concluded that positive affect was related to physical health, potentially via physiological processes such as cardiovascular and immune functioning. This is an important finding, given the obvious importance of physical health for evolution. In another review, Lindfors (2013) found that positive affect is associated with processes in the prefrontal cortex, heightened cardiovascular activity, and both immune and endocrine system functioning. Lindfors also found physiological correlates with a sense of meaning in life. Specifically, Lindfors concluded that allostatic load, or the cumulative effects of stressors that influence cardiovascular functioning, for example, was linked to sense of meaning in life.

Behavioral Evidence

Research also connects evolutionary processes to behaviors and responses linked to well-being. For example, the experience of orgasm is obviously pleasurable and is relevant to human happiness. There is a rather obvious evolutionary function to male orgasms: reward for procreative behavior (Wallen & Lloyd, 2011; Zietsch & Santtila, 2011). Although there has been intense debate about the potential evolutionary function of female orgasms (see Lloyd, 2005), recent accumulating evidence supports an evolutionary perspective (Puts, Dawood, & Welling, 2012). First, female orgasm appears to promote conception. A woman's orgasmic contractions promote the flow of semen toward the ovum and may also encourage ejaculation. Female orgasm also places the cervix in an optimal position to accept semen. Interestingly, orgasm is more likely when women are in the fertile phase of their cycle (Puts et al., 2012).

Second, data indicate that orgasms help women "choose" to conceive with healthy men who are likely to provide good genetic material to their children, a prediction known as the "sire choice" hypothesis (Puts et al., 2012). Obviously, women do not make a conscious decision to conceive during orgasm, but the idea is that orgasm facilitates conception and is more likely when women unconsciously sense that their partner is a good mate. Puts, Welling, Burriss, and Dawood (2012) confirmed the sire choice hypothesis among a sample of heterosexual student couples from the northeastern United States. Women with masculine and dominant partners orgasmed more frequently and were more likely to orgasm during or after their partner's ejaculation than other women. These results are important because masculinity and dominance are indicators that men can contribute good genetic material to potential children. Therefore, our female ancestors who were more likely to orgasm with such men probably had more genetically fit offspring. Furthermore, the timing of female orgasm predicts the probability of conception. Women who orgasm slightly before or after male ejaculation are more likely to conceive (Baker & Bellis, 1993).

There are other ties between happiness and evolutionary pressures. For instance, altruism predicts, and quite possibly even causes, increased well-being, health, and longevity. Furthermore, the connection between altruism and well-being is likely driven by evolutionary considerations, particularly among family members (Post, 2005).

Another example is laughter, a definite signal of happiness. Recent research suggests that rats make a chirping sound that may be an ancestral form of human laughter. For instance, rats chirp during play and positive social interactions (Panksepp, 2007). Rats and humans also share similar brain circuitry that controls both rat chirping and human laughter (Panksepp, 2007; Panksepp & Burgdorf, 2003). Panksepp (2007) argues in a review of the literature that

> The evidence so far is remarkably consistent with the possibility that human laughter and rat 50 kHz chirping are rewarding and share an

executive infrastructure that at the very least, has homologous components. We have empirically evaluated this relationship from many perspectives; we have encountered no major disconfirmations that compel us to change our minds on the hypothesis that they are *evolutionarily* related. (p. 241, emphasis added)

Thus, Panksepp (2007) argues that evolutionary processes produced both human laughter and rat chirping. The finding that rats have something like primitive laughing behaviors strengthens the evolutionary argument because we would not expect rats to have "minds" separated from the physiology of their brains.

Yet another example is that political conservatives have higher levels of well-being than do liberals (Napier & Jost, 2008). Vigil (2010) argues for an evolutionary explanation of this difference. He demonstrated that liberals report being more dissatisfied with their level of social support and less trusting of their relationships. These findings support an evolutionary perspective because social support and relationships were essential components of survival among our hominid ancestors (Baumeister & Leary, 1995; Buss, 1990; DeWall & Bushman, 2011). Thus, if evolution has influenced how humans find happiness, we would expect those with less satisfactory relationships (in this case, liberals) to be less happy.

As a final example, who do you think is the first to say "I love you" in a romantic heterosexual relationship: men or women? Ackerman, Griskevicius, and Li (2011) investigated this question. They found that although most people assume women are the first to declare love for their romantic partner, in reality men usually profess love before women do. Professions of love by a romantic partner also increased men's happiness more than it did women's.

Interestingly, although these relationships apply in general, the timing of the statement of love makes a great deal of difference. Ackerman et al. (2011) also found that confessions of love *before* sexual intimacy were greeted with more happiness by men than by women. However, *after* sexual intimacy had entered the relationship, women were somewhat happier when their partner expressed love than were men.

Can you see how these results are consistent with evolutionary psychology? A bit more background about the theory may be helpful. The evolutionary argument here is based on the idea of *differential parental investment* (Trivers, 1972), which predicts that women will be more cautious about entering sexual relationships than men because of their necessarily higher "investment" in any potential children. Women are hypothesized to be high in parental investment because of the relatively small number of children they can produce (relative to men), and the physiological investments that are necessary for carrying a fetus to term. On the other hand, men are hypothesized to be less choosy about sexual partners, and more willing to engage in low commitment sex. Therefore, the evolutionary argument predicts that men should be more eager to profess love before sexual intimacy as a way of convincing women (who are high in parental investment) that they will be good and committed partners. However, after sexual intimacy has begun, men should be less happy about professions of love, because these professions of commitment limit their sexual options with other women (Ackerman et al., 2011). This pattern of results, and the fact that it contradicts cultural assumptions (that women would profess love first), support the evolutionary view.

A Preference for Nature

Another line of evidence also supports the evolutionary interpretation of human well-being. This research is loosely based on Wilson's (1984) *Biophilia* hypothesis: Because humans evolved in natural environments, we should have an affinity for them. Further-more, exposure to natural environments should increase psychological well-being. Note that this is an evolutionary hypothesis because it predicts that natural selection pres-sures built our preference for natural environments and also explain why and how they increase our well-being. Kaplan and Kaplan (1989) developed a more psychological inter-pretation of this idea with their theory that nature restores attentional resources. Kaplan and Kaplan hypothesized that nature is inherently fascinating to humans, and there-fore, we can focus attention on it without effort. As a result, exposure to nature is hypoth-esized to replenish our attentional capacities and energy levels.

An abundance of research is consistent with the attention restoration hypothesis. For instance, Hartig, Evans, Jamner, Davis, and Gärling (2003) found that participants who were randomly assigned to an attention-depleting task, and then given a chance to take a short walk in nature, had greater attentional capacity than participants who walked in an urban environment after the attention depleting task. Similarly, van den Berg, Koole, and van der Wulp (2003) showed all participants a frightening film (*Faces of Death*, which contained images of a farmer's wife decapitating a rooster, and so on), and then ran-domly assigned them to watch videos of walks through either an urban or natural envi-ronment. Results indicated that nature video participants had somewhat better attentional capacities than did urban video participants. Both of these results are consistent with the restoration hypothesis because they demonstrate that "depleted" participants (because of an earlier task or a frightening video) were "restored" after nature exposure. These results are also consistent with the notion that evolutionary factors can influence human feelings of happiness.

Research also demonstrates that exposure to nature is related to happiness. For instance, nature-exposed participants had more positive moods than urban-exposed participants in both the studies described previously. In addition, research indicates higher levels of happiness for participants led on a nature walk versus an urban walk (Mayer, Frantz, Bruehlman-Senecal, & Dolliver, 2009; Nisbet & Zelenski, 2011; Ryan et al., 2010), who feel "connected" to nature (Capaldi, Dopko, & Zelenski, 2014; Howell, Dopko, Passmore, & Buro, 2011), who live in urban areas with more green space (White, Alcock, Wheeler, & Depledge, 2013), who view slides of nature (Ryan et al., 2010; Weinstein, Przybylski, & Ryan, 2009), and who imagined themselves in nature (Ryan et al., 2010).

Although the data are consistent with the evolutionary perspective of well-being, we should be careful when drawing causal conclusions. Can you think of potential counter explanations for these results? Are there reasons other than a naturally selected and innate affinity for nature that might explain these findings? Think about it for a minute before reading the next paragraph.

One problem with much of this research is the potential for participants' expectations to influence their responses (technically referred to as "demand characteristics"). Participants led on a nature walk, or shown pictures of nature, might expect to be happier, and/or they might think that the researcher expects them to be happier. This could very easily influence participant responses on self-report questionnaires. Another problem is that it is difficult to control for all the potential differences between a natural and urban environment. Noise levels, temperature and humidity, activity level, colors, pollution levels, novelty, and other factors are all likely to differ between a walk in urban versus natural environment. Similar problems are likely when comparing pictures of natural and urban environments. Have the researchers been able to fully control for the quality of the photographs, color content, activity levels of people and animals, and so on?

We also need to see more cross-cultural research. If this effect is driven by evolution, then it should affect all peoples and have some universal influence independent of local culture. However, most of the data come from samples of Westerners. Do non-Westerners show the same preferences? We do not have enough data yet to know for sure. But a skeptic could justifiably wonder whether individuals who did not grow up in a culture of National Geographic specials on television, and without a history of idolizing the "frontier" the way Americans do, would show similar responses to exposure to nature.

Finally, the hypothesis needs sharpening. What do we mean by *nature*? In most of the literature, nature is defined as any place that is green. However, evolutionarily speaking, nature should specifically refer to the savannah/forest edge environments in which our hominid ancestors began to become what we recognize as human (Walter, 2013). Should we expect natural affinities toward beautiful, but resource-scarce alpine environments and deserts? Relatedly, none of the research has exposed participants to any of the harsher elements of the natural environment. What would we predict if participants were in a bug-infested environment with extreme temperatures, precipitation, and hungry predators?

There is more work to be done in this area. The evidence is consistent with the evolutionary perspective, but it is unclear whether the apparent nature affinity is caused by evolution or by other factors. However, this area of research is interesting and promising, and the problems are potentially surmountable.

BEHAVIOR IS RARELY A FUNCTION OF GENES ALONE

It is clear that happiness is heritable. The twin studies described earlier demonstrate this, and evidence from the nature–urban comparison studies are also consistent with this conclusion, as are the behavior/response studies. Our genes have an important influence on our feelings of well-being. However, some researchers may have overstated this point. Tellegen and colleagues (1988), who conducted the first twin study we reviewed in this chapter, estimated that about half the differences in individuals' personalities is explained by genetic factors (see also Lykken & Tellegen, 1996). Furthermore, they concluded that because of measurement error inherent in psychological scales, ". . . the environmentally based trait variance may not amount to more than 20 to 35% [of the differences between individuals' personalities]. . . . It seems reasonable to conclude that personality differences are more influenced by genetic diversity than they are by environmental diversity" (Tellegen et al., 1988, p. 1036). Later in their article, they claim that environments make a "very modest" (p. 1037) contribution to personality. Stated more clearly and bluntly, it might not be possible to increase individuals' happiness because of the overpowering effects of genetics (Franz et al., 2012).

But as I have hinted, this is not the case. Genes matter, but environments do also. Evolutionary psychologists have long recognized that human behavior is the interactive product of both genes and environment. Specifically, social and physical environments can affect the expression of genetic factors (Buss, 2004; Kenrick, 1987; Kenrick, Li, & Butner, 2003; Kenrick, Maner, Butner, Li, Becker, & Schaller, 2002).

This essential insight also applies to human well-being. *Epigenetics*, the study of how developmental processes affect the expression of genes (Holliday, 1987, 2006), indicates that environmental events can influence whether genes are activated or not, thus providing an example of gene–environment interaction. Research on both humans and animals indicate that this process is partly caused by stressors, leading to the addition of certain alkyls to elements of DNA. This is referred to as *methylation*. These alkyls then influence whether genes express themselves or not (Hing, Gardner, & Potash, 2014). For example, Hing et al. (2014) concluded from their review of the literature that the process of methylation plays a role in some suicides and that it also mediates the relationship between chronic work stress and burnout among nurses and between child abuse and depression. Thus, although genes are important, the environment matters too.

Genetic *variability* may also produce interactions between genes and the environment. Duncan, Pollastri, and Smoller's (2014) review of the literature found that genetic variability in serotonin functioning interacted with the environment to affect human moods. Although there has been difficulty replicating some findings (Munafò, Durrant, Lewis, & Flint, 2009; Risch et al., 2009), Duncan and her colleagues found preliminary support for three separate gene/environment interactions involving serotonin that predicted antisocial behavior, anxiety, and depression. For example, Cicchetti, Rogosch, and Sturge-Apple (2007) found higher levels of depression and anxiety among low socioeconomic youths who had *both* a genetic marker for this malady *and* a history of sexual abuse.

Here are important details about Cicchetti et al.'s study. They identified whether these adolescents had been maltreated (physically abused, sexually abused, neglected, or not maltreated). They also classified them as having differing alleles of a gene known to influence serotonin levels, a neurotransmitter associated with well-being. Previous research indicated that the "short" allele and other alleles that are functionally equivalent promoted lower levels of serotonin than did the "long" allele. Interestingly, a history of sexual abuse was associated with more symptoms of depression and anxiety for all the youth, regardless of which version of the gene they had. And even more importantly, environmental influences *interacted* with genetic traits such that the short allele (the marker for depression and anxiety) was associated with higher levels of symptoms *only* for the youth who had been sexually abused.

Thus, this research shows that genetics can produce a vulnerability factor that can predispose an individual toward an emotional state. But, in this case genetics alone does not produce anxiety and depression. Cicchetti et al. (2007) and other researchers (e.g.,

Dalton, Hammen, Najman, & Brennan, 2014) have even examined combinations of genetic markers for depression and anxiety, and still found that predictions of anxiety and depression were improved by also considering environmental factors. And remember that there was no relationship between allele type and symptoms in Cicchetti et al.'s study. Instead, the genetic marker expressed itself only in a particular environment (when the youth had been sexually abused). All of this research is consistent with an interactionist perspective. The important point is that our genes are not our destiny, and that our environment matters.

Here is another example of how genetics and our social environment can interact. Marital status (and cohabitation) affect the strength of the relationship between genes and happiness. Nes, Røysamb, Harris, Czajkowski, and Tambs (2010) examined a large sample of fraternal and identical twin pairs (4,462 individuals) in Norway and replicated earlier findings that genetic similarities were related to similarities in well-being. However, they also found that these genetic influences were larger among single men and women than they were among married individuals of both sexes.

Why would this be? Nes et al. (2010) explain the decrease in genetic influence on happiness among marrieds by arguing that the marriage environment is high in *social control*. That is, in marriage there are rather strict social constraints on behavior. As such, the environment can minimize the effect of genetically influenced personality differences on behavior and emotions. This is a classic case of how genes and environments can interact. When the social environment is strong enough to constrain behaviors, individuals respond more strongly according to the influences of that environment, and genes have a reduced influence.

We learn in this and later chapters that our own behaviors also matter. We can significantly increase our happiness. I describe some suggestions made by evolutionary psychologists at the end of this chapter. Later in the book we meet Dr. Sonja Lyubomirsky, a leading researcher in positive psychology, who estimates that about 40% of our happiness is under our control (Lyubomirsky, 2008). Lyubomirsky has conducted important research testing this idea and demonstrated that intentional choices we make about how we construe the world around us have a large impact on our happiness.

CONTRIBUTIONS OF THE EVOLUTIONARY PERSPECTIVE TO UNDERSTANDING HAPPINESS

Now that we have established the validity of the evolutionary perspective, what does this idea contribute to our understanding of happiness? One answer is a different understanding of "The Core Dilemma of Modernity" (Nesse, 2004, 2005). The dilemma is that happiness has apparently stopped increasing, particularly in the West, despite tremendous gains in human health and wealth. Nesse argues that because of our technologies, most Westerners no longer suffer from material wants such as hunger, cold, pain, and sickness the way people did only a relatively short time ago. However, these wondrous technological miracles have not led to general and widespread happiness. The question then is, why not, and what can be done to increase happiness? Nesse argues that evolutionary psychology offers a promising roadmap for answering these questions.

The short answer, according to the evolutionary perspective, is twofold (Hill & Buss, 2008; Nesse, 2004, 2005). First, although basic safety and comfort concerns are central to an evolutionary understanding of behavior, they are not the ultimate human motivations. Affiliation with peers and strategic allies and successful reproduction, including close and meaningful mentoring contact with children and grandchildren, are vitally important from an evolutionary perspective. These activities may not be a prominent feature of modern life (Hill & Buss, 2008). Second, evolution probably selected for certain negative emotions, making them potentially part of the human condition. This does not mean that happiness is unattainable, but it does imply that specific strategies might be needed to address these features of human psychology. I discuss these issues in more detail later in the chapter, but let us first consider the general contributions and the roadmap offered by evolutionary psychology.

New Questions About Core Motivations

One important contribution made by evolutionary psychology is that it prompts us to examine and ask questions about core human goals (Nesse, 2004, 2005). For example, rather than merely addressing proximal mechanisms such as, "Are people happier when they have certain kinds of social relationships?" evolution can help us ask why these relationships are fulfilling. Is it because they fulfill adaptive needs? This emphasis on core motivations can provide a deeper understanding. We can know more than merely whether two variables are related (do social relations predict well-being?); we can begin to understand why this relationship exists. It can also help frame and guide future research. We can refer to evolution for suggestions about other factors that may influence human well-being.

One example is a reinterpretation of Maslow's (1943) famous hierarchy of human needs by Kenrick, Griskevicius, Neuberg, and Schaller (2010). You may remember that Maslow's hierarchy proceeds in sequence from the base need of immediate physiological needs to safety, love, esteem, and, finally, self-actualization. Kenrick, Griskevicius, et al.'s (2010) alternative hierarchy again starts with immediate physiological needs and continues in sequence to self-protection, affiliation, status/esteem, mate acquisition, mate retention, and, finally, parenting. Note the emphasis on evolutionary motives with affiliation, which was important to survival for our relatively weak-limbed hominid ancestors, to status/esteem, which would have helped our ancestors acquire and protect resources and mating opportunities, and the final three mating needs, which are obviously important in evolution (Buss, 2004).

Kenrick, Griskevicius, et al. (2010) make only general references to human well-being, but the implications of their model are clear. Satisfying our base physiological needs is necessary for happiness, but it is only a start (remember the core dilemma of modernity). We also need to affiliate with others and to receive status and esteem from our peers. And, to be fully happy, we need to be involved in the reproductive process that includes love, cooperation, and parenting/mentoring behaviors. The important point is that Kenrick, Griskevicius, et al.'s model is an example of how evolutionary psychology's focus on core motivations might help shape research in the psychology of happiness.

Negative emotions offer another example of how the examination of core motivations might increase our understanding of human happiness. Outside of an evolutionary framework, the typical theoretician's response to negative emotions seems to be a puzzled exasperation based on the assumption that negative emotions are somehow "unnatural" and unnecessary. However, according to evolutionary psychology, negative (and positive) emotions are quite "natural" and understandable (they solved adaptive needs of our ancestors) if core motivations are considered (Hill & Buss, 2008; Nesse, 2004, 2005).

Dissatisfied by Design

Why are people so often unhappy and dissatisfied, even in the United States, with our material abundance? As I have hinted several times in this chapter, the evolutionary perspective suggests that negative emotions have been selected for because they offered adaptive advantages to our ancestors (Hill & Buss, 2008; Nesse, 2004, 2005). This prompted Hill and Buss (2008) to coin the subtitle I borrowed for this section: Dissatisfied by Design. This insight is so important that you should take a moment to let it soak in.

Think about it for a moment: Our ancestors who were inclined to some degree of unhappiness were more likely to survive and successfully reproduce. The hypothesis is that we would not be here if our ancestors had not been this way. And we now have their genes, and their emotional inclinations. The implication is that negative emotions are not an "unnatural" condition, at least in the sense that at one time they were adaptive. Evolution "designed" us to have some degree of unhappiness and dissatisfaction.

The "smoke detector principle" is an example of this logic (Nesse, 2004, 2005). Nesse (2004) argues that "false alarms" would have been evolutionarily advantageous even at the cost of low level generalized anxiety and the resultant unnecessary expenditure of energy.

> . . . if successful panic flight costs 200 calories but being clawed by a tiger costs the equivalent of, say, 20 000 calories, then it will be worthwhile to flee in panic whenever the probability of a tiger being present is greater than 1%. This means that the normal system will express 99 false alarms for every time a tiger is actually present; the associated distress is unnecessary in almost all individual instances. Blocking the tendency to panic would be an unalloyed good. Except, that is, for that 1 time in 100. This has been called the "smoke detector principle" after our willingness to accept false alarms from making toast because we want a smoke detector that will give early warning about any and every actual fire. (Nesse, 2004, p. 1338)

Therefore, the negative emotion of anxiety is quite normal, at least at certain levels. Evolution "designed" humans to have this unpleasant characteristic.

Similar logic applies to other negative emotions such as envy and greed. Emotions are not "good" or "bad," but are simply a method that evolution uses to communicate pending adaptive successes or failures to individuals (Cosmides & Tooby, 2000; Hill & Buss, 2008). Buss (1989a; Hill & Buss, 2008) proposed Strategic Interference Theory to explain these effects. The theory posits that negative emotions such as anger, jealousy, and upset result when our efforts to obtain evolutionarily relevant goals are blocked (i.e., there is strategic interference). The resulting negative emotions are evolved reactions that signal interference and motivate us to remove or reduce that interference. In other words, negative emotions tell us that something is wrong and that we need to fix the problem. Hill and Buss (2008) note a host of emotions that evidence indicates have evolved because of their ability to signal interference with evolutionary goals: envy, anxiety, depression, fears and phobias, sexual jealousy, low self-esteem, anger, and upset.

Evolution also appears to diminish happiness because of natural selection pressures on mating and reproduction. These pressures may produce tension between men and women because of the potential for the sexes to use different mating strategies (Buss, 1995, 2000, 2004). We have already discussed the principle of differential parental investment (Trivers, 1972), which predicts that women will be sexually choosy compared to men. This result suggests evolutionary processes behind the often recognized tendency for men to be more casual about sex than women (Buss, 1989b, 2004; Clark & Hatfield, 1989). It may also be a source of conflict between men and women because they are pursuing different goals. Unhappiness is likely to result if commitment-averse men interact with commitment-seeking women.

These evolutionary mating pressures may also produce *intra*-sexual tension. That is, evolution may produce tension between men competing among themselves for women, as well as among women competing among themselves for men (Buss, 2004). Again, let me provide a little background theory. *Sexual selection* was one of Darwin's (1859) hypotheses, and a close cousin of natural selection. Sexual selection occurs when individuals show preferences for (heterosexual) sexual partners with specific characteristics. These preferences then determine which individuals are most likely to mate. For example, research indicates that women tend to select male sexual partners who are physically and socially dominant (Sadalla, Kenrick, & Vershure, 1987) and who have acquired resources (Buss, 1989b; Kenrick & Keefe, 1992; Kenrick, Sadalla, Groth, & Trost, 1990). Thus, men are set in competition among themselves to establish dominance and acquire financial resources in order to attract women (Buss, 2004). Although men are relatively less choosy, they prefer younger and more physically attractive women (Buss, 1989b; Kenrick & Keefe, 1992). Therefore, women compete among themselves to establish hierarchies of beauty (Buss, 2004). All this competition is also likely to produce unhappiness.

In fact, this sort of competition is such a general phenomenon that Hill and Buss (2006, 2008) refer to it as the *positional bias*, in which individuals are hypothesized to be more concerned with their relative status in a variety of domains than they are with their absolute level of standing. For example, the positional bias predicts that I care more about how much money I have compared to how much you have than about my absolute level of wealth.

You can probably see the evolutionary logic here. It is all about competition for resources and mates. If I have more than you, I have an advantage over you and more access to mates (Hill & Buss, 2008). This topic is explored further in Chapter 6, but there is an unfortunate consequence that goes beyond mere competition and the strife that it may bring. Hill and Buss (2008) argue that the positional bias also makes it hard for us to *ever* be completely satisfied with our level of material wealth. Because relative position is so important, we always have the feeling that there is more out there to acquire and that someone else may get it before we do.

This is not a recipe for long-term happiness, but it does make evolutionary sense. Our (in this case male) ancestors who acted as if they were motivated by the positional bias were probably more likely to survive because of the resources they acquired. They were also likely to mate more often, again because of the resources they acquired. Knowing whom to blame for the source of such unhappiness (some distant great grandfather × $10^{1,000}$) may be some consolation, but it probably does not reduce the harm the positional bias causes. Fortunately, Hill and Buss (2008) offer some evolutionarily based suggestions for defeating the positional bias that I discuss toward the end of this chapter.

Evolutionary Pathways Are Likely Indirect

It is important to realize that happiness is not likely "directly encoded in the genes" (Nesse, 2004, p. 1335, see also Nesse, 2005). Therefore, the effects of genes on well-being, although they are real and important, are likely indirect. The positional bias is an example. We probably all inherit the tendency to have difficult-to-satisfy material desires, although there are also probably individual differences in how strongly we have this trait. This behavioral tendency then leads us to engage in behaviors that are likely to affect our happiness (Nesse, 2005). As I mentioned, there is not likely to be "a gene" or a set of genes that directly influences our happiness, particularly without some input from the environment. Another example of the indirect effect of our genes is that we may inherit a tendency to experience various life events (Nesse, 2004). This again argues against the direct gene-to-happiness hypothesis. Instead, genes may steer us (but not command us) toward certain environmental experiences, which then affect our happiness.

EVOLUTIONARY PATHS TO HAPPINESS

Find Your Inner Caveperson

So, what can be done? As I have indicated, evolutionary psychologists have some suggestions for increasing our happiness. These suggestions generally involve recapturing our inner caveperson, and thinking about what made our prehistoric ancestors happy (Hill & Buss, 2008; Nesse, 2005). You might already be thinking about some of these suggestions.

According to evolution (Hill & Buss, 2008), our ancestors were happy when they had satisfying relationships with close family members, when they had healthy and thriving children and grandchildren, and when they felt integrated into larger social networks that were really extended kinship groups of between 50 and 200 people. In other words, our ancestors were surrounded by close allies and a strong sense of community. They also did work that was directly relevant to their survival, including activities such as hunting and foraging, building shelter, making clothing, and attending to illnesses.

Finally, it is also constructive to think about things they did *not* do, one of which was attend to electronic media. Hill and Buss (2008) argue that our distant ancestors were not exposed to media portrayals of others who were impossibly rich and/or impossibly attractive. Remember the positional bias? Think about what motivations and emotions common media images might spark in us today. However, our ancestors were likely surrounded by others who were fairly similar to themselves. Although there were certainly individual differences in wealth and attractiveness, these differences were probably relatively narrow. They were not subjected to the tricks of modern video imagery, including camera angles, lighting, and makeup, that can produce impressions of attractiveness that few, if any, of us can compete with.

Social Connections Are Paramount

What are the evolutionary strategies for enhancing happiness? Hill and Buss (2008) suggest several strategies, including generally trying to reduce the discrepancies between how we live and how our prehistoric ancestors lived. Fortunately, their suggestions do not include wearing loinclothes, giving up indoor plumbing and penicillin, and chasing deer and bunny rabbits with clubs. They do suggest trying to recapture the sense of community and social connection that our ancestors must have had. For instance, they argue that our modern way of living in isolated suburban lots, disconnected from extended family and other allies, is not a recipe for well-being. They also suggest using modern technology to enhance and maintain social relationships. For instance, airplanes and social media may help us nurture and maintain social ties with others who are distant from us, either because of geography or because of lack of time. Modern Internet dating sites might help us create new satisfying relationships that are evolutionarily meaningful.

It is also important to emphasize cooperation with other individuals. Much of this chapter has focused on the competitive motivations we inherited via evolution, such as the positional bias. These motivations are real and are an essential product of the struggle for survival in evolution (Axelrod & Hamilton, 1981; Buss, 2004; Nowak, 2006). However, cooperation is also an important part of human behavior, and it likely has evolutionary roots (Axelrod & Hamilton, 1981; Buss, 2004; Henrich & Henrich, 2006; Nowak, 2006; Tomasello, Melis, Tennie, Wyman, & Herrmann, 2012; Walter, 2013). Remember that humans evolved in close kinship groups and that cooperation within these groups was likely essential for individual and group survival (Buss, 2004; Tomasello et al., 2012; Walter, 2013). Although cooperation might seem unlikely in the savage and amoral universe of evolution by natural selection (if you help me, you are helping a potential competitor and my genes), evolutionists have discovered several mechanisms that favor cooperative behavior. For instance, helping kin, and reciprocal helping, in which partners trade favors, can both be favored by evolution (Axelrod & Hamilton, 1981; Buss, 2004; Nowak, 2006; Tomasello et al., 2012).

And cooperation, rather than unmitigated competition, is likely to foster happiness because our ancestors relied on it, and because it is essential for establishing meaningful social connections. And deep and meaningful social connections are essential for human happiness (Baumeister & Leary, 1995). In short, cooperation is likely to often be satisfying in and of itself because it helps address innate goals (as discussed in the next section), and because it leads to friendship. However, keep in mind that in an evolutionary sense cooperating is not the same thing as being taken advantage of. Evolutionists would not expect us to be happy if we cooperated with pirates bent solely on exploiting us. Again, cooperation with kin or similar others, and in a reciprocating fashion, is likely to be rewarding.

Satisfy Innate Desires and Goals

We can also increase our happiness by recognizing and moving to satisfy evolutionarily relevant goals (Hill & Buss, 2008). For instance, we are evolved toward desiring physical and material security, respect from our peers, and strong social ties, particularly with kin. Hill and Buss (2008) argue that accomplishing these tasks elevates our well-being. Furthermore, they conclude from their review of the literature that moving toward these goals may be as important for our happiness as actually accomplishing them. As long as we perceive that we are making progress toward accomplishing these evolutionary relevant goals, our happiness increases.

We should also consider how the pursuit of modern goals matches that of ancestral goals (Nesse, 2005). Nesse argues that the size and duration of modern goals is very different than those of our ancestors. For instance, our ancestors might have a goal to gather nuts or fruit. This goal might take a few days, and the results of their efforts would be readily apparent and immediately satisfying. Compare this task to someone training to be an Olympic athlete, pursuing a PhD, studying to be a concert pianist, or climbing the corporate ladder.

According to Nesse (2005), these modern pursuits are long and open ended and contain relatively few satisfying, readily apparent, and evolutionarily meaningful rewards along the way. Therefore, they are less satisfying. Furthermore, these modern goals require greater levels of commitment and therefore may be harder to give up on than were ancestral goals. For instance, our prehistoric ancestors who were having trouble finding fruits and nuts one day might easily have decided to switch to foraging for roots and berries that day instead. But think about how difficult and psychologically painful it might be to give up on a PhD program after investing several years of study with little tangible benefit to show for it. The PhD student has learned and presumably acquired some new skills but does not have a store full of berries gathered to show for the efforts. In fact, Nesse argues that modern goals often require so much commitment that they detract from other important evolutionary priorities. For instance, our starving piano student might spend so much time practicing that little time is left for family and friends.

The implication here is that we need to be careful pursuing modern goals of success. If our happiness is important to us, we need to make sure that our success goals do not interfere with other important goals such as nurturing family life. In addition, we need to find ways to tangibly recognize and celebrate incremental successes. For instance, although the life of a PhD student can be lonely and isolating, graduate students typically celebrate when a peer passes the first statistics test, finishes the first year in the program, completes a master's thesis, publishes a first journal article, completes the comprehensive exams, finishes and defends a dissertation, and lands a first teaching job. These incremental celebrations are rewarding and perhaps mimic the smaller scale successes of our ancestors.

Defeat the Positional Bias

Interestingly, the positional bias does not occur in all areas of human life (Hill & Buss, 2008). For instance, people do not show the positional bias in terms of the length of time they wish to remain married and the length of their vacations (Hill & Buss, 2008). Hill and Buss suggest shifting attention away from positional bias-threatened domains to other areas of life. They also suggest that we should look for ways to minimize the threat of the positional bias in areas like wealth and beauty. Specifically, they suggest we consider "media fasts" in which we limit our exposure to modern media (e.g., some television shows, fashion and lifestyle magazines, and so on) that depict unrealistic examples of wealth and beauty.

Some psychologists have begun to develop evolutionarily based psychotherapies. For example, an approach building on attachment theory (Bowlby, 1970, 1977; Gilbert, 2002) proposes that evolution has produced two basic systems for the human brain to organize information. One is the *defense system*, which monitors and responds to threats. The other is the *safeness system*, which seeks and responds to potential rewards. According to Gilbert, these systems of organizing information and thought were essential for human survival in our prehistoric past. Furthermore, because of our early socio-conditioning history as children and because of roles we currently occupy, we can feel relatively optimistic and safe, or we can feel defensive (Gilbert, 2002). This potential to feeling overly defensive can create psychological problems. Gilbert suggests that cognitive therapies designed to defuse this defensiveness can benefit many individuals.

SUMMARY

Evolution offers a unique perspective on the psychology of happiness, suggesting that dissatisfaction with our lives may be a normal part of the human experience. For instance, our ancestors may have needed to be anxious and envious in order to survive and reproduce successfully. We may have those same traits because we inherited their genes. An impressive array of research examining twins, human physiology, and human behavior is consistent with this perspective.

Therefore, the evolutionary perspective offers key insights into humans' core motivations. These involve attempts to solve basic evolutionary problems such as creating secure social bonds, finding mates, and maintaining physical safety. Evolution also offers concrete suggestions for improving our happiness. According to this perspective we are happier when we are surrounded by close social relationships, when our physical needs are met, and when we are not tempted by modern society to be overly envious of others.

REFERENCES

Ackerman, J. M., Griskevicius, V., & Li, N. P. (2011). Let's get serious: Communicating commitment in romantic relationships. *Journal of Personality and Social Psychology, 100*(6), 1079–1094.

Anderson, K. G., Kaplan, H., & Lancaster, J. (1999). Paternal care by genetic fathers and stepfathers I: Reports from Albuquerque men. *Evolution and Human Behavior, 20*(6), 405–431.

Axelrod, R., & Hamilton, W. (1981). The evolution of cooperation. *Science, 211*, 1390–1396.

Baker, R. R., & Bellis, M. A. (1993). Human sperm competition: Ejaculate manipulation by females and a function for the female orgasm. *Animal Behaviour, 46*(5), 887–909.

Baumeister, R. F., & Leary, M. R. (1995). The need to belong: Desire for interpersonal attachments as a fundamental human motivation. *Psychological Bulletin, 117*(3), 497–529.

Bowlby, J. (1970). Disruption of affectional bonds and its effects on behavior. *Journal of Contemporary Psychotherapy, 2*(2), 75–86.

Bowlby, J. (1977). The making and breaking of affectional bonds: I. Aetiology and psychopathology in the light of attachment theory. *British Journal of Psychiatry, 130*, 201–210.

Buss, D. M. (1989a). Conflict between the sexes: Strategic interference and the evocation of anger and upset. *Journal of Personality and Social Psychology, 56*(5), 735–747.

Buss, D. M. (1989b). Sex differences in human mate preferences: Evolutionary hypotheses tested in 37 cultures. *Behavioral and Brain Sciences, 12*, 1–49.

Buss, D. M. (1990). The evolution of anxiety and social exclusion. *Journal of Social and Clinical Psychology, 9*(2), 196–201.

Buss, D. M. (1995). Evolutionary psychology: A new paradigm for psychological science. *Psychological Inquiry, 6*(1), 1–30.

Buss, D. M. (2000). The evolution of happiness. *American Psychologist, 55*(1), 15–23.

Buss, D. M. (2004). *Evolutionary psychology: The new science of the mind* (2nd ed.). Needham Heights, MA: Allyn & Bacon.

Capaldi, C. A., Dopko, R. L., & Zelenski, J. M. (2014). The relationship between nature connectedness and happiness: A meta-analysis. *Frontiers in Psychology, 5*, 1–15.

Cicchetti, D., Rogosch, F., & Sturge-Apple, M. (2007). Interactions of child maltreatment and serotonin transporter and monoamine oxidase A polymorphisms: Depressive symptomatology among adolescents from low socioeconomic status backgrounds. *Development and Psychopathology, 19*, 1161–1180.

Clark, R. D., & Hatfield, E. (1989). Gender differences in receptivity to sexual offers. *Journal of Psychology and Human Sexuality, 2*(1), 39–55.

Cosmides, L., & Tooby, J. (2000). Evolutionary psychology and the emotions. In M. Lewis & J. M. Haviland-Jones (Eds.), *Handbook of emotions* (2nd ed., pp. 91–115). New York, NY: Guilford Press.

Dalton, E., Hammen, C., Najman, J., & Brennan, P. (2014). Genetic susceptibility to family environment: BDNF Val66met and 5-HTTLPR Influence Depressive Symptoms. *Journal of Family Psychology, 28*(6), 947–956.

Darwin, C. (1859). *On the origin of the species.* London, UK: Murray.

DeWall, C. N., & Bushman, B. J. (2011). Social acceptance and rejection: The sweet and the bitter. *Current Directions in Psychological Science, 20*(4), 256–260.

Duncan, L. E., Pollastri, A. R., & Smoller, J. W. (2014). Mind the gap: Why many geneticists and psychological scientists have discrepant views about gene–environment interaction (GxE) research. *American Psychologist, 69*(3), 249–268.

Franz, C. E., Panizzon, M. S., Eaves, L. J., Thompson, W., Lyons, M. J., Jacobson, K. C., . . . Kremen, W. S. (2012). Genetic and environmental multidimensionality of well- and ill-being in middle aged twin men. *Behavior Genetics, 42*(4), 579–591.

Gangestad, S. W., Garver-Apgar, C. E., Simpson, J. A., & Cousin, A. J. (2007). Changes in women's mate preferences across the ovulatory cycle. *Journal of Personality and Social Psychology, 92*, 151–163.

Gilbert, P. (2002). Evolutionary approaches to psychopathology and cognitive therapy. *Journal of Cognitive Psychotherapy, 16*(3), 263–294.

Hartig, T., Evans, G. W., Jamner, L. D., Davis, D. S., & Gärling, T. (2003). Tracking restoration in natural and urban field settings. *Journal of Environmental Psychology, 23*(2), 109–123.

Henrich, J., & Henrich, N. (2006). Culture, evolution and the puzzle of human cooperation. *Cognitive Systems Research, 7*(2–3), 220–245.

Hill, S. E., & Buss, D. M. (2006). Envy and positional bias in the evolutionary psychology of management. *Managerial and Decision Economics, 27*(2–3), 131–143.

Hill, S. E., & Buss, D. M. (2008). Evolution and subjective well-being. In M. Eid & R. J. Larsen (Eds.), *The science of subjective well-being* (pp. 62–79). New York, NY: Guilford Press.

Hing, B., Gardner, C., & Potash, J. B. (2014). Effects of negative stressors on DNA methylation in the brain: Implications for mood and anxiety disorders. *American Journal of Medical Genetics Part B: Neuropsychiatric Genetics, 165*(7), 541 554.

Holliday, R. (1987). The inheritance of epigenetic defects. *Science, 238*(4824), 163–170.

Holliday, R. (2006). Epigenetics: A historical overview. *Epigenetics, 1*(2), 76–80.

Howell, A. J., Dopko, R. L., Passmore, H., & Buro, K. (2011). Nature connectedness: Associations with well-being and mindfulness. *Personality and Individual Differences, 51*(2), 166–171.

Kaplan, R., & Kaplan, S. (1989). *The experience of nature: A psychological perspective.* New York, NY: Cambridge University Press.

Kenrick, D. T. (1987). Gender, genes, and the social environment: A biosocial interactionist perspective. In P. Shaver & C. Hendrick (Eds.), *Sex and gender* (pp. 14–43). Thousand Oaks, CA: Sage.

Kenrick, D. T., Griskevicius, V., Neuberg, S. L., & Schaller, M. (2010). Renovating the pyramid of needs: Contemporary extensions built upon ancient foundations. *Perspectives on Psychological Science, 5*(3), 292–314.

Kenrick, D. T., & Keefe, R. C. (1992). Age preferences in mates reflect sex differences in mating strategies. *Behavioral and Brain Sciences, 15*, 75–91.

Kenrick, D. T., Li, N. P., & Butner, J. (2003). Dynamical evolutionary psychology: Individual decision rules and emergent social norms. *Psychological Review, 110*(1), 3–28.

Kenrick, D. T., Maner, J., Butner, J., Li, N., Becker, D., & Schaller, M. (2002). Dynamical evolutionary psychology: Mapping the domains of the new interactionist paradigm. *Personality and Social Psychology Review, 6*(4), 347–356.

Kenrick, D. T., Neuberg, S. L., Griskevicius, V., Becker, D. V., & Schaller, M. (2010). Goal-driven cognition and functional behavior: The fundamental-motives framework. *Current Directions in Psychological Science, 19*(1), 63–67.

Kenrick, D. T., Sadalla, E. K., Groth, G., & Trost, M. R. (1990). Evolution, traits, and the stages of human courtship: Qualifying the parental investment model. *Journal of Personality, 58*(1), 97–116.

Keyes, C. L. M., Myers, J. M., & Kendler, K. S. (2010). The structure of the genetic and environmental influences on mental well-being. *American Journal of Public Health, 100*(12), 2379–2384.

Krebs, D. (2011). *The origins of morality: An evolutionary account.* New York, NY: Oxford University Press.

Lindfors, P. (2013). *Physiological correlates of mental well-being.* New York, NY: Springer Science + Business Media.

Lloyd, E. A. (2005). *The case of the female orgasm: Bias in the science of evolution.* Cambridge, MA: Harvard University Press.

Lykken, D., & Tellegen, A. (1996). Happiness is a stochastic phenomenon. *Psychological Science, 7*(3), 186–189.

Lyubomirsky, S. (2008). *The how of happiness: A new approach to getting the life you want.* New York, NY: Penguin Press.

Maslow, A. (1943). A theory of human motivation. *Psychological Review, 50,* 370–396.

Mayer, F. S., Frantz, C. M., Bruehlman-Senecal, E., & Dolliver, K. (2009). Why is nature beneficial? The role of connectedness to nature. *Environment and Behavior, 41*(5), 607–643.

McDermott, R., Fowler, J. H., & Smirnov, O. (2008). On the evolutionary origin of prospect theory preferences. *The Journal of Politics, 70*(2), 335–350.

Munafò, M. R., Durrant, C., Lewis, G., & Flint, J. (2009). Gene × environment interactions at the serotonin transporter locus. *Biological Psychiatry, 65*(3), 211–219.

Napier, J. L., & Jost, J. T. (2008). Why are conservatives happier than liberals? *Psychological Science, 19*(6), 565–572.

Nes, R. B., Røysamb, E., Harris, J. R., Czajkowski, N., & Tambs, K. (2010). Mates and marriage matter: Genetic and environmental influences on subjective well-being across marital status. *Twin Research and Human Genetics, 13*(4), 312–321.

Nes, R. B., Røysamb, E., Tambs, K., Harris, J. R., & Reichborn-Kjennerud, T. (2006). Subjective well-being: Genetic and environmental contributions to stability and change. *Psychological Medicine, 36*(7), 1033–1042.

Nesse, R. (2004). Natural selection and the elusiveness of happiness. *Philosophical Transactions of the Royal Society B: Biological Sciences, 359,* 1333–1347.

Nesse, R. M. (2005). Natural selection and the regulation of defenses: A signal detection analysis of the smoke detector principle. *Evolution and Human Behavior, 26*(1), 88–105.

Nisbet, E. K., & Zelenski, J. M. (2011). Underestimating nearby nature: Affective forecasting errors obscure the happy path to sustainability. *Psychological Science, 22*(9), 1101–1106.

Nowak, M. (2006). Five rules for the evolution of cooperation. *Science, 314,* 1560–1563.

Panksepp, J. (2007). Neuroevolutionary sources of laughter and social joy: Modeling primal human laughter in laboratory rats. *Behavioural Brain Research, 182*(2), 231–244.

Panksepp, J., & Burgdorf, J. (2003). "Laughing" rats and the evolutionary antecedents of human joy? *Physiology and Behavior, 79*(3), 533–547.

Post, S. G. (2005). Altruism, happiness, and health: It's good to be good. *International Journal of Behavioral Medicine, 12*(2), 66–77.

Puts, D. A., Dawood, K., & Welling, L. L. M. (2012). Why women have orgasms: An evolutionary analysis. *Archives of Sexual Behavior, 41*(5), 1127–1143.

Puts, D. A., Welling, L. L. M., Burriss, R. P., & Dawood, K. (2012). Men's masculinity and attractiveness predict their female partners' reported orgasm frequency and timing. *Evolution and Human Behavior, 33*(1), 1–9.

Risch, N., Herrell, R., Lehner, T., Liang, K., Eaves, L., Hoh, J., . . . Merikangas, K. (2009). Interaction between the serotonin transporter gene (5-HTTLPR), stressful life events, and risk of depression: A meta-analysis. *Journal of the American Medical Association, 301*(23), 2462–2471.

Ryan, R. M., Weinstein, N., Bernstein, J., Brown, K. W., Mistretta, L., & Gagné, M. (2010). Vitalizing effects of being outdoors and in nature. *Journal of Environmental Psychology, 30*(2), 159–168.

Sadalla, E., Kenrick, D., & Vershure, B. (1987). Dominance and heterosexual attraction. *Journal of Personality and Social Psychology, 52*, 730–738.

Schaller, M., & Park, J. H. (2011). The behavioral immune system (and why it matters). *Current Directions in Psychological Science, 20*(2), 99–103.

Steptoe, A., Dockray, S., & Wardle, J. (2009). Positive affect and psychobiological processes relevant to health. *Journal of Personality, 77*(6), 1747–1775.

Tellegen, A., Lykken, D. T., Bouchard, T. J., Wilcox, K. J., Segal, N. L., & Rich, S. (1988). Personality similarity in twins reared apart and together. *Journal of Personality and Social Psychology, 54*(6), 1031–1039.

Tomasello, M., Melis, A., Tennie, C., Wyman, E., & Herrmann, E. (2012). Two key steps in the evolution of human cooperation. *Current Anthropology, 53*(6), 673–692.

Tooby, J., Cosmides, L., & Price, M. E. (2006). Cognitive adaptations for n-person exchange: The evolutionary roots of organizational behavior. *Managerial and Decision Economics, 27*(2–3), 103–129.

Trivers, R. L. (1972). Parental investment and sexual selection. In B. Campbell (Ed.), *Sexual selection and the descent of man, 1871–1971* (pp. 136–179). Chicago, IL: Aldine-Atherton.

van den Berg, A. E., Koole, S. L., & van der Wulp, N. Y. (2003). Environmental preference and restoration: (How) are they related? *Journal of Environmental Psychology, 23*(2), 135–146.

Vigil, J. M. (2010). Political leanings vary with facial expression processing and psychosocial functioning. *Group Processes and Intergroup Relations, 13*(5), 547–558.

Wallen, K., & Lloyd, E. A. (2011). Female sexual arousal: Genital anatomy and orgasm in intercourse. *Hormones and Behavior, 59*(5), 780–792.

Walter, C. (2013). *Last ape standing: The seven-million-year story of how and why we survived.* New York, NY: Walker & Company/Bloomsbury Publishing.

Weinstein, N., Przybylski, A., & Ryan, R. (2009). Can nature make us more caring? Effects of immersion in nature on intrinsic aspirations and generosity. *Personality and Social Psychology Bulletin, 35*(10), 1315–1329.

White, M. P., Alcock, I., Wheeler, B. W., & Depledge, M. H. (2013). Would you be happier living in a greener urban area? A fixed-effects analysis of panel data. *Psychological Science, 24*(6), 920–928.

Wilson, E. (1984). *Biophilia.* Cambridge, MA: Harvard University Press.

Zietsch, B. P., & Santtila, P. (2011). Genetic analysis of orgasmic function in twins and siblings does not support the by-product theory of female orgasm. *Animal Behaviour, 82*(5), 1097–1101.

CHAPTER **3**

Personality

Happiness depends on ourselves.

—Aristotle

We all know people who are characterologically happy or unhappy. One of the strongest memories of my childhood is of my grade school bus driver, Mr. Echols. His son and I played together on a baseball team one summer in the small Alabama city where I grew up. We didn't just play Little League; we played "Dixie Youth" baseball. We lived in a town where our family doctor had separate waiting rooms for Whites and Blacks. My family and I were White; Mr. Echols and his family, Black.

Mr. Echols was strong and dignified. He was also optimistic and positive. He always had a smile and a story for us to start the day, and he was a great whistler. He was kind and understanding to schoolchildren, even when we didn't deserve it. He was this way despite many circumstances in life that were stacked against him. First, he was a Black man living in a time and place constrained by rigid segregation. He was also poor. But he wasn't a pushover, and he didn't allow people to demean him.

My impression was (and is) that Mr. Echols was genuinely happy, despite his circumstances. He worked hard and had a loving family. He treated others with respect, as he expected to be treated. He found joy someplace in each day. He wasn't part of the White stereotype of a happy Black man who simply smiled to appease the White power structure. Instead, he actively resisted that power structure. I have often wondered how he found within himself the ability to find happiness despite these circumstances. What in his personality allowed him to do this? In this chapter I offer some clues.

PERSONALITY AND HAPPINESS

Important Personality Predictors of Happiness

In psychological parlance, *personality* refers to stable behavioral patterns within an individual that remain fairly consistent across differing circumstances (Kenrick & Funder,

1988). As you have probably observed, some people are naturally happier than others, despite external circumstances. Perhaps you know someone like Mr. Echols. There are individuals who remain consistently happy, or unhappy, largely regardless of life circumstances. These individuals tend to have a consistent and predictable set of traits that are associated with their happiness levels. We also see that these people have a uniform way of viewing and interpreting the world around them. Thus, we find that there is a personality of happiness.

We begin by looking at the evidence for happy personalities, people who maintain consistent levels of happiness largely regardless of their environment. One way to think about the importance of personality in forming happiness is to consider the impact of personality's opposite force, the environment. While personality is a stable force within a person, the environment is, by definition, outside the person. Therefore, knowing something about the environmental impact on happiness may tell us something about the importance of personality. And researchers have generally concluded that life circumstances and environmental factors have relatively little impact on happiness. For example, Lyubomirsky, Sheldon, and Schkade (2005) reviewed this literature and concluded that life circumstances, such as demographic characteristics, accounted for only about 10% in the differences in individuals' happiness levels.

Being a warm weather transplant to God-forsaken frozen western New York, I have often wondered whether I would be happier if I returned to a warmer climate. Many of the people around me dream of moving to Florida or North Carolina, thinking that they would be much happier. Surely this environmental/life circumstance variable has big effects on our happiness, right?

Surprisingly, the data say otherwise. Lucas and Lawless (2013) examined daily weather data from all 50 of the United States and representative samples of more than a million individuals living in those states. Data collection covered a 5-year period. Results showed that weather was not reliably associated with well-being. So, weather and similar environmental variables do not seem to be strongly associated with well-being. By implication, this suggests that personality is important.

Furthermore, examining the question more directly, research indicates that personality is an important predictor of well-being (DeNeve & Cooper, 1998; Ozer & Benet-Martinez, 2006). A *meta-analysis* (a literature review that statistically combines the results of studies in an area) by DeNeve and Cooper (1998) indicates that personality is a more powerful predictor of well-being than demographic characteristics such as marital status, and is as important as socioeconomic status (defined as a composite of income, education, and occupational status). Furthermore, personality predicts life satisfaction (cognitive well-being) and positive affect equally well but predicts negative affect less well.

In summary, there is evidence for a personality of happiness: stable and consistent levels of happiness within individuals. Environmental factors that include life circumstances seem to have fairly minimal effects on happiness, and personality is predictive. But so far we have discussed personality in a global sense. We now turn to identifying the specific features of personality that predict well-being.

The Big Five

Personality researchers have identified a "Big Five" set of traits that are important predictors of behavior (Costa & McCrae, 1992). This model proposes five independent dimensions[1]:

▶ Agreeableness

▶ Extraversion

▶ Conscientiousness

▶ Neuroticism

▶ Openness to experience

Happiness researchers have extended this research by using the Big Five to predict well-being.

For example, DeNeve and Cooper (1998), who conducted the meta-analysis described previously, found that the Big Five predicted well-being. Specifically, their results indicate that neuroticism predicts all three domains of well-being (life satisfaction and positive and negative affect) more strongly than any other dimension. Of course, neuroticism is negatively related to well-being. Conscientiousness has the strongest positive association with well-being. Extraversion and agreeableness predict positive affect with equal accuracy, and both predict better than do the other dimensions. Openness to experience is not related to well-being. More recent work (Boyce, Wood, & Powdthavee, 2013) has strengthened the conclusion that the Big Five are related to well-being by demonstrating that changes in these personality dimensions predict changes in well-being.

These results for the Big Five dimensions have been confirmed by other research (e.g., Albuquerque, de Lima, Matos, & Figueiredo, 2012; Chamorro-Premuzic, Bennett, & Furnham, 2007; Hayes & Joseph, 2003). The Big Five predict happiness on a societal level as well. McCann (2011) acquired state-level polling data from the 48 contiguous United States. Results indicate that state-level Big Five personality dimension scores predict states' well-being levels. This conclusion is possible because previous researchers had conducted phone surveys of representative samples within each state, assessing state-level personality and well-being characteristics.

Consistent with DeNeve and Cooper's (1998) results, McCann (2011) found that state-level neuroticism is a good predictor of states' well-being. You may be interested to learn that in McCann's findings, New York State had the highest levels of neuroticism and was slightly more than half a standard deviation below average in well-being. Colorado had the lowest level of neuroticism and was about a quarter of a standard deviation above the mean in well-being.

Facets of the Big Five

Each dimension of the Big Five is made up of a number of single measures. DeNeve and Cooper (1998) found that the single measures that best predict life satisfaction are trust, desire for control, emotional stability, and repressive defensiveness. All these correlations were positive, except for repressive defensiveness, which DeNeve and Cooper (1998, p. 216) define as "nonconscious avoidance of threatening information that leads to a denial of the experience and the expression of negative emotions associated with that experience." All of these measures are moderately correlated with life satisfaction.

These findings led subsequent researchers to investigate how *facets*, or subdivisions, of the Big Five personality factors predict well-being. The effort here is to see whether predictions can be strengthened by using a more precisely tailored measure of personality. For instance, the global dimension called "neuroticism" consists of the following six individual measures: anxiety, anger, depression, self-consciousness, impulsiveness, and vulnerability. Scores on each of these measures are compiled in order to form a neuroticism score. The question is whether some subset of these six measures might predict well-being more accurately.

Results show that subdivisions of the Big Five personality dimensions predict well-being more strongly than does the entire dimension. For example, Albuquerque et al. (2012) found that depression and vulnerability, subcomponents of neuroticism, predicted life satisfaction more strongly than does neuroticism as a whole. Specifically, depression and vulnerability account for 21% of the variance in life satisfaction, while the entire neuroticism dimension accounts for only 15%. You may wonder how it can be that fewer measures can predict more accurately. Albuquerque et al. explain that one of the reasons is that items that do not predict well add "error" to the measurement, which reduces the strength of the overall prediction. Similar results were obtained by Quevedo and Abella (2011).

These findings are important because they give a more detailed picture of the specific aspects of personality that are relevant to well-being. For instance, rather than merely knowing that neuroticism in general is negatively related to life satisfaction, Albuquerque et al. (2012) found that vulnerability and depression are particularly important, and more important than the other measures of neuroticism. In addition, Albuquerque et al. found that positive emotions are the most important component of extraversion, and that competence, order, and self-discipline are the most important components of conscientiousness in predicting life satisfaction.

How and Why the Big Five Predict Well-Being

Researchers have wondered how personality combines with other variables to affect well-being. Before I explain the findings here, we need to make a brief methodological side trip. Researchers use a technique called *mediation analysis* that allows them to understand *why* two variables are related.

The basic logic is simple, and I use a metaphor to explain it. We are pretty sure there is a relationship between studying and grades, but no one really thinks that studying directly influences grades. Instead, we realize that (hopefully) studying increases learning, which then directly influences grades. Therefore we can hypothesize a causal chain that looks like the following:

Studying → Learning → Grades

From this diagram we can see that the reason why studying leads to higher grades is that it first increases learning. In fancy terminology, "studying" is the predictor variable, "grades" is the outcome variable, and "learning" is the *mediating variable* (mediator) that explains why the predictor is related to the outcome. We can say that learning *mediates* the relationship between studying and grades.

Finally, it is possible to have either no mediation, partial mediation, or full mediation. No mediation means that the potential mediator we have tested does not explain why the predictor and the outcome are related. Full mediation means that the mediator *fully explains* the relationship between the predictor and the outcome. For instance, if the *only* reason studying leads to better grades is increased learning, then we say the relationship between studying and grades is fully mediated by learning. However, it is possible that the mediator explains only part of the reason why the predictor and outcome are related. For instance, suppose studying increases grades both because it increases learning *and* because it increases students' confidence that they will do well on a test. Here we would say that both learning and confidence partially mediate the relationship.[2] The resulting diagram would look like this:

Emotional Intelligence

Why does personality predict well-being? There appear to be several answers to this question, but one reason is that it promotes *emotional intelligence*. You may already know that emotional intelligence refers to the ability to use information about our own and others' emotions when we interact with others (Mayer, DiPaolo, & Salovey, 1990). Chamorro-Premuzic et al. (2007) found that emotional intelligence partially mediates the relationship between both neuroticism and conscientiousness and happiness, and fully mediates the relationship between agreeableness and happiness.

Thus, the reason why agreeable individuals—that is, people who have traits such as cooperativeness—are happy is that their agreeableness leads them to develop high levels of emotional intelligence. This high level of emotional intelligence is then the *immediate* cause of their happiness. In other words, agreeableness is an important, but distant cause of happiness. It is related to happiness only because it first produces high levels of emotional intelligence.

In addition, *part* of the reason that neuroticism and conscientiousness are related to happiness is that these first lead to higher (in the case of conscientiousness) or lower (in the case of neuroticism) levels of emotional intelligence. Because the relationship between both conscientiousness and neuroticism with happiness is only partially mediated, there are other reasons why these predictors are associated with well-being. However, the current data set did not identify what that other reason(s) might be.

Personal Projects

Other research has investigated the question of how and why personality predicts happiness from a different angle. One effort has examined how our "personal projects" might mediate the relationship between personality and happiness. *Personal projects* are conscious and purposive sets of actions that can be mundane (taking out the trash) or entail great passion and commitment (help Mom deal with her Alzheimer's; Little, 2014).

Albuquerque, de Lima, Matos, and Figueiredo (2013) asked participants to identify all their current and planned personal projects and then to pick seven that best defined who they were. Participants then appraised these projects on a set of cognitive dimensions including importance, challenge, competence, and absorption. These appraisals were then combined to form a measure of personal projects' efficacy. High scores on personal projects' efficacy indicated that participants felt control over their projects and that they expected them to be successful. The interrelations between personal project efficacy, the Big Five personality dimensions, and well-being were then assessed.

Consistent with predictions, Albuquerque et al. (2013) found that personal projects' efficacy mediate the relationship between the Big Five and well-being. Figure 3.1 shows the complete mediation results. The numbers along the lines are path coefficients that indicate the strength and direction (positive or negative) of the relationships.

Note that there are both *indirect* paths from the various dimensions of the Big Five to well-being that pass through personal projects' efficacy (indicating mediation), and *direct* paths from personality to well-being. The presence of direct and indirect paths from a personality dimension to well-being indicates partial mediation, while the presence of only indirect paths indicates full mediation. Take a moment to examine the diagram and see if you can make sense of it.

One interesting finding in Albuquerque et al.'s (2013) results is that relationships of openness to experience, agreeableness, and conscientiousness to life satisfaction are fully mediated. Furthermore, the "paths" from these variables to life satisfaction are positive, indicating that more agreeableness, and so on, are associated with higher levels of life satisfaction. Another interesting finding is that the relationship between neuroticism and life satisfaction is negative and is also partially mediated. What do these results suggest, and why might they be important?

Remember that we started with the question of how and why personality may be related to well-being. Because the relations for openness, agreeableness, and conscientiousness are fully mediated, our feelings that our personal projects are going well and that we are in control of them explain the relationship between these personality variables and life satisfaction. In other words, having a personality that is open, agreeable, and conscientious leads us to feel in control of our personal projects and to feel that they are likely to be successful. These feelings about our personal projects then are the apparent immediate cause of life satisfaction. On the other hand, neuroticism is associated with weaker feelings of being in control over our projects and confidence that

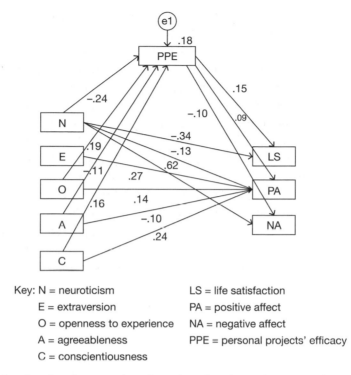

Key: N = neuroticism   LS = life satisfaction
     E = extraversion   PA = positive affect
     O = openness to experience   NA = negative affect
     A = agreeableness   PPE = personal projects' efficacy
     C = conscientiousness

FIGURE 3.1. Results of mediation path analysis show the relationship among the Big Five personality domains (on the left) and the components of a sense of well-being (on the right). Personal projects' efficacy (at the top of the diagram) is a mediator between the Big Five and sense of well-being. Estimates are standardized ($n = 396$).
Adapted from Albuquerque et al. (2013)

they will be successful. This lack of control over our projects and low confidence about their success is then an immediate contributor to low life satisfaction.

I hope this explanation allows you to understand why these mediational analyses are so important. It is important to know that personality predicts life satisfaction. However, this understanding by itself does not tell us anything about why that relationship exists. Merely observing the correlation between personality and well-being does not tell us about the *mechanism* that connects personality to life satisfaction. The mediational analyses allow us to get a glimpse of these mechanisms. Knowing that personality is associated with higher levels of life satisfaction because it helps us feel confident about our life-defining projects and be confident that they will be successful is much more satisfying than knowing only that there is some connection between the two.

Work on identifying mediational relationships between personality and well-being continues to progress. For instance, Pollock, Noser, Holden, and Zeigler-Hill (2016) found that an orientation toward happiness in which individuals look for meaning in their life partially mediated the relationship between extraversion and life satisfaction. In other words, part of the reason why extraverts are more satisfied with their lives is that they look for happiness by trying to find life meaning. All these efforts to identify mediators are exciting and interesting. Researchers will probably start integrating these disparate findings regarding mediators soon. We can expect a comprehensive model that includes all these separate findings to emerge. This model, when it is developed, will give us a much better understanding of why and how personality is associated with well-being.

In summary, the Big Five personality traits are importantly related to well-being. Neuroticism, extraversion, conscientiousness, openness to experience, and agreeableness make up important aspects of the personality of happiness. In addition, facets, or subcomponents, of these major dimensions are also important predictors.

But the most interesting and scientifically fruitful research has examined how and why the Big Five might predict well-being. Although this research has not yet been fully systematized into a single coherent theory, some promising findings have emerged. The Big Five personality traits are related to individuals' ability to understand their own and others' emotions, and this ability facilitates well-being. In addition, the Big Five are also associated with confidence that our own important personal projects are going well. This sense of success enhances well-being. Other research indicates that the Big Five are associated with a sense of life meaning and purpose, which also enhances well-being.

DIFFERENCES BETWEEN HAPPY AND UNHAPPY PEOPLE

Another research tradition has identified individuals who are naturally happy or unhappy, and then compared them to understand how they are different. This is an interesting approach that stands in stark contrast to efforts to identify characteristics that might *predict* who is happy or not. For example, Diener and Seligman (2002) collected a sample of 222 college students and assessed their happiness levels using a variety of measures. They then compared the upper and lower 10% of individuals with individuals in the middle of the happiness distribution.

Results indicated that happy and unhappy individuals had differing personal traits, but not experiences. For instance, the happiest 10% of participants had significantly stronger social ties, were more extraverted and agreeable, and were also less neurotic than other participants. However, the happiest participants did not exercise more, did not participate in more religious activities, and, importantly and perhaps surprisingly, did not experience more positive life events. Thus, the two groups did not differ in their experiences (except perhaps in terms of social ties), but they did differ in the way they interacted with the world: The happier group was more outgoing and agreeable.

Other research further demonstrates that happy individuals view, *interpret,* and interact with the world differently than do the less happy. Otake, Shimai, Tanaka-Matsumi, Otsui, and Fredrickson (2006) found that happy individuals were more focused on gratitude and kindness than were less happy individuals. These researchers divided a sample of Japanese college students at the median on a scale of subjective happiness to create "happy" and "less happy" groups. Happy participants experienced more positive events, and rated those events as more emotionally intense. However, happy and less happy participants did not differ in the number or intensity of negative events. In addition, the content of the happy experiences were very telling. Most of the happy experiences involved positive interactions with other people, particularly involving acts of kindness. The happy individuals recognized these acts and felt gratitude for them.

Thus, the happy individuals did not reach this state because they had fewer bad things happen to them. Instead, they had more good things happen to them, and they recognized these events involved acts of kindness from others. This is such an important point that I want to bring us back to the word *interpret* in the first sentence of the previous paragraph. There is an abundance of evidence, much of which we discuss toward the end of the chapter, that one of the primary differences between happy and unhappy people is how they interpret events around them. The Otake et al. (2006) study is a great example of this research because it demonstrates that happy people appear to be more likely to remember kindnesses, and they also feel more gratitude for these acts.

Other researchers have found similar findings in American samples. For example, Gilman and Huebner (2006) found that happy adolescents were more hopeful and had a stronger sense of control over events than did less happy teens. Similarly, Proctor, Linley, and Maltby (2010) found that happy American adolescents had a stronger sense of life meaning and felt more gratitude than did less happy youth. These results reinforce the idea that the way we view the world and understand the events around us has a strong bearing on our happiness levels. We discuss additional research comparing happy and less happy individuals later in the chapter when we consider a theory of why happier individuals are happier.

There is, indeed, a personality of happiness. Traits and individual differences distinguish between the happy and the less happy, and these traits are largely impervious to situations and are constant over time. Specifically, the Big Five predict well-being, and descriptive studies comparing the traits of happy and less happy individuals indicate marked differences between these two groups. However, it is also important to realize that at this point researchers have not identified a single, unified set of predictors that define *the* personality of happiness. Instead, there is a personality of happiness in the sense that personality is an important contributor to well-being, and not in the sense that there is one set of personality characteristics that is all-powerful.

DOES HAPPINESS CHANGE?

So, there is a personality of happiness. Although the personality of happiness is complex and is certainly not unidimensional, there are multiple personality characteristics that predict well-being. This conclusion may suggest that happiness is therefore fixed and unchangeable, because personality implies consistent and stable traits that do not vary much across situations.

This consideration leads to one of the most fundamentally important questions about happiness. Is happiness changeable? Can we improve our happiness? Or, is our happiness fixed or set within a specific narrow range by personality and genetic factors, such that it bounces up or down slightly from circumstance to circumstance, and from day to day, but always stays within this predetermined range, and always returns to a previous baseline?

These questions have interesting and important philosophical and practical implications. They also get to the heart of any study of personality and happiness. In this section we investigate Set Point Theory, which posits that happiness is not changeable.

Although this theory has been firmly embraced by researchers in the recent past, it is probably no longer tenable. Happiness can and does change.

Keep in mind though that this does not negate the conclusions about personality we have reached in our discussion so far. The fact that happiness can change does not imply that personality does not matter. Instead, most of the time our happiness is fairly stable. But the fact that it can change opens up exciting avenues for research and possible interventions to improve well-being that we discuss later in this chapter.

SET POINT THEORY

For a long time psychologists thought that happiness was relatively fixed, and the idea of a happiness *set point* dominated the field (Headey, 2013). The idea of happiness set points was originally proposed by Lykken and Tellegen (1996), who found strong genetic influences of happiness. The thinking was that because genetics is so important, we adapt quickly to any environmental influence that might jolt our happiness. According to this theory, we experience a transient increase or decrease in happiness because of ongoing events around us but then quickly return to our natural baseline level of well-being.

Therefore, Set Point Theory predicts that happiness is relatively stable across time and across situations. Once an individual's personality becomes well-developed, Set Point Theory predicts that the individual's happiness will not change much over long periods of time. It also predicts that major life events such as marriage, divorce, getting a prestigious new job, or becoming disabled will have only temporary effects on happiness. Although these events will likely raise or lower happiness in the short term, the theory predicts that happiness will return to the previous baseline range relatively quickly. We examine these predictions in the following sections.

How Stable Is Happiness?

Contrary to Set Point Theory, happiness (particularly life satisfaction) is only moderately stable over time (Fujita & Diener, 2005; Lucas & Donnellan, 2007). For example, Fujita and Diener (2005) observed the characteristics such as height, weight, personality, and life satisfaction of a large and representative longitudinal sample of German adults. Some of their results are catalogued in Figure 3.2. The y-axis represents the correlation between a characteristic (inches, pounds, body mass index [BMI], and so on) at the beginning of the study and in a subsequent year. For example, height (inches) was correlated a little over .6 with the original measurement 1 year later. By the end of the study 16 years later, the correlation with the original measure of height (inches) was only a little more than .2. Of course, correlations approaching 1.0 indicate a perfect relationship, and those approaching zero indicate no relationship.

Look at the correlations over time for life satisfaction, and compare them with the other measurements. What jumps out at you from Figure 3.2?

You have probably noticed that, contrary to Set Point Theory, the relationship between any year's life satisfaction measurement and the original measure drops precipitously over time. One year later, life satisfaction still correlates almost .6 with the original

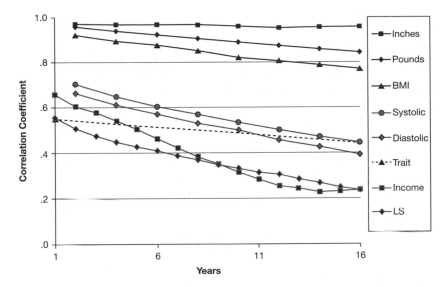

FIGURE 3.2. Comparison of stability of psychological, biological, and financial individual differences in a representative sample of adults.

BMI, body mass index; LS, life satisfaction.

Source: Fujita and Diener (2005).

measure, but 16 years later, the correlation is only a little above .2. This is consistent with quite a bit of instability in life satisfaction. In other words, the data indicate that life satisfaction changes over time. Fujita and Diener (2005) conclude that about 10% of their sample experienced "large" changes in life satisfaction.

In addition, "trait" refers to personality measures. Note that life satisfaction is less stable than personality over time. Fujita and Diener (2005) note that personality affects life satisfaction. They also note that the fact that life satisfaction is less stable than personality traits suggests that environment influences life satisfaction. This observation is also inconsistent with Set Point Theory.

Furthermore, life satisfaction has about the same stability as does income. The authors note that this is a useful comparison because we all have intuitive ideas about how income changes over a life span. Fujita and Diener (2005) argue that although relative income has some stability because social class and education funnels individuals into income groups, we know that some people lose their jobs, for instance, and others do not, and that some individuals advance up the career ladder faster than others with similar backgrounds. This disparity in income level is about the same as the disparity in life satisfaction among individuals. Thus, some people experience significant changes in well-being.

Other research has reinforced this conclusion (Headey, 2013; Li, Yin, Jiang, Wang, & Cai, 2014). Headey (2006, 2008b, 2010) found marked fluctuations in individuals' happiness levels over time. For example, Headey (2010) observed happiness levels among a large representative and longitudinal sample of German adults. He observed changes in happiness of one standard deviation or more among a quarter to a third of the sample of adults aged 25 to 69, the group who is supposed to have the most stability in happiness. This is a large change and is equivalent to moving from the 30th to the 65th percentile in well-being (or vice versa).

Similarly, Yang and Waliji (2010) also found large changes in happiness in a longitudinal sample. These authors found that about 20% of happy participants became unhappy during their lifetimes, and, encouragingly, about 50% of unhappy participants later became happy. These changes can be further illustrated by the authors' statistical modeling results. As seen in Table 3.1, happy 30-year-old women from this sample could expect to live another 50.2 years. They could also expect 38.5 of those years to be happy, and 11.8 to be unhappy. There are several interesting points here, but first note the variability in individuals' happiness levels over their lifetimes. Both happy and unhappy individuals could expect years of happiness and unhappiness ahead of them. However, happy 30-year-olds could expect more happy future years than could unhappy individuals, indicating some stability and predictability in happiness.

Personality characteristics are associated with these major changes in well-being. For instance, Headey (2008b) found that neuroticism and extraversion predict changes in happiness, and argues that this might be because extraverts experience more positive life events and neurotics experience more negative events. In addition, Headey (2008a) and Headey, Muffels, and Wagner (2010) found that life choices and goals, including commitment to family and to social and political involvement, predict well-being and also appear to explain changes in well-being over time.

In addition, research indicates that personality can change over time. This is important because personality is an important predictor of well-being. Therefore, if personality changes, we would expect well-being to also change. For example, Boyce et al. (2013) followed almost 9,000 Australian adults for 4 years, and found that their personalities changed about as much as did income, marital status, and other demographic factors. These personality changes were associated with changes in well-being, demonstrating that happiness is changeable.

Finally, there is evidence that the neurological substrates of happiness are malleable (Rickard & Vella-Brodrick, 2014). These structures can respond to environmental

TABLE 3.1 Life Expectancies for 30-Year-Old Women and Men, Including Expectations for Happy and Unhappy Future Years

	Happy Participants			Unhappy Participants		
	Total Life Expectancy (at age 30)	Happy Years Expected	Unhappy Years Expected	Total Life Expectancy (at age 30)	Happy Years Expected	Unhappy Years Expected
Women	50.2	38.5	11.8	50.1	34.7	15.4
Men	44.8	36.6	8.2	44.4	32.9	11.5

Source: Adapted from Yang and Waliji (2010).

influences. Therefore, neurophysiological structures that influence well-being are not fixed, and do not unwaveringly constrain happiness within certain limits or to a specific direction. Instead, this physiological malleability of happiness processes implies that happiness can change (Rickard & Vella-Brodrick, 2014).

For instance, Rickard and Vella-Brodrick (2014) reviewed the literature and pointed out that even heritable physical structures related to happiness, such as genes that regulate serotonin transport, interact with, and are changed by, the environment. Therefore, environmental factors can influence genetic expressions, and lead to changes in happiness. Again, this can happen even in cases in which there originally were physiological mechanisms that constrained happiness within certain limits.

Furthermore, developmental processes that form neurophysiological mechanisms that regulate happiness are somewhat slow. Rickard and Vella-Brodrick report that they are still developing well after puberty, thus providing a wide window of opportunity for happiness interventions in childhood and through adolescence. Finally, there is "neuroplasticity" in some happiness-related structures even late into adulthood. In fact, some interventions specifically designed to increase happiness have been shown to produce physiological modifications.

The data we have reviewed in this section strongly suggest that happiness is not stable. Instead, happiness seems to change over time, and this emerging conclusion is important because it contradicts the most basic prediction of Set Point Theory. However, Cummins, Li, Wooden, and Stokes (2014) have disputed these findings and defend Set Point Theory. Their main empirical argument is that researchers have not always allowed enough time for happiness levels to return to their previous baselines. In other words, Cummins et al. argue that although happiness changes, given enough time, it does tend to return to an initial baseline.

Cummins et al. (2014) raise an interesting empirical question that can be answered only with more data. Once again, it will be interesting to see where the data lead. However, for practical purposes, the argument against Set Point Theory seems compelling. Researchers have tracked changes in happiness over appreciable time spans. If happiness does return to some previous baseline, it does not appear that this happens quickly.

Do We Adapt to Life Events?

A Study of Lottery Winners and Paralysis Victims

This question of whether humans adapt to life events is tremendously important to Set Point Theory, because the theory predicts that our happiness is based on our genetics and our fixed personality traits, and are therefore largely unchangeable. Thus, environmental events, even major ones like becoming disabled or winning the lottery, should just bounce off of us without significantly affecting our happiness. The idea of adapting to environmental events is perhaps most clearly exemplified by a famous study by Brickman, Coates, and Janoff-Bulman (1978). In fact, this study is so well known that it may already be familiar to you. Consistent with Set Point Theory, Brickman et al. seemed to demonstrate that individuals adapt to even the most extreme circumstances.

TABLE 3.2 Mean General Happiness and Mundane Pleasure Ratings				
Condition	General Happiness			Mundane Pleasure
	Past	Present	Future[a]	
Study 1 — Winners	3.77	4.00	4.20	3.33
Study 1 — Controls	3.32	3.82	4.14	3.82
Study 1 — Victims	4.41	2.96	4.32	3.48

[a]Some participants did not complete this measure.
Source: Brickman et al. (1978).

Brickman et al. (1978) interviewed a sample of accident victims who became at least partially paralyzed, lottery winners,[3] and control participants. All participants were asked how happy they were 6 months earlier, and how happy they were currently. They were also asked how happy they expected to be in a couple of years. Finally, participants reported how pleasant they found a set of mundane activities, including talking with a friend, watching television, eating breakfast, hearing a funny joke, getting a compliment, and reading a magazine.

The results are shown in Table 3.2. Keep in mind that these data come from individuals who have experienced extreme circumstances (paralysis or winning the lottery), so it offers a potential test of humans' ability to adapt to circumstances. What patterns do you see in the data?

These results seem to support the adaptation and set point hypotheses. Accident victims and lottery winners, people with wildly differing circumstances, experienced mundane pleasure similarly and did not differ in their expectations of future happiness. And both these groups were similar to control participants who experienced neither winning the lottery nor becoming paralyzed on both measures. In addition, 2.5 was the mid-point of all the scales, so accident victims were somewhat above neutral in happiness, even when considering the present. It seems astounding that paraplegic and quadriplegic accident victims were at least neutral in terms of present happiness, and expected to be just as happy as did lottery winners in the future. These findings are consistent with the notion that we adapt to events and return to our original set point of happiness. They seem to suggest that events do not affect happiness.

These results were widely interpreted as strongly supporting the idea that we humans can adapt to anything, and also suggested that individual happiness is relatively fixed. But it turns out that this conclusion was unwarranted (see later discussion). In addition, there are hints in this data set that should have caused people to be cautious in how they interpreted the results.

You have probably realized already that this study was not an experiment, because Brickman et al. (1978) were unable to randomly assign participants to "control," "victim," and "winner" conditions. Therefore, we cannot know whether winners and the control participants were comparable to the victims before they had the accident/winning/control experiences. For instance, perhaps the controls' scores for future happiness expectations were similar to the victims' because they were naturally pessimistic people? Brickman et al. tried to address this concern in a second study but were still unable to adequately match participants in the various conditions.

Another serious problem involves questions about humans' ability to predict accurately how happy they will be in the future or in hypothetical situations. This is called *affective forecasting* and humans are not very good at it (Gilbert, 2006), as we will see in Chapter 4. So there is serious doubt about whether participants' predictions about their future happiness are meaningful.

Finally, the ultimate test of the adaptation hypothesis is not whether people *expect* to become happier, but whether they actually *do* become happier. The only way to address this question is to conduct a *longitudinal* study in which individuals' happiness is followed over time. Brickman et al.'s (1978) study was a *cross-sectional* study in which participants were assessed at only one point in time.

Longitudinal Studies of Adaptation

Subsequent studies did track happiness over time and found that we adapt to some life events better than others (Diener, 2012; see also Luhmann, Hofmann, Eid, & Lucas, 2012). Specifically, individuals seem to adapt reasonably quickly and fully to marriage, the birth of a child,[4] and to divorce (Anusic, Yap, & Lucas, 2014a, 2014b; Clark, Diener, Georgellis, & Lucas, 2008; Clark & Georgellis, 2013; Lucas, 2005, 2007a; Lucas & Clark, 2006; Yap, Anusic, & Lucas, 2012). These results are consistent with Set Point Theory because they indicate that happiness returns to preevent levels.

However, and inconsistent with Set Point Theory, we do not seem to adapt to unemployment, disability, and, possibly, to bereavement. The evidence concerning adaptation for each of these life events is discussed separately, later in this chapter, but let us start with unemployment. Several studies (Anusic et al., 2014a, 2014b; Clark et al., 2008; Lucas, 2007b; Lucas, Clark, Georgellis, & Diener, 2004; Yap et al., 2012) indicate that happiness declines when a person becomes unemployed. Furthermore, happiness generally does not return to its preunemployment level, even after a substantial passage of time. Finally, these relations are particularly strong for men.

Although this is clear evidence that men (and women) do not adapt to unemployment, the story is a bit more complicated. It also turns out that the happiness trajectories for individuals who will in the future[5] become unemployed trend downward. When Yap et al. (2012) and Anusic et al. (2014a) examined data sets in Great Britain and Australia, respectively, they found that the happiness levels of the unemployed eventually matched their predicted levels *even if they had not become unemployed*. Examine Figure 3.3 from Anusic et al.'s (2014a) paper to get a better idea of what this means.

The figure on the right is the key. The solid line represents the actual happiness results for the unemployed. Note that happiness goes down and does not return to the level at

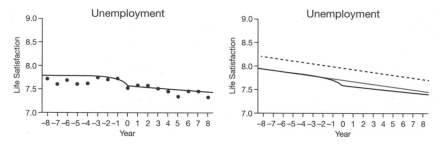

FIGURE 3.3. Estimated trajectories of life satisfaction from traditional models (left) and models that included normative changes over time (right). Points indicate raw means of life satisfaction of people who experienced a major life event. Solid black lines show estimated trajectories in event groups. Dashed lines show estimated trajectories in control groups. Solid gray lines estimate what the trajectories would be for people who experienced a major event if they did not go on to experience the event.
Source: Anusic et al. (2014a).

year "zero" when unemployment occurred. However, also note that these individuals' happiness levels were trending down anyway, even before unemployment occurred. The light gray line projects their happiness into the future even if they had not become unemployed, and, after a number of years, "catches up" with their actual happiness level.

What do we make of these results? It is unclear whether we should call this "adaptation." But this is really a definitional, rather than an empirical, issue. It is important that adaptation, if we call it that, does not occur for several years after unemployment. The gray and solid lines of the figure to the right do not begin to merge until at least 5 or 6 years after unemployment.

Thus, at the very least, adaptation effects in response to unemployment are not as quick and painless as suggested by Brickman et al. (1978) in their study of lottery winners and the disabled. It is also important that Anusic et al.'s (2014a) results are inconsistent with Set Point Theory. Whether we call these results adaptation or not, the findings clearly indicate that happiness changes over time.

Findings concerning bereavement and adaptation are decidedly mixed. Although some researchers find evidence of complete adaptation to bereavement (Clark et al., 2008; Clark & Georgellis, 2013), others find the opposite (Anusic et al., 2014a; Yap et al., 2012). In addition, researchers have also compared the actual happiness results of the bereaved to their projected happiness levels based on prebereavement trends, as has been done for unemployment. These studies also yield mixed results. Yap et al. (2012) found in a sample from Great Britain that bereaved individuals' happiness levels are lower than what would be expected from their prebereavement trajectories. However, Anusic et al. (2014a) found this is not the case in a sample of Australians. Future research may find that these mixed results are due to differences in culture, sex of the bereaved, and/or conditions surrounding bereavement. But there is enough evidence already to indicate that happiness changes in response to bereavement to cast serious doubt on Set Point Theory.

The data for disability are complex, but indicate that individuals do not adapt, at least not nearly with the ease that Brickman et al. (1978) suggested. Some of the few studies to show adaptation to disability were conducted by Pagán-Rodriguez (2010, 2012). And even these studies indicated that complete adaptation in overall life satisfaction was not reached until 5 or 6 years following the disability. Furthermore, Pagán-Rodriguez (2012) found that individuals reached only about 50% adaptation in terms of their satisfaction with their job and health after 7 years. In other words, they recovered only about half the job and health satisfaction they lost immediately following the disability.

Several other authors have also found less than complete adaptation in overall happiness in response to disability (Anusic et al., 2014b; Lucas, 2007a, 2007b; Powdthavee, 2009). Anusic et al. (2014b) also found that disabled individuals' happiness levels were even less than what was predicted by their predisabled trends in happiness. In addition, Braakmann (2014) found only partial adaptation to one's one disability and no adaptation to one's romantic partner's disability.

Other evidence also indicates that individuals do not adapt well to disability. For instance, previous evidence indicates that adaptation is weaker the more severe the disability (Lucas, 2007a, 2007b). Consistent with this finding, assuming that pain is associated with more severe disability, McNamee and Mendolia (2014) found no evidence of adaptation for life satisfaction among male chronic pain sufferers, and only partial adaptation among women in Australia. Similarly, Binder and Coad (2013) found partial adaptation in response to some medical conditions (e.g., heart problems, cancer diagnosis), and little or no adaptation to others (e.g., disability involving the arms, strokes). Taken together, these studies tracking the disabled over time and gauging the effects of pain and physical conditions tell us that our ability to adapt to disability is limited at best.

In conclusion, the longitudinal data offer mixed support for the adaptation hypothesis. We adapt more readily to some life events (e.g., marriage, divorce, childbirth) than others (e.g., unemployment and disability). Adaptation to bereavement is somewhat uncertain at this point. Interestingly, the adaptation effects are not a function of the positivity of the event (Luhmann et al., 2012). Note, for example, that individuals adapt to both positive events like marriage and childbirth, and also to seemingly negative events such as divorce.

Note that the disability findings directly contradict those of Brickman et al. (1978). It is clear that asking participants to estimate their future happiness (as did Brickman et al.) does not yield the same results as actually tracking happiness over time. It is also clear that Brickman et al. (1978) overstated the extent to which individuals can adapt to all situations, particularly disability. These results are inconsistent with Set Point Theory because they indicate that happiness changes.

Are There Individual Differences in Adaptation?

Agreeableness, one of the Big Five personality characteristics, can moderate or change the rate of adaptation to disability. For example, Boyce and Wood (2011) examined a cohort of individuals over time, some of whom became disabled. Consistent with other research, they found that disability was strongly negatively related to life satisfaction for everyone, at least initially. However, moderately agreeable individuals showed signs of complete adaptation to their disability within 4 years, while low agreeable individuals showed almost no signs of adaptation.

Over time, individuals with moderate levels of agreeableness were about a third of a standard deviation higher in life satisfaction than moderately disagreeable individuals. In other words, moderately agreeable individuals returned to their predisability level of well-being, while low agreeable individuals did not. Boyce and Wood argued that these results make sense because agreeableness is associated with kindness, sympathy, affection, and cooperation, all of which are conducive to fostering social support and good relationships, in addition to positive coping strategies. The resulting benefits for social support, relationships, and positive coping should help disabled individuals maintain their well-being.

Research also shows that dimensions of the Big Five other than agreeableness do not moderate adaptation patterns to life events (e.g., Anusic et al., 2014a; Yap et al., 2012). However, other individual difference variables do moderate adaptation patterns. For example, Mancini, Bonanno, and Clark (2011) found that sociodemographic variables such as age, income, and health predicted individual differences in response to divorce, marriage, and bereavement. Interestingly, they found that most individuals were not affected by these life events, showing no significant changes at all, even in the short run. However, their results also indicated that a sizable minority of respondents were affected, and that these effects varied depending on these sociodemographic characteristics.

Figure 3.4 is from Mancini et al.'s (2011) results for bereavement. Note that 59% of the individuals experienced no significant change in well-being (the resilient were "unperturbed" in the researchers' words), but that there were three other trajectories of responses. This figure illustrates the importance of considering individual differences in adaptation, just as did Boyce and Wood's (2011) results. Specifically, note that merely stating that the bereaved do not fully adapt to their experience does not describe the

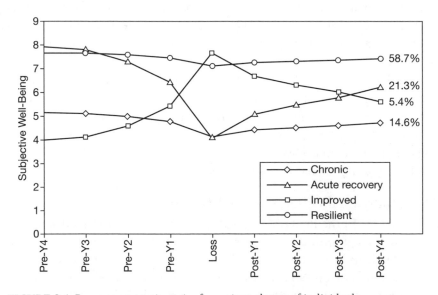

FIGURE 3.4. Bereavement trajectories for various classes of individuals.
Source: Reproduced with permission from Mancini et al. (2011). ©2011 Hogrefe Publishing www.hogrefe.com

complete reality of this experience, although it is technically true when the data are massed together and individual differences are ignored.

Mancini et al. (2011) found similar patterns for marriage and divorce, although the percentages of the "unperturbed" were even higher: 72% of respondents experienced no change in well-being after divorce, and 72% experienced no change after marriage. In addition, there were two other trajectories for divorce and three for marriage. Age, health dysfunction, and change in income predicted individual trajectories for bereavement, while income and health dysfunction predicted trajectories for marriage. Health dysfunction and years of education predicted trajectories for divorce.

In conclusion, there are individual differences in adaptation. However, no unified theoretical understanding explains differences in adaptation among individuals or adaptation more readily to some life events than to others. Why does agreeableness predict adaptation to disability but not to other life events, while the other dimensions of the Big Five seem unrelated to adaptation at all? What explains the individual trajectories in Mancini et al.'s (2011) findings? These are empirical questions that can be answered scientifically but will require more data.

Current Status of Set Point Theory

Set Point Theory has undergone some important revisions. Diener, Lucas, and Scollon (2006) noted that set points, if they exist, are not neutral. Instead, most people are happy (their happiness level is above scale neutral points). Another revision is that we do not all have the same level of happiness. Some people are simply happier than others. Finally, happiness levels differ depending on the domain of happiness assessed. For instance, measures of cognitive well-being, positive affect, and negative affect consistently yield differing values. Diener et al.'s review was perhaps an effort to salvage the theory, but that seems no longer possible because the theory's major prediction is that happiness is stable over time and situations, and the evidence clearly shows that happiness changes. We see this with the studies of the stability of happiness over time, and with the studies examining reactions of major life events. However, it is still possible that some additionally revised Set Point Theory, one that hypothesizes that happiness is difficult to change and that specifies the conditions under which it changes, might be possible.

This is not to say that happiness necessarily *must* change. There is some evidence that, barring changes in an individual's "normal or predictable pattern of life events," happiness remains relatively stable (Headey, 2013, p. 890). However, the fact that happiness often does change invalidates Set Point Theory (Headey, 2013).

This discarding of Set Point Theory has tremendously important implications. How would you feel if you learned that happiness was fixed by our (your!) personality and genetic endowment, and could not change? You might feel discouraged to learn that you could not expect to increase your own happiness, nor that of those you care about, nor society's in general. Headey (2010, p. 8) even refers to Set Point Theory as "stultifying," because it denies the possibility of changes in happiness. Encouragingly, this is not the case (although it does leave open the possibility that happiness can decrease too).

The next question is, what then does lead to changes in human happiness? Headey (2013) argues that "*preferences*, including life goals/priorities, and religion, and behavioral *choices*" are more important than most life events (p. 897, emphasis in the original). In other words, factors under our control can influence our happiness. The choices we make about how to live our lives, and particularly regarding how we prioritize things in our lives, are very important. This is a liberating and empowering thought.

There is plenty of evidence that happiness can change. The data on the stability of happiness that we reviewed at the beginning of the section clearly shows this. We also saw that life events can affect happiness and that there are individual differences in how people react to these life events. Thus, Set Point Theory, at least in its present form, is not valid.

LYUBOMIRSKY'S THEORY OF CONSTRUAL

It is clear that there is a *personality of happiness*. There are personal traits that make some individuals happier than others. These traits are associated with different ways of *interpreting* life events, and it seems that these interpretations are crucial for helping some individuals be happier than others. For instance, recall that Otake et al. (2006) found that happy participants were more likely to feel gratitude and recognize kindnesses from others. Happy individuals *interpret* events in ways that make them feel grateful for what they have, and this seems to be one of the reasons they are happy.

These findings, paired with the findings that happiness is not fixed, but instead is changeable, open up some exciting avenues for research. If happiness can change, and if the happy differ from the less happy because of the way they interpret events, is it possible to build interventions to increase happiness by altering how individuals interpret events? This is the focus of the rest of this chapter.

Researchers use the term *construal* as jargon for what I call *interpretation*, but the meaning is the same (Abbe, Tkach, & Lyubomirsky, 2003; Layous, Chancellor, & Lyubomirsky, 2014; Lyubomirsky et al., 2001). Lyubomirsky (2001) developed *a construal theory of happiness* that focuses on the cognitive and emotional processes that happy individuals use to interpret and understand events. These researchers study how individuals *construe* (i.e., interpret) events. For example, upon reviewing the literature, Lyubomirsky (2001) found that happy individuals are less negatively affected by social comparison information (i.e., the relative performance of peers), are more likely to remember events in positive or otherwise adaptive ways (e.g., temper the recall of negative events with humor), are more appreciative, and are less likely to dwell on negative events. Thus, Lyubomirsky's (2001) theory of construal postulates that the way we think about events has huge implications for our happiness.

All of these cognitive and motivational strategies are examples of adaptive *psychological reactions* to objective events. This insight led Lyubomirsky (2001, p. 240) to ask whether any event can be "truly objective." Her point is that everything that happens to a person is forced through his or her own psychological filters. It is ". . . construed and framed, evaluated and interpreted, contemplated and remembered . . . so that each individual may essentially live in a separate subjective world" (Lyubomirsky, 2001, p. 240).

Lyubomirsky's (2001) theory is that happiness is primarily in our heads. Think about that statement for a moment. What happens around us may be less important than how we interpret or construe those happenings. Events matter, but their impact is largely indirect and by means of our cognitive and motivational structures that interpret those events. Therefore, personality matters, because individuals differ in their interpretations and construals of events.

I often tell my students that psychologists are not really interested in reality. I get some knowing smiles and smirks, as if they always suspected as much about these crazy psychology professors. But I use this statement to help them understand Lyubomirsky's (2001) point about construal. To a psychologist, the events around us (i.e., reality) are mainly important in terms of how they affect thoughts, emotions, and motivations. Imagine that it is 90° Fahrenheit right now. That reality may or may not make you happy, depending on how you process that information. Your current location and goals, and the associations you make with warm weather, cause you to interpret this temperature differently. The fact of 90° does not matter as much as how you construe that information.

Empirical Support

Social Comparisons

There is strong empirical support for Lyubomirsky's (2001) theory. For instance, the differences in how happy and less happy individuals respond to social comparisons are particularly striking. Lyubomirsky and Ross (1997) had happy and less happy female college students work on unscrambling anagrams side by side with another female college student who was actually a research confederate. The female confederate was instructed to complete the anagrams either 50% faster or slower than the participant. Lyubomirsky and Ross then examined participants' perceptions of their own abilities. The "peer" in Figure 3.5 refers to the confederate's speed in completing the anagrams. "Before" and "After" refer to whether participants gave estimates of their own ability before or after receiving the false feedback about their performance on the anagram task. What do you make of the results?

Happy and unhappy participants responded identically to the slower peer, as depicted in the top graph (the slopes of the two lines are statistically the same and we should think of them as lying on top of each other). But note the striking difference between happy and unhappy participants in the bottom graph. Happy participants were not bothered by the faster "peer" and even became more confident in their own abilities, while unhappy participants became less confident. Thus, happy participants evaluated their performance against an internal standard, and not against another person. Despite the fact that happy and unhappy participants experienced identical external events (i.e., the faster peer), happy participants processed these events consistently with Lyubomirsky's (2001) hypothesis that happy individuals construe the world adaptively.

Subsequent research indicated that unhappy participants react more negatively to social comparisons when working in teams. Lyubomirsky et al. (2001) asked participants to work on a "word generation task" as part of a team competition. False feedback was then given about each participant's score and the team's score. The results are shown

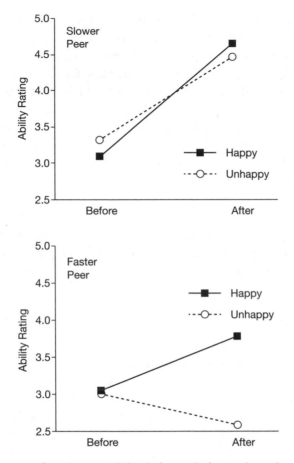

FIGURE 3.5. Assessments of participants' ability before and after working alongside a slower (top graph) versus faster peer (bottom graph) (study 1).
Source: Lyubomirsky and Ross (1997).

in Figure 3.6. "Self-Assessments" refer to participants' ratings of their own performance. Participants competed on four-person teams, so coming in fourth place indicates the worst performance on the team.

Note that unhappy participants were more strongly affected when they received negative feedback (they came in fourth place on the team). In addition, unhappy participants responded more extremely to their team winning. Finally, unhappy participants experienced a greater positive mood if their team lost, but they had the best score on the team, while happy participants' mood decreased in this condition. Notice again that unhappy participants appear to respond more strongly to social comparisons, both in terms of individual feedback and in terms of team performance. This, again, is consistent with Lyubomirsky's (2001) theory.

Memory for Events and Dwelling

Research also indicates that happy and unhappy individuals remember and cope with events differently. For example, Liberman, Boehm, Lyubomirsky, and Ross (2009) found

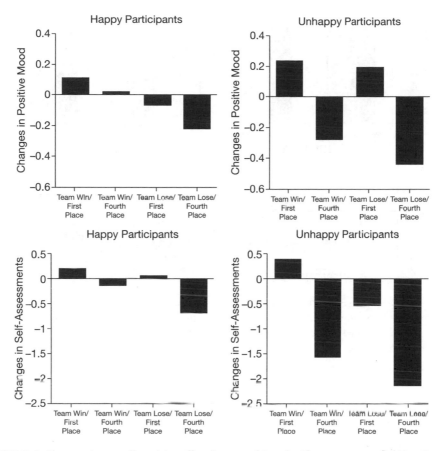

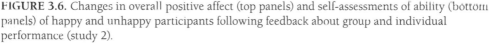

FIGURE 3.6. Changes in overall positive affect (top panels) and self-assessments of ability (bottom panels) of happy and unhappy participants following feedback about group and individual performance (study 2).

Source: Lyubomirsky et al. (2001).

that happy students in both Israel and the United States were more likely to savor positive past events and to avoid dwelling on past negative events. Thus, happy and unhappy individuals differ in how they remember or, in other words, construe events by either dwelling on negatives or savoring positives.

Other research has experimentally manipulated happy and unhappy participants' opportunities to dwell, and have confirmed these results. Lyubomirsky, Boehm, Kasri, and Zehm (2011) found that unhappy participants dwell on bad news, and that this dwelling is associated with both poorer performance and negative mood. Lyubomirsky et al. (2011) randomly assigned happy and unhappy college students to receive false feedback that they had performed either poorly or very well compared to other college students (relative success/failure conditions) on a task. All participants were then given a reading comprehension task. The results in Figure 3.7 describe participants' performance on this task. Participants were scored for how much of the passage they read (question screen on which interrupted), the number of questions about the passage they answered

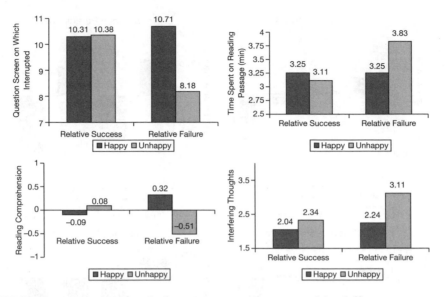

FIGURE 3.7. Question screen on which participants were interrupted (top left), time spent on reading passage (top right), reading comprehension (bottom left), and interfering thoughts (bottom right) in response to relative success versus relative failure (study 2).
Source: Lyubomirsky et al. (2011).

correctly (reading comprehension), the time spent reading, and number of off-task thoughts they had that interfered with the task (interfering thoughts).

Interpreting data from graphs is an acquired skill that takes practice but is very worthwhile. What do the results shown in Figure 3.7 indicate about the effects of dwelling? Can you see the pattern in which unhappy participants' performance is lower following negative feedback, and that this lowered performance is associated with dwelling?

Remember that everything you see in this figure has happened after participants were told that they did relatively well or relatively poorly on the anagram task. Notice that unhappy students who received negative feedback performed poorly on the subsequent reading comprehension task. Specifically, they completed less of the reading comprehension task (top left graph) and comprehended the passage less well (bottom left graph). This poor performance among unhappy, negative feedback-receiving participants was paired with dwelling. They spent more time reading the passage (top right graph), and had more interfering and off-task thoughts (bottom right graph).

Coping With Events

Happy and unhappy individuals also differ in terms of how they cope with events. Lyubomirsky and Tucker (1998) asked college students to nominate close friends who were especially happy or unhappy. These happy or unhappy nominees then described recent positive and negative life events and also chose how they coped with or reacted to these events from a list of potential strategies. Happy and unhappy participants differed in terms of how they tried to cope with negative events. Happy participants were particularly likely to view the negative event with a sense of humor and to think about how much better things are at present than were less happy participants.

Appreciation

Other research shows that happy and unhappy individuals differ in their appreciation for life events. Tucker (2007) randomly assigned college students to think of events within the past 24 hours that had either frustrated them or that they were appreciative of. Participants described these events in detail and were asked to indicate how appreciative they were of the elements of each event (for example, participants in the frustration condition might rate how much they appreciated a friend that had frustrated them recently).

As expected, there were clear differences between happy and unhappy participants in the appreciative condition. Happy participants recalled more events for which they were appreciative, demonstrated higher levels of appreciation for these events, expected these events to lead to longer duration of happiness, and were more appreciative in general (on most other days in addition to the previous 24 hours) than were unhappy participants. There were no differences between happy and unhappy participants in the frustration condition, perhaps because it was difficult for all participants to appreciate anything involving frustrating events. Regardless, once again researchers demonstrated that happy and unhappy individuals construe the world differently.

The data are clear. Consistent with Lyubomirsky's (2001) theory of construal, happy and unhappy individuals view, understand, and interpret the world very differently. Happy participants are less likely to notice and are less affected by social comparisons. Happy individuals also remember events more positively and are less likely to dwell on negative experiences. Finally, happy individuals are more likely to use humor to soften negative experiences and show more appreciation for life events. Notice again the importance of construal. Happy individuals see the world in more positive ways.

You may be wondering about causality here. After all, researchers have not randomly assigned some participants to be happy and others to be less so. Could there be something other than construal that explains the differences between the happy and unhappy? Because this is correlational research, another explanation is always possible. However, our confidence in construal theory is strengthened by subsequent intervention research (e.g., Layous et al., 2014; Lyubomirsky & Layous, 2013; Lyubomirsky et al., 2005) that experimentally assigns unhappy individuals to act like (i.e., construe the world like) happy individuals.

For example, Lyubomirsky et al. (2011) ran another study in the paper examining dwelling. The methods were similar (false feedback on performance on an anagram task, followed by measuring performance, and so forth, on a reading comprehension task), but this time unhappy participants were randomly assigned to either a "dwelling" or a "distraction" condition. Participants in the distraction condition were instructed to think of things (e.g., how clouds form) that drew their attention away from the feedback on the earlier anagram task. Dwelling participants were instructed to think about their feelings and attributes. Results indicated that the distracted unhappy participants performed very much like happy participants.

Thus, because the behaviors of happy people seem to cause more productive construals among the less happy, we can be relatively confident that these construal patterns are causal agents. We review similar findings in much more detail in Chapter 11. Lyubomirsky's (2001) theory and the subsequent supporting research give some important and effective strategies for improving happiness. As Lyubomirsky (2008, 2013) has written in two books on happiness for popular audiences, our happiness really is largely up to us. Individuals can be taught to construe the world more effectively.

FURTHER THOUGHTS

The data are clear that construals are undeniably important. We have remarkable powers to control and grow our own happiness. However, I sometimes worry that this message might get stretched too far, even to the point of blaming unhappy individuals for their plight. Is it possible that we might wag our fingers at unhappy people and chastise them?

Would this ever be appropriate? And would our knowledge of the importance of construals ever make it difficult for us to recognize that some unhappy people are in bad marriages, have chronic pain, are biologically depressed, have a child who is deathly ill, or live in an oppressive political and economic system? Will it perpetuate a "blame the victim" mentality? Clearly, Lyubomirsky does not think this would ever be appropriate. Her tone in the two books she has written on happiness for popular audiences is very kind, compassionate, and helpful, and she specifically singles out biological-based depression for special discussion (Lyubomirsky, 2008, 2013).

Others share my concerns in this area. Remember our discussion in Chapter 1 about the political implications of the psychology of happiness? The social critics Ehrenreich (2009) and Davies (2015) were both concerned that the (in their view overly) individualistic emphasis of positive psychology might place too much responsibility on individuals to solve their own happiness problems and suppress calls for important social reforms.

These questions are interesting because of the obvious implications and because of the nature of the field of psychology. My students are often surprised when I say that psychology is a rather politically conservative discipline. Think about this. Psychology is the study of individuals, and therefore tends to locate agency (i.e., control or causality), for both good and bad, within individuals rather than within the political and economic systems in which they live. This focus on individual rights and responsibilities is also the basis of conservative political philosophy. This approach is very different from a liberal outlook, which more heavily emphasizes the importance of social and political structures.

You can easily see the conservatism in psychology courses in which students are taught how individuals can adjust to the systems in which they live rather than how to adjust the system. A course in the "psychology of adjustment," the psychology of will power, and the psychology of self-control emphasize the importance of individuals maintaining appropriate behaviors rather than adjusting political systems to human needs.

Psychology, by its very nature, is likely to emphasize the individual's role in achieving happiness, while other social science disciplines, such as sociology, are more likely to emphasize the importance of culture and economic systems. My point here is not to criticize one approach and laud the other, but to draw attention to the distinctions. Both approaches are worth considering. The data on these perspectives are examined in more detail as we progress through the book.

FURTHER THEORETICAL DEVELOPMENT

Architecture of Sustainable Happiness

Lyubomirsky and her colleagues have refined the construal theory of happiness in recent years. Lyubomirsky et al. (2005) posited an *architecture of sustainable happiness model* in which construals are recognized as important contributors to happiness, along with genetics/personality and life circumstances. This model offers several advances from Lyubomirsky's (2001) earlier paper.

First, Lyubomirsky et al. (2005) strengthen the theoretical basis for the importance of construals. These authors reviewed the literature and concluded that 50% of the variability in people's happiness is due to genetic factors, 10% due to circumstances, and 40% the result of *intentional activities* that reflect individuals' behavior and cognitions (i.e., construals). This conclusion challenges the conventional view that happiness is mostly fixed and unchangeable.

Second, Lyubomirsky et al. (2005) expand on the idea of construals, as indicated by the phrase "intentional activities." Intentional activities are freely chosen and are done with the intention of increasing happiness. They require effort and will eventually lead to happiness-sustaining habits. Thus, intentional activities include positive construals, but they also have a strategic element in which the individual chooses to put effort toward establishing positive habits. These intentional activities form Lyubomirsky et al.'s "architecture of sustainable happiness." We discuss this in more detail in Chapter 11.

Third, and finally, Lyubomirsky et al.'s (2005) theory offers encouragement that happiness can be increased. All individuals have the ability to take up these intentional activities that can increase happiness. Furthermore, Lyubomirsky argues that a full 40% of the differences in people's happiness is under personal control, rather than being fixed by life circumstances or the genetic lottery.

Lyubomirsky and colleagues (2005) offer support for this last point by describing their own studies. In one study, some participants were encouraged to consider their blessings or to act kindly toward others. This intervention is an example of the construal/intentional activities approach because it requires effort, and so on, and because it can shape how participants view the world. Considering blessings is similar to the appreciation research noted earlier, and acts of kindness may also increase appreciation for one's own good fortune. As expected, participants in both conditions generally increased their well-being.

Positive Activity Model

Subsequent research further refined how and why intentional activities foster well-being. Lyubomirsky and Layous (2013) developed the *positive activity model* (Figure 3.8). The premise of this model is that intentional activities, now renamed "positive activities" to emphasize their links to well-being, increase happiness indirectly by first developing

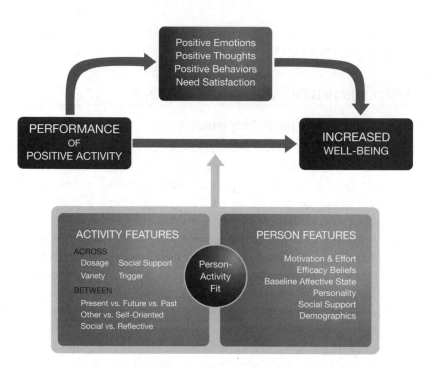

FIGURE 3.8. The positive activity model, which aims to explain how and why performing positive activities makes people happier. As illustrated at the top, positive activities increase positive emotions, positive thoughts, positive behaviors, and need satisfaction, all of which, in turn, enhance well-being. Features of positive activities (e.g., dosage and variety) and of the person (e.g., motivation and effort) influence the degree to which the activities improve well-being. An optimal *person–activity fit* (i.e., the overlap between activity and person features) further predicts increases in well-being.

Source: Lyubomirsky and Layous (2013).

positive emotions, thoughts, and behaviors, and by satisfying basic human needs. Note the importance of construal. Positive activities improve well-being by first altering emotions and thoughts. In addition, the authors propose that positive activities affect basic human needs such as feelings of autonomy, connectedness, and competence, which also reflect how individuals view and process social information.

The model also posits that specific features of the positive activities, which the authors refer to as person/activity fit, are crucial. For example, the dosage and variety of positive activities need to be fine-tuned, and the individual must be motivated and exert effort. Once again we discuss more of the specifics of the model in Chapter 11. But for now it is important to understand how Lyubomirsky's (2001) construal model has evolved to explain how and why construals affect well-being.

A new development in the model is that positive activities may also protect against factors that threaten well-being. Layous et al. (2014) argue that positive activities can protect well-being by leading to the development of skills that help individuals deal with negative events and emotional challenges. Thus, positive activities can be beneficial in both immediate and long-term contexts. They are helpful immediately in that they aid construal right now, but they can also build more permanent construal skills that are portable across situations and time.

For instance, positive activities can reduce rumination (i.e., dwelling), defined as "repetitively focusing attention on oneself and one's problems without taking action to resolve them" (Layous et al., 2014, p. 6) that is empirically linked to several psychological problems. Positive activities can draw an individual's attention away from himself or herself and toward more positive emotions. Positive activities can also reduce other emotional challenges such as loneliness. For instance, acts of kindness and feeling gratitude can help individuals feel and become more socially integrated. Finally, positive activities might also aid coping by helping individuals construe events more positively (Layous et al., 2014).

SUMMARY

There are fascinating relationships between personality and well-being. Ongoing research is exploring how and why these personality characteristics affect happiness. This research suggests that personality characteristics, such as the Big Five, affect how we approach the world, and that these approaches have powerful impacts on well-being. However, although our personalities affect our happiness, happiness levels can change, particularly if we regulate how we interpret the world around us. We are not trapped by dispositional and genetic forces within a narrow range of possible happiness levels.

Therefore, more than anything else, the message in this chapter is a hopeful one. Happiness levels are malleable, independent of the whirl of life circumstances that buzz around us. It is possible to become happier by mimicking the thoughts and behaviors of dispositionally happy people.

NOTES

1. Agreeableness refers to traits related to high-quality interpersonal relationships (e.g., cooperativeness), neuroticism refers to traits related to lack of adjustment (e.g., anxiety), and openness to experience refers to traits related to cognitive complexity (e.g., creativity).

2. There are rather complex statistics that will allow us to determine whether some form of mediation has occurred, but it is not necessary to explain the specifics of how this works.

3. All the lottery winners won at least $50,000, and the majority won $400,000 or more.

4. Parents tend to experience a temporary increase in well-being leading up to and shortly after the birth of a child. This increase dissipates quickly though. Many studies show that the overall long-term effect of parenthood on happiness is negative.

5. Remember that these are longitudinal studies, so researchers can look back in the past and identify individuals who will become unemployed in later data sets.

REFERENCES

Abbe, A., Tkach, C., & Lyubomirsky, S. (2003). The art of living by dispositionally happy people. *Journal of Happiness Studies, 4*(4), 385–404.

Albuquerque, I., de Lima, M. P., Matos, M., & Figueiredo, C. (2012). Personality and subjective well-being: What hides behind global analyses? *Social Indicators Research*, *105*(3), 447–460.

Albuquerque, I., de Lima, M. P., Matos, M., & Figueiredo, C. (2013). The interplay among levels of personality: The mediator effect of personal projects between the Big Five and subjective well-being. *Journal of Happiness Studies*, *14*(1), 235–250.

Anusic, I., Yap, S. C. Y., & Lucas, R. E. (2014a). Does personality moderate reaction and adaptation to major life events? Analysis of life satisfaction and affect in an Australian national sample. *Journal of Research in Personality*, *51*, 69–77.

Anusic, I., Yap, S. C. Y., & Lucas, R. E. (2014b). Testing Set-Point Theory in a Swiss national sample: Reaction and adaptation to major life events. *Social Indicators Research*, *119*(3), 1265–1288.

Binder, M., & Coad, A. (2013). "I'm afraid I have bad news for you . . ." estimating the impact of different health impairments on subjective well-being. *Social Science and Medicine*, *87*, 155–167.

Boyce, C. J., & Wood, A. M. (2011). Personality prior to disability determines adaptation: Agreeable individuals recover lost life satisfaction faster and more completely. *Psychological Science*, *22*(11), 1397–1402.

Boyce, C. J., Wood, A. M., & Powdthavee, N. (2013). Is personality fixed? Personality changes as much as "variable" economic factors and more strongly predicts changes to life satisfaction. *Social Indicators Research*, *111*(1), 287–305.

Braakmann, N. (2014). The consequences of own and spousal disability on labor market outcomes and subjective well-being: Evidence from Germany. *Review of Economics of the Household*, *12*(4), 717–736.

Brickman, P., Coates, D., & Janoff-Bulman, R. (1978). Lottery winners and accident victims: Is happiness relative? *Journal of Personality and Social Psychology*, *36*(8), 917–927.

Chamorro-Premuzic, T., Bennett, E., & Furnham, A. (2007). The happy personality: Mediational role of trait emotional intelligence. *Personality and Individual Differences*, *42*(8), 1633–1639.

Clark, A. E., Diener, E., Georgellis, Y., & Lucas, R. E. (2008). Lags and leads in life satisfaction: A test of the baseline hypothesis. *Economic Journal*, *118*(529), F222–F243.

Clark, A. E., & Georgellis, Y. (2013). Back to baseline in Britain: Adaptation in the British household panel survey. *Economica*, *80*(319), 496–512.

Costa, P. T., & McCrae, R. R. (1992). The five-factor model of personality and its relevance to personality disorders. *Journal of Personality Disorders*, *6*(4), 343–359.

Cummins, R. A., Li, N., Wooden, M., & Stokes, M. (2014). A demonstration of set-points for subjective wellbeing. *Journal of Happiness Studies*, *15*(1), 183–206.

Davies, W. (2015). *The happiness industry: How the government and big business sold us well-being*. London, UK: Verso.

DeNeve, K. M., & Cooper, H. (1998). The happy personality: A meta-analysis of 137 personality traits and subjective well-being. *Psychological Bulletin*, *124*(2), 197–229.

Diener, E. (2012). New findings and future directions for subjective well-being research. *American Psychologist*, *67*(8), 590–597.

Diener, E., Lucas, R. E., & Scollon, C. N. (2006). Beyond the hedonic treadmill: Revising the adaptation theory of well-being. *American Psychologist*, *61*(4), 305–314.

Diener, E., & Seligman, M. E. P. (2002). Very happy people. *Psychological Science*, *13*(1), 81–84.

Ehrenreich, B. (2009). *Bright-sided: How the relentless promotion of positive thinking has undermined America*. New York, NY: Metropolitan Books.

Fujita, F., & Diener, E. (2005). Life satisfaction set point: Stability and change. *Journal of Personality and Social Psychology, 88*(1), 158–164.

Gilbert, D. (2006). *Stumbling on happiness*. New York, NY: Alfred A. Knopf.

Gilman, R., & Huebner, E. S. (2006). Characteristics of adolescents who report very high life satisfaction. *Journal of Youth and Adolescence, 35*(3), 311–319.

Hayes, N., & Joseph, S. (2003). Big 5 correlates of three measures of subjective well-being. *Personality and Individual Differences, 34*(4), 723–727.

Headey, B. (2006). Subjective well-being: Revisions to dynamic equilibrium theory using national panel data and panel regression methods. *Social Indicators Research, 79*(3), 369–403.

Headey, B. (2008a). Life goals matter to happiness: A revision of Set-Point Theory. *Social Indicators Research, 86*(2), 213–231.

Headey, B. (2008b). The Set-Point Theory of well-being: Negative results and consequent revisions. *Social Indicators Research, 85*(3), 389–403.

Headey, B. (2010). The Set Point Theory of well-being has serious flaws: On the eve of a scientific revolution? *Social Indicators Research, 97*(1), 7–21. doi:10.1007/s11205-009-9559-x

Headey, B. (2013). Set-Point Theory may now need replacing: Death of a paradigm? *The Oxford handbook of happiness* (pp. 887–900). New York, NY: Oxford University Press.

Headey, B., Muffels, R., & Wagner, G. G. (2010). Long-running German panel survey shows that personal and economic choices, not just genes, matter for happiness. *Proceedings of the National Academy of Sciences of the United States of America, 107*(42), 17922–17926.

Kenrick, D. T., & Funder, D. C. (1988). Profiting from controversy. Lessons from the person-situation debate. *American Psychologist, 43*(1), 23–34.

Layous, K., Chancellor, J., & Lyubomirsky, S. (2014). Positive activities as protective factors against mental health conditions. *Journal of Abnormal Psychology, 123*(1), 3–12.

Li, Z., Yin, X., Jiang, S., Wang, M., & Cai, T. (2014). Psychological mechanism of subjective well-being: A stable trait or situational variability. *Social Indicators Research, 118*(2), 523–534.

Liberman, V., Boehm, J. K., Lyubomirsky, S., & Ross, L. D. (2009). Happiness and memory: Affective significance of endowment and contrast. *Emotion, 9*(5), 666–680.

Little, B. R. (2014). *Me, myself, and us: The science of personality and the art of well-being*. New York, NY: Public Affairs Books.

Lucas, R. E. (2005). Time does not heal all wounds: A longitudinal study of reaction and adaptation to divorce. *Psychological Science, 16*(12), 945–950.

Lucas, R. E. (2007a). Adaptation and the set-point model of subjective well-being: Does happiness change after major life events? *Current Directions in Psychological Science, 16*(2), 75–79.

Lucas, R. E. (2007b). Long-term disability is associated with lasting changes in subjective well-being: Evidence from two nationally representative longitudinal studies. *Journal of Personality and Social Psychology, 92*(4), 717–730.

Lucas, R. E., & Clark, A. E. (2006). Do people really adapt to marriage? *Journal of Happiness Studies, 7*(4), 405–426.

Lucas, R. E., Clark, A. E., Georgellis, Y., & Diener, E. (2004). Unemployment alters the set point for life satisfaction. *Psychological Science, 15*(1), 8–13.

Lucas, R. E., & Donnellan, M. B. (2007). How stable is happiness? Using the STARTS model to estimate the stability of life satisfaction. *Journal of Research in Personality, 41*(5), 1091–1098.

Lucas, R. E., & Lawless, N. M. (2013). Does life seem better on a sunny day? Examining the association between daily weather conditions and life satisfaction judgments. *Journal of Personality and Social Psychology, 104*(5), 872–884.

Luhmann, M., Hofmann, W., Eid, M., & Lucas, R. E. (2012). Subjective well-being and adaptation to life events: A meta-analysis. *Journal of Personality and Social Psychology, 102*(3), 592–615.

Lykken, D., & Tellegen, A. (1996). Happiness is a stochastic phenomenon. *Psychological Science, 7*(3), 186–189.

Lyubomirsky, S. (2001). Why are some people happier than others? The role of cognitive and motivational processes in well-being. *American Psychologist, 56*(3), 239–249.

Lyubomirsky, S. (2008). *The how of happiness: A new approach to getting the life you want.* New York, NY: Penguin Press.

Lyubomirsky, S. (2013). *The myths of happiness: What should make you happy, but doesn't, what shouldn't make you happy, but does.* New York, NY: Penguin Press.

Lyubomirsky, S., Boehm, J. K., Kasri, F., & Zehm, K. (2011). The cognitive and hedonic costs of dwelling on achievement-related negative experiences: Implications for enduring happiness and unhappiness. *Emotion, 11*(5), 1152–1167.

Lyubomirsky, S., & Layous, K. (2013). How do simple positive activities increase well-being? *Current Directions in Psychological Science, 22*(1), 57–62.

Lyubomirsky, S., & Ross, L. (1997). Hedonic consequences of social comparison: A contrast of happy and unhappy people. *Journal of Personality and Social Psychology, 73*(6), 1141–1157.

Lyubomirsky, S., Sheldon, K. M., & Schkade, D. (2005). Pursuing happiness: The architecture of sustainable change. *Review of General Psychology, 9*(2), 111–131.

Lyubomirsky, S., & Tucker, K. L. (1998). Implications of individual differences in subjective happiness for perceiving, interpreting, and thinking about life events. *Motivation and Emotion, 22*(2), 155–186.

Lyubomirsky, S., Tucker, K. L., & Kasri, F. (2001). Responses to hedonically conflicting social comparisons: Comparing happy and unhappy people. *European Journal of Social Psychology, 31*(5), 511–535.

Mancini, A. D., Bonanno, G. A., & Clark, A. E. (2011). Stepping off the hedonic treadmill: Individual differences in response to major life events. *Journal of Individual Differences, 32*(3), 144–152. doi:10.1027/1614-0001/a000047

Mayer, J. D., DiPaolo, M., & Salovey, P. (1990). Perceiving affective content in ambiguous visual stimuli: A component of emotional intelligence. *Journal of Personality Assessment, 54*(3–4), 772–781.

McCann, S. J. H. (2011). Emotional health and the Big Five personality factors at the American state level. *Journal of Happiness Studies, 12*(4), 547–560.

McNamee, P., & Mendolia, S. (2014). The effect of chronic pain on life satisfaction: Evidence from Australian data. *Social Science and Medicine, 121*, 65–73.

Otake, K., Shimai, S., Tanaka-Matsumi, J., Otsui, K., & Fredrickson, B. L. (2006). Happy people become happier through kindness: A counting kindnesses intervention. *Journal of Happiness Studies*, *7*(3), 361–375.

Ozer, D. J., & Benet-Martinez, V. (2006). Personality and the prediction of consequential outcomes. *Annual Review of Psychology*, *57*, 401–421.

Pagán-Rodriguez, R. (2010). Onset of disability and life satisfaction: Evidence from the German socio-economic panel. *The European Journal of Health Economics*, *11*(5), 471–485.

Pagán-Rodriguez, R. (2012). Longitudinal analysis of the domains of satisfaction before and after disability: Evidence from the German socio-economic panel. *Social Indicators Research*, *108*(3), 365–385.

Pollock, N. C., Noser, A. E., Holden, C. J., & Zeigler-Hill, V. (2016). Do orientations to happiness mediate the associations between personality traits and subjective well-being? *Journal of Happiness Studies*, *17*(2), 713–729.

Powdthavee, N. (2009). What happens to people before and after disability? Focusing effects, lead effects, and adaptation in different areas of life. *Social Science and Medicine*, *69*(12), 1834–1844.

Proctor, C., Linley, P. A., & Maltby, J. (2010). Very happy youths: Benefits of very high life satisfaction among adolescents. *Social Indicators Research*, *98*(3), 519–532.

Quevedo, R. J. M., & Abella, M. (2011). Well-being and personality: Facet-level analyses. *Personality and Individual Differences*, *50*(2), 206–211.

Rickard, N. S., & Vella-Brodrick, D. (2014). Changes in well-being: Complementing a psychosocial approach with neurobiological insights. *Social Indicators Research*, *117*(2), 437–457.

Tucker, K. L. (2007). Getting the most out of life: An examination of appreciation, targets of appreciation, and sensitivity to reward in happier and less happy individuals. *Journal of Social and Clinical Psychology*, *26*(7), 791–825.

Yang, Y., & Waliji, M. (2010). Increment-decrement life table estimates of happy life expectancy for the U.S. population. *Population Research and Policy Review*, *29*(6), 775–795.

Yap, S. C. Y., Anusic, I., & Lucas, R. E. (2012). Does personality moderate reaction and adaptation to major life events? Evidence from the British household panel survey. *Journal of Research in Personality*, *46*(5), 477–488.

CHAPTER 4

Joy and Positive Emotions

Walk as if you are kissing the Earth with your feet.
— Thich Nhat Hanh, *Peace Is Every Step: The Path of Mindfulness in Everyday Life*

Laughter is wine for the soul—laughter soft, or loud and deep, tinged through with seriousness—the hilarious declaration made by man that life is worth living.
— Seán O'Casey (By kind permission of the Estate of Seán O'Casey)

MOST OF US ARE AT LEAST MILDLY HAPPY

One of the most striking findings from happiness research is that most of us are at least mildly happy most of the time. Diener, Kanazawa, Suh, and Oishi (2015) refer to this as the *positive mood offset* and cite several lines of evidence in support of this idea. For instance, a recent Gallup World Poll (GWP) found that 82% of respondents from 160 countries and almost one million individuals around the world reported feeling some positive emotion much of the previous day. This is an important finding because the poll examined a representative sample of almost all of humanity. Thus, positive emotions are the default for most of us.

Diener et al. (2015) also reanalyzed existing data sets to investigate baseline levels of happiness. One was a study of American college students whose mood was assessed at random times each day for 6 weeks. Students reported being happy 94% of the time, and even the least happy student reported at least some happy feelings 68% of the time. They found similar results in another study that examined peer reports of individuals' happiness levels. Only 2% of 200 target individuals were rated as unhappy by peers.

The positive mood offset even applies to prisoners and to individuals who have gone hungry, lacked shelter, and have been assaulted in the past year. The GWP found that 57% of participants in the least happy nations reported feeling at least some positive emotion the previous day. In addition, 53% of individuals who had been hungry, *and* who did not have enough money for housing, *and* who had been assaulted in the past year reported enjoying most of the previous day. Sixty percent of these individuals reported they laughed and smiled a lot the previous day. Thus, even individuals living in difficult circumstances tend to be at least mildly happy (Diener et al., 2015).

Diener et al. (2015) suggest this widespread positive mood has evolutionary roots. These authors argue that positive moods are associated with behaviors that were probably adaptive to our prehistoric ancestors. They cite evidence that happy individuals are more sociable and cooperative and have more supportive social relationships. Happiness is also associated with positive energy and optimism. All these characteristics would have been evolutionarily advantageous to our distant ancestors who relied on tight-knit social networks to survive.

Most people around the world are at least moderately happy. There is a strong argument that this chronic level of moderate happiness is evolutionarily adaptive. We explore why positive emotions and happiness might be adaptive in more detail in the next section. There we consider Fredrickson's (1998, 2001) Broaden and Build Theory (BBT), which hypothesizes that positive emotions (happiness) help us build useful skills and live better and happier lives.

THE BROADEN AND BUILD THEORY

Positive emotions—short-lived, pleasant reactions to a circumstance—make powerful contributions to our overall well-being. Feelings of joy, contentment, love, or interest, for example, are not just signs that we are flourishing. They are also *causes* of flourishing (Conway, Tugade, Catalino, & Fredrickson, 2013; Fredrickson, 1998, 2001). We examine this and other features of the positive emotion–well-being relationship in this chapter.

Imagine that you were one of the participants in a study on positive emotions conducted by Fredrickson and Branigan (2005) and were lucky enough to be randomly assigned to view a film clip that aroused amusement or contentment, rather than negative emotions. You are then asked to list up to 20 things you would like to do right now.

Fredrickson and Branigan (2005) found that participants who watched the positive emotion-inducing film clips thought more broadly. They listed significantly more things they would like to do right at that moment. The positive mood from the film opened participants up to possibilities that they would not have otherwise considered. This broadened thinking has tremendously important consequences. It kicks off a cascade of escalating positivity. Other research shows that if we were in the positive movie condition, our broadened thinking would help us get over psychological hurts, build skills, and raise defenses against future negative events (Conway et al., 2013; Fredrickson, 1998, 2001).

Positive emotions are good for us. Pursued with the right attitude and motivations, seeking out a slobbery kiss from a puppy, a fresh-baked chocolate chip cookie, a warm smile from a friend, a funny movie, or whatever makes us really smile can lead to real improvements in our well-being. We will even see research considering the appropriate ratio of positive to negative emotions that maximizes our well-being.

The Theory

The BBT has four essential elements (Conway et al., 2013; Fredrickson, 1998, 2001). First, positive emotions *broaden* the scope of thoughts and actions. When we are feeling positive, we are more likely to consider a range of possible actions, rather than focusing closely on any specific behavior. This increased range of possible behaviors produces new personal resources that we can use for long-term benefit. For example, Fredrickson (2001) notes that joy produces the urge to play, along with other behaviors. Play then builds physical and social resources, such as friendships, that can be helpful later.

A second element is that positive emotions can *undo* the effects of negative emotions. Positive and negative emotions are incompatible, so positive emotions crowd out any lingering effects, both psychological and physiological, of negative emotions. A third element is that positive emotions increase our *resilience.* This most directly gets at the "build" part of the theory, because positive emotions help us acquire or "build" skills and resources that we can use to better deal with life's negative experiences (Fredrickson, 2001).

The final element is that positive emotions lead to an *upward spiral* of positivity that increases well-being (Fredrickson, 2001, p. 223). The broadened thought and action patterns, the undoing of the effects of negative emotions, and the increased resiliency all combine to fuel this upward spiral. Positive emotions lead to good results, which then foster more positive emotions and more good results, and so on. Specifically, the new resources, additional resiliency, and the undoing of the effects of negative emotion all build on and reinforce each other. Each produces more positive emotion and allows us to find positive meaning in our lives, which further builds resources and resiliency and further undoes the effects of negative emotions.

Evidence for the Broaden and Build Theory

Broadening of Thoughts and Actions

Fredrickson (1998, 2001) drew on earlier work by Isen and colleagues for support for the hypothesis that positive emotions broaden thought and action patterns. For instance, Isen and Daubman (1984) found that positive emotions are linked to more flexible patterns of thought, and Isen, Daubman, and Nowicki (1987) found they are linked to creativity. Later research by Fredrickson and Branigan (2005), which I briefly described at the beginning of this section, tested the broadening hypothesis more directly. Recall that participants randomly assigned to view a positive emotion-inducing film clip showed broadened thought and action patterns by listing more things they would like to do right at that moment than did participants in the negative film clip condition.

Fredrickson and Branigan (2005) also measured broadened thoughts and actions in other ways. Take a look at Figure 4.1. If you were a participant in this study, your job would be to identify which of the two figures at the bottom of the picture are more like the one at the top. Your choice could identify something about your present emotional state. If you thought the figure on the bottom left most resembled the one at the top, the chances are good that you have positive emotions right now.

FIGURE 4.1. This image was used to measure the breadth of viewers' thoughts and actions, which can be linked to emotional state.
Source: Fredrickson and Branigan (2005).

The image on the bottom right resembles the top image in terms of *local detail*. Both figures are made up of squares. Noticing this similarity is an indicator that you are attending to specific narrow details about the figures, and this is associated with negative emotions. However, the image at the bottom left resembles the top image in terms of its *global shape*. Even though the specific details of the two images are very different (triangles versus squares), their general shape is similar. Noticing this similarity is an indication of broadened thought patterns and is associated with positive emotions (Fredrickson & Branigan, 2005).

Results were consistent with Fredrickson and Branigan's (2005) hypothesis that positive emotions led to broader thinking patterns. Participants who viewed the positive emotion-inducing film clips were more likely to say that the image on the bottom left most resembled the top image. Those who viewed the negative film clips were more likely to note the similarity between the bottom right image and the top image. Several other studies have replicated this effect, showing that positive emotion expands attentional focus and thought processes (Conway et al., 2013; see Garland et al., 2010 for a review).

The Undo Hypothesis

The undo hypothesis predicts that positive emotions can "undo" the effects of negative emotions. Fredrickson, Mancuso, Branigan, and Tugade (2000) confirmed this by subjecting college students to a stressful experience and then observing whether the positive emotions generated by pleasant film clips could aid physiological recovery. All participants were told that they had 1 minute to prepare a 3-minute speech. Furthermore, there was a 50% chance that the computer would select them to give the speech in front of a video camera, and that their speech would be evaluated by students in another study.

Of course, the threat of the speech under such unreasonable conditions was just a cover story to arouse negative emotions among the participants. No participants were actually selected to deliver their speech. Participants' cardiovascular responses were assessed before they learned about the speech requirement and then tracked throughout the study. These cardiovascular measures showed that participants were significantly aroused (presumably negatively) as they prepared their speech (Fredrickson et al., 2000).

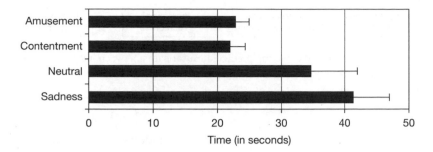

FIGURE 4.2. Mean duration of cardiovascular reactivity by participants viewing positive film clips. Error bars represent standard errors of the means.
Source: Fredrickson et al. (2000).

Participants were then randomly assigned to see a film clip that pilot studies had shown produced amusement, contentment, sadness, or neutral emotions. Figure 4.2 shows that the positive film clips (amusement and contentment) restored participants' cardiovascular activities to baseline levels (i.e., to the levels before participants received the speech instructions), significantly more quickly than did the neutral or sad film clips, supporting the hypothesis that positive emotions can undo the effects of negative events.

These results have been replicated several times (Conway et al., 2013), including studies that have tested the theory in more naturalistic conditions. For instance, Gloria, Faulk, and Steinhardt (2013) examined the positive affect and well-being of public school teachers in Texas. They found that teachers who reported feeling the most positive emotions (e.g., amused, calm, content) experienced lower levels of burnout and more psychological resiliency, for example, saying "Under pressure, I stay focused and think clearly" (Gloria et al., 2013, p. 188), even after controlling for level of work stress.

Positive Emotions Build Resiliency

In addition to supporting the undo hypothesis, the Gloria et al. (2013) study shows that positive emotions are associated with greater resiliency. This effect has been replicated several times. For instance, positive emotions are associated with increased resilience and this predicts fewer symptoms of depression (e.g., Loh, Schutte, & Thorsteinsson, 2014).

Other research shows that positive emotions can fuel resiliency in a self-perpetuating cycle. Cohn, Fredrickson, Brown, Mikels, and Conway (2009) assessed college students' levels of life satisfaction and resilience ("I quickly get over and recover from being startled," p. 363) at the beginning of a 28-day study. Participants then completed measures of their positive and negative emotions once a day for 28 days on a secure website. Finally, participants again indicated their resilience and life satisfaction at the end of the 28 days.

Consistent with predictions, positive emotions predicted both resiliency and life satisfaction at the end of the study, even after controlling for initial levels of resiliency and life satisfaction. Thus, participants who experienced the most positive emotions throughout the month had the highest levels of resiliency at the end of the month. Positive emotions also mediated the relationship between beginning- and end-of-the-month resiliency.

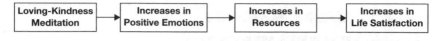

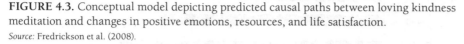

FIGURE 4.3. Conceptual model depicting predicted causal paths between loving kindness meditation and changes in positive emotions, resources, and life satisfaction.
Source: Fredrickson et al. (2008).

Thus, resiliency was associated with more positive emotions, which led to greater levels of resiliency, linking positive emotions and resiliency in a potentially self-perpetuating cycle (Cohn et al., 2009).

Other research demonstrated the connection between positive emotions and resiliency by showing that positive emotions help build important personal resources. Recall that this is an important part of the theory: Positive emotions should increase resiliency because they help us acquire skills and resources we can draw from in tough times (Fredrickson, 2001; see Garland et al., 2010 for a review). The relationship between positive emotions and resources has been shown in several studies. For instance, Fredrickson, Cohn, Coffey, Pek, and Finkel (2008) demonstrated that a meditation practice increased positive emotions in a sample of working adults. As shown in Figure 4.3, this increase in positive emotions was then associated with increases in personal resources (increased resilience, faster recovery from stress, optimism, better social relationships, better sleep, and so on), which then led to increases in life satisfaction.

Chaves, Hervas, Garcia, and Vazquez (2016) demonstrated this relationship in a sample of severely ill children (average age of 12 and suffering from cancer or other life-threatening illness). Results showed that positive emotions built resiliency by helping the children build and acquire important resources. Positive emotions at the beginning of the study predicted higher levels of gratitude, vitality, benefit finding, and love during the course of the study. These resources were associated in turn with higher levels of life satisfaction. Thus, as predicted, these resources mediated the relationship between positive emotions and life satisfaction, indicating that positive emotions contribute to life satisfaction by association with resource building. Furthermore, these results were significant even after controlling for the children's initial levels of life satisfaction, health, and other factors.

Positive Emotions Promote an Upward Spiral of Well-Being

Studies support the hypothesis that positive emotions promote an upward spiral of well-being by showing that positive emotions form reciprocal and escalating relationships with coping and interpersonal trust. Fredrickson and Joiner (2002) found that positive emotion predicted greater use of broad-minded coping tactics (for example, participants think of a new way to solve a problem) across a 5-week study of college students. First, positive emotions increased broadened thought patterns in terms of coping. Second, the broad-minded coping produced by positive emotions led to more positive emotions in the future.

Other results further supported the upward spiral by showing that positive emotions reinforce themselves and that they are closely intertwined with coping. Specifically, broad-minded coping mediated the relationship between initial levels of positive emotions (at the beginning of the study) and the level of positive emotions at the end of the study. Similarly, changes in positive emotions mediated the relationship between levels of broad-minded coping at the beginning of the study and broad-minded coping at the end of the study[1] (Fredrickson & Joiner, 2002) as the following progressions show:

Positive Emotions   →   Changes in Broad-Minded Coping   →   Positive Emotions

(at the beginning of the 5-week study)   (across the 5-week study)   (at the end of the 5-week study)

Broad-Minded Coping   →   Change in Positive Emotions   →   Broad-Minded Coping

(at the beginning of the 5-week study)   (across the 5-week study)   (at the end of the 5-week study)

As Fredrickson (1998, 2001) predicted, positive emotions lead to more positive emotions because they build resources and skills such as broad-minded coping. The fact that positive emotions and broad-minded coping mediate each other shows how closely intertwined they are. Burns et al. (2008) replicated these results using a different measure of coping and a measure of interpersonal trust as mediators. Once again, positive emotions at the beginning of the study predicted higher levels of resources (this time changes in the different measures of coping and changes in the measure of interpersonal trust). These resources then predicted higher levels of positive emotion at the end of the study. Other work by Fredrickson and her colleagues links the upward spiral of positive emotions to physical health as well as psychological well-being (e.g., Kok et al., 2013).

Evidence for the upward spiral of positive emotions leading to upward spirals of resource building and psychological well-being is still somewhat tentative. Although the pieces of the model have been tested separately, no study has tested the entire model at one time.

But research as a whole has confirmed all the individual elements of the model.

Updates to the Broaden and Build Theory

Brain Plasticity

Brain plasticity refers to the ability of our brains to change their structures in response to experiences. Garland et al. (2010) hypothesized that positive emotions' ability to broaden patterns of thought and action can alter the physical structures of our brains. They cited evidence from the emerging field of affective neuroscience to support their case. For instance, they noted that adults who engage in enriching experiences such as playing a musical instrument, memorizing routes, and learning to juggle experience changes in their brains' neuronal structures. They also noted that differences in the structure of the prefrontal cortex are associated with differences in resiliency. Furthermore, these structures can change with repeated experiences of positive or negative events.

Garland et al.'s (2010) review also found that positive emotions can have some of the same influences on brain structures that research has noted for enriching experiences such as playing a musical instrument. These include strengthening the connections between neurons, as well as the development of new neurons. Some of these changes seem to be at least partly caused by the association between positive emotion and the release of dopamine within certain parts of the brain.

Finally, Garland et al. (2010) noted that the development of mood and anxiety disorders is associated with changes in brain structures. This finding further demonstrates the possibility that emotions can alter the way our brains structure themselves and suggest implications for encouraging individuals to seek out positive emotions. In sum, there is good evidence that positive emotions do not just alter our psychological states. They also change the physical nature of our brains.

Changes in Appraisals

Positive emotions are beneficial in part because they crowd out negative ones. Garland et al. (2010) systemize this hypothesis by suggesting that positive emotions decrease negative patterns of behavior by changing the way individuals appraise events. Specifically, positive emotions may reduce distorted, inaccurate, or inappropriate thinking processes, such as the likelihood that we inappropriately think that an event poses a threat, and thus, positive emotions reduce the likelihood of an inappropriately anxious or depressed response.

This positive mood/reappraisal hypothesis has led Fredrickson and her colleagues (e.g., Cohn & Fredrickson, 2010) to explore mindfulness and meditation interventions to produce positive mood and greater psychological well-being. The logic here is that these interventions produce positive emotions and also directly help individuals reappraise events more appropriately.

Implications of the Broaden and Build Theory

Positivity Ratios

Positive emotions are clearly associated with well-being. Should we therefore try to seek out and cultivate positive emotions? If so, how many should we try to get? Is there an optimal ratio of positive to negative emotions? The answers to these questions are important, although complicated. For one thing, we see in a later section that "seeking out" positive emotions can be a risky enterprise. Our motivations matter very much (Catalino, Algoe, & Fredrickson, 2014).

But Fredrickson (2012, 2013a) suggests that we try to cultivate positive emotions in order to improve our well-being. How much positive emotion do we need? In a review of the literature, Fredrickson (2013b) found that individuals who are the most psychologically healthy, those she calls "flourishers," experience at least three times as many positive emotions as they do negative emotions. The ratio of positive to negative emotions for nonflourishers is closer to two to one.

For instance, Fredrickson and Losada (2005) compared flourishers to nonflourishers in two separate studies and found remarkably similar patterns of differences between the two groups. The positive to negative emotions ratio in the two studies were 3.2:1 and 3.4:1 for flourishers, compared to significantly lower ratios for nonflourishers: 2.3:1 and 2.1:1. In addition, Waugh and Fredrickson (2006) found that incoming university students with positivity ratios of at least 2.9:1 developed stronger relationships with their new peers over time, while students with lower positivity ratios did not.

Other research finds a similar pattern of different positivity ratios separating psychologically thriving individuals from those who are not. Fredrickson (2013b) found in her review that happy marriages are marked by positivity ratios of about 5:1, while those headed toward divorce have ratios of only 1:1. Similarly, depressed individuals have a positivity ratio of about 1:1, while those making the strongest recovery from depression experience four positive emotions for every negative emotion. In addition, individuals who are very creative have positivity ratios of about 3.6:1. Other data suggest that positive emotions have little or no benefit for mental health when positivity ratios are less than 3:1. Thus, Fredrickson (2013b) suggests a possible nonlinear relation between positive emotions and well-being in which the benefits of positive emotions "kick in" only above a critical positivity ratio.

So, the answer to the question, *should we try to seek out and cultivate positive emotions?* is a definite *yes!* Although there is still uncertainty about the optimum positivity ratio, Fredrickson (2013b, p. 819) makes her answer clear:

> . . . striving to raise one's positivity ratio from a low level to a moderately high level in hopes of attaining flourishing mental health remains a reasonable and healthy goal. Indeed, the now-ample evidence for the long-range benefits of positive emotions . . . assures that this advice is both on point and evidence-based.

Furthermore, Fredrickson (2013a) stresses that positive emotions are not an end in themselves but also help build long-term happiness.

> . . . unlocking more momentary experiences of positive emotions *is not simply the end-goal of a desire to feel good*, but rather, doing so is an important vehicle for reshaping people's abiding levels of resilience, health and well-being, as well as a host of other resources and personality traits that make life more satisfying and meaningful. . . . (Fredrickson, 2013a, p. 155, emphasis added)

Generating Positivity

Fredrickson not only advises that we raise our positivity ratios; she offers suggestions about how to do this. Garland et al. (2010, p. 856, emphasis added) speculate that many who suffer poor mental health "are not aware that positive emotions can be *intentionally self-generated.*" Note the emphasis I placed in the quotation. These authors argue that it is a mistake to think that positive emotions must be "natural" or must arise spontaneously. Instead, they maintain that we can actively seek out positive events that produce positive emotions.

Garland et al. (2010) offer a series of suggestions for generating positive emotions, including drawing upon the "character strengths" developed by positive psychology. For instance, they refer to Lyubomirsky, Sheldon, and Schkade (2005), who also emphasize intentional activities, such as practicing kindness, that can produce well-being. Lyubomirsky (2008, 2013) is the author of two books for popular audiences about how to use positive psychology principles such as optimism, gratitude, and savoring to intentionally cultivate happiness.

Fredrickson and her colleagues (e.g., Cohn & Fredrickson, 2010; Fredrickson, 2012; Fredrickson et al., 2008; Garland et al., 2010) also find that the practice of *mindfulness meditation* is a good way of intentionally producing positive emotions. Mindfulness meditation is a focused state of attention on the present moment in which the individual monitors but does not react to or evaluate his or her emotions and thoughts. This meditation produces positive emotions and broadens patterns of thoughts and behaviors (Garland et al., 2010). Fredrickson and her colleagues have typically operationalized mindfulness meditation by training research participants to practice loving kindness meditation (LKM) from Buddhism.

In one example of this research, Fredrickson et al. (2008) recruited employees from a large computer company in Detroit to participate in a series of LKM workshops. More than 100 employees volunteered for the study. About half were randomly assigned to begin the program right away, and the other half served as waitlisted controls who began the program later.

Participants completed six 1-hour workshops in which they were taught LKM techniques by an experienced instructor. The first week's session included a meditation directed toward love and compassion toward the self. The meditations in later sessions were directed toward loved ones, friends, strangers, and all living beings. Participants were also instructed to practice LKM at home at least 5 days each week. LKM caused a cascade of increasing positive emotions, resources, and life satisfaction.

Fredrickson et al.'s (2008) study is important not only because it validates BBT, but also because it demonstrates that intentional activities can produce well-being. One of the features of LKM is that it teaches individuals to cultivate positive emotions during the meditation and during the rest of one's ordinary life (Fredrickson et al., 2008). We can intentionally produce positivity to increase our well-being.

Regardless of the type of intervention, Garland et al. (2010) argue that intentionally seeking positive experiences/positive emotions activates the upward spiral predicted by BBT. These positive experiences, and the resulting positive emotions, can decrease negative emotions, and allow individuals to experience stress in more positive and productive ways. This intentional behavior facilitates the upward spiral by helping to activate pleasure and reward centers in the brain, which then leads to more positive emotions.

Some research suggests that more mundane intentional activities like eating ice cream can generate worthwhile positive emotions that stimulate well-being (e.g., Hurling, Linley, Dovey, Maltby, & Wilkinson, 2015; Linley et al., 2013). However, Fredrickson (2009) tends to downplay efforts like eating ice cream in her excellent book for popular audiences describing her work. This is because things like ice cream eating are likely to lead to momentary pleasures rather than real positive emotions. She advises us to look for positive meaning in our everyday experiences. In her book and in several videos available on YouTube (www.youtube.com/watch?v=Ds_9Df6dK7c; www.youtube.com/watch?v=_hFzxfQpLjM), she urges us to be open, appreciative, kind, curious, and real.

By "open" Fredrickson (2009) means that we should be open to the good around us, which includes beauty and the everyday humane and charitable acts of others. We should notice and embrace this goodness and let it produce positive emotions for us. She also emphasizes the importance of genuineness and sincerity with the keyword "real." It is important that we do not fake or pretend to have positive emotions. Instead, we should seek out things that we are genuinely curious about and that we sincerely think are beautiful.

And this is the clear bottom line that Fredrickson (2009) wants her readers to understand. She urges us to give ourselves permission to seek out positive experiences every day, even though doing so might seem trivial or difficult to prioritize in our busy lives. These must be "real," sincere, and genuine, but Fredrickson's (2009) research shows that they are worthwhile.

Positivity as Treatment for Psychopathology

Clinical therapies emphasizing positive emotions may also help those suffering from anxiety, depression, and even schizophrenia. Garland et al. (2010) note a *downward spiral* of negative emotions in depression and anxiety. In this process, negative emotions narrow the focus of attention, making individuals more sensitive to potential threats, and thereby producing even more negative emotions that prompt the downward spiral. Garland et al. (2010) suggest that in addition to traditional cognitive behavioral therapies, positive psychology interventions (practicing kindness, savoring, and so on) that encourage individuals to seek out positive emotions and that aim for a positivity ratio of at least three to one can help treat anxiety and depression. The logic here is straightforward: Replacing negative emotions with positive emotions can broaden thought and action patterns and thereby replace the downward spiral of depression and anxiety with an upward spiral of positivity.

Garland et al. (2010) also suggest that more favorable positivity ratios may help some schizophrenics, a particularly interesting and even startling idea, given the current emphasis on pharmacological treatments of the disease. A significant number of schizophrenics suffer from *negative symptoms*, which include decreased motivation, pleasure, emotional expression, and desire for social contact. Schizophrenics also experience less *anticipatory pleasure* (the likelihood of anticipating pleasure in potential future activities) than do control participants.. These negative symptoms and the difficulty anticipating future pleasure amount to a deficit of positive emotions that might be addressed with the BBT. Therefore, training schizophrenics to self-generate positive emotions could help relieve at least some of their symptoms.

Too Much Positivity?

Positive emotions, much like ice cream, pizza, and statistics classes, are subject to the universal law that too much of a good thing is not so good. Too much positive emotion does not seem to be good for us (Fredrickson, 2013b; see also Forgas, 2014). There seem to be two factors at work here. One concerns the level or intensity versus the frequency of positive emotion. While frequent (and relatively mild) positive emotions seem to benefit us, too high a level of positive emotion does not seem to work well. For instance, the *frequency* of (relatively mild) positive mood is a better predictor of life satisfaction than is the *intensity* or level of positive mood (Fredrickson, 2013b).

There is an inverted "U"-shaped relationship between levels of positive mood and adaptive behaviors. Increasing positive mood predicts greater creativity, income, longevity, and other behaviors, but only until one reaches moderate levels of positive mood. After moderate levels of positive mood are exceeded, the levels of these behaviors begin to diminish. Bipolar disorder, with its dramatic mood swings between depression and mania, offers an example. The destructive manic phase of bipolar disorder is characterized by very high levels of positive emotions (Fredrickson, 2013b).

A second factor is that (relatively mild) negative emotions can be surprisingly valuable. For instance, feeling anger in contexts in which it might be useful (e.g., arguing with someone who has caused you harm) is associated with happiness (Kim, Ford, Mauss, & Tamir, 2015; Tamir & Ford, 2012). Psychologically healthy individuals want to feel anger during confrontations with others, but want to feel happy when they work collaboratively with others (Kim et al., 2015). Similarly, negative emotions that are not so high that they become debilitating can help motivate us to deal with dangerous events such as a serious illness (Fredrickson, 2013b). Also, mild levels of stress can improve performance (Robertson, 2016). It is also interesting that "flourishers," those particularly psychologically healthy individuals, have as many *negative emotions* as do nonflourishers (Catalino & Fredrickson, 2011). The two groups differed only in the number of positive emotions. Thus, some minimal level and frequency of negative emotion does not seem to retard flourishing and even seems to be valuable to human functioning.

VALUING AND PURSUING HAPPINESS: POTENTIAL PROBLEMS?

Not all researchers fully accept the position of Fredrickson and her colleagues favoring the value of positive emotions and their argument that positive emotions, and therefore happiness defined more broadly and generally, can be intentionally pursued and cultivated.

Some argue that people in much of the world, particularly individuals who live in Eastern cultures, are actually "averse" to happiness. Findings in this area question Fredrickson's call to encourage the pursuit of positive emotions and greater happiness. In addition, other researchers argue that valuing and pursuing happiness can often "backfire" by making individuals *less* happy. Let us sort through these arguments, and discuss Fredrickson's response.

Aversion to Happiness

Are some people averse to happiness? Do they really not want to be happy, at least in the way that most of us in the Western world understand happiness? Joshanloo and

Weijers (2014) think so, and their findings are presented in this section. They conclude from a review of the literature that many individuals in Eastern cultures, and at least some individuals in all cultures, share this aversion to happiness, or at least have negative views about happiness. Contrary to Western assumptions that happiness is the supreme goal and motivator of all people, many individuals around the world view happiness with at least some caution and suspicion, seeing it as a potentially dangerous feeling.

For instance, East Asians value social harmony and belongingness more than they do individual happiness and consider individual happiness to be a possible threat to social harmony. As a result, East Asian cultures deemphasize individuals' "need" for personal happiness. Joshanloo and Weijers also point out other evidence of cultural differences in reactions to happiness. For instance, Asians are less likely to focus on and savor positive emotions than are Westerners. There are also noticeable levels of "fear of happiness" (i.e., the feeling that joy is usually followed by sadness) even among individuals from Western cultures.

Why Might Some Be Averse to Happiness?

There are several reasons why some individuals are averse to happiness. Some believe that happiness and sadness are linked, with happiness believed to cause, or at least be associated with, future sadness. This belief is common in many Asian cultures, and it also has a presence in the West as indicated by various proverbs and sayings such as "what goes up, must come down" (Joshanloo & Weijers, 2014, p. 723). Also, some believe that happiness makes one a bad person. For instance, some strains of Christianity warn that pleasure in this world could be a sign that one is falling away from God. Parts of Islam have similar elements. Furthermore, many mistakenly believe that unhappiness is necessary for creativity and productivity. Therefore, unhappiness is mistaken as a sign that one is a productive citizen.

Individuals may also be wary of expressing happiness. Acting happy may arouse envy and jealousy in others, which could lead to negative social consequences. Both Eastern and Western cultures warn against unrestrained expressions of happiness.

Finally, others believe that actively pursuing happiness is not a worthy goal, because it could lead to negative outcomes for the one who pursues happiness and for those around him or her. Buddhist tradition maintains that pursuing individual happiness is self-centered and self-defeating, and that it can encourage selfishness. Western thinkers have made similar arguments: The pursuit of happiness can cause individuals to become poorer critical thinkers and less concerned about injustices and the plight of others. Similarly, others in the West warn that the extreme individualism prompted by the pursuit of happiness can lead to materialism, the break-down of community ties, and selfishness.

In summary, directly pursuing happiness is looked upon with suspicion by many around the world. There is a moral component here that suggests that happiness is not a morally worthy pursuit. Embedded in these reasons, and touched upon only briefly earlier, is also the belief that the pursuit of happiness can be self-defeating. Happiness, perhaps like romantic love and some subatomic particles known to physics, may be a slippery concept that escapes us if we try too hard to capture it. We examine this idea more closely in the next section.

Valuing Happiness Can Backfire

Many scholars suggest that happiness is best pursued indirectly. These thinkers argue that instead of actively pursuing happiness, we should strive toward other goals. Ironically, and even paradoxically, this indirect path will increase our happiness. This line of thought is very important to our discussion because it contradicts much of what is written in this chapter. The implication is that we cannot find happiness by directly seeking it by, for instance, cultivating positive emotions.

For instance, Aristotle argued that happiness is the result of a lifetime of virtuous living. The more modern philosopher Henry Sidgwick (1874/1981) developed the phrase *paradox of hedonism* (sometimes called the paradox of pleasure) to capture the idea that happiness cannot be achieved directly. Instead, Sidgwick (1874/1981) argued that we should do things we enjoy for their own sake, and that these pursuits will bring us happiness. In other words, it is useless to engage in hobbies or other activities simply because we expect them to make us happy. However, if we pick up a hobby because it is inherently interesting to us, this hobby will then increase our happiness.

Others have also urged us to seek an indirect path to happiness. Holocaust survivor and psychiatrist Victor Frankl (1946/2006, 1986, 1988) argues that happiness is a by-product of our successful search for meaning in our lives. He also argues that serving and loving others is the highest form of life meaning. And finally, Kay (2012), a contemporary author and economist, combines arguments and data from philosophy and several social sciences to maintain that many goals, including happiness, are best pursued indirectly.

Evidence

Several studies demonstrate that strongly pursuing and highly valuing happiness can *lower* one's happiness. In other words, pursuing happiness can backfire. Although this paradoxical effect is not inevitable, it does occur. It is even associated with clinical levels of mental disturbances. Taken as a whole, these findings are consistent with the idea that directly pursuing happiness can be a fool's errand.

For instance, valuing happiness is associated with depression symptoms among normally functioning adults. It also predicts clinical levels of depression, even after controlling for demographic variables (Ford, Shallcross, Mauss, Floerke, & Gruber, 2014). In addition, extreme levels of valuing happiness predict bipolar disorder, again even after controlling for demographic characteristics (Ford, Mauss, & Gruber, 2015).

Valuing happiness also negatively affects us in less dramatic ways. For instance, it may set us up for disappointment. Mauss, Tamir, Anderson, and Savino (2011) hypothesize that those who seek and highly value happiness would set happiness goals for themselves that would be hard to reach. These higher happiness goals would then lead to disappointment and a loss of happiness. They further speculate that this effect primarily occurs in positive circumstances when there is no apparent external reason for less than stellar levels of happiness. However, these authors hypothesize that negative circumstances, such as experiencing high stress, would provide a readily available reason for diminished happiness. Therefore, seeking and valuing happiness is not expected to lower happiness in these negative circumstances.

These hypotheses were tested and confirmed in two studies by Mauss et al. (2011). The first study measured the extent to which participants (adult women living in Denver) valued happiness. As predicted, life stresses moderated (i.e., changed) this relationship. Specifically, valuing happiness was associated with less experienced happiness only among the women who felt low levels of life stress, not among the women who reported high levels of life stress.

The second study experimentally manipulated valuing happiness by telling half of the subjects that happiness has social, professional, and health benefits. Participants were also randomly assigned to watch a film clip that pretests had shown produced either sad or happy emotions. This manipulation allowed the researchers to again test whether valuing happiness reduces experienced happiness only under positive circumstances. Once again, participants who highly valued happiness were less happy in the positive emotion condition (happy film clip), and had no effect on happiness in the negative emotion condition.

Results also demonstrated that disappointment fully mediated the relationship between valuing happiness and actual experienced happiness. Specifically, participants manipulated to highly value happiness felt more disappointed about their current level of happiness. This disappointment fully explained the relationship between valuing happiness and how much happiness participants actually experienced.

Other research shows that pursuing happiness can cause loneliness. Mauss et al. (2012) hypothesize that the pursuit of happiness can be a personal quest that might isolate individuals and damage social relationships. They tested this by asking adults to keep daily diaries of stress and loneliness. Consistent with predictions, valuing of happiness was associated with higher levels of loneliness when participants experienced stress. This result was significant even after controlling for participants' normal levels of stress and happiness and also for demographic variables. A subsequent study demonstrated that participants who were randomly assigned to value happiness were lonelier than participants in a control group.

Theory

The importance of culture   Other research shows that culture affects the extent to which we value happiness. Ford, Dmitrieva, et al. (2015) examined samples from cultures that differed along the individualism-collectivism continuum. They found that valuing happiness is negatively related to experienced happiness in the United States. However, it is unrelated to experienced happiness in Germany, and predicts *higher* levels of happiness in Russia and East Asia.

These results are consistent with the hypothesis that actively pursuing happiness would be negatively related to happiness only in individualistic cultures such as in the United States. As hypothesized, the pursuit of happiness increased happiness in the more collectivist cultures (Ford, Dmitrieva, et al., 2015). Therefore, cultural differences are one explanation for how and when pursuing happiness can influence actual experienced happiness.

The way happiness is pursued   Another set of reasons why pursuing happiness can lead us to feel less happy appears to be less culturally bound. Ford and Mauss (2014) suggest a trio of reasons surrounding the *way* in which we pursue happiness. The first is that pursuing happiness can lead us to expect to be very happy. This expectation can lead to disappointment. Paradoxically, we can feel unhappy even in circumstances that would otherwise make us feel quite happy.

The other two reasons are new to us. The second is that we often do not understand what makes us happy (Ford & Mauss, 2014). This phenomenon is called making *affective forecasting errors* ("affective" refers to emotions here), and we explore this topic in depth later in this chapter. An example is that individuals can spend precious time and energy pursuing wealth and fame, mistakenly thinking that these pursuits will make them happy. In the process they ignore or undervalue friends and family. We see in later chapters that social relationships are actually much more predictive of happiness than are fame and fortune.

Finally, Ford and Mauss (2014) argue that the pursuit of happiness changes happiness from a spontaneous state to one that is a goal. Naturally, we tend to monitor our progress toward achieving happiness, as we would monitor our progress toward achieving any goal. However, closely monitoring our happiness and how close we are to achieving our happiness goal is counterproductive. For example, trying to measure the air pressure in a bicycle tire inevitably releases some air from the tire. Likewise, trying to measure (monitor) our happiness inevitably lets some of our happiness escape.

Ford and Mauss (2014) describe research in which participants were asked to explain why a joke was funny. These participants enjoyed the joke less than did controls who were simply told the joke. Why does monitoring happiness erode our happiness? Ford and Mauss (2014) argue that monitoring takes us out of the "present moment" and forces us to analyze our emotional state instead of simply experiencing it. The potential goal orientation of pursuing happiness is perhaps the key. Monitoring our efforts to achieve happiness may remind us that we have not fully reached this goal and lead to disappointment.

Does Pursuing Happiness Always Cause Backfire?

Some Evidence Contradicting Backfire

Several authors argue that happiness can be actively pursued with success. Fredrickson's thinking and research (Cohn & Fredrickson, 2010; Garland et al., 2010; Fredrickson, 2009, 2013a, 2013b) that positive emotions create upward spirals that increase our happiness is certainly consistent with this idea. In addition, Lyubomirsky (2008, 2013) has written two popular self-help books describing how to do this. Unlike most self-help books, these are solidly based on rigorous scientific research (much of it her own). We see in the next section that it is important to go about this in the right way, but Lyubomirsky makes a convincing case that it is possible to increase our happiness by active pursuit. In fact, there is direct evidence from Lyubomirsky's research that motivation to improve happiness and the amount of effort we put into this pursuit are helpful, which contradicts some of the backfire effect reviewed earlier (Lyubomirsky, Dickerhoof, Boehm, & Sheldon, 2011; Lyubomirsky & Layous, 2013; Sin & Lyubomirsky, 2009).

Other research has more directly challenged the backfire findings. Luhmann, Necka, Schönbrodt, and Hawkley (2016) found that the scale previous researchers (e.g., Mauss et al., 2011) used to measure valuing happiness is not unidimensional. In other words, the scale measures distinct psychological constructs. One of these is the extent to which individuals worry about being unhappy ("If I don't feel happy, maybe there is something wrong with me," Luhmann et al., 2016, p. 49). While this part of the scale (worry about happiness) negatively predicts happiness, other parts of the scale are either positively related or not related at all to happiness.

Luhmann et al. (2016) conclude that while valuing happiness can lead to lower happiness, this effect is limited to a specific manner of valuing happiness that involves worrying about happiness. Valuing happiness in other ways may not limit our happiness. For instance, one set of items from the valuing happiness scale seemed to reflect participants' thinking that happiness meant their life was worthwhile. This set of items positively predicted both positive emotions and life satisfaction. Another set of items reflected the extent to which happiness was important to participants. This set of items was positively associated with positive emotions.

Fredrickson and her colleagues have also directly challenged the backfire findings. Catalino et al. (2014) developed a "prioritizing positivity" scale that measures individuals' motivation to seek out positive experiences when planning their day ("I structure my day to maximize my happiness," p. 1158). Consistent with the BBT, they hypothesized and found that individuals who sought out positive emotions were happier. Specifically, high scores on the prioritizing positivity scale were associated with high life satisfaction and less depression in a sample of adults.

The results from the studies by Luhmann et al. (2016) and Catalino et al. (2014) suggest that *the way* we pursue happiness matters quite a bit. Although the research in this area is still evolving, it does appear that happiness is something we can directly pursue, although we have to be careful about how we pursue happiness. Ford and Mauss (2014), who find that actively pursuing happiness can backfire, also think that this backfire effect is not inevitable. They present the model in Figure 4.4 as a guide to how pursuing happiness sometimes does and sometimes does not lead to greater happiness. As you can see, pursuing happiness is effective if we set realistic goals for happiness that are not likely to lead to disappointment, pursue activities (i.e., have goals) that really do increase happiness, and do not closely monitor our emotional state. So we can take some comfort here. Pursuing happiness can pay off if we go about it the right way.

Lyubomirsky and Layous make a similar argument that happiness can be pursued effectively if we set about it the right way (Layous & Lyubomirsky, 2014; Lyubomirsky & Layous, 2013). For instance, individuals need specific suggestions about what to do.

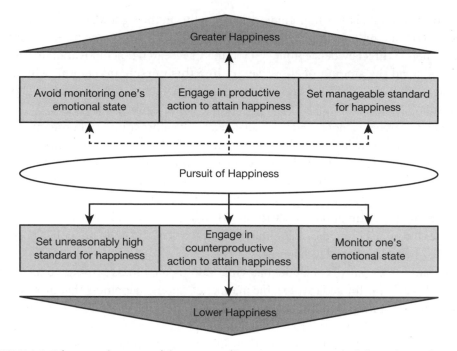

FIGURE 4.4. Schematic depiction of the pursuit of happiness, as interpreted through a goal-pursuit framework.

Source: Adapted from Ford and Mauss (2014).

Layous and Lyubomirsky (2014) give the example that simply instructing someone to exercise in order to increase his or her health is not effective. Instead, telling the person to walk at least 30 minutes each day works much better. Similarly, these authors argue that individuals need specific suggestions, such as expressing gratitude, that are shown to work by empirical studies. This is similar to Ford and Mauss's (2014) observation that we might not always know what makes us happier.

Layous and Lyubomirsky (2014) also recommend care concerning the timing and "dosage levels" of happiness-increasing activities. They describe research showing that pursuing potential happiness-increasing activities the right number of times a week, with the right intensity, is critical. Engaging in a variety of activities, rather than repeating the same activity over and over, is also important. They also review evidence that happiness-increasing activities must fit with a person's personality and situation.

Catalino et al. (2014, p. 1160), the authors who developed and tested the prioritizing positivity scale, also urge caution in the way we pursue happiness, ". . . it would be misleading not to acknowledge that the pursuit of happiness appears to be a delicate art." In the next paragraph they add, "The pursuit of happiness is complex because there appear to be effective and ineffective ways of doing it. This notion that it is not what you do, but the way that you do it, resonates with other research in positive psychology." Thus, it seems that happiness can be intentionally enhanced, but we must pursue it the right way.

AFFECTIVE FORECASTING

How good are humans at predicting or forecasting what will and will not make us happy in the future? We have already seen arguments that we cannot do this very well, and that this is one of the reasons our efforts to pursue happiness consciously sometimes backfire. In this section, we examine the theoretical and empirical basis for this claim.

The act of predicting future emotions is referred to as *affective forecasting*. Remember that *affect* is the word psychologists often use for emotions. It turns out that we are not very good at this important task. Much like the beleaguered weather reporter on your local television station, we are not very good at forecasting whether specific events are going to bring emotionally sunny or cloudy skies tomorrow[2] (Wilson & Gilbert, 2005).

In one of the first direct investigations of the topic, Gilbert, Pinel, Wilson, Blumberg, and Wheatley (1998) examined how happy or unhappy college students expected to be after (a) the breakup or the beginning of a romantic relationship, (b) receiving negative personal feedback, (c) facing rejection during a job interview, (d) reading an account of a child's death, or (e) discovering one's favorite candidate won or lost an election. In an additional study, they asked college professors how happy or unhappy they expected to be after being granted or denied tenure, which is a critical career step in academia.

The results showed that participants often made inaccurate predictions about how happy they were likely to be in response to these events. In other words, participants often made affective forecasting errors. For instance, a group of students currently in a romantic relationship, the *Luckies*, estimated how (un)happy they would be if their relationship ended. Not surprisingly, the *Luckies* expected to be quite unhappy if this happened. The researchers then compared the *Luckies' estimates* of happiness at the ending of their relationship with the *actual* happiness of *Leftovers*, students whose relationships had recently ended. Interestingly, the *Luckies' estimates* of their happiness were significantly lower than the *actual* happiness of the *Leftovers* (Gilbert et al., 1998).

Overestimating Happiness and Unhappiness

Negative Events

Gilbert et al. (1998) found similar results for the other events. The college professors overestimated how unhappy they would be during the 5-year period after being denied tenure. Furthermore, students whose candidate lost an election overestimated how unhappy this event would make them, as did other students who either unexpectedly received negative personal information, read a story about the death of a child, or were rejected in a job interview.

Other research reinforces these findings. In fact, affective forecasting errors are more likely in response to negative events than to positive events (Coteţ & David, 2016). Here are some other examples. Competitive runners strongly overestimate how unhappy they will feel if they fail to meet their personal performance goals (van Dijk, Finkenauer, & Pollmann, 2008). Also, pro-football fans overestimate how unhappy they will be if their team loses the Super Bowl (Meyvis, Ratner, & Levav, 2010). Other research (Loehr & Baldwin, 2014) shows that physically inactive individuals (who exercise less than

60 minutes per week) do not expect to enjoy exercise. However, they reported enjoying exercise more than they thought they would, again reflecting an affective forecasting error. Still other research replicated Gilbert et al.'s (1998) findings (e.g., Eastwick, Finkel, Krishnamurti, & Loewenstein, 2008; Meyvis et al., 2010; Norris, Dumville, & Lacy, 2011).

Finally, we also overestimate the happiness-producing potential of revenge, at least in some circumstances. Carlsmith, Wilson, and Gilbert (2008) randomly assigned participants the ability to punish a greedy and unscrupulous research confederate in a cooperative decision-making game that offered the chance for participants to win money. Results showed that participants made affective forecasting errors by overestimating how happy they would be after punishing the greedy research confederate. Perversely, participants who tried to get revenge by punishing the confederate actually felt *worse* than those who were not allowed the opportunity to get revenge.

Carlsmith et al. (2008) found that revenge has this negative effect because it traps participants into ruminating or obsessing about the offender, rather than moving on to more pleasant concerns. Subsequent research (Funk, McGeer, & Gollwitzer, 2014) demonstrates that participants can accurately forecast (predict) the effects of revenge, and these effects can be positive. However, this occurs only if the offender (the greedy and unscrupulous confederate) acknowledges the punishment, and, especially, if the offender promises to act morally in the future.

Positive Events

Do we also overestimate effects of positive events? The answer is that we often do. For instance, college students overestimate how happy they will be if they receive a higher than expected grade for an assignment (Sevdalis & Harvey, 2007) or if their school wins a football game against a rival (Wilson, Wheatley, Meyers, Gilbert, & Axsom, 2000). Furthermore, college students assigned to desirable on-campus housing were not as happy as they expected to be after 1 year (Dunn, Wilson, & Gilbert, 2003). Individuals also overestimate how happy they will be after making an important purchase (Meyvis et al., 2010). And couples expecting or considering having children overestimate how happy they will be after the birth of their child (Powdthavee, 2009). Sadly, our expectations about vacations are also overly "rosy" (Mitchell, Thompson, Peterson, & Cronk, 1997).

And still other research shows that highly desirable and extraordinary experiences that others are unlikely to have can have a surprisingly negative effect on happiness. The logic here is that extraordinary experiences, even if they are highly positive, are by definition not shared by many people (Cooney, Gilbert, & Wilson, 2014). The very unusual nature of extraordinary experiences may cause feelings of social isolation that, in turn, may cause a net decrease in happiness because social relationships are so important for human happiness (Baumeister & Leary, 1995).

Underestimating Happiness and Unhappiness

We also *underestimate* the effects of some actions and events on our happiness. For instance, we underestimate the pleasure of rediscovering mundane, everyday experiences from our past. Zhang, Kim, Brooks, Gino, and Norton (2014) asked participants to write about a recent conversation. Participants also indicated how enjoyable it would be to read what they wrote sometime in the future. Participants were contacted 7 months later and were shown what they had written about the conversation. Results showed that they enjoyed reading about their conversation more than they had anticipated.

Zhang et al. (2014) obtained similar results in several other studies, including one in which participants constructed a "time capsule" at the beginning of the summer containing information about recent social experiences, including social events, songs they had listened to, conversations, an inside joke, and so on. Participants again underestimated the pleasure of rediscovering this information at the end of the summer. Zhang et al. suggest that we under-appreciate our present mundane experiences. This causes us to fail to document the present (e.g., by keeping a journal), and leads us to fail to recognize how much we would enjoy rediscovering these experiences in the future.

There are other examples of underestimations of the effects of events on happiness. Commuters underestimate the enjoyment of taking a bus to work (and overestimate the pleasure of taking their car; Comerford, 2011). This affective forecasting error has important implications for the environment. It might be possible to pry people out of their cars and into more environmentally friendly public transportation if they were aware of results like these (Comerford, 2011). Other research related to the environment shows that we underestimate the pleasure of walking outdoors in an urban park setting (Nisbet & Zelenski, 2011).

Finally, consider the happiness-producing effects of virtuous or prosocial behaviors. In a review of the literature, Sandstrom and Dunn (2011) conclude that behaving virtuously—for instance, practicing generosity, gratitude, or forgiveness, or acting with integrity—unexpectedly increases our happiness. That is, these behaviors make us happier even though we do not expect them to do so. Dunn, Aknin, and Norton (2008) found that individuals expected to reap more happiness by spending money on themselves than by spending it on others. However, they found the opposite was true in a series of additional studies.

Causes of Affective Forecasting Errors

Immune Neglect

One explanation of affective forecasting errors is *immune neglect*. Gilbert et al. (1998) proposed that humans have a *psychological immune system* that protects us from the psychological consequences of negative events. Our psychological immune system reinterprets negative events so that they do not damage our self-image. According to Gilbert et al. (1998, p. 619), the human mind is artful in the ways it, ". . . ignores, augments, transforms, and rearranges information in its unending battle against the affective [emotional] consequences of negative events." Thus, our psychological immune system allows us to rationalize away or otherwise minimize negative events that threaten our happiness. Because negative events are fairly common, this immune system allows us to continue on with our lives without feeling gloomy all the time.

Gilbert et al. (1998) hypothesize that we are largely unaware of our psychological immune system because the system functions best when we are not closely observing.

The trickery involved in transforming and rearranging information to protect our self-image works best if we do not analyze it too closely.

We make forecasting errors about negative events precisely because we are unaware of the psychological immune system. Because of immune neglect, we do not realize that our minds come with special equipment designed to protect us from gloom-inducing negativity. Thus, if you ask me how I expect I would feel if I lost my job, my answer is that I would feel terrible. But the data suggest I would not feel as badly or for as long as I expect I would. According to Gilbert et al. (1998), this is largely because I am unaware of my psychological immune system that would quickly kick in to salvage at least a large part of my happiness. For instance, I would convince myself that I never really liked my job, that there are better opportunities elsewhere, that I should have left a long time before, that sleeping on my brother's couch really won't be so bad, and so on.

To sum up, our psychological immune systems equip us with the means to deal with negative events. But we are largely unaware of this marvelous feature of our brains. Thus, we make forecasting errors in which we overestimate the emotional impact of negative events. Finally, note that immune neglect can explain responses only to negative events. It cannot explain why we overestimate the emotional effects of positive events (Gilbert et al., 1998).

Focalism

Another explanation for affective forecasting errors is that we focus too much attention on the event, and fail to consider other things that are likely to affect our happiness. This explanation, called *focalism* (Wilson et al., 2000), can potentially explain forecasting errors in response to both positive and negative events. Whether you ask me how I expect to feel if I lost my job or if I won the lottery, I am probably going to be thinking only about the event itself, and not about other important factors.

Losing my job would obviously be bad, and if I am asked to think of this prospect, my mind will likely be laser-focused on that event. I am unlikely to think about related events that might increase my happiness. For instance, I might enjoy spending more time with my family, and I might find another job that is even better than the one I had. I also might make new friends or learn rewarding new skills during my job search. The prospect of losing my job focuses my mind so that I do not think about ongoing factors that bring me happiness apart from my job. For instance, I will still enjoy the love of my family and the support of my friends, along with mundane pleasures such as good food, beautiful sunsets, and so on. Therefore, because of my limited focus, I erroneously predict that I will be much unhappier than I am likely to be.

Focalism applies similarly to my expectations about positive events such as winning the lottery. Ask me how happy I expect to be upon winning the lottery, and my mind is fixated on that big check. I do not also think about how the money could change my relationships with friends and family in negative ways, for instance, or the ongoing pain in my knees that will still be there even after I cash the check. Thus, my estimate of future happiness relies too heavily on the positives surrounding the big check, and not enough on the potential negatives, and this focus causes me to overestimate how happy I will be.

Motivated Reasoning

A third explanation for affective forecasting errors is that they motivate individuals to accomplish goals. Specifically, I might be very motivated, and work very hard, to accomplish a goal that I expect to make me happy, or to avoid an outcome I expect to be disastrous. I might unconsciously make affective forecasting errors to motivate myself. Some evidence supports this perspective (Morewedge & Buechel, 2013).

Note the motivational tone here. Affective forecasting errors are linked to our desire to achieve a goal. These errors occur in strategic ways that can aid goal achievement: when we are committed to the goal, and if we think we have influence over the outcome. Furthermore, affective forecasting errors are likely to increase effort toward achieving the goal. Thus, one of the reasons we make affective forecasting errors is that these mistakes help motivate us. If we believe that an event will make us very happy or unhappy, we are more likely to try to influence its outcome.

Memory Failure

If we regularly make these affective forecasting errors, why don't we ever learn? It seems that eventually we would realize that our forecasts have been wrong so many times, and that insight would prod us toward a correction that would eventually lead to fewer of these errors. But that does not seem to be the case.

Meyvis et al. (2010) suggest that we do not learn from our affective forecasting mistakes because we forget them. They demonstrated that individuals made affective forecasting mistakes and then did not accurately remember their original forecast. For instance, in one study pro-football fans overestimated how unhappy they would be if their team lost the Super Bowl. However, after the loss they (mis)remembered their loss/unhappiness prediction as being less extreme that it actually was. Thus, we fail to learn from our forecasting mistakes because we erroneously think that our forecast was accurate.

Why does this misremembering of the original forecast happen? You might have learned that humans construct memories rather than pulling them out of their heads fully intact, the way one retrieves a file from a computer. Instead of being a snapshot that we simply recover, our memories are constructed by numerous factors, including our present environment and mood (Loftus, 1979). Meyvis et al. (2010) hypothesized and confirmed that after an event has occurred (e.g., participants' team has lost the Super Bowl), individuals construct memories of their affective forecasts about the event based on their *current* feelings. These memories accurately reflect the individuals' current experience, but not their *predictions* of their current experience.

Individual Differences

Neuroticism and extraversion from the Big Five personality inventory moderate (that is, change) affective forecasts. Specifically, neurotics are likely to underestimate, and extraverts overestimate, how happy they will be after an event (Hoerger & Quirk, 2010). Other research shows that introverts make affective forecasting errors by underestimating the positive effects of extraversion (sociability and outgoingness) that lead to greater happiness. Thus, introverts might be happier if they did not make this forecasting error (Zelenski et al., 2013).

Individuals high in emotional intelligence are more accurate affective forecasters (Dunn, Brackett, Ashton-James, Schneiderman, & Salovey, 2007; Hoerger, Chapman, Epstein, & Duberstein, 2012). *Emotional intelligence* is the capacity to perceive, regulate, and understand emotions and to use this ability to think more clearly (Mayer & Salovey, 1997). Emotionally intelligent individuals are more accurate affective forecasters because of their ability to identify emotions and to understand factors that produce them. Specifically, they are better at predicting future emotional states because they are able to recognize emotions, understand their causes, and know how long these emotions are likely to last (Dunn et al., 2007).

Some Implications: Ethics

You can probably think of many important implications of the affective forecasting errors. For instance, you may have considered the implications of underestimating how happy we will be if we exercise or overestimating the happiness associated with revenge. Anyone interested in increasing happiness can find some nuggets to work with in this literature.

But affective forecasting errors also influence ethical decisions. Specifically, individuals sometimes act unethically because they overestimate how unhappy they will be if they fail at a task. This overestimation of unhappiness, an affective forecasting error, can then lead them to drastic measures, such as cheating, in order to avoid failure (Noval, 2016).

Noval (2016) confirmed this hypothesis with college student participants considering an upcoming exam. Results indicated that students were *less* likely to consider cheating when they were focused on nonacademic aspects of their lives. Furthermore, these nonacademically focused students were less likely to make the affective forecasting error of thinking that a poor exam performance would make them unhappy. Thus, focalism and affective forecasting errors are linked to ethical behaviors. Noval (2016) replicated these findings in two other studies using hypothetical scenarios (for example, participants imagined they had a chance to land their dream job after college), and a fourth study in which real cheating behavior was assessed.

Noval (2016, p. 11) refers to the implications of these results as "profound." These results demonstrated that we may cheat in order to achieve a goal that we (perhaps incorrectly) think will increase our happiness. Noval argues that most organizations try to promote ethical behavior by hiring or otherwise selecting individuals with strong moral character traits, and by inspiring such behavior within the organization. However, this approach is limited because it is difficult to identify these character traits, and because situational factors can strongly affect behaviors. Therefore, Noval suggests that we should address the reasons for unethical behaviors instead. One of these reasons is that individuals overpredict how happy they will be after gaining rewards such as a raise or a promotion at work.

In summary, affective forecasting errors occur across a variety of situations, although they are more likely in response to negative than to positive events (Coteţ & David, 2016). There are several reasons why we make these mistakes. One is that we often direct too much attention and emphasis toward a specific event when we try to predict our future happiness. A student who lands a dream job right out of college might focus almost completely on that single fact when thinking about how happy he or she is likely to be in the future. As a result, the student might not recognize the many other factors that will also affect future happiness.

Affective forecasting errors also occur because we do not fully appreciate the power of our "psychological immune systems" to maintain our happiness when negative events occur. Memory failure, the fact that we forget how we have felt when previous events occurred, also contributes to forecasting errors. Finally, there may be an adaptive, motivational component that produces forecasting errors. Expecting that bad events will make us very unhappy and positive events will make us very happy may motivate us to work hard to avoid the bad events and achieve the good ones.

There are also some interesting individual differences in affective forecasting. For instance, depressives are not only inaccurate; they are also more likely to be negatively biased in their forecasts. They are more likely to expect a negative event to make them unhappy and less likely to think a positive event will make them happy. On the other hand, emotionally intelligent individuals are more accurate in their forecasting than other individuals.

Affective forecasting has important implications, including the possibility that we might sometimes make unethical choices because we overestimate how much happiness success might bring us. There are other implications as well. For instance, if we overestimate the unhappiness brought on by a romantic breakup, we might stay in the relationship longer than is necessary or healthy. Likewise, if we overestimate the happiness produced by career success, we might devote so much energy to our career that we have little left over for other important parts of our lives.

Finally, it is important to recognize that no one is saying that we make forecasting mistakes in every situation. Although affective forecasting errors are common, we do not make mistakes every time we think about our future happiness. As Gilbert et al. (1998, p. 617) eloquently observe, we make accurate forecasts in many situations:

> But are these [affective] forecasts correct? In some ways they undoubtedly are. For example, most people recognize that a weekend in Paris would be more enjoyable than gallbladder surgery, and few people fear chocolate or tingle in anticipation of next year's telephone directory.

FLOW

Have you ever felt like you were "in the zone" when you were doing something that really interested you? Maybe you were learning to play a musical instrument or were working on a complicated puzzle. Perhaps you were doing something that took physical skill, like rock climbing or juggling. You may even have been studying for a class that particularly interested you. Whatever the activity, you may have felt that you were completely involved in what you were doing and that time just melted away without your noticing. You may have also felt that the activity was extremely challenging, but you were also confident you could complete your tasks if you kept trying. If so, you were probably experiencing something called *flow*. The experience of flow is an important component of positive emotions, and it predicts long-term happiness (Csikszentmihalyi, 1979, 1999).

For some necessary background to understanding flow, consider the work of Csikszentmihalyi[3] (1975), who wondered what led creative individuals to doggedly persist in their craft despite difficult circumstances. What made artists, for instance, keep painting for long hours, seemingly ignoring fatigue and hunger, with little regard for any direct external reward they could receive from their intense labors? Furthermore, why did these individuals seemingly lose interest in their projects once they were completed (Nakamura & Csikszentmihalyi, 2002)?

To find out, Csikszentmihalyi interviewed creative and dedicated individuals. He realized that there was something immensely compelling about activities that were intrinsically or naturally interesting and that contained just the right amount of challenge. He adopted the term *flow* to describe these experiences because it was used spontaneously by many of those he interviewed. For instance, a poet who was also an experienced rock climber used the term to describe the self-contained motivation of writing poetry and rock climbing.

> . . . The justification of climbing is climbing, like the justification of poetry is writing; you don't conquer anything except things in yourself. . . . The act of writing justifies poetry. Climbing is the same: recognizing that you are a flow. The purpose of the flow is to keep on flowing, not looking for a peak or utopia but staying in the flow . . . you move up only to keep the flow going. There is no possible reason for climbing except the climbing itself. . . . (Csikszentmihalyi, 1975, pp. 47–48)

Csikszentmihalyi (1975, 1999) eventually collected interviews from more than 10,000 individuals from many walks of life, including athletes, surgeons, artists, writers and academics, business professionals, and blue-collar workers. These individuals described remarkably similar flow experiences (Csikszentmihalyi, 1975, 1999). First, there was a close match between the demands of the task and respondents' skill sets, such that the task was extremely challenging, but doable. Second, respondents accomplished a series of goals and closely monitored their progress and changed their behaviors as necessary to complete these goals. And finally, respondents entered a particular state of consciousness with the following properties:

- ▶ Intense concentration on the task at hand
- ▶ Full awareness of the actions taken to complete the task
- ▶ Fading of awareness of oneself, with focus solely on the task
- ▶ Feeling of control over the task
- ▶ Loss of sense of time (time usually seems to slip by quickly)
- ▶ Intense intrinsic interest in the task

The final point regarding intrinsic interest is particularly important. Csikszentmihalyi (1975) notes that it was the inherent interest in the task at hand that largely drove the experience. Individuals seeking external rewards did not experience flow, and external rewards were incompatible with experiencing flow. This is why individuals in flow quickly lose interest in the task once it is completed. It is the pursuit of the task that really matters, not whatever comes after the task is completed. To emphasize the importance of intrinsic interest, he refers to flow experiences as *autotelic experiences*, a phrase derived from the Greek language (*autos* "self"; *telos* "goals"). He later also proposed the idea of an autotelic personality type, indicating individuals were predisposed to experience flow because they sought out activities that were inherently interesting to them (Nakamura & Csikszentmihalyi, 2002).

Remember the 10,000 interviews of individuals from all walks of life that forms to the basis of Csikszentmihalyi's (1975, 1999) theory? He found that individuals in all these professions, or with differing hobbies, could experience flow when they worked on tasks that were intrinsically interesting and challenging. This led Csikszentmihalyi (1999, p. 826) to a major conclusion about happiness, "People are happy not because of what they do, but because of how they do it." For instance, assembly line workers can be in flow, while someone at a luxury resort may not be. Thus, flow, and by consequence happiness as well, is available to all of us if and when we find intrinsic interests to pursue.

Flow and Positive Emotions

The immediate experience of flow can be positive, but is not necessarily so. Remember the poet/rock climber quoted about his flow experiences? That person also had this to say about flow and climbing, "The mystique of rock climbing is climbing; you get to the top of a rock glad it's over but really wish it would go forever" (Csikszentmihalyi, 1975, p. 47). There is often an element of flow that is hard work, stressful, or both. This is largely because we experience the highest levels of flow when challenges do not quite exceed our skill level.

So why are we discussing flow in a chapter about joy and positive emotions? There are two reasons. One is that to reach maximal flow, we have to be confident that our skills, though taxed to the limit, are enough to complete the task. This is often associated with positive feelings (Csikszentmihalyi, 1975). Fredrickson also notes that flow is similar to many positive emotions such as interest because interest and the intrinsic motivation required to produce flow are almost interchangeable (Catalino & Fredrickson, 2011; Fredrickson, 1998, 2001). Fredrickson (2013a) reports that she used parts of Csikszentmihalyi's (1990) theory to support the BBT when it was first under development.

The second reason to link flow and positive emotions is that flow can build *psychological capital* that can be useful later, and can foster future positive emotions. Csikszentmihalyi (2003) describes how this works by thinking about the choices available to him when he comes home from work. He can sit and watch television, or he can do something more active like read a book, volunteer at a hospital, learn to play the guitar, and so on. The latter activities are more likely to build important psychological skills that can be used later. These skills are a resource or capital that can build future positive emotions.

Do you notice a similarity between the idea of psychological capital and Fredrickson's (2001) notion of *resiliency* from the BBT? Like positive emotions, flow can build resources that can be beneficial later (Csikszentmihalyi, 2003). These resources can potentially make us more resilient. Therefore, flow can build positive emotions in a similar way that Fredrickson (2001) describes. Although it is not always the case, flow is often experienced as a positive emotion (Nakamura & Csikszentmihalyi, 2002). Fredrickson also notes that flow is similar to many positive emotions such as interest (Catalino & Fredrickson, 2011; Fredrickson, 1998, 2001).

Empirical Evidence

Research from a number of different laboratories working from multiple perspectives confirms Csikszentmihalyi's (1975) flow hypothesis. Much of this research has relied on *experience sampling*, in which respondents are queried (via pagers or cell phones) about their current experiences several times during the day as they go through their normal routines. This gives researchers a glimpse of respondents' "natural" life and experiences. Research using this method shows that the flow experience is relatively common among creative individuals (Nakamura & Csikszentmihalyi, 2002). It also generally shows that a close match between challenge and skills is an important component of flow. Individuals must feel challenged to enter a flow state, but they cannot feel overwhelmed (Fong, Zaleski, & Leach, 2015).

Flow also predicts happiness (Csikszentmihalyi, 1999, 2000; Robinson, Kennedy, & Harmon, 2012). For instance, quality of Chicagoans' psychological experience was more strongly predicted by flow than it was by whether they were at work or were pursuing a leisure activity (Csikszentmihalyi & LeFevre, 1989). In addition, quality of flow experience predicted greater life satisfaction and positive affect, as well as less negative affect, in a sample of adults aged 70 and older (Collins, Sarkisian, & Winner, 2009). It also predicted life satisfaction in a sample of adults from India (Sahoo & Sahu, 2009), and American adolescents (Csikszentmihalyi & Hunter, 2003). It was also associated with happiness among mountain climbers in Taiwan (Tsaur, Yen, & Hsiao, 2013) and white water kayakers in West Virginia (Jones, Hollenhorst, & Perna, 2003).

Some Applications

Schools

Introducing more opportunities for flow could be of great benefit to our educational systems (Csikszentmihalyi, 1999). Students who feel flow in school perform better and are more committed to their schoolwork. Schoolwork can, and sometimes does, consist of high challenge/high skill activities that produce flow. School can also contribute to the development of the autotelic personality type (individuals who are particularly good at finding flow). However, and unfortunately, schoolwork can also consist of high challenge/ low skill activities in which students are subjected to high pressure testing with inadequate preparation. This combination builds stress and deflates intrinsic motivation and flow (Nakamura & Csikszentmihalyi, 2002).

Literature reviews of student interests and motivations indicate that young children are often eager to learn but often lose this interest early in their school careers. Instead of being active learners, they often seem bored and disengaged from school. This may be because schools have difficulty sparking the intrinsic interests of children. In other words, students may not have adequate opportunities to experience flow in school (Shernoff & Csikszentmihalyi, 2009).

Are there ways to solve this problem? The flow perspective suggests that there are two critical components to engaging students optimally in their learning. One is that the subject matter needs to be challenging and relevant. The second is that conditions must be right so that students can have a positive emotional experience from their academic work. This positive emotional experience requires that students feel they have some control over their learning and that they have the skills to meet academic challenges. They must also feel actively involved in their learning. For example, passively listening to lectures tends to undermine positive reactions to academics. Instead, the ability to interact with peers and teachers is more conducive to optimal engagement (Shernoff & Csikszentmihalyi, 2009).

Finally, teachers' sense of engagement (flow) can also be important and can contribute to students' positive emotional experiences in schools. Some research suggests that teachers' sense of flow can be contagious and cross over to their students. Taken together, these positive emotional learning experiences promote a sense of self-esteem, enjoyment, and enhanced intrinsic motivation among students. Teachers' influence can lead students to more fully enjoy school and also improve students' performance (Shernoff & Csikszentmihalyi, 2009).

Consumerism and Materialism

Flow—or more accurately, the lack of flow—may also be related to our unhappy reactions to Western consumer culture. Csikszentmihalyi (2000, 2003) observes that much of his experience sampling data indicates that many Americans spend little time in flow or otherwise actively engaged in something that is intrinsically interesting. He hypothesizes from these observations that many individuals may use consumerism and materialism (seeking consumer products) as a way to compensate for the lack of flow in their lives.

Csikszentmihalyi (2000) argues that the pursuit of consumer products is depicted by marketers as an effective way to become socially engaged and to meet important psychological needs for mastery, control, and self-esteem. These appeals can be persuasive to those who are not often in flow. However, the promises of marketers are quite hollow, and material pursuits do not offer effective long-term ways to meet these needs. As a result, consumerism is a poor substitute for flow, and the long-term consequence of pursuing consumer products rather than active engagement in interesting pursuits is lowered happiness.

According to Csikszentmihalyi (2003), a big part of the problem is that material pursuits, such as coveting and acquiring just the right clothes or car, can bring momentary pleasure, but not long-term enjoyment or happiness. The reason relates to the idea of psychological capital. Simply buying something, or simply watching television, does not build skills that will help one more effectively pursue happiness or build psychological capital, and will not make one happy in the long run. Csikszentmihalyi (2003) argues that we need to reject materialism and work toward a world in which we strive to meet psychological needs for belongingness and self-esteem by seeking flow through active pursuit of intrinsic interests.

As we have seen, the experience of flow is a special category of positive emotions and is associated with skill development and well-being. The important characteristics of this experience are intrinsic motivation and a close match between skills and challenges. There are several important applications of flow, including ways to improve student engagement and learning in schools.

SUMMARY

Positive emotions are not only pleasurable; they are also essential for our long-term happiness. Positive emotions help us build skills and develop resiliencies that help us cope with life challenges. The appropriate ratio of positive to negative emotions can also lead to an upward spiral of positivity that increases well-being.

In addition, it appears that we can intentionally, and successfully, pursue positive emotions and happiness. However, we must be careful to conduct our pursuit in the right way. One critical feature of this pursuit is that we must recognize that we are not always very accurate at recognizing what will truly make us happy (or sad). We often make affective forecasting errors. Therefore, we must choose our happiness goals carefully.

NOTES

1. Both of these results were partial mediations, indicating that some of the relationship between the predictor and the outcome variable did not go through the mediator.

2. There has been some controversy about the legitimacy of the affective forecasting effect. See Levine, Lench, Kaplan, and Safer (2012) and Wilson and Gilbert (2013) for a review. However, the basic effect appears well supported. For instance, reviews by Coteţ and David (2016) and Mathieu and Gosling (2012) show that there are errors in affective forecasting.

3. Pronounced "Cheek—sent—me—high."

REFERENCES

Baumeister, R. F., & Leary, M. R. (1995). The need to belong: Desire for interpersonal attachments as a fundamental human motivation. *Psychological Bulletin, 117*(3), 497–529.

Burns, A. B., Brown, J. S., Sachs-Ericsson, N., Plant, E. A., Curtis, J. T., Fredrickson, B. L., & Joiner, T. E. (2008). Upward spirals of positive emotion and coping: Replication, extension, and initial exploration of neurochemical substrates. *Personality and Individual Differences, 44*(2), 360–370.

Carlsmith, K. M., Wilson, T. D., & Gilbert, D. T. (2008). The paradoxical consequences of revenge. *Journal of Personality and Social Psychology, 95*(6), 1316–1324.

Catalino, L. I., Algoe, S. B., & Fredrickson, B. L. (2014). Prioritizing positivity: An effective approach to pursuing happiness? *Emotion, 14*(6), 1155–1161.

Catalino, L. I., & Fredrickson, B. L. (2011). A Tuesday in the life of a flourisher: The role of positive emotional reactivity in optimal mental health. *Emotion, 11*(4), 938–950.

Chaves, C., Hervas, G., Garcia, F. E., & Vazquez, C. (2016). Building life satisfaction through well-being dimensions: A longitudinal study in children with a life-threatening illness. *Journal of Happiness Studies, 17*(3), 1051–1067.

Cohn, M. A., & Fredrickson, B. L. (2010). In search of durable positive psychology interventions: Predictors and consequences of long-term positive behavior change. *The Journal of Positive Psychology, 5*(5), 355–366.

Cohn, M. A., Fredrickson, B. L., Brown, S. L., Mikels, J. A., & Conway, A. M. (2009). Happiness unpacked: Positive emotions increase life satisfaction by building resilience. *Emotion, 9*(3), 361–368.

Collins, A. L., Sarkisian, N., & Winner, E. (2009). Flow and happiness in later life: An investigation into the role of daily and weekly flow experiences. *Journal of Happiness Studies, 10*(6), 703–719.

Comerford, D. A. (2011). Attenuating focalism in affective forecasts of the commuting experience: Implications for economic decisions and policy making. *Journal of Economic Psychology, 32*(5), 691–699.

Conway, A. M., Tugade, M. M., Catalino, L. I., & Fredrickson, B. L. (2013). *The broaden-and-build theory of positive emotions: Form, function, and mechanisms.* New York, NY: Oxford University Press.

Cooney, G., Gilbert, D. T., & Wilson, T. D. (2014). The unforeseen costs of extraordinary experience. *Psychological Science, 25*(12), 2259–2265.

Coteţ, C. D., & David, D. (2016). The truth about predictions and emotions: Two meta-analyses of their relationship. *Personality and Individual Differences, 94*, 82–91.

Csikszentmihalyi, M. (1975). Play and intrinsic rewards. *Journal of Humanistic Psychology, 15*(3), 41–63.

Csikszentmihalyi, M. (1979). Play is real, work is escape. *Contemporary Psychology, 24*(4), 313–314.

Csikszentmihalyi, M. (1990). The domain of creativity. In M. A. Runco & R. S. Albert (Eds.), *Theories of creativity* (pp. 190–212). Thousand Oaks, CA: Sage.

Csikszentmihalyi, M. (1999). If we are so rich, why aren't we happy? *American Psychologist, 54*(10), 821–827

Csikszentmihalyi, M. (2000). The costs and benefits of consuming. *Journal of Consumer Research, 27*(2), 267–272.

Csikszentmihalyi, M. (2003). Legs or wings? A reply to R. S. Lazarus. *Psychological Inquiry, 14*(2), 113–115.

Csikszentmihalyi, M., & Hunter, J. (2003). Happiness in everyday life: The uses of experience sampling. *Journal of Happiness Studies, 4*(2), 185–199.

Csikszentmihalyi, M., & LeFevre, J. (1989). Optimal experience in work and leisure. *Journal of Personality and Social Psychology, 56*(5), 815–822.

Diener, E., Kanazawa, S., Suh, E. M., & Oishi, S. (2015). Why people are in a generally good mood. *Personality and Social Psychology Review, 19*(3), 235–256.

Dunn, E. W., Aknin, L. B., & Norton, M. I. (2008). Spending money on others promotes happiness. *Science, 319*(5870), 1687–1688.

Dunn, E. W., Brackett, M. A., Ashton-James, C., Schneiderman, E., & Salovey, P. (2007). On emotionally intelligent time travel: Individual differences in affective forecasting ability. *Personality and Social Psychology Bulletin, 33*(1), 85–93.

Dunn, E. W., Wilson, T. D., & Gilbert, D. T. (2003). Location, location, location: The misprediction of satisfaction in housing lotteries. *Personality and Social Psychology Bulletin, 29*(11), 1421–1432.

Eastwick, P. W., Finkel, E. J., Krishnamurti, T., & Loewenstein, G. (2008). Mispredicting distress following romantic breakup: Revealing the time course of the affective forecasting error. *Journal of Experimental Social Psychology, 44*(3), 800–807.

Fong, C. J., Zaleski, D. J., & Leach, J. K. (2015). The challenge–skill balance and antecedents of flow: A meta-analytic investigation. *The Journal of Positive Psychology, 10*(5), 425–446.

Ford, B. Q., Dmitrieva, J. O., Heller, D., Chentsova-Dutton, Y., Grossmann, I., Tamir, M., . . . Mauss, I. B. (2015). Culture shapes whether the pursuit of happiness predicts higher or lower well-being. *Journal of Experimental Psychology: General, 144*(6), 1053–1062.

Ford, B. Q., & Mauss, I. B. (2014). The paradoxical effects of pursuing positive emotion: When and why wanting to feel happy backfires. In J. Gruber & J. T. Moskowitz (Eds.), *Positive emotion: Integrating the light sides and dark sides* (pp. 363–381). New York, NY: Oxford University Press.

Ford, B. Q., Mauss, I. B., & Gruber, J. (2015). Valuing happiness is associated with bipolar disorder. *Emotion, 15*(2), 211–222.

Ford, B. Q., Shallcross, A. J., Mauss, I. B., Floerke, V. A., & Gruber, J. (2014). Desperately seeking happiness: Valuing happiness is associated with symptoms and diagnosis of depression. *Journal of Social and Clinical Psychology, 33*(10), 890–905.

Forgas, J. P. (2014). On the downside of feeling good: Evidence for the motivational, cognitive and behavioral disadvantages of positive affect. In J. Gruber & J. T. Moskowitz (Eds.), *Positive emotion: Integrating the light sides and dark sides* (pp. 301–322). New York, NY: Oxford University Press.

Frankl, V. (1986). *The doctor and the soul* (3rd ed.). New York, NY: Vintage Books.

Frankl, V. (1988). The will to meaning: Foundations and applications of logotherapy. New York, NY: Penguin Books.

Frankl, V. (2006). *Man's search for meaning.* Boston, MA: Beacon Press. (Original work published 1946)

Fredrickson, B. L. (1998). What good are positive emotions? *Review of General Psychology, 2*(3), 300–319.

Fredrickson, B. L. (2001). The role of positive emotions in positive psychology: The broaden-and-build theory of positive emotions. *American Psychologist, 56*(3), 218–226.

Fredrickson, B. L. (2009). *Positivity: Groundbreaking research reveals how to embrace the hidden strength of positive emotions, overcome negativity, and thrive.* New York, NY: Crown Publishers/Random House.

Fredrickson, B. L. (2012). *Building lives of compassion and wisdom.* New York, NY: Guilford Press.

Fredrickson, B. L. (2013a). Learning to self-generate positive emotions. In D. Hermans, B. Rimé, & B. Mesquita (Eds.), *Changing emotions* (pp. 151–156). New York, NY: Psychology Press.

Fredrickson, B. L. (2013b). Updated thinking on positivity ratios. *American Psychologist, 68*(9), 814–822.

Fredrickson, B. L., & Branigan, C. (2005). Positive emotions broaden the scope of attention and thought-action repertoires. *Cognition and Emotion, 19*(3), 313–332.

Fredrickson, B. L., Cohn, M. A., Coffey, K. A., Pek, J., & Finkel, S. M. (2008). Open hearts build lives: Positive emotions, induced through loving-kindness meditation, build consequential personal resources. *Journal of Personality and Social Psychology, 95*(5), 1045–1062.

Fredrickson, B. L., & Joiner, T. (2002). Positive emotions trigger upward spirals toward emotional well-being. *Psychological Science, 13*(2), 172–175.

Fredrickson, B. L., & Losada, M. F. (2005). Positive affect and the complex dynamics of human flourishing. *American Psychologist, 60*(7), 678–686.

Fredrickson, B. L., Mancuso, R. A., Branigan, C., & Tugade, M. M. (2000). The undoing effect of positive emotions. *Motivation and Emotion, 24*(4), 237–258.

Funk, F., McGeer, V., & Gollwitzer, M. (2014). Get the message: Punishment is satisfying if the transgressor responds to its communicative intent. *Personality and Social Psychology Bulletin, 40*(8), 986–997.

Garland, E. L., Fredrickson, B., Kring, A. M., Johnson, D. P., Meyer, P. S., & Penn, D. L. (2010). Upward spirals of positive emotions counter downward spirals of negativity: Insights from the broaden-and-build theory and affective neuroscience on the treatment of emotion dysfunctions and deficits in psychopathology. *Clinical Psychology Review, 30*(7), 849–864.

Gilbert, D. T., Pinel, E. C., Wilson, T. D., Blumberg, S. J., & Wheatley, T. P. (1998). Immune neglect: A source of durability bias in affective forecasting. *Journal of Personality and Social Psychology, 75*(3), 617–638.

Gloria, C. T., Faulk, K. E., & Steinhardt, M. A. (2013). Positive affectivity predicts successful and unsuccessful adaptation to stress. *Motivation and Emotion, 37*(1), 185–193.

Hoerger, M., Chapman, B. P., Epstein, R. M., & Duberstein, P. R. (2012). Emotional intelligence: A theoretical framework for individual differences in affective forecasting. *Emotion, 12*(4), 716–725.

Hoerger, M., & Quirk, S. W. (2010). Affective forecasting and the Big Five. *Personality and Individual Differences, 49*(8), 972–976.

Hurling, R., Linley, A., Dovey, H., Maltby, J., & Wilkinson, J. (2015). Everyday happiness: Gifting and eating as everyday activities that influence general positive affect and discrete positive emotions. *International Journal of Wellbeing, 5*(2), 28–44.

Isen, A. M., & Daubman, K. A. (1984). The influence of affect on categorization. *Journal of Personality and Social Psychology, 47*(6), 1206–1217.

Isen, A. M., Daubman, K. A., & Nowicki, G. P. (1987). Positive affect facilitates creative problem solving. *Journal of Personality and Social Psychology, 52*(6), 1122–1131.

Jones, C., Hollenhorst, S., & Perna, F. (2003). An empirical comparison of the Four Channel Flow Model and Adventure Experience Paradigm. *Leisure Sciences, 25*(1), 17–31.

Joshanloo, M., & Weijers, D. (2014). Aversion to happiness across cultures: A review of where and why people are averse to happiness. *Journal of Happiness Studies, 15*(3), 717–735.

Kay, J. (2012). *Obliquity*. New York, NY: Penguin Press.

Kim, M. Y., Ford, B. Q., Mauss, I., & Tamir, M. (2015). Knowing when to seek anger: Psychological health and context-sensitive emotional preferences. *Cognition and Emotion, 29*(6), 1126–1136.

Kok, B. E., Coffey, K. A., Cohn, M. A., Catalino, L. I., Vacharkulksemsuk, T., Algoe, S. B., . . . Fredrickson, B. L. (2013). How positive emotions build physical health: Perceived positive social connections account for the upward spiral between positive emotions and vagal tone. *Psychological Science, 24*(7), 1123–1132.

Layous, K., & Lyubomirsky, S. (2014). The how, why, what, when, and who of happiness: Mechanisms underlying the success of positive activity interventions. In J. Gruber & J. T. Moskowitz (Eds.), *Positive emotion: Integrating the light sides and dark sides* (pp. 473–495). New York, NY: Oxford University Press.

Levine, L. J., Lench, H. C., Kaplan, R. L., & Safer, M. A. (2012). Accuracy and artifact: Reexamining the intensity bias in affective forecasting. *Journal of Personality and Social Psychology, 103*(4), 584–605.

Linley, P. A., Dovey, H., de Bruin, E., Transler, C., Wilkinson, J., Maltby, J., & Hurling, R. (2013). Two simple, brief, naturalistic activities and their impact on positive affect: Feeling grateful and eating ice cream. *Psychology of Well-Being: Theory, Research and Practice, 3*(6), 1–14.

Loehr, V. G., & Baldwin, A. S. (2014). Affective forecasting error in exercise: Differences between physically active and inactive individuals. *Sport, Exercise, and Performance Psychology, 3*(3), 177–183.

Loftus, E. F. (1979). The malleability of human memory. *American Scientist, 67*(3), 312–320.

Loh, J. M. I., Schutte, N. S., & Thorsteinsson, E. B. (2014). Be happy: The role of resilience between characteristic affect and symptoms of depression. *Journal of Happiness Studies, 15*(5), 1125–1138.

Luhmann, M., Necka, E. A., Schönbrodt, F. D., & Hawkley, L. C. (2016). Is valuing happiness associated with lower well-being? A factor-level analysis using the valuing happiness scale. *Journal of Research in Personality, 60*, 46–50.

Lyubomirsky, S. (2008). *The how of happiness: A new approach to getting the life you want.* New York, NY: Penguin Press.

Lyubomirsky, S. (2013). *The myths of happiness: What should make you happy, but doesn't, what shouldn't make you happy, but does.* New York, NY: Penguin Press.

Lyubomirsky, S., Dickerhoof, R., Boehm, J. K., & Sheldon, K. M. (2011). Becoming happier takes both a will and a proper way: An experimental longitudinal intervention to boost well-being. *Emotion, 11*(2), 391–402.

Lyubomirsky, S., & Layous, K. (2013). How do simple positive activities increase well-being? *Current Directions in Psychological Science, 22*(1), 57–62.

Lyubomirsky, S., Sheldon, K. M., & Schkade, D. (2005). Pursuing happiness: The architecture of sustainable change. *Review of General Psychology, 9*(2), 111–131.

Mathieu, M. T., & Gosling, S. D. (2012). The accuracy or inaccuracy of affective forecasts depends on how accuracy is indexed: A meta-analysis of past studies. *Psychological Science, 23*(2), 161–162.

Mauss, I. B., Savino, N. S., Anderson, C. L., Weisbuch, M., Tamir, M., & Laudenslager, M. L. (2012). The pursuit of happiness can be lonely. *Emotion, 12*(5), 908–912.

Mauss, I. B., Tamir, M., Anderson, C. L., & Savino, N. S. (2011). Can seeking happiness make people unhappy? Paradoxical effects of valuing happiness. *Emotion, 11*(4), 807–815.

Mayer, J. D., & Salovey, P. (1997). What is emotional intelligence? In P. Salovey & D. J. Sluyter (Eds.), *Emotional development and emotional intelligence: Educational implications* (pp. 3–34). New York, NY: Basic Books.

Meyvis, T., Ratner, R. K., & Levav, J. (2010). Why don't we learn to accurately forecast feelings? How misremembering our predictions blinds us to past forecasting errors. *Journal of Experimental Psychology: General, 139*(4), 579–589.

Mitchell, T. R., Thompson, L., Peterson, E., & Cronk, R. (1997). Temporal adjustments in the evaluation of events: The "rosy view." *Journal of Experimental Social Psychology, 33*(4), 421–448.

Morewedge, C. K., & Buechel, E. C. (2013). Motivated underpinnings of the impact bias in affective forecasts. *Emotion, 13*(6), 1023–1029.

Nakamura, J., & Csikszentmihalyi, M. (2002). *The concept of flow*. New York, NY: Oxford University Press.

Nisbet, E. K., & Zelenski, J. M. (2011). Underestimating nearby nature: Affective forecasting errors obscure the happy path to sustainability. *Psychological Science, 22*(9), 1101–1106.

Norris, C. J., Dumville, A. G., & Lacy, D. P. (2011). Affective forecasting errors in the 2008 election: Underpredicting happiness. *Political Psychology, 32*(2), 235–249.

Noval, L. J. (2016). On the misguided pursuit of happiness and ethical decision making: The roles of focalism and the impact bias in unethical and selfish behavior. *Organizational Behavior and Human Decision Processes, 133*, 1–16.

Powdthavee, N. (2009). Think having children will make you happy? *The Psychologist, 22*(4), 308–310.

Robertson, I. (2016). *The stress test: How pressure can make you stronger and sharper*. London, UK: Bloomsbury.

Robinson, K., Kennedy, N., & Harmon, D. (2012). The flow experiences of people with chronic pain. *OTJR: Occupation, Participation and Health, 32*(3), 104–112.

Sahoo, F. M., & Sahu, R. (2009). The role of flow experience in human happiness. *Journal of the Indian Academy of Applied Psychology, 35*, 40–47.

Sandstrom, G. M., & Dunn, E. W. (2011). The virtue blind spot: Do affective forecasting errors undermine virtuous behavior? *Social and Personality Psychology Compass, 5*(10), 720–733.

Sevdalis, N., & Harvey, N. (2007). Biased forecasting of postdecisional affect. *Psychological Science, 18*(8), 678–681.

Shernoff, D. J., & Csikszentmihalyi, M. (2009). *Flow in schools: Cultivating engaged learners and optimal learning environments*. New York, NY: Routledge/Taylor & Francis.

Sidgwick, H. (1981). *Methods of ethics* (7th [Hackett reprint] ed.). Indianapolis, IN: Hackett. (Original work published 1874)

Sin, N. L., & Lyubomirsky, S. (2009). Enhancing well-being and alleviating depressive symptoms with positive psychology interventions: A practice-friendly meta-analysis. *Journal of Clinical Psychology, 65*(5), 467–487.

Tamir, M., & Ford, B. Q. (2012). When feeling bad is expected to be good: Emotion regulation and outcome expectancies in social conflicts. *Emotion, 12*(4), 807–816.

Tsaur, S., Yen, C., & Hsiao, S. (2013). Transcendent experience, flow and happiness for mountain climbers. *International Journal of Tourism Research, 15*(4), 360–374.

van Dijk, W. W., Finkenauer, C., & Pollmann, M. (2008). The misprediction of emotions in track athletics: Is experience the teacher of all things? *Basic and Applied Social Psychology, 30*(4), 369–376.

Waugh, C. E., & Fredrickson, B. L. (2006). Nice to know you: Positive emotions, self-other overlap, and complex understanding in the formation of a new relationship. *The Journal of Positive Psychology, 1*(2), 93–106.

Wilson, T. D., & Gilbert, D. T. (2005). Affective forecasting: Knowing what to want. *Current Directions in Psychological Science, 14*(3), 131–134.

Wilson, T. D., & Gilbert, D. T. (2013). The impact bias is alive and well. *Journal of Personality and Social Psychology, 105*(5), 740–748.

Wilson, T. D., Wheatley, T., Meyers, J. M., Gilbert, D. T., & Axsom, D. (2000). Focalism: A source of durability bias in affective forecasting. *Journal of Personality and Social Psychology, 78*(5), 821–836.

Zelenski, J. M., Whelan, D. C., Nealis, L. J., Besner, C. M., Santoro, M. S., & Wynn, J. E. (2013). Personality and affective forecasting: Trait introverts underpredict the hedonic benefits of acting extraverted. *Journal of Personality and Social Psychology, 104*(6), 1092–1108.

Zhang, T., Kim, T., Brooks, A. W., Gino, F., & Norton, M. I. (2014). A "present" for the future: The unexpected value of rediscovery. *Psychological Science, 25*(10), 1851–1860.

CHAPTER 5

Social Relationships

No road is long with good company.

—Turkish Proverb

Have you ever spent any appreciable amount of time alone? Do you usually feel like you belong to a group of other people? How have you felt during these times?

These are important questions because they address a fundamental aspect of human psychology, the extent to which humans are social creatures. We need other people, not just for practical assistance like someone to care for our pets while we are out of town, but for the deep emotional closeness that others can provide. Emotional connections to others are essential for our well-being. Interestingly, the number of mere acquaintances we have—people we know casually, but do not feel strongly connected to—does not matter as much as whether we have a few people in our lives with whom we feel a close emotional bond.

In this chapter, we also explore fascinating questions about whether marriage improves happiness, and whether romantic relationships are necessary to feel happy. In addition, we investigate the effect of parenthood on happiness and marital satisfaction. Social relationships are such a fundamental area in the study of human happiness, and romantic relationships and parenthood are especially interesting and important.

THE NEED TO BELONG

A Theory

The focal point of research in this area is a ground-breaking theoretical paper hypothesizing that humans have an innate "need to belong" by Baumeister and Leary (1995). They proposed that this need to belong is a fundamental human motive that is evolutionarily based and is therefore prevalent cross-culturally. This motivation has two essential elements. First, we need frequent, emotionally pleasant interactions with the same person over a period of time. Second, the interactions must include a feeling of emotional bondedness. There must be a perception of caring for each other's welfare. We also need these caring interactions to recur frequently at predictable intervals, and we must have the expectation that they will continue into the future.

The Need to Belong Theory includes several important predictions. Perhaps the most important is that human happiness is dependent on satisfying this need to belong. The authors hypothesized that forming meaningful relationships increases well-being, and that a deficit of caring relations harms well-being. The theory also predicts that any threats to our feelings of belongingness should affect our attention and thought processes.

Another prediction follows closely from these elements of the theory. We are specifically motivated to form *caring and emotionally bonded relationships*. This is not a theory of mere affiliation. Mere acquaintances are not expected to be satisfying. For example, there are several people I say hello to during my walk to work every day. Although we are friendly with each other, I do not know these people well. I do not socialize with them and do not know much about their families. We do not have the sense of mutual caring and concern for each other's welfare beyond the usual goodwill people feel for others who live in the same neighborhood. The theory predicts that I could have dozens of these kinds of relationships and not satisfy my need to belong. The *quality* of the relationships matters much more than the *quantity*.

The theory also predicts that our need to belong will be satisfied by a relatively small number of close emotional bonds. We will become *satiated* after forming just a few bonds. Although the precise tipping point is not specified (three close friends, four?), Baumeister and Leary emphasize that our motivation to form close relationships will diminish as we approach some critical number. At that point we will even begin to resist forming new relationships.

Other important predictions are that we will form social bonds easily (before satiation) and that we will resist breaking them. Furthermore, we will readily *substitute* relationship partners when a bond does decay. Baumeister and Leary predict that relationship partners are interchangeable. There is not a particular type of person we need to satisfy our need to belong. Finally, these authors predict that our perceptions and cognitions are closely attuned to finding and maintaining relationships.

This brings us to some important distinctions between Baumeister and Leary's theory and other theories. For instance, the Need to Belong Theory's insistence that our relationship partners are interchangeable differs markedly from both attachment theory (Bowlby, 1969) and Freudian theory (Freud, 1962), both of which specify that our relationship with an early caregiver (typically our mother) is essential to our well-being. The theory is also unique in that it characterizes the need to belong as a fundamental human motivation, as opposed to other motivational theories that emphasize sex (Freud, 1962, 2002), consistency (Festinger, 1957), attachment (Bowlby, 1969), or meaning (Baumeister, 1991), to give some examples.

Initial Support for the Theory

Baumeister and Leary (1995) support their theory with a strong array of evidence. For instance, their review of the literature indicates that people around the globe form social bonds easily, and that they resist breaking them. They also found that human cognitive processes are focused interpersonally. For instance, we think about our group differently (often more favorably) than we do about other groups. We make more extreme judgments about out-group members than we do in-group members, and we are more likely to forget the bad things that members of our group do. And our cognitive processes are driven by our relationships with others. For example, we are more likely to attend to the characteristics of individuals when we are considering a close relationship with them.

Importantly, the strength of the emotional bond matters. Baumeister and Leary (1995) found no convincing evidence that mere affiliation is satisfying. But they did find that we are happier when we experience close emotional bonds and that we suffer when we do not. Finally, they also found support for their substitution (that we readily form new bonds when old ones are broken) and satiation hypotheses.

Strong initial support for the theory has been confirmed by subsequent research. For instance, Gere and MacDonald (2010) recently reviewed the literature and concluded that it was broadly supported. The Need to Belong Theory has held up well over the years.

Subsequent Research

Before we dive into the details of the research I would like to offer a notion of caution and support. Understanding subsequent research is crucial for our understanding of the fundamental question about whether humans have a basic motivation to belong. Think about how relevant the following questions are to our personal lives and to the societies in which we live. Are we happier having lots of acquaintances, or do we need emotionally close friendships? Are we limited in the number of friendships we are capable of supporting? What happens when we are socially excluded?

The research details are important, but do not lose sight of the big picture. We are examining cognitive processes, for instance, in order to see whether humans respond as if there is a fundamental need to belong. Do the data support this hypothesis? Keeping this basic question in mind will help you make sense of the details.

Cognitive Processes

Subsequent research confirms that threats to our sense of belonging affect our thought processes. For instance, Knowles (2014) found that the experience of social exclusion affected participants' social memories and caused them to take another person's perspective. Similarly, O'Connor and Gladstone (2015) found that social exclusion caused participants to see social networks and social connections that did not actually exist.

These results are consistent with Baumeister and Leary's (1995) hypothesis that threats to belongingness change thought processes. Both results also show that we respond to social exclusion in ways that could be associated with rebuilding social ties, either by taking the perspective of others or by looking closely for social connections. Furthermore, these results support the contention that the need to belong is a basic motivation that is wired into human psychology, because it affects important cognitive processes. Almost all the behaviors described in subsequent sections involve accompanying thought processes.

Satiation Hypothesis

The satiation hypothesis (that there is a relatively low number of individuals to whom we seek to become closely emotionally attached) has not been fully tested. However, DeWall, Baumeister, and Vohs (2008) provided evidence consistent with this hypothesis. DeWall et al. reason that motivations that are satisfied become weaker. For example, we feel less motivated to eat after a large meal. Consequently, they hypothesize that individuals are less motivated to work toward social relationship goals when they feel satiated or secure in their relationships.

They tested this in a series of six studies by, for instance, giving participants false feedback (positive or negative) about their prospects for satisfying relationships in the future. All participants then played a game that required effort and concentration. Before beginning the game, half the participants were told performance on the game was "diagnostic" of social skills, and the other half were not. The design was therefore a 2 (future alone or with others) × 2 (game diagnostic of social skills or not), with four conditions. The outcome measure was how accurately and quickly participants completed the game.

Consistent with predictions that need to belong motivations can be satiated, only those participants who were told they would not have satisfying relationships in the future, and who thought the test was diagnostic of social skills, worked hard to demonstrate social skills (they performed well in the game). This was presumably because they were not relationally satiated, and because they thought that a good performance would indicate they had the social skills necessary for good relationships. As expected, participants who expected satisfying relationships in the future and those who did not think the game was a diagnostic did not perform well, presumably because the game did not offer an opportunity to improve their prospects for social relationships.

This is not a direct test of the satiation hypothesis. That would require demonstrating that individuals with existing emotionally close relationships reject opportunities for additional similar relationships. But DeWall et al.'s (2008) study is important because it demonstrates that individuals lose motivation to pursue goals relevant to relationships when they are satiated.

Other evidence (e.g., Waytz & Epley, 2012) demonstrates that socially connected (i.e., satiated) individuals are more likely to dehumanize others. Again, the evidence here is indirect, but it is consistent with the satiation hypothesis. That the socially satiated dehumanize others is consistent with the notion that they are not looking to form additional social relationships.

In conclusion, more research is needed on this topic, although the satiation hypothesis has received indirect support. It would be interesting to see a direct test of the hypothesis in which satiated individuals had a chance to forgo other social contacts, if this could be done ethically. If confirmed, research should also investigate the psychological mechanisms that produce satiation. For instance, what emotional signals tell us we are satiated? How is the experience of satiation perceived?

The implications of this hypothesis are worth considering. What does it say about human happiness if it turns out that we become satiated after a relatively small number of close emotional relationships? Perhaps the answer to this question is more philosophical than scientific. But it also may impact thinking about ways to improve human happiness, suggesting that societies must titrate the balance between human needs for emotional closeness and emotional privacy.

Quality of Relationships

Some clever research supports Baumeister and Leary's contention that the depth of our relationships matters. For example, Mehl, Vazire, Holleran, and Clark (2010) persuaded undergraduates to wear an "electronically activated recorder" (EAR) for 4 days. The EAR is an unobtrusive audio recorder designed to capture samples of conversation during a person's day. Results showed that substantive conversations, with meaningful social exchanges (e.g., "She fell in love with your dad? So, did they get divorced soon after?" Mehl et al., 2010, p. 539), predicted overall well-being and happiness even after controlling for personality differences.

In addition, Anderson, Kraus, Galinsky, and Keltner (2012) found that sociometric status, ". . . the respect and admiration one has in face-to-face groups (e.g., among friends or coworkers" (p. 1), was more strongly related to well-being than was socionomic status, a measure that includes income. Furthermore, attachment patterns, a measure of the quality of relationships, are also strongly linked to happiness (Mikulincer & Shaver, 2013). Finally, perceptions of social support are also important predictors of happiness. Interestingly, the perception of social support is more important than the actual support given (Lakey, 2013).

Other evidence shows that the *quality* of relationships is more important than the *quantity* of relationships. For example, Demir and Özdemir (2010) examined friendship patterns among college students and found that quality of friendship is positively associated with happiness, and that emotionally meaningful friendships are more predictive of happiness than are casual friendships. Similarly, Saphire-Bernstein and Taylor (2013) conclude from a literature review that while marriage is not a strong predictor of happiness, marital *quality* predicts much more strongly.

Social Exclusion and Happiness

Evidence is mixed concerning whether threats of social exclusion (i.e., threats to our need to belong) produce unhappiness (Gere & MacDonald, 2010). Recall that serious negative consequences of this threat are an important conclusion of Baumeister and Leary's theory. Consistent with this conclusion, literature reviews find that long-term social exclusion in real-world settings is associated with increased risk of dying by as much as 400% and that the increased mortality risk is equivalent to the risk posed by smoking (Tay, Tan, Diener, & Gonzalez, 2013).

However, Gere and MacDonald's (2010) review indicates that some studies show no effect of social exclusion on happiness, while others show either decreases in positive affect or increases in negative affect. The potential for null effects here is important because it would constitute a major disconfirmation of the Baumeister and Leary's theory of the need to belong. These are puzzling findings, because, in addition to contradicting the theory, it just seems odd that social exclusion would not lower happiness.

And they are particularly puzzling given the findings for the correlation of social exclusion and mortality in the findings of Tay et al. (2013).

There are several potential explanations for these findings. Gere and MacDonald (2010) suggest that personality differences may explain these inconsistent results. Baumeister and Leary hypothesized the possibility of personality differences in the *degree* to which individuals feel the need to belong, so Gere and MacDonald's (2010) interpretation of these results could be consistent with the original theory.

Several other explanations of these puzzling findings are also consistent with the theory. One possibility is that individuals feel emotional numbness in response to exclusion that may not register as a negative emotion (Baumeister & DeWall, 2005). Another is that there may be different reactions to *social exclusion* versus *ostracism*. Mere social exclusion may not always bring unhappiness because there may be opportunities to repair the relationship or find new relationships.

However, ostracism is a more absolute form of social exclusion, and it therefore might be more painful. Researchers find that ostracism is universally unpleasant (Wölfer & Scheithauer, 2013). In fact, van Beest, Williams, and van Dijk (2011) found that unhappiness is such a pervasive response to ostracism that the only exception to this rule they could manufacture was to ostracize participants from a simulated game of Russian roulette!

Researchers have addressed the possibility that social exclusion may not always lead to unhappiness because of opportunities to repair the relationship or find new ones by considering the timing of the outcome measure. Both Richman and Leary (2009) and Williams (Williams, 2007; Williams & Carter-Sowell, 2009) theorize that immediate responses to exclusion are emotionally negative, but that later responses, or when participants are asked to project into the future, may not necessarily be negative.

For example, Richman and Leary (2009) developed a model in which, although the immediate emotional response to exclusion is always negative, this initial response is tempered by how the individual interprets ("construes" in Richman and Leary's terminology) the exclusion. For instance, an excluded individual who perceives that the relationship can be repaired or replaced will respond more positively to the exclusion.

In conclusion, it is important to recognize that these explanations are not competing with the Need to Belong Theory. If confirmed, these explanations would indicate that social exclusion does produce unhappiness unless there is a way to quickly find other relationships. The emotional numbness hypothesis is also consistent with the theory in that numbness is a sort of pain that researchers have not yet been able to measure adequately. In addition, the hypothesis regarding personality differences in need to belong motivation is also consistent with Baumeister and Leary's theory.

Social Exclusion and Behavior

We would also expect that behavior, and not just emotions like happiness, would respond to social exclusion. However, behavioral responses to exclusion are curiously inconsistent. Gere and MacDonald (2010) note that the expected prediction from Baumeister and Leary's model is that excluded individuals would act to gain social inclusion and that this effort would presumably include socially desirable and norm-appropriate responding.

However, they conclude that research often indicates that individuals respond to social exclusion with aggression and retaliation.

Gere and MacDonald (2010) note that these antisocial responses to exclusion might be the result of artificial laboratory conditions in many of these studies. Specifically, in many studies, participants are not given an opportunity to repair social relationships or create new ones. Gere and MacDonald note that other studies indicate that when given an opportunity, excluded participants often look for chances to join social groups (such as Maner, DeWall, Baumeister, & Schaller, 2007; Twenge, Baumeister, Tice, & Stucke, 2001). If confirmed, this insight about the artificial lab conditions would indicate that social exclusion does move behavior in the direction predicted by the Need to Belong Theory.

Social Exclusion and Pain

Research indicates that social exclusion is painful and that humans experience this pain similarly to the way we experience physical pain (Bernstein & Claypool, 2012; Eisenberger, Lieberman, & Williams, 2003; Gere & MacDonald, 2010; MacDonald & Leary, 2005). This finding is important because it confirms the fundamental human motivation hypothesis for the need to belong. After all, if the need to belong is a basic motivation, then there should be some built in punishment system that alerts us when the motivation is not satisfied.

That we experience emotional and physical pain in similar ways is also consistent with the need to belong as a fundamental motivation because it ties emotional pain to evolutionarily derived physiological architecture. MacDonald and Leary (2005) argued that the physiology for emotional pain evolved on top of the already developed architecture for physical pain. When inclusion in social groups became important to their survival, social animals underwent selection pressures that favored individuals who experienced exclusion as unpleasant. Research has confirmed this hypothesis (Bernstein & Claypool, 2012; DeWall & Bushman, 2011; Riva, Romero-Lauro, DeWall, & Bushman, 2012).

Let's consider two studies as a sample of the evidence relating social and physical pain. First, Eisenberger et al. (2003) gathered images of brain activity while participants were socially excluded. Those images indicated that socially excluded participants showed brain activity that was similar to that typically shown by participants experiencing physical pain. Specifically, both the anterior cingulate cortex and the right ventral prefrontal cortex were active in excluded participants. This activity also predicted self-reports of distress.

DeWall et al. (2010) demonstrated the overlap between physical and social pain centers in the brain by finding that acetaminophen reduces social pain. They found that participants randomly assigned to take 1,000 milligrams of acetaminophen each day for 3 weeks reported lower levels of hurt feelings than did a placebo control group. A second study found that acetaminophen reduced brain activity in the dorsal anterior cingulate cortex, an area previously associated with physical/emotional pain overlap.

In conclusion, social exclusion literally hurts, similarly to the way physical pain hurts (Riva et al., 2012; Vangelisti, Pennebaker, Brody, & Guinn, 2014). If we are motivated to belong, we would expect social exclusion to be unpleasant, and we would also expect it to be tied to our basic physiology. Take note of the practical implications of this important insight for the psychology of happiness. Our bodies are constructed to feel pain when we are socially excluded. Any attempts to increase happiness, either on the personal or societal level, must take this finding seriously.

Personality Differences and the Need to Belong

Personality affects individuals' need to belong motivation (Gere & MacDonald, 2010). Baumeister and Leary (1995) acknowledge this possibility and frame this as differences in the *degree* to which individuals differ in the need to belong. In fact, Leary, Kelly, Cottrell, and Schreindorfer (2013) developed a scale to measure individual differences in the need to belong, and research shows that there are important individual differences in this motivation (Lavigne, Vallerand, & Crevier-Braud, 2011).

For instance, individuals who are poorly attached, have low self-esteem, are socially anxious and/or depressed, and who are hypersensitive to rejection show strong need to belong motivation. This heightened sensitivity perversely causes increased difficulty in forming and maintaining relationships, because such individuals feel a persistent need for social reassurance, among other challenges. Sensitive individuals also react to social contact as a potential *threat*, in that they constantly feel that it will be withdrawn. Other individuals see social contact as differentially *rewarding*. For example, avoidantly attached individuals, who perceive relationships as unrewarding, do not evidence need to belong motivations as strongly as do other individuals (Gere & MacDonald, 2010).

Some theoretical work has integrated and formalized how individuals see social contact as a threat or as a potential reward. Lavigne et al. (2011) hypothesized two ways that individuals express belongingness needs. *Growth-oriented* individuals actively seek relationships and social commitments, because they view relationships as *enriching*. Such individuals are nondefensive and relatively unafraid of opening up to others, because they do not fear negative judgments. Lavigne et al. propose that growth orientation is associated with higher levels of well-being. On the other hand, while *deficit reduction–oriented* individuals also seek social relationships, their motivation is not based on enrichment, but to fill a social void because of a lack of social acceptance. These individuals are characterized by loneliness, social anxiety, eagerness for social acceptance, and lower levels of well-being.

Lavigne et al. (2011) show that the two orientations are statistically distinct and valid. For instance, both orientations predict belongingness motivations, but deficit reduction orientation is more strongly associated with avoiding social rejection than is growth orientation. Second, the two orientations predict well-being in different ways. As expected, growth orientation is positively associated with well-being, while deficit reduction is negatively associated. In conclusion, these results indicate that all individuals are motivated by a need to belong. However, the underlying reasons for this motivation and the way this motivation manifests itself can differ markedly across individuals with important implications for well-being. These results have been replicated by other researchers, including Pillow, Malone, and Hale (2015).

There is ample evidence that humans universally feel a need to belong (Lavigne et al., 2011), and that this is a basic human motivation (DeWall et al., 2008, 2010). In fact, some researchers suggest that a major contributor to the Facebook epidemic is a general human need to belong (Nadkarni & Hofmann, 2012), in which Facebooking is a modern expression of this motivation. Social exclusion, which blocks our need to belong, affects thinking patterns (Gere & MacDonald, 2010), probably reduces well-being (Richman & Leary, 2009; Williams, 2007; Williams & Carter-Sowell, 2009), causes something akin to real physical pain (DeWall et al., 2010), and alters behavior (Gere & MacDonald, 2010).

Although we all seem to feel the need to belong, we can experience this motivation in different ways, and these differences influence our well-being (Lavigne et al., 2011). Depending on the level of attachment or growth orientation, individuals can feel greater or smaller amounts of the motivation, although all individuals appear to feel this motivation, at least to some degree. It is also interesting that personality differences can cause the belongingness motivations to hinder or facilitate positive relationships.

Finally, the quality of our social contacts matters more than the quantity (Demir, Orthel, & Andelin, 2013), and we appear to become satiated by a relatively low number of close and emotionally meaningful social relationships (DeWall et al., 2008). Overall, Baumeister and Leary's (1995) theory is well supported.

A MARRIAGE "BENEFIT"?

We would expect marriage to strongly increase well-being, thus providing a "marriage benefit." This makes sense, given our discussion of evolution, and the Need to Belong Theory. After all, marriage can satisfy evolutionary motivations to reproduce, and it should also provide the emotionally close relationship humans are so motivated to find. There are other reasons to expect marriage to increase well-being. For instance, it can provide meaningful social roles that are recognized and encouraged by cultural institutions that help foster life purpose. It can also strengthen the commitment between relationship partners (Musick & Bumpass, 2012).

Research shows that there is a relationship between marriage and happiness (Diener, Suh, Lucas, & Smith, 1999; Wadsworth, 2016). But it is a big jump to go from observing this relationship to being confident that marriage is a cause of happiness. There are several alternative (i.e., noncausal) explanations for this relation. And there are other qualifications we need to consider. For instance, the quality of the marriage is crucial, as is the quality of single persons' relationships. Bad marriages do not increase happiness, and single people can be quite happy if they cultivate other (i.e., nonmarital) relationships.

Does Marriage Cause Happiness?

Although marriage predicts happiness, it may not *cause* happiness. Obviously, researchers cannot randomly assign some individuals to get married, and others to remain single, so it is difficult to eliminate other explanations for the marriage–happiness relationship (DePaulo, 2011). For example, the direction of causality is unclear. Married individuals might be happier because they are just naturally happy, at least as compared to singles. The idea that happiness causes marriage (rather than marriage causing happiness) is called the *selection hypothesis* (i.e., happier people are *selected* into marriage).

It is also possible that marriage and happiness are only coincidentally related because of their common ties to some third variable. For instance, there could be a personality variable that causes people both to be happy and to get married. If so, this would coincidentally create a relationship between marriage and happiness.

Another related question concerns whether, if marriage does cause happiness, the relation is permanent or only temporary. As we shall see in Chapter 6, we can become adapted to a given level of income. What seemed at one time to be lots of money can seem ordinary or even unsatisfactory after a while. Does the same thing happen for marriage? If marriage does cause a happiness boost, does this wear off? Do we adapt to marriage and feel less happy about being married over time?

Researchers have made a lot of progress toward answering these questions. Cross-sectional studies that compare married and single individuals at a single point in time have found that marrieds are happier than singles, even after statistically controlling for variables like income and age (Diener et al., 1999). This helps to eliminate the third variable question. Our confidence that the marriage/happiness relationship is not the result of third variables is further strengthened by longitudinal studies we discuss next. These studies have also instituted careful statistical controls for third variables.

Selection

The selection hypothesis explains at least part of the happiness differences between married and single people (Lucas & Clark, 2006). Stutzer and Frey (2006) found support for selection in a German longitudinal study. Because they obtained measurements of happiness over time, Stutzer and Frey could observe that singles who eventually marry are happier than those who never marry. This difference remains even after statistically controlling for sociodemographic factors. Stutzer and Frey reported that the happiness gap between individuals who never marry and those who eventually marry is "substantial," but they also state that selection effects likely do not completely explain the happiness differences between married and single individuals.

There is also genetic evidence for selection effects. Horn, Xu, Beam, Turkheimer, and Emery (2013) examined identical and fraternal twins who were either married or single. Recall that identical twins are genetically identical, and fraternal twins share 50% of their DNA, just as non-twin siblings do. The design allowed the authors to control for both shared genetic and environmental influences. Therefore, they could more precisely estimate the extent to which "happier" individuals are more likely to get married, and the effect this has on well-being.

Horn et al. (2013) found that the health benefits of marriage are completely due to selection. Happier and healthier people are more likely to get married, which explained the relationship between these variables. However, similar to Stutzer and Frey's (2006) results, selection explains only part of the relationship between marriage and psychological well-being. Some of the marriage/happiness relationship is explained by the "protective effect" of marriage. For example, among sets of identical twins in which one member was married and the other was single, the married twin scored 0.13 standard deviations lower on a depression index than the unmarried co-twin. Thus, the evidence shows a bidirectional relationship between marriage and happiness: Happiness is both a cause and a consequence of marriage (Braithwaite & Holt-Lunstad, 2017).

Adaptation

There is quite a bit of support for the marriage adaptation hypothesis from longitudinal studies (e.g., Frijters, Johnston, & Shields, 2011; Lucas & Clark, 2006; Lucas, Clark, Georgellis, & Diener, 2003; Luhmann, Hofmann, Eid, & Lucas, 2012; Stutzer & Frey, 2006). Luhmann et al. (2012) conducted a meta-analysis, a literature review in which the results of various studies were statistically combined, which showed that life satisfaction rises as the wedding approaches, is higher after weddings than immediately before, but then decreases in the following months, even returning to the original baseline level individuals feel before the approach of the wedding. Interestingly, marriage has no effect on affective well-being (i.e., cheerfulness).

These adaptation effects appear fairly quickly. Most of the decline in life satisfaction toward premarriage baseline levels occurs within 4 years of marriage (Luhmann et al., 2012). The effects are consistent for age and gender: Adaptation rates are similar for men and women, and individuals' age at marriage does not influence adaptation. Interestingly, adaptation is less pronounced among couples who did not separate during the time of the study. However, even couples who do not separate show adaptation effects.

Subsequent research has challenged these conclusions in favor of adaptation. This research suggests that evidence for or against the adaptation effect depends on when the first measure of happiness is taken. Qari (2014) examined longitudinal data from Germany, and found that individuals who were married for at least 5 years were happier than they were when they were single. This finding contradicts the adaptation hypothesis.

But, Qari (2014) used the period of 5 years before marriage to define singlehood, rather than 1 or 2 years before marriage. The reasoning for choosing this time period is made apparent by Figure 5.1. Note that happiness starts to increase dramatically 2 years before marriage. Qari argues that this increase is part of the boost of happiness that comes from marriage, because individuals are typically enjoying relationships with their future

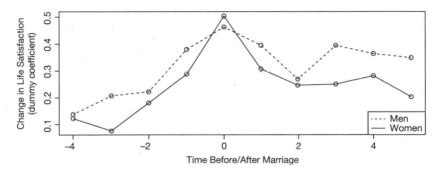

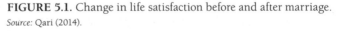

FIGURE 5.1. Change in life satisfaction before and after marriage.
Source: Qari (2014).

spouse during this time. In other words, individuals are not really single at this time, but they were single 5 years before marriage. The figure shows that individuals do not completely adapt to marriage if the baseline time period for singlehood is moved back to a time when they presumably had not yet begun a relationship with their future spouse. Note that the lines at 5 years after marriage do not return to the happiness levels (on the y-axis) experienced 3 or 4 years before marriage.

Also note that the lines do slope down after the wedding (the 0 on the x-axis), so some adaptation occurs, although this adaptation is not complete. Qari estimates the size of the adaptation effect as 60% for women and 25% for men. In other words, after 5 years of marriage, women lose 60% of the increase in happiness they experienced leading up to marriage and men lose 25% of this happiness. So by these estimates marriage does offer a lasting boost in happiness.

And this happiness boost is large. Qari estimates that the impact of marriage on happiness is two or three times larger than the happiness difference of being employed versus unemployed! In monetary terms, it would take about €32,000 to replace the happiness a woman who was married for 5 years would lose if she were no longer married. The equivalent for a man married for 5 years is about €53,000.

The question about whether marriage is a cause of happiness seems to come down to our views about adaptation. Given the combination of cross-sectional and longitudinal research, all including careful statistical controls, it seems unlikely (but still possible) that a third variable is creating the relationship between marriage and happiness, just by coincidence. And, while it is true that happy individuals are more likely to get married, this finding cannot explain the entire relationship between marriage and happiness. Longitudinal studies also show that marriage is associated with increased happiness. Thus, selection cannot entirely explain the marriage/happiness relationship.

If we accept Qari's (2014) argument that marriage really begins about 2 years before the wedding, it appears that individuals do not fully adapt to marriage. Instead, they have long-lasting and meaningful increases in happiness compared to when they were single (5 years before marriage). As a result, there is a strong argument that marriage causes happiness.

Potential Solutions to the Adaptation Problem

Many of my students are disillusioned when they read about adaptation and marriage. Even partial adaptation undermines the romantic ideal of "happy ever after" that we associate with marriage. However, adaptation is probably not inevitable. Sonja Lyubomirsky, a distinguished psychological scientist, has studied well-being extensively and has written two informative and readable books that give advice about preventing or minimizing adaptation effects. I highly recommend both of these: Lyubomirsky, 2008, 2013.

Based on her own extensive research and that of many of her colleagues, Lyubomirsky (2008) advises us to consciously cherish and enjoy our relationships, in addition to looking for ways to keep them fresh. Also, Sheldon and Lyubomirsky (2012) proposed a Hedonic Adaptation Prevention Model, which emphasizes appreciation of life changes and seeking variety in events surrounding a life change. The model helped college students resist hedonic adaptation to various positive events they were experiencing (Sheldon & Lyubomirsky, 2012). Bao and Lyubomirsky (extended the model by specifically applying it to romantic relationships.

Recent research from another lab is consistent with Lyubomirsky's recommendations. Coulter and Malouff (2013) recruited 101 Australian couples by using newspaper, radio, and social media sources. Half the couples were randomly assigned to list 10 "exciting" activities they could do together (they were given examples from different domains including "adventurous," "sexual," "interesting," and "spontaneous" as prompts). These couples then set aside 90 minutes a week for 4 weeks to enable them to engage in one of these activities each week. The other half of the couples were wait-listed, completed the intervention 4 weeks later, and served as controls.

Results support the idea that adaptation can be resisted. Intervention couples experienced greater positive affect and relationship satisfaction than controls. Furthermore, intervention couples showed benefits from the program 4 weeks after the study was completed. Interestingly, levels of excitement mediated the relationship between the intervention and increased relationship satisfaction. In other words, the intervention apparently worked because it increased couples' sense of shared excitement, and this increased excitement was the direct cause of greater relationship satisfaction. Consistent with Lyubomirsky's suggestions, couples need not necessarily experience adaptation to their marriage (Lyubomirsky, 2008; Sheldon & Lyubomirsky, 2012). But it often takes conscious effort to build in excitement and other emotional characteristics that are necessary to forestall adaptation.

Individual Differences

Depression

The effect of marriage seems to depend, at least in part, on personality factors and other individual differences. You may have noticed that marriages differ among the people you know in lots of ways, including happiness. For example, depression level has an ironic relation to happiness in marriage. Frech and Williams (2007) found that individuals showing signs of depression prior to marriage showed the largest *gains* in well-being following marriage in a large and nationally representative longitudinal sample of American adults.

It is important to note that these "depressed" individuals were not necessarily clinically depressed, but they did evidence more symptoms than the general population (they scored at or above the 80th percentile on the measurement scale). Frech and Williams (2007) suggest that their "depressed" participants showed a larger marriage effect because they were more likely to benefit from the companionship that is inherent in marriage. Regardless, the larger point for our purposes is that individuals experience differing "marriage benefits" depending on their personal characteristics.

Marriage Quality

Marriage quality was another important factor that influenced well-being in the Frech and Williams (2007) study. Their results indicate that individuals' happiness is affected by the quality of their marriage (as measured by marital quality and conflict). Not surprisingly, individuals are happier when they are in a low-conflict, high-quality marriage. This was the case regardless of the level of depressive symptomatology participants in the study showed before entering marriage.

Although Frech and Williams (2007) did not explicitly measure well-being, they argued on theoretical and methodological grounds that their measures of depression qualify as an indicator of the "absence" of well-being. Again, the larger point: The happiness effect of marriage depends, this time, on the quality of the marriage. Frech and Williams conclude:

> These findings call into question the assumption that marriage is always a good choice for all individuals. What appear to be strong average benefits of marriage are actually highly dependent on a range of individual, interpersonal and structural characteristics. (2007, p. 149)

These conclusions about the importance of marriage quality are reinforced by other research. A meta-analysis of 93 studies by Proulx, Helms, and Buehler (2007) showed that higher marital quality predicted greater well-being. Furthermore, Bourassa, Sbarra, and Whisman (2015) found that women in low-quality marriages had higher life satisfaction after they divorced.

Other research shows that marriages have different trajectories that are linked to well-being, thus further supporting the idea that not all marriages are the same, and that marital quality matters. For instance, Dush, Taylor, and Kroeger (2008) found three separate trajectories of marital happiness—low, middle, and high—in a large nationally representative longitudinal sample of American adults, consistent with the idea that not all marriages are experienced the same way. These marital happiness trajectories were linked to overall well-being. Specifically, every 1 point increase in overall well-being (on a 3-point scale of well-being) resulted in a 247% increase in the probability of being in the high marital happiness trajectory, and a 77% decreased probability of being in the low marital happiness trajectory. Described another way, Dush et al.'s (2008) results show an association between marital happiness and overall well-being. In addition, overall well-being for low marital happiness individuals significantly decreased over time, while it did not decrease, or decreased only slightly, for high marital happiness individuals.

Some recent research indicates that high-quality marriages are associated with increased overall well-being, at least among certain populations. Carr, Freedman, Cornman, and Schwarz (2014) examined a sample of older adults (at least 60 years old with a spouse who was at least 50 years old) in the United States. These authors found that marital satisfaction was strongly related to overall life satisfaction.

In fact, in Carr et al.'s (2014) study, a 1 point increase on a 4-point marital satisfaction scale was associated with a 0.45 point increase in life satisfaction. However, being nondisabled was associated with only a 0.23 point increase in life satisfaction (the authors also collected data on the effects of disability). Marital happiness does have a comparatively large effect on life satisfaction. In addition, the husband's life satisfaction was increased when his wife was satisfied with the marriage, but decreased when his wife was less satisfied. Interestingly, the wife's life satisfaction was not related to her husband's marital satisfaction.

Individuals in happy marriages have higher levels of well-being than those in less happy marriages. The former begin marriage happier, and their happiness does not decline over time as much as for individuals in less satisfactory marriages. Again, marriage as a whole does not affect happiness in the same way. *Happy* marriages are associated with higher levels of well-being, but not all marriages show this association.

Is Marriage Essential? The Cohabitation Question

An interesting accompanying question concerns whether couples who cohabitate without marriage are as happy as those who marry. Social science research has traditionally supported the value of marriage (DePaulo & Morris, 2005, 2006; Musick & Bumpass, 2012). However, recent work suggests that cohabitation may not negatively affect older American adults. For instance, Musick and Bumpass (2012) found that married and cohabitating individuals over 50 years of age had similar levels of well-being in a longitudinal study in the United States. In addition, individuals who cohabitated before marriage were not less happy than participants who did not.

The cohabitation effect may also depend on culture. Soons, Liefbroer, and Kalmijn (2009) examined a longitudinal study of Dutch young adults, and found that married and cohabitating individuals were similarly happy and that cohabitating before marriage did not decrease well-being after marriage. Gender norms and other cultural factors may explain the different findings in the United States and the Netherlands. For example, Soons and Kalmijn (2009) found that happiness differences between the married and cohabiters was smaller in countries that were more accepting of cohabitation, and almost zero in countries where cohabitation is fully accepted (see also Wiik, Keizer, & Lappegård, 2012). Other research has produced similar findings, showing that cohabitants were similar in happiness to marrieds in countries that are more gender egalitarian and less religious (e.g., Lee & Ono, 2012; Stavrova, Fetchenhauer, & Schlösser, 2012).

Still other research suggests that the ratio of married versus cohabitating individuals within a society matters. Wadsworth (2016) examined census data in the United States and found that the differences between married and single individuals' life satisfaction scores approximately doubles when 80% of their peers are married versus only 20% of their peers are married. It is not clear whether this is a cultural effect or a universal effect of conformity or a similar process. It would be interesting to try to replicate these effects in other cultures. If they do replicate (i.e., similar effects of ratios are found in other cultures), that would suggest that psychological process-like conformity or social comparisons affect marriage's ability to boost happiness.

All the results refer to *psychological well-being* measures such as life satisfaction. However, individuals who cohabitate may be lower in *social well-being* than are married individuals. Social well-being assesses social adjustment (does the individual feel integrated into a coherent social structure, does the person have a place in society, and can he or she make a contribution to society?) and perceived social support. This makes sense because marriage is such a strongly held social and cultural institution. Cohabiters, particularly in the United States, might be socially marginalized, and this might explain why they feel less socially integrated (Shapiro & Keyes, 2008).

Are Ongoing Sexual Partnerships Essential?

Happy Singles?

Popular culture promotes the idea that real happiness is not possible without a sexual partnership (DePaulo & Morris, 2005). But is this true? DePaulo and Morris (DePaulo, 2011; DePaulo & Morris, 2005, 2006) do not think so.

Instead, DePaulo (2011) and DePaulo and Morris (2005) reviewed the evidence and found that singles, defined as individuals without a sexual *partnership*,[1] can be as happy as those engaged in ongoing sexual relationships, including marrieds. How can this be? How can stereotypically "lonely" singles be just as happy as individuals cocooned in committed relationships, particularly given the evidence for Baumeister and Leary's (1995) Need to Belong Theory?

DePaulo and Morris (2005) argue that, consistent with the Need to Belong Theory, singles ". . . typically *do* have lasting, positive, and significant relationships" (p. 71, emphasis in the original) that are essential for human well-being. Furthermore, they argue that friends and siblings are likely to meet the belongingness needs of singles. For instance, they review evidence that singles are particularly likely to be close to their siblings, nephews, and nieces and that they find sibling relationships particularly rewarding. In another review, DePaulo (2011) found that singles work harder to maintain relationship ties than marrieds do. For instance, they are more likely to visit and spend time with friends and relatives. DePaulo's (2011) review also found that singles had as many strong attachments to others as did married individuals.

Modern Marriage

DePaulo and Morris (2005) also criticize modern conceptions of marriage as having unrealistic expectations that one partner will satisfy all of an individual's emotional needs, including needs for sexual and emotional intimacy, along with needs such as those for recreation and intellectual stimulation. They argue that marriage can stifle well-being because it can unduly limit individuals' options for having their needs met. It is worth quoting DePaulo and Morris (2005, pp. 76–77, bracketed expression added) at length here.

> In the cult of the couple, the [sexual partnership] roles include sexual playmate, best friend, soul mate, and many others. The contemporary couple, in scientific theory as well as in the cultural imagination, is the ultimate all-in-one solution. It is the human equivalent of the phone that takes pictures, sends e-mails, records messages, receives faxes, and also functions as a conventional phone. When it works, it is efficient and convenient. But when it breaks down, then the owner suddenly has no camera, no e-mail, no answering machine, no fax, and no phone.
>
> It might be argued that in a couple, each person is a backup for the other, and it is singles who have to provide everything for themselves. The couple, the argument goes, has two all-in-one phones, whereas the single has just one. But

that argument harkens back to the caricature of the single person as isolated and alone. Our argument is that both singles and couples are likely to benefit from having a number of significant people in their lives rather than just one. No one person is ever present at all times, psychologically engaged at all times, or repositories for all manner of ideas, skills, or advice.

Other theorists have supported DePaulo and Morris' (2005) critique of the potentially limiting effect of marriage. Finkel, Hui, Carswell, and Larson's (2014) "The Suffocation of Marriage" proposes that Americans are increasingly (in a long-term historical sense) looking to marriage to fulfill higher order Maslovian needs for self-actualization. Furthermore, any desire to use marriage to fulfill these needs naturally requires a larger investment of time and emotional energy in the marriage. However, modern Americans have reduced their emotional investments in marriage over time, and this has led to lower levels of marital satisfaction and overall well-being.

Finkel et al. (2014) use the term "suffocation" intentionally, of course, as part of a metaphor. We are largely dependent on our romantic partner as we seek to climb "Mount Maslow" in modern America. We depend on our spouse almost exclusively for many things, including helping to facilitate our own personal growth and well-being. According to Finkel et al., it is possible for romantic partners to play this role, but it is not easy, because of the huge emotional investment required. Thus, DePaulo and Morris (2005) might add, are we not asking a lot out of this one relationship? Do singles have a self-actualization advantage because they are not constrained to one relationship to fulfill various needs?

Finally, DePaulo and Morris (2005) argue that it is difficult to think of singles as happy because American culture fosters an "Ideology of Marriage and Family" that stigmatizes singles. For instance, our culture views couples as the default or normal status for living, and singlehood as something deficient, and research shows that singles are negatively stereotyped (Morris, Sinclair, & DePaulo, 2007). This belief may cause unfortunate consequences: Both men and women are less choosey about a romantic partner the more they fear being single (Spielmann et al., 2013). Perhaps this finding reflects the marriage and family ideology that happiness is possible only via coupledom. DePaulo and Morris (2005) also criticize social scientists, "including the best in the business" (p. 65) whom they view as greatly exaggerating the association between marriage and well-being.

In summary, although marriage probably does increase happiness, it is also true that happy individuals are more likely to get married. If we begin measuring the effect of marriage a couple years before the wedding, it seems that individuals do not adapt to the happiness increases associated with marriage. These findings strongly suggest that marriage is a cause of happiness.

But marriage is not a magic ticket to happiness. Individual differences, such as the quality of the marriage, also matter quite a bit. In some cases cohabitating couples might be as happy as marrieds. In addition, some critics have questioned the expectations we place on marriage, and wonder if it can really fulfill them. There are also questions about whether a romantic or sexual relationship is necessary for happiness. But it is clear that the prototypical average person is happier being married than being single.

PARENTHOOD

Relationship Satisfaction

Parenthood is related to romantic relationship satisfaction differently than it is to over-all well-being. Therefore, we examine these two outcome measures separately. Litera-ture reviews show that the transition to parenthood, particularly the time through early infancy, is associated with declining relationship satisfaction (Mitnick, Heyman, & Smith Slep, 2009; Twenge, Campbell, & Foster, 2003). Several authors note that this is a very challenging time in a couple's relationship (e.g., Trillingsgaard, Baucom, & Heyman, 2014), so it is perhaps not surprising that there is a toll on relationship satisfaction.

However, even though parenthood is *associated* with declines in relationship satisfac-tion, there is some confusion about whether it *causes* these declines. There are also some important exceptions to this pattern of relationship satisfaction decline among parents. Relationship satisfaction declines on average, but it does not, at least to the same extent, for all parents. There are important qualifying variables that moderate the relationship between parenthood and satisfaction with relationships. We examine these issues next.

Causality?

Selection

The question of causality is tricky. Obviously, researchers cannot randomly assign some couples to have children and others to remain nonparents, so a true experiment is not possible. One noncausal explanation is that any decline in relationship satisfaction fol-lowing childbirth might be due to normal adaptation effects. Recall that we have already learned that couples "adapt" to each other, and experience less satisfaction from their relationship, even without the addition of a child.

Could it be that most couples have their first child at about the same time that these adaptation effects are presenting themselves? This coincidence would mean that chil-dren do not cause declines in relationship satisfaction. Instead, it would indicate that these declines are just a normal process that couples experience, and that it just hap-pens to occur at the same time as most couples become parents. This possibility is impor-tant because it illustrates how difficult it is to attribute causality in nonexperimental research done in naturalistic settings.

One way that researchers have addressed this problem is by moving from longitudi-nal designs that track only future parents and their relationship satisfaction to designs that include control samples of couples who do not become parents.[2] There are some mixed results, but parenthood generally causes relationship decline over and above the normal adaptation effects. Although a meta-analysis by Mitnick et al. (2009) reveals no differences between parents and nonparents in relationship satisfaction decline, another meta-analysis does show differences (Twenge et al., 2003).

The Slope of the Decline

In addition, several empirical studies conducted after Mitnick et al.'s (2009) paper indi-cate that parenthood causes relationship satisfaction to decline (that is, it is not just a matter of adaptation). For example, both Keizer and Schenk (2012) and Castellano, Velotti, Crowell, and Zavattini (2014) track longitudinal samples of both future parents and nonparents and found greater relationship decline among parents. In addition, Doss, Rhoades, Stanley, and Markman (2009) found that parenthood speeds up relationship satisfaction decline. Although parents and nonparents experienced equivalent amounts of decline over an 8-year period, the decline was sudden for parents and much more gradual for nonparents. Lawrence, Rothman, Cobb, Rothman, and Bradbury (2008) also found similar results.

The finding of immediate decline in relationship satisfaction is important. First, the potential shock of the sudden decline among parents might have important implications for parental and child well-being even if the *overall* amount of decline is equivalent among parents and nonparents. Second, the sudden nature of the decline of parents' relationship satisfaction following childbirth leads Doss et al. (2009) to conclude that the transition to parenthood is a casual factor and is unlikely to be a coincidence.

Third, Mitnick et al. (2009) might have missed this sudden decline among parents because most of the studies they reviewed did not measure satisfaction often enough and use the appropriate statistical techniques to assess the shape of the relationship function (sudden versus gradual). This could explain the differences between Mitnick et al.'s conclusion that relationship declines among parents are merely adaptation effects that affect all couples, and Doss et al.'s (2009) conclusion that parenthood causes declines in relationship satisfaction.

The evidence is mixed but supports the premise that the transition to parenthood causes decreases in relationship functioning. The Doss et al. (2009) finding of the sudden decrease in relationship satisfaction is particularly important, both in terms of sorting out the causality issues and in terms of understanding the process of this decline. It appears that adaptation effects do *eventually* produce the same amount of decline in nonparents that parents experience. But these adaptation effects may take as long as 8 years to manifest among nonparents (Doss et al., 2009), while parenthood causes an almost immediate decline.

Finally, these changes in relationship satisfaction are described by most researchers as large enough to be both statistically and practically meaningful, although not overpowering. Research also indicates that relationship satisfaction is related to overall life satisfaction during pregnancy and infancy. In fact, during this time, relationship satisfaction impacts life satisfaction more strongly than life satisfaction impacts relationship satisfaction (Dyrdal, Røysamb, Nes, & Vittersø, 2011). Therefore, parenthood-induced declines in relationship satisfaction affect individuals' overall well-being.

Qualifying Variables

Parents' Gender

The decline in relationship satisfaction for parents depends on a number of factors. There are so many of these qualifying (i.e., moderating) factors that it is difficult to categorize them all. In fact, some authors (e.g., Holmes, Sasaki, & Hazen, 2013) question the usefulness of examining average relationship satisfaction scores in response to parenthood because of the amount of variability in these scores. But one interesting qualifying variable is parent gender. Do mothers and fathers experience the same reaction to parenthood?

Twenge et al.'s (2003) meta-analytic review indicates that relationship satisfaction drops following the birth of a first child for both men and women. However, the effect is larger for women, particularly women with infant children, than it is for men. In addition, the size of the parent versus nonparent differences in satisfaction are meaningful. For instance, 62% of childless women are likely to have high relationship satisfaction, while this is true for only 38% of women with infants.

Twenge et al. (2003) suggested that these gender differences for parents might be due to traditional child-rearing roles, given that mothers still take major responsibility for caring for children. Although this idea has been challenged (Keizer & Schenk, 2012), recent research has replicated the gendered effect (Bower, Jia, Schoppe-Sullivan, Mangelsdorf, & Brown, 2013; Castellano et al., 2014; Dew & Wilcox, 2011). In addition, Dew and Wilcox (2011) found that changes in the perceived fairness of housework allotments are related to mothers' relationship satisfaction decline. This finding is consistent with Twenge et al.'s supposition that traditional gender roles affect parents' satisfaction with each other.

You may recall the previous discussion showing that couples are naturally linked together emotionally. You might then wonder how mothers and fathers can have different levels of relationship satisfaction. After all, wouldn't mothers' dissatisfaction cause fathers to be dissatisfied also? Holmes et al. (2013) suggest that mothers' and fathers' satisfaction levels are synchronized in just this way. When one parent becomes less satisfied, the other parent will also. But there may be a time lag before synchronization when parents report uneven levels of satisfaction. This explanation would mean that mothers are less satisfied than fathers only relatively early in their children's lives. This reasoning is consistent with Twenge et al.'s (2003) finding that mothers of infants are particularly dissatisfied.

Parents' Attachment and Personality

Attachment style is another important qualifying variable. Bowlby (1969) theorizes that early relationships with a caregiver can establish attachment styles that can affect our relationships later in life. Recent research indicates that a parent's poor or insecure attachment is associated with greater declines in relationship satisfaction (Castellano et al., 2014; Kohn et al., 2012), particularly if the future father has poor attachment (Bouchard, 2014; Don & Mickelson, 2014). Other personality factors, including depression (Bower et al., 2013; Trillingsgaard et al., 2014), neuroticism, particularly among future fathers (Bouchard & Poirier, 2011), negative emotionality (Bower et al., 2013), lower feelings or parental efficacy (Biehle & Mickelson, 2011), and less spiritual attitudes toward marriage (Kusner, Mahoney, Pargament, & DeMaris, 2014), also predict more decline in relationship satisfaction.

Situational Circumstances

Situational factors also moderate the effects of parenthood on relationship satisfaction. Individuals who cohabitated before marriage (Kamp Dush, Rhoades, Sandberg-Thoma,

& Schoppe-Sullivan, 2014; Mortensen, Torsheim, Melkevik, & Thuen, 2012), mothers whose parents had divorced (Doss et al., 2009), parents of easily aroused or distressed infants (Holmes et al., 2013), parents with unplanned pregnancies (Lawrence et al., 2008), and parents of girls (Doss et al., 2009; Holmes et al., 2013) all show greater declines in relationship satisfaction when they became parents.

In addition, higher socioeconomic class parents, and parents who have had children in recent years, also show more relationship satisfaction decline (Twenge et al., 2003). These results are apparently because of higher levels of individualism among wealthier and more educated parents, and among parents in recent decades. These parents are more likely to experience young children as hindering their own personal freedom (Twenge et al., 2003).

Finally, relationship quality is also an important moderator. Low relationship quality before birth predicts steeper declines in satisfaction after the birth of a child. Prebirth relationship conflict positively predicts postbirth conflict (Doss et al., 2009), and perceptions of positive spousal support are associated with smaller declines in relationship satisfaction (Don & Mickelson, 2014). Interestingly, higher levels of prebirth *positive* relationship functioning (e.g., high levels of relationship satisfaction and dedication) also predict *steeper* declines in relationship functioning after birth (Doss et al., 2009; Lawrence et al., 2008). These results suggest that couples at the extremes of positive and negative relationship functioning are particularly vulnerable to relationship satisfaction decline (Doss et al., 2009).

Can you see why some authors write that it is useless to discuss *average* effects of parenthood on relationship satisfaction? Certainly there are so many factors that it makes it difficult to discuss the effects of parenthood in general. However, another way to think about this issue is that there are many different *risk factors* for declines in relationship satisfaction. Furthermore, Trillingsgaard et al. (2014) found that these risk factors apply in an additive function rather than interactively. What this means is that the more of the risk factors we have, the greater the probability of poor relationship quality. Also, because the factors do not seem to interact, it is not the case that particular combinations of factors are especially important. Again, the quantity of risk factors is the major issue.

Therefore, there are a lot of different paths to get to a poor relationship with the partner with whom you are parenting. And because there are so many of these paths, the likelihood that you or I will stumble down at least a few of them is also relatively high. Thus, by and large, parents are less satisfied with their romantic relationships than nonparents.

These conclusions are not necessarily meant to discourage anyone from having children. The authors of several of the papers I cite make this point explicitly, and they also discuss the joys of parenting. (Being a parent myself, I certainly concur.) However, parenthood is not easy, and it should not be romanticized. Perhaps knowing about some of the risk factors for relationship satisfaction decline can help you avoid at least some of the problem.

Finally, have you noticed some of the things that are missing from this literature? For one thing, we need more data on the timing of relationship satisfaction decline. At what precise stages of our children's lives does this happen? Furthermore, most of the data examine parents with relatively young children. It would be useful and interesting to learn more about parental relationship satisfaction throughout the entire course of their children's lives. In addition, much of the data I reviewed comes from Europe and the United States. As a result, there is a need for more data from more diverse samples and cultures.

WELL-BEING

It is interesting that happier people are more likely to become parents (Cetre, Clark, & Senik, 2016; Kim & Hicks, 2016). However, research shows that parenthood is either associated with the loss of some of this happiness (e.g., Hansen, 2012; Luhmann et al., 2012) or with no change in happiness (e.g., Stanca, 2012). The relationship is also more negative for mothers than it is for fathers, although fathers are also less happy than men without children (Stanca, 2012). There is also no evidence of hedonic adaptation working in parents' favor. Parents do not seem to adapt to having children such that their happiness returns to the more positive levels they enjoyed before having children (Luhmann et al., 2012; see also Myrskylä & Margolis, 2014). These are startling conclusions. Despite the cultural myths surrounding the joy of being a parent (Hansen, 2012), and despite (or perhaps because of) the tremendous amount of time and effort it takes to be a parent, the best typical parents can hope for is that parenthood will not strongly decrease their overall happiness.

These conclusions are based on several reviews of the literature, including Luhmann et al.'s (2012) meta-analysis of 313 longitudinal samples examining almost 66,000 individuals and on samples from around the world, including one study (Stanca, 2012) that drew data from 94 different nations. Therefore, the conclusion that, overall, parenthood is associated with less happiness (or at least does not increase happiness) stands on pretty firm ground.

In addition, at least one author (Stanca, 2012) suggests that parenthood is a *cause*, and not merely a predictor, of lower well-being. There are a variety of reasons why parenthood may cause lower well-being. These include the financial cost of children (Beja, 2015; Myrskylä & Margolis, 2014; Pollmann-Schult, 2014; Stanca, 2012), the personal sacrifices made necessary by childcare (Beja, 2015; Pollmann-Schult, 2014), and the negative effects of parenthood on relationship satisfaction (Beja, 2015).

And there are only a few hints of a silver lining hidden among these dark parenting clouds. Some studies suggest that the *direct* relationship between parenthood and happiness is positive, but that this effect is offset by the way parenthood affects other facets of life, including relationship strain, financial cost, and the efforts and sacrifices necessary to care for children (Beja, 2015; Pollmann-Schult, 2014). A silver lining is that it may be possible to change public policy so that societies are more supportive of parents, and thus increase parents' well-being (Beja, 2015). For instance, any efforts to reduce the financial burdens of childcare should increase parents' happiness. Parents may also choose to decide to have children under circumstances that are least likely to cause these countervailing pressures (Nelson, Kushlev, & Lyubomirsky, 2014).

Another silver lining is that parental happiness increases as birth approaches, although it recedes quickly afterward (Myrskylä & Margolis, 2014). Also, the negative relationship between parenthood and happiness applies to the majority of parents, but not to all parents. For instance, parents younger than 45 years old are less happy than their childless peers, but there is no relationship between parenthood and happiness for individuals between the ages of 45 and 64. Interestingly, parents 65 and older are happier than individuals without children. Widowers are also happier if they have children (Stanca, 2012; for similar findings see Myrskylä & Margolis, 2014; Pollmann-Schult, 2014).

In summary, having children either reduces, or fails to improve, the overall happiness of most parents. And the happiness reduction associated with parenthood appears to last. Parents do not hedonically adapt to parenthood. But an important positive hidden among these negatives is that they are the result of indirect effects of parenthood, such overwhelming factors as the strain to our finances and our romantic relationship. Being a parent itself seems to make us happier. Finally, these effects do not generalize to all parents. The strongest exception is probably that older parents are happier than their childless counterparts.

These results are often met with surprise and a certain amount of denial. Most people seem to expect that parenthood will increase happiness, at least for themselves (Hansen, 2012; Powdthavee, 2009). Why is there a disconnect between what people think and the empirical reality? We address this question in the next section.

WHY WE WANT TO BE PARENTS, DESPITE THE EVIDENCE

Hansen (2012) argues that there are folk theories on parenthood that mistakenly connect it with greater happiness. For example, childless adults are seen as sad, lonely hedonists. There is also a strong cultural belief that children improve happiness. According to Hansen, these folk beliefs are perpetuated because we do not recognize that parenting involves large emotional and financial costs, that there are advantages to not having children, and that nonparents adapt to their circumstances and find other rewarding roles and life paths. Hansen also argues that there may be cognitive biases that lead us to believe parenthood will lead us to happiness.

Perhaps no one who has not been a parent can truly understand the emotional costs of cradling a crying baby at two in the morning without having had a good night's sleep in what seems like months, when one has to be at work early the next morning. Or the costs of not having time for a few minutes alone with one's partner for weeks or months on end. And it is perhaps easy to forget until becoming a parent that one's nonparent friends have time to go to movies, eat dinner together, and so on, and still get a good night's sleep. It is hard for nonparents to understand these facts, particularly when culture prioritizes parenthood as the noblest of goals.

Which leads us to the cognitive bias. Hansen (2012) argues that culture has so ingrained the value of parenthood into our minds that we move toward it reflexively, without thinking. Furthermore, Hansen refers to the *focusing illusion* (Gilbert, 2006) that causes us to remember only the positive aspects of an event. Thus, when we consider parents, we selectively recall positive parenting examples we have observed (such as thinking, "Boy, my friend sure seemed to enjoy playing baseball with his son when he became a father"). This selective recall is aided by the fact that culture reinforces and widely publicizes these positive memories.

So the desire to be a parent is not completely rational, although it is understandable for cultural, not to mention evolutionary, reasons. But most people do become parents, so it is important to think about the conditions that are most likely to help parents be happy. We discuss this issue in the next section.

WHEN PARENTHOOD CAN INCREASE WELL-BEING

It is important to recognize these facts about parenthood. I have two children, and, next to meeting my wife, becoming a father is probably the best thing that has ever happened to me. But being a parent is not easy, and I think couples considering the prospect should try to learn all they can about how to do it right, including how to be parents while maintaining or increasing their individual and joint happiness. Nelson et al. (2014) provide a great service by attempting to outline the factors that predict happy parenting.

Sleep deprivation, financial costs, strains on the relationship with one's partner, and negative emotions related to frustrations that inevitably arise with child rearing are identified as paths that reduce happiness among parents. However, the purpose and meaning in life that comes from raising children, satisfaction of basic human needs (e.g., the evolutionary drive to reproduce), positive emotions, and the heavily rewarded social roles that parents can play all predict increased happiness among parents. There were also a number of demographic (e.g., parents' ages and marital and socioeconomic status) and psychological (e.g., social support and child temperament) characteristics that predicted parental well-being (Nelson et al., 2014).

Nelson et al. developed a model that proceeds straightforwardly from these findings. They predicted that parents will be happier to the extent to which they get enough sleep, maintain a strong relationship with their partner, and receive social support, among other factors. In fact, Nelson et al. composed a useful table that I like to show my students— who are almost always unmarried—in class (see Table 5.1). I ask them to use the table to find which parents are happiest and least happy. Students also imagine themselves as parents and envision where they will stand on the characteristics shown in the table. It is a fun exercise and good way to think about the important variables.

Other research has begun to add to the knowledge base established by Nelson et al. (2014). Luthar and Ciciolla (2015) studied the well-being of more than 2,000 upper-middle-class mothers and found that their perceptions of support were important predictors. Women who felt they had high-quality and supportive relationships with their partners and with friends reported greater well-being. These findings reinforce the idea that parenting can be a positive experience under the right circumstances.

In conclusion, parenthood tends to decrease overall well-being. However, this does not have to be the case. There is a lot more work to be done, as you can see by the number of question marks in Table 5.1, but there is hope that we might eventually be able to predict (and improve) parental happiness with some degree of precision.

TABLE 5.1 Overview of the Moderators of Parents' Well-Being		
Moderator Variable	**Type of Parent**	**Association With Well-Being**
Parent demographic characteristics		
Parent age	Young	−
	Middle-aged	0/+
	Old	0/+
Parent gender	Male	+
	Female	+/−
Employment status	Employed	?
	Unemployed	?
	Stay-at-home	+/−
SES	Low SES	?
	Middle SES	?
	High SES	−
Marital status	Unmarried	−
	Married	0/+
Family structure	Biological	+/−
	Step	0/+/−
	Adoptive	+/−
Culture	Non-Western	?
	Western	+/−
Parent psychological characteristics		
Social support	With high social support	+
	With low social support	−

(*continued*)

TABLE 5.1 Overview of the Moderators of Parents' Well-Being *(continued)*		
Moderator Variable	**Type of Parent**	**Association With Well-Being**
Parenting style	With an intensive parenting style	+/−
Parent attachment style	Securely attached	+
	Insecurely attached	−
Child demographic characteristics		
Child age	With young child(ren)	−
	With middle-childhood child(ren)	?
	With adolescent child(ren)	?
	With adult child(ren)	+/−
Family residence	Noncustodial	−
	Custodial	+/−
	Empty nest	+
Child psychological characteristics		
Child problems	With at least one child with problems	−
	With no children with problems	+
Child temperament	With child(ren) with difficult temperament	−
	With child(ren) with easy temperament	+

Note: (+), parents in this group report higher levels of happiness than nonparents; (−), parents in this group report lower levels of happiness than nonparents; (0), parents in this group report similar levels of happiness to nonparents; (+/−), findings for this group are mixed; (?), findings for this group are scarce or inconclusive; SES = socioeconomic status.

Source: Nelson et al. (2014).

SUMMARY

We have covered a lot of ground in this chapter, but there is one especially important take-away to keep in mind: Humans are constructed to need a few emotionally intimate social relationships in order to be happy. We not only feel unhappy when this need is thwarted; we feel something akin to physical pain. Any serious attempt to improve the happiness of a society must consider this basic human need.

Another take-away concerns marriage and parenthood. Both have wonderful potential to greatly enrich our lives and make us much happier. But neither of these, and particularly parenthood, is guaranteed to increase our happiness. If we want to be happy, it is important not to romanticize these relationships but instead to try to think clearly about the conditions under which marriage and parenthood are most likely to bring joy and meaning to our lives.

NOTES

1. To be clear, the term *partnership* is critical here. DePaulo and Morris (2005) recognize that singles participate in varying amounts of sex, but that they are defined by their lack of an ongoing, committed sexual relationship.

2. You may be wondering how researchers track relationship satisfaction of "future" parents. This is not magic. Researchers simply acquire a large sample of couples and then follow them over time. Some of these couples become parents, and others do not.

REFERENCES

Anderson, C., Kraus, M. W., Galinsky, A. D., & Keltner, D. (2012). The local-ladder effect: Social status and subjective well-being. *Psychological Science, 23*(7), 764–771.

Bao, K. J., & Lyubomirsky, S. (2013). Making it last: Combating hedonic adaptation in romantic relationships. *The Journal of Positive Psychology, 8*(3), 196–206.

Baumeister, R. F. (1991). *Meanings of life.* New York, NY: Guilford Press.

Baumeister, R. F., & DeWall, C. N. (2005). The inner dimension of social exclusion: Intelligent thought and self-regulation among rejected persons. In K. D. Williams, J. P. Forgas, & W. von Hippel (Eds.), *The social outcast: Ostracism, social exclusion, rejection, and bullying* (pp. 53–73). New York, NY: Psychology Press.

Baumeister, R. F., & Leary, M. R. (1995). The need to belong: Desire for interpersonal attachments as a fundamental human motivation. *Psychological Bulletin, 117*(3), 497–529.

Beja, E. L. (2015). Direct and indirect impacts of parenthood on happiness. *International Review of Economics, 62*(4), 307–318.

Bernstein, M. J., & Claypool, H. M. (2012). Not all social exclusions are created equal: Emotional distress following social exclusion is moderated by exclusion paradigm. *Social Influence, 7*(2), 113–130.

Biehle, S. N., & Mickelson, K. D. (2011). Preparing for parenthood: How feelings of responsibility and efficacy impact expectant parents. *Journal of Social and Personal Relationships, 28*(5), 668–683.

Bouchard, G. (2014). The quality of the parenting alliance during the transition to parenthood. *Canadian Journal of Behavioural Science/Revue Canadienne Des Sciences Du Comportement*, 46(1), 20–28.

Bouchard, G., & Poirier, L. (2011). Neuroticism and well-being among employed new parents: The role of the work–family conflict. *Personality and Individual Differences*, 50(5), 657–661.

Bourassa, K. J., Sbarra, D. A., & Whisman, M. A. (2015). Women in very low quality marriages gain life satisfaction following divorce. *Journal of Family Psychology*, 29(3), 490–499.

Bower, D., Jia, R., Schoppe-Sullivan, S., Mangelsdorf, S. C., & Brown, G. L. (2013). Trajectories of couple relationship satisfaction in families with infants: The roles of parent gender, personality, and depression in first-time and experienced parents. *Journal of Social and Personal Relationships*, 30(4), 389–409.

Bowlby, J. (1969). Disruption of affectional bonds and its effects on behavior. *Canada's Mental Health Supplement*, 59, 12.

Braithwaite, S., & Holt-Lunstad, J. (2017). Romantic relationships and mental health. *Current Opinion in Psychology*, 13, 120–125.

Carr, D., Freedman, V. A., Cornman, J. C., & Schwarz, N. (2014). Happy marriage, happy life? Marital quality and subjective well-being in later life. *Journal of Marriage and Family*, 76(5), 930–948.

Castellano, R., Velotti, P., Crowell, J. A., & Zavattini, G. C. (2014). The role of parents' attachment configurations at childbirth on marital satisfaction and conflict strategies. *Journal of Child and Family Studies*, 23(6), 1011–1026.

Cetre, S., Clark, A. E., & Senik, C. (2016). Happy people have children: Choice and self-selection into parenthood. *European Journal of Population*, 32(3), 445–473.

Coulter, K., & Malouff, J. M. (2013). Effects of an intervention designed to enhance romantic relationship excitement: A randomized-control trial. *Couple and Family Psychology: Research and Practice*, 2(1), 34–44.

Demir, M., Orthel, H., & Andelin, A. K. (2013). Friendship and happiness. In S. A. David, I. Boniwell, & A. Conley Ayers (Eds.), *The Oxford handbook of happiness* (pp. 860–870). New York, NY: Oxford University Press.

Demir, M., & Özdemir, M. (2010). Friendship, need satisfaction and happiness. *Journal of Happiness Studies*, 11(2), 243–259.

DePaulo, B. (2011). Living single: Lightening up those dark, dopey myths. In W. R. Cupach & B. H. Spitzberg (Eds.), *The dark side of close relationships II* (pp. 409–439). New York, NY: Routledge/Taylor & Francis.

DePaulo, B. M., & Morris, W. L. (2005). Singles in society and in science. *Psychological Inquiry*, 16(2–3), 57–83.

DePaulo, B. M., & Morris, W. L. (2006). The unrecognized stereotyping and discrimination against singles. *Current Directions in Psychological Science*, 15(5), 251–254.

Dew, J., & Wilcox, W. B. (2011). If momma ain't happy: Explaining declines in marital satisfaction among new mothers. *Journal of Marriage and Family*, 73(1), 1–12.

DeWall, C. N., Baumeister, R. F., & Vohs, K. D. (2008). Satiated with belongingness? Effects of acceptance, rejection, and task framing on self-regulatory performance. *Journal of Personality and Social Psychology*, 95(6), 1367–1382.

DeWall, C. N., & Bushman, B. J. (2011). Social acceptance and rejection: The sweet and the bitter. *Current Directions in Psychological Science*, 20(4), 256–260.

DeWall, C. N., MacDonald, G., Webster, G. D., Masten, C. L., Baumeister, R. F., Powell, C., . . . Eisenberger, N. I. (2010). Acetaminophen reduces social pain: Behavioral and neural evidence. *Psychological Science, 21*(7), 931–937.

Diener, E., Suh, E. M., Lucas, R. E., & Smith, H. L. (1999). Subjective well-being: Three decades of progress. *Psychological Bulletin, 125*(2), 276–302.

Don, B. P., & Mickelson, K. D. (2014). Relationship satisfaction trajectories across the transition to parenthood among low-risk parents. *Journal of Marriage and Family, 76*(3), 677–692.

Doss, B. D., Rhoades, G. K., Stanley, S. M., & Markman, H. J. (2009). The effect of the transition to parenthood on relationship quality: An 8-year prospective study. *Journal of Personality and Social Psychology, 96*(3), 601–619.

Dush, C. M. K., Taylor, M. G., & Kroeger, R. A. (2008). Marital happiness and psychological well-being across the life course. *Family Relations: An Interdisciplinary Journal of Applied Family Studies, 57*(2), 211–226.

Dyrdal, G. M., Røysamb, E., Nes, R. B., & Vittersø, J. (2011). Can a happy relationship predict a happy life? A population-based study of maternal well-being during the life transition of pregnancy, infancy, and toddlerhood. *Journal of Happiness Studies, 12*(6), 947–962.

Eisenberger, N. I., Lieberman, M. D., & Williams, K. D. (2003). Does rejection hurt? An fMRI study of social exclusion. *Science, 302*(5643), 290–292.

Festinger, L. (1957). *A theory of cognitive dissonance*. Palo Alto, CA: Stanford University Press.

Finkel, E. J., Hui, C. M., Carswell, K. L., & Larson, G. M. (2014). The suffocation of marriage: Climbing Mount Maslow without enough oxygen. *Psychological Inquiry, 25*(1), 1–41.

Frech, A., & Williams, K. (2007). Depression and the psychological benefits of entering marriage. *Journal of Health and Social Behavior, 48*(2), 149–163.

Freud, S. (1962). *Three essays on the theory of sexuality* (James Strachey, Trans.). New York, NY: Basic Books.

Freud, S. (2002). *Civilization and its discontents*. London, UK: Penguin.

Frijters, P., Johnston, D. W., & Shields, M. A. (2011). Life satisfaction dynamics with quarterly life event data. *Scandinavian Journal of Economics, 113*, 190–211.

Gere, J., & MacDonald, G. (2010). An update of the empirical case for the need to belong. *The Journal of Individual Psychology, 66*(1), 93–115.

Gilbert, D. (2006). *Stumbling on happiness*. New York, NY: A. A. Knopf.

Hansen, T. (2012). Parenthood and happiness: A review of folk theories versus empirical evidence. *Social Indicators Research, 108*(1), 29–64.

Holmes, E. K., Sasaki, T., & Hazen, N. L. (2013). Smooth versus rocky transitions to parenthood: Family systems in developmental context. *Family Relations: An Interdisciplinary Journal of Applied Family Studies, 62*(5), 824–837.

Horn, E. E., Xu, Y., Beam, C. R., Turkheimer, E., & Emery, R. E. (2013). Accounting for the physical and mental health benefits of entry into marriage: A genetically informed study of selection and causation. *Journal of Family Psychology, 27*(1), 30–41.

Kamp Dush, C. M., Rhoades, G. K., Sandberg-Thoma, S., & Schoppe-Sullivan, S. (2014). Commitment across the transition to parenthood among married and cohabiting couples. *Couple and Family Psychology: Research and Practice, 3*(2), 126–136.

Keizer, R., & Schenk, N. (2012). Becoming a parent and relationship satisfaction: A longitudinal dyadic perspective. *Journal of Marriage and Family, 74*(4), 759–773.

Kim, J., & Hicks, J. A. (2016). Happiness begets children? Evidence for a bi-directional link between well-being and number of children. *Journal of Positive Psychology, 11*(1), 62–69.

Knowles, M. L. (2014). Social rejection increases perspective taking. *Journal of Experimental Social Psychology, 55*, 126–132.

Kohn, J. L., Rholes, W. S., Simpson, J. A., Martin, A. M., Tran, S., & Wilson, C. L. (2012). Changes in marital satisfaction across the transition to parenthood: The role of adult attachment orientations. *Personality and Social Psychology Bulletin, 38*(11), 1506–1522.

Kusner, K. G., Mahoney, A., Pargament, K. I., & DeMaris, A. (2014). Sanctification of marriage and spiritual intimacy predicting observed marital interactions across the transition to parenthood. *Journal of Family Psychology, 28*(5), 604–614.

Lakey, B. (2013). Perceived social support and happiness: The role of personality and relational processes. In S. A. David, I. Boniwell, & A. Conley Ayers (Eds.), *The Oxford handbook of happiness* (pp. 847–859). New York, NY: Oxford University Press.

Lavigne, G. L., Vallerand, R. J., & Crevier-Braud, L. (2011). The fundamental need to belong: On the distinction between growth and deficit-reduction orientations. *Personality and Social Psychology Bulletin, 37*(9), 1185–1201.

Lawrence, E., Rothman, A. D., Cobb, R. J., Rothman, M. T., & Bradbury, T. N. (2008). Marital satisfaction across the transition to parenthood. *Journal of Family Psychology, 22*(1), 41–50.

Leary, M. R., Kelly, K. M., Cottrell, C. A., & Schreindorfer, L. S. (2013). Construct validity of the need to belong scale: Mapping the nomological network. *Journal of Personality Assessment, 95*(6), 610–624.

Lee, K. S., & Ono, H. (2012). Marriage, cohabitation, and happiness: A cross-national analysis of 27 countries. *Journal of Marriage and Family, 74*(5), 953–972.

Lucas, R. E., & Clark, A. E. (2006). Do people really adapt to marriage? *Journal of Happiness Studies, 7*(4), 405–426.

Lucas, R. E., Clark, A. E., Georgellis, Y., & Diener, E. (2003). Reexamining adaptation and the set point model of happiness: Reactions to changes in marital status. *Journal of Personality and Social Psychology, 84*(3), 527–539.

Luhmann, M., Hofmann, W., Eid, M., & Lucas, R. E. (2012). Subjective well-being and adaptation to life events: A meta-analysis. *Journal of Personality and Social Psychology, 102*(3), 592–615.

Luthar, S. S., & Ciciolla, L. (2015). Who mothers mommy? Factors that contribute to mothers' well-being. *Developmental Psychology, 51*(12), 1812–1823.

Lyubomirsky, S. (2008). *The how of happiness: A new approach to getting the life you want.* New York, NY: Penguin Press.

Lyubomirsky, S. (2013). *The myths of happiness: What should make you happy, but doesn't, What shouldn't make you happy, but does.* New York, NY: Penguin Press.

MacDonald, G., & Leary, M. R. (2005). Why does social exclusion hurt? The relationship between social and physical pain. *Psychological Bulletin, 131*(2), 202–223.

Maner, J. K., DeWall, C. N., Baumeister, R. F., & Schaller, M. (2007). Does social exclusion motivate interpersonal reconnection? Resolving the "porcupine problem." *Journal of Personality and Social Psychology, 92*(1), 42–55.

Mehl, M. R., Vazire, S., Holleran, S. E., & Clark, C. S. (2010). Eavesdropping on happiness: Well-being is related to having less small talk and more substantive conversations. *Psychological Science*, 21(4), 539–541.

Mikulincer, M., & Shaver, P. R. (2013). Adult attachment and happiness: Individual differences in the experience and consequences of positive emotions. In S. A. David, I. Boniwell, & A. Conley Ayers (Eds.), *The Oxford handbook of happiness* (pp. 834–846). New York, NY: Oxford University Press.

Mitnick, D. M., Heyman, R. E., & Smith Slep, A. M. (2009). Changes in relationship satisfaction across the transition to parenthood: A meta-analysis. *Journal of Family Psychology*, 23(6), 848–852.

Morris, W. L., Sinclair, S., & DePaulo, B. M. (2007). No shelter for singles: The perceived legitimacy of marital status discrimination. *Group Processes and Intergroup Relations*, 10(4), 457–470.

Mortensen, Ø., Torsheim, T., Melkevik, O., & Thuen, F. (2012). Adding a baby to the equation. Married and cohabiting women's relationship satisfaction in the transition to parenthood. *Family Process*, 51(1), 122–139.

Musick, K., & Bumpass, L. (2012). Reexamining the case for marriage: Union formation and changes in well-being. *Journal of Marriage and Family*, 74(1), 1–18.

Myrskylä, M., & Margolis, R. (2014). Happiness: Before and after the kids. *Demography*, 51(5), 1843–1866.

Nadkarni, A., & Hofmann, S. G. (2012). Why do people use Facebook? *Personality and Individual Differences*, 52(3), 243–249.

Nelson, S. K., Kushlev, K., & Lyubomirsky, S. (2014). The pains and pleasures of parenting. When, why, and how is parenthood associated with more or less well-being? *Psychological Bulletin*, 140(3), 846–895.

O'Connor, K. M., & Gladstone, E. (2015). How social exclusion distorts social network perceptions. *Social Networks*, 40, 123–128.

Pillow, D. R., Malone, G. P., & Hale, W. J. (2015). The need to belong and its association with fully satisfying relationships: A tale of two measures. *Personality and Individual Differences*, 74, 259–264.

Pollmann-Schult, M. (2014). Parenthood and life satisfaction: Why don't children make people happy? *Journal of Marriage and Family*, 76(2), 319–336.

Powdthavee, N. (2009). Think having children will make you happy? *The Psychologist*, 22(4), 308–310.

Proulx, C. M., Helms, H. M., & Buehler, C. (2007). Marital quality and personal well-being: A meta-analysis. *Journal of Marriage and Family*, 69(3), 576–593.

Qari, S. (2014). Marriage, adaptation and happiness: Are there long-lasting gains to marriage? *Journal of Behavioral and Experimental Economics*, 50, 29–39.

Richman, L., & Leary, M. R. (2009). Reactions to discrimination, stigmatization, ostracism, and other forms of interpersonal rejection: A multimotive model. *Psychological Review*, 116(2), 365–383.

Riva, P., Romero-Lauro, L. J., DeWall, C. N., & Bushman, B. J. (2012). Buffer the pain away: Stimulating the right ventrolateral prefrontal cortex reduces pain following social exclusion. *Psychological Science*, 23(12), 1473–1475.

Saphire-Bernstein, S., & Taylor, S. E. (2013). Close relationships and happiness. In S. A. David, I. Boniwell & A. Conley Ayers (Eds.), *The Oxford handbook of happiness* (pp. 821–833). New York, NY: Oxford University Press.

Shapiro, A., & Keyes, C. L. M. (2008). Marital status and social well-being: Are the married always better off? *Social Indicators Research*, 88(2), 329–346.

Sheldon, K. M., & Lyubomirsky, S. (2012). The challenge of staying happier: Testing the Hedonic Adaptation Prevention Model. *Personality and Social Psychology Bulletin*, 38(5), 670–680.

Soons, J. P. M., & Kalmijn, M. (2009). Is marriage more than cohabitation? Well-being differences in 30 European countries. *Journal of Marriage and Family*, 71(5), 1141–1157.

Soons, J. P. M., Liefbroer, A. C., & Kalmijn, M. (2009). The long-term consequences of relationship formation for subjective well-being. *Journal of Marriage and Family*, 71(5), 1254–1270.

Spielmann, S. S., MacDonald, G., Maxwell, J. A., Joel, S., Peragine, D., Muise, A., & Impett, E. A. (2013). Settling for less out of fear of being single. *Journal of Personality and Social Psychology*, 105(6), 1049–1073.

Stanca, L. (2012). Suffer the little children: Measuring the effects of parenthood on well-being worldwide. *Journal of Economic Behavior and Organization*, 81(3), 742–750.

Stavrova, O., Fetchenhauer, D., & Schlösser, T. (2012). Cohabitation, gender, and happiness: A cross-cultural study in thirty countries. *Journal of Cross-Cultural Psychology*, 43(7), 1063–1081.

Stutzer, A., & Frey, B. S. (2006). Does marriage make people happy, or do happy people get married? *The Journal of Socio-Economics*, 35(2), 326–347.

Tay, L., Tan, K., Diener, E., & Gonzalez, E. (2013). Social relations, health behaviors, and health outcomes: A survey and synthesis. *Applied Psychology: Health and Well-Being*, 5(1), 28–78.

Trillingsgaard, T., Baucom, K. J. W., & Heyman, R. E. (2014). Predictors of change in relationship satisfaction during the transition to parenthood. *Family Relations: An Interdisciplinary Journal of Applied Family Studies*, 63(5), 667–679.

Twenge, J. M., Baumeister, R. F., Tice, D. M., & Stucke, T. S. (2001). If you can't join them, beat them: Effects of social exclusion on aggressive behavior. *Journal of Personality and Social Psychology*, 81(6), 1058–1069.

Twenge, J. M., Campbell, W. K., & Foster, C. A. (2003). Parenthood and marital satisfaction: A meta-analytic review. *Journal of Marriage and Family*, 65(3), 574–583.

van Beest, I., Williams, K. D., & van Dijk, E. (2011). Cyberbomb: Effects of being ostracized from a death game. *Group Processes and Intergroup Relations*, 14(4), 581–596.

Vangelisti, A. L., Pennebaker, J. W., Brody, N., & Guinn, T. D. (2014). Reducing social pain: Sex differences in the impact of physical pain relievers. *Personal Relationships*, 21(2), 349–363.

Wadsworth, T. (2016). Marriage and subjective well-being: How and why context matters. *Social Indicators Research*, 126(3), 1025–1048.

Waytz, A., & Epley, N. (2012). Social connection enables dehumanization. *Journal of Experimental Social Psychology*, 48(1), 70–76.

Wiik, K. A., Keizer, R., & Lappegård, T. (2012). Relationship quality in marital and cohabiting unions across Europe. *Journal of Marriage and Family*, 74(3), 389–398.

Williams, K. D. (2007). Ostracism. *Annual Review of Psychology*, 58, 425–452.

Williams, K. D., & Carter-Sowell, A. (2009). Marginalization through social ostracism: Effects of being ignored and excluded. In F. Butera & J. M. Levine (Eds.), *Coping with minority status: Responses to exclusion and inclusion* (pp. 104–122). New York, NY: Cambridge University Press.

Wölfer, R., & Scheithauer, H. (2013). Ostracism in childhood and adolescence: Emotional, cognitive, and behavioral effects of social exclusion. *Social Influence*, 8(4), 217–236.

CHAPTER 6

Money

*Those who say that money can't buy happiness, just don't know
how to spend it.*
—Unknown Author

"Money doesn't buy happiness." Uh, do you live in America?
—Comedian Daniel Tosh

These are clever sayings and we chuckle at them. Intuitively, it seems that it must be true that more money would make us happier. Most people probably think, "Surely if I had a bit more money, there would be less stress in my life, and I could do more things that would make me happier."

The assumption that wealth increases well-being also forms the basis of most economic thought and social policy in the capitalist world. Economic and social policy is predicated on the assumption that both individual citizens and society as a whole benefit as a nation becomes wealthier. But does a society become happier as it becomes wealthier, and, if so, is this a powerful and straightforward relationship? Are wealthier individuals necessarily happier than poorer ones? Is economic growth an effective way to increase happiness in all societies? Let's look at the evidence.

THE EASTERLIN PARADOX

The first major empirical challenge to the assumption that money increases well-being was presented by Richard Easterlin in a now famous paper titled "Does Economic Growth Improve the Human Lot?" (Easterlin, 1974). Easterlin noted three important and paradoxical relationships (Table 6.1). First, income and wealth clearly predict higher well-being *within* a country. This is true across many countries, including the United States and other Westernized cultures (e.g., West Germany) and in non-Western cultures as well (e.g., India). It was also true across time, in the period that Easterlin studied, ranging from the mid-1940s to 1970. Easterlin also noted that many more of the very wealthy

TABLE 6.1 Easterlin Paradox	
Finding 1	Income is associated with more happiness *within* a country.
Finding 2	Individuals in wealthier countries are not necessarily happier than individuals in poorer countries.
Finding 3	Economic growth does not necessarily increase happiness within a country.
Rationales	Easterlin proposed two primary reasons for these findings: ▶ *Relative* income affects happiness more strongly than does *absolute* income. ▶ Humans *adapt* to their present circumstances. Therefore, any happiness boost provided by income is relatively short-lived.

than of the very poor report feeling very satisfied in the United States and that the proportion of "very satisfied" responses increases steadily with income.

The paradox arises with Easterlin's second and third findings. Contrary to the comparisons *within* a country, his second finding indicates that wealth is not a strong predictor of well-being *across different* countries. Average satisfaction levels in wealthy countries (as measured by gross national product [GNP] per capita) are not consistently higher than satisfaction levels in less wealthy countries. Furthermore, Easterlin noted that if there is any relationship at all between national wealth and average well-being, it is much weaker than the relationship between income and well-being within a country.

Finally, Easterlin's (1974) third finding is even more startling. He concluded that economic growth does not improve long-term happiness. For instance, he found that Americans did not become noticeably happier between 1946 and 1970, despite the fact that the country became much wealthier during this time.

Easterlin suggested that *relative wealth*, rather than *absolute wealth*, explains these results. He argued that growth of our national economy (e.g., increasing national wealth) does not produce greater happiness because it is difficult to feel wealthier if everyone around us is getting wealthier at the same rate we are. Because we are not advancing compared to our peers, Easterlin argued that we do not feel wealthier. He also hypothesized that individuals *adapt* to their present circumstances, and therefore cease to feel the benefit of increased income and wealth over time.[1] According to Easterlin, we simply become accustomed to the trappings of wealth and they no longer deliver the same happiness they once did.

Easterlin argued for the importance of relative income and adaptation by pointing out that definitions of wealth and poverty radically change as societies become richer. Not surprisingly, it takes more to be considered rich than it once did in many societies. Similarly, definitions of poverty today might have seemed affluent to people of the past. He noted the minimal material requirements for happiness demanded by individuals from India and the United States. As you might imagine, citizens of India, who were relatively poor, had relatively low aspirations. These people wanted clean tap water, electricity, and a future free of disease. However, Americans sought expensive products and services such as a new car, a boat, and private schools for their children. Thus, consistent with the adaptation and relative income hypotheses, comparatively wealthy Americans were no longer satisfied with outcomes that would delight comparatively poor Indian nationals.

These results are certainly paradoxical. Income and wealth are associated with more well-being within a country, but richer countries are not happier than poorer ones, and happiness does not increase within a country as it becomes wealthier (at least not in a wealthy country like the United States). We explore these relationships and the potential explanations for them more fully in the sections that follow. But first, it is important to briefly consider the implications of the Easterlin Paradox.

The most important implication is that Easterlin's findings question the assumption that economic growth boosts well-being. Furthermore, his results challenge the central assumption of economists' standard model that wealth is a proxy measure of well-being. Economists equate wealth with happiness because they assume that individuals will make rational, happiness-increasing choices with additional wealth. Keep these implications in mind as we explore additional data and theory in the rest of this chapter. Let's see whether Easterlin is right.

Challenges to Easterlin

There is general agreement with Easterlin's first conclusion regarding the effects of wealth within countries. Researchers consistently find that your rich neighbors are happier than you are (Lucas & Schimmack, 2009). But several researchers have challenged Easterlin's second and third conclusions. Sacks, Stevenson, and Wolfers (2012) and Stevenson and Wolfers (2008) conclude that citizens of wealthy nations are, on average, happier than citizens of poorer nations. Similarly, Diener, Tay, and Oishi (2013), along with Sacks et al. and Stevenson and Wolfers, argue that economic growth increases the well-being of the average citizen within a country.

These challengers make compelling arguments that must be carefully considered. We examine each of Easterlin's points and subsequent challenges to them in the next sections.

Income and Happiness Within a Country

The Size of the Income–Happiness Relationship

Although income does predict well-being within countries, discussion of the relationship between income and happiness within countries centers on the size of this relationship. Is this relationship large enough to be meaningful? Would we be meaningfully happier if our income increased? The conclusion we reach is that money is important, but it is not overwhelmingly important. Factors other than money matter as much or more for our happiness. In addition, the amount by which most people can increase their income—for instance, by getting a raise at work or finding a better paying job—are not likely to have meaningful and long-lasting impacts on their happiness. However, this is not the same thing as saying that poverty is psychologically benign. Poverty clearly lowers well-being (Wood, Boyce, Moore, & Brown, 2012).

The satiation hypothesis   Increasing income is a questionable strategy for increasing the well-being of most nonpoor individuals. One of the reasons for this is that income's effect on well-being is one of diminishing marginal utility (Diener, Ng, Harter, & Arora, 2010, p. 54), which is a phrase economists use to indicate that the effect of a variable weakens at higher levels. For instance, a moderate amount of pizza will probably be quite tasty. But it will not taste as good after we have eaten a truckload of pizza. In other words, we become *satiated* on pizza at some amount below truckload.

A similar effect happens with income and well-being, although the relationship differs depending on the type of measure. For instance, Kahneman and Deaton (2010) found that income has a weak or nonexistent relation to emotional well-being after it reaches about $75,000 per year (in 2009 dollars). This is sometimes referred to as the *satiation hypothesis* (Sacks et al., 2012). Thus, income-based strategies for increasing positive and negative emotions are effective mainly at relatively low levels of income.

Direct comparisons of income   The size of the money/happiness relationship has been hotly debated. But the happiness difference appears to be small unless the very rich and very poor are being compared. For instance, Angeles (2011) found that income accounts for only 3.6% of the differences in individuals' well-being scores. However, Lucas and Schimmack (2009) conclude that researchers have underestimated the size of the money/happiness relationship. They examined a representative sample of Germans and found that individuals who earned the equivalent of more than $200,000 were as much as 0.88 standard deviations higher in life satisfaction than were those who earned the equivalent of less than $10,000. Furthermore, the $200,000 earner was between 0.5 and 0.67 standard deviations higher in life satisfaction than an individual in the middle of the distribution who earned about $55,000.

But, is it surprising that someone who earns more than $200,000 a year is more satisfied with life than someone who earns less than $10,000, or even $55,000? More importantly, are these differences meaningful? Lucas and Schimmack (2009) establish that huge jumps in income have noticeable impacts on life satisfaction. The rich are more satisfied with life than the poor, and there are important social policy implications for this finding. But perhaps a more meaningful question involves advice we can give individuals who seek to increase their own well-being. Should we advise them to seek more income?

As you can see from Figure 6.1, which Lucas and Schimmack (2009) generated from their data, moving up several tiers in income usually has only small effects on life satisfaction. For example, increasing income by $10,000 per year, which would be a rare achievement for most people, has almost no meaningful effect on life satisfaction at almost any point of initial income. Even moving from the $50,000 to $60,000 income range up to the $80,000 to $90,000 range in income, which would be a huge jump rarely

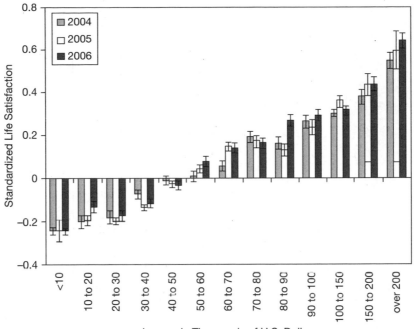

FIGURE 6.1. Average standardized life satisfaction scores (with standard errors) for different income groups in the 2004, 2005, and 2006 waves of the German Socioeconomic Panel Study.
Source: Lucas and Schimmack (2009).

experienced by most people, produces only about 0.2 standard deviations increase in life satisfaction.

Kahneman and Deaton (2010) also reported a relatively strong relationship between income and life evaluation ratings. However, a close look at their data reveals that although this relationship is statistically significant, it is also small at higher levels of income, which is consistent with the satiation hypothesis. Individuals earning more than $120,000 a year score only 0.23 points higher on an 11-point life evaluation scale than those who earn between $90,000 and $120,000. Similarly, the $90,000 to $120,000 group is also only 0.23 points higher on the life evaluation scale than those who earn between $60,000 and $90,000.

Figure 6.2 displays some of Kahneman and Deaton's (2010) data. The "ladder" line refers to measures of life evaluation, and the other three lines refer to aspects of emotional well-being. Note the evidence of "diminishing marginal utility." The slopes for all the lines are much steeper at lower levels of income. In the next paragraphs, which compare national differences in wealth, this satiation effect is discussed in more detail, but clearly the effect of income on well-being is weaker at higher levels of income. This is important to remember whenever we consider the size of the income/well-being effect.

This is not to say that money and income do not matter at all for happiness. Some studies have found monetary issues to be important predictors. For instance, Ng and

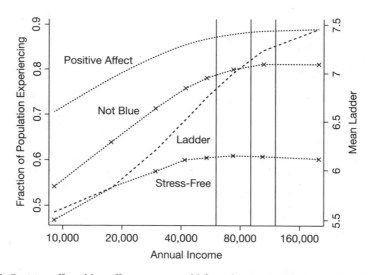

FIGURE 6.2. Positive affect, blue affect, stress, and life evaluation in relation to household income. Positive affect is the average of the fractions of the population reporting happiness, smiling, and enjoyment. "Not blue" is 1 minus the average of the fractions of the population reporting worry and sadness. "Stress free" is the fraction of the population that did not report stress for the previous day. These three hedonic measures are marked on the left-hand scale. The ladder is the average reported number on a scale of 0 to 10, marked on the right-hand scale.
Source: Kahneman and Deaton (2010).

Diener (2014) found that financial satisfaction and income were strong predictors of "life evaluation" (i.e., how positively respondents evaluated their lives) in a representative sample of about 95% of the world's population obtained from the Gallup World Poll.

Comparisons to other predictors The role of money in explaining happiness should not be overstated and should be compared to other factors. For example, Ng and Diener (2014) argued that financial and nonfinancial factors should be considered when making policy decisions about well-being. They found that financial satisfaction predicted life evaluation more than twice as strongly as did actual income in both the 15 wealthiest and the 15 poorest nations on Earth. These results are important because financial satisfaction is not a straightforward reflection of income. It is also affected by psychological constructs such as relative income and adaptation effects. We are more likely to be financially satisfied when we make more than others and before we have had a chance to adapt to our current level of income. Therefore, financial satisfaction is an important predictor of well-being, and it cannot be maximized by simply increasing income. This conclusion highlights the need to consider the relative importance of money (i.e., relative to other factors, including psychological processes) in predicting well-being.

There are other interesting perspectives on the strength of the money/satisfaction relationship. How much money would it take to compensate for the loss of happiness caused by, for example, losing important social relationships? It is possible to make such a calculation. Similarly to what you may remember from a high school algebra course, researchers can find the equation describing the relationship between any *x* and *y* values by solving for the slope of the function and the y intercept. Our researcher could then plug in a value for x (income) and estimate y (well-being). This procedure could then be repeated for another, higher value of x in order to see how much well-being (y) would increase. We might then know that increasing income by $10,000 would increase well-being by an average of 1 point on a 7-point scale. We might also know, from similar procedures, that a reduction in social relationships reduces well-being by 2.5 points on the same scale.

Therefore, researchers can estimate how much money it might take to replace lost happiness. Powdthavee (2008) determined from a national sample of British households that individuals who could no longer meet with friends and relatives on most days would lose so much happiness that they would require an annual payment of £62,400 for the rest of their lives to make up for this loss. And this is in 1996 British pounds! Similarly, Blanchflower and Oswald (2004) found from a representative sample of American households that it would take $100,000 per year to compensate someone for widowhood, $60,000 per year for being unemployed, and $30,000 per year for being Black.

Of course, these numbers are not meant to be taken literally. I would hope that my suddenly widowed and presumably grieving wife would not accept a fat check and then say, "Jim who?" Obviously, the psychological reaction to loss cannot be erased with money. But the figures do present an interesting way to consider the relative impact of various factors on our happiness. It is remarkable that it takes so much money to make up for these negative experiences. These figures suggest that the money effect size is not overwhelming.

In summary, money predicts well-being, particularly when comparing individuals within the same country. But, we should be careful not to overestimate the strength of this effect. Maximizing income is not an efficient way to increase happiness. The size of income increases that are likely available to most individuals are not likely to produce large increases in happiness. Also, other factors can be as important as or more important than money.

Wealth Differences Between Countries

Shape of the Curve

Debate about whether wealthy countries are happier than poor ones has generated even more research. For instance, Ingelhart and Klingemann (2000) found a strong relationship between national wealth (GNP^2) and national happiness when considering a range of rich and poor nations. However, as seen in Figure 6.3, the relationship is not linear, at least as far as the raw data are concerned.

Note that the relationship between wealth and happiness is very steep for poor countries on the left end of the x-axis, but that it plateaus past the middle of the x-axis. In fact, Ingelhart and Klingemann find no relationship between national wealth and happiness once wealth reaches the equivalent of $13,000 per person in 1995 U.S. dollars. To put this into perspective, per capita income in the United States was $28,782 in 1995 according to the World Bank (http://data.worldbank.org/indicator/NY.GDP.PCAP.CD ?locations=US). Thus, national wealth begins to have a diminishing effect on individual

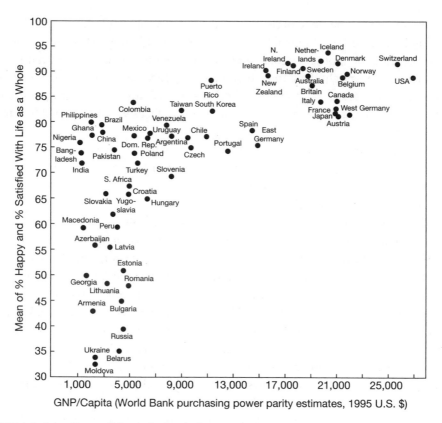

FIGURE 6.3. Subjective well-being by level of economic development.
$r = 0.70$; $n = 65$; $p < .0000$.

Source: Inglehart and Klingemann (2000). Figure 7.2 on page 168, © 2000 Massachusetts Institute of Technology, by permission of The MIT Press.

well-being in countries that are well below the level of wealth we have in the United States. A country does not have to be terribly wealthy before further increases in wealth begin to have only small effects on happiness.

This conclusion is consistent with Need Theory, which posits that wealth is important for happiness to the extent that it allows individuals and countries to meet basic survival needs (Howell & Howell, 2008), a perspective that is consistent with Maslow's (1943) Hierarchy of Needs Theory (Diener et al., 2010). Thus, once basic survival needs such as food and shelter are satisfied, increasing wealth does little or nothing to increase happiness, according to this perspective. This conclusion has important policy implications. What is the point of a country becoming substantially wealthier if, after a certain point, wealth has little or no impact on happiness? We discuss this issue in Chapter 11.

However, later researchers challenge the conclusion that national wealth has diminishing returns for happiness. Deaton (2008) found results that at first seem similar to those of Inglehart and Klingemann. Note Figure 6.4, which again includes raw data, and the apparent *inflection point* at incomes above $10,000, at which the curve begins to have

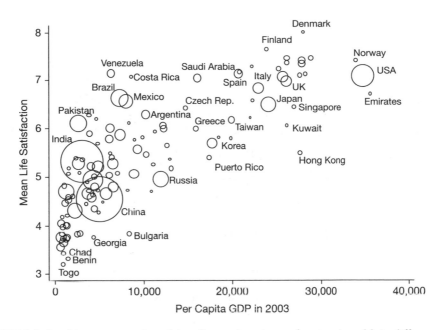

FIGURE 6.4. Graphic representation of the effect on happiness of national wealth in different countries. Each circle is a country, with diameter proportional to population. GDP in 2003 is adjusted to reflect prices of consumer products (purchasing power parity).

GDP, gross domestic product.

Source: Deaton (2008). Copyright American Economic Association, reproduced with permission. https://www.ncbi.nlm.nih .gov/pmc/articles/PMC2680297

a flatter slope and plateau. These data appear to replicate Inglehart and Klingemann's (2000) conclusion that the effect of wealth diminishes at higher levels. However, Deaton (2008) then subjects the raw gross domestic product (GDP) data on the *x*-axis to a logarithmic transformation, and obtains Figure 6.5. Note the striking differences between the two figures.

The nontransformed data indicate a nonlinear relationship between wealth (i.e., GDP) and well-being, but that the log-transformed data indicate a linear relationship, without an apparent inflection point. This pattern is not specific to Deaton's (2008) study. Jorm and Ryan (2014), in a review of the literature, observe almost identical patterns.

The implications of these differing patterns are enormous. Figure 6.4 indicates that wealth stops facilitating meaningful increases in well-being (when comparing across countries) at a fairly low level of GDP. Figure 6.5 indicates that the effect of wealth does not diminish at higher levels. Wealth continues to facilitate well-being even when comparing rich nations. In fact, if you look closely at Figure 6.5, you can see that, if anything, the slope is even steeper at higher levels of GDP, indicating that the effect of wealth is even stronger when comparing wealthy nations (Deaton, 2008). Other researchers, including Sacks et al. (2012) and Stevenson and Wolfers (2013), have found similar results. Therefore, the policy implication of these data is that nations should continue to increase their wealth because of the beneficial effects on well-being.

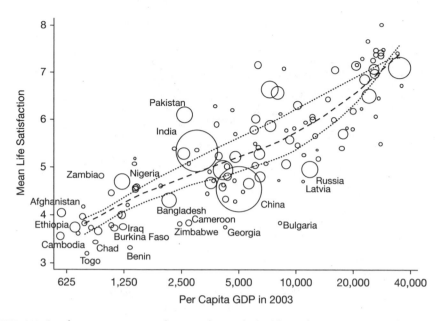

FIGURE 6.5. Graphic representation showing that each doubling of GDP is associated with a constant increase in life satisfaction. Note that each circle is a country, with diameter proportional to population. The scale on the x-axis is logarithmic. The middle line shows average life satisfaction for each level of per capita GDP, while the outer two lines show the same thing, but for two age groups, ages 15 to 25—the upper line for most of the figure—and ages 60 and older—which is usually the lower line. GDP per capita in 2003 is measured in purchasing power parity chained dollars at 2000 prices.

GDP, gross domestic product.

Source: Deaton (2008). Copyright American Economic Association; reproduced with permission. https://www.ncbi.nlm.nih .gov/pmc/articles/PMC2680297

Interpretations

Which version of the data is correct? First, there is nothing necessarily inappropriate about transforming data. There are legitimate statistical reasons to do so, because transformations can force recalcitrant data into distributions that more closely match basic statistical assumptions (Diener et al., 2013). In addition, transformations can often help interpret data (Diener et al., 2010).

It is this second point about interpretation that is crucial. The log transformation allows us to see that there is no inflection point, and no diminishing marginal utility of wealth, in relation to happiness. Specifically, happiness changes by the same amount every time wealth doubles, regardless of whether we compare two poor countries or two rich countries, one of which is twice as wealthy as the other. Because of this constant change in happiness, increasing wealth increases happiness, even when comparing wealthy countries. In this sense, Inglehart and Klingemann (2000) were wrong, and Easterlin's (1974) second point that there is no meaningful difference in the well-being of poor and rich nations is also incorrect.

But, and this is a big but, read the third sentence in the previous paragraph again: Happiness changes by the same amount every time wealth *doubles*. Diener et al. (2010,

p. 60, bracketed expression added), who also examined data on this topic, explain this clearly:

> . . . differences in raw absolute income [non-log transformed] produce larger effects for the poor than for the rich . . . an increase from $10,000 to $20,000 will have more of an impact than an increase from $80,000 to $90,000. In using log income as our measure . . . an increase from $10,000 to $20,000 dollars is equivalent in log terms to an increase from $80,000 to $160,000—in both cases a doubling of one's income. Viewed from this perspective, income has an effect on life evaluations even in wealthy nations, although the raw amount of income required to produce noticeable change is much larger.

Sacks et al. (2012) show the same important caution regarding interpretations of log-transformed data as do Diener et al. (2010; see also Stevenson & Wolfers, 2013). Sacks et al. (2012) argue as follows:

> Well-being rises with income at all levels of income; satiation does not occur in our data. But of course, the logarithmic relationship implies that each percent of increase in income raises measured well-being by a similar amount, and hence each extra dollar raises well-being less than the previous. That is, going from $1,000 to $2,000 raises satisfaction by twice as much as going from $2,000 to $3,000 and by the same amount as going from $10,000 to $20,000. (p. 1183)

Finally, Diener and Tay (2015), analyzing data from a representative sample of 98% of the world's population, find that income positively predicts well-being. Although they find the same log-linear relationship, they explain the proper interpretation well in the caption to Figure 6.6. I include their graph along with those from previously described publications because it clearly lists country names and indicates population sizes.

Deaton (2008) and Sacks et al. (2012) are correct that the citizens of richer nations are more satisfied than the citizens of poorer nations. Easterlin's (1974) conclusion that richer nations are not happier than poorer ones is wrong. But, it is also clear that higher levels of wealth produce diminishing returns (Jorm & Ryan, 2014). As Sacks et al. state, the logarithmic scale means that there are equal elevations in well-being every time national wealth *doubles*.

Other data illustrate how little national wealth increases well-being once a wealth threshold is crossed. For instance, individuals in poorer nations whose per capita GDP was below $5,600 are 12% less likely to report the highest level of life satisfaction than were citizens of richer nations whose per capita GDP was more than $15,000. However, consistent with the satiation hypothesis that the effect of additional wealth decreases in wealthy countries, any increase in per capita GDP past $17,000 increases the odds of citizens reporting the highest levels of life satisfaction by less than 2% (Proto & Rustichini, 2015).

Therefore, technically, there is no diminishing return on wealth's effect on well-being. However, in a practical sense a much smaller *absolute* gain in wealth would benefit the

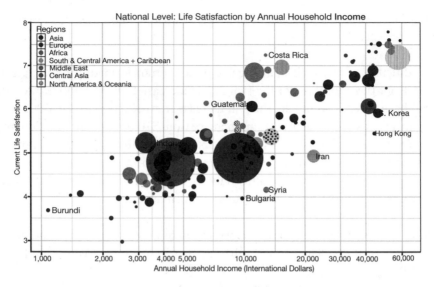

FIGURE 6.6. Cross-section association of national mean life satisfaction by annual household income. Note that the size of the circles represents the population of each nation. Although there is a declining marginal utility, with more money being required the higher the current income to make the same difference to life satisfaction, the pattern here is linear because of the logarithmic scaling of income on the *x*-axis.

Source: Diener and Tay (2015).

happiness of poorer countries more than it would richer ones. Thus, wealth increases have only relatively small effects on happiness in richer countries.

Need Theory

Recall that Need Theory predicts that wealth is important because it helps individuals meet basic physiological needs such as food and shelter (Howell & Howell, 2008). The major implication is that wealth will be more important for the well-being of the poor than of the rich. This supposition is at least partly supported by findings that smaller absolute amounts of wealth have greater impacts on the well-being of the poor than on the rich.

Some researchers have examined Need Theory even more specifically. Howell and Howell (2008) confirmed the theory in a meta-analysis of 56 studies, which examined 54 countries at different stages of development and with differing levels of national education. Economic development status was more strongly associated with well-being in the developing than in economically developed countries. The association between wealth and well-being was also stronger in the poorest countries and those that had the lowest levels of education. Thus, consistent with both Need Theory and the satiation hypothesis, wealth matters the most for the poorest and least educated countries.

Similarly, Tay and Diener (2011) found that income does not add significant predictive power to well-being after psychological needs have been accounted for in a sample of 123 countries around the world. These needs include those for basic survival, safety, social needs, respect, mastery, and autonomy. In addition, individuals living in nations that help provide for these needs among their citizenry have higher levels of well-being, further implicating the importance of meeting psychological needs.

These results are important because of what they indicate about national wealth and happiness. Recall that Easterlin argued that differences in national wealth do not predict well-being. An extension of Easterlin's argument is that increasing wealth will have more effect on happiness in poor than in wealthy countries. Howell and Howell's (2008) and Tay and Diener's (2011) results are consistent with these perspectives.

Size of the Relationship

Research has compared national wealth to other predictors of well-being and found that these other factors are also very important. Helliwell (2003) found that health status, unemployment status, being married, and belief in God predict life satisfaction more strongly than does national income. Furthermore, living in a country with high rates of social memberships, in which people frown on cheating and trust each other, and which have a trustworthy and functional government predict life satisfaction roughly as strongly as does national income. And relative income predicts well-being about as well as does absolute income.

Similarly, Fischer and Boer (2011) found that societal support for individualism predicts negative well-being (e.g., anxiety or stress), even after controlling for national wealth (GDP) in samples of 63 countries widely dispersed around the world. Consistent with Tay and Diener's (2011) findings, wealth adds little predictive power over and above that of societal values of individualism. Fischer and Boer (2011) conclude that if wealth does influence well-being, it is probably because it increases individual freedom and autonomy (i.e., individualism), which is then a more immediate cause of well-being.

The implications of these findings are important. Although wealth is one predictor of national happiness, there are other predictors that are at least as important. It is important to keep this in mind when considering ways to increase national happiness. It is especially worth noting the importance of nonmaterialistic predictors such as belief in God, social membership, and trust when weighing the impact of monetary policy on well-being.

Types of Well-Being Measures

The discussion has focused on life satisfaction measures of well-being. However, other measures show even weaker relationships with wealth. For instance, wealth is only weakly related to positive and negative feelings such as worry or enjoyment (Diener et al., 2010; Howell & Howell, 2008; Ng & Diener, 2014). Positive and negative feelings are more strongly predicted by "social psychological prosperity" (Diener et al., 2010, p. 59), which includes feeling respected and psychologically fulfilled. Other research finds that emotional well-being is better predicted by factors such as health and loneliness than it is by income (Kahneman & Deaton, 2010).

Also, daily mood is better predicted by fulfillment of psychological and nonmaterialistic needs, consistent with Ryan and Deci's (2000) self-determination theory (Ng & Diener, 2014). Ng (2013) argues that social psychological prosperity is more likely to satisfy basic psychological needs for feelings of competence, autonomy, and relatedness speci-fied by self-determination theory. Fulfillments of these basic psychological needs are then likely to lead to positive emotional reactions such as those observed earlier.

In summary, the shape of the relationship between income/wealth and well-being has generated a lot of debate, particularly regarding cross-country comparisons. The log-transformed data indicate that this relationship is linear. A doubling of income at any point of the income scale is associated with an equivalent increase of well-being (Sacks et al., 2012). In this sense, there is truly no point of "satiation" in which income ceases its association with well-being.

However, it is important to remember that the absolute amount of income needed to provide the same increase in well-being is much larger for wealthy countries than it is for poor ones. In this perhaps more practical sense, there are diminishing effects of national wealth on happiness. There is a good argument that there is a practical satia-tion point in the national wealth/well-being relationship.

The probability of national wealth substantially increasing well-being in wealthy coun-tries appears small (Proto & Rustichini, 2015). Also, at least two studies (Fischer & Boer, 2011; Tay & Diener, 2011) found that fulfillment of psychological needs and expe-riencing individualism are so important for well-being that money ceases to contribute to happiness once these needs are fulfilled. In addition, although wealth is related to cognitive measures of well-being such as life satisfaction and evaluation, it is only weakly if at all connected to emotional or affective happiness (Ng, 2013). Taken together, these results caution us against overemphasizing the importance of national wealth as a tool to increase well-being.

ECONOMIC GROWTH AND HAPPINESS

The question of whether economic growth increases happiness has huge implications for how we might choose to order our societies. Easterlin (Easterlin, 1995; Easterlin, 2005; Easterlin, McVey, Switek, Sawangfa, & Zweig, 2010; Easterlin, Morgan, Switek, & Wang, 2012) argues that economic growth does not reliably increase well-being, at least over the long term. Easterlin maintains that researchers who claim to find this relation-ship have made important errors, particularly assessing the effects of economic growth by comparing different countries with different-sized economies. Easterlin argues that the only way to measure the effect of economic growth is to track the same country over time to see whether happiness increases or decreases as its economy grows. His second objection is based on the tendency for individuals to adapt to increased wealth over time. Easterlin grants that there may be short-term increases in well-being that accom-pany economic growth, but he finds that adaptation effects erase these happiness boosts in about 10 to 12 years (Easterlin, 2013; Easterlin et al., 2010).

Studies Showing Economic Growth Predicts Well-Being

Two studies seem to satisfy Easterlin's (2013) methodological requirements of studying individual nations over time and to disconfirm Easterlin's (1974) argument that economic growth does not promote well-being. Sacks et al. (2012) examined nations over considerable lengths of time and found that economic growth was associated with increases in well-being. Sacks et al. argue that they find the relationship when Easterlin has not because they use larger samples of countries with better measures of well-being.

Interestingly, Sacks et al. (2012) did not find this relationship in the United States, which has experienced strong economic growth and a slight decline in psychological well-being over the past several decades. Somewhat curiously, they describe the United States, at the time the world's largest economy, as ". . . more of an interesting outlier than a key example" (Sacks et al., 2012, p. 1184). However, in an earlier working paper published by the National Bureau of Economics Research that worked with the same data set used by Sacks et al. (2012), Stevenson and Wolfers (2008) explained the results for the United States in terms of income inequality. Stevenson and Wolfers (2008) calculate that the average American has experienced very little increase in economic well-being because of this inequality, and therefore conclude that it is not surprising that this average American does not also experience an increase in psychological well-being.

Diener et al. (2013) also found that economic growth is associated with increases in well-being in a sample of 135 countries. Well-being is more closely associated with changes in household income than with changes in national GDP, perhaps because GDP does not closely reflect the economic experience of the average person in a country. Furthermore, Diener et al. (2013) found a linear relationship between log-transformed household income and well-being, indicating that the effect of income growth is the same for both rich and poor nations (at least in log units). There is also evidence (available because this is a longitudinal study) that household income causes future well-being, rather than merely being associated with this variable.

These results show that economic growth can increase well-being, contrary to Easterlin's (1974) hypothesis. However, the exception for the United States is curious, and it is difficult to simply ignore this important country as a simple outlier. It is also worth noting the conditions that must apparently be met in order for growth to increase happiness. For instance, recall that Stevenson and Wolfers (2008) cite income inequality as the reason growth has not led to greater happiness in the United States, and Diener et al. (2013) found that growth in average household income, rather than GDP, predicts well-being.

Concerns About the Economic Growth Hypothesis

Shape of the Relationship

Sacks et al. (2012) and Diener et al. (2013) make convincing arguments that economic growth can predict increases in well-being, but there are still concerns about this hypothesis. One concern is the shape of the relationship. These researchers used log transformations of economic growth in their calculations. Therefore, even though their results have yielded straight line relationships between the economic growth and well-being across countries at different stages of development, we know from our previous discussion that it takes a much larger absolute amount of growth to promote increases in happiness in richer countries than it does in poorer ones. For instance, Beja (2014) found only a very weak relationship between economic growth and well-being among citizens of economically developed European countries. Other authors have reported similar results (Becchetti, Corrado, & Rossetti, 2011; Becchetti & Rossetti, 2009). Thus, economic growth has stronger happiness benefits for poor countries than for rich ones (Jorm & Ryan, 2014).

How Strongly Does Economic Growth Affect Well-Being?

The effects of economic growth on well-being are small (Becchetti & Rossetti, 2009; Becchetti et al., 2011). For instance, Beja (2014) notes that researchers, including Easterlin and his colleagues, the members of the Stevenson–Wolfers group, and others have generally found significant but small relationships between economic growth and well-being. Consistent with these earlier results, Beja indicates that economic growth is positive and significantly associated with well-being, but that the size of the relationship is "very small" (p. 229). Beja concludes that GDP would have to grow at a steady 2% per year for 20.5 years in order to move average happiness from 3.15 to 3.20 on a 4-point well-being scale. Alternatively, these economies could grow at 5% per year for 8.2 years in order to achieve the same 0.05-point increase in well-being.

Beja's (2014) study is limited to only nine countries, all of which are European and economically developed, and it uses per capita GDP as the measure of economic growth. Recall that Diener et al. (2013) found that changes in household income more closely track changes in well-being than does GDP, although GDP is still a significant predictor. Diener et al. (2013) might argue that Beja's results are weak because of the use of a less sensitive measure of economic progress.

But Beja's study also had the positive characteristics of examining this relationship over a long time span (1973–2012) and controlling for adaptation and social comparison effects. Again recall that this is noteworthy because of Easterlin et al.'s (2010) contention that effects of economic growth on well-being dissipate over time, because individuals adapt to their new standard of living, and because they compare themselves to others who also have a correspondingly high new standard of living. Thus, it is difficult to dismiss Beja's findings.

Other evidence supports Beja's (2014) conclusions. Happiness rose in the United States along with economic growth, but this rise was counteracted by changes in divorce rates and by the effects of health on happiness. Furthermore, the effects of income are small. Using surveys from the United States that record well-being from 1972 to 2006, Angeles (2011, p. 71) found that "the predicted change in average happiness due to raising average incomes in the United States between the 1970s and the early 2000s is a mere 0.07 units on a 0–10 scale." This gain in happiness is quite small in response to a real, inflation adjusted increase in average family income of 37%.

Data From China and Other "Transitioning" Countries

Results from studies of China present additional concerns by showing that well-being has not increased despite impressive economic growth. Easterlin et al. (2012) found a U-shaped pattern in Chinese life satisfaction from 1990 to 2010. Despite a 400% rise in per capita GDP during this time, life satisfaction dropped sharply from 1990 to about 2005 and then began to recover. However, the net change in life satisfaction was either zero or slightly negative. Tang (2014) and Li and Raine (2014) found similar patterns.

Easterlin et al. (2012) note that this U-shaped pattern is typical of emerging economies. Almost identical patterns of GDP growth and resulting life satisfaction levels were observed in the former Soviet Union and countries in Eastern Europe as they transitioned from communism to capitalism. Graham (2009, p. 146) refers to similar patterns in Latin America as the pattern of "unhappy growth." The similarity in these patterns in Eastern Europe and China increases confidence that economic growth does not reliably bolster well-being (Easterlin et al., 2012). These authors note that the case of China is particularly remarkable because this country experienced an immediate increase in GDP, rather than the bust then boom cycle experienced by the former communist countries in Eastern Europe. It is remarkable that life satisfaction has not increased in China, given the consistent growth in its GDP (Easterlin et al., 2012).

Therefore, it seems that economic growth is not associated with increased well-being in China. Given the amount of growth China has experienced in the past several decades, and the central place it now holds in the world economy, this result strongly suggests that there is no straightforward positive effect of economic growth on well-being. Easterlin et al. (2012), Tang (2014), and Li and Raine (2014) suggest that factors such as social disruption, income inequality, unemployment, and political freedom, which are all often associated with economic growth, can mitigate any benefits for life satisfaction.

Other Factors

It is useful to compare the influence of economic growth to that of other variables. These comparisons indicate that the effects of economic growth are not extraordinary when compared to variables such as marital separation, number of social contacts, and relative income (Becchetti & Rossetti, 2009). Becchetti et al. (2011) found that individuals from a representative sample from Great Britain showed little increase in life satisfaction after experiencing growth in yearly income. The reason for the small increase in life satisfaction is that any positive effect of income growth is counteracted by social and psychological factors such as relative income status and changes in social contacts.

Other research confirms the importance of *social capital*, a person's ability to connect with others, in promoting well-being and suggests that economic growth can undermine this important contributor to happiness (Bartolini, 2007b). For example, Bartolini (2007a, 2007b) argues that economic growth can create "relational poverty" (Bartolini, 2007b, p. 351) by disrupting social relationships, including by emphasizing the market economy over social relations and by requiring or encouraging long work hours.[3] Similarly, Layard (2005) argues that economic growth can disrupt family relationships and the delicate balance in time and energy allotment between work and family. Family relationships are one of the important happiness-increasing factors in our lives. But this avenue for happiness is undermined if we spend too much time at work because of an overemphasis on economic advancement.

Social capital also contributes to well-being independently of economic growth. Abbott and Wallace (2014) find that social integration (e.g., marital status and contact with parents, children, and friends) and social cohesion (e.g., general trust and trust in the government) predict life satisfaction even after controlling for economic measures such as household income and respondents' ability to make ends meet among new members of the European Union. These results are important because these countries experienced economic growth during this time period (2003–2007). Thus, even during a time of economic growth, social factors contributed to life satisfaction.

Income inequality can also counteract the potential for economic growth to increase well-being. Tang (2014) concludes that income inequality accounts for much of the drop in Chinese life satisfaction since it moved to a free-market economy. Interestingly, Tang also found that inequality seems to have had a diminishing effect over time in China, perhaps because citizens have become accustomed to it. Diener et al. (2013), who conducted the study of 135 countries described earlier, suggest that income growth will not increase well-being unless it is evenly distributed such that the average individual in a society experiences increased prosperity. Similarly, Gruen and Klasen (2013) found that in wealthy countries, reductions in income inequality have a larger effect on well-being than increases in economic growth. Literature reviews by Jorm and Ryan (2014) and by Senik (2014) and an empirical study by Abbott and Wallace (2014) reach similar conclusions. In addition, very fast economic growth, particularly if it creates inequality, is also associated with lower well-being (Graham, 2009).

Relative income is worth noting. Individuals do not base their judgments of well-being merely on their own *absolute* economic position, but largely on how they stand *relative* to others. I can feel poor even if my income is rising, if your income is rising even faster. The benefits of economic growth can be at least partially counteracted by perceptions of relative income (Becchetti & Pelloni, 2013).

Still other research makes it clear that the effects of money, including economic growth, are fully psychologically mediated. In other words, money does not automatically increase well-being. Instead of economic growth and other monetary stimuli directly affecting our happiness, they first affect our perceptions, emotions, and behaviors. These psychologically based processes then determine our well-being. The effects of relative income are one example of this sequence of influences.

Thus, what individuals perceive about economic growth is important, not economic growth itself. Diener et al. (2013) found that economic growth prompts increased well-being when individuals become optimistic about their future and satisfied with their current finances. Individuals must also temper their aspirations for additional income. Economic growth does not inevitably spur optimism and satisfaction, and it often fails to temper aspirations.

> Our findings indicate that for rising income to be most likely to influence SWB [subjective well-being] it must lead to greater optimism, financial satisfaction, and household material prosperity. In the cases where these factors move in the opposite direction from income, they can mask the effects of income on SWB. Thus, where optimism about the future is low, or aspirations for income are rising very quickly, higher incomes may not be associated with higher SWB. (Diener et al., 2013, p. 275)

Thus, while income growth can increase well-being, it does not inevitably do so. In fact, the relationship between economic growth and psychological well-being is quite complicated. There are noneconomic factors that can match the potential happiness-boosting effects of economic growth (Becchetti & Pelloni, 2013). The United States may be a good example. Although we have experienced strong economic growth over several decades, our happiness has not increased.

The relationship is probably small for nations that are at least moderately prosperous, but quite a bit stronger for poor countries, although the case of China indicates that economic growth does not inevitably increase well-being, even in impoverished nations. The relationship is further complicated by the potential for growth to damage a nation's social fabric and to create high levels of economic inequality, both of which decrease well-being. Similarly, economic growth is associated with greater happiness only when it first creates optimism about the future. Therefore, it is clear that economic growth is not a panacea for well-being. Although economic growth can potentially increase happiness, it remains to be seen whether growth can occur without also producing inequalities and other social disruptions that lower well-being.

Conclusions About the Easterlin Paradox

Remember the questions that started this chapter: Is the relationship between money and happiness powerful and straightforward? Is economic growth an effective way to increase the well-being of all societies? We have some answers now. In general, the effects of money on well-being are not powerful, and they are not straightforward. For the most part, Easterlin (1974) was correct.

Easterlin's (1974) first point was correct. Income predicts well-being within a country (although the effect is small). His second point that it does not predict across countries was incorrect, although, again, the effect is small when comparing between rich countries or between poor countries. The effect is large only when poor countries are compared to rich ones. The conclusions regarding these first two points resolves the "paradox" that Easterlin (1974) observed (income predicts well-being within countries but not between them). Income seems to predict in both cases. Finally, his third point that economic growth does not increase well-being is also technically false, but the effect that economic growth does have is small for wealthy countries, and complicated for all countries.

In short, money has only a weak relation to well-being once basic needs for shelter and food, and psychological needs for companionship, self-direction, and feelings of competence, are met. There are several reasons for this, including the importance of relative income, which we discuss next.

RELATIVE INCOME AND SOCIAL COMPARISONS

What matters most for happiness, the absolute amount of our wealth and income, or how our wealth and income compare to that of others? Easterlin (1974) speculates that the effects of relative income are at the root of his famous paradoxical findings. Easterlin is right that relative income matters quite a bit. People regularly make judgments by whether something is "big" or "small" or "enough" by comparing it to other things. For instance, we are less happy if we think we have sex less frequently than our peers (Wadsworth, 2014). A similar effect occurs with money (Blanchflower & Oswald, 2004).

But before we get to the data, we need to consider two important points about the relative income/happiness hypothesis. First, this hypothesis proposes that psychological processes influence economic behavior in ways that economists have been reluctant to consider (Layard, 2005). Traditional economic theory argues that humans are "rational actors" (O'Boyle, 2005). As rational actors, we should think of money in absolute terms, not relative to our neighbors, because it is the absolute amount of money that determines what we can buy.

Second, the answer to this question has profound policy implications, because the potential importance of relative income calls into question the ability of economic growth to increase happiness, at least in wealthy countries. If relative income matters, then only the few at the very top of the income distribution will be made happier by growth. Happiness for the rest of us will either remain unchanged, because our relative position does not change, or will drop, because others are getting ahead of us. We consider both of these points in detail in Chapter 11.

Challenges to the Hypothesis

Some recent research has challenged the relative income hypothesis with findings from broad international data sets. Diener et al. (2013) found that relative income does not meaningfully predict well-being after controlling for absolute income in their study of 135 nations. Sacks et al. (2012) reach similar conclusions. However, Diener et al. (2013, p. 273) offer a somewhat qualified conclusion. Although they conclude that there is no evidence that "income relative to others in one's country" affects life evaluations, they think it is possible that a global standard for income does influence well-being. Specifically, rising income that lags behind a global standard of income might still result in lower well-being.

Findings Consistent With the Hypothesis

Other research uses more direct measures of relative income than do Diener et al. (2013) and Sacks et al. (2012). For instance, researchers have measured perceptions of relative deprivation, asked participants to compare themselves to their neighbors, and have ranked participants' self-reports of income relative to a reference group. These more direct measures generally support the relative income hypothesis.

Some of this research uses broad national or international data sets in which a national-level reference group defines relative income. Other research examines neighborhood-level reference groups, computing relative income in terms of how individuals compare with those living close by. Interestingly, results from both types of reference groups support the relative income hypothesis.

National- and International-Level Reference Groups

Several studies show that relative income predicts well-being. Blanchflower and Oswald (2004) found this to be true even after controlling for absolute income in large representative samples from the United States and Great Britain. Interestingly, income relative to the top earners seems more predictive than does income relative to average earners. Similarly, Brockmann, Delhey, Welzel, and Yuan (2009) used financial dissatisfaction as a proxy measure of relative income because it was the best available measure in their data set, and because other authors found that it was highly correlated with relative income. They found that this measure predicted why well-being in China has fallen so drastically since its move to a free-market economy: "people directly derive dissatisfaction from being poorer than others, and not from simply being poor" (Brockmann et al., 2009, p. 396).

Still other research further strengthens our confidence in the importance of relative income. Using a representative sample from Great Britain, Boyce, Brown, and Moore (2010) demonstrated that household income rank predicts life satisfaction more powerfully than does absolute income, even after controlling for important demographic variables. These results were replicated with samples from Taiwan (Chang, 2013), Germany (D'Ambrosio & Frick, 2007), and China (Mishra, Nielsen, & Smyth, 2014).

Other studies have added interesting qualifications to these findings. Relative income is more important in poor countries than in rich ones (Gruen & Klasen, 2013), and among relatively poor individuals in Germany (Budria, 2013). Furthermore, relative income is more important during times of economic crisis in Turkey than during times of growth, although it predicts well-being during both time periods (Caner, 2014).

Neighborhood-Level Reference Groups

Findings with measures at the neighborhood level of analysis, which employ more precise measures of relative income and social comparisons, show that relative income is an important predictor of well-being. Dittmann and Goebel (2010) examined a representative sample from East and West Germany and found that individuals who were less wealthy than their neighbors were less satisfied with their lives. Does this mean that middle-income individuals are happier if they live among the poor? The answer is no, because individuals seek not only relative status, but also social amenities such as good schools for their children. But it is true that Americans living abroad are happier if they live in wealthy neighborhoods within poor countries, which is consistent with the relative income hypothesis (Firebaugh & Schroeder, 2009).

Other research demonstrates that even the relatively wealthy are less happy if they live among the very wealthy. This research examines neighborhoods in terms of average income, not in terms of socioeconomic status, as did Dittmann and Goebel (2010). For example, Stutzer (2004) examined Swiss citizens and found that individuals living in wealthy neighborhoods had higher aspirations for future income, a variable reliably associated with lower life satisfaction.

Other research has explicitly highlighted the social comparison nature of this effect. In a paper evocatively titled "Neighbors as Negatives," Luttmer (2005) examined a nationally representative sample from the United States. Consistent with previous results, Luttmer found that living in a wealthy neighborhood was associated with lower life satisfaction, even after controlling for household income. Once again, even the wealthy are, on average, less happy when they live among the wealthy. And, the decrease in life satisfaction associated with living in a wealthy neighborhood was even more pronounced among those who socialized with neighbors at least once a month. However, socializing with relatives *outside* the neighborhood did not change the detrimental effects of living in a wealthy neighborhood.

Note the strength of the evidence supporting social comparison here. We are likely to compare ourselves to our neighbors. When we live among rich neighbors, we are less happy, and this effect is exacerbated when we socialize with them fairly frequently (and therefore have more chances for comparisons). But this seems to be an effect of comparison, and not merely socialization, because socializing outside our rich neighborhood, with those less likely to be wealthy, does not alter the relationship between where we live and our happiness. Luttmer (2005) is explicit about the importance of the social comparison effect, and his "Neighbors as Negatives" thesis.

> The size of the effect is economically meaningful. An increase in neighbor's earnings, and a similarly sized decrease in own income have roughly about the same negative effect on well-being. (p. 990)

This "Neighbors as Negatives" effect was replicated in a sample of poor rural Chinese, extending the cross-cultural generality of the findings. Knight and Gunatilaka (2012) found that life satisfaction was negatively predicted by household income below the village average. However, life satisfaction was positively related to having a current income above the village average. These results were obtained after statistically controlling for current income, indicating that the effects were not merely a product of having a high or low income. Thus, the effects of income are largely relative. Additional research further extends the cross-cultural generality of these findings. Relative income, as measured by village-level comparisons, predicts well-being in poor countries in Eastern Europe (Cojocaru, 2016). Similar results are reported in samples from Brazil (Gori-Maia, 2013), Bangladesh (Asadullah & Chaudhury, 2012), and Great Britain (Distante, 2013).

There are mixed findings regarding the influence of relative income on well-being. Results from the Sacks et al. (2012) and Diener et al. (2013) studies are inconsistent with the hypothesis. However, neither of these directly assessed individuals' income relative to some standard. Studies that more directly measure relative income support the hypothesis with remarkable cross-cultural consistency. Therefore, it seems wise to accept that relative income affects happiness.

It seems that attempts to raise well-being by increasing economic growth will be undercut by the relative income effect, particularly in societies that are at least moderately prosperous. Any potential happiness boost that might result from a uniform increase in income will be dampened by social comparison effects. Perhaps these social comparison effects should not be much of a surprise. Recall from our discussion of evolutionary psychology that humans seem to be naturally selected to compete (and also to cooperate) with each other. As a result, tendencies to constantly monitor the wealth of others, to try to compete in the "wealth race," and not to feel easily satisfied with present circumstances may be part of our nature.

THE HEDONIC TREADMILL

Another important factor related to the potential effects of economic growth is humans' tendency to adapt to circumstances. Similar to the effects of relative income discussed, we do not experience a stimulus in isolation, but instead compare it to our previous experience. This is documented in terms of both physical and social stimuli. For example, if you place your hand in a bucket of cold water, then move it to a bucket of normal room temperature water, the second bucket will feel warmer than usual.

This adaptation effect was dubbed "The Hedonic Treadmill," or "Hedonic Adaptation" by Brickman and Campbell (1971; see also Brickman, Coates, & Janoff-Bulman, 1978). In terms of money, this means that we can become accustomed to a level of income that formerly seemed quite satisfying. I vividly remember wondering how I could ever possibly spend all the money I would be making in my position as an assistant professor fresh out of graduate school. After years living on graduate student wages, it seemed like a princely sum. But alas, within a short time my salary seemed only adequate.

There is some disagreement about whether individuals adapt to rising incomes, but the bulk of the research indicates that they do. Keep in mind the potential policy implications of this hypothesis. If we do adapt to rising income, what does this suggest about the potential for economic growth to increase happiness?

Challenges to the Hedonic Adaptation Hypothesis

Some evidence suggests that individuals do not adapt to increases in income. For instance, Sacks et al. (2012), Diener et al. (2013), and Stevenson and Wolfers (2013) argue against adaptation because log-transformed income data show a linear relationship between income and well-being. The Stevenson and Wolfers (2013) data are less helpful because they compare different individuals who have differing levels of income, instead of following the same individuals across time. Obviously, it is necessary to see how individuals react to the experience of increasing wealth over time in order to determine whether adaptation occurs.

However, Sacks et al. (2012) and Diener et al. (2013) do make cross-time comparisons for the same individuals. The crucial point is understanding how to interpret their findings for log-transformed income. By now the elements of the discussion should be familiar. Recall that the log-transformation/linear relationship results in any doubling of income producing the same change in well-being. This is technically contrary to the hedonic adaptation hypothesis. However, it also means that the absolute level of income needed to achieve the same increase in happiness is much larger for rich individuals than it is for the poor. In practical terms, it means that the ability for increases in income to increase happiness essentially levels off after some point, which is consistent with hedonic adaptation.

Confirmations of Hedonic Adaptation

Other evidence supports the hypothesis. Beja (2014), whose study of nine Western European countries we considered earlier, found evidence of complete adaptation to creases in GDP in about 4 years. Other researchers have specifically examined how rising income affects individuals' *aspirations* for more income. Stutzer (2004) found that Swiss participants with higher household incomes had higher aspirations for earnings in the future. And this relationship held even after controlling for level of household income. Thus, consistent with the hedonic treadmill hypothesis, no matter how much money we make, we want to make more. Stutzer (2004) also found that aspiring to earn more is associated with lower life satisfaction.

Thus, we run on the treadmill to make more money, but the more we run (and make) the more we think we need to make. And the more we think we need to make, the less happy we are. In fact, Stutzer's (2004) data indicate that a one-dollar increase in income leads to a 40 cent increase in required minimum income. We experience a greatly diminished "happiness effect" from increased income simply because we adapt to our improved circumstances (Layard, 2005).[4] Once again, the relationship between income and well-being is not straightforward.

Research using a poor rural sample in China partially replicated Stutzer's (2004) results. Knight and Gunatilaka (2012) found that household income positively predicted aspirations (i.e., perceived minimum income needed). Consistent with the hedonic adaptation hypothesis, the more participants made, the more they thought they needed to make in order to maintain basic household needs. Furthermore, and also consistent with adaptation theory, aspirations negatively predicted life satisfaction. However, participants in this sample did not adapt to higher income as strongly as did those in Stutzer's (2004) study, perhaps because they were much poorer than Stutzer's Swiss participants.

In summary, the evidence supports hedonic adaptation theory, at least in a practical sense. Sacks et al. (2012) and Diener et al. (2013) found that the slope between income and well-being is linear when income is log-transformed. In this sense, they are correct that there is no satiation point in which income fails to bring additional well-being. However, the absolute amount of increased income necessary to produce a comparable change in well-being is much larger among the rich than the poor. Thus, in a practical sense, there does seem to be a satiation point in wealthy nations.

There is also direct support for hedonic adaptation in studies that include statistical terms in their models, that specifically test for adaptation, and that also examine how income affects aspirations and then how these aspirations influence well-being. Although it is not clear whether adaptation effects can completely wipe out the potential increases in happiness given by boosts in income, it is clear that adaptation happens and its effects are significant.

INCOME AND WEALTH INEQUALITY

Income Inequality Lowers Well-Being

Our discussion of the effects of economic growth and relative income demonstrates that income inequality has potentially important consequences for well-being. Income inequality is probably one reason why economic growth has not fostered increased happiness in China, for example.

Social Indicators

Income inequality also has interesting psychological consequences in itself. For example, income inequality is associated with a host of social miseries, including higher rates of imprisonment, mental illness, infant mortality, obesity, and lower life expectancies in the United States[5] and around the world (Pickett & Wilkinson, 2007; Wilkinson & Pickett, 2009). Inequality also predicted alcohol problems in nationally representative samples from the United States (Karriker-Jaffe, Roberts, & Bond, 2013), and bullying rates in a study of 37 countries around the world (Elgar, Craig, Boyce, Morgan, & Vella-Zarb, 2009). Furthermore, state-level inequality predicts child abuse in the United States (Eckenrode, Smith, McCarthy, & Dineen, 2014), and country-level inequality predicts child injury mortality rates in Europe (Sengoelge, Hasselberg, Ormandy, & Laflamme, 2014).

Wealth and income inequality are also associated with disruptions of a nation's social fabric. These factors predict weaker support for democracy around the world, except among individuals with very low incomes. When inequality is high, wealthy individuals show less support for democracy than do poorer individuals (Andersen, 2012). Income inequality also predicts lower voter turnout in Italy (Scervini & Segatti, 2012), lowered civic and social participation among the poor (Lancee & van de Werfhorst, 2012), and less "willingness to improve the living conditions of other people" in one's country in a European sample (Paskov & Dewilde, 2012).

Alert readers probably wonder whether this relationship is causal, because the data are correlational. However, Wilkinson and Pickett's (2009) findings hold even when per capita income is controlled, and apply to wealthy industrial countries as well as poorer and less developed countries. The relationship also holds when immigration rates, ethnic diversity, and level of social services and spending are considered (Pickett & Wilkinson, 2007). Although we can never be absolutely sure about causality when considering correlational data, the authors make a strong argument that income inequality is a cause of social dysfunction.

Finally, the negative effects of inequality are not trivial. If inequality could be halved in the United Kingdom, we could expect that murder rates would decrease by 50%, while mental illness could be reduced by two thirds, imprisonment and teen births would both fall by 80%, and levels of trust could increase by 85%. Furthermore, although decreasing inequality would improve the well-being of lower income individuals the most, it would also positively affect the well-being of wealthy individuals because the reduction in the social problems listed would benefit everyone, rich and poor (Wilkinson & Pickett, 2009).

Subjective Well-Being

Other data extend these findings using measures of happiness. Both longitudinal and cross-sectional (i.e., nonlongitudinal) studies of representative samples in the United States have replicated the relationship (e.g., Alesina, Di Tella, & MacCulloch, 2004; Oishi, Kesebir, & Diener, 2011). The relationship has also been replicated in nonrepresentative U.S. samples (e.g., Di Domenico & Fournier, 2014; Neville, 2012). Other studies find a negative relationship between income inequality and well-being in representative samples of the world's population (e.g., Beja, 2014[6]; Delhey & Kohler, 2011; Diener & Tay, 2015; Oishi, Schimmack, & Diener, 2012[7]; Verme, 2011). The relationship is found in Brazil (e.g., Filho, Kawachi, Wang, Viana, & Andrade, 2013) and throughout Europe (e.g., Alesina et al., 2004; Delhey & Dragolov, 2014). Finally, Ferrer-i-Carbonell and Ramos (2014) reviewed much of the literature in this area and concluded that income inequality is associated with lowered well-being, at least in Western countries.

These findings are sizable and meaningful. Filho et al. (2013) found that Brazilians living in areas of high inequality were 76% more likely to report depression. Furthermore, Alesina et al. (2004) found that a 10% increase in inequality in Europe would be associated with a 21% decrease in individuals reporting the top level of well-being and 27% increase in those reporting the lowest level of well-being. They found similar results for the United States. A 10% increase in U.S. inequality would be associated with an 18.5% decrease in those reporting the highest level of well-being and a 26% increase in those reporting the lowest level of well-being.

Political Ideology

Still other data find a relationship between income inequality and well-being is qualified by individual differences pertaining to political affiliation and perceptions of economic opportunity. Specifically, those who believe that their society offers opportunities for economic advancement tend to have greater tolerance for income inequality. For example, Napier and Jost (2008) examined a representative sample of Americans and found that the negative effects of inequality on well-being depended on political ideology. As shown in Figure 6.7, political conservatives' happiness did not decline significantly as inequality increased. However, liberals' happiness did. Overall, there was a negative relationship between inequality and happiness, but it was significant only among liberals. Other researchers have found similar results (e.g., Alesina et al., 2004; Bjornskov, Dreher, Fischer, Schnellenbach, & Gehring, 2013; Hajdu & Hajdu, 2014).

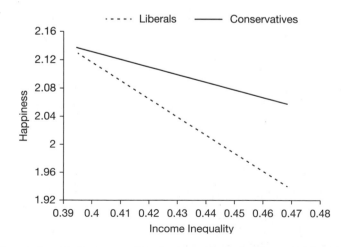

FIGURE 6.7. The relationship between political orientation and self-reported happiness as a function of the Gini coefficient, a common measure of income inequality, 1974 through 2004 (study 3). *Source:* Napier and Jost (2008).

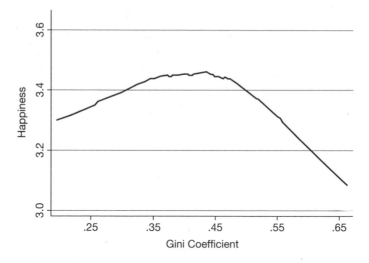

FIGURE 6.8. The Gini coefficient shows an inverse relationship between income inequality and happiness in China.
Source: Wang et al. (2015).

Napier and Jost (2008) also found that conservatives are happier than liberals because they rationalize or justify inequalities. This finding led them to conclude that conservatives' happiness is not sensitive to income inequality because they do not perceive inequality as problematic. Similarly, Davidai and Gilovich (2015) found that American conservatives are more likely to believe there is social mobility such that individuals can move up or down the income ladder with hard work and dedication.

Other research is consistent with Napier and Jost's (2008) hypothesis that social perceptions create individual differences in reaction to inequality. Studies from Germany (Schneider, 2012), from industrialized and emerging economies around the world (Beja, 2014), from China (Zhao, 2012), and from Europe (Ravazzini & Chávez-Juárez, 2015; see also Bjornskov et al., 2013) replicated their basic findings. One additional interesting finding comes from Wang, Pan, and Luo (2015), who observed an inverted U-shaped relationship between income inequality and well-being throughout China. As seen in Figure 6.8, happiness was higher in areas with moderately high levels of inequality than it was in areas with little or no inequality. The Gini coefficient is a standard measure of inequality. However, areas with high levels of inequality are less happy than areas with moderate levels, thus the inverted U shape.

Wang et al. (2015) suggest that moderate levels of inequality are a hopeful sign in an emerging economy such as China. Individuals may see inequality as a signal that it is possible to become prosperous, because they begin to see others doing so. However, high levels of inequality may signal that prosperity is harder to reach. The important point for our purposes is that this explanation is consistent with the idea that individuals' perceptions of inequality are what matters. Similar to Zhao's (2012) results, individuals become happier with inequality if they think it signals upward social mobility.

This research shows that income or wealth inequality differentially affects well-being depending on individuals' views of social conditions. Inequality does not significantly lower well-being for those who think of it as "good" or who are able to rationalize its existence with beliefs about upward social mobility and economic opportunity. Furthermore, individuals' perceptions of whether they themselves are moving up or down the social and economic ladder also affect the relationship between inequality and well-being.

These qualifications to the inequality effect probably should not surprise us. Humans rarely act uniformly to any stimulus. Instead, stimuli are filtered through our perceptions, which are influenced by our experiences and values.

Challenges to the Inequality Hypothesis

There are some empirical challenges to the inequality hypothesis. Zagorski, Evans, Kelley, and Piotrowska (2014) found no relationship between income inequality and well-being after controlling for wealth (i.e., GDP) in a study of 28 European countries. Zagorski et al. argue that nations with high levels of inequality tend to be poor. These nations have lower well-being not because of their inequality, but because of their poverty. Therefore, inequality is only coincidently, and noncausally, related to well-being because of its association with low national economic output. Somewhat similarly, Berg and Veenhoven (2010) found in a study of 119 countries around the world that countries with high levels of inequality are *happier* than those with lower inequality, again after controlling for GDP. Rözer and Kraaykamp (2013) obtained similar results in a study of 85 nations around the world.

Although any failures to replicate previous findings should be taken seriously, it is difficult to know what to make of these studies. When examined closely, it is clear that Berg and Veenhoven's (2010) and Rözer and Kraaykamp's (2013) results are heterogeneous and in many ways match our discussion of individual differences, as previously discussed. For instance, although Rözer and Kraaykamp (2013) found a positive relationship between inequality and well-being overall, this relationship changes depending on individuals' preferences for inequality and trust in others and in social institutions. Specifically, and consistent with the findings reported in the earlier discussion of individual differences, inequality is negatively associated with well-being among those who prefer more equal division of wealth and income. We can also expect that highly trusting individuals would have higher expectations of fairness.

Berg and Veenhoven's (2010) results are similarly heterogeneous. Although these authors found a positive relationship between inequality and well-being overall, this effect varies by level of economic development. Inequality negatively predicts well-being among Western developed countries and is positively related in Asia, Latin America, and Eastern Europe. There was no relationship in Africa. The reasons for these differences are not clear, but they may reflect stronger preferences for equality among citizens of developed nations.

We need to seriously consider the criticisms of the inequality/well-being hypothesis raised by these authors, but the weight of the existing evidence does seem to indicate that inequality lowers the well-being of at least a great many people, depending on some individual difference characteristics. Let us keep a close eye on future research as it develops.

Why Inequality Is Related to Well-Being

Inequality seems to promote social comparisons among children by making them more aware of differences in status. Children are aware of status differences, and they respond to these differences similarly to the way adults do. Status differences evoke changes in performance and behavior, including violence. For example, both juvenile and adult homicide rates are correlated with inequality, and are best explained by ". . . loss of face and people's sensitivity to feeling disrespected and looked down on" (Pickett & Wilkinson, 2007, p. 1084). This triangular connection among inequality, loss of face and feeling disrespected, and social problems is what we would expect if inequality produced ill effects because of social comparison processes (Pickett & Wilkinson, 2007).

Research provides broad conceptual support for the hypothesis that inequality lowers happiness by encouraging social comparisons. For instance, income inequality is associated with lower levels of trust in others in Europe (Olivera, 2014). In addition, Oishi et al. (2011) examined representative samples from the United States between 1972 and 2008 and found that "General Trust" and "Perceived Fairness" fully mediate the relationship between income inequality and happiness for lower income Americans, but not for high-income earners. Specifically, income inequality leads to lower levels of trust and perceived fairness, which is then associated with lower levels of happiness. Finally, Neville (2012) examined state-level data of Internet traffic at websites that peddle term papers and demonstrated that "generalized trust" (indicated by responses to the question, "Would you say that most people can be trusted?") fully mediates the relationship between income inequality and academic dishonesty.

Income inequality is also positively associated with "self-enhancement," even after controlling for age, gender, and cultural values. Loughnan et al. (2011) examined 1,625 individuals from 15 countries across five continents, and found that those from unequal societies are more likely to view themselves as superior to others. Although these authors did not directly test a mediator, they hypothesized that inequality fosters a greater sense of superiority, and that this leads to more self-enhancement.

Inequality is also linked to political trust. Although this research does not explicitly assess well-being, it links inequality to aspects of political trust that are likely associated with well-being. For instance, income inequality is associated with less trust in political institutions such as national governments, the judiciary, and political parties among Latin Americans, even after controlling for GDP (Zmerli & Castillo, 2015). It is also linked to lowered trust in others and political apathy in Eastern Europe (Loveless, 2013).

These studies are conceptually consistent with the hypothesis that social comparison/status differentiation mediates the relationship between inequality and well-being. Just as we would expect if inequality lowered happiness because it increased social comparisons and recognition of status differences, these studies demonstrate that income inequality lowers trust in others and the perception that others are fair, and that these factors mediate its relationship to happiness and academic dishonesty.[8] The academic dishonesty finding is particularly interesting because it is a behavior that might be expected when social status differences are noticeable and acute. Furthermore, inequality also increases individuals' feelings of superiority, possibly because they feel increased competition pressure, which would also be expected if status concerns are highly salient.

Although some research questions the causal link between income inequality, trust, and well-being (e.g., Bergh & Bjørnskov, 2014), most of the research supports this pathway between inequality and well-being. These studies provide evidence from separate research teams, with separate methodologies and measures, which all converge to support a unified explanation of why income inequality is associated with ill effects. These data also broaden the level of analysis by demonstrating that the inequality/happiness relationship occurs at both the group (average level of happiness in states and countries) and the individual level (e.g., measures of individual's happiness in the studies just reviewed). This convergence of methods, measures, and levels of analysis increases our confidence that inequality lowers happiness by encouraging social comparisons.

Although it is always difficult to be certain about causality when considering these sorts of variables, it is clear that income inequality is associated with lower well-being, particularly among relatively wealthy Western nations. Inequality is not just associated with lower personal well-being. It also predicts myriad social problems, such as incarceration rates, infant mortality, and rates of mental illness. It is also associated with rifts in the social fabric such as lowered trust, poor voter participation, and lack of civic engagement.

It seems likely that this relationship is causal, given the number of longitudinal studies conducted with controls for national wealth. However, the path connecting inequality to well-being is not completely clear. It appears that inequality lowers well-being because it creates status differentials that cultivate competition among individuals and erodes trust in others, faith in democracy, and trust in national institutions. This inequality-caused distrust seems to be the proximal cause of lower well-being.

There are also interesting individual differences in the inequality/well-being relationship. Remarkably, in some poor countries, inequality can serve as a signal of economic opportunity and can therefore raise individual well-being. Those who believe they are likely to advance on the economic ladder are often heartened by inequality. Inequality is less likely to affect political conservatives because they are able to rationalize inequity as a matter of individual choices and responses to opportunity. On the other hand, political liberals are less happy when inequality is high.

UNEMPLOYMENT

Basic Findings

Unemployment is consistently associated with lower well-being. Literature reviews demonstrate that unemployment predicts suicide rates (Milner, Spittal, Page, & LaMontagne, 2014; Uutela, 2010), psychiatric admissions (Simone, Carolin, Max, & Reinhold, 2013), substance abuse (Henkel, 2011), all-cause mortality (Roelfs, Shor, Davidson, & Schwartz, 2011; Roelfs, Shor, Blank, & Schwartz, 2015), and poor mental health and lower subjective well-being (Clark, 2003; Eichhorn, 2014; Luhmann, Hofmann, Eid, & Lucas, 2012; Paul & Moser, 2009; Reneflot & Evensen, 2014). Similarly, a recent empirical study of a representative sample in Great Britain found that unemployment reduces the amount of time respondents report being in good health by 19% (Cooper, McCausland, & Theodossiou, 2015).

These associations are large and meaningful. A 1% *rise* in unemployment corresponds with a 5% rise in schizophrenia admissions, while a 1% *fall* in unemployment is associated with a 2% decrease in schizophrenia admissions (Simone et al., 2013). Similarly, unemployed men face a 51% higher risk of suicide than do employed men (Milner et al., 2014). Also, more than twice as many of the unemployed (34%) report psychological distress as compared to the employed (16%; Paul & Moser, 2009). Finally, the all-cause mortality risk for the unemployed is 62% higher than it is for employed individuals (Roelfs et al., 2015).

Causality?

You have probably noted that all this research is correlational. Therefore, it is smart to wonder whether unemployment causes unhappiness. For instance, do personality traits cause individuals to become unemployed and to also be unhappy? Does unemployment cause happiness, or does happiness cause unemployment?

These are good questions. However, a careful look at the research indicates that unemployment is probably a cause of (un)happiness. Personality differences cannot account for the negative relationship between unemployment and happiness. Schimmack, Schupp, and Wagner (2008) found that unemployment is negatively related to happiness even after controlling for the "Big Five" personality characteristics. Also, studies of factory closures, in which individuals become unemployed regardless of their personalities, show negative effects of unemployment on mental health (Paul & Moser, 2009). In addition, longitudinal studies (e.g., Lucas, Clark, Georgellis, & Diener, 2004) demonstrate that individuals become less happy after they become unemployed. These results point toward unemployment as a cause of (un)happiness.

Findings of a "dose–response" relationship between unemployment and well-being also suggest a causal relationship. Paul and Moser (2009) reviewed the literature and concluded that happiness drops when individuals become unemployed and then rises when they find new employment. It is unlikely that any third variable can explain this dose–response linkage between employment and happiness. Studies of unemployment and suicide show similar dose–response relationships (Milner et al., 2014).

Our confidence that unemployment is a cause of unhappiness is further strengthened by results controlling for demographic factors such as age, gender, and marital status (e.g., Blanchflower & Oswald, 2004). Simple loss of income does not appear to account for the negative effects of unemployment either. Unemployment lowers well-being even after controlling for income (Blanchflower & Oswald, 2004) and relative income (Helliwell, 2003). Therefore, it seems that something about unemployment itself, and not simply the associated loss of income, causes lowered well-being.

Scarring

The negative effects of unemployment persist even after individuals become reemployed, further demonstrating the meaningfulness of this experience. We do not seem to adapt fully to the experience of unemployment. Daly and Delaney (2013) refer to this effect as psychological *scarring*. Consistent with the scarring hypothesis, Daly and Delaney found that the amount of time during adulthood that individuals spend unemployed predicts well-being at age 50, even after controlling for childhood distress levels and current employment status. Thus, individuals who experience longer terms of unemployment appear *scarred* by this experience. Similarly, Strandh, Winefield, Nilsson, and Hammarström (2014) found that youth unemployment produces long-lasting negative psychological consequences. Daly and Delaney (2013) speculate that this scarring effect occurs because unemployment produces persistent insecurity about future employment, even among those who currently have a job.

Unemployment also scars individuals' sense of trust. Laurence (2015) found that 50-year-old individuals who involuntarily lost a job between the ages of 33 and 50 were 4.5% less likely to "think that most people could be trusted" (p. 50). This finding is significant even after controlling for demographic variables and initial levels of trust at age 33. Furthermore, this decrease in trust lasts for at least 9 years and is specific to those who involuntarily lost a job. For instance, trust decreases among individuals who have been laid off or who lose their jobs because the company closed. However, it does not decrease among those who leave jobs for family or health reasons or who decide to take a career break. These results are interesting because trust is linked directly to happiness (Helliwell, 2003). Trust is also linked indirectly to happiness via its connection with income inequality (Loveless, 2013).

Mitigating Factors

The severity of the negative effects of unemployment changes depending on social class and other demographic factors. For example, minimally and medium-skilled unemployed Americans have about two and a half times the risk of all-cause mortality as do similar employed American workers. However, there is no elevated mortality risk among unemployed highly skilled American workers. Likewise, unemployed German workers at any skill level who were educated in West Germany also do not face elevated mortality risks (McLeod, Lavis, MacNab, & Hertzman, 2012).

Therefore, job skill level affects reactions to unemployment in the United States, but not in Germany. It is not clear what accounts for these cross-cultural differences. Differences in the level of unemployment benefits are one possibility, but the evidence is mixed. For instance, some research indicates that the provision and quality of unemployment benefits do not affect psychological reactions to unemployment (Eichhorn, 2014). However, other research finds that the level of unemployment benefits among states in the United States has a small but statistically significant relationship with suicide rates (Cylus, Glymour, & Avendano, 2015). Another explanation is that Germany provides more support for reemployment than does the United States. This may explain why highly skilled, and therefore readily reemployable, American workers have mortality risks that are similar to German workers (McLeod et al., 2012).

In addition, the more highly educated (Galić, 2007; Mandemakers & Monden, 2013) are less negatively affected by unemployment. The more educated apparently fare better in response to unemployment because of their likely greater financial resources and prospects for future employment (Galić, 2007; Mandemakers & Monden, 2013). Other research demonstrates more negative effects of unemployment among men (van der Meer, 2014) and those who perceived high levels of social support at their previous jobs (Backhans & Hemmingsson, 2012). Finally, unemployment is more psychologically damaging in individualistically oriented cultures that have an ethic of individual responsibility for success (Mikucka, 2014).

The fact that the effects of unemployment change depending on various mitigating factors indicates that the psychology of unemployment is important. As we see in other chapters, individuals' perceptions and construal of an event affect their responses. This suggests that policy interventions can be effective in reducing the negative psychological effects of unemployment. We explore some possible policies in the following section.

Social Norms

Our reactions to unemployment are also affected by the number of other people who are also unemployed, thus further illustrating the psychological nature of our response to unemployment. Unemployment is less distressing if others like us are also unemployed (Clark, 2003; Flint, Bartley, Shelton, & Sacker, 2013). Clark (2003) argues that unemployment rates establish social norms that affect well-being. If many other people like us are unemployed, then our unemployment is more "normative" and therefore less distressing.

The data are consistent with Clark's (2003) hypothesis. As expected, employed individuals have higher well-being than do the unemployed. However, analyses of local unemployment rates show that this well-being difference in favor of the employed is significantly larger when the local unemployment rate is low (around 5%) than when it is higher (around 15%). Thus, if relatively few people are unemployed, workers are much happier than are the unemployed. However, if the unemployment rate is high, then the happiness difference between the employed and unemployed is much reduced. It even appears that there would be no well-being difference between the employed and the unemployed once the unemployment rate reaches 24%. Thus, consistent with the social norm hypothesis, individuals are less distressed by their own unemployment if many of their peers are also unemployed (Clark, 2003).[9] Also, these relations are significant when considering both men and women, but are much stronger for men.

Although these are correlational data and causality is uncertain, there is a strong argument that social norms are the active ingredient in this recipe. These results hold after controlling for income, health, and demographic characteristics. There are also no regional differences in unemployment compensation in Great Britain (Clark, 2003). It is difficult to imagine an alternative explanation for the results that can successfully compete with Clark's (2003) social norm hypothesis.

Clark's (2003) data also show that the well-being of the unemployed is related to the employment status of others in their own household. For instance, if I am unemployed and my partner is employed, the probability that I have the highest level of well-being is 31%. However, that probability jumps to 40% if both myself and my household partner are unemployed. Similarly, if I am unemployed and no one else in my household is unemployed, the probability I will have the highest level of well-being is 36%. However, if everyone else in my household is also unemployed, that probability is 46%.

These data do not make sense unless we assume that a social norm of unemployment lightens the blow of unemployment on our own well-being. After all, a household in which everyone is unemployed should suffer much more than one in which I am the only one unemployed. Yet, I am happier when the rest of my household joins me in unemployment. Flint et al. (2013) replicated these findings, but noted that the unemployed have lower well-being than employed individuals regardless of the local unemployment rate. Therefore, although we are less hurt by unemployment when it is a "norm," unemployment lowers well-being.

SUMMARY

Unemployment is strongly and negatively associated with well-being, and the relationship appears to be causal. Interestingly, the negative effects of unemployment are less severe if many other individuals are also unemployed at the same time. It also appears that unemployment leaves permanent emotional scars. These results indicate that serious policy considerations should be given to reducing unemployment if a society wishes to increase the happiness of its citizens.

The overall message from this chapter is that the relationship between money and happiness is relatively weak once individuals climb up to an income level that provides for basic physical and emotional needs. This relationship is also tremendously complicated and not at all straightforward. Hedonic adaptation, relative income, income inequality, and individual difference variables among other factors all affect the relationship. But it is clear that increased wealth, either on a personal or a national level, is not an efficient strategy for increasing the happiness of those who already have their basic needs met. Instead, there are a variety of other factors, such as improving our social relationships, that offer a much more promising path to greater happiness.

NOTES

1. Easterlin (1974) does not separate this point cleanly from his argument about relative income, but he does make the argument.

2. Gross national product (GNP, sometimes measured as gross domestic product [GDP]) is an estimate of the total wealth in a society as indicated by the sum of all goods and services in that country.

3. But see Sarracino (2012) for a partial rebuttal.

4. It is clear that increasing income has some potential to increase our well-being. After all, our required minimum income does not increase at the same rate as our actual income. But, the 40% erosion of the potential effect of income speaks to the effect size question we discussed earlier in the chapter. Also, remember that social comparison processes are likely to further erode any positive contributions that income might make to happiness.

5. The United States is one of the more unequal countries in the world. The top 10% of earners claimed 50.4% of all pretax income in the United States in 2012. The bottom 90% of wage earners in the United States earned less than half the county's total income. And, the top 1% of earners took about 23% of total U.S. income that same year (Saez, 2013).

6. Beja (2014) found that higher levels of inequality are associated with lower subjective well-being in both industrial and "emerging" economies. However, low levels of inequality are not related to well-being in industrial economies, and are positively related in emerging economies.

7. Oishi et al. (2011) just report the basic correlation between income inequality and life evaluation without controlling for other factors, such as national wealth or household income.

8. However, see Fairbrother and Martin (2013) for a partial exception to these findings.

9. You may wonder about the small well-being difference between the employed and unemployed when regional unemployment is high. Is this small difference because the unemployed become *less* unhappy in these circumstances? Or, could it indicate that working individuals become *more* unhappy when they see so many of their fellow citizens become unemployed? The answer is that the unemployed become less unhappy when regional unemployment is high. We know this because the regional unemployment rate is not related to well-being.

REFERENCES

Abbott, P., & Wallace, C. (2014). Rising economic prosperity and social quality: The case of new member states of the European Union. *Social Indicators Research, 115*(1), 419–439.

Alesina, A., Di Tella, R., & MacCulloch, R. (2004). Inequality and happiness: Are Europeans and Americans different? *Journal of Public Economics, 88*(9–10), 2009–2042.

Andersen, R. (2012). Support for democracy in cross-national perspective: The detrimental effect of economic inequality. *Research in Social Stratification and Mobility, 30*, 389–402.

Angeles, L. (2011). A closer look at the Easterlin paradox. *Journal of Socio-Economics, 40*(1), 67–73.

Asadullah, M. N., & Chaudhury, N. (2012). Subjective well-being and relative poverty in rural Bangladesh. *Journal of Economic Psychology, 33*(5), 940–950.

Backhans, M. C., & Hemmingsson, T. (2012). Unemployment and mental health—who is (not) affected? *European Journal of Public Health, 22*(3), 429–433.

Bartolini, S. (2007a). Beyond accumulation and technical progress: Negative externalities as an engine of economic growth. In M. Basili, M. Franzini, & A. Vercelli (Eds.), *Environment, inequality and collective action* (pp. 51–70). New York, NY: Routledge.

Bartolini, S. (2007b). Why are people so unhappy? Why do they strive so hard for money? Competing explanations of the broken promises of economic growth. In L. Bruni & P. L. Porta (Eds.), *Handbook on the economics of happiness* (pp. 337–364). Northampton, MA: Edward Elgar.

Becchetti, L., Corrado, L., & Rossetti, F. (2011). The heterogeneous effects of income changes on happiness. *Social Indicators Research, 104*(3), 387–406.

Becchetti, L., & Pelloni, A. (2013). What are we learning from the life satisfaction literature? *International Review of Economics, 60*(2), 113–155.

Becchetti, L., & Rossetti, F. (2009). When money does not buy happiness: The case of "frustrated achievers." *The Journal of Socio-Economics, 38*(1), 159–167.

Beja, E. L., Jr. (2014). Subjective well-being analysis of income inequality: Evidence for the industrialized and emerging economies. *Applied Research in Quality of Life, 9*(2), 139–156.

Berg, M., & Veenhoven, R. (2010). Income inequality and happiness in 119 nations: In search for an optimum that does not appear to exist. In B. Greve (Ed.), *Happiness and social policy in Europe* (pp. 174–194). Cheltenham, UK: Edward Elgar.

Bergh, A., & Bjørnskov, C. (2014). Trust, welfare states and income equality: Sorting out the causality. *European Journal of Political Economy, 35,* 183–199.

Bjornskov, C., Dreher, A., Fischer, J. A. V., Schnellenbach, J., & Gehring, K. (2013). Inequality and happiness: When perceived social mobility and economic reality do not match. *Journal of Economic Behavior and Organization, 91,* 75–92.

Blanchflower, D. G., & Oswald, A. J. (2004). Well-being over time in Britain and the USA. *Journal of Public Economics, 88* (7–8), 1359–1386.

Boyce, C. J., Brown, G. D. A., & Moore, S. C. (2010). Money and happiness: Rank of income, not income, affects life satisfaction. *Psychological Science, 21*(4), 471–475.

Brickman, P., & Campbell, D. T. (1971). Hedonic relativism and planning the good society. In M. H. Appley (Ed.), *Adaptation level theory: A symposium* (pp. 287–302). New York, NY: Academic Press.

Brickman, P., Coates, D., & Janoff-Bulman, R. (1978). Lottery winners and accident victims: Is happiness relative? *Journal of Personality and Social Psychology, 36*(8), 917–927.

Brockmann, H., Delhey, J., Welzel, C., & Yuan, H. (2009). The China puzzle: Falling happiness in a rising economy. *Journal of Happiness Studies, 10*(4), 387–405.

Budria, S. (2013). Are relative-income effects constant across the well-being distribution? *Journal of Happiness Studies, 14*(4), 1379–1408.

Caner, A. (2014). Happiness, comparison effects, and expectations in Turkey. *Journal of Happiness Studies, 16*(5), 1323–1345.

Chang, W. (2013). Climbing up the social ladders: Identity, relative income, and subjective well-being. *Social Indicators Research, 113*(1), 513–535.

Clark, A. E. (2003). Unemployment as a social norm: Psychological evidence from panel data. *Journal of Labor Economics, 21*(2), 323–351.

Cojocaru, A. (2016). Does relative deprivation matter in developing countries: Evidence from six transition economies. *Social Indicators Research, 125*(3), 735–756.

Cooper, D., McCausland, W. D., & Theodossiou, I. (2015). Is unemployment and low income harmful to health? Evidence from Britain. *Review of Social Economy, 73*(1), 34–60.

Cylus, J., Glymour, M. M., & Avendano, M. (2015). Health effects of unemployment benefit program generosity. *American Journal of Public Health, 105*(2), 317–323.

Daly, M., & Delaney, L. (2013). The scarring effect of unemployment throughout adulthood on psychological distress at age 50: Estimates controlling for early adulthood distress and childhood psychological factors. *Social Science and Medicine, 80,* 19–23.

D'Ambrosio, C., & Frick, J. R. (2007). Income satisfaction and relative deprivation: An empirical link. *Social Indicators Research, 81*(3), 497–519.

Davidai, S., & Gilovich, T. (2015). Building a more mobile America—one income quintile at a time. *Perspectives on Psychological Science, 10*(1), 60–71.

Deaton, A. (2008). Income, health, and well-being around the world: Evidence from the Gallup World Poll. *Journal of Economic Perspectives, 22*(2), 53–72.

Delhey, J., & Dragolov, G. (2014). Why inequality makes Europeans less happy: The role of distrust, status anxiety, and perceived conflict. *European Sociological Review, 30*(2), 151–165.

Delhey, J., & Kohler, U. (2011). Is happiness inequality immune to income inequality? New evidence through instrument-effect-corrected standard deviations. *Social Science Research, 40*(3), 742–756.

Di Domenico, S. I., & Fournier, M. A. (2014). Socioeconomic status, income inequality, and health complaints: A basic psychological needs perspective. *Social Indicators Research, 119*(3), 1679–1697.

Diener, E., Ng, W., Harter, J., & Arora, R. (2010). Wealth and happiness across the world: Material prosperity predicts life evaluation, whereas psychosocial prosperity predicts positive feeling. *Journal of Personality and Social Psychology, 99*(1), 52–61.

Diener, E., & Tay, L. (2015). Subjective well-being and human welfare around the world as reflected in the Gallup World Poll. *International Journal of Psychology, 50*(2), 135–149.

Diener, E., Tay, L., & Oishi, S. (2013). Rising income and the subjective well-being of nations. *Journal of Personality and Social Psychology, 104*(2), 267–276.

Distante, R. (2013). Subjective well-being, income and relative concerns in the UK. *Social Indicators Research, 113*(1), 81–105.

Dittmann, J., & Goebel, J. (2010). Your house, your car, your education: The socioeconomic situation of the neighborhood and its impact on life satisfaction in Germany. *Social Indicators Research, 96*(3), 497–513.

Easterlin, R. A. (1974). Does economic growth improve the human lot? In P. A. David & M. W. Reder (Eds.), *Nations and households in economic growth: Essays in honor of Moses Abramovitz* (pp. 89–126). New York, NY: Academic Press.

Easterlin, R. A. (1995). Will raising the incomes of all increase the happiness of all? *Journal of Economic Behavior and Organization, 27*(1), 35–47.

Easterlin, R. A. (2005). Feeding the illusion of growth and happiness: A reply to Hagerty and Veenhoven. *Social Indicators Research, 74*(3), 429–443.

Easterlin, R. A. (2013). Cross-sections are history. *Population and Development Review, 38*(Suppl. 1), 302–308.

Easterlin, R. A., McVey, L. A., Switek, M., Sawangfa, O., & Zweig, J. S. (2010). The happiness–income paradox revisited. *Proceedings of the National Academy of Sciences of the United States of America, 107*(52), 22463–22468.

Easterlin, R. A., Morgan, R., Switek, M., & Wang, F. (2012). China's life satisfaction, 1990–2010. *Proceedings of the National Academy of Sciences of the United States of America, 109*(25), 9775–9780.

Eckenrode, J., Smith, E. G., McCarthy, M. E., & Dineen, M. (2014). Income inequality and child maltreatment in the United States. *Pediatrics, 133*(3), 454–461.

Eichhorn, J. (2014). The (non-)effect of unemployment benefits: Variations in the effect of unemployment on life-satisfaction between EU countries. *Social Indicators Research, 119*(1), 389–404.

Elgar, F. J., Craig, W., Boyce, W., Morgan, A., & Vella-Zarb, R. (2009). Income inequality and school bullying: Multilevel study of adolescents in 37 countries. *Journal of Adolescent Health, 45*(4), 351–359.

Fairbrother, M., & Martin, I. W. (2013). Does inequality erode social trust? Results from multilevel models of US states and counties. *Social Science Research*, 42(2), 347–360.

Ferrer-i-Carbonell, A., & Ramos, X. (2014). Inequality and happiness. *Journal of Economic Surveys*, 28(5), 1016–1027.

Filho, A. D. P. C., Kawachi, I., Wang, Y. P., Viana, M. C., & Andrade, L. H. S. G. (2013). Does income inequality get under the skin? A multilevel analysis of depression, anxiety and mental disorders in São Paulo, Brazil. *Journal of Epidemiology and Community Health*, 67(11), 966–972.

Firebaugh, G., & Schroeder, M. B. (2009). Does your neighbor's income affect your happiness? *American Journal of Sociology*, 115(3), 805–831.

Fischer, R., & Boer, D. (2011). What is more important for national well-being: Money or autonomy? A meta-analysis of well-being, burnout, and anxiety across 63 societies. *Journal of Personality and Social Psychology*, 101(1), 164–184.

Flint, E., Bartley, M., Shelton, N., & Sacker, A. (2013). Do labour market status transitions predict changes in psychological well-being? *Journal of Epidemiology and Community Health*, 67(9), 796–802.

Galić, Z. (2007). Psychological consequences of unemployment: The moderating role of education. *Review of Psychology*, 14(1), 25–34.

Gori-Maia, A. (2013). Relative income, inequality and subjective wellbeing: Evidence for Brazil. *Social Indicators Research*, 113(3), 1193–1204.

Graham, C. (2009). *Happiness around the world: The paradox of happy peasants and miserable millionaires*. New York, NY: Oxford University Press.

Gruen, C., & Klasen, S. (2013). Income, inequality, and subjective well-being: An international and intertemporal perspective using panel data. *Jahrbuch Fur Wirtschaftsgeschichte*, 54(1), 15–35.

Hajdu, T., & Hajdu, G. (2014). *Reduction of income inequality and subjective well-being in Europe* (Economics Discussion Papers No 2014–22). Kiel Institute for the World Economy. Retrieved from http://www.economics-ejournal.org/economics/discussionpapers/2014-22/file

Helliwell, J. (2003). How's life? Combining individual and national variables to explain subjective well-being. *Economic Modelling*, 20(2), 331–360.

Henkel, D. (2011). Unemployment and substance use: A review of the literature (1990–2010). *Current Drug Abuse Reviews*, 4(1), 4–27.

Howell, R. T., & Howell, C. J. (2008). The relation of economic status to subjective well-being in developing countries: A meta-analysis. *Psychological Bulletin*, 134(4), 536–560.

Inglehart, R., & Klingemann, H. D. (2000). Genes, culture, democracy, and happiness. In E. Diener & E. M. Suh (Eds.), *Culture and subjective well-being* (pp. 165–183). Cambridge, MA: MIT Press.

Jorm, A. F., & Ryan, S. M. (2014). Cross-national and historical differences in subjective well-being. *International Journal of Epidemiology*, 43(2), 330–340.

Kahneman, D., & Deaton, A. (2010). High income improves evaluation of life but not emotional well-being. *Proceedings of the National Academy of Sciences of the United States of America*, 107(38), 16489–16493.

Karriker-Jaffe, K., Roberts, S. C. M., & Bond, J. (2013). Income inequality, alcohol use, and alcohol-related problems. *American Journal of Public Health*, 103(4), 649–656.

Knight, J., & Gunatilaka, R. (2012). Income, aspirations and the hedonic treadmill in a poor society. *Journal of Economic Behavior and Organization*, 82(1), 67–81.

Lancee, B., & van de Werfhorst, H. G. (2012). Income inequality and participation: A comparison of 24 European countries. *Social Science Research, 41*(5), 1166–1178.

Laurence, J. (2015). (Dis)placing trust: The long-term effects of job displacement on generalised trust over the adult lifecourse. *Social Science Research, 50*, 46–59.

Layard, R. (2005). *Happiness: Lessons from a new science*. London, UK: Allen Lane.

Li, J., & Raine, J. W. (2014). The time trend of life satisfaction in China. *Social Indicators Research, 116*(2), 409–427.

Loughnan, S., Kuppens, P., Allik, J., Balazs, K., de Lemus, S., Dumont, K., . . . Haslam, N. (2011). Economic inequality is linked to biased self-perception. *Psychological Science, 22*(10), 1254–1258.

Loveless, M. (2013). The deterioration of democratic political culture: Consequences of the perception of inequality. *Social Justice Research, 26*(4), 471–491.

Lucas, R. E., & Schimmack, U. (2009). Income and well-being: How big is the gap between the rich and the poor? *Journal of Research in Personality, 43*(1), 75–78.

Lucas, R. E., Clark, A. E., Georgellis, Y., & Diener, E. (2004). Unemployment alters the set point for life satisfaction. *Psychological Science, 15*(1), 8–13.

Luhmann, M., Hofmann, W., Eid, M., & Lucas, R. E. (2012). Subjective well-being and adaptation to life events: A meta-analysis. *Journal of Personality and Social Psychology, 102*(3), 592–615.

Luttmer, E. F. P. (2005). Neighbors as negatives: Relative earnings and well-being. *Quarterly Journal of Economics, 120*(3), 963–1002.

Mandemakers, J. J., & Monden, C. W. S. (2013). Does the effect of job loss on psychological distress differ by educational level? *Work, Employment and Society, 27*(1), 73–93.

Maslow, A. H. (1943). A theory of human motivation. *Psychological Review, 50*(4), 370–396.

McLeod, C. B., Lavis, J. N., MacNab, Y. C., & Hertzman, C. (2012). Unemployment and mortality: A comparative study of Germany and the United States. *American Journal of Public Health, 102*(8), 1542–1550.

Mikucka, M. (2014). Does individualistic culture lower the well-being of the unemployed? Evidence from Europe. *Journal of Happiness Studies, 15*(3), 673–691.

Milner, A., Spittal, M. J., Page, A., & LaMontagne, A. D. (2014). The effect of leaving employment on mental health: Testing "adaptation" versus "sensitisation" in a cohort of working age Australians. *Occupational and Environmental Medicine, 71*(3), 167–174.

Mishra, V., Nielsen, I., & Smyth, R. (2014). How does relative income and variations in short-run well-being affect wellbeing in the long run? Empirical evidence from China's Korean minority. *Social Indicators Research, 115*(1), 67–91.

Napier, J. L., & Jost, J. T. (2008). Why are conservatives happier than liberals? *Psychological Science, 19*(6), 565–572.

Neville, L. (2012). Do economic equality and generalized trust inhibit academic dishonesty? Evidence from state-level search-engine queries. *Psychological Science, 23*(4), 339–345.

Ng, W. (2013). The duality of wealth: Is material wealth good or bad for well-being? *Journal of Social Research and Policy, 4*(2), 7–19.

Ng, W., & Diener, E. (2014). What matters to the rich and the poor? Subjective well-being, financial satisfaction, and postmaterialist needs across the world. *Journal of Personality and Social Psychology, 107*(2), 326–338.

O'Boyle, E. J. (2005). Homo socio-economicus: Foundational to social economics and the social economy. *Review of Social Economy, 63*(3), 483–507.

Oishi, S., Kesebir, S., & Diener, E. (2011). Income inequality and happiness. *Psychological Science, 22*(9), 1095–1100.

Oishi, S., Schimmack, U., & Diener, E. (2012). Progressive taxation and the subjective well-being of nations. *Psychological Science, 23*(1), 86–92.

Olivera, J. (2014). Changes in inequality and generalized trust in Europe. *Social Indicators Research, 124*(1), 21–41.

Paskov, M., & Dewilde, C. (2012). Income inequality and solidarity in Europe. *Research in Social Stratification and Mobility, 30*, 415–432.

Paul, K. I., & Moser, K. (2009). Unemployment impairs mental health: Meta-analyses. *Journal of Vocational Behavior, 74*(3), 264–282.

Pickett, K. E., & Wilkinson, R. G. (2007). Child wellbeing and income inequality in rich societies: Ecological cross sectional study. *British Medical Journal, 335*(7629), 1080–1085.

Powdthavee, N. (2008). Putting a price tag on friends, relatives, and neighbours: Using surveys of life satisfaction to value social relationships. *The Journal of Socio-Economics, 37*(4), 1459–1480.

Proto, E., & Rustichini, A. (2015). Life satisfaction, income and personality. *Journal of Economic Psychology, 48*, 17–32.

Ravazzini, L., & Chávez-Juárez, F. (2015). Which inequality makes people dissatisfied with their lives? *Evidence of the link between life satisfaction and inequalities.* Retrieved from https://ssrn.com/abstract=2577694

Reneflot, A., & Evensen, M. (2014). Unemployment and psychological distress among young adults in the Nordic countries: A review of the literature. *International Journal of Social Welfare, 23*(1), 3–15.

Roelfs, D. J., Shor, E., Blank, A., & Schwartz, J. E. (2015). Misery loves company? A meta-regression examining aggregate unemployment rates and the unemployment-mortality association. *Annals of Epidemiology, 25*(5), 312–322.

Roelfs, D. J., Shor, E., Davidson, K. W., & Schwartz, J. E. (2011). Losing life and livelihood: A systematic review and meta-analysis of unemployment and all-cause mortality. *Social Science and Medicine, 72*(6), 840–854.

Rözer, J., & Kraaykamp, G. (2013). Income inequality and subjective well-being: A cross-national study on the conditional effects of individual and national characteristics. *Social Indicators Research, 113*(3), 1009–1023.

Ryan, R. M., & Deci, E. L. (2000). Self-determination theory and the facilitation of intrinsic motivation, social development, and well-being. *American Psychologist, 55*, 68–78.

Sacks, D. W., Stevenson, B., & Wolfers, J. (2012). The new stylized facts about income and subjective well-being. *Emotion, 12*(6), 1181–1187.

Saez, E. (2013). Striking it richer: The evolution of top incomes in the United States (Updated with 2012 preliminary estimates). Retrieved from http://eml.berkeley.edu//~saez/saez-UStopincomes-2012.pdf

Sarracino, F. (2012). Money, sociability and happiness: Are developed countries doomed to social erosion and unhappiness? Time-series analysis of social capital and subjective well-being in western Europe, Australia, Canada and Japan. *Social Indicators Research, 109*(2), 135–188.

Scervini, F., & Segatti, P. (2012). Education, inequality and electoral participation. *Research in Social Stratification and Mobility, 30*, 403–413.

Schimmack, U., Schupp, J., & Wagner, G. G. (2008). The influence of environment and personality on the affective and cognitive component of subjective well-being. *Social Indicators Research, 89*(1), 41–60.

Schneider, S. M. (2012). Income inequality and its consequences for life satisfaction: What role do social cognitions play? *Social Indicators Research, 106*(3), 419–438.

Sengoelge, M., Hasselberg, M., Ormandy, D., & Laflamme, L. (2014). Housing, income inequality and child injury mortality in Europe: A cross-sectional study. *Child: Care, Health and Development, 40*(2), 283–291.

Senik, C. (2014). The French unhappiness puzzle: The cultural dimension of happiness. *Journal of Economic Behavior and Organization, 106*, 379–401.

Simone, C., Carolin, L., Max, S., & Reinhold, K. (2013). Associations between community characteristics and psychiatric admissions in an urban area. *Social Psychiatry and Psychiatric Epidemiology, 48*(11), 1797–1808.

Stevenson, B., & Wolfers, J. (2008, Spring). *Economic growth and subjective well-being: Reassessing the Easterlin paradox* (Working Paper No. 14282). Cambridge, MA: National Bureau of Economic Research.

Stevenson, B., & Wolfers, J. (2013). Economic growth and subjective well-being: Reassessing the Easterlin paradox. In B. S. Frey & A. Stutzer (Eds.), *Recent developments in the economics of happiness* (pp. 133–219). Northampton, MA: Edward Elgar.

Strandh, M., Winefield, A., Nilsson, K., & Hammarström, A. (2014). Unemployment and mental health scarring during the life course. *European Journal of Public Health, 24*(3), 440–445.

Stutzer, A. (2004). The role of income aspirations in individual happiness. *Journal of Economic Behavior and Organization, 54*(1), 89–109.

Tang, Z. (2014). They are richer but are they happier? Subjective well-being of Chinese citizens across the reform era. *Social Indicators Research, 117*(1), 145–164.

Tay, L., & Diener, E. (2011). Needs and subjective well-being around the world. *Journal of Personality and Social Psychology, 101*(2), 354–365.

Uutela, A. (2010). Economic crisis and mental health. *Current Opinion in Psychiatry, 23*(2), 127–130.

van der Meer, P. H. (2014). Gender, unemployment and subjective well-being: Why being unemployed is worse for men than for women. *Social Indicators Research, 115*(1), 23–44.

Verme, P. (2011). Life satisfaction and income inequality. *Review of Income and Wealth, 57*(1), 111–127.

Wadsworth, T. (2014). Sex and the pursuit of happiness: How other people's sex lives are related to our sense of well-being. *Social Indicators Research, 116*(1), 115–135.

Wang, P., Pan, J., & Luo, Z. (2015). The impact of income inequality on individual happiness: Evidence from China. *Social Indicators Research, 121*(2), 413–435.

Wilkinson, R. G., & Pickett, K. E. (2009). Income inequality and social dysfunction. *Annual Review of Sociology, 35*, 493–511.

Wood, A. M., Boyce, C. J., Moore, S. C., & Brown, G. D. A. (2012). An evolutionary based social rank explanation of why low income predicts mental distress: A 17 year cohort study of 30,000 people. *Journal of Affective Disorders, 136*(3), 882–888.

Zagorski, K., Evans, M. D. R., Kelley, J., & Piotrowska, K. (2014). Does national income inequality affect individuals' quality of life in Europe? Inequality, happiness, finances, and health. *Social Indicators Research, 117*(3), 1089–1110.

Zhao, W. (2012). Economic inequality, status perceptions, and subjective well-being in China's transitional economy. *Research in Social Stratification and Mobility, 30*(4), 433–450.

Zmerli, S., & Castillo, J. C. (2015). Income inequality, distributive fairness and political trust in Latin America. *Social Science Research, 52,* 179–192.

CHAPTER 7

Materialism

Stay together, learn the flowers, go light.

—Gary Snyder

Have you noticed the themes running through ads and commercials—that buying something will ease emotional pain, improve our relationships, or bring us love and happiness? Commercials might suggest that buying the right digital devices will keep your whole family happily occupied playing games, communicating, or watching different programs simultaneously, each on his or her own device, or promise happiness from driving a particular brand of car. Ads may suggest that possessions indicate how successful we are or tell us that we can have higher social status if we own the right consumer products.

Such ads and commercials are not really selling a physical product; they give little or no information about the product's qualities or capabilities. Instead, they suggest that the products can satisfy our unfulfilled emotional needs: My family will love me if I buy this car; I can dull the pain of loneliness if I buy these shoes.

Attempts to use material objects to satisfy emotional needs are referred to as *materialistic behaviors*. Materialism can also involve valuing material goods more highly than interpersonal relationships. As you might imagine, materialistic strategies do not work very well. As the comedian George Carlin once said, "Trying to be happy by accumulating possessions is like trying to satisfy hunger by taping sandwiches all over your body." Materialistic individuals are less happy than those who cultivate genuinely close relationships with others. In this chapter we learn why a great number of our fellow citizens are materialistic, and we also investigate why materialism is negatively related to happiness.

DEFINING MATERIALISM

The empirical literature generally defines *materialism* as ". . . individual differences in people's long-term endorsement of values, goals, and associated beliefs that center on the importance of acquiring money and possessions that convey status" (Dittmar, Bond, Hurst, & Kasser, 2014, p. 880). In other words, materialism is a kind of personality trait or statement of values. Materialistic individuals feel that it is important to acquire things in order to demonstrate their social status. If this makes you think about the Ferengi from Star Trek, then you understand the idea.

Materialism is measured in a variety of ways. Representative scale items used to measure materialism include, "I value money very highly," "Money is a symbol of success," and "I would be happier if I had more money to buy things for myself" (Dittmar et al., 2014, p. 881). Researchers have also subcategorized the value orientations. For example, Richins and Dawson (1992) developed separate subscales measuring "acquisition centrality," "acquisition as the pursuit of happiness," and "possession defined success" (p. 304). By acquisition centrality, Richins and Dawson mean that the quest for material possessions dominates the lives of high materialistic individuals.

A second approach to measuring materialism emphasizes individuals' *goals* for acquiring wealth and material objects (Dittmar et al., 2014). These materialistic goals are often measured relative to other, nonmaterialistic goals, such as striving for community involvement or personal relationships. Representative scale items include the goal of having ". . . many expensive possessions" as compared to the goal of having ". . . deep, enduring relationships" (Dittmar et al., 2014, p. 881).

A variation of the goals approach to measuring materialism distinguishes between intrinsic and extrinsic goals. Intrinsic goals are those that seek to satisfy basic psychological needs. They are also directly satisfying in the sense that satisfaction of these goals does not depend on the approval of others. Intrinsic goals are nonmaterialistic, whereas extrinsic goals are not directly satisfying and do not automatically satisfy basic psychological needs. Instead, these goals seek public approval and status (Kasser & Ryan, 2001).

MATERIALISM AND HAPPINESS

Basic Findings

The scientific literature clearly demonstrates that materialism is negatively associated with well-being. Dittmar et al. (2014) conducted a meta-analysis, in which they statistically combined the results of all the pertinent studies (151 studies with 278 independent samples). According to their findings, materialistic values and beliefs predict compulsive buying particularly strongly, followed in the strength of the prediction by risky behaviors, such as alcohol consumption and smoking, and negative self-image. Materialism also predicts depression, lower levels of life satisfaction, negative affect, anxiety, and physical health problems. Thus, materialism does not seem to have a narrow or specific effect on happiness. Individuals with materialistic values are less happy across several dimensions of well-being.

The meta-analysis showed that the negative relationship between materialism and well-being is remarkably stable across various participant characteristics and economic and cultural variables (Dittmar et al., 2014). For example, results were consistent regardless of the publication date of the various studies, indicating that results have not strengthened or weakened over time. Similarly, results did not change depending on participants' personal or household income, ethnicity, or education level and were consistent regardless of whether the sample was composed of college students or adults from the general population. Likewise, results were similar regardless of national wealth (as measured by gross domestic product [GDP]), the presence of a free-market economy (vs. a controlled economy), and cultural values of materialism. To emphasize, materialistic individuals, regardless of these variables, all showed similarly low levels of well-being (Dittmar et al., 2014).

The relationship between materialism and well-being did change across some other variables. But it is important to recognize that these changes were only in the strength of the relationship, and not in its direction. In no case did materialism ever predict *increases* in well-being (Dittmar et al., 2014). For example, the relationship is weaker, but still negative, for samples with a higher proportion of male participants and for samples drawn from educational or professional environments that were probably supportive of materialism. For example, some authors (e.g., Kasser & Ahuvia, 2002) have specifically sought out samples of business students because their environment is probably supportive of materialism. But even in studies of these subjects, materialism is always negatively associated with happiness (Dittmar et al., 2014).

Example Studies

Materialism, Vitality, and Self-Image

Here are some example studies to help describe the flavor of these findings. Kasser and Ryan (1993) found that materialistic aspirations (i.e., goals) are negatively associated with a range of well-being measures. College students rated each of four categories of aspirations in terms of how important each was to them personally: self-acceptance (rated by agreement with such statements as "You will know and accept who you really are"), affiliation (such as, "You will have good friends that you can count on"), community feeling (for example, "You will work to make the world a better place"), and financial success (exemplified by "You will be financially successful"; Kasser & Ryan, 1993, p. 422).[1]

Results indicate that materialistic aspirations for financial success are negatively related to well-being, while most of the nonmaterialistic aspirations are positively related to well-being. For instance, participants who placed more importance on meeting financial success goals were lower in self-actualization and vitality. However, participants who thought goals for self-acceptance and community feeling were very important were higher on these outcome measures. Affiliation did not significantly predict the outcome measures. These results are replicated in two other studies that include the additional outcome measures of anxiety and depression.

Materialistic values are also associated with negative self-image. Frost, Kyrios, McCarthy, and Matthews (2007) measure materialistic values using measures of acquisitiveness (e.g., possessions define success). Results show that materialistic values are positively associated with negative self-image and with compulsive (i.e., uncontrollable and repetitive) buying. However, materialism is not associated with acquiring free possessions. This is consistent with the premise that materialism is directed toward status enhancement, because only possessions that must be purchased are likely to be envied by others.

Materialism, Extrinsic Motivation, and Well-Being

Materialistic goals are ones that are extrinsically motivated (Kasser & Ryan, 1996). Unlike intrinsic goals, which are nonmaterialistic, extrinsic goals are oriented toward gaining approval from others, a means to an end, or both (Kasser & Ryan, 1993). For instance, someone might pursue medical school not because of a love of medicine or desire to help others, but because a medical degree can support a luxurious lifestyle.

Research shows that the pursuit of extrinsic goals is less satisfying. Kasser and Ryan (1996, p. 281) persuaded adults living in an urban neighborhood in a city in the Northeastern United States to rate the personal importance of seven different types of goals:

- ▶ Self-acceptance

- ▶ Affiliation

- ▶ Community feeling

- ▶ Physical fitness ("Feel healthy and free of illness")

- ▶ Financial success

- ▶ Social recognition ("Be famous, well-known, and admired")

- ▶ Appealing appearance ("Look attractive in terms of body, clothing, and fashion")

Participants rated the importance of items representing each goal, and these ratings were then subjected to a statistical procedure, which looks for commonalities among the items. Results indicated that self-acceptance, affiliation, community feeling, and physical fitness form a common "factor" that suggests items from these goals are all measuring the same intrinsic, nonmaterialistic motivation. Items from the financial success, social recognition, and appealing appearance goals form a second common factor that assesses extrinsic, materialistic goals (Kasser & Ryan, 1993).

Consistent with predictions, participants who placed strong importance on the extrinsic, materialistic goals reported lower levels of self-actualization and vitality. They also reported more physical symptoms such as headaches and faintness. Results for those with intrinsic, nonmaterialistic goals were starkly reversed. These participants reported higher levels of self-actualization and vitality, fewer physical symptoms, and less depression. These results were replicated in a second study using a sample of college students (Kasser & Ryan, 1993).

These results are important not only because they replicate Kasser and Ryan's (1993) earlier findings showing that materialism is related to lower well-being. They also confirm that the essential nature of materialistic goals is that they are extrinsic. That is, they are controlled by forces outside the individual, and are directed toward satisfying demands from others rather than satisfying intrinsic psychological needs. Interestingly, other research shows that these extrinsic goals do not bring happiness even when they are met (Kasser & Ryan, 2001). Thus, the unhappiness associated with chasing extrinsic/materialistic goals is not because they are hard to reach. Instead, the very pursuit of these goals seems to breed unhappiness.

Why Materialism Affects Well-Being

Dittmar et al. (2014) identified several hypotheses for why materialism lowers well-being. The Negative Self-Appraisal Model comes from the consumer marketing literature and suggests that advertising and consumer culture purposefully produce feelings of inadequacy. Advertisements suggest that we are not beautiful enough or cool enough, and so on, but that we could be if we bought the right product. Although these messages promote materialism as an antidote to our inadequacy, we are never able to overcome these negative feelings because of the constant barrage of new advertising suggesting other ways in which we are inadequate. Thus, the materialism engendered by these advertisements leads to negative self-appraisals, which then lower our well-being (Dittmar et al., 2014).

Self-Determination Theory (SDT; Ryan & Deci, 2000) offers another explanation. This perspective argues that materialism is incompatible with other, more satisfying values and goals because of its focus on extrinsic goals such as status seeking. As a result, materialistic individuals' basic psychological needs for competence, relatedness, and autonomy are unsatisfied. Research shows that failure to satisfy these basic psychological needs is associated with lower well-being (Dittmar et al., 2014).

The Financial Satisfaction Model proposes that materialists are likely dissatisfied with their financial standing. This dissatisfaction results from social comparisons with others. Particularly in our world of modern media, we are always aware of others who are richer and more successful. If materialism is an important value, then witnessing others with a richer material life will presumably lead to financial dissatisfaction. The model further proposes that this financial dissatisfaction affects overall life satisfaction and happiness (Dittmar et al., 2014).

The Psychological Insecurities Model (Kasser, Ryan, Couchman, & Sheldon, 2004) suggests a dual process model of materialism. Specifically, cultural models of materialism, including advertising, along with unmet emotional needs (e.g., a lack of nurturance during childhood) combine to produce materialism. According to this model, we learn from advertisements and other cultural messages that owning material objects that signal status and security can heal emotional insecurities. However, this coping strategy does not work, because the quest for material objects undermines basic psychological needs such as autonomy, competence, and relatedness, thereby lowering our well-being (Dittmar et al., 2014).

The Psychological Insecurities Model overlaps heavily with SDT and with the Negative Self-Appraisal Model. The Insecurity Model emphasizes the importance of meeting basic psychological needs, as does SDT, which also theorizes that materialism is related to the development of feelings of inadequacy, as does the Negative Self-Appraisal Model. The key difference is that, unlike the other two models, the Psychological Insecurities Model sees materialistic values and behaviors as ineffective *coping strategies* directed toward reducing insecurities.

Meta-Analytic Tests of Models

Dittmar et al. (2014) tested the financial satisfaction and the SDT perspectives in their meta-analysis. Specifically, they tested whether satisfaction with financial status, and satisfaction of basic psychological needs, mediated the relationship between materialism and well-being. However, they were unable to test the other two perspectives. There were not enough data regarding materialism and emotional insecurities and negative self-appraisals to test the other two models.

Dittmar et al.'s (2014) results support the SDT account. Satisfaction of the basic psychological needs for autonomy, relatedness, and competence partially mediates the relationship between materialism and well-being. In other words, changes in levels of satisfaction of these basic needs partially (but not fully) explain the relationship between materialism and well-being. There is no support for the Financial Satisfaction Model.

You may wonder what it means to "partially mediate" a relationship. It means that a mediator accounts for a significant part of the relationship between the predictor and outcome variable, but not for the entire relationship. In this case, need satisfaction accounts for only part of the relationship between materialism and well-being.

What accounts for the rest of the relationship between materialism and well-being? Dittmar et al. (2014) cannot identify the factor or factors that mediate the rest of the relationship between these two variables because research has not sufficiently investigated other possible mediators. But the Psychological Insecurities and the Negative Self-Appraisal Models are likely candidates. Dittmar et al. (2014) note that the support they found for SDT and the importance of meeting basic psychological needs is not incompatible with Kasser et al.'s (2004) model suggesting that materialism is associated with psychological insecurities and resultant coping attempts.

Another Possibility: Gratitude

Materialists may also be less happy because they lack gratitude for the things they do have. Tsang, Carpenter, Roberts, Frisch, and Carlisle (2014) tested this possibility in a sample of marketing students attending college in the United States. They also considered whether a materialistically driven lack of gratitude might inhibit need satisfaction, thereby ultimately leading to less happiness. Thus, Tsang et al.'s (2014) model is similar to the SDT.

Results demonstrate the importance of gratitude. As seen in Figure 7.1, the relationship between materialism and life satisfaction is "double mediated" by gratitude and need satisfaction. Materialists are lower in gratitude (note the coefficient between these two variables is negative), and low gratitude individuals are also low in need satisfaction (note that the coefficient between these two variables is positive). Finally, those low in need satisfaction are also low in life satisfaction (because of the positive coefficient). Therefore, materialism suppresses life satisfaction because it also suppresses gratitude, which then leads to lower levels of need satisfaction.

It is also interesting that there is a mediated pathway that does not include need satisfaction. Materialism is associated with lower levels of gratitude, which is then directly linked to life satisfaction. Thus, gratitude is also a direct mediator between materialism and life satisfaction. Interestingly, there is no direct relationship between materialism and

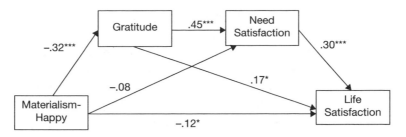

FIGURE 7.1. Mediational analysis of the links between materialism and life satisfaction.
* $p < .05$; *** $p < .001$.
Source: Tsang et al. (2014).

need satisfaction (this path is nonsignificant). Thus, need satisfaction is not a direct result of materialism, as suggested by SDT. Instead, materialism influences need satisfaction only by first lowering gratitude (Tsang et al., 2014).

Gratitude and need satisfaction explain about 50% of the relationship between materialism and life satisfaction. It is unclear what accounts for the other half of this relationship. Regardless, the data suggest interventions that might increase materialists' happiness. For instance, a gratitude-based therapy might break the negative connection between materialism and life satisfaction (Tsang et al., 2014).

Causality?

Our discussion shows that materialism is related to well-being and that there are clear theoretical reasons to think that it is a cause of well-being. However, much of the research we have reviewed is correlational, so we now must consider whether the relationship is causal. It is possible that these two variables are only coincidentally related because they both happen to be related to a third variable, such as personality. It is also possible that unhappiness causes materialism, or that these two variables cause each other at the same time. We see in the following section that this last possibility is correct: There is evidence for a bidirectional relationship between these two variables in which both cause each other.

Evidence That Materialism Causes Low Well-Being

It seems likely that there is a causal relationship between materialism and well-being, because researchers have statistically controlled for many personality characteristics that might create a coincidental relationship between these two variables. For example, in the Frost et al. (2007) study, described earlier, materialism was negatively correlated with well-being even after statistically controlling for participants' depression levels, indecisiveness, and uncertainty about relating with other people. In addition, Chan and Joseph (2000) found the negative materialism–well-being relationship after controlling for age, gender, extraversion, neuroticism, psychoticism, and participants' attempts to fake positive or negative responses.

However, these statistical controls do not guarantee that there is a causal relationship. There may be an additional factor that researchers have not yet controlled that coincidentally links materialism and well-being. These statistical control techniques also do not indicate the direction of causality.

Some studies have experimentally manipulated materialism. Bauer, Wilkie, Kim, and Bodenhausen (2012) randomly assigned participants to receive either consumeristic cues (pictures of luxury goods) or control cues, and found that participants who received the consumeristic cues responded more materialistically and also reported more depression, anxiety, and shame. These results were later replicated by Li, Lim, Tsai, and O (2015). The experimental manipulations of materialism greatly increase our confidence that it is a cause of a low sense of well-being.

Longitudinal studies, which examine whether *changes* in materialism are associated with changes in well-being, also help identify causality. Hellevik (2003) found that Norwegians' well-being decreased as their national level of materialism increased during the 1990s. Similarly, Twenge et al. (2010) identified a broad cultural shift toward more extrinsic rather than intrinsic goals across much of the 20th century in the United States. This shift was associated with increases in national psychopathological symptoms (e.g., antisocial behavior) among college and high school students, even after controlling for national economic conditions.

Other research examined changes in materialism on an individual level. Across four studies, Kasser et al. (2014) found that changes in individuals' materialism are associated with changes in their well-being. One of these studies followed adults from age 18 until age 30, another tracked college students for 2 years after graduation, and another tracked Icelandic adults for 6 months during the severe economic recession in 2009. All three found that individuals who became more materialistic over time developed lower well-being, while the opposite was true for those who decreased in materialism.

The fourth study contained an intervention in which adolescents were either given nonmaterialistic messages or were assigned to a control group. No changes in well-being were expected or found among participants who were low in materialism at the beginning of the study. However, and consistent with predictions, intervention participants who were highly materialistic at the beginning of the study became less materialistic over time and also experienced increases in self-esteem. Control participants who were initially high in materialism experienced increased materialism and decreased self-esteem, which was also consistent with predictions (Kasser et al., 2014). Taken together, this research supports the hypothesis that materialism is a cause of poor well-being.

Evidence That Low Well-Being Causes Materialism

There is also evidence that low well-being causes materialism. This makes theoretical sense because Kasser et al. (2004) hypothesized that materialism is a coping strategy designed to heal psychological insecurities. This section describes some of the findings showing that low well-being can cause materialism.

Sheldon and Kasser (2008) capitalized on previous findings (e.g., Rosenblatt, Greenberg, Solomon, Pyszczynski, & Lyon, 1989) that reminders of one's own mortality cause existential insecurity and anxiety about the meaning of life. Consistent with the hypothesized link between emotional insecurity and materialism, Sheldon and Kasser

(2008) found that participants reminded of mortality expressed stronger extrinsic (i.e., materialistic) goals than did control participants. In another study, these authors found that interpersonal threat (i.e., receiving conditional acceptance from another person) produced similar effects.

Other studies have demonstrated similar relationships between psychological insecurity/threat and materialism. Kasser, Ryan, Zax, and Sameroff (1995) found that 18-year-olds who reported having nonnurturing mothers also valued financial goals more highly than less materialistic goals. In addition, Jiang, Zhang, Ke, Hawk, and Qiu (2015) found that participants primed to remember being rejected by a peer were more materialistic.

Gao, Wheeler, and Shiv (2009) linked psychological threats and insecurities to clear behavioral measures of materialism. These authors developed a Model of the Shaken Self, in which individuals can become temporarily less confident about their self-image if they receive even mild threats. This lack of confidence can lead them to act materialistically by choosing specific consumer products that reestablish their self-image. Consistent with this hypothesis, these authors found that participants with a threatened self-image who were not given other ways to restore their self-image chose consumer products that specifically addressed their self-image concern. For example, participants who had their self-image as intelligent threatened were more likely to choose a "gift" of a fountain pen (prerated as associated with intelligence) than a pack of candy.

Finally, economic threat is also related to higher materialism. Sheldon and Kasser (2008) also found that participants randomly assigned to think that their future employment prospects were bleak were more materialistic than were those assigned to think they had excellent employment prospects. Similarly, Zhang, Tian, Lei, Yu, and Liu (2015) found that participants made to feel that others had more economic resources were more materialistic.

Note the consistency of these findings. Feelings of emotional insecurity, including feeling anxious about the meaning of one's life, feeling unnurtured as a child, not feeling confident about a self-identity, or feeling economically threatened, are all examples of lowered well-being. In addition, all these examples of emotional insecurity and lowered well-being appear to cause increased materialistic behavior.

It seems that there is a reciprocal relationship between materialism and well-being in which they both cause and affect each other. This reciprocal relationship seems consistent with Kasser et al.'s (2004) Psychological Insecurities Model. Specifically, cultural models and psychological insecurities (a form of low well-being) can produce materialistic coping strategies that then further lower well-being. As a result, materialism might well be both a cause and a consequence of low well-being.

In summary, a large empirical literature has investigated the relationship between materialism and well-being. This literature demonstrates that materialism is associated with lower well-being across a variety of measures. This finding is remarkably consistent and generalized across education and income levels, ethnicities, and cultural and economic conditions. Although there are some variables that alter (i.e., moderate or make the relationship stronger or weaker) the relationship between materialism and

... ᴜᴄing, there is no evidence that materialism is ever associated with greater well-being.

There is also evidence for a bidirectional relationship between materialism and well-being that is consistent with Kasser et al.'s (2004) Psychological Insecurities Model of materialism and well-being. This model predicts that psychological insecurities, along with cultural models of materialism, lead to the development of materialistic values. These values then lead to lower levels of well-being.

However, there has not been an adequate test of Kasser et al.'s (2004) full Model of Psychological Insecurities. The currently definitive literature review in the area (namely, Dittmar et al., 2014) supports the SDT explanation for the materialism/well-being relationship, and is not able to test Kasser et al.'s (2004) Psychological Insecurities Model. However, the SDT account only partially explains the relationship between materialism and well-being. Kasser et al.'s (2004) Psychological Insecurities Model is compatible with SDT and may help fully explain the relationship between materialism and well-being. Finally, there is also evidence that gratitude can help explain some of the relationship between these two variables.

MATERIALISM AND CORPORATE VALUES

The Importance of Economic Systems

We have not fully discussed where materialism comes from. The Psychological Insecurity Model (Kasser et al., 2004) predicts that unmet emotional needs and cultural models of materialism such as advertising combine to produce materialistic individuals. But this model does not fully explain how culture can lead to materialistic values.

However, Kasser, Cohn, Kanner, and Ryan (2007) suggest that economic systems can influence the development of materialistic cultures. Economic systems are ideologies, or sets of beliefs, that pervade much of our lives. These sets of beliefs about, for example, the appropriateness of advertising, what can be legally bought and sold, how prices are determined, how financial resources are distributed, and the role of competition and cooperation in our society likely shape our behaviors and emotional reactions to events. Thus, Kasser et al. (2007) found it odd that psychologists have largely neglected to study the psychological effects of capitalism, the economic system that dominates much of the modern world.

American Corporate Capitalism

Capitalism is a form of economic organization in which property is owned privately rather than shared communally. This economic system leads to the development of a class-based society in which *capitalists*, individuals with financial resources, invest in businesses and earn a share of the profits from these enterprises. On the other hand, workers earn most of their living from selling their labor to those businesses (Kasser et al., 2007).

As with any economic system or other ideology, capitalism promotes a set of basic assumptions about human nature and motivation. Chief among these are that competition and the pursuit of individual self-interest enhance the well-being of both individuals and society. According to capitalist theory, we are all better-off when bakers, for instance, compete with each other to sell their bread. This competition ensures that the price of bread is kept low, and the quality kept high, because consumers will not purchase inferior bread if there are better and cheaper alternatives available. Similarly, we are also better-off when workers compete with each other to sell their labor. This competition limits wages (because other workers may be willing to work for lower wages), and therefore lowers the price of production of essential consumer products such as bread (Kasser et al., 2007).

Kasser et al. (2007) also argue that capitalism, like any economic system, has varying features. They focus on what they refer to as American Corporate Capitalism (ACC) because they see it as the most dominant variant of modern capitalism. ACC is characterized by several specific features. One of these is the development of large corporations, which concentrate enormous political and financial power into relatively few hands. Another is a commitment by both government and industry to steady economic growth as an important national priority. Among other reasons, economic growth is essential because it produces new markets and investment opportunities for capitalists. Finally, ACC promotes advertising of consumer products. Advertising is essential in order to create demand for consumer products so that businesses remain profitable.

Capitalism, Values, and Happiness

What does modern capitalism have to do with happiness? ACC involves more than money and prices. It promotes a particular set of beliefs, including the value of competition, the consumption of consumer products, and the pursuit of self-interest. Kasser et al. (2007) recognize that capitalism clearly increases a society's wealth. But they also argue that the ideology of capitalism interferes with happiness, because it promotes materialistic and extrinsic values. Furthermore, the values of self-interest and competition overwhelm or crowd out other nonmaterialistic values that increase happiness (Kasser et al., 2007).

Research from around the world examining human values has identified a core set of values and how they are interrelated. As seen in Figure 7.2 (Schwartz, 1992), these values include two dimensions: self-transcendence versus self-enhancement, and openness to change versus conservatism. These are subdivided into the "slices of the pie" within the circumplex. For instance, self-enhancement versus self-transcendence includes the subdimensions of both achievement and power at the self-enhancement end of the continuum, and benevolence (e.g., caring for others) and universalism (e.g., tolerance, interest in social justice) on the self-transcendence end (Schwartz, 1992).

Results from several labs using a variety of cross-cultural data sets indicate that we are unlikely to hold beliefs at both ends of either of these two dimensions (Kasser et al., 2007). For example, individuals who value achievement and power are unlikely also to value benevolence and universalism. This finding has significance for Kasser et al. (2007). ACC's emphasis on self-interest and competition leads to the development of the self-enhancing values of power and achievement and the weakening of values for universalism and benevolence.

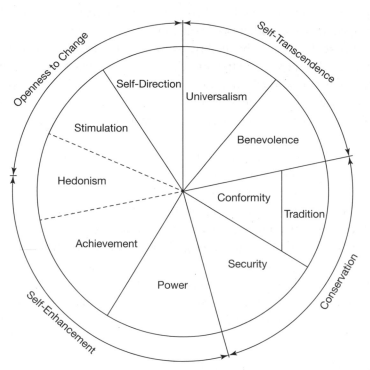

FIGURE 7.2. Circumplex model of values.
Source: Schwartz (1992).

Kasser et al. (2007) argue that ACC's emphasis on competition, and the resulting development of power and achievement values, lower happiness because these values undermine basic psychological needs such as relatedness. For instance, heavy emphasis on self-interest and competition makes it difficult to feel a common bond with others, thus undermining the happiness-inducing feelings of community. Consistent with this notion, the materialistic values of ACC are associated with less agreeableness, prosocial behavior, empathy, and generosity.

Another important need undermined by ACC is self-worth. ACC's values lower our self-worth because success is defined narrowly, in terms of material goods. Our possessions signal how well we have done in this materialistic, highly competitive and self-interested culture. However, because ACC produces such vast inequalities in wealth, most of us will lose the status race for possessions, thus wounding our sense of self-worth (Kasser et al., 2007).

Finally, ACC can also undermine our needs for autonomy or self-direction and the sense that we are free to choose our own goals. Kasser et al.'s (2007) argument here is largely based on SDT (Ryan & Deci, 2000) and its prediction that the pursuit of extrinsic goals is unsatisfying. Specifically, ACC's emphasis on acquiring material possessions and its narrow definition of success drive us to try to win the game of social comparison. Therefore, one of our primary goals under ACC is to impress others and win their approval. This pursuit of external rewards (i.e., approval) inhibits the pursuit of intrinsic goals that are based on our own personal interests and values that are more likely to enhance our happiness.

ACC and Suppression of Transcendent Values

Other theorists also question the effects of ACC on psychological values. For example, George (2014) urged researchers to investigate how ACC might lower compassion, which is closely related to the self-transcendent values of benevolence and universalism, in business organizations. Citing wealth inequality, corporate layoffs, and the working conditions of factory laborers in third world countries, George (2014) asks whether ACC's dominant control over international business might play a causal role in modern social and economic problems. Might these problems result, at least in part, because ACC's emphasis on economic performance, self-interest, and competition undermines compassion (George, 2014)?

Other findings support Kasser et al.'s (2007) contention that ACC undermines the self-transcendent values of universalism and benevolence. Pulfrey and Butera (2013) examined whether the self-enhancing values associated with American capitalism are related to cheating. This research is important because cheating contradicts the value of universalism (a subcomponent of self-transcendence) because of its likely interference with social justice and equality. Consistent with Kasser et al.'s (2007) theorizing, Pulfrey and Butera (2013) found that self-enhancing values predicted whether university students cheated on a test of problem solving and whether they condoned academic cheating in general. Furthermore, they found that priming self-transcendent values eliminates this relationship. Specifically, and consistent with the idea that activating one side of the circumplex of values shown in Figure 7.2 deactivates values on the other side of the circumplex, self-enhancing values no longer predicted cheating on the problem-solving test when participants were reminded of self-transcendent values.

Other research shows that cueing economic concepts can suppress transcendent values. Molinsky, Grant, and Margolis (2012) found that cuing economic thoughts lowers compassion and empathy. Interestingly, economics was cued in one of their studies in a way that explicitly primed the values of ACC. Economic cue participants wrote a story using words such as *self-interested, cost–benefit analysis, fiscally responsible,* and *profitable,* while control participants wrote a story using neutral words. Economic cue participants showed less compassion and empathy in a letter they wrote informing hypothetical students that their scholarship had been defunded. Other research has conceptually replicated these results (e.g., Guéguen & Jacob, 2013; Kouchaki, Smith-Crowe, Brief, & Sousa, 2013).

Molinsky et al.'s (2012) results are important because lowered compassion and empathy suggest that values of benevolence and universalism are weakened. In addition, all the research reviewed in this section shows that self-transcendent values are weakened by ACC. This weakening is empirically linked to lower well-being (Kasser et al., 2007).

ACC and Happiness

National values Research also directly connects ACC's values with lowered happiness. For instance, Kasser (2011) found that national values that justify hierarchy and the unequal distribution of wealth (that is, favoring competition and self-interest) rather than caring and cooperation are negatively related to children's well-being.

Similarly, another study showed that as the United States became increasingly materialistic during the 20th century, there was a corresponding increase in the number of high school and college students with significant mental health problems. Twenge et al. (2010) examined archival data that included 131 separate samples of American students gathered at various times during the 20th century. The students completed the Minnesota Multiphasic Personality Inventory (MMPI), a widely used and strongly validated measure of psychopathology. The researchers also tracked changes in American cultural values over the same period by assessing, for instance, the importance students placed on being wealthy.

Results showed that psychopathology increased along with materialism during this time period. There was a six- to eight-fold increase in unrealistic positive self-appraisal, overactivity, and low self-control; a five- to six-fold increase in narcissism and antisocial behavior; a five- to seven-fold increase in feelings of isolation; and a six-fold increase in depression among college students between 1938 and 2007. Anxiety and obsessiveness also increased significantly. Similar results were found for high school students. Thus, there were notable increases in psychological problems as our culture increased its emphasis on money and individual achievement, and deemphasized social relationships and community. The authors suggested that these figures may even underestimate the actual rise in psychopathology because the introduction of psychotropic drugs may hide symptoms that would otherwise show on the MMPI (Twenge et al., 2010).

Further analyses rule out several potentially plausible alternative explanations. For instance, the changes in psychopathology did not track national unemployment rates, thus suggesting that economic changes cannot account for the results. Nor were the increases in psychopathology due to increasing numbers of women attending colleges, as pathology increased for both men and women. The increases in pathology were also evenly spread geographically throughout the entire country. Finally, the results do not appear to reflect any changes in the nature of college students (other than materialism) over time, because the pattern was replicated among high school students. Therefore, it is unlikely that the mere fact that a greater proportion of our population now attends college can account for these results.

Politics and public policy In its purest forms, capitalism is characterized by hostility toward labor unions, treating human labor as a commodity to be bought and sold, and relatively politically conservative governing policies and parties. Unfortunately, these characteristics are negatively associated with well-being. Radcliff (2001) examined life satisfaction data from industrialized countries, mainly in North America and Europe.[2] Results indicate that more socialist governments (less strongly free-market capitalist governments typical of ACC) are associated with higher life satisfaction scores, while conservative governments are associated with lower scores. These results are significant after controlling for national wealth and unemployment rates, along with sociodemographic variables such as education levels. Research by Alvarez-Diaz, Gonzalez, and Radcliff (2010) has replicated these findings.

Research by Radcliff (2001) and his colleagues (Flavin & Radcliff, 2009; Pacek & Radcliff, 2008) also shows that strong social welfare programs (which are not typical of capitalist societies) such as unemployment and medical benefits and direct assistance to needy families are associated with greater well-being, again after controlling for a number of factors. Radcliff and his colleagues use the term *decommodification* (borrowed from Esping-Andersen, 1990) to measure the overall strength of social welfare programs. Decommodification reflects the extent to which an individual is freed from being treated merely as a commodity, such as a bushel of corn or a ton of steel, whose worth and welfare is defined strictly by the economics of market forces.

If the welfare protections are strong enough so that individuals can "freely opt out of work, when necessary, without risking their jobs, income or general welfare" they are thought to be decommodified (Pacek & Radcliff, 2008, p. 183). Decommodified individuals are not dependent on market forces in three critical domains: unemployment, disability, and retirement status. They are entitled to a decent standard of living if they lose their jobs, become disabled, or can no longer work because of advancing age.

Entitled is a key word here. Decommodified individuals are entitled to this standard of living, and it is provided by the social welfare system, even if they do not have paid employment or substantial savings. Radcliff and his colleagues (Flavin & Radcliff, 2009; Pacek & Radcliff, 2008; Radcliff, 2001) demonstrate that decommodification is associated with higher well-being. These results reinforce the hypothesis that the characteristics associated with ACC, in which values and worth are completely shaped by market forces, are negatively associated with well-being.

Labor unions are also associated with greater well-being. Flavin, Pacek, and Radcliff (2010) found that the presence of labor unions is associated with increased life satisfaction for both union and nonunion members. The positive relationship between union density and life satisfaction is strongest among the poor. There is a weak negative relationship between union density and well-being among the wealthy, but the relationship is positive for most of the population. Again, these findings hold after statistically controlling for a variety of factors. These results again show that characteristics associated with ACC (i.e., lack of strong labor unions) negatively predict well-being.

Extrinsically oriented microenvironments   One of the hallmarks of ACC, according to Kasser et al. (2007), is that it emphasizes extrinsic motivation. Under ACC we are driven to seek financial success and other extrinsic rewards. So it is interesting to test Kasser et al.'s (2007) hypotheses by investigating the happiness of individuals who inhabit microenvironments that stress extrinsic versus intrinsic motivations.

Sheldon and Krieger (2014) compare the happiness of "service" lawyers, whose jobs are more focused on helping others than on personal advancement, and "money" lawyers, whose jobs focus relatively heavily on personal advancement, power, and prestige. Service lawyer jobs include public defender, legal services to the poor, and local government lawyer; whereas money lawyer jobs include malpractice attorneys, corporate lawyers, and tax lawyers. Because of the nature of these jobs, Sheldon and Krieger (2014) argue that money and service lawyer jobs can be categorized as extrinsic and intrinsic, respectively. In other words, service and money lawyers inhabit different microenvironments, one of which resembles ACC (money lawyers) more than the other (service lawyers).

Results are consistent with predictions drawn from Kasser et al.'s (2007) theory regarding ACC and happiness: Service lawyers are happier than money lawyers. Service lawyers reported lower levels of negative affect and drinking frequency and amount of alcohol consumed than did money lawyers. They also reported greater positive affect, life satisfaction, and overall well-being than did money lawyers. Furthermore, these differences persisted even after controlling for differences in income, number of years working as a lawyer, class rank upon graduation from law school, and personal intrinsic and extrinsic values (Sheldon & Krieger, 2014).

Other research demonstrates the link between extrinsically oriented culture and happiness by examining individuals who choose to reject that culture. Consistent with Kasser et al.'s (2007) expectations, individuals who consciously reject extrinsically oriented cultural materialism are happier than those who remain in the mainstream of the culture. Brown and Kasser (2005) compared Americans committed to the lifestyle of voluntary simplicity, which deemphasizes material goals, to "mainstream" Americans. The two groups were similar in terms of age, gender, and ethnicity. However, the voluntary simplifiers had clearly rejected the material culture of ACC by making conscious decisions to earn and spend less money. As expected, the voluntary simplifiers reported greater life satisfaction, even though their incomes and spending levels were below what we would expect based on their education levels alone.

Nurturing environments   There is also evidence that nurturing environments promote well-being. These environments have little in common with capitalistic values. Biglan, Flay, Embry, and Sandler (2012) concluded from a literature review that nurturing environments (a) minimize harmful environmental effects, (b) encourage prosocial behavior, (c) limit the opportunity for negative behaviors, and (d) make individuals mindful of their own individual values. Furthermore, Biglan et al. (2012) concluded that environments with these nurturing characteristics are most likely to minimize emotional and behavioral disorders.

Although all four characteristics of nurturing environments are relevant to ACC, the first two are particularly important. First, nurturing environments limit harmful environmental experiences by providing a sense of emotional as well as physical safety and the opportunity to meet basic psychological needs, such as positive self-regard, relatedness, and community. However, ACC's focus on competition and self-enhancement can erode feelings of community and self-worth. Second, nurturing environments encourage prosocial behavior by prompting individuals to consider the needs and feelings of others, and to value helping. This encouragement of prosocial behavior obviously contradicts ACC's mantra of competition and self-enhancement (Biglan et al., 2012).

Third, nurturing environments limit the opportunity for antisocial behaviors. And fourth, nurturing environments allow individuals the psychological flexibility to be mindful of their own personal values despite competing demands from that environment (Biglan et al., 2012). ACC's overwhelming emphasis on self-enhancement, competition, and consumerism may promote antisocial behavior and seems unlikely to allow the flexibility to choose nonmarketplace values. Therefore, although nurturing environments are empirically associated with greater well-being, there are good reasons to suspect that ACC inhibits the development of these environments.

Biglan (2015) expands on these ideas and connects them to ACC even more explicitly in a recently published book. He describes how corporate advertising of tobacco and junk food produce nonnurturing environments that ultimately lower well-being. For instance, he includes a chapter titled "Harmful Corporate Marketing Practices" and asserts that nurturance requires protecting children from corporate advertising.

> Successful nurturance includes protecting our children from everything that could damage their health and well-being throughout life. One of the influences that is most important yet also most difficult to control is the marketing of harmful products. If you've ever been in a supermarket with a young child, you've probably had the experience of your child demanding candy at the checkout counter and getting upset when it wasn't forthcoming. Of course, stores put candy there because they know how little kids work—and because they know how hesitant most parents are to refuse and risk a tantrum. (Biglan, 2015, p. 143)

Biglan (2015) also discusses national economic policies that have increased poverty and inequality in the United States and the consequences of these policies for Americans' well-being. In Biglan's (2015, pp. 160, 164) words, poverty and inequality "damage" individuals' well-being, particularly children's. Among other negative results, poor kids receive lower quality parenting and are negatively stigmatized. Inequality damages well-being by increasing a host of social problems including increased mental illness rates and lower levels of social trust.

While not explicitly implicating ACC for these problems, Biglan (2015) points to corporate-friendly policies as culprits. These include changes in tax law that favor the wealthy, lagging minimum wage levels, and weak regulations on businesses. These policies reflect many of the characteristics of ACC-dominated culture noted by Kasser et al. (2007). Biglan (2015) also traces efforts of business groups to positively influence public opinion about free-market capitalism since the early 1970s. These efforts have resulted in multitudes of probusiness think tanks, whose members regularly appear in the media and attempt to influence public opinion and public policy. This research is again consistent with Kasser et al.'s (2007) contention that ACC has fully penetrated our culture.

In summary, Kasser et al. (2007) suggest that any economic system promotes its own set of values that support that system. They then theorize about the values associated with ACC, because this is the dominant economic system in the world, and conclude that ACC's values emphasize self-enhancement rather than self-transcendence. Furthermore, they cite evidence that activation of one set of values deactivates or weakens alternative values. This is important because research shows that self-enhancing values are associated with lower well-being, while self-transcendent values are associated with greater well-being.

Although it is difficult to fully test a theory about how an entire economic system may affect happiness, the existing data are consistent with Kasser et al.'s (2007) theory. Data indicate that ACC suppresses self-transcendent values and that this is associated with lower well-being. The well-being data come from a variety of levels of analysis, and all are consistent with Kasser et al.'s (2007) predictions. Specifically, societal level data comparing across countries (Kasser, 2011) and examining time trends within the United States (Twenge et al., 2010) are consistent with other data comparing individuals in microenvironments that are either high or low in extrinsic and corporatist values (e.g., Brown and Kasser's 2005 study of voluntary simplifiers and Sheldon and Krieger's 2014 study of service and money lawyers).

MATERIALISM, CONSUMERISM, AND CHILDREN'S WELL-BEING

Children as Consumers

The data reviewed in the previous section highlight the need to carefully consider consumer culture, the advertising that promotes it, and their effects on children's well-being. A 2004 Task Force report by the American Psychological Association (APA) estimated that companies spend $12 billion each year advertising to children, and that kids see more than 40,000 commercials a year (Wilcox et al., 2004). Furthermore, the Task Force reported that several professional books directly teach how to market to children. Sporting titles such as *What Kids Buy and Why: The Psychology of Marketing to Kids* (Acuff & Reiher, 1997), these books draw upon sophisticated psychological theory to lure kids into becoming shoppers. Obviously, consumer culture is an important element in children's lives.

The relation between materialism and well-being demonstrated in adult participants also extends to children. For instance, Kasser (2005) found a negative correlation between materialism and well-being in a sample of middle and high school students from a rural community in Illinois. Materialism is associated with less happiness and lower levels of self-esteem, along with more anxiety, alcohol use, and physical fighting in this sample.

The APA Task Force report showed that materialism and consumer culture can negatively affect children's well-being. The report reviewed the literature and found that advertisements are related to increased parent–child conflict (as kids appeal to parents for products they have seen advertised), more favorable attitudes toward alcohol and tobacco, increases in obesity, and more acceptance of materialistic values (Wilcox et al., 2004).

For example, Schor (2004) demonstrated that 10- to 13-year-old Bostonian children's involvement in consumer culture was linked to depression, anxiety, low self-esteem, and psychosomatic symptoms such as headaches. Easterbrook, Wright, Dittmar, and Banerjee (2014) conceptually replicated Schor's (2004) study with a sample of British schoolchildren aged 8 to 13. Still other research shows that children's self-esteem has been "commodified" by consumer culture. Isaksen and Roper (2012) examined a sample of British adolescents and found that their self-esteem largely depended on obtaining the right possessions. The adolescents saw these possessions as necessary for gaining the social acceptance and friendships that supported their self-esteem. Thus, self-esteem is "commodified" in the sense that it is largely dependent on what one owns and buys.

Consumer Culture, Extrinsic Motivation, and Learning

Research also connects consumer culture and children's learning. Vansteenkiste, Simons, Lens, Soenens, and Matos (2005) found that 11- and 12-year-old Belgian children performed worse on a learning task if it was presented as extrinsically rather than intrinsically motivated. More specifically, researchers had obese children read information about healthy eating, and told half the sample that following the guidelines in the text was important for achieving physical health (intrinsic motivation). The other half were told that following the guidelines would increase their physical attractiveness (extrinsic motivation). These results indicate that extrinsic motivation designed to win approval from others based on physical appearance is one of the hallmarks of materialistic and consumerist culture (Kasser et al., 2007).

Research has extended these results by examining students' motives and their school grades. Ku, Dittmar, and Banerjee (2014) found that students' materialism levels in both Britain and Hong Kong were negatively associated with final exam grades in English and math. Furthermore, this relationship between materialism and grades was mediated by performance and mastery goals. Low materialists were higher in mastery goals such as wanting to learn as much of the material as possible. This was then associated with higher exam scores. However, high materialists were higher in performance goals, such as wanting to show others they can perform well. This goal was then associated with lower exam scores.

These results were replicated in three subsequent studies (Ku et al., 2014). In a second study, examining students from the first study 1 year later, the initial materialism scores from the first study were negatively associated with exam scores 1 year later. The third and fourth studies experimentally manipulated materialistic or nonmaterialistic values. Participants who were materialistically primed were more likely to endorse performance goals, which were associated with lower exam performance in the first study (Ku et al., 2014). Finally, Ku et al. (2014) found similar results in samples of teenagers from Britain and Hong Kong.

Ethics

Research findings such as the aforementioned ones led the APA Task Force to single out psychologists who worked for the advertising industry. The Task Force noted "an increasing number of companies headed by people trained as child psychologists that specialize in market research on children" (Wilcox et al., 2004, p. 38). It suggested that psychologists who use psychological research in service of advertising should think carefully about their ethical responsibilities (Wilcox et al., 2004).

One particularly important ethical issue concerns whether younger children are able to recognize whether a media message is an advertisement or not. The Task Force found from its review of the literature that children younger than 4 or 5 years old have trouble recognizing the differences between advertisements and regular programming. Furthermore, children as old as 7 or 8 have difficulty understanding the *persuasive intent* of the advertisers, which involves,

> . . . the recognition that the advertiser has a perspective different from [that of] the viewer and that advertisers intend to persuade their audience to want to buy their products, . . . that such persuasive communication is biased, and that biased messages must be interpreted differently than unbiased messages. (Wilcox et al., 2004, p. 5)

The Task Force repeatedly refers to advertising to young children as "unfair" because it takes advantage of individuals who are not cognitively developed enough to fully understand the influences acting upon them (see, for example, Wilcox et al., 2004, pp. 7, 9–12, 17, 19–20). Some may argue that modern children are not helpless in the face of this advertising onslaught. Instead, these skeptics may argue that kids are savvy enough to recognize and resist advertising because they have grown up in a media-saturated age. Unfortunately, this is not the case.

Developmental psychologists such as Jean Piaget (1952) have shown that children do not have the same intellectual capacities as adults. Regardless of how relatively savvy, intelligent, or mature they are, children younger than 8 are simply incapable of thinking fully critically and rationally about an advertisement (Levin & Linn, 2004). In addition to exploiting children's cognitive vulnerabilities, advertisers also take advantage of kids' natural developmental needs for control and independence. For example, Erikson (1964) theorized that children progress through natural psychosocial stages, one of which involves the need to develop an independent identity from their parents. Advertisers recognize this and market their products so as to take advantage.

Levin and Linn (2004) cite Kraft Lunchables, trays of processed meats, cheese, and crackers that kids can assemble themselves at lunch time, as an example. They argue that although many parents prefer that their kids not eat Lunchables, marketers appeal directly to kids' desire for independence to thwart parents' wishes. Further highlighting the role of psychological theory and data in marketing, Levin and Linn (2004) note that the child marketing handbook *What Kids Buy and Why* cites the work of Piaget and Erikson when instructing advertisers how to sell their products to children.

Results of many studies thus confirm that consumer and materialistic culture is negatively related to well-being. Negative consequences include more favorable attitudes toward alcohol and tobacco, lower self-esteem and happiness, greater anxiety, and decreased school performance. Research even shows that teenagers' sense of self-esteem has been commodified in the sense that it is largely dependent on which consumer product they purchase (Isaksen & Roper, 2012).

These negative consequences raise important ethical issues. Should we restrict advertising directed toward young children? Is it ethical to market products directly toward children who are too young to fully understand the persuasive intent of advertisers? What are the responsibilities of psychological scientists and other experts? Are there ethical limits to their participation in the advertising industry?

These are tough questions that cannot be answered scientifically because their answers depend on value judgments. Science tells us that advertising and consumerism lower children's well-being, but it cannot tell us whether we ought to act on these findings. In a democracy such as ours, that decision is presumably left to citizens.

POSITIVE WAYS TO SPEND MONEY

We have seen that blind pursuit of possessions diminishes our happiness. But are there more positive ways to spend money so that it can help increase our happiness? The answer is yes. Dunn, Gilbert, and Wilson (2011) offer some advice in an article provocatively titled "If Money Doesn't Make You Happy, Then You Probably Aren't Spending It Right."

But we must remember that any discussion of this topic must first acknowledge the importance of the "bread line" distinction made by Layard (2005) and others. Refer to the evidence in Chapter 6 that money predicts well-being much more strongly among the poor than it does among the wealthy. Thus, the following discussion is not meant to imply that the poor who seek basic material necessities such as food or shelter are somehow diminishing their own happiness.

So how can we spend money to make ourselves happier? Dunn et al. (2011) make eight suggestions. We discuss six of them here and go into more detail about the other two (buying experiences rather than material products and giving money away) later in the chapter. We also discuss two other ideas, the potential value of thrift and the importance of time.

Six of Dunn et al.'s (2011) suggestions seem particularly applicable to purchases of material goods such as a new car or wardrobe. These suggestions involve altering how we think about material purchases and the happiness we expect to receive from them. As we see in the next section, experiential purchases (e.g., going on a trip or to an amusement park) do not seem to involve the same thinking processes and expectations.

1. *Shift purchasing to provide a stream of less-expensive pleasures.* Dunn et al. (2011) suggest spending smaller amounts of money on several lesser pleasures instead of lots of money on a few large pleasures. They argue that this strategy reduces the speed at which we adapt to purchases. Do you remember the hedonic treadmill from Chapter 6? Humans become accustomed to all sorts of stimuli, including income and material objects, and these bring less pleasure over time. However, we do not adapt quickly to events that are unexpected, new to us, uncertain (difficult to explain), or those that keep changing. The authors use the example of an expensive new dining room table. The table remains the same over time, is no longer new after a short time, and is expected. Therefore, we adapt to it and quickly lose the pleasure we originally gained from its purchase. However, a constant stream of small pleasures is more likely to be unexpected, changing, and so on, and thus, in an overall sense, more resistant to adaptation.

2. *Avoid unnecessary insurance.* Another suggestion is to avoid buying unnecessary insurance, particularly for expensive consumer products. The idea here is that we fail to recognize how quickly we can adapt to the loss of those products. In the same way that we adapt to pleasures, we also adapt to losses. In addition, insurance for many consumer products is overpriced and therefore not a good way to spend our money to maximize our happiness.

3. *Delay consumption.* We should also seek to delay consumption when possible. Not only does this practice help keep us out of debt, it also leads to anticipation, which is positively related to happiness. Waiting to make the purchase or otherwise consume the product can also lead us to make better choices. When we choose products for immediate consumption, we tend to choose those that give immediate gratification but are unhealthy in the long term. However, when we choose between products that we will consume in the future, we tend to make healthier choices. Finally, products that we will consume later may involve more uncertainty, which delays any adaptation effects.

4. *Carefully consider purchases.* Dunn et al. recommend that we think through material purchases very carefully. They offer the example of buying a lakeside cottage. When considering this purchase, we naturally think about sunsets, pleasant family gatherings, and fun activities like boating and fishing. The unpleasant details of owning the cottage may not pop out at us, for example, the cost, headache, and labor involved in maintaining it. Nor do we think about the potential stress and aggravation of commuting to the cottage, and so on. Although certain features of the cottage are bound to give us pleasure, others are likely to detract from our happiness. We need to consider whether the pleasures will outweigh the pains.

5. *Avoid the traps of comparison shopping.* Comparison shopping can be another happiness-detracting trap (Dunn et al., 2011). Imagine a couple shopping for a new home. Comparisons between alternative choices might lead them to overestimate the happiness they are likely to feel from living in a large and beautiful home. As a result, they might overextend themselves financially in order to make the down payment on the larger home.

6. *Consider the happiness of others with a purchase.* Finally, when considering a purchase, we should look to see how happy other people who have previously made the same purchase are. Perhaps surprisingly, other people's happiness with a product or experience predicts our own quite well. In Dunn et al.'s words, purchases are more likely to bring happiness when you "follow the herd instead of your head" (2011, p. 123).

Experiential Versus Material Purchases
Evidence That Experiential Purchases Make Us Happier

Buying experiences (e.g., a trip to the beach) rather than material goods (e.g., expensive sunglasses) can also make us happier. For instance, van Boven and Gilovich (2003) asked college students to recall a recent material or experiential purchase they had made that cost at least $100. Students who recalled an experiential purchase remembered the purchase as bringing more happiness than did students who recalled a material purchase. These researchers followed up this study by asking a largely representative sample of American adults to recall an experiential and a materialistic purchase. Consistent with the previous results, participants reported that the experiential purchase made them happier than the material purchase.

Van Boven and Gilovich (2003) also found that participants who thought about an experiential purchase expressed more *current* happiness and positive mood than did participants who thought about a material purchase. This last study is important because it assesses current mood and happiness rather than past emotional states. The authors noted that we often inaccurately recall past emotional states. Subsequent research has replicated these findings, showing that experiential purchases bring more happiness than do material purchases, for instance, by showing that material purchases are more often associated with regrets (Gilovich, Kumar, & Jampol, 2015; van Boven, 2005).

Why Experiential Purchases Bring More Happiness

Researchers quickly turned their focus to the question of why experiential purchases make us happier. Gilovich et al. (2015) point to three primary factors: (a) experiences facilitate social relationships, (b) we are less likely to compare our experiences with alternative experiences, and (c) experiences are central to our identities. Emerging research also suggests that experiential purchases are more pleasurable to anticipate (Gilovich et al., 2015).

Experiences and social relationships   We learned in Chapter 5 that positive relationships with others are crucial for happiness. Gilovich et al. (2015) argue that experiences lead to more happiness than do material possessions because they are more likely to be "consumed" with other people. For example, we typically go to concerts and on vacations with other people, while material possessions such as new clothes are not as likely to facilitate social interaction. We also feel more connected to others with similar experiences, even if we did not have those experiences at the same time and place. Furthermore, experiences may make us feel more connected to other people in general.

These ideas are empirically supported. For instance, social relationships mediate the relationship between type of purchase and happiness. Specifically, experiential (as opposed to materialistic) purchases lead to stronger social bonds, and these stronger social bonds then predict greater happiness (Howell & Hill, 2009).

Experiences and social comparisons   As discussed in Chapter 6, social comparisons can have a corrosive effect on our happiness. Evidence indicates that experiences are less likely to provoke social comparisons than are material possessions. We are less likely to compare our experiences to those of others, and to other alternative experiences we might have had.

Research supports this hypothesis by showing that experiential purchases are negatively associated with social comparisons. Experiential participants are less likely to strongly endorse items indicating concern about the perception of others (e.g., "I am concerned about how others will perceive this purchase," Howell & Hill, 2009, pp. 513–514). This reduction in social comparisons is then associated with greater happiness (Howell & Hill, 2009).

Other research shows even more directly that experiential purchases lead to fewer social comparisons. Carter and Gilovich (2010) found that participants who imagined making a materialistic purchase were more upset than those who imagined an experiential purchase by the thought that a rival may have gotten the same purchase at a better price. They also found that participants who actually received a materialistic (pen) versus experiential (Sun Chips) prize were more affected by knowing that more desirable prizes were available.

Experiences and social identity   Our experiences also help to define who we are. As a crucial component of our self-definitions, experiences might bring us emotional comfort, and they might also help us express our identity to others. Experiences might also perform these functions much better than do material possessions. After all, our possessions are always separated from ourselves in ways that experiences are not. In some sense, we become the sum of our experiences (Gilovich et al., 2015).

Research supports these hypotheses by demonstrating that participants consider experiential purchases as more central representations of their identity than materialistic purchases (Carter & Gilovich, 2010). Gilovich et al. (2015) argue that we naturally positively evaluate things that are central to our sense of self. By extension, these central representations of ourselves bring us enjoyment. This logic is supported by research showing that individuals expressed more satisfaction with experiential purchases than materialistic ones (Carter & Gilovich, 2010).

Anticipation   Gilovich et al. (2015) note that anticipation might also explain the happiness differences between material and experiential purchases. Kumar, Killingsworth, and Gilovich (2014) found that participants waiting to make an anticipated experiential purchase were happier than those waiting to make a material purchase and were also happier than those who were not anticipating any purchase. Thus, experiential purchases make us happier before we even acquire the experience, while material purchases do not.

Some Additional Findings

Purchasing an experiential *product*, such as a guitar instead of a shirt, also typically brings more happiness than does the purchase of a materialistic product. This is interesting because we usually think of a product as being materialistic, but that is not always the case. The reasons experiential products bring more happiness are similar to those identified by Gilovich et al. (2015) concerning experiential versus materialistic purchases. Experiential products are more likely to satisfy basic needs for identity, competence, and social relatedness (Guevarra & Howell, 2015).

There are also some important moderators of these effects. Remember that moderating variables are ones that change the relationship between two other variables. Some research (e.g., Guevarra & Howell, 2015; Nicolao, Irwin, & Goodman, 2009) suggests that experiential purchases are associated with more happiness only when they are perceived as positive and enjoyable. The experience may have to turn out well before it brings more happiness than a materialistic purchase.

There is also some evidence that personality moderates the effect. Nicolao et al. (2009) found that individuals with strong materialistic values were not influenced by the type of purchase. Instead, materialists were equally happy with material and experiential purchases that turned out well, and equally unhappy with both types of purchases when they turned out poorly.

In addition, Zhang, Howell, Caprariello, and Guevarra (2014) found evidence that happy, sociable individuals are more likely to benefit from experiential purchases.

Finally, having a wealth of *extraordinary* experiences, ones that are fantastic and unusual, may reduce our ability to savor and enjoy more mundane experiences. For instance, Quoidbach, Dunn, Hansenne, and Bustin (2015) found that the number of countries a person had visited is *negatively* associated with the expectations of savoring a visit to an ordinary but pleasant country of the person's choosing. In addition, the number of countries visited is also negatively associated with savoring of even extraordinary destinations. Thus, the most traveled among us, those of us with the greatest wealth of travel experiences, appear less able to enjoy future trips, particularly a trip to an agreeable but mundane locale.

These studies are noteworthy because they indicate that the hedonic treadmill (Brickman & Campbell, 1971) can apply to experiences as well as possessions. We adapt to experiences, just as we do to possessions, such that previous experiences affect our ability to enjoy future ones. Experiences are a net positive for all of us, regardless of our level of wealth of previous experiences. But it is important to recognize the effects of our previous history and perhaps to look for ways to fully savor all of our experiences.

In summary, we are happier when we pursue and anticipate experiences rather than material products. Experiential purchases are also more likely to satisfy our needs to establish social ties and our social identity. We are also less likely to make harmful social comparisons about our experiential purchases. These factors explain why experiential pursuits are more likely to lead to happiness than are materialistic ones.

Spend for the Benefit of Others Rather Than Ourselves

Spending money on others can increase our happiness (Dunn, Aknin, & Norton, 2014). For example, researchers find that *prosocial spending*, the combination of charitable donations and money spent on presents for others, positively predicted well-being among a representative sample of American adults (Dunn, Aknin, & Norton, 2008). These results were significant even after controlling for income, thus undermining the possibility that prosocial spenders were happier simply because they were wealthier. In addition, the relationship between prosocial spending and well-being was almost identical to that of income and well-being. In other words, our happiness is as much affected by how much we spend on others as it is by the size of our own income. Finally, the amount participants spent to pay bills and for gifts to themselves were unrelated to their happiness.

These results appear to generalize to people from all over the world. Prosocial spending has positively predicted well-being in samples from Tanna Island, a small island in the South Pacific, northeast of Australia (Aknin, Broesch, Hamlin, & van de Vondervoort, 2015); India (Aknin, Barrington-Leigh, et al., 2013); Uganda and South Africa (Aknin, Barrington-Leigh, et al., 2013); the United States (e.g., Dunn et al., 2008); and Canada (e.g., Aknin, Dunn, & Norton, 2012). Another study found the relationship using a small sample of individuals from 10 different countries: the United States, India, Turkey, and seven European countries (Surana & Lomas, 2014). But most impressively, Aknin, Barrington-Leigh, et al. (2013) found that prosocial spending predicted well-being in a representative sample of 95% of the world's population that included participants from 136 different countries. Their results show a positive relationship between prosocial spending and happiness in 120 of the 136 countries, and this relationship was statistically significant in 59% of those 120 countries.

Furthermore, when Aknin, Barrington-Leigh, et al. (2013) made statistical corrections to account for small sample sizes, they found a significant prosocial spending/well-being relationship in 87% of the 120 countries. This relationship did not seem to be a function of national or individual wealth, was not concentrated in any particular geographical area of the world, and was also not dependent on culture, level of political freedom, or quality of national government. Finally, the size of the relationship was meaningful; the relationship between charitable donations and happiness was roughly equivalent to the happiness associated with doubling one's household income.

Evidence for Causality

You might be wondering whether prosocial spending is a *cause* of happiness, or if it is merely coincidentally related. After all, the research described so far is correlational, indicating only that individuals who happen to give money away also happen to be happy. Could there be some other explanation for this relationship? For instance, perhaps the direction of causality goes the other way, and being happy causes people to give money away.

Individuals in a good mood are more charitable (Cialdini, Schaller, Houlihan, Arps, Fultz, & Beaman, 1987), so happy people are probably more likely to be charitable. But there is also reason to think the causal flow goes from charity to happiness. Some of this evidence comes from the statistical controls mentioned earlier (e.g., Aknin, Barrington-Leigh, et al., 2013). Several experimental studies also demonstrate that prosocial spending can increase happiness (e.g., Aknin, Dunn, Whillans, Grant, & Norton, 2013; Dunn et al., 2008). These studies typically give some individuals a chance to donate part of the compensation they received for participating in a study to a charity. Results show that participants randomly assigned to have the opportunity to make charitable donations are happier.

Why Does Prosocial Spending Increase Happiness?

In a review of the literature, Dunn et al. (2014) argued that prosocial spending leads to greater well-being when it satisfies the innate psychological needs outlined by SDT (Ryan & Deci, 2000): relatedness (connectedness with others), competency (mastery), and autonomy (free choice and self-direction). Consistent with this hypothesis, Hill and Howell (2014) found that psychological need satisfaction (measured as the average of relatedness, competency, and autonomy) mediates the relationship between prosocial spending and well-being. In other words, prosocial spending is related to greater happiness because it first satisfies basic psychological needs, which then directly increase happiness.

Individuals with self-transcendent values are more likely to gain happiness from prosocial spending (Hill & Howell, 2014). Recall from our earlier discussion that self-transcendent values involve caring for others and tolerance for differing viewpoints. Hill and Howell asked participants to recall how much they typically spent each month on bills, gifts for themselves, gifts for others, and charitable donations. They found that prosocial spending enhanced well-being only for high self-transcendence participants. Thus, it appears that prosocial spending is only associated with happiness if the individual values caring for others and tolerance.

In summary, spending on others increases our happiness. There is good evidence that this relationship is bidirectional and causal: spending on others causes our happiness to increase, and being happy causes us to spend more on others. Spending on others also makes us happy because it helps satisfy basic psychological needs for competence, autonomy, and relatedness, and because it is consistent with self-transcendent values.

THRIFT

It may seem strange to read about thrift as a way to spend money to increase happiness. After all, being thrifty implies that we limit our spending and carefully and wisely manage our money. But thrift can also involve spending money to pay down debt before making new purchases (Chancellor & Lyubomirsky, 2011) and moving it to a savings account (Kasser, 2011). In this section, we discuss other examples of thrifty spending and how they can improve happiness.

Chancellor and Lyubomirsky (2011, 2014) catalogued many ways that thrifty spending can improve happiness. For instance, we receive more happiness by preventing bad things from happening to us than we do from experiencing good things. In Chancellor and Lyubomirsky's (2014) words, "bad is stronger than good" (p. 21), and we should "cure ills before seeking thrills" (p. 20). In fact, the research Chancellor and Lyubomirsky (2014) reviewed indicates that negative events have three to five times more impact on happiness than do positive events because they attract more attention. We also adapt to positive events more quickly than we do to negative ones. Thus, thriftiness, in the sense of thinking twice before buying expensive pleasures, can increase our happiness (Chancellor & Lyubomirsky, 2014). Instead of indiscriminately spending on pleasures, we should concentrate on eliminating negatives in our lives first. A modestly priced, but warmly functional, winter coat is likely to bring us more happiness than a more expensive highly advertised brand-named coat that does not keep us as warm.

Similarly, we should carefully distinguish between our wants and our needs (Chancellor & Lyubomirsky, 2014). Our true needs are fairly basic, and generally it does not cost much for most of us to meet these needs. We need basic sustenance and shelter, along with a sense of physical safety. Psychologically, we need to feel competent, in control of our own lives, and connected to other people (Chancellor & Lyubomirsky, 2014). Directing our spending toward necessities rather than luxuries not only saves money; it also makes us happier. Once we have a basic automobile to commute to work (allowing us to meet our sustenance needs) and visit friends (allowing satisfaction of our social connectedness needs), any additional luxurious add-ons (e.g., leather seats and a sun roof) contribute only minimally to our happiness (Chancellor & Lyubomirsky, 2014).

Thrift Strategies
Thrift and Debt
We are also happier if we avoid debt. Chancellor and Lyubomirsky's (2014) review indicates that the psychological costs of debt, measured in terms of anxiety, family conflict, the negative consequences of being unable to pay off debt (e.g., home foreclosure), and our general happiness, is much higher than the happiness benefits of acquiring expensive items. These authors acknowledge that debt makes sense when the cost of a loan is cheaper than the benefit we expect to receive from the loan. For instance, we expect that borrowing money for college is a good investment because the cost of the loan will be less than the life-time earnings boost provided by our education. Still, these types of long-term debt are relatively rare in an individual's life, and a thrifty person who avoids debt is likely to be happier (Chancellor & Lyubomirsky, 2014).

Frugal Shopping Habits
Frugal shopping habits can also make us happier. Chancellor and Lyubomirsky (2014) found in their review that coupon clippers and bargain hunters can experience a thrill from saving money on purchases. Frugal shoppers also delay purchases instead of succumbing to impulse buying. This restraint allows them to consider whether the purchase really is both a good deal and something they really want, and it allows them the pleasure of anticipation.

Other Thrift-Based Strategies
Chancellor and Lyubomirsky (2011) identified several other thrift-based, happiness-increasing strategies. For instance, renting a vacation cabin is cheaper than owning one that we rarely use. We can also practice thrift and increase our happiness by feeling grateful for the material possessions we already have and focusing on our appreciation for them (Chancellor & Lyubomirsky, 2014). Gratitude increases our happiness (Lyubomirsky, Dickerhoof, Boehm, & Sheldon, 2011), and in this case it can reduce our felt need to buy more stuff. Finally, we would be happier if we directed our discretionary spending toward

things we truly enjoy and away from stuff that is meant only to impress others (Chancellor & Lyubomirsky, 2011, 2014). We can save money and make ourselves happier by spending on things that help us satisfy intrinsic goals that are directly and personally meaningful, such as meeting with friends and pursuing hobbies and other sincere interests.

A General (Tentative) Theory of Thrift

The thrift literature is somewhat confusing. Kasser (2011) found mixed results concerning the relationship between thrift and happiness in his literature review. Thrift is often associated with more happiness. For example, measures of frugality predict well-being. Other research indicates that followers of voluntary simplicity, who purposefully decide to take lower paying jobs in order to live simpler, less stressful, and less consumptive lives, are also happier than more mainstream and less frugal individuals (Kasser, 2011). However, research also shows that thrift can lower well-being. Those who are obsessive about saving or who are extremely reluctant ever to spend money tend to be less happy (Kasser, 2011).

Kasser (2011) offered a tentative theory about thrift and happiness by arguing that thrift can increase happiness when it helps to satisfy basic psychological needs for safety, competence, relatedness, and autonomy. Although his theory has not been fully tested, it seems to make sense out of the mix of findings.

For instance, we might resort to thrift if we feel unsafe or insecure, either physically or psychologically. In this case, thrift is a reaction to an unmet need. Thrifty individuals may also feel separated from our mainstream, materialistic culture, and therefore have difficulty developing and maintaining close relationships. In this case, thrift might detract from well-being. In both cases, thrifty individuals are likely to feel less happy (Kasser, 2011).

However, thrift can also give a person a feeling of competence and self-direction. The feelings associated with finding bargains, developing thrifty do-it-yourself skills, and successfully practicing good money skills can be very rewarding. These can increase well-being by satisfying needs for autonomy and competence (Kasser, 2011). Thrift can also increase well-being by strengthening relationships. Specifically, thrifty individuals may have more time and energy to invest in relationships because they have voluntarily exited high stress, high time-demand jobs (Kasser, 2011). In conclusion, thrift can either raise or lower our well-being, depending on how it is associated with our basic needs.

In summary, there are several reasons why thrift can increase happiness. One of the most powerful reasons is that being thrifty can often shield us from bad consequences. It is important to remember the power that bad things have in our lives (Chancellor & Lyubomirsky, 2014). Thriftiness can also bring us a sense of competence, because it takes skill to find good bargains, and so on. In addition, the thrifty habits of voluntary simplifiers may also bring happiness because they reduce materialism. However, thrift is unlikely to bring happiness to a desperately poor individual who is forced into frugality in order to survive. The key may be whether thrift is a means to meeting basic psychological needs. Thrift that increases our sense of competence, relatedness, and autonomy seems most likely to increase our happiness.

TIME

Time Affluence

We may also be able to increase our happiness by buying ourselves more time. This is because *time affluence*, the feeling that we have an abundant supply of time, is associated with happiness. Kasser and Sheldon (2009) found that time affluence predicts life satisfaction as well as job and family satisfaction. Furthermore, this relationship between time affluence and well-being is partially mediated by mindfulness and by satisfaction of the basic psychological needs for competence, autonomy, and relatedness. Thus, time affluence makes us happier because it helps us meet basic psychological needs.

They also found that while both material and time affluence are related to well-being, the shape of the curve is linear for time affluence, but curvilinear for material affluence. The linear relationship between time affluence and well-being means that time affluence continues to predict higher well-being, even among individuals with high levels of time affluence. There is no diminishing return of time. More time, at any level, means more well-being. But the positive effects of material affluence on well-being level off at higher levels of affluence. Material wealth stops predicting greater well-being once a certain level of wealth is reached (Kasser & Sheldon, 2009).

These results were obtained in four separate studies that included a nationally representative sample of American adults, two nonrepresentative convenience samples of American adults, and one sample of college students. The results held even after controlling for material affluence and the personality characteristics of sensation seeking, need to keep busy, and need for achievement. Thus, the relationship between feeling that we have an abundance of time and happiness does not imply that those of us who have more time are richer, or higher in achievement (Kasser & Sheldon, 2009).

Other research has produced similar results. Howell and Buro (2015) found that time affluence predicted flourishing (e.g., "I lead a purposeful and meaningful life," p. 907) and positive and negative emotions, even after controlling for material affluence, in a sample of Canadian college students. Similarly, Manolis and Roberts (2012) found that time-affluent American high school students had higher well-being than did their more hurried peers.

Manolis and Roberts (2012) also found that moderate levels of time affluence seemed to blunt the negative effects of materialism on well-being. Highly materialist teens in this study who also had moderate levels of time affluence were less unhappy than were other materialist teens. Manolis and Roberts suggest that this may be because a moderate level of time affluence lessens materialistic desires. Interestingly, this buffering effect of time affluence occurred only for moderately time-affluent participants. Highly materialistic/high time affluent teens had relatively low well-being.

Time scarcity at work is also related to lower well-being (Guillen-Royo, 2010; Promislo, Deckop, Giacalone, & Jurkiewicz, 2010). Other research shows a particularly steep drop in life satisfaction for those who work more than 40 hours per week (Brown & Kasser, 2005). These findings have led several theorists (e.g., Coote, Franklin, & Simms, 2010; Reisch, 2001; Schor, 2010) to suggest that reducing work hours can increase well-being. The newfound time can then be used to cultivate stronger social relationships and to pursue leisure activities or intrinsically motivating hobbies, all of which are likely to substantially increase our happiness. These nonwork activities are likely to benefit our happiness more than any likely monetary reward we receive from working long hours (Coote et al., 2010; Reisch, 2001; Schor, 2010).

Implications

This research shows that our time is precious. In fact, merely thinking about time affects our happiness. Mogilner (2010) found that simply reminding experimental participants about time led them to spend more time socializing and less time working. On the other hand, reminders about money led to decreased socializing and more work. These results are important, because our social relationships and other intrinsic pursuits bring us more happiness than does our work.

Using our time to pursue intrinsic interests such as hobbies and to meet basic psychological needs for relatedness, competence, and autonomy tends to increase our happiness. However, using our time to chase purely monetary, materialistic, and extrinsic (i.e., keeping up with the Joneses) goals detracts from our happiness unless we are very poor. Mogilner (2010) suggests that American society may be particularly likely to stimulate thoughts about money rather than time, and this might have consequences for our happiness.

Feeling rich in time is connected to happiness. Data show that this relationship is likely because having time allows us to reflect and be more mindful. But time is scarce for many of us. Work's demands on time seem particularly destructive for many. Perhaps it is time to consider changes in public policy that will allow us more and better time away from work.

SUMMARY

Materialistic behaviors and values reduce our happiness, probably because they make it more difficult to meet important and basic psychological needs for autonomy, competence, and relatedness. Unfortunately, our culture of consumerism promotes materialism and also seems to teach us that buying the right consumer products can heal psychological insecurities. Our capitalist economic culture also promotes materialism by encouraging extrinsic values such as self-enhancement and dampening more happiness-producing intrinsic values such as self-transcendence.

Psychologists are faced with ethical dilemmas when offered positions within, or support from, the advertising industry. Although these positions and support can be lucrative, the APA has urged psychologists to carefully consider their ethical responsibilities when working within this industry, especially in advertising to children.

Interestingly, there are many positive ways to spend money that are associated with increased happiness. For instance, we can spend money on others, or buy experiences rather than products. These methods largely sidestep consumer culture and do not lead us toward materialism. We can also sidestep materialistic culture by seeking out nurturing environments that promote intrinsic values and prosocial behaviors. Thrifty behavior and buying time are also related to increased well-being.

NOTES

1. Financial success is a materialistic aspiration, and the other three are nonmaterialistic.

2. The countries are Austria, Belgium, Canada, Denmark, Finland, France, Germany, Great Britain, Ireland, Italy, Japan, the Netherlands, Norway, Sweden, and the United States.

REFERENCES

Acuff, D. S., & Reiher, R. H. (1997). *What kids buy and why: The psychology of marketing to kids.* New York, NY: Free Press.

Aknin, L. B., Barrington-Leigh, C., Dunn, E. W., Helliwell, J. F., Burns, J., Biswas-Diener, R., . . . Norton, M. I. (2013). Prosocial spending and well-being: Cross-cultural evidence for a psychological universal. *Journal of Personality and Social Psychology, 104*(4), 635–652.

Aknin, L. B., Broesch, T., Hamlin, J. K., & van de Vondervoort, J. W. (2015). Prosocial behavior leads to happiness in a small-scale rural society. *Journal of Experimental Psychology: General, 144*(4), 788–795.

Aknin, L. B., Dunn, E. W., & Norton, M. I. (2012). Happiness runs in a circular motion: Evidence for a positive feedback loop between prosocial spending and happiness. *Journal of Happiness Studies, 13*(2), 347–355.

Aknin, L. B., Dunn, E. W., Whillans, A. V., Grant, A. M., & Norton, M. I. (2013). Making a difference matters: Impact unlocks the emotional benefits of prosocial spending. *Journal of Economic Behavior and Organization, 88*, 90–95.

Alvarez-Diaz, A., Gonzalez, L., & Radcliff, B. (2010). The politics of happiness: On the political determinants of quality of life in the American states. *Journal of Politics, 72*(3), 894–905.

Bauer, M. A., Wilkie, J. E. B., Kim, J. K., & Bodenhausen, G. V. (2012). Cuing consumerism: Situational materialism undermines personal and social well-being. *Psychological Science, 23*(5), 517–523.

Biglan, A. (2015). *The nurture effect: How the science of human behavior can improve our lives and our world.* Oakland, CA: New Harbinger.

Biglan, A., Flay, B. R., Embry, D. D., & Sandler, I. N. (2012). The critical role of nurturing environments for promoting human well-being. *American Psychologist, 67*(4), 257–271.

Brickman, P., & Campbell, D. T. (1971). Hedonic relativism and planning the good society. In M. H. Appley (Ed.), *Adaptation level theory: A symposium* (pp. 287–302). New York, NY: Academic Press.

Brown, K. W., & Kasser, T. (2005). Are psychological and ecological well-being compatible? The role of values, mindfulness, and lifestyle. *Social Indicators Research, 74*(2), 349–368.

Carter, T. J., & Gilovich, T. (2010). The relative relativity of material and experiential purchases. *Journal of Personality and Social Psychology, 98*(1), 146–159.

Chan, R., & Joseph, S. (2000). Dimensions of personality, domains of aspiration, and subjective well-being. *Personality and Individual Differences, 28*(2), 347–354.

Chancellor, J., & Lyubomirsky, S. (2011). Happiness and thrift: When (spending) less is (hedonically) more. *Journal of Consumer Psychology, 21*(2), 131–138.

Chancellor, J., & Lyubomirsky, S. (2014). Money for happiness: The hedonic benefits of thrift. In M. Tatzel (Ed.), *Consumption and well-being in the material world* (pp. 13–47). New York, NY: Springer Science + Business Media.

Cialdini, R. B., Schaller, M., Houlihan, D., Arps, K., Fultz, J., & Beaman, A. L. (1987). Empathy-based helping: Is it selflessly or selfishly motivated? *Journal of Personality and Social Psychology, 52*(4), 749–758.

Coote, A., Franklin, J., & Simms, A. (2010). *21 hours: Why a shorter working week can help us all to flourish in the 21st century.* London, UK: New Economics Foundation. Retrieved from https://b.3cdn.net/nefoundation/f49406d81b9ed9c977_p1m6ibgje.pdf

Dittmar, H., Bond, R., Hurst, M., & Kasser, T. (2014). The relationship between materialism and personal well-being: A meta-analysis. *Journal of Personality and Social Psychology, 107*(5), 879–924.

Dunn, E. W., Aknin, L. B., & Norton, M. I. (2008). Spending money on others promotes happiness. *Science, 319*(5870), 1687–1688.

Dunn, E. W., Aknin, L. B., & Norton, M. I. (2014). Prosocial spending and happiness: Using money to benefit others pays off. *Current Directions in Psychological Science, 23*(1), 41–47.

Dunn, E. W., Gilbert, D. T., & Wilson, T. D. (2011). If money doesn't make you happy, then you probably aren't spending it right. *Journal of Consumer Psychology, 21*(2), 115–125.

Easterbrook, M. J., Wright, M. L., Dittmar, H., & Banerjee, R. (2014). Consumer culture ideals, extrinsic motivations, and well-being in children. *European Journal of Social Psychology, 44*(4), 349–359.

Erikson, E. H. (1964). *Childhood and society.* New York, NY: W. W. Norton.

Esping-Andersen, G. (1990). *The three worlds of welfare capitalism.* Princeton, NJ: Princeton University Press.

Flavin, P., Pacek, A. C., & Radcliff, B. (2010). Labor unions and life satisfaction: Evidence from new data. *Social Indicators Research, 98*(3), 435–449.

Flavin, P., & Radcliff, B. (2009). Public policies and suicide rates in the American states. *Social Indicators Research, 90*(2), 195–209.

Frost, R. O., Kyrios, M., McCarthy, K. D., & Matthews, Y. (2007). Self-ambivalence and attachment to possessions. *Journal of Cognitive Psychotherapy, 21*(3), 232–242.

Gao, L., Wheeler, S. C., & Shiv, B. (2009). The "shaken self". Product choices as a means of restoring self-view confidence. *Journal of Consumer Research, 36*(1), 29–38.

George, J. M. (2014). Compassion and capitalism: Implications for organizational studies. *Journal of Management, 40*(1), 5–15.

Gilovich, T., Kumar, A., & Jampol, L. (2015). A wonderful life: Experiential consumption and the pursuit of happiness. *Journal of Consumer Psychology, 25*(1), 152–165.

Guéguen, N., & Jacob, C. (2013). Behavioral consequences of money: When the automated teller machine reduces helping behavior. *Journal of Socio-Economics, 47*, 103–104.

Guevarra, D. A., & Howell, R. T. (2015). To have in order to do: Exploring the effects of consuming experiential products on well-being. *Journal of Consumer Psychology, 25*(1), 28–41.

Guillen-Royo, M. (2010). Realising the "wellbeing dividend": An exploratory study using the human scale development approach. *Ecological Economics, 70*(2), 384–393.

Hellevik, O. (2003). Economy, values and happiness in Norway. *Journal of Happiness Studies, 4*(3), 243–283.

Hill, G., & Howell, R. T. (2014). Moderators and mediators of pro-social spending and well-being: The influence of values and psychological need satisfaction. *Personality and Individual Differences, 69*, 69–74.

Howell, A. J., & Buro, K. (2015). Measuring and predicting student well-being: Further evidence in support of the flourishing scale and the scale of positive and negative experiences. *Social Indicators Research, 121*(3), 903–915.

Howell, R. T., & Hill, G. (2009). The mediators of experiential purchases: Determining the impact of psychological needs satisfaction and social comparison. *The Journal of Positive Psychology, 4*(6), 511–522.

Isaksen, K. J., & Roper, S. (2012). The commodification of self-esteem: Branding and British teenagers. *Psychology and Marketing, 29*(3), 117–135.

Jiang, J., Zhang, Y., Ke, Y., Hawk, S. T., & Qiu, H. (2015). Can't buy me friendship? Peer rejection and adolescent materialism: Implicit self-esteem as a mediator. *Journal of Experimental Social Psychology, 58*, 48–55.

Kasser, T. (2005). Frugality, generosity, and materialism in children and adolescents. In K. A. Moore & L. H. Lippman (Eds.), *What do children need to flourish: Conceptualizing and measuring indicators of positive development* (pp. 357–373). New York, NY: Springer Science + Business Media.

Kasser, T. (2011). Cultural values and the well-being of future generations: A cross-national study. *Journal of Cross-Cultural Psychology, 42*(2), 206–215.

Kasser, T., & Ahuvia, A. (2002). Materialistic values and well-being in business students. *European Journal of Social Psychology, 32*(1), 137–146.

Kasser, T., Cohn, S., Kanner, A. D., & Ryan, R. M. (2007). Some costs of American corporate capitalism: A psychological exploration of value and goal conflicts. *Psychological Inquiry, 18*(1), 1–22.

Kasser, T., Rosenblum, K. L., Sameroff, A. J., Deci, E. L., Niemiec, C. P., Ryan, R. M., . . . Hawks, S. (2014). Changes in materialism, changes in psychological well-being: Evidence from three longitudinal studies and an intervention experiment. *Motivation and Emotion, 38*(1), 1–22.

Kasser, T., & Ryan, R. M. (1993). A dark side of the American dream: Correlates of financial success as a central life aspiration. *Journal of Personality and Social Psychology, 65*(2), 410–422.

Kasser, T., & Ryan, R. M. (1996). Further examining the American dream: Differential correlates of intrinsic and extrinsic goals. *Personality and Social Psychology Bulletin, 22*, 280–287.

Kasser, T., & Ryan, R. M. (2001). Be careful what you wish for: Optimal functioning and the relative attainment of intrinsic and extrinsic goals. In P. Schmuck & K. M. Sheldon (Eds.), *Life goals and well-being: Towards a positive psychology of human striving* (pp. 116–131). Ashland, OH: Hogrefe & Huber.

Kasser, T., Ryan, R. M., Couchman, C. E., & Sheldon, K. M. (2004). Materialistic values: Their causes and consequences. In T. Kasser & A. D. Kanner (Eds.), *Psychology and consumer culture: The struggle for a good life in a materialistic world* (pp. 11–28). Washington, DC: American Psychological Association.

Kasser, T., Ryan, R. M., Zax, M., & Sameroff, A. J. (1995). The relations of maternal and social environments to late adolescents' materialistic and prosocial values. *Developmental Psychology, 31*(6), 907–914.

Kasser, T., & Sheldon, K. M. (2009). Time affluence as a path toward personal happiness and ethical business practice: Empirical evidence from four studies. *Journal of Business Ethics, 84*, 243–255.

Kouchaki, M., Smith-Crowe, K., Brief, A. P., & Sousa, C. (2013). Seeing green: Mere exposure to money triggers a business decision frame and unethical outcomes. *Organizational Behavior and Human Decision Processes, 121*(1), 53–61.

Ku, L., Dittmar, H., & Banerjee, R. (2014). To have or to learn? The effects of materialism on British and Chinese children's learning. *Journal of Personality and Social Psychology, 106*(5), 803–821.

Kumar, A., Killingsworth, M. A., & Gilovich, T. (2014). Waiting for merlot: Anticipatory consumption of experiential and material purchases. *Psychological Science, 25*(10), 1924–1931.

Layard, R. (2005). *Happiness: Lessons from a new science.* London, UK: Allen Lane.

Levin, D. E., & Linn, S. (2004). The commercialization of childhood: Understanding the problem and finding solutions. In T. Kasser & A. D. Kanner (Eds.), *Psychology and consumer culture: The struggle for a good life in a materialistic world* (pp. 213–232). Washington, DC: American Psychological Association.

Li, N. P., Lim, A. J. Y., Tsai, M.-H., & O, J. (2015). Too materialistic to get married and have children? *PLOS ONE, 10*(5). doi:10.1371/journal.pone.0126543

Lyubomirsky, S., Dickerhoof, R., Boehm, J. K., & Sheldon, K. M. (2011). Becoming happier takes both a will and a proper way: An experimental longitudinal intervention to boost well-being. *Emotion, 11*(2), 391–402.

Manolis, C., & Roberts, J. A. (2012). Subjective well-being among adolescent consumers: The effects of materialism, compulsive buying, and time affluence. *Applied Research in Quality of Life, 7*(2), 117–135.

Mogilner, C. (2010). The pursuit of happiness. Time, money, and social connection. *Psychological Science, 21*(9), 1348–1354.

Molinsky, A. L., Grant, A. M., & Margolis, J. D. (2012). The bedside manner of homo economicus: How and why priming an economic schema reduces compassion. *Organizational Behavior and Human Decision Processes, 119*(1), 27–37.

Nicolao, L., Irwin, J. R., & Goodman, J. K. (2009). Happiness for sale: Do experiential purchases make consumers happier than material purchases? *Journal of Consumer Research, 36*(2), 188–198.

Pacek, A. C., & Radcliff, B. (2008). Welfare policy and subjective well-being across nations: An individual-level assessment. *Social Indicators Research, 89*(1), 179–191.

Piaget, J. (1952). *The origins of intelligence in children.* New York, NY: International Universities Press.

Promislo, M. D., Deckop, J. R., Giacalone, R. A., & Jurkiewicz, C. L. (2010). Valuing money more than people: The effects of materialism on work–family conflict. *Journal of Occupational and Organizational Psychology, 83*(4), 935–953.

Pulfrey, C., & Butera, F. (2013). Why neoliberal values of self-enhancement lead to cheating in higher education: A motivational account. *Psychological Science, 24*(11), 2153–2162.

Quoidbach, J., Dunn, E. W., Hansenne, M., & Bustin, G. (2015). The price of abundance: How a wealth of experiences impoverishes savoring. *Personality and Social Psychology Bulletin, 41*(3), 393–404.

Radcliff, B. (2001). Politics, markets, and life satisfaction: The political economy of human happiness. *American Political Science Review, 95*(4), 939–952.

Reisch, L. A. (2001). Time and wealth: The role of time and temporalities for sustainable patterns of consumption. *Time and Society, 10*(2–3), 367–385.

Richins, M. L., & Dawson, S. (1992). A consumer values orientation for materialism and its measurement: Scale development and validation. *Journal of Consumer Research, 19*(3), 303–316.

Rosenblatt, A., Greenberg, J., Solomon, S., Pyszczynski, T., & Lyon, D. (1989). Evidence for terror management theory: I. The effects of mortality salience on reactions to those who violate or uphold cultural values. *Journal of Personality and Social Psychology, 57*(4), 681–690.

Ryan, R. M., & Deci, E. L. (2000). Self-determination theory and the facilitation of intrinsic motivation, social development, and well-being. *American Psychologist, 55,* 68–78.

Schor, J. (2004). *Born to buy: The commercialized child and the new consumer culture*. New York, NY: Scribner.

Schor, J. (2010). *Plentitude: The new economics of true wealth*. New York, NY: Penguin Press.

Schwartz, S. H. (1992). Universals in the content and structure of values: Theoretical advances and empirical tests in 20 countries. *Advances in Experimental Social Psychology, 25*, 1–65.

Sheldon, K. M., & Kasser, T. (2008). Psychological threat and extrinsic goal striving. *Motivation and Emotion, 32*(1), 37–45.

Sheldon, K. M., & Krieger, L. S. (2014). Service job lawyers are happier than money job lawyers, despite their lower income. *The Journal of Positive Psychology, 9*(3), 219–226.

Surana, P. K., & Lomas, T. (2014). The power of charity: Does giving away money improve the well-being of the donor? *Indian Journal of Positive Psychology, 5*(3), 223–230.

Tsang, J., Carpenter, T. P., Roberts, J. A., Frisch, M. B., & Carlisle, R. D. (2014). Why are materialists less happy? The role of gratitude and need satisfaction in the relationship between materialism and life satisfaction. *Personality and Individual Differences, 64*, 62–66.

Twenge, J. M., Gentile, B., DeWall, C. N., Ma, D., Lacefield, K., & Schurtz, D. R. (2010). Birth cohort increases in psychopathology among young Americans, 1938–2007: A cross-temporal meta-analysis of the MMPI. *Clinical Psychology Review, 30*(2), 145–154.

Van Boven, L. (2005). Experientialism, materialism, and the pursuit of happiness. *Review of General Psychology, 9*(2), 132–142.

Van Boven, L., & Gilovich, T. (2003). To do or to have? That is the question. *Journal of Personality and Social Psychology, 85*(6), 1193–1202.

Vansteenkiste, M., Simons, J., Lens, W., Soenens, B., & Matos, L. (2005). Examining the motivational impact of intrinsic versus extrinsic goal framing and autonomy-supportive versus internally controlling communication style on early adolescents' academic achievement. *Child Development, 76*(2), 483–501.

Wilcox, B., Kunkel, D., Cantor, J., Dowrick, P., Linn, S., & Palmer, E. (2004). Report of the APA Task Force on *advertising and children*. Retrieved from http://www.apa.org/pi/families/resources/advertising -children.pdf

Zhang, H., Tian, Y., Lei, B., Yu, S., & Liu, M. (2015). Personal relative deprivation boosts materialism. *Basic and Applied Social Psychology, 37*(5), 247–259.

Zhang, J. W., Howell, R. T., Caprariello, P. A., & Guevarra, D. A. (2014). Damned if they do, damned if they don't: Material buyers are not happier from material or experiential consumption. *Journal of Research in Personality, 50*, 71–83.

CHAPTER 8

Work

I put my heart and soul into my work, and I have lost my mind in the process.
—Vincent Van Gogh

HAPPINESS AND CAREER SUCCESS

Does Happiness Lead to Success at Work?

Are happy people successful at work? Do they produce more, and do their careers advance faster and farther? Or does happiness drain motivation and make us too easily contented? We examine these important questions in this section. First, though, consider that, as discussed in Chapter 4, happiness is generally good for us. We see here that happy workers also tend to be good workers.

Review of the Evidence

Much of what we know about this topic comes from a meta-analysis review by Lyubomirsky, King, and Diener (2005). These authors proposed that happiness and success in a variety of areas are bidirectionally related. That is, happiness causes success, and success also causes happiness. Furthermore, they hypothesized that happiness leads to success because it first produces thoughts, emotions, and behaviors that help us succeed. In other words, happiness-related thoughts, emotions, and behaviors mediate the relationship between happiness and success.

Building on Fredrickson's (2001) Broaden and Build Theory (BBT), Lyubomirsky et al. (2005) hypothesized that happiness creates feelings of confidence, optimism, and positive energy, among other positive emotions. These emotions are then expected to encourage individuals to approach goals and actively work to achieve them. Happiness is also expected to encourage positive behaviors such as creativity and appropriate conflict resolution strategies, which also increase the probability of success. Furthermore, and closely following Fredrickson's (2001) model, happy individuals' previous experience with positive moods should allow them to acquire many important skills that naturally follow from positive emotions. Therefore, they should have the skills necessary to complete their tasks (Lyubomirsky et al., 2005).

Lyubomirsky et al. (2005) used positive affect (i.e., emotion) as their primary definition of happiness. However, they also used measures of life satisfaction when those were the only measures available in the well-being–success literature. Although life satisfaction involves more of a cognitive appraisal of happiness than an emotional evaluation, Lyubomirsky et al. noted that life satisfaction and positive affect are moderately to highly correlated. They therefore argue that life satisfaction is a good substitute measure for positive affect.

Results of their literature review indicated that happy individuals are successful workers. For instance, happy individuals are more likely to graduate from college and obtain job interviews. They are also more productive at work, receive better job evaluations from their supervisors, and perform better as managers. Happy workers are also better organizational citizens. They are more likely to help coworkers and to go beyond the minimum requirements of their job. They also generate feelings of goodwill at the work site, and are better at resolving conflict.

Finally, happy individuals are often more creative. However, the research results conflict regarding whether happy individuals perform better on complex mental tasks: Happy individuals were found to perform better, worse, or similarly to nonhappy individuals on these tasks. Lyubomirsky et al. suggested that the reason for these conflicting results is that happy individuals use more *heuristics*, or cognitive shortcuts, to solve problems. For instance, they rely on formulas or methods that have worked well in the past, rather than carefully analyzing each problem to see which approach is best. The apparent reason for this approach is that happy individuals are more optimistic and are confident that they can solve problems fairly quickly.

As a result, Lyubomirsky et al. suggested that happy individuals are efficient at solving complex mental problems when their heuristics or cognitive shortcuts apply appropriately to the problem. They also seem to be good complex problem solvers when cues signal that careful thought is necessary. In this case, happy individuals are likely to avoid automatic responses based on simple heuristics. However, if such cues are not available, and/or if the problem is unusual or requires a new approach, happy individuals may perform more poorly. Lyubomirsky et al.'s review of the evidence supports each of these assertions.

There is also support for the larger model. Remember that Lyubomirsky et al. proposed that happiness produces optimism and other positive emotions and behaviors that then lead to success in many domains, including work. Consistent with this hypothesis, Lyubomirsky et al.'s (2005) review showed that happiness activates a series of emotions and behaviors that likely lead to success at work. Among these are emotions such as positive self-perceptions. In addition, the review shows that happy individuals are more cooperative, likable, and creative, and are also better problem solvers. All of these features are likely to enhance one's probability of being successful at work.

Finally, the review also suggested that happiness is a cause of worker success. Evidence from experiments shows that manipulations of happiness are a cause of the hypothesized mediators. Specifically, experimental evidence shows that participants randomly assigned to experience positive emotions are more creative and better able to resolve conflicts than control participants. Furthermore, longitudinal studies, in which participants are followed over time, show that past happiness is associated with work success that occurs later. In other words, happiness that happens before a measure of work success predicts that success. Because happiness is measured before success, these studies make us more confident that happiness is a cause of success, and not merely a consequence of it.

Later reviews led to similar conclusions. Boehm and Lyubomirsky (2008) conducted a literature review focused exclusively on whether happiness might increase career success, rather than general life success. Similarly to the Lyubomirsky et al. (2005) review, Boehm and Lyubomirsky examined experimental, correlational, and longitudinal studies on the topic. They concluded that happiness is likely a cause of career success and that happy workers are more productive, are more helpful and cooperative with coworkers, and exhibit less absenteeism.

Subsequent reviews (e.g., De Neve, Diener, Tay, & Xuereb, 2013; Diener, Oishi, & Lucas, 2015; Erdogan, Bauer, Truxillo, & Mansfield, 2012; Fisher, 2010; Reichard, Avey, Lopez, & Dollwet, 2013; Shockley, Ispas, Rossi, & Levine, 2012), including several meta-analyses, reinforced these conclusions and added other important information. For instance, the level of average positive mood of workers within a work unit predicts positive outcomes for the organization (Fisher, 2010). Thus, not only does positive mood predict performance of individual workers; it also predicts performance on an organizational level. There is also evidence that positive mood can cause important work performance variables (Fisher, 2010).

In addition, changes in individuals' daily positive moods also predict increased creativity and workplace citizenship behaviors (Fisher, 2010). This implies that it is not just that already happy workers are better workers, but that all workers are better workers when they are in a better mood. Thus, attempts by an organization to improve happiness may be beneficial. Although some literature review authors (e.g., Fisher, 2010) have concluded that the size of the positive mood effect is often modest, others have concluded that it is large enough to be financially meaningful to companies. For instance, De Neve et al. (2013) concluded from their review that positive mood can have a large impact on a company's financial success, and Shockley et al. (2012) suggested that companies look for ways to improve their workers' happiness. In conclusion, research clearly shows that positive mood produces benefits for both individual workers and for the companies they work for.

Why Does Happiness Lead to Success?

Now that we know that happiness seems to lead to success, the next question is why does it do so? Haase, Poulin, and Heckhausen (2012) suggested several potential answers, all of which may have some role in the relationship. Positive affect may enhance our sense that our life is meaningful. This sense of life meaning could lead to success because it is associated with better coping skills (King, Hicks, Krull, & Del Gaiso, 2006). Positive affect may also make us more focused on the future (Foo, Uy, & Baron, 2009), which might also have positive consequences for success.

There are some additional reasons why positive affect may foster success (Haase et al., 2012). We discussed Fredrickson's (2001) BBT at the beginning of this section. It is likely that life satisfaction and positive emotions lead to success because they first broaden thoughts so that individuals are more creative and open to new information and experiences. They also help individuals build personal resources and develop new skills that can be applied later. All of these influences would lead happy individuals to have more successes.

Another possibility is that happiness makes us more motivated. Haase et al. (2012) hypothesized that positive affect increases our willingness to commit time and effort to reach goals and makes us more determined to overcome obstacles that stand between us and our goals. Haase et al. (2012) drew their hypothesis from Mood as Information Theory (Schwarz & Clore, 1983), which suggests that we use our present mood as an indicator of the likelihood of future success. According to this theory, positive moods make us think that we have control over our outcomes, and this makes us more motivated to reach our goals. This could also help happy individuals be more successful.

A final possibility is that positive moods help us make controlled, positive, and adaptive behavioral choices, and this increase in self-control might also be part of the reason why positive affect is associated with success (Haase et al., 2012). *Self-control*, defined as the ability to modify our behavior to help us reach long-term goals, is an important factor in life success (Baumeister, Vohs, & Tice, 2007). For instance, we are better able to reach our long-term weight goals if we have the self-control to resist the cookies in front of us right now. Similarly, workers with the self-control to resist distractions are probably more likely to achieve professional success.

Does Career Success Lead to Happiness?

Happy workers are also likely to be successful workers. Happiness does not steal our motivations, nor does it morally corrupt our work ethic. But what about the flip side of this relationship? If happy workers are also better, more efficient workers, is it also true that career success leads to greater happiness? Given the amount of time and energy we devote to work, it seems important to know whether success at work is likely to increase our happiness.

It is surprising how little research is devoted to this question and how much of this research investigates the relationship between salary and income and well-being. As discussed in Chapter 6, this relationship is positive, but modest (Abele-Brehm, 2014).

Aside from salary and income, career success might contribute to happiness in several ways. Certainly individuals might feel proud of their success and might also benefit from having a reputation as a successful person (Abele-Brehm, 2014). Career success might also help meet needs for autonomy and competence (Abele, Hagmaier, & Spurk, 2016), two of the basic psychological needs specified by Self-Determination Theory (SDT; Ryan & Deci, 2000). Successful people are also likely to feel competent and to have a sense of autonomy in that they feel self-directed and in control of their own life decisions. However, work success may also require a huge investment of time and energy, which might take away from attention to family and other relationships. If so, we would expect career success to reduce happiness (Abele et al., 2016).

The limited data on this topic show that career success can both raise and lower happiness in ways explained previously. For instance, some research shows a moderately sized positive relationship between career success and well-being. Leung, Cheung, and Liu (2011) find that career success was associated with higher psychological and physical well-being among professional workers in Hong Kong. These results are significant even after controlling for age, gender, salary, family cohesion, and self-esteem. However, it is also important to know that, for these subjects, social connectedness had a similarly sized relationship to physical well-being and was somewhat more strongly related to psychological well-being than was career success.

Other research shows that career success can also negatively impact well-being. For example, the amount of time one commits to work, and the extent to which one feels that there is not enough time to get work done, are both positively associated with stress via the mediator work-to-family conflict (Parasuraman, Purohit, Godshalk, & Beutell, 1996). These findings suggest that, to the extent that career success requires heavy time commitment to work, career success can be associated with lower personal and family well-being.

Finally, the mixed effects of career success on well-being are apparent in the results of a study of professional workers by Abele et al. (2016). As you can see in Figure 8.1, career success had both positive and negative impacts on their participants' life satisfaction. Career success, which is assessed as a combination of income and work responsibility (e.g., whether the participant could delegate work, whether the participant was in charge of a project), is directly and negatively associated with life satisfaction.

You can also see in this figure that career success is positively related to life satisfaction via the mediator's self-referent and other-referent success evaluations. Self-referent

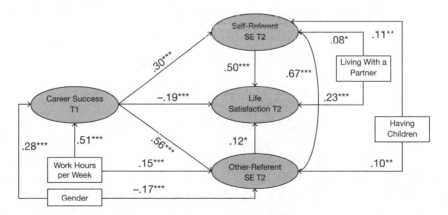

FIGURE 8.1. First mediation model for the association between career success and life satisfaction.
Note: Effects of nonsignificant control variables are not displayed.

SE, success evaluation; $n = 900$.

*$p < .05$; **$p < .01$; ***$p < .001$.

Source: Abele et al. (2016).

success evaluations assess the participant's perceptions of his or her own career success, and other referent assesses the participant's perceptions of his or her career success relative to others with similar credentials (e.g., other college graduates). It is also interesting to note that hours worked each week contributed to career success, and, indirectly, to life satisfaction. Although hours worked each week was rather weakly and positively associated with life satisfaction via other referent, it was more strongly, and negatively, related to life satisfaction via career success (Abele et al., 2015).

In conclusion, Abele et al. (2016) noted that career success is positively, but weakly, related to life satisfaction overall when the effects of the direct path and the two mediated paths are all combined. Therefore, career successful individuals have only slightly greater life satisfaction than do less successful workers. The other research described earlier leads to similar conclusions. So, the take-away here is that striving for career success appears to be a poor method of increasing our life satisfaction. There may be other reasons to strive for a certain level of career success, but we are much more likely to maximize our life satisfaction by concentrating on other goals, such as trying to find satisfying social relationships.

In summary, happiness is not only related to work success; it also appears to cause it. Happy workers are generally more creative, productive, and cooperative. Research even shows that organizational efforts to increase workers' happiness could increase company-wide productivity. Happiness has these positive effects on worker success for several reasons. Consistent with Fredrickson's (2001) BBT, happiness produces thoughts and emotions that make individuals more open to new information and ideas, produces positive energy in the form of optimism and self-confidence, and helps develop new skills. Happiness also benefits workers because it enhances meaning in life, increases motivation, and increases self-control.

It is also true that work success causes happiness, so the relationship is bidirectional. Successful task completions contribute to our happiness. But the effect of career success on happiness appears small. The increased salary that can follow career success, along with feelings of competence, autonomy, and social respect, positively influence happiness. However, these effects appear to be largely cancelled out by the work time commitment and loss of personal and family time that career success often demands.

HOW AND WHY WORK CAN AFFECT HAPPINESS

Work is a vitally important part of most people's lives, and not just because it offers a way to make money to pay the bills. Although the ability to pay our bills obviously affects happiness, work affects our well-being in other ways as well. Caza and Wrzesniewski (2013) catalogue many of these ways, including the sheer amount of time we spend at our jobs. Caza and Wrzesniewski cite evidence that adults spend one third of their waking lives at work. Also, modern communication technology has blurred the lines between home and work for many of us, further increasing work's presence in our lives. We should therefore expect such a dominant force in our lives to have a strong effect on our well-being.

Many of us also spend a tremendous amount of time and energy preparing and training for work before we ever get our first job as an adult, further underlining the importance of work and its ability to affect our happiness. Given the amount of time we spend training for our eventual work lives and then actually working, it is no surprise that work defines many individuals' sense of identity. Self-identity is another pathway by which work can affect our happiness (Caza & Wrzesniewski, 2013).

Work also offers a way to form social relationships, an important source of happiness, and to meet other psychological needs. Work can also help satisfy needs for achievement, meaning, and life purpose, which are also related to better well-being. Therefore, it is clear that work can affect our happiness in many ways. We discuss some of these next using Caza and Wrzesniewski's (2013) categories of "Work as a Contract," "Work Itself," and "Work Context."

General Pathways From Work to Happiness

Work as a Contract

Work is a contract between employees and management, and workers' perceptions of the fairness in the workplace affects their well-being. An important part of the contract involves wages and salaries. The money we earn at work can affect our happiness because it allows us to meet important material needs. However, as we saw in Chapter 6, the direct relationship between income and well-being is rather modest. But money also has important symbolic power (Zhou, Vohs, & Baumeister, 2009) that is reflected in the way that perceptions of the fairness of salaries and wages affect happiness (Caza & Wrzesniewski, 2013). These perceptions, along with perceptions of whether employees are also fairly and justly recognized for their contributions in nonmonetary ways, are known as *distributive justice* (Colquitt, 2001).

However, there are other components of fairness. *Procedural justice* refers to a more general sense of whether employees feel appreciated and that their needs and inputs are considered by the organization. *Interpersonal justice* reflects whether workers feel they are treated respectfully. Finally, *informational justice* is the extent to which workers feel informed about organizational policies and strategies (Colquitt, 2001). All of these perceptions of justice are related to employee well-being (Herr et al., 2015; Ndjaboué, Brisson, & Vézina, 2012; Robbins, Ford, & Tetrick, 2012; Ybema & van den Bos, 2010).

Work Itself

The job satisfaction pathway   The actual work we perform also affects our well-being via several different pathways. One pathway involves job and career satisfaction (Caza & Wrzesniewski, 2013). Job satisfaction does not predict life satisfaction as strongly as do nonwork factors such as social relationships. However, it is positively related to overall life satisfaction and significantly predicts life satisfaction even when personality and nonwork experiences are controlled for (Abele-Brehm, 2014).

What factors predict job and career satisfaction? Jobs with *autonomy* (i.e., opportunity to decide how and when work is completed), *skill variety* (use of a range of skills), *task identity* (focus on the larger whole, not just on subcomponents of the finished product), and *task significance*[1] (work that benefits others) are associated with increased job satisfaction (Grant, Christianson, & Price, 2007). Satisfaction with these job features is also linked to greater life satisfaction (Caza & Wrzesniewski, 2013).

However, work features can sometimes increase some aspects of job satisfaction and overall well-being while simultaneously undermining others. For instance, jobs that give workers lots of responsibility (e.g., autonomy and skill variety) can increase job satisfaction and psychological well-being but decrease physical health by increasing stress. Thus, we see that the relationship between the nature of the actual work we do and our well-being is often complex (Grant et al., 2007). There are other examples of complexity. For instance, many features of work show either an upside-down "U"- or plateau-shaped relationship with well-being, indicating that well-being increases only until job autonomy, skill variety, and so on, reach moderate levels. Once moderate levels of these job features are surpassed, happiness either stops increasing or begins to decrease (Warr, 2013).

There are several reasons why these relationships are not linear. One is that moderate levels of control and other similar job features can appear to be an opportunity, but high levels can seem like a requirement. An employee might be delighted at having moderate control over his or her job, but complete control might lead to an overwhelming sense of responsibility and stress (Warr, 2013).

The meaningfulness pathway   Another pathway that connects work to well-being involves meaningfulness (Caza & Wrzesniewski, 2013; Searle & Parker, 2013). May, Gilson, and Harter (2004) found that measures of task identity, skill variety, task significance, autonomy, and feedback predicted psychological meaningfulness (e.g., "My job activities are personally meaningful to me," p. 36), which is related to general well-being (Caza & Wrzesniewski, 2013). Other research links meaningful work directly to well-being. Steger, Dik, and Duffy (2012) found that a multidimensional measure of meaning in work that assessed "positive meaning" (e.g., "I understand how my work contributes to my life's meaning"), "meaning through work" (e.g., "I view my work as contributing to my personal growth"), and "greater good motivations" ("I know my work makes a positive difference in the world") predicted life satisfaction among a sample of university employees with several different occupations (p. 330). These results were significant even after controlling for job satisfaction and other work-related satisfaction variables.

The structured time pathway   A final pathway is that work can provide a way to structure our time and create a rhythm for our daily lives that gives us a sense of control (Caza & Wrzesniewski, 2013). Jahoda (1981) suggested that income provides an obvious motivation for individuals to work, but that there are also latent, or largely hidden, motivations other than income. Along with the prestige and self-identity we gain from work, these latent motivations include the time structure that work places on our day.

For instance, Jahoda suggested that happiness decreases for the unemployed, and often for retired individuals, because they lose the ability to have a purposeful and predictable schedule in their day. As a result, they cannot enjoy their leisure time.

Research supports Jahoda's hypothesis regarding the importance of time structure. A meta-analysis of the literature by McKee-Ryan, Song, Wanberg, and Kinicki (2005) found that unemployed individuals who reported time-structured and purposeful days were more mentally healthy than those who reported less time structure and purpose in their days.

Work Context

The physical and social environments in which work takes place also affect happiness. Certainly, safe and pleasant physical working environments are essential for well-being (Caza & Wrzesniewski, 2013). But the social environment is also important. Opportunities to give and receive social support and to form meaningful relationships with others can enhance employee well-being (Caza & Wrzesniewski, 2013).

This section focuses on how social environments influence workers' well-being. The amount of practical and emotional support, referred to as *social support*, is an important aspect of the work environment. For instance, social support at work is related to fewer sleeping difficulties (Nordin, Westerholm, Alfredsson, & Åkerstedt, 2012; Sinokki et al., 2010). Social support at work also predicts greater job satisfaction and general well-being and less conflict between work and family roles. A meta-analytic review of the literature by Michel, Mitchelson, Kotrba, LeBreton, and Baltes (2009) found that work-related social support is positively related to satisfaction with family life and is more strongly associated with life satisfaction and job satisfaction. Social support from both supervisors and coworkers are associated with greater well-being.

Data published after Michel et al. (2009) finished their review lead to similar conclusions. Blackmore et al. (2007) found lack of social support at work predicted elevated risk of depression in a sample of almost 37,000 Canadian workers. The sample was largely representative of noninstitutionalized Canadians who were not in the military and did not live in an Indian reservation.

Results showed the importance of social support. Canadian men reporting low work social support were 2.7 times more likely to have had a major depressive episode during the previous 12 months than were their peers with high levels of work related social support. Similarly, Canadian women with low levels of work social support were 2.4 times more likely to have experienced major depression in the previous 12 months than were their peers who experienced high levels of work social support (Blackmore et al., 2007). Stansfeld, Shipley, Head, Fuhrer, and Kivimaki (2013) reported similar results from a sample of more than 5,000 civil servants in Britain. Both studies controlled for sociodemographics, health, and other variables.

The data reported so far largely represent middle-class workers. Other data suggest that social support is not as important for the working poor. Simmons and Swanberg (2009) found no relationship between work social support and depressive symptoms for "working poor" Americans (i.e., those who worked but earned less than two and a half times the federal poverty line). However, social support was associated with fewer depressive symptoms among higher earners. Similarly, Griggs, Casper, and Eby (2013) examined low-wage workers in the Southeastern United States, and found that social support from coworkers was not associated with work-to-family interference, a common measure of the extent to which work interferes with family life. However, social support from work supervisors was associated with less work-to-family interference.

Individual Differences, Work, and Happiness

Work as a Job, a Career, or a Calling

Stable individual traits such as personality, social class, and demographic characteristics also predict work's relationship to happiness (Caza & Wrzesniewski, 2013). One important personality factor is how individuals think of their work. Those who think of their work as a *job* see it as a way to pay the bills and support their family. Other workers, who think of their work as a *career,* seek not only financial rewards, but also the social power and prestige that comes with occupational advancement (Caza & Wrzesniewski, 2013).

Finally, others see their work as a *calling.* These individuals see their work as a part of who they are as a person, and as an important part of their identity. They view their work as vitally important, find it personally fulfilling and meaningful, and think that it can make the world better. As you have probably guessed, individuals who see their work as a calling are generally happier than other workers (Caza & Wrzesniewsk, 2013). For example, Hagmaier and Abele (2015) examined two samples of professionally employed German adults and found that a calling was associated with higher life satisfaction. As seen in Figure 8.2, this relationship was both direct and mediated. The mediated pathway suggests that work as a calling increases self-congruence (i.e., feeling that our actual and idealized selves are closely related) and engagement (i.e., feeling absorbed and challenged by daily tasks), which then increase life satisfaction.

While work calling is associated with greater happiness, having an unanswered calling predicts less happiness. Gazica and Spector (2015) examined a sample of professors

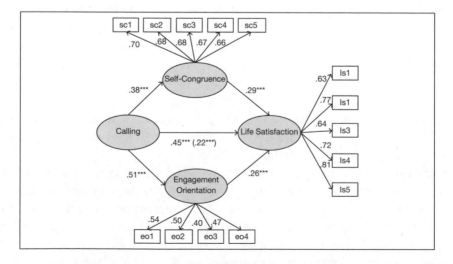

FIGURE 8.2. Structural equation model examining the direct and indirect (see coefficient in parentheses) effects of the realization of one's calling on life satisfaction.
Source: Hagmaier and Abele (2015).

currently employed in public universities around the United States, and found that those with a professional calling had higher well-being than those with no calling. But they also found that professors with an unanswered calling (i.e., those who felt a calling, but did not feel it was their present occupation) had even lower life satisfaction than professors who had felt no professional calling at all.

However, high levels of work as a calling have also been linked to job burnout and other stressors (Caza & Wrzesniewski, 2013). For example, Bunderson and Thompson (2009) examined job calling among American and Canadian zookeepers. The zookeepers felt a strong calling to their profession (the mean calling score was a 6 on a 7-point scale), but there was variability around this mean with some individuals experiencing a stronger calling for their work than others. The results showed the same happiness benefits of a calling demonstrated in other research. For instance, individuals with the highest calling scores found their work the most meaningful and important. However, calling was also associated with the willingness to sacrifice their free time (without pay) to work and to sacrifice personal finances and physical comfort for work. Therefore, workers with a calling were more easily exploited by management. In addition, high calling individuals were more suspicious of the motivations of management.

The Big Five Personality Inventory

Researchers have explored how the Big Five personality inventory (agreeableness, openness to experience, neuroticism, extraversion, and conscientiousness) predicts workers' well-being. For example, Grant and Langan-Fox (2007) found that neuroticism predicted more health problems in a sample of Australian department store managers. The relationship was both direct and indirect. The indirect, or mediated, pathway went through job role conflict, a measure of whether differing employment roles seem to conflict with each other. Thus, neurotics are more likely to view their various job roles (e.g., manager, peer, and subordinate) as conflicting, and this conflict is associated with poorer health.

Other research shows that workers' reactions to job stress can depend on their level of conscientiousness. Lin, Ma, Wang, and Wang (2015) found in a sample of Chinese professional workers that high conscientiousness was associated with greater well-being only if work stressors were low. As seen in Figure 8.3, workers with all levels of conscientiousness had similar levels of (low) well-being if work stress was high. Challenge stressors, the variable on the x-axis of the figure, refer to stress caused by work responsibilities (e.g., the number of projects awaiting completion). A similar pattern was obtained for hindrance stressors, that is, stress caused by workplace obstacles such as office politics.

Lin et al. (2015, p. 105) suggest that conscientiousness is a double-edged sword with a dark side, because the well-being of highly conscientious workers fluctuates so dramatically depending on stress level (although overall, highly conscientious workers have higher well-being). Therefore, conscientiousness is not necessarily a resource that always helps workers, as had been suggested by other researchers. Instead, conscientious workers apparently take their jobs so seriously that they suffer significantly when workplace stress interferes with their ability to perform (Lin et al., 2015).

Other research suggests that positive personality traits in general, rather than specific factors from the Big Five Inventory, are important for workers' well-being.

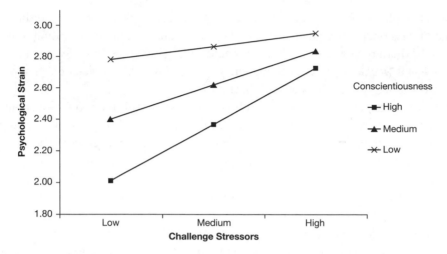

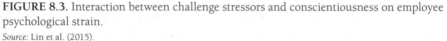

FIGURE 8.3. Interaction between challenge stressors and conscientiousness on employee psychological strain.
Source: Lin et al. (2015).

Braunstein-Bercovitz, Frish-Burstein, and Benjamin (2012) found that Israeli working women who were low in neuroticism and high on all four of the other dimensions of the Big Five had the highest well-being. Rogers, Creed, and Searle (2012) found similar results in a sample of medical students, whose schooling is similar to professional employment.

Thus, we see that work affects happiness via several pathways including perceptions of fairness (work as a contract), the work itself, and the social context in which we work. A sense of fairness at work includes workers' perceptions of being respected and fairly rewarded and has implications for both emotional and physical health. Work that allows freedom to make decisions, use skills, and work on meaningful tasks are most likely to promote happiness, although moderate levels of some of these variables seem most desirable.

Personality, social class, and demographics influence the relationship between work and happiness. Perhaps one of the most interesting of these factors is the extent to which individuals see their work as a calling, or an extension of their identity, rather than as a job or a career. These individuals receive an important sense of life meaning and purpose from their work. Feeling a calling from our work can increase happiness as long as we do not sacrifice too much for our work. Research also shows relationships between happiness, work, and the Big Five personality traits and positive personality traits in general.

WORK AND FAMILY CONFLICT

Work is an important part of our lives. But other aspects of our lives, particularly family life for many of us, are also important. Unfortunately, work often demands a great deal of time and energy that is sometimes subtracted from what we have available for our families. Work can also be stressful, and we sometimes bring this home at the end of the day. This spillover can damage our well-being, including our satisfaction with our family life.

The spillover of fatigue and negative emotions from work to home is referred to as work interference with family (WIF). WIF is high when work roles and expectations are incompatible with those for family (Amstad, Meier, Fasel, Elfering, & Semmer, 2011). This conflict can occur because work expectations take time, energy, and/or psychological resources away from family. The following measures of WIF (Goh, Ilies, & Wilson, 2015, p. 68) are representative of those used in the research we discuss in this section:

► "My work took up time that I would like to spend with family or friends today."

► "The demands of my job made it difficult for me to be relaxed at home today."

► "After work, I came home too tired to do some of the things I would have liked to do."

Why study WIF? Evidence quite securely links it to well-being. WIF also seems to be growing. Williams, Berdahl, and Vandello (2016) report that it has reached an all-time high. Other authors note evidence that workers' hours are increasing and that there are more dual earner couples, which makes it more difficult to juggle careers and families (e.g., Beauregard, 2011; Matias & Fontaine, 2015). Therefore, WIF seems like a potent threat to workers' well-being that deserves close study.

Work Interference With Family (WIF) and Well-Being

Meta-analytic reviews confirm our suspicion that WIF damages well-being. For instance, Amstad et al. (2011, see also Byron, 2005) reviewed 261 separate WIF findings from peer-reviewed studies and found consistently negative associations with various measures of well-being. WIF is most strongly related to work-related measures of well-being such as work-related stress and exhaustion/burnout. However, WIF is also associated with family stress, low life satisfaction, and health problems and is positively related to depression. Thus, well-being is significantly harmed when fatigue and negative emotions spill over from work to family.

You might wonder about the direction of these effects. After all, WIF and well-being are correlational variables, so it is not clear whether well-being is a cause or a consequence of WIF. Fortunately, numerous longitudinal studies have examined the relationship between these variables repeatedly over time to determine how levels of WIF (or well-being) at the beginning of a study predict well-being (or WIF) at the end, thus indicating which variable is the cause and which is the effect.

The results show that the causal flow is *bidirectional* (Nohe, Meier, Sonntag, & Michel, 2015). Thus, when work interferes with family life (for example, because we are tired and stressed), it damages our well-being. At the same time, having low well-being to begin with also increases work's ability to interfere with family life.

Causes of WIF

WIF is predicted by various factors. Michel, Kotrba, Mitchelson, Clark, and Baltes's (2011) meta-analysis of 178 studies found that work role stressors (job stressors, work role ambiguity or conflict, and so on) and work time demands are relatively strongly, and positively, related to WIF. Work social support is consistently related to WIF, although these relationships are weaker and negative. Interestingly, some features of family life (e.g., family stress and family climate) also predict WIF. Additionally, the individual difference factors neuroticism and negative mood predict WIF. Finally, work characteristics (such as salary) are weakly and inconsistently associated with WIF.

There are some interesting twists in the findings. Both work social support and work schedule flexibility predict lower levels of WIF for workers who are either married or are parents than they do for other workers. Similarly, the (negative) relationship between family-friendly organizational policies and WIF is strongest for workers who are parents. Also, the relationship between job stress and WIF is higher (and more positive) for nonparents than for parents, and work time demands are more strongly (positively) related to WIF for nonmarried workers than for marrieds (Michel et al., 2011).

Why would job stress and the amount of time spent at work increase WIF life more for nonparents and nonmarried workers, respectively, than for workers who are parents and married? Michel et al. suggest that these findings reflect the importance of having multiple social roles. Citing Self-Complexity Theory (Linville, 1985), they argue that individuals with multiple social roles (e.g., spouse, parent, and worker) might feel less threatened by stress in one specific domain of their lives. A person with multiple social roles is likely to be a multi-"selved" person, so problems in one category of the self—as a worker, for instance—are less likely to threaten that person's global self-evaluation. Therefore, because the multiple social roles occupied by workers who are also parents buffer or protect their global self-evaluations from threats in any one domain, job stress does not increase WIF as much for them. This is an important hypothesis that we take up again later when we discuss the well-being of women in and out of the workforce.

More recent research by Ilies, Huth, Ryan, and Dimotakis (2015) shows that emotional fatigue is an important mediator that facilitated WIF among a sample of professional teaching, administrative, and support staff from three schools in the midwestern United States. As seen in Figure 8.4, both job demands and stress (affective distress) predicted WIF via the mediator emotional fatigue. Interestingly, neither cognitive nor physical fatigue acted as mediators.[2]

Other research is consistent with these findings. For instance, emotional exhaustion was associated with WIF among a sample of Greek medical doctors, even after controlling for demographic variables, hours worked, and job demands (Montgomery, Panagopolou, & Benos, 2006). Furthermore, research on emotional labor has examined the effects of workplace demands that employees display particular emotions while at work. For example, service workers are often required to smile while at work, regardless of their personal mood. Jobs that require *surface acting*, in which workers pretend to show the organization's desired emotions, are associated with higher levels of WIF and lower levels of well-being (Cheung & Tang, 2009; Montgomery, Panagopolou, de Wildt, & Meenks, 2006). These findings are consistent with the idea that emotional exhaustion is an important predictor of WIF if we assume that the task of faking a smile at work is emotionally draining.

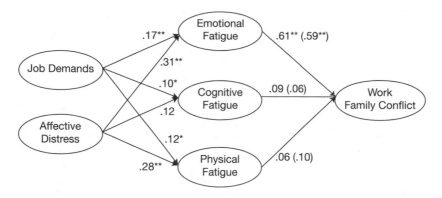

FIGURE 8.4. Parameter estimates obtained from hierarchical linear modeling (HLM). Parameter estimates were estimated with multiple HLM analyses. All regression coefficients are standardized. The coefficients provided in parentheses concern spouse-reported work–family conflict.
*p < .05; **p < .01.
Source: Ilies et al. (2015).

These findings have important implications. Neither having a sore back from lifting heavy objects all day nor having a sore brain from a day spent lifting heavy thoughts at work is likely to interfere with family life. However, coming home emotionally exhausted is another matter, borne out by a story a colleague of mine tells of his days working in a preschool early in his married life. After a long day spent with 4-year-olds, who, by their very nature, do not respect physical space boundaries and need constant emotional attention, he often told his wife that he did not want to be touched for a little while once he got home. What a great example of work interfering with family life!

How WIF Is Related to Well-Being

WIF, Gender, and Exhaustion

Sheer exhaustion is part of why WIF reduces well-being. Demerouti, Bakker, and Schaufeli (2005) confirm the model shown in Figure 8.5, using a sample of Dutch dual-earner parents. As you can see, exhaustion mediates the relationship between WIF (listed in the figure as WFI for work–family interference) and life satisfaction for both men and women. For both genders,[3] WIF is associated with more exhaustion, which is then related to lower life satisfaction. Thus, WIF seems to lower well-being by causing exhaustion.

But you have probably also noticed that these results are gendered in interesting ways. For instance, women's exhaustion predicts men's exhaustion, but the reverse does not seem to be the case. Also, men's life satisfaction predicts women's, but again the reverse does not seem to be true (Demerouti et al., 2005). Thus, exhaustion and life satisfaction relationships cross over from one gender to the other, but they do not do so symmetrically.

What can explain these gender differences? First, the path from women's to men's exhaustion was weak, so we have to be careful interpreting this result (Demerouti et al., 2005). However, Demerouti et al. (2005) hypothesized that both the life satisfaction and

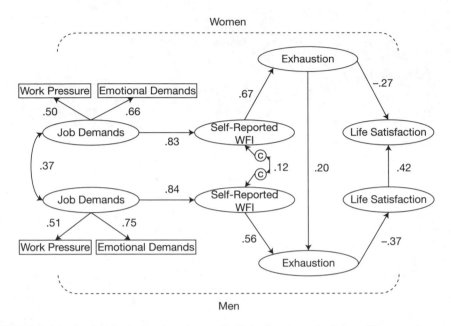

FIGURE 8.5. Standardized solution (maximum likelihood estimates) of the spillover and crossover model for self-reported WFI, $n = 191$ couples.
Source: Demerouti et al. (2005).

the exhaustion crossover relationships are based in gender socialization processes. Regardless of whether they are employed outside the home, women may still be expected to do a greater share of housework and childcare than are men. When working wives become exhausted, a greater share of this household work may shift to their husbands, which would then increase their own exhaustion. Similarly, women may also be socialized to evaluate their own well-being based on the well-being of those around them. However, men may be socialized to evaluate their well-being more individualistically. Thus, husbands' well-being may predict their wives' well-being, but the causal arrow may not flow in the other direction.

Our Use of Work Time

WIF may also reduce our well-being because it makes us use our work time less efficiently (Dahm, Glomb, Manchester, & Leroy, 2015). The logic for this hypothesis goes like this: WIF is emotionally and perhaps even physically draining, even exhausting. This drain on cognitive, emotional, and physical resources is likely to reduce workers' capacity to self-regulate (Baumeister & Vohs, 2007). In other words, workers who are depleted by WIF may find it difficult to control impulses, defer gratification, and focus attention on complex mental tasks (Dahm et al., 2015).

As a result, workers who are emotionally depleted because they are swimming in WIF-induced stress may not have enough impulse control, attentional focus, or ability to delay gratification to complete major, long-term tasks that are essential for their career. The importance of focus and impulse control may be obvious, but it is also important to recognize the role of delayed gratification. Long-term tasks, by definition, mean that the sense of accomplishment, reward, and gratification that comes from completing a task is a long way off in the future.

So WIF-depleted workers may focus on smaller, short-term tasks instead. This type of task may seem very attractive because it requires fewer attentional resources. It also promises the reward of more immediate satisfaction because it can be completed more quickly, and that sense of immediate accomplishment may relieve some WIF-induced stress. The problem is that complicated long-term projects are likely critical for workers' long-term career success and consequent long-term well-being.

Dahm et al. (2015) tested this hypothesis using a sample of American university professors. These professors were required to divide their time between teaching, research, and committee work, but their career prospects were largely dependent on their research productivity. Pilot testing indicated that professors considered research activities to require the most self-regulation. Research tasks were the most complex, were more long-term in nature, and required the most delayed gratification.

Professors were asked how much time they spent on teaching, research, and committee work, and also how much time they ideally would like to spend on each. The difference between actual and ideal time spent on research was calculated to reflect the extent to which professors avoided research tasks for tasks that required less self-regulation. Consistent with hypotheses, the difference between ideal/actual research time partially mediated the relationship between WIF and well-being. Specifically, high WIF professors spent less time conducting research than they ideally would like to. This discrepancy was then related to lower well-being. Thus, the evidence supported the proposition that individuals avoid complex, long-term tasks when experiencing WIF, and that this avoidance is associated with lower well-being (Dahm et al., 2015).

Interestingly, there was a stronger relationship between WIF and idea/actual research time allocations for female than for male professors. Dahm et al. (2015) hypothesize that this is because WIF is more depleting for women than it is for men. Social role conventions that work should not interfere with family seem to apply more strongly to women than to men. The authors also argue that high WIF women may find that alternatives to research, such as committee work, replenish emotional resources particularly well. Committee work is often referred to as "service to the institution," a role that women may be especially socialized for.

Household Labor

The previous discussion shows that WIF depletes workers. As a result, and consistent with the material we discussed earlier, the way we experience work affects our home life. Work affects our happiness not just at work, but also at home. One pathway by which work affects happiness at home is that WIF depletion is often amplified by the way household labor is divided within a couple. Chores such as house cleaning and meal preparation must get done, and young children need care and attention, no matter how drained one feels after work. So couples have to make decisions about how to divide this workload. Research shows that these decisions predict marital satisfaction and general well-being.

For instance, data from a representative sample of adults in the Netherlands found that respondents' mental health rose with the amount of time their family partner spent taking care of children and performing housework (Oomens, Geurts, & Scheepers, 2007). These results were significant even after controlling for family and work characteristics, and demonstrate how important the division of housework and childcare duties are for well-being.

Other research confirms that the division of housework predicts marital satisfaction. A survey of a largely representative sample of American adults by Frisco and Williams (2003) found that those who feel that they do more than their fair share of the housework are less satisfied with their marriage. This relationship was significant for both husbands and wives, although it was stronger for wives. This may be because women continue to do most of the housework, even in developed countries, and this gender difference has persisted even as women have joined the paid workforce (Treas & Lui, 2013).

Frisco and Williams (2003) also found that wives who felt that they did more than their fair share were more than twice as likely to divorce than were wives who felt that housework was fairly divided. Husbands' feelings that they did more than their fair share of housework were unrelated to their odds of divorce. All these findings held after controlling for demographic, family, and work characteristics (Frisco & Williams, 2003).

Several other studies reach similar conclusions (e.g., Claffey & Mickelson, 2009; Kamp Dush & Taylor, 2012; Mikula, Riederer, & Bodi, 2012). So there is a lot of evidence that unfair divisions of household labor lower marital happiness. But there is also evidence that equitable sharing of housework is associated with greater happiness. Specifically, "wives and husbands who spend more hours in housework and paid work report more frequent sex" (Gager & Yabiku, 2010, p. 135).

Importance of National Policies and Culture

Much of the research has focused on individual- and organizational-level causes of WIF. For instance, in the meta-analysis by Michel et al. (2011) described earlier, stress, personality, and family and work characteristics were identified as predictors of WIF. Other research (e.g., Ilies et al., 2015) showed that individuals' emotional fatigue predicted WIF. We also saw that research links WIF to well-being through individual factors such as exhaustion (Demerouti et al., 2005), use of work time (Dahm et al., 2015), and various family factors (Bakker, Demerouti, & Burke, 2009).

Following this tradition, much of the research examining potential ways to reduce WIF and increase well-being has focused on individual factors or on local work settings. For example, Versey (2015, pp. 1673, 1674) examined whether *positive reappraisals* (e.g., "When I am faced with a bad situation, it helps to find a different way of looking at things") and *lowered aspirations* (e.g., "When my expectations are not being met, I lower my expectations") might protect employees from the negative results of WIF. Results indicated that reappraisals offered some well-being protection against WIF. Similarly, Matias and Fontaine (2015) found that workers' planning and management skills protect well-being against WIF. As a final example of the relatively local approach to addressing WIF's negative relationship to well-being, a meta-analysis by Kossek, Pichler, Bodner, and Hammer (2011) showed that workers' impressions of supervisor and organizational (i.e., company) support for family concerns predicted well-being.

However, other research examines how structural factors predict WIF and well-being. Specifically, researchers have studied how national cultural norms about work (e.g., Williams et al., 2016) and national policies, such as laws regarding parental leave (e.g., Allen et al., 2014), are related to WIF and well-being. Writing in the *Annual Review of Psychology*, Williams et al. (2016) specifically note the lack of research focus on these structural issues, and urge that more attention be drawn to these.

National Policies

National policies toward sick leave and family leave are examples of structural variables that can have important influences on WIF. For instance, some countries have national labor policies requiring employers to grant maternity and paternity leave to workers, while others do not have such policies. Some countries also have national policies mandating a minimum number of paid sick leave days. Is WIF less of a problem in countries with such policies?

Allen et al. (2014) found that some national labor policies were related to WIF. However, we will also see that the effects of these national policies depended heavily upon local organizational culture and policies. They addressed this question by sampling workers from a variety of industrialized countries. All participants were managers, married, and had young children at home.

Specifically, workers in countries with stronger national parental leave policies experienced *less* WIF if they felt that their workplace was not supportive of family concerns ("The way to advance is to keep non-work matters out of the workplace," Allen et al., 2014, p. 12). However, national parental leave policy was *not related* to WIF for workers who perceived that their work organization was supportive of family concerns. The pattern was reversed concerning nationally mandated sick leave policy. National sick leave policy was *not related* to WIF if workers felt that their workplace was unsupportive of family concerns. However, national sick leave policy predicted *less* WIF if workers perceived that their workplace was supportive of family concerns (Allen et al., 2014).

The most important point is that national family leave policies were not independently related to WIF. Instead, their effect was moderated by (in other words, depended upon) the organization's policies and culture at local workplaces. For instance, national parental leave policies only reduced WIF for workers whose companies were not supportive of family concerns, and national sick leave policies only reduced WIF for workers whose companies were supportive of family concerns. These findings led Allen et al. (2014) to conclude that national leave policies are not a cure-all for WIF concerns. Obviously, local company policies and cultures are also important.

Cultural Norms

Williams et al. (2016) argue that American cultural norms directed toward white-collar professional workers define a "good person," a "good man," and a "good woman" in terms of their commitment to their work. This results in the *work devotion schema*, which is the idea that cultural definitions of being a "good" and even a "moral" person require such a devotion to work that it becomes the central focus of life. Family concerns are not supposed to distract from this focus on work. As a result, WIF soars because the boundaries between work and home become heavily blurred. In the process, workers' individual identities become defined by their work. As we will see, this identity as someone devoted to work makes it difficult to solve WIF-related well-being problems (Williams et al., 2016).

The work devotion schema applies most straightforwardly to professional, white-collar men. There are several reasons for this (Williams et al., 2016). First, devotion to work for these men can reflect moral purity. For men in this social class, cultural norms dictate that "good" men are those who work extremely hard, are productive, and are financially successful. Second, devotion to work also signals elite social class status of professional men. Blue-collar men want to be seen as "good providers" for their families, but they resist defining themselves by their work, and they tend to want to keep strict boundaries between work and home. Therefore, work devotion is something that separates blue-collar men from professional men, and serves as a marker of social class.

Finally, the work devotion schema applies particularly well to professional men because it is closely linked to the masculinity in this social class. For instance, Williams et al. (2016) reviewed studies of male engineers and surgeons who think of their long work hours as evidence of their "iron man" status, and a signal of their ranking in a machismo work culture. Williams et al. (2016) also cited evidence that men who took advantage of family leave programs, or discussed their family caregiving responsibilities while at work, suffered from a *flexibility stigma*. Their masculinity was questioned because they seemed less committed to work. This resulted in a loss of interpersonal status at work and career penalties from their companies.

The same logic of cultural norms aggrandizing work also applies to professional women, but in more complicated ways. Professional women face the same "work devotion" pressures to prioritize work over home as do professional men. However, cultural forces catch women in a difficult push/pull dynamic that also demands that they be devoted mothers and wives. This situation is further complicated by conflict between professional working women who are parents and those who are not parents. Both groups can feel that the other has violated an important social norm. Working mothers can cite the importance of being available for their children, while nonparents can cite the importance of being devoted to work. Importantly, regardless of which side of the divide a professional woman is on, the work devotion norm creates the potential for WIF (Williams et al., 2016).

Norms, Identity, and Their Implications

Williams et al. (2016) argue that these cultural norms celebrating work devotion help to cement in patterns of overwork that become central to an individual's identity. These authors also argue that overwork as an identity makes it difficult to reduce WIF. Identities are psychologically comforting and, once established, are difficult to change. Also, challenges to our identity, almost by definition, seem like a direct threat to our very selves. Therefore, if I see myself as a devoted worker who admirably puts in long hours at the office, I am likely to react negatively to any reforms (such as reducing work hours or instituting a flexible work schedule) aimed at reducing WIF.

As a result, Williams et al. (2016) argue that many professional workers themselves are likely to resist efforts to reduce WIF, even when data indicate that WIF lowers their well-being. These workers' personal identities are simply too heavily defined by devotion to work to tolerate suggestions that they should reduce work hours and prioritize family time. Similarly, business leaders also resist efforts to reduce WIF. For example, there is a long-standing, data-driven, "business case" for addressing WIF that suggests that companies can save money by helping their workers live more balanced lives. Yet companies are not persuaded. Williams et al. (2016) hypothesized that this is because businesses have also been captured by the social norms and psychological identity pressures surrounding work devotion.

What can be done? Williams et al. (2016) suggest that structural changes that address work culture are necessary. To these authors, WIF cannot be adequately addressed without also addressing cultural norms that demand devotion to work, and that define moral purity, masculinity, and social status in terms of prioritizing work over family. Although structural issues such as culture are typically the domain of sociologists, there are ample opportunities for psychologists to make important contributions.

But according to Williams et al. (2016), these contributions are not likely to come from research on strictly individual difference variables such as optimism and self-efficacy. Williams et al. (2016) acknowledge that personality variables such as these predict WIF such that less optimistic workers are likely to suffer more from work pressures. However, they also maintain that even psychologically healthy workers are likely to become maladjusted if they remain in work devotion schema cultures for very long. Instead, Williams et al. (2016) argue that psychologists should address workers' identity concerns. Identity is a psychological issue, and it is the crucial connector between social norms and individual behavior. According to these authors, workers who avoid forming work devotion identities are likely to have greater well-being.

Women, Work, and Happiness

It seems appropriate to end this section about work and family conflict with a discussion of work and the happiness of women with children. Are women with children happier if they work outside the home? This question is likely critical to understanding work-to-family conflict. Women still devote substantially more time toward domestic tasks than do men (Treas & Lui, 2013). This imbalance persists even among dual earner couples and becomes stronger after the birth of a child (Yavorsky, Dush, & Schoppe-Sullivan, 2015).

This gender imbalance in family workload suggests that families with working mothers are seething in work-to-family conflict. As a result, we might expect these mothers to be unhappy. In fact, the *role strain hypothesis* (Goode, 1960) predicts just that. This idea is that multiple roles will often conflict with each other. For instance, our duties as a parent, spouse, and worker often pull us in widely differing directions: We might feel the need to work late, but we would also like to attend our child's play at school, or have dinner with our spouse.

According to the Role Strain Theory, the strain of fulfilling these conflicting roles produces stress. There is some real truth here, as an even casual observer of modern life can easily see. It is stressful to juggle the demands of work, family, personal interests and hobbies, and so on, and this stress can affect our happiness. The theory also predicts that a certain amount of role strain is an inevitable part of modern life. However, the clear implication is that individuals would be happier if they could reduce the number of *conflicting* roles they fulfill. This suggests that mothers who work outside the home should be less happy because of their often conflicting roles.

However, the Role Accumulation Theory (Sieber, 1974) predicts that multiple roles enhance well-being overall, even if they do lead to some stress when they conflict with each other. The important idea here is that multiple roles such as being a spouse, worker, parent, volunteer, and so on, provide benefits that outweigh any stress caused by role conflict. These benefits include a buffer against the psychological consequences of failure in any one role.

For instance, if a woman is both a mother and a worker, a setback at work may not be as psychologically painful as it might have been if she were only a worker. Because her identity includes more than one dimension, she can "fall back" on other dimensions when things are not going well in one aspect of her life. This same process may also help protect an individual's social status. A setback in one role may not undermine one's social status as much if he or she occupies several social roles and can demonstrate competence in other roles (Sieber, 1974).

Another potential benefit in occupying multiple roles is that this connects us to more people. For example, a woman who is both a mother and a worker is likely to know individuals at her work and at her child's preschool. These connections can offer tangible and emotional benefits including business and social opportunities and additional sources of friendship and social support (Sieber, 1974).

Finally, multiple roles may offer opportunities for excitement and "change of pace" that help keep us mentally and emotionally stimulated in ways that a person who occupies only a single role may find hard to do. The additional opportunities provided by multiple roles to meet new people, see and learn new things, and have different experiences could be quite valuable. These opportunities can also help us build new skills that may transfer across roles. As a result, we may be able to develop a synergy in which activities in our various roles benefit our performance in other roles (Sieber, 1974).

I wade into this discussion cautiously, because it concerns emotional issues that touch upon deeply held values. Because of this, it is important to emphasize that the data cannot tell us whether women *should* work outside the home or not. This is a personal choice best left up to each individual woman. But we can still examine the data on the happiness of women who make different choices.

Data: Mental and Physical Health

So, what does the data say? We will start by discussing findings for happiness, and will discuss findings for health later. For happiness at least, the data generally indicate that mothers with romantic partners and paid employment outside the home are as happy, or happier, than their stay-at-home, romantically partnered counterparts (Barnett, 2004; Castro & Gordon, 2012; Klumb & Lampert, 2004; Plaisier, de Bruijn, et al., 2008; Roos, Burström, Saastamoinen, & Lahelma, 2005). A lot depends on the quality of their jobs (Plaisier, Beekman, et al., 2008). For instance, mothers with low-quality jobs that do not allow them to use their skills do not benefit from the additional role of paid employment (Oomens et al., 2007). These findings lend at least partial support to the role strain hypothesis. The addition of a low-quality role appears to add to a woman's stress, and does not increase her happiness (Oomens et al., 2007).

However, a high-quality job—for instance, one that allows her to use skills—can increase a mother's happiness relative to that of a stay-at-home mom (Barnett, 2004; Castro & Gordon, 2012; Oomens et al., 2007). Although this appears to offer partial support for the role accumulation hypothesis (although not all new roles can boost happiness, ones that are of high quality can and often do), this support is weak. First, several researchers conclude that the number of a woman's roles is not the central issue, but rather the quality of those roles (e.g., Barnett, 2004; Gervais & Millear, 2014; Plaisier, Beekman, et al., 2008; Scalea et al., 2012; Sumra & Schillaci, 2015). Contrary to a strict interpretation of the role accumulation hypothesis, becoming an employee, and therefore gaining an additional role, does not automatically increase happiness.

Second, the *combination* of being a romantic partner, and a mother, and a worker, rarely predicts greater happiness (Klumb & Lampert, 2004; Oomens et al., 2007; Plaisier, Beekman, et al., 2008; Plaisier, de Bruijn, et al., 2008). Instead, work itself seems to have a singular positive effect on happiness, regardless of which other roles a woman occupies. In other words, (high-quality) work is beneficial regardless of whether a woman is a mother or in a romantic relationship, and so on. This finding offers only weak support for the role accumulation hypothesis. This is because the hypothesis predicts that it is the *combination* of multiple roles, and not any particular role, that enhances happiness.

So far we have discussed the happiness only of employed moms. Interestingly, quite a bit of evidence suggests that employed moms are healthier than their stay-at-home counterparts (e.g., Janzen & Muhajarine, 2003; Lahelma, Arber, Kivelä, & Roos, 2002; McMunn, Bartley, & Kuh, 2006; Wahrendorf, 2015). For instance, McMunn et al. (2006) found that homemakers (stay-at-home moms) were 88% more likely to report poor health at age 54 than were women who occupied the roles of mother, spouse, and worker. These results come from a longitudinal study of British women, and are significant even after controlling for work quality, family and work stress, and social class. Table 8.1 gives another interesting perspective on their findings.

Some researchers conclude that the quality of employment matters for women's health, and thus find partial evidence for the role strain hypothesis (e.g., Castro & Gordon, 2012; Janssen et al., 2012). However, McMunn et al. (2006) attribute their findings that working moms are healthier as support for the Role Accumulation Theory (they refer to it as *role enhancement*). In their view, multiple roles, including paid work outside the home, increases health by increasing a woman's sense of *agency*, or her power to act freely. McMunn et al. (2006) argue that agency is a basic human need that affects both psychological and physical health. Janzen and Muhajarine (2003), who also found

TABLE 8.1 Self-Reported Health at Age 54 by Role Histories Among Women in the NSHD 1946 Birth Cohort

Self-Reported Health	n	Multiple Roles (%)	Homemakers (%)	Lone Mothers (%)	Childless (%)	Remarried Mothers (%)	Intermittent Employed Married Mothers (%)
Excellent	125	13.0	2.6	11.4	11.3	7.9	11.2
Good	665	60.5	55.6	52.2	52.5	58.9	53.6
Fair	322	23.0	33.3	32.1	28.4	27.2	31.2
Poor	59	3.5	8.5	4.3	7.8	6.0	4.0
Total	1,171	100	100	100	100	100	100

NSHD, National Study of Health and Development.

a link between women's multiple roles and health among a sample of Canadian women, likewise interpret their own results in terms of the Role Accumulation Theory.

In conclusion, mothers who work outside the home are generally not less happy than stay-at-home moms, and may be happier. The quality of their work life is a critically important determinant of their happiness. Moms with high-quality jobs that allow them to use their skills are particularly likely to experience a happiness benefit. It also appears though that working moms are generally healthier than stay-at-home moms.

These results offer mixed support for the two theoretical perspectives discussed earlier. The fact that job quality is important lends partial support to the role strain hypothesis. However, research on working moms and health lend support for the role accumulation hypothesis. I should note, however, that this review of the multiple roles hypotheses is limited to research about working versus stay-at-home moms, and should not be taken as a statement about the overall validity of either theory.

Work can interfere with family life and this can lower happiness. Research indicates that WIF is increasing. Stressful and demanding work is likely to increase WIF. Emotional fatigue is a primary contributor in WIF, and it also explains much of WIF's effects on life satisfaction.

WIF also affects well-being through the division of household chores among romantic partners. Perhaps because of increasing work stress in recent years, the distribution of housework and childcare predicts several measures of well-being, including the probability of divorce. Interestingly, family dynamics can alter these relationships. For instance, feelings of gratitude and appreciation from one's partner can lessen perceptions that housework is distributed unfairly.

Much of the research on lessening the negative effects of WIF has concentrated on ways in which individuals can reappraise their situation; thus, emphasizing individuals' responsibility makes them happier by changing their responses to WIF. However, some research has examined the effects of national policies such as family leave, and how these might reduce WIF and its negative consequences. Some of this research shows promising results, but the effects of national policies depend heavily on the culture of the local workplace. Cultural norms about how a "good person" and a "good worker" are defined are also important. It will be difficult to lessen WIF as long as there is a "work devotion schema" that overly emphasizes work among professionals.

Finally, the happiness of working moms is an important and controversial issue. Mothers with paid employment outside the home are as happy as, or happier than, stay-at-home moms. Evidence suggests that working moms are also healthier. However, the quality of a mother's paid employment is quite important. Most of the well-being benefits for working outside the home are associated with high-quality work that allows women to use skills and that provide them some control over their working lives.

SUMMARY

Work can bring happiness under the right circumstances. It is also true that happy individuals are better and more generally successful workers. However, career success is an inefficient method of improving happiness: Its effects on happiness are very small. Thus, it is wonderful when we find meaning, joy, and happiness from our work, but this is most likely to happen when we find work that is intrinsically interesting. Pursuing a successful career for its own sake (absent intrinsic interest in the work) is not likely to markedly improve our happiness.

Several features of work, including characteristics of the work itself and of the social environment at work, can promote our happiness. But it is also important to recognize the tremendous power work has to interfere with our family lives and thereby erode our happiness. Finding ways to protect ourselves from this possibility is an essential component of a positive work–happiness relationship.

NOTES

1. Definitions of italicized terms are from Grant et al. (2007).

2. Note that there are not any significant paths (marked by asterisks) that go all the way from job demands or affective distress to WIF in Figure 8.4.

3. Note that the results for women are listed in the top half of Figure 8.5, and the results for men are listed in the bottom half.

REFERENCES

Abele, A. E., Hagmaier, T., & Spurk, D. (2016). Does career success make you happy? The mediating role of multiple subjective success evaluations. *Journal of Happiness Studies, 17*(4), 1615–1633.

Abele-Brehm, A. (2014). The influence of career success on subjective well-being. In A. C. Keller, R. Samuel, M. M. Bergman, & N. K. Semmer (Eds.), *Psychological, educational, and sociological perspectives on success and well-being in career development* (pp. 7–18). New York, NY: Springer Science + Business Media.

Allen, T. D., Lapierre, L. M., Spector, P. E., Poelmans, S. A. Y., O'Driscoll, M., Sanchez, J. I., . . . Woo, J. (2014). The link between national paid leave policy and work–family conflict among married working parents. *Applied Psychology: An International Review, 63*(1), 5–28.

Amstad, F. T., Meier, L. L., Fasel, U., Elfering, A., & Semmer, N. K. (2011). A meta-analysis of work–family conflict and various outcomes with a special emphasis on cross-domain versus matching-domain relations. *Journal of Occupational Health Psychology, 16*(2), 151–169.

Bakker, A. B., Demerouti, E., & Burke, R. (2009). Workaholism and relationship quality: A spillover-crossover perspective. *Journal of Occupational Health Psychology, 14*(1), 23–33.

Barnett, R. C. (2004). Women and multiple roles: Myths and reality. *Harvard Review of Psychiatry, 12*, 158–164.

Baumeister, R. F., & Vohs, K. D. (2007). Self-regulation, ego depletion, and motivation. *Social and Personality Psychology Compass, 1*(1), 115–128.

Baumeister, R. F., Vohs, K. D., & Tice, D. M. (2007). The strength model of self-control. *Current Directions in Psychological Science, 16*(6), 351–355.

Beauregard, T. A. (2011). Direct and indirect links between organizational work–home culture and employee well-being. *British Journal of Management, 22*(2), 218–237.

Blackmore, E. R., Stansfeld, S. A., Weller, I., Munce, S., Zagorski, B. M., & Stewart, D. E. (2007). Major depressive episodes and work stress: Results from a national population survey. *American Journal of Public Health*, 97(11), 2088–2093.

Boehm, J. K., & Lyubomirsky, S. (2008). Does happiness promote career success? *Journal of Career Assessment*, 16(1), 101–116.

Braunstein-Bercovitz, H., Frish-Burstein, S., & Benjamin, B. A. (2012). The role of personal resources in work–family conflict: Implications for young mothers' well-being. *Journal of Vocational Behavior*, 80(2), 317–325.

Bunderson, J. S., & Thompson, J. A. (2009). The call of the wild: Zookeepers, callings, and the double-edged sword of deeply meaningful work. *Administrative Science Quarterly*, 54(1), 32–57.

Byron, K. (2005). A meta-analytic review of work–family conflict and its antecedents. *Journal of Vocational Behavior*, 67(2), 169–198.

Castro, Y., & Gordon, K. H. (2012). A review of recent research on multiple roles and women's mental health. In P. K. Lundberg-Love, K. L. Nadal, & M. A. Paludi (Eds.), *Women and mental disorders* (pp. 37–54). Santa Barbara, CA: Praeger/ABC-CLIO.

Caza, B. B., & Wrzesniewski, A. (2013). How work shapes well-being. In S. A. David, I. Boniwell, & A. Conley Ayers (Eds.), *The Oxford handbook of happiness* (pp. 693–710). New York, NY: Oxford University Press.

Cheung, F. Y., & Tang, C. S. (2009). The influence of emotional intelligence and affectivity on emotional labor strategies at work. *Journal of Individual Differences*, 30(2), 75–86.

Claffey, S. T., & Mickelson, K. D. (2009). Division of household labor and distress: The role of perceived fairness for employed mothers. *Sex Roles*, 60(11–12), 819–831.

Colquitt, J. A. (2001). On the dimensionality of organizational justice: A construct validation of a measure. *Journal of Applied Psychology*, 86(3), 386–400.

Dahm, P. C., Glomb, T. M., Manchester, C. F., & Leroy, S. (2015). Work–family conflict and self-discrepant time allocation at work. *Journal of Applied Psychology*, 100(3), 767.

Demerouti, E., Bakker, A. B., & Schaufeli, W. B. (2005). Spillover and crossover of exhaustion and life satisfaction among dual-earner parents. *Journal of Vocational Behavior*, 67(2), 266–289.

De Neve, J.-E., Diener, E., Tay, L., & Xuereb, C. (2013). The objective benefits of subjective well-being. In J. Helliwell, R. Layard, & J. Sachs (Eds.), *World Happiness Report 2013*. New York, NY: UN Sustainable Development Solutions Network. Retrieved from https://ssrn.com/abstract=2306651

Diener, E., Oishi, S., & Lucas, R. E. (2015). National accounts of subjective well-being. *American Psychologist*, 70(3), 234–242.

Erdogan, B., Bauer, T. N., Truxillo, D. M., & Mansfield, L. R. (2012). Whistle while you work: A review of the life satisfaction literature. *Journal of Management*, 38(4), 1038–1083.

Fisher, C. D. (2010). Happiness at work. *International Journal of Management Reviews*, 12(4), 384–412.

Foo, M., Uy, M. A., & Baron, R. A. (2009). How do feelings influence effort? An empirical study of entrepreneurs' affect and venture effort. *Journal of Applied Psychology*, 94(4), 1086–1094.

Fredrickson, B. L. (2001). The role of positive emotions in positive psychology: The broaden-and-build theory of positive emotions. *American Psychologist*, 56(3), 218–226.

Frisco, M. L., & Williams, K. (2003). Perceived housework equity, marital happiness, and divorce in dual-earner households. *Journal of Family Issues, 24*(1), 51–73.

Gager, C. T., & Yabiku, S. T. (2010). Who has the time? The relationship between household labor time and sexual frequency. *Journal of Family Issues, 31*(2), 135–163.

Gazica, M. W., & Spector, P. E. (2015). A comparison of individuals with unanswered callings to those with no calling at all. *Journal of Vocational Behavior, 91*, 1–10.

Gervais, R. L., & Millear, P. (2014). The well-being of women at work: The importance of resources across the life course. *Journal of Organizational Change Management, 27*(4), 598–612.

Goh, Z., Ilies, R., & Wilson, K. S. (2015). Supportive supervisors improve employees' daily lives: The role supervisors play in the impact of daily workload on life satisfaction via work–family conflict. *Journal of Vocational Behavior, 89*, 65–73.

Goode, W. J. (1960). A theory of role strain. *American Sociological Review, 25*, 483–496.

Grant, A. M., Christianson, M. K., & Price, R. H. (2007). Happiness, health, or relationships? Managerial practices and employee well-being tradeoffs. *The Academy of Management Perspectives, 21*(3), 51–63.

Grant, S., & Langan-Fox, J. (2007). Personality and the occupational stressor-strain relationship: The role of the Big Five. *Journal of Occupational Health Psychology, 12*(1), 20–33.

Griggs, T. L., Casper, W. J., & Eby, L. T. (2013). Work, family and community support as predictors of work–family conflict: A study of low-income workers. *Journal of Vocational Behavior, 82*(1), 59–68.

Haase, C. M., Poulin, M. J., & Heckhausen, J. (2012). Happiness as a motivator: Positive affect predicts primary control striving for career and educational goals. *Personality and Social Psychology Bulletin, 38*(8), 1093–1104.

Hagmaier, T., & Abele, A. E. (2015). When reality meets ideal: Investigating the relation between calling and life satisfaction. *Journal of Career Assessment, 23*(3), 367–382.

Herr, R. M., Loerbroks, A., van Vianen, A. E. M., Hoffmann, K., Fischer, J. E., & Bosch, J. A. (2015). Injustice at work and leukocyte glucocorticoid sensitivity: Findings from a cross-sectional study. *Psychosomatic Medicine, 77*(5), 527–538.

Ilies, R., Huth, M., Ryan, A. M., & Dimotakis, N. (2015). Explaining the links between workload, distress, and work–family conflict among school employees: Physical, cognitive, and emotional fatigue. *Journal of Educational Psychology, 107*(4), 1136–1149.

Jahoda, M. (1981). Work, employment, and unemployment: Values, theories, and approaches in social research. *American Psychologist, 36*(2), 184–191.

Janssen, I., Powell, L. H., Jasielec, M. S., Matthews, K. A., Hollenberg, S. M., Sutton-Tyrrell, K., & Everson-Rose, S. (2012). Progression of coronary artery calcification in Black and White women: Do the stresses and rewards of multiple roles matter? *Annals of Behavioral Medicine, 43*(1), 39–49.

Janzen, B. L., & Muhajarine, N. (2003). Social role occupancy, gender, income adequacy, life stage and health: A longitudinal study of employed Canadian men and women. *Social Science and Medicine, 57*(8), 1491–1503.

Kamp Dush, C. M., & Taylor, M. G. (2012). Trajectories of marital conflict across the life course: Predictors and interactions with marital happiness trajectories. *Journal of Family Issues, 33*(3), 341–368.

King, L. A., Hicks, J. A., Krull, J. L., & Del Gaiso, A. K. (2006). Positive affect and the experience of meaning in life. *Journal of Personality and Social Psychology, 90*(1), 179–196.

Klumb, P. L., & Lampert, T. (2004). Women, work, and well-being 1950–2000: A review and methodological critique. *Social Science and Medicine, 58*(6), 1007–1024.

Kossek, E. E., Pichler, S., Bodner, T., & Hammer, L. B. (2011). Workplace social support and work–family conflict: A meta-analysis clarifying the influence of general and work–family-specific supervisor and organizational support. *Personnel Psychology, 64*(2), 289–313.

Lahelma, E., Arber, S., Kivelä, K., & Roos, E. (2002). Multiple roles and health among British and Finnish women: The influence of socioeconomic circumstances. *Social Science and Medicine, 54*(5), 727–740.

Leung, A. S. M., Cheung, Y. H., & Liu, X. (2011). The relations between life domain satisfaction and subjective well-being. *Journal of Managerial Psychology, 26*(2), 155–169.

Lin, W., Ma, J., Wang, L., & Wang, M. (2015). A double-edged sword: The moderating role of conscientiousness in the relationships between work stressors, psychological strain, and job performance. *Journal of Organizational Behavior, 36*(1), 94–111.

Linville, P. W. (1985). Self-complexity and affective extremity: Don't put all of your eggs in one cognitive basket. *Social Cognition, 3*(1), 94–120.

Lyubomirsky, S., King, L., & Diener, E. (2005). The benefits of frequent positive affect: Does happiness lead to success? *Psychological Bulletin, 131*(6), 803–855.

Matias, M., & Fontaine, A. M. (2015). Coping with work and family: How do dual-earners interact? *Scandinavian Journal of Psychology, 56*(2), 212–222.

May, D. R., Gilson, R. L., & Harter, L. M. (2004). The psychological conditions of meaningfulness, safety and availability and the engagement of the human spirit at work. *Journal of Occupational and Organizational Psychology, 77*(1), 11–37.

McKee-Ryan, F. M., Song, Z., Wanberg, C. R., & Kinicki, A. J. (2005). Psychological and physical well-being during unemployment: A meta-analytic study. *Journal of Applied Psychology, 90*(1), 53–76.

McMunn, A., Bartley, M., & Kuh, D. (2006). Women's health in mid-life: Life course social roles and agency as quality. *Social Science and Medicine, 63*(6), 1561–1572.

Michel, J. S., Kotrba, L. M., Mitchelson, J. K., Clark, M. A., & Baltes, B. B. (2011). Antecedents of work–family conflict: A meta-analytic review. *Journal of Organizational Behavior, 32*(5), 689–725.

Michel, J. S., Mitchelson, J. K., Kotrba, L. M., LeBreton, J. M., & Baltes, B. B. (2009). A comparative test of work–family conflict models and critical examination of work–family linkages. *Journal of Vocational Behavior, 74*(2), 199–218.

Mikula, G., Riederer, B., & Bodi, O. (2012). Perceived justice in the division of domestic labor: Actor and partner effects. *Personal Relationships, 19*(4), 680–695.

Montgomery, A. J., Panagopolou, E., & Benos, A. (2006). Work–family interference as a mediator between job demands and job burnout among doctors. *Stress and Health, 22*(3), 203–212.

Montgomery, A. J., Panagopolou, E., de Wildt, M., & Meenks, E. (2006). Work–family interference, emotional labor and burnout. *Journal of Managerial Psychology, 21*(1), 36–51.

Ndjaboué, R., Brisson, C., & Vézina, M. (2012). Organisational justice and mental health: A systematic review of prospective studies. *Occupational and Environmental Medicine, 69*(10), 694–700.

Nohe, C., Meier, L. L., Sonntag, K., & Michel, A. (2015). The chicken or the egg? A meta-analysis of panel studies of the relationship between work–family conflict and strain. *Journal of Applied Psychology, 100*(2), 522–536.

Nordin, M., Westerholm, P., Alfredsson, L., & Åkerstedt, T. (2012). Social support and sleep: Longitudinal relationships from the WOLF study. *Psychology, 3*(12A), 1223–1230.

Oomens, S., Geurts, S., & Scheepers, P. (2007). Combining work and family in the Netherlands: Blessing or burden for one's mental health? *International Journal of Law and Psychiatry, 30*(4–5), 369–384.

Parasuraman, S., Purohit, Y. S., Godshalk, V. M., & Beutell, N. J. (1996). Work and family variables, entrepreneurial career success and psychological well-being. *Journal of Vocational Behavior, 48*(3), 275–300.

Plaisier, I., Beekman, A. T. F., de Bruijn, J. G. M., de Graaf, R., ten Have, M., Smit, J. H., . . . Penninx, B. W. J. H. (2008). The effect of social roles on mental health: A matter of quantity or quality? *Journal of Affective Disorders, 111*(2–3), 261–270.

Plaisier, I., de Bruijn, J. G. M., Smit, J. H., de Graaf, R., ten Have, M., Beekman, A. T. F., . . . Penninx, B. W. J. H. (2008). Work and family roles and the association with depressive and anxiety disorders: Differences between men and women. *Journal of Affective Disorders, 105*(1–3), 63–72.

Reichard, R. J., Avey, J. B., Lopez, S., & Dollwet, M. (2013). Having the will and finding the way: A review and meta-analysis of hope at work. *The Journal of Positive Psychology, 8*(4), 292–304.

Robbins, J. M., Ford, M. T., & Tetrick, L. E. (2012). Perceived unfairness and employee health: A meta-analytic integration. *Journal of Applied Psychology, 97*(2), 235–272.

Rogers, M. E., Creed, P. A., & Searle, J. (2012). Person and environmental factors associated with well-being in medical students. *Personality and Individual Differences, 52*(4), 472–477.

Roos, E., Burström, B., Saastamoinen, P., & Lahelma, E. (2005). A comparative study of the patterning of women's health by family status and employment status in Finland and Sweden. *Social Science and Medicine, 60*(11), 2443–2451.

Ryan, R. M., & Deci, E. L. (2000). Self-determination theory and the facilitation of intrinsic motivation, social development, and well-being. *American Psychologist, 55,* 68–78.

Scalea, T. L., Matthews, K. A., Avis, N. E., Thurston, R. C., Brown, C., Harlow, S., & Bromberger, J. T. (2012). Role stress, role reward, and mental health in a multiethnic sample of midlife women: Results from the study of women's health across the nation (SWAN). *Journal of Women's Health, 21*(5), 481–489.

Schwarz, N., & Clore, G. L. (1983). Mood, misattribution, and judgments of well-being: Informative and directive functions of affective states. *Journal of Personality and Social Psychology, 45*(3), 513–523.

Searle, B. J., & Parker, S. K. (2013). Work design and happiness: An active, reciprocal perspective. In S. A. David, I. Boniwell, & A. Conley Ayers (Eds.), *The Oxford handbook of happiness* (pp. 711–732). New York, NY: Oxford University Press.

Shockley, K. M., Ispas, D., Rossi, M. E., & Levine, E. L. (2012). A meta-analytic investigation of the relationship between state affect, discrete emotions, and job performance. *Human Performance, 25*(5), 377–411.

Sieber, S. D. (1974). Toward a theory of role accumulation. *American Sociological Review, 39*(4), 567–578.

Simmons, L. A., & Swanberg, J. E. (2009). Psychosocial work environment and depressive symptoms among US workers: Comparing working poor and working non-poor. *Social Psychiatry and Psychiatric Epidemiology, 44*(8), 628–635.

Sinokki, M., Ahola, K., Hinkka, K., Sallinen, M., Härmä, M., Puukka, P., . . . Virtanen, M. (2010). The association of social support at work and in private life with sleeping problems in the Finnish health 2000 study. *Journal of Occupational and Environmental Medicine, 52*(1), 54–61.

Stansfeld, S. A., Shipley, M. J., Head, J., Fuhrer, R., & Kivimaki, M. (2013). Work characteristics and personal social support as determinants of subjective well-being. *PLOS ONE, 8*(11). doi:10.1371/journal .pone.0081115

Steger, M. F., Dik, B. J., & Duffy, R. D. (2012). Measuring meaningful work: The work and meaning inventory (WAMI). *Journal of Career Assessment, 20*(3), 322–337.

Sumra, M. K., & Schillaci, M. A. (2015). Stress and the multiple-role woman: Taking a closer look at the "superwoman." *PLOS ONE, 10*(3). doi:10.1371/journal.pone.0120952

Treas, J., & Lui, J. (2013). Studying housework across nations. *Journal of Family Theory and Review, 5*(2), 135–149.

Versey, H. S. (2015). Managing work and family: Do control strategies help? *Developmental Psychology, 51*(11), 1672–1681.

Wahrendorf, M. (2015). Previous employment histories and quality of life in older ages: Sequence analyses using SHARELIFE. *Ageing and Society, 35*(9), 1928–1959.

Warr, P. (2013). Jobs and job-holders: Two sources of happiness and unhappiness. In S. A. David, I. Boniwell, & A. Conley Ayers (Eds.), *The Oxford handbook of happiness* (pp. 733–750). New York, NY: Oxford University Press.

Williams, J. C., Berdahl, J. L., & Vandello, J. A. (2016). Beyond work–life "integration." *Annual Review of Psychology, 67*, 515–539.

Yavorsky, J. E., Dush, C. M. K., & Schoppe-Sullivan, S. J. (2015). The production of inequality: The gender division of labor across the transition to parenthood. *Journal of Marriage and Family, 77*(3), 662–679.

Ybema, J. F., & van den Bos, K. (2010). Effects of organizational justice on depressive symptoms and sickness absence: A longitudinal perspective. *Social Science and Medicine, 70*(10), 1609–1617.

Zhou, X., Vohs, K. D., & Baumeister, R. F. (2009). The symbolic power of money: Reminders of money alter social distress and physical pain. *Psychological Science, 20*(6), 700–706.

CHAPTER 9

Religion

No matter how much we try to run away from this thirst for the answer to life,
for the meaning of life, the intensity only gets stronger and stronger. We cannot escape
these spiritual hungers.

—Source unknown

Humans have many basic emotional needs, but our needs to find meaning and to build social relationships seem particularly powerful. Several prominent psychological theories emphasize these needs for meaning (see, for example, Baumeister, 1991; Lawford & Ramey, 2015; Rosenblatt, Greenberg, Solomon, Pyszczynski, & Lyon, 1989; Snyder, 2002) and for social relationships (Baumeister & Leary, 1995). Therefore, it makes sense that religion is psychologically important because it offers a pathway to fill these needs. Obviously, religion binds individuals together in faith communities, and it also speaks to the meaning and purpose of human existence.

Indeed, many religious individuals are happier than their nonbelieving counterparts, and it is clear that faith plays an important role in this happiness gap. However, the role of religion in producing happiness is wonderfully complex (Pargament, 2002; Thoresen & Harris, 2002). The relationship depends on a number of factors, including cultural values, individual level of religious commitment, the type of religious practice, and whether the individual feels stressed by economic and cultural factors (Pargament, 2002).

In this chapter, we also investigate some interesting findings regarding the happiness of atheists. Because faith influences happiness, we might expect that atheists, those who reject religious faith, would be less happy, perhaps because they have less meaning in their lives. But it turns out that the happiness of atheists is generally equivalent to that of religious believers. The certainty with which individuals hold their faith, or nonfaith, is also an important predictor, and can help explain this apparent paradox (along with some other factors).

We also find that the religion–happiness relationship is rarely direct, but instead is mediated by several psychological variables (e.g., Powell, Shahabi, & Thoresen, 2003).

Recall that a mediated relationship means that there is an intervening variable between the predictor and outcome that explains the relationship between the two. It is not merely religion itself that produces happiness. Instead, faith can produce psychological states that then affect our happiness.

RELIGION AND WELL-BEING

Psychological and Physical Well-Being

Religion is often positively related to happiness. Myers (2008, p. 324) reviewed the literature and concluded, "In survey after survey, actively religious people have reported markedly greater happiness and somewhat greater life satisfaction than their irreligious counterparts." The literature shows that spiritual commitment, feeling close to God, and frequency of attending religious services are all strongly related to psychological well-being and physical health.

Subsequent research confirms Myers's (2008) conclusions. For instance, religion predicts better psychological well-being among older adults in the United States (Wilmoth, Adams-Price, Turner, Blaney, & Downey, 2014), and is associated with greater well-being among younger and middle-aged adults (Berthold & Ruch, 2014; Byron & Miller-Perrin, 2009; Wilmoth et al., 2014). Other literature reviews reach similar conclusions (e.g., Koole, McCullough, Kuhl, & Roelofsma, 2010; Larson & Larson, 2003; Seybold & Hill, 2001; Tay, Li, Myers, & Diener, 2014; Vishkin, Bigman, & Tamir, 2014).

Religious belief also often predicts better physical health (Headey, Hoehne, & Wagner, 2014; Krause, 2010; Seybold & Hill, 2001). In addition, religious and spiritual individuals live longer than their less religious counterparts (Headey et al., 2014; Powell et al., 2003), with church attendance a particularly important predictor (Masters & Hooker, 2013). This relationship can be quite strong. Headey et al. (2014) found that men 52 years or older were 38% less likely to die within 8 years if they attended church regularly compared to men who never or seldom attended. We see later in this chapter that the religion–health relationship is complex (Thoresen & Harris, 2002). For instance, the relationship is stronger for religious individuals living in religious rather than nonreligious cultures (Stavrova, 2015). However, religion does provide an overall health benefit (Headey et al., 2014).

Religion also seems to protect the well-being of some individuals experiencing stressful situations (Pargament, 2002). Schreiber and Brockopp (2012) found in a review of the literature that religious belief can help maintain or increase well-being among women diagnosed with breast cancer. In another literature review, Hollywell and Walker (2009) found that private prayer is related to lower rates of depression and anxiety among hospitalized patients. Similarly, Eytan (2011) found that religious belief predicts less frequent and severe episodes of depression among prison inmates. Yet another literature review (Larson & Larson, 2003) concludes that religiosity aids individuals suffering from mental illnesses, including depression and substance abuse.

Religious faith can also at least partially protect against the well-being–destroying effects of unemployment. Lechner and Leopold (2015) examined the happiness of

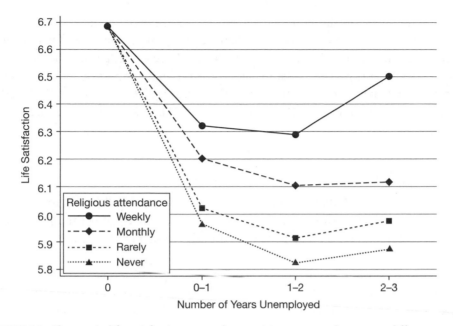

FIGURE 9.1. Changes in life satisfaction across the transition to unemployment at different rates of religious attendance.

Note: Germany's Socio-Economic Panel Study 1990–2012, release 2013. *n* = 5,446 individuals; *n* = 13,979 observations (person/years). The *y*-axis shows life satisfaction scores (0 = completely dissatisfied; 10 = completely satisfied).

Source: Lechner and Leopold (2015)

5,446 unemployed German adults from 1990 to 2012. As seen in Figure 9.1, although unemployment negatively affected well-being, regular church attendance softened the blow. Those who attended religious services each week (represented by the solid line in the figure) were the only respondents to show evidence of adapting to unemployment. These results are significant even after controlling for sociodemographic characteristics.

These conclusions regarding the benefits of religion during stressful circumstances are supported by a massive cross-national study of economic conditions by Diener, Tay, and Myers (2011). These authors conducted two separate studies, one of which included a sample of more than 350,000 American adults. They also examined a worldwide sample of 427,540 individuals from 153 different countries that was representative of 79% of the world's population (China was not sampled because of difficulties in asking questions about religion). In both studies, Diener et al. (2011) assessed participants' experience of difficult life circumstances, including whether basic needs for safety, security, and sustenance were met. They also recorded national measures of life expectancy and participants' level of education.

Results showed that religion's ability to increase well-being depends on the difficulty of life within a country (Diener et al., 2011). Religious individuals living in one of the 25% of nations with the most difficult life circumstances had *higher* well-being than did their nonreligious fellow citizens. Religious citizens of these poor and unstable countries rated their lives more positively, had stronger positive emotions, and had weaker negative emotions than did nonreligious citizens. Citizens of countries with the most life difficulties were also more religious than were citizens of the 25% of nations with the most wealth and stability (Diener et al., 2011). However, religiosity had little or no impact on well-being in wealthy countries. These findings support the notion that religious practice benefits those who are under stress. A literature review by Paul (2012) and other empirical work (e.g., Delamontagne, 2010; Paul, 2009) have reached similar conclusions.

Causality?

There is reason to think that religious faith may be a cause of well-being. You may have already wondered about this possibility, given that researchers cannot randomly assign some participants to have religious faith and others to be nonbelievers. Therefore, the research is necessarily correlational.

This limitation on research means that there are several alternative explanations for the hypothesis that religious faith causes well-being. For instance, could personality characteristics such as conscientiousness or agreeableness cause both religious faith and well-being, with a coincidental rather than causal relationship being a reasonable explanation for the findings? Researchers' careful statistical controls for several potential alternative explanations, while not perfect, do add to our confidence that religious faith and well-being are causally related.

Some examples may be helpful. Edara (2013) demonstrated that spirituality is associated with higher levels of both life satisfaction and positive affect among a sample of American adults. This relationship is significant even after statistically controlling for personality traits such as extraversion, agreeableness, and conscientiousness and the cultural values of individualism and collectivism. Thus, these controls show that it is unlikely that the link between spirituality and better well-being is simply a coincidence of values or personality.

Other research using similar statistical control techniques confirms the idea that religion and spirituality can cause higher levels of well-being. For instance, Mochon, Norton, and Ariely's (2011) results show a significant overall relationship between religiosity and well-being even after statistically controlling for education level, age, gender, marital status, ethnicity, income, political affiliation, and religious denomination in a sample of more than 6,000 individuals from all 50 states in the United States.

In addition, recall Diener et al.'s (2011) massive cross-national study (described earlier). These authors found that individual religiosity positively predicts well-being in poor and unstable nations, even after controlling for a variety of negative life circumstances. These factors are important because they also represent possible alternatives to the hypothesis that religion causes well-being. The control for education level seems particularly noteworthy. Perhaps high (or low) levels of education cause both religious observance and happiness?

Once again, the finding that religiosity was connected to greater well-being even after statistically controlling for plausible alternative explanations adds to our confidence that religiosity is a cause of well-being. However, we must also remember that the research in this area is correlational. Therefore, the results *suggest* rather than *confirm* causality.

These findings make it clear that religious faith is connected to well-being. And there is reason to suspect that the relationship may be causal. However, the research also found that, while the positive association between faith and well-being is valid in a general sense, this association is rarely straightforward.

In the following sections we explore reasons why religion is often associated with well-being and the complexities involved in this often indirect relationship, which can be mediated by other variables. It also turns out that religion and spirituality have uneven effects depending on cultural factors and features of specific religious beliefs. We explore these complexities in the rest of the chapter.

THE COMPLEXITIES: RELIGION DOES NOT ALWAYS PREDICT GREATER WELL-BEING

Although there is an overall positive relationship between religious practice and well-being, the relationship is complex, and some forms of religious and spiritual practice seem to decrease happiness. Pargament (2002, p. 168; see also Weber & Pargament, 2014) argued that the question of whether religious belief and practice aid well-being is too simplistic:

> . . . religion is a richer, more complex process than psychologists have imagined, one that has the potential both to help and to harm. Questions about the general efficacy of religion should give way to the more difficult but more appropriate question: How helpful or harmful are particular forms of religious expression for particular people dealing with particular situations in particular social contexts . . .?

Pargament (2002) gives the frustrating but common answer to many psychological questions, "It depends" (p. 169). The answer depends on several factors including social context, the extent to which individuals struggle with spiritual questions, the nature of their beliefs about God, and the extent to which religious beliefs are fully integrated into their lives.

Features of Belief

Fundamentalism

Religious fundamentalism is defined as belief in the literal interpretation of religious documents, acceptance of strict regulation of everyday behaviors (Sethi & Seligman, 1993), and the belief that there is one "true God" (Altemeyer & Hunsberger, 2004). Although fundamentalism is sometimes associated with negative outcomes, including prejudice, social anxiety, and psychopathology (Carlucci, Tommasi, Balsamo, Furnham, & Saggino, 2015; Pargament, 2002), it also predicts greater well-being.

For instance, fundamentalism predicted greater life satisfaction among a sample of Italian Catholic college students (Carlucci et al., 2015). Another study (Sethi & Seligman, 1993) linked fundamentalism to greater optimism, a personality characteristic often associated with happiness (Lyubomirsky, 2008). Furthermore, Green and Elliott (2010) found that fundamentalism predicted greater happiness in a largely representative sample of American adults. These last results were significant even after controlling for demographic and life circumstance factors, and for religious affiliation. Finally, a meta-analysis by Hackney and Sanders (2003) indicated that fundamentalism predicts higher life satisfaction and self-actualization.

Why is fundamentalism associated with greater happiness? It may help maintain a sense of meaning and purpose for life (Kinnvall, 2004). Pargament (2002) argued that fundamentalism also provides a sense of community, meaning and purpose in life, and hopefulness, all of which are psychologically satisfying. These features then offer distinct psychological advantages including,

> . . . [providing] individuals with an unambiguous sense of right and wrong, clear rules for living, closeness with like-minded believers, a distinctive identity, and, most important, the faith that their lives are sanctioned and supported by God. (p. 172)

Believing That God Is Harsh and Punitive

Belief that God is punitive, or that God has abandoned us, is often associated with lower well-being (Weber & Pargament, 2014). Silton, Flannelly, Galek, and Ellison (2014) found that belief that God is punishing and wrathful was associated with higher levels of social anxiety, paranoia, obsession, and compulsion in a sample of 1,426 American adults. These findings were significant even after statistically controlling for demographic characteristics, religiousness, and whether participants believed in God. However, belief that God is benevolent (not severe or critical) was associated with lower levels on all these measures.

Other studies report similar results. Research from the Netherlands also reports that believing that God is punishing is related to higher levels of guilt (Braam et al., 2008). Belief in a punishing God is also related to a hostile interpersonal style that predicts lower levels of health and emotional well-being (Jordan, Masters, Hooker, Ruiz, & Smith, 2014). Worry that God abandoned them predicted both emotional distress and problematic Internet use (i.e., obsessive use) among college students at a private Christian college (Knabb & Pelletier, 2014). Feeling that God is challenging (the item, "God has never asked me to do hard things," Lawrence, 1997, p. 226, is reverse scored) predicted higher levels of anxiety and depression among Iranian college students (Koohsar & Bonab, 2011). Finally, participants who wondered whether God had abandoned them were more depressed while dealing with problems in their lives (Braam et al., 2008). Although some research shows conflicting results (e.g., Krause, Emmons, & Ironson, 2015), the literature as a whole seems to indicate that belief in a hostile or punishing God is negatively related to well-being.

Intrinsic and Integrated Religiosity

Religious belief that is deeply and genuinely felt offers the strongest well-being benefits. Pargament (2002, p. 168) reviewed the literature and concluded that,

> Well-being has been linked positively to a religion that is internalized, intrinsically motivated, and based on a secure relationship with God and negatively to a religion that is imposed, unexamined, and reflective of a tenuous relationship with God and the world.

Intrinsically religious individuals are those who *live* their religion, as opposed to those who *use* their religion to gain external rewards such as social approval (Allport & Ross, 1967). The intrinsically religious are motivated by a sincere commitment to their faith.

Similarly, those who have internalized their religion have freely chosen it, rather than having it forced upon them by social or other pressures (Ryan, Rigby, & King, 1993). Internalization of belief has several subdimensions. One of these is the extent to which religious beliefs are integrated into larger social and cultural contexts. Religious beliefs that are culturally supported are more likely to bring well-being. Religious beliefs must also be appropriately integrated into an individual's problem-solving strategies. For instance, well-being is likely to suffer if prayer is used as a complete substitute for medical care. In addition, religious beliefs must integrate well with other beliefs, both religious and nonreligious, in order to give individuals a sense of coherence and consistency (Pargament, 2002).

Thus, the nature of belief is critically important. Simply going through the motions of being religious is unlikely to increase well-being. Instead, belief must be sincere, deeply felt, intrinsic, and internalized.

Spiritual Struggles

Negative consequences of spiritual struggle Pargament and colleagues (e.g., Abu-Raiya, Pargament, & Krause, 2016; Pargament, Murray-Swank, Magyar, & Ano, 2005) have consolidated much of the research reported earlier by investigating *spiritual struggles* and how they relate to well-being. These authors define *spiritual struggle* as tension and conflict concerning spiritual topics. Such struggles are fairly common among believers, with as many as two thirds of some samples experiencing spiritual struggles (Desai & Pargament, 2015).

Spiritual struggles can include tension between individuals and themselves, other people, or with God (Abu-Raiya et al., 2016). Feeling punished or abandoned by God is referred to as *divine struggle* (Fitchett, Winter-Pfändler, & Pargament, 2014), and researchers have identified several other types of struggle including demonic (worry that the Devil causes one's problems), interpersonal (feeling that one's beliefs are not respected by others), moral (worry that one's actions are sinful), ultimate meaning (concerns about lack of meaning in life; Abu-Raiya, Pargament, Krause, & Ironson, 2015), and intrapsychic (doubts about one's own spiritual beliefs; Faigin, Pargament, & Abu-Raiya, 2014). These measures are implemented by asking participants to think of an event or problem they have experienced. Participants then rate the extent to which their reactions reflect spiritual struggle (e.g., did they think that God was punishing them; Faigin et al., 2014).

Faigin et al. (2014) found that a combination of divine, interpersonal, and intrapsychic struggles predict a series of addictive behaviors that include gambling, food starving, drug use, sex, and shopping. The study was longitudinal, and followed a sample of American college students for about 5 weeks. The results were significant even after statistically controlling for participants' level of neuroticism, stress, religious behaviors and level of commitment, and addictive behavior at the beginning of the study. Thus, this study suggests that ongoing spiritual struggle may cause additional addictive behavior.

Other research has replicated and extended these findings. Fitchett et al. (2014) found similar results in a sample of hospitalized Swiss adults experiencing divine struggle. In addition, Abu-Raiya et al. (2015) found that divine, demonic, interpersonal, moral, and ultimate meaning spiritual struggles all predicted higher levels of depression and anxiety in a sample of 2,208 American adults who professed belief in God. All struggles except interpersonal also predicted lower life satisfaction and happiness. The results were significant even after statistically controlling for religious commitment, neuroticism, social isolation, ethnicity, and multiple demographic variables. These controls again support the hypothesis that spiritual struggles among believers cause lower well-being.

Some might wonder whether these results simply show that believers who struggle and *lose* their faith are prone to problems. This would not be very surprising or interesting because, as noted earlier, religious belief is associated with greater well-being. However, it does not seem that spiritually struggling participants in this study lost their faith (Abu-Raiya et al., 2016). Participants were moderately religious and spiritual, and only about 10% expressed no religious preference. Furthermore, remember that the results were significant even after controlling for religious commitment. Instead, these individuals were likely believers who were simply struggling. The implication here is that these results are not about losing faith. Instead, the combination of being religious *and* experiencing spiritual struggle is related to poorer well-being.

Recent reviews of the literature further show the importance of spiritual struggles. Exline and Rose (2013) concluded from their review that spiritual struggles were negatively associated with emotional well-being and physical health. Furthermore, longitudinal studies suggest that the chronic and reoccurring nature of spiritual struggles is most important. Temporary struggles do not have the same negative impact. Mediators are also beginning to emerge, one of which is social support; spiritual struggles seem to reduce well-being because they make it more difficult for individuals to access usually reliable social support networks.

Longitudinal studies point toward spiritual struggles as a cause and lower well-being as an effect. However, the lack of experimental research makes the direction of causality still somewhat unclear. It is also possible that there is a bidirectional causal relationship between struggles and well-being (Exline & Rose, 2013).

Religious coping as protection against spiritual struggle   Other data show that some aspects of faith can buffer the negative effects of spiritual struggles. Desai and Pargament (2015) assessed the well-being and spiritual growth of college students who were experiencing some degree of spiritual struggle. Results indicated that positive aspects of religious coping (e.g., thinking of God as benevolent) were related to greater well-being and to greater spiritual growth, even after controlling for demographic variables. Desai and Pargament concluded that factors that strengthen an individuals' *religious orienting system* (Pargament, 1997), a system of religiously oriented experiences and resources that can be used to cope with stress, are associated with greater well-being. Thus, positive religious coping helps build a support system that can buffer the effects of stressful events.

Other research examines these issues even more specifically. Abu-Raiya et al. (2016) assess participants' degree of religious struggles, and of several other variables, including *religious commitment*, the extent to which their spiritual beliefs guide their lives; *religious hope*, the extent to which their spiritual beliefs make them optimistic about the future; and their level of *life sanctification*, the extent to which they felt that part of them was sacred. Participants also indicated their level of *religious support*, the extent to which they dealt with stressful life events by seeking support from God. Participants were 2,140 American adults who had experienced at least one significant negative life event during the previous year and a half.

Results showed that religious hope and life sanctification moderated or buffered the negative effects of religious struggle on depression (Abu-Raiya et al., 2016). In addition, all four potential moderators (i.e., religious commitment, hope, and support, along with life sanctification) buffer the effects of religious struggles on happiness Figures 9.2 and 9.3 illustrate the results and describe more fully what is meant by buffering the effects of spiritual struggles.

For instance, Figure 9.2 shows that depression increases as individuals experience greater levels of spiritual struggle. However, the rate of this increase is significantly lower for high life-sanctification individuals. Thus, feeling that part of oneself is sacred offers some protection against the negative effects of spiritual struggle. The buffering effects are even clearer in Figure 9.3, representing happiness levels. Note that participants who

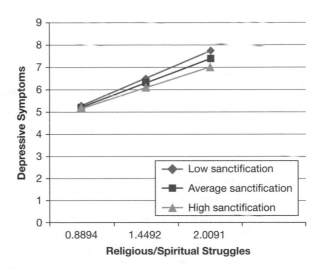

FIGURE 9.2. Simple slopes of depressive symptoms on religious/spiritual struggles at values of life sanctification.

Source: Abu-Raiya et al. (2016).

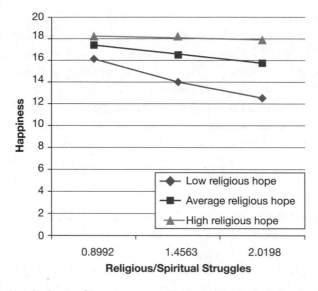

FIGURE 9.3. Simple slopes of happiness on religious/spiritual struggles at values of hope. *Source:* Abu-Raiya et al. (2016).

are high in religious hope show no negative effects of spiritual struggle, which those who are low or average in hope do.

Abu-Raiya et al. point out the importance of their findings. Religious faith can dampen the effect of many negative life events, including struggles with faith and spirituality. The results further illustrate the complicated relationship between faith and well-being (Pargament, 2002). Faith can lessen well-being when individuals struggle with their belief systems. However, those very belief systems (e.g., religious commitment) can offer protection against this spiritual struggle. Abu-Raiya et al. (brackets and italics for emphasis added) place an accent on the complicated nature of the religion–well-being relationship:

> . . . Equipped with a well-developed, well integrated religious orienting system [i.e., strong religious commitment], the person may be better positioned to deal effectively with the negative implications of r/s [religious/spiritual] struggle for distress and well-being. *In this paradoxical sense, religion becomes both the problem and the solution.* (p. 1272)

Aspects of faith that provide protection   You may have noticed a consistency concerning faith as a protection against spiritual struggle. The aspects of faith that provide protection all provide positive coping strategies. For example, in the Abu-Raiya et al. (2016) study, participants who felt religious hope, sanctification, support, and commitment all had better outcomes.

A review by Pargament, Falb, Ano, and Wachholtz (2013) confirms these findings for the literature as a whole. Positive religious coping, such as seeking spiritual support, is helpful. However, negative religious coping, such as rethinking God's powers, simply continues the spiritual struggle and lowers well-being. These findings remain significant even after controlling for demographic variables and for nonreligious coping methods.

Thus, those with spiritual struggles have higher well-being if they recommit themselves to their faith (Pargament et al., 2013). The key to greater well-being is to stop the spiritual struggle and reach some sense of certainty about one's beliefs (Weber, Pargament, Kunik, Lomax, & Stanley, 2012). Ordinarily, this approach means using positive religious coping strategies. But we see when we discuss atheism that it could also involve increasing certainty by an alternative strategy of abandoning faith.

Culture

Important Cultural Factors

The relationship between religious practice and well-being also depends on the surrounding culture. Religion is most strongly related to positive well-being if it is normative or common in the culture, and if there is little cultural hostility toward religion (Diener et al., 2011; Stavrova, Fetchenhauer, & Schlösser, 2013).

Social hostility toward religion and religious socialization   Lun and Bond (2013) examined the cultural factors of social hostility toward religion and support for religious socialization in countries around the world. Social hostility was measured using reports from several human rights organizations that documented violence or intimidation toward religious practices. This measure, assessed by the Social Hostility Index (SHI), does not necessarily reflect governmental hostility toward religion. It also reflects hostility between majority and minority status religions within a country. Support for religious socialization reflects citizens' beliefs that it is important to teach faith to children. Religiosity was measured as practicing a religion or by believing in religious authorities.

Lun and Bond examined a sample of almost 50,000 participants from 42 countries. Results show that the relationship between religiosity and well-being is affected by cultural factors.[1] For instance, examine the graphs for life satisfaction and happiness in Figures 9.4 through 9.7. Note that the relationship between well-being and religiosity depends on cultural attitudes toward religion (i.e., religious socialization or social hostility toward religion).

For instance, spiritual practice (i.e., practicing a religion) is associated with lower well-being in cultures with low support for religious socialization (i.e., cultures that do not value teaching faith to children). You can see this relationship by closely examining the two white bars for the spiritual practice/happiness data (Figure 9.6). Note that those who do not practice any religion are happier than those who do in cultures with low support for religious socialization. In other words, the relationship between religious practice and well-being is dependent on whether religion is accepted in the larger culture. Thus, religion is not always associated with greater well-being.

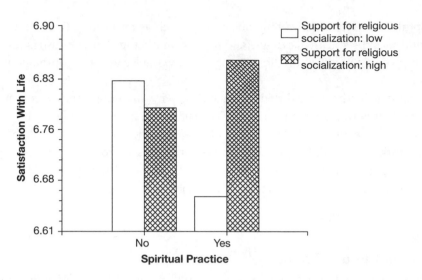

FIGURE 9.4. Interaction between spiritual practice and cultural support for religious socialization on the prediction of life satisfaction.

Source: Lun and Bond (2013).

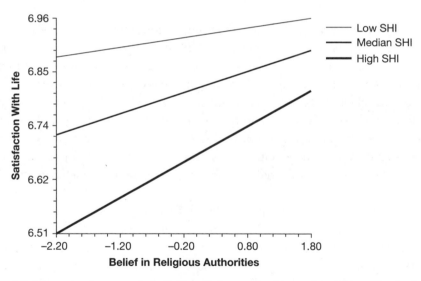

FIGURE 9.5. Interaction between the belief in religious authorities and social hostility on the prediction of life satisfaction.

SHI, Social Hostility Index.

Source: Lun and Bond (2013).

The results for belief in religious authorities (Figures 9.5 and 9.7) are also interesting. Recall that the SHI score reflects hostility toward specific religions that comes from both the government and from other religions. Note that everyone has more happiness and life satisfaction in cultures that are low in social hostility toward religion. Also, religiosity, as measured by belief in religious authorities, is also associated with more

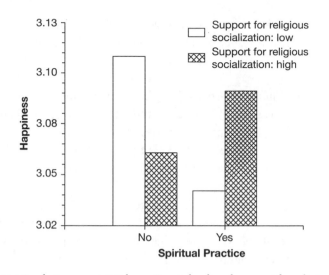

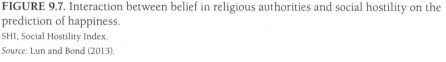

FIGURE 9.6. Interaction between spiritual practice and cultural support for religious socialization on the prediction of happiness.

Source: Lun and Bond (2013).

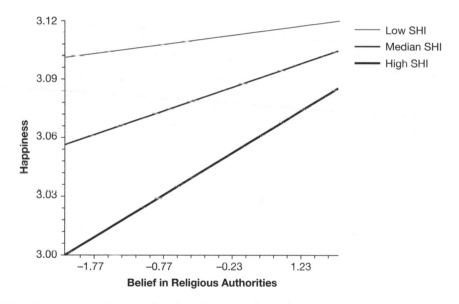

FIGURE 9.7. Interaction between belief in religious authorities and social hostility on the prediction of happiness.

SHI, Social Hostility Index.

Source: Lun and Bond (2013).

happiness and life satisfaction. But, belief in religious authorities (again, a measure of religiosity) does not matter as much for well-being if the culture is either low or around the median in social hostility toward religion.

Specifically, the slopes for the low and median SHI lines are relatively flat, indicating that belief in religious authorities does not matter much in those cultural conditions.

But it matters much more if the culture is high in social hostility, as shown by a steeper slope for the high SHI line. Once again, the relationship between religiosity and well-being depends on cultural values.

Religion as a cultural norm   Other research confirms and extends Lun and Bond's results using different measures of cultural attitudes toward religion. Diener et al.'s (2011) massive international study classifies countries in terms of the percentage of individuals who believed that religion was an important part of their daily lives. Countries with a high percentage of individuals with that belief are seen as having a cultural norm that favored religion.

Diener et al. then examined how this measure of cultural religiosity affected the relationship between individual religious practice and well-being. Similar to Lun and Bond's (2013) results, Diener et al. found that the relationship between religiosity and well-being depends on cultural factors. Figure 9.8 depicts Diener et al.'s results. First, note the results for individuals living in one of the nations among the top 25% of the most religious in the sample (the two left-hand bars in each panel). Similar to previous findings, religious individuals living in one of these religious countries are higher in life evaluation and positive feelings, and lower in negative feelings, than are low religiosity individuals.

Now examine the results for the least religious nations (the two bars on the right in each panel). Note that the well-being differences between religious and nonreligious individuals are much smaller in these relatively nonreligious countries. In fact, religious and nonreligious individuals are virtually identical in terms of life evaluation and positive feelings (the differences are significant only because of the extremely large sample size) although there is a more meaningful difference in terms of negative feelings. These results confirm the notion that religious practice is particularly beneficial when conducted within religious cultures but that the benefits of religiosity can diminish if the larger culture is less religious.

Other research shows that cultural norms favoring religion affect the relationship between individual religiosity and health. Stavrova (2015) measured cultural norms favoring religion in samples of 59 countries around the world and within regions of the United States. Consistent with other findings reported in this section, the positive relationship between individual religiosity and health was stronger in countries and in regions of the United States that were highly religious. Figures 9.9 and 9.10 describe the results.

These figures are structured in an unusual way. The x-axis is straightforward; it represents the strength of cultural norms favoring religion in a nation or in a region of the United States. The y-axis represents the size of the association[2] between individual religiosity and health, with higher scores indicating stronger relationships. Figures 9.9 and 9.10 show that the strength of the relationship between individual religiosity and health is strongest (i.e., have the highest values on the y-axis) in cultures that are more religious (i.e., those farther to the right on the x-axis).

Note that the association between individual religiosity and health is near zero in cultures that have relatively weak norms favoring religion. Finally, health is defined by self-reports in the cross-national sample and by mortality statistics in the data from the

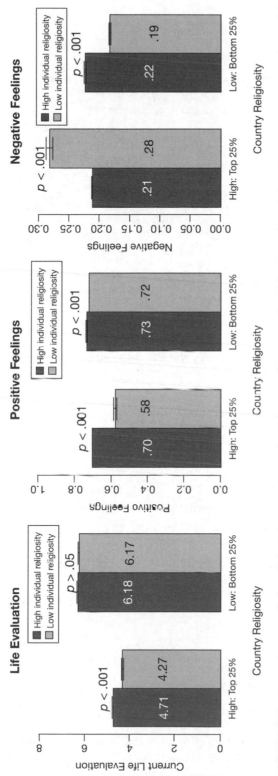

FIGURE 9.8. Person–environment fit for religiosity's association with subjective well-being. Individuals who indicated that religion is important and attended a religious meeting in the past week are categorized as high individual religiosity. Conversely, individuals who indicated that religion is not important and did not attend a religious meeting in the past week are categorized as low individual religiosity.

Source: Diener et al. (2011).

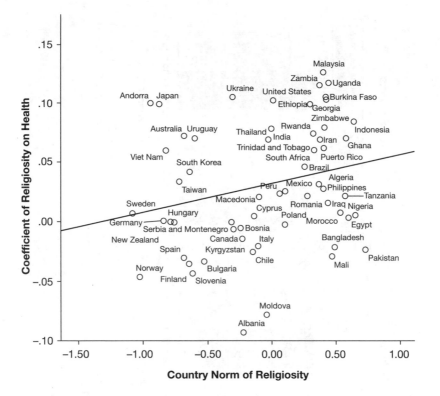

FIGURE 9.9. Effect of religiosity on self-rated health as a function of the country norm of religiosity.

$r = .24$; $n = 59$; $p = .067$. The coefficients (β) were obtained from country-specific ordinary least squares (OLS) regression, and the models included all individual-level control variables.

Source: Stavrova (2015).

United States. For the U.S. data, a large number of individuals were repeatedly sampled over a long period of time, so Stavrova was able to investigate how individual religiosity and cultural norms regarding religion were related to death rates. It is remarkable that these factors do not just predict what individuals say about their own health, but also the probability of death. To put this in stark terms, religious individuals in the United States live longer if they reside in a region of the country that has cultural norms favoring religion.

Social Dysfunction

Finally, to come back to the Diener et al. (2011) study one more time, recall that this is a large-scale cross-national study. The findings that religiosity is associated with higher well-being among citizens living in the poorest, most unstable nations support the idea that religion helps well-being in stressful circumstances.

But now let us look at how the effect of religion might change depending on the level of social dysfunction within a culture (nation). As seen in Figure 9.11, Diener et al.'s results also show that the religious benefit to well-being is largely limited to poorer and

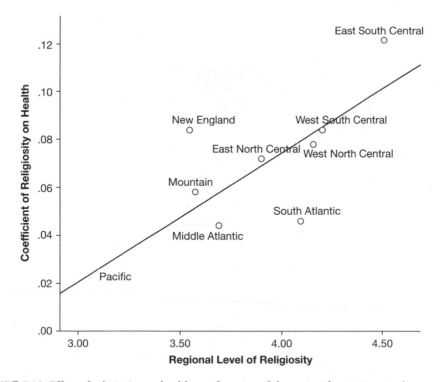

FIGURE 9.10. Effect of religiosity on health as a function of the regional variations in the mean level of religiosity.

r = .76; *n* = 9.

Source: Stavrova (2015).

less stable nations (see the two bars on the right side of each frame). Although religious citizens living in nations among the top 25% in wealth and stability reported more positive emotions, they also reported more negative emotions and lower life evaluations (see the two bars on the left side of each frame).

These results again show that the happiness benefits of religion depend on cultural context. Diener et al. (2011) speculate that this pattern might explain why large numbers of people are abandoning formal religion in economically developed nations and areas. That is, individuals in developed and secure societies do not need to rely as much on religion to achieve their well-being goals. This idea is supported by other research showing that individuals living in less economically developed areas are more religious. For instance, Barber (2013) reported this finding in a cross-national study of 114 nations, and replicated it (Barber, 2015) in an examination of states within the United States.

Subsequent research fortified confidence that wealth affects both the level of religiosity and resulting well-being. Oishi and Diener (2014) analyzed cross-cultural data from more than 100 nations and found that religiosity mediated the relationship between national wealth and suicide rates. Specifically, poorer nations were more religious, and higher levels of religion were associated with lower suicide rates, once again showing the interplay among level of wealth, religiosity, and well-being.

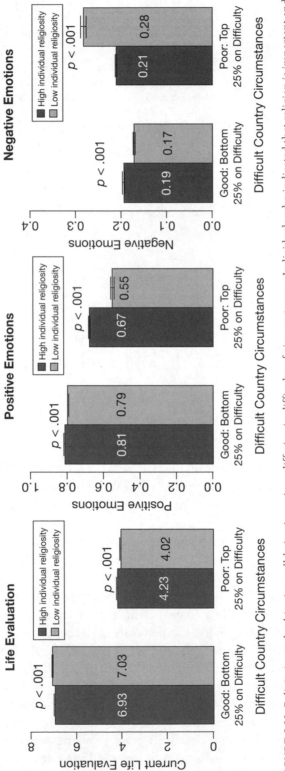

FIGURE 9.11. Religiosity and subjective well-being in nations differing in difficulty of circumstances. Individuals who indicated that religion is important and attended a religious meeting in the past week are categorized as high individual religiosity. Conversely, individuals who indicated that religion is not important and did not attend a religious meeting in the past week are categorized as low individual religiosity.

Note: Error bars represent the standard errors.

Source: Diener et al. (2011).

Why Does Culture Matter?

Religious individuals have higher well-being when they reside in a religious culture because of the respect and support they receive in such cultures (Diener et al., 2011; Stavrova et al., 2013). For instance, Diener et al. also examined individuals' perceptions of social support (i.e., whether friends and family would help them if needed), of feeling respected, and of feeling that there was meaning and purpose in their lives. Results showed that these perceptions mediate the relationship between individual religiosity and well-being. Thus, religion enhances well-being if it is coupled with social support and respect, which culture can largely affect.

Other research reaches similar conclusions. Stavrova et al. (2013) also found that individual religiosity and cultural religiosity combine to predict well-being. As in other studies, religious individuals were happiest when they resided within a religious culture. Furthermore, social recognition (feeling that one is respected, treated fairly, and appropriately recognized) partially mediates the relationship between religiosity and well-being.

Being individually religious within a religious culture is associated with greater feelings of social recognition, which then explains part of the relationship between individual religiosity and well-being (Stavrova et al., 2013). Note that this mediational pattern is somewhat different from the one found by Diener et al. (2011), who used only individual religiosity as the predictor. Stavrova et al. (2013) used the combination of individual religiosity and cultural religiosity as their predictor. Stavrova et al.'s results are particularly important because they are directly related to the central question of this section: Why does religious culture affect the happiness of religious individuals? Again, the answer seems to be, in part, that religious cultures increase the respect and social recognition given to religious individuals.

However, it is also important to consider how national wealth and stability influence the effects of religion on well-being. Practicing religion is associated with greater feelings of social support, respect, and meaning, which in turn was associated with greater well-being (Diener et al., 2011). But it appears that individuals in wealthy and secure nations have other, nonreligious ways of attaining social support and respect. Therefore, most people are relatively happy in these wealthy and secure nations, regardless of their religious inclinations.

But religion offers important advantages to those living in poor and unstable nations. Those individuals can find respect, meaning, and social support via religion that might not otherwise be available to them, all important positive effects on their well-being. As a result, religion seems particularly important for the well-being of people living in difficult and challenging circumstances (Diener et al., 2011).

Meaning in life seems to play a particularly important role in how religion promotes well-being in poorer nations. Recall Oishi and Diener's (2014) cross-cultural study connecting wealth, religion, and well-being. They found that meaning in life is more important than social support and respect in explaining how religion is related to well-being in poor nations. According to these authors, ". . . a central reason for the link between religiosity and meaning in life is that religion gives a system that connects daily experiences with the coherent whole and a general structure to one's life" (Oishi & Diener, 2014, p. 428). They also maintain that religion helps individuals find meaning in difficult circumstances.

Atheism and Happiness

Atheists Are Generally as Happy as Believers

Given our discussion so far, we might expect atheists to be particularly unhappy. However, that generally does not seem to be the case. Instead, several recent literature reviews conclude that atheists and believers are roughly equally happy (e.g., Brewster, Robinson, Sandil, Esposito, & Geiger, 2014; Streib & Klein, 2013; Weber et al., 2012). Weber et al. reviewed 10 papers comparing believers and nonbelievers. Seven of these papers produced at least some data showing that nonbelievers feel roughly equal or *lower* levels of psychological distress than do believers. Furthermore, only 2 of the 10 papers consistently show more distress among nonbelievers, and these two studies assess spiritual distress rather than well-being. For example, these two studies found that nonbelievers had more anger toward God and had more difficulty forgiving God than did believers (many of the nonbelievers had previously been religious but lost their faith).

Therefore, the data indicate no overall differences in the well-being of atheists and believers. However, this area is acutely understudied, and more research is needed (Brewster et al., 2014). There is also an interesting exception to the conclusion that atheists are *generally* as happy as are believers. Atheists do appear to have lower well-being than the faithful when they experience discrimination and social rejection.

Obstacles to Atheists' Happiness

Interestingly, a study with a novel research methodology that was published too recently to be included in the previously cited literature reviews found evidence that atheists are *less* happy than believers. Although these results do not seem strong enough to change the conclusions from the three literature reviews cited earlier, they are still worth considering. Ritter, Preston, and Hernandez (2014) examined the Twitter messages of thousands of individuals who followed either public atheists (e.g., Richard Dawkins) or Christian leaders (e.g., Pope Benedict). The authors assumed that followers shared the beliefs of those whom they followed. The authors then examined the frequency of words used in the followers' messages that suggested positive or negative emotions or life events.

Results indicate that atheist tweets contained more words related to unhappiness, thus suggesting that atheists are less happy than Christians. What do you think about this research methodology? Certainly it has the advantage of eliminating the possibility that either atheists' or believers' behavior (that is, the messages they tweet) is intended to influence the conclusions of the research.

But does the content of Twitter messages reflect an individual's overall happiness? As discussed later, atheists are discriminated against. Perhaps this discrimination, rather than their overall happiness, affects the words they use in public tweets. We do not know the answers to these questions, but this study opens up an interesting line of research that will be important to follow.

Anti-atheist discrimination Atheists are less happy than believers when they are targets of discrimination and social rejection. And it is clear that atheists suffer from discrimination, particularly in religious countries (Stavrova et al., 2013). For instance, Gervais, Shariff, and Norenzayan (2011) found that atheists are distrusted, and Gervais (2014) showed that much of the public sees atheists as immoral. Across five separate studies, when participants were asked whether the perpetrator of an immoral act such as incest was more likely to be an atheist or a member of some other cultural or religious group, they consistently thought the immoral actor was more likely an atheist (Gervais et al., 2014).

Literature reviews also show that atheists are perceived negatively and are often socially rejected. Weber et al. (2012) concluded that atheists are often distrusted. For instance, they cite instances from the empirical literature in which atheists were rated negatively even after performing prosocial behaviors such as showing generosity. They also cite polling data indicating that respondents would not approve of their children marrying an atheist.

Discrimination against atheists lowers their happiness Weber et al. (2012), whose literature review showing that atheists are distrusted and socially rejected was previously discussed, theorized that anti-atheist discrimination is a significant source of psychological distress for atheists for the same reasons that discrimination lowers the well-being of other social groups. Specifically, atheists must deal with social exclusion, inequality, and the potential to internalize the negative perceptions others have of them.

Other research more specifically links social rejection and discrimination with atheists' (un)happiness. Kugelmass and Garcia (2015) found that nonbelieving adolescents are almost twice as likely overall to experience mental disorders (mood, anxiety, substance abuse, or behavioral disorders) as their faithful counterparts, even after controlling for family sociodemographic characteristics. However, these mental disorders suffered by nonbelieving adolescents hinge on the adolescents' parents' beliefs.

Specifically, a nonbelieving adolescent whose parents were believers was 136% *more likely* to experience a mental disorder than a believing adolescent. However, a nonbelieving adolescent whose parents were also nonbelievers was *no more likely* to experience a mental disorder than an adolescent who believed in God. Can we assume that nonbelieving youth in religious households feel a certain amount of rejection and exclusion that those who grow up in a nonreligious household do not? If so, these results are consistent with the perspective that atheists' lower well-being is due primarily to feeling socially excluded and perhaps discriminated against.

Some research (e.g., Diener et al., 2011; Stavrova et al., 2013) shows that nonreligious individuals receive less respect, particularly if they live in a highly religious culture, and that this lack of respect is associated with lower levels of well-being. Although not specifically comparing atheists with believers (religiosity is measured on a scale from high to low), these findings are consistent with the notion that discrimination causes nonbelievers to be less happy than believers.

Other research specifically comparing atheists to believers show similar results. Remember Ritter et al.'s (2014) finding that atheists tweeted more unhappiness-related words than did Christians. They also found that "social connection" along with "analytic thinking" mediate the relationship between belief and happiness. That is, Christians also tweeted more words suggesting social connection (e.g., mate or friend), and this, in turn, predicts more happiness-related words. Thus, as is always the case with mediation, the social connection-related tweets explain why Christians used more happiness-related words and atheists used fewer. These results are consistent with the hypothesis that atheists are less happy than believers when they experience less social respect.

Other research directly measures atheists' perceptions of discrimination, and how this relates to their well-being. Doane and Elliott (2015) collected a sample of 960 atheists by recruiting on a website belonging to an international organization of atheists. Consistent with expectations, and as shown in Figure 9.12, perceived discrimination is negatively associated with well-being. Interestingly, perceived discrimination also strengthens atheists' identification with atheism (i.e., they feel more committed to their atheist identity). This strengthened atheist identity is then positively associated with well-being.

Thus, discrimination both decreased and increased atheists' well-being through separate pathways shown in Figure 9.12. Perceived discrimination decreased well-being via the direct path between discrimination and well-being, but it also increased well-being via the indirect path through atheist identification.[3] However, the direct path from perceived discrimination to well-being was stronger, making the overall relationship between perceived discrimination and well-being negative. Thus, when atheists do have lower well-being than believers, discrimination and lack of social acceptance seem to account for some of this deficit.

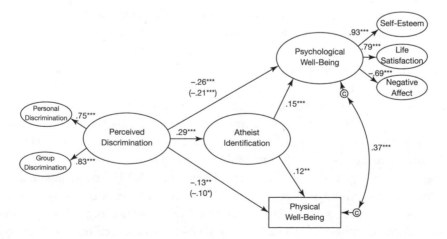

FIGURE 9.12. Structural model of the rejection-identification process.

This figure displays standardized regression coefficients. Total effects of perceived discrimination on well-being are in parentheses. *n* = 960.

*p < .05; **p < .01; ***p < .001.

Source: Doane and Elliott (2015).

Influences on Both Atheists and Believers

The importance of belief certainty   There is a paradox here. We have seen evidence that religious belief is generally associated with higher well-being. But we also see that atheists, at least when not persecuted, have levels of well-being comparable to those of believers. What accounts for this paradox?

Certainty of belief is one key. Weber et al. (2012) note that belief certainty predicts well-being for both believers and atheists. Religious individuals with little certainty about their beliefs are often less happy than nonbelievers who are certain about their convictions. However, Christians and atheists who are firmly convinced of their spiritual positions have comparable well-being.

For example, Galen and Kloet (2011) found the "U"-shaped relationship between belief certainty and well-being shown in Figure 9.13. Note that there are separate lines for two different outcome measures, with higher scores indicating greater well-being for each. Emotional stability includes items such as "I am relaxed most of the time" (Galen & Kloet, 2011, p. 677). The results indicate that participants have roughly equal well-being regardless of whether they believe in God or not, as long as they are certain of their beliefs. However, the uncertain participants, represented in the middle of the x-axis, reported lower well-being than did either the certain believers or certain atheists.

Galen and Kloet obtained their sample from email lists from two mainstream churches in the midwestern United States, and from the email list of a local branch of the Center for Inquiry, a secular organization committed to science, reason, and related concerns. The results are significant even after controlling for demographic variables and for respondents' perceived social support. This sample is skewed toward believers in that 49% of the overall sample were absolutely certain that God exists. However, Galen and Kloet

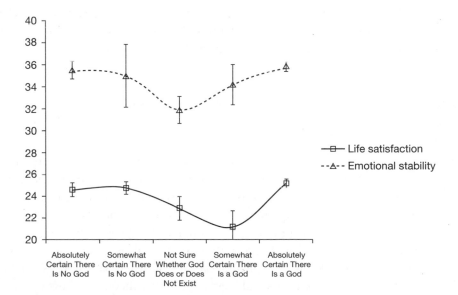

FIGURE 9.13. Life satisfaction and emotional stability as a function of belief certainty.
Source: Galen and Kloet (2011).

performed a second study with a separate sample that skews in the other direction (40% of respondents were absolutely certain that God does not exist) and found a similar pattern. A literature review by Streib and Klein (2013) reached similar conclusions about a "U"-shaped relationship between belief certainty and well-being.

The importance of spiritual struggles   Another reason why believers and nonbelievers have similar well-being is that they both experience spiritual struggles that affect well-being. For instance, both the faithful and nonbelievers must manage their relationships with others whose spiritual beliefs inevitably differ from their own to some degree. Both must also struggle to find purpose and meaning in life. It is important to emphasize that everyone probably experiences these struggles, regardless of their religious beliefs (Weber et al., 2012). Therefore, it is perhaps not surprising that they experience similar levels of happiness.

This brings us back to the importance of certainty. Some religious individuals and some nonreligious individuals struggle with their convictions and are not completely certain about the meaning of their lives, for example. However, we are all happier when we find certainty in our beliefs.

It is clear that the relationship between religion and well-being is complicated although positive overall. For instance, features of specific belief systems matter a great deal, and the way they matter is complicated. One example is that while fundamentalists are generally happy, those who believe in a strict and punishing God are not. Another example is that atheists, as long as they are not persecuted, are generally as happy as believers. Cultural attitudes toward religion further complicate matters, and spiritual struggles add another dimension of complexity. Research shows that religion can lower well-being when individuals struggle with their spirituality, *and* increase well-being if positive religious coping strategies are used in the face of spiritual struggles.

These findings highlight the importance of Pargament's (2002) statement that we should avoid simplistic questions about whether religion is good or bad for happiness. Instead, we should recognize that religion can be both. The important question is whether specific forms of religion are helpful to specific individuals in specific circumstances.

WHY MIGHT RELIGION PREDICT WELL-BEING?

Life Meaning and Purpose

Religion might increase well-being by enhancing our sense of life purpose and meaning, thereby leading to more happiness. In other words, life meaning and purpose might mediate the relationship between religious faith and well-being. In this section, we discuss the theoretical argument that religion can provide a sense of meaning. In the next section we examine data connecting religious faith, meaning, and well-being.

As noted in the beginning of this chapter, the search for meaning and purpose in our lives is a strong motivational force (e.g., Baumeister, 1991; Rosenblatt et al., 1989). Many social scientists have recognized this and have constructed theories of how this search for meaning might explain the relationship between religious belief and well-being. Park,

Edmondson, and Hale-Smith (2013) synthesize much of this research by proposing that humans have a need for a "functional meaning system" (p. 157) that can

> . . . serve as the filter through which people attend to and perceive stimuli; organize their behavior; conceptualize themselves, others and interpersonal relationships; remember their past; and anticipate their future. (p. 158)

Thus, creating and understanding life's meaning is a critical function of human psychology. Our meaning systems influence how we understand events and the actions of both ourselves and of others. They help us make sense of our past and to make the future seem more predictable and understandable.

Our meaning systems also help us manage all the individual threats to meaning that plague humanity. These threats include wondering what happens to us after we die, the uncertainty of human experience (i.e., difficulty predicting the future and understanding the present), a nagging sense of purposefulness many of us feel, and the various absurdities of human existence. By meeting all these functions, our meaning systems also help us establish a stable sense of self and identity (Park et al., 2013). Although Park et al. (2013) do not explicitly state this, a clear implication of their meaning systems hypothesis is that a functional meaning system that helps build a sense of purpose in life will be associated with greater well-being.

But what is most important about Park et al.'s paper is that they specifically argue that religion offers a uniquely effective way for individuals to meet their needs for meaning. They support this claim first by pointing to how common religion is cross-culturally, and to how many individuals practice religion. Furthermore, these individuals and cultures view religion as the most important part of their meaning systems.

Park et al. also argue that religious meaning systems are more effective at addressing existential questions than are alternative meaning systems such as science and the scientific method. Existential questions go to the nature of existence. Questions such as, "Why do we exist?" and "What happens to us after we die?" are existential questions These questions may not be answerable with science. How can we gather data on *why* we exist?

Therefore, appeals to supernatural events and God may give particularly satisfying answers to these existential questions. Park et al. refer to research showing that beliefs in supernatural powers of gods are comforting. They also argue that such beliefs have the advantage of being largely immune to disproof. This may make religious meaning systems especially comforting. Because they rely on subjective experiences and other nonobservables, religious believers can be confident that their belief systems will not be invalidated by others.

Religion can also provide a sense of coherence and control that reduces feelings of uncertainty. Belief in a supernatural power can make the world seem more understandable by providing explanations for events. The faithful can understand events as being caused by God, and as a part of God's will. Furthermore, such a belief opens the opportunity to influence events either by following God's will or by making appeals to God for special help. All of these factors can help individuals develop a sense of life meaning and purpose.

Finally, religion can also be very beneficial in times of distress. It can both provide meaning and protect our existing sense of meaning. Park et al. refer to data indicating that religious faith is comforting during times of stress, assuring the faithful that God will protect them during difficult times and referring to God's actions to provide an understanding of why difficult times occur.

Empirical Evidence

Several studies (among them, Cranney, 2013; Stroope, Draper, & Whitehead, 2013; van Tongeren, Hook, & Davis, 2013) show that at least some forms of religiosity are associated with a greater sense of purpose in life. Other research (e.g., Diener, Fujita, Tay, & Biswas-Diener, 2012; García-Alandete, 2015; Sumner, Burrow, & Hill, 2015) indicates that meaning and purpose in life predict well-being. However, while this research is consistent with the idea that meaning and purpose mediate the relationship between religiosity and well-being, none of it tests the entire model.

But three studies using college samples, two from the United States (Byron & Miller-Perrin, 2009; Kashdan & Nezlek, 2012) and the other from Australia (Sillick & Cathcart, 2014), do confirm this idea. These studies found that some form of religiosity is associated with life purpose, which then predicts well-being. Another study from the United States (Krok, 2015) that examined a sample of 19- to 62-year-old adults found similar results using religious coping as a measure of religiosity.

One of the studies with a sample of U.S. college students is worth describing in some detail because it is longitudinal. Kashdan and Nezlek (2012) asked 87 college students to report their levels of *daily* spirituality, life meaning and positive affect, and self-esteem for 2 weeks. The longitudinal nature of this study allows more confidence than we have in the other studies that spirituality is a cause, and not an effect, of life meaning and well-being.

But the strongest evidence that purpose or meaning in life mediates the relationship between religiosity and well-being comes from Diener et al. (2011). This is the massive study, discussed earlier, that examined a representative sample of 153 nations representing 79% of the world's people. The results support the model among both rich and poor nations on well-being measures of life evaluation, and for positive and negative emotions. Also, purpose and meaning in life more strongly mediate the religion–well-being relationship for life evaluation than do two other potential mediators, social support and social respect. However, social support and social respect are stronger mediators than were life purpose/meaning for the well-being measures of positive and negative emotions (Diener et al., 2011).

These results are conceptually replicated by a later cross-cultural study examining suicide rates. Oishi and Diener (2014) examine measures of religiosity, meaning of life, and national suicide rates in more than 100 countries from around the world. Results once again show that meaning in life mediates the relationship between religiosity and well-being, this time measured as national suicide rates. Therefore, data from both convenience samples of college students and from international survey studies are consistent with the model that religion increases well-being because it first increases a sense of meaning in life and/or life purpose, which then have direct relations to well-being.

Social Relationships

Social relationships provide another potential explanation for why religion can enhance well-being. Most of us are familiar with scenes of church suppers, potlucks, and ice cream socials and with references to church or religious "communities." These are real and thriving social communities that offer support and a way to form the social relationships that are so vital to our well-being.

Given that social and collective behaviors are a very important part of most religions (Graham & Haidt, 2010) and that social relationships are a crucial determinant of well-being (Baumeister & Leary, 1995), the mediational model of religion is very plausible.

Before we examine the data, it is worth describing the argument that social and collective behaviors are essential for religion. Graham and Haidt (2010) make this argument in a review of the literature. They found that collective actions such as group singing, dancing, and praying increase liking, trust, and cooperation among group members. Furthermore, these types of collective behaviors are common religious practices and are used to build commitment to fellow believers and to the religion as a whole. In fact, Graham and Haidt conclude from their review that the social aspects of religious practice are more important in predicting well-being than are beliefs. Specifically, the amount of time individuals spend in group worship, the number of times they attend services, the degree to which they are embedded in religious social communities, and so on, predict well-being better than does the strength of their religious beliefs.

A similar argument comes from the perspective of Social Identity Theory (Tajfel & Turner, 1986), which maintains that we often think of ourselves in terms of our group memberships. This is important because we draw self-esteem from these group memberships if they are socially respected. Ysseldyk, Matheson, and Anisman (2010) argue that religious group identities are particularly attractive from this perspective. First, religious group membership offers social support, respect, and status in ways that are similar to other social groups. However, religious groups also claim exclusive knowledge of ultimate truth that cannot be disproven (because of the nature of faith). Such group membership can therefore offer protection against uncertainty and existential anxiety. It may also offer the perceived ability to control events via appeals to God. This sense of certainty and control has obvious benefits for self-esteem and other aspects of well-being.

There are strong self-esteem benefits from belonging to a religious group that flow from the social support that goes with membership in any group. But the benefits for religious group membership are particularly strong because of the sense of certainty, control, and truth offered by religious faith (Ysseldyk et al., 2010).

Evidence That Social Relations Mediate Between Religion and Well-Being

On to the evidence, which shows that social relationships can mediate the relationship between religion and well-being. First, church-based social support is associated with improvements in self-ratings of health. Krause (2006) examined a longitudinal sample of elderly Black and White Americans who were either practicing Christians or lapsed Christians or who did not follow any faith. Consistent with the hypothesis that religion promotes well-being by providing social support, respondents who anticipated the most support from church members reported the most positive changes in health over time.

These results were significant even after controlling for sociodemographic variables and for church attendance, the frequency of private prayer, and self-rated health at the beginning of the study. Results were also significant after controlling for the amount of enacted support, the support actually delivered by church members (Krause, 2006).

These results are noteworthy because they point toward the power of social support. Note that what matters is the degree to which participants *think* other church members will support them, even after considering how much they actually do offer support. Thus, the *perception* of social support is particularly important. Similarly, why does it matter that improvements in health are related to anticipated support even after also controlling for prayer and church attendance? These results are also very important because they confirm Graham and Haidt's contention that social support is the most important component of the religion–well-being relationship—even more important than religious belief or practice.

Religion and social relationships   Recall that Ritter et al. (2014) found that followers of Christian public figures were more likely to include words suggesting social connections in their tweets than were followers of atheist public figures. This use of tweets containing social connection words mediated the relationship between religious affiliation and well-being. Likewise, Diener et al. (2011) conducted the massive international study that found that social support mediated the relationship between religiosity and well-being, although social support was a weaker mediator than was life meaning. Other, smaller scale research (e.g., Salsman, Brown, Brechting, & Carlson, 2005) also supports this mediational model.

Other studies also show that social relationships mediate the religion–well-being connection. Hopkins et al. (2016) studied 416 religiously devoted Hindu pilgrims as they attended an annual religious festival in northern India. The pilgrims ritually bathed in the Ganges River, attended religious meetings, and prayed, while living a simple life that rejects ordinary cares and pleasures.

Hopkins et al. found that shared identity (i.e., a feeling of "we-ness" with the other pilgrims) partially mediated the relationship between religiosity and respondents' positive experiences at the festival. Remember that partial mediation means that some of the relationship goes through the mediator, but that there is also a direct relationship between the predictor and outcome variable (in this case, religiosity and positive experience, respectively). The findings of this study are consistent with the hypothesis that religion increases well-being by enhancing social relationships.

However, social support may not mediate the relationship between religion and well-being for members of all faiths. Pirutinsky et al. (2011) tested the mediational model among a sample of Orthodox and non-Orthodox Jews. The non-Orthodox sample replicates the pattern shown in previous research. I am simplifying the results a bit for clarity, but results from the non-Orthodox respondents show that social support mediated the relationship between intrinsic religiosity and depression (such that religiously infused social support predicted lower levels of depression).

But this was not the case among the Orthodox respondents. For these individuals, religiosity was not related to social support. Although social support did predict lower levels of depression, it did not mediate the relationship between religiosity and depression.

Pirutinsky et al. explain these findings by noting that Orthodox Judaism has a strong focus on religious mental states. There are strict rules and beliefs that members must follow, and these are emphasized more strongly than interpersonal relationships. On the other hand, the non-Orthodox Jews are a part of a much more communal religion. Social participation is emphasized more heavily than specific religious states. As a result, social support may not be as strongly connected to religious practice for Orthodox Jews as it is for non-Orthodox Jews.

Once again, more research is needed. But this is certainly an interesting issue, and it calls into question Graham and Haidt's hypothesis that social relations are an essential part of the religion–well-being relationship for all religions. If Pirutinsky et al.'s results replicate those for other religions that are similar to Orthodox Judaism, it would suggest that Graham and Haidt are at least partly wrong, and that the nature of the specific religion must be considered.

Other Potential Mediators

Psychological Attachment

Psychological attachment (Bowlby, 1988) might also mediate the relationship between religion and well-being. Attachment Theory maintains that children need to form secure emotional connections with a primary caregiver early in life. Furthermore, this connection must be continued in order for individuals to feel secure and thrive psychologically.

Several features of secure attachment are particularly important. Among these is that attachment provides a sense of security in times of stress. Another is that it provides a safe setting from which the child can explore and begin to develop important life skills. Third, the loss of attachment, or separation from the attachment figure, is stressful and anxiety producing. Thus, secure attachment is important for well-being (Bowlby, 1988).

Religion might increase well-being via a form of psychological attachment to God. Granqvist and Kirkpatrick (2013) theorize that much of human religious behavior can be understood as a symbolic attachment to God. For instance, humans form emotional bonds with God that are expressed in terms of love and caring. God is thought to provide security and to help us find wisdom. God also protects us in times of stress, and separation from God is anxiety producing. Granqvist and Kirkpatrick reviewed the literature and found support for each of these assertions. This suggests a mediational model in which religion produces symbolic attachment to God, which then enhances well-being similarly to the way attachment to a human caregiver does.

Self-Control and Self-Regulation

Another possible mediational model is that religion increases individuals' ability for self-control and self-regulation. These characteristics then increase well-being. McCullough and Carter (2013) note that believers in "moral" religions, whose gods stipulate rules of correct behavior, must internalize and follow those rules. Therefore, followers of religions such as Judaism, Islam, and Christianity learn to control impulsive urges relatively well. The self-control that may flow from religious practice then increases well-being by reducing the temptations of drugs, alcohol, and crime, and by helping individuals plan for the future (McCullough & Carter, 2013).

This argument is based on both biological and cultural evolution. McCullough and Carter argue that as societies shifted from mobile hunter gatherers to more sedentary farming communities, there was strong natural selection pressure in favor of self-control. Living in sedentary farming communities required higher levels of cooperation and patience. For instance, population densities increased in these farming communities, so there were simply more people with whom each individual had to interact successfully. There were also more group projects such as digging wells and farming large fields. Each of these features required cooperation and patience. As a result, individuals with higher levels of self-control would have a selective advantage.

The form of religion began to change at about the same time because of cultural evolution, according to McCullough and Carter. Cultures that developed "moral" religions with strict rules of appropriate behavior were better able to encourage self-control in general. This cultural change acted along with evolutionary pressures to enhance individuals' ability to control and self-regulate.

McCullough and Carter reviewed the literature and found support for their hypotheses. For instance, religiosity is positively associated with self-control. Religiosity is also positively related to respect for others and self-discipline, and negatively correlated with self-indulgence. They also argue that self-control may explain many of the religion–well-being associations noted in the literature. For instance, it may explain why religion is associated with less crime, delinquency, and substance abuse, and with higher school performance.

One important point though is that McCullough and Carter's hypothesis applies only to "moral" religions. These are religions that believe God cares about the actions of individuals, and that issue strict rules that followers must obey. Therefore, these hypotheses do not apply to individuals who are merely "spiritual" or who belong to a religion that suggests God is not interested in ordinary human affairs. Another important point is that the theory has not been widely tested. There have been few formal tests of a mediational model that connect this specific type of religion to well-being via a self-control mediator. Instead, research has connected only parts of the model at a time by showing, for instance, that moral religion is associated with self-control.

In summary, the relationship between religion and well-being is not direct. Instead, religion enhances a number of positive psychological states, including meaning in life, social relationships, attachment, and self-control, which mediate the relationship. Meaning in life appears to have attracted the most theoretical attention and research. This research confirms theorists' predictions that meaning in life mediates the relationship between religion and well-being.

The relative strength of each mediator is unknown. Diener et al. (2011) found that meaning in life is a stronger mediator than social relations when life evaluation is the measure of well-being, but few other studies have compared the strength of various mediators. Given the importance of social relations for happiness (Baumeister & Leary, 1995), we might expect social relations to be important relative to other mediators, but this theory is just a hypothesis at present. As always, there is a need for more research, but it is exciting to know something about the mechanisms by which religion can improve well-being.

SUMMARY

Religion is often, but not always, associated with greater well-being. Studies using statistical control techniques suggest that this relationship may be causal, although we cannot be sure without experimental evidence. However, it is important to remember that it is difficult to make an accurate summary statement about such a complex overall relationship.

For instance, atheists, who reject religion completely, can be just as happy as religious individuals. Specific features of religious beliefs are also important. Culture also influences whether religious practice increases well-being. Religion is particularly beneficial for well-being in cultures that support religion and in poor and unstable countries.

There is a good chance that religion is, or at least was at one point, at least indirectly evolutionarily adaptive. However, it could have also developed as an evolutionary by-product. This question has important implications for happiness. If religion developed as a biological adaptation, the implication is that its purpose was to aid survival and reproduction, and not to increase happiness. Therefore, religion-related happiness would occur only when evolutionary needs are satisfied.

The relationship between religion and happiness is not direct, but instead is mediated by a number of factors. Meaning in life appears to be a particularly important mediator, although other variables also mediate. Thus, religion's primary role in happiness may be in enhancing our sense of meaning and purpose in life, which then increases our well-being.

NOTES

1. As with all the results discussed in this section on religious culture, these authors controlled for a variety of demographic variables, along with variables assessing individual religious preference or denomination. Although not guaranteeing that the results reflect causal relationships, these controls make us more confident that they might.

2. β is the standardized slope of the regression line showing the relationship between individual religiosity and health.

3. This indirect path from discrimination to identity to well-being is not unique. Doane and Elliott (2015) note similar findings regarding the effects of discrimination on African Americans' well-being.

REFERENCES

Abu-Raiya, H., Pargament, K. I., & Krause, N. (2016). Religion as problem, religion as solution: Religious buffers of the links between religious/spiritual struggles and well-being/mental health. *Quality of Life Research*, 25(5), 1265–1274.

Abu-Raiya, H., Pargament, K. I., Krause, N., & Ironson, G. (2015). Robust links between religious/spiritual struggles, psychological distress, and well-being in a national sample of American adults. *American Journal of Orthopsychiatry*, 85(6), 565–575.

Allport, G. W., & Ross, J. M. (1967). Personal religious orientation and prejudice. *Journal of Personality and Social Psychology*, 5(4), 432–443.

Altemeyer, B., & Hunsberger, B. (2004). A revised religious fundamentalism scale: The short and sweet of it. *International Journal for the Psychology of Religion*, 14(1), 47–54.

Barber, N. (2013). Country religiosity declines as material security increases. *Cross-Cultural Research: The Journal of Comparative Social Science*, 47(1), 42–50.

Barber, N. (2015). Why is Mississippi more religious than New Hampshire? Material security and ethnicity as factors. *Cross-Cultural Research: The Journal of Comparative Social Science*, 49(3), 315–325.

Baumeister, R. F. (1991). *Meanings of life*. New York, NY: Guilford Press.

Baumeister, R. F., & Leary, M. R. (1995). The need to belong: Desire for interpersonal attachments as a fundamental human motivation. *Psychological Bulletin*, 117(3), 497–529.

Berthold, A., & Ruch, W. (2014). Satisfaction with life and character strengths of non-religious and religious people: It's practicing one's religion that makes the difference. *Frontiers in Psychology*, 5, 1–9.

Bowlby, J. (1988). *A secure base: Parent–child attachment and healthy human development*. New York, NY: Basic Books.

Braam, A. W., Schaap-Jonker, H., Mooi, B., De Ritter, D., Beekman, A. T. F., & Deeg, D. J. H. (2008). God image and mood in old age: Results from a community-based pilot study in the Netherlands. *Mental Health, Religion and Culture*, 11(2), 221–237.

Brewster, M. E., Robinson, M. A., Sandil, R., Esposito, J., & Geiger, E. (2014). Arrantly absent: Atheism in psychological science from 2001 to 2012. *Counseling Psychologist*, 42(5), 628–663.

Byron, K., & Miller-Perrin, C. (2009). The value of life purpose: Purpose as a mediator of faith and well-being. *The Journal of Positive Psychology*, 4(1), 64–70.

Carlucci, L., Tommasi, M., Balsamo, M., Furnham, A., & Saggino, A. (2015). Religious fundamentalism and psychological well-being: An Italian study. *Journal of Psychology and Theology*, 43(1), 23–33.

Cranney, S. (2013). Do people who believe in God report more meaning in their lives? The existential effects of belief. *Journal for the Scientific Study of Religion*, 52(3), 638–646.

Delamontagne, R. G. (2010). High religiosity and societal dysfunction in the United States during the first decade of the twenty-first century. *Evolutionary Psychology*, 8(4), 617–657.

Desai, K. M., & Pargament, K. I. (2015). Predictors of growth and decline following spiritual struggles. *International Journal for the Psychology of Religion*, 25(1), 42–56.

Diener, E., Fujita, F., Tay, L., & Biswas-Diener, R. (2012). Purpose, mood, and pleasure in predicting satisfaction judgments. *Social Indicators Research*, 105(3), 333–341.

Diener, E., Tay, L., & Myers, D. G. (2011). The religion paradox: If religion makes people happy, why are so many dropping out? *Journal of Personality and Social Psychology, 101*(6), 1278–1290.

Doane, M. J., & Elliott, M. (2015). Perceptions of discrimination among atheists: Consequences for atheist identification, psychological and physical well-being. *Psychology of Religion and Spirituality, 7*(2), 130–141.

Edara, I. R. (2013). Spirituality's unique role in positive affect, satisfaction with life, and forgiveness over and above personality and individualism-collectivism. *Research in the Social Scientific Study of Religion, 24*, 15–41.

Exline, J. J., & Rose, E. D. (2013). Religious and spiritual struggles. In R. F. Paloutzian & C. L. Park (Eds.), *Handbook of the psychology of religion and spirituality* (2nd ed., pp. 380–398). New York, NY: Guilford Press.

Eytan, A. (2011). Religion and mental health during incarceration: A systematic literature review. *Psychiatric Quarterly, 82*(4), 287–295.

Faigin, C. A., Pargament, K. I., & Abu-Raiya, H. (2014). Spiritual struggles as a possible risk factor for addictive behaviors: An initial empirical investigation. *International Journal for the Psychology of Religion, 24*(3), 201–214.

Fitchett, G., Winter-Pfändler, U., & Pargament, K. I. (2014). Struggle with the divine in Swiss patients visited by chaplains: Prevalence and correlates. *Journal of Health Psychology, 19*(8), 966–976.

Galen, L. W., & Kloet, J. D. (2011). Mental well-being in the religious and the non-religious: Evidence for a curvilinear relationship. *Mental Health, Religion and Culture, 14*(7), 673–689.

García-Alandete, J. (2015). Does meaning in life predict psychological well-being? *The European Journal of Counselling Psychology, 3*(2), 89–98.

Gervais, W. M. (2014). Everything is permitted? People intuitively judge immorality as representative of atheists. *PLOS ONE, 9*(4). doi:10.1371/journal.pone.0092302

Gervais, W. M., Shariff, A. F., & Norenzayan, A. (2011). Do you believe in atheists? Distrust is central to anti-atheist prejudice. *Journal of Personality and Social Psychology, 101*(6), 1189–1206.

Graham, J., & Haidt, J. (2010). Beyond beliefs: Religions bind individuals into moral communities. *Personality and Social Psychology Review, 14*(1), 140–150.

Granqvist, P., & Kirkpatrick, L. A. (2013). Religion, spirituality, and attachment. In K. I. Pargament, J. J. Exline, & J. W. Jones (Eds.), *APA handbook of psychology, religion, and spirituality (Vol. 1): Context, theory, and research* (pp. 139–155). Washington, DC: American Psychological Association.

Green, M., & Elliott, M. J. (2010). Religion, health, and psychological well-being. *Journal of Religion and Health, 49*, 149–163.

Hackney, C. H., & Sanders, G. S. (2003). Religiosity and mental health: A meta-analysis of recent studies. *Journal for the Scientific Study of Religion, 42*(1), 43–55.

Headey, B., Hoehne, G., & Wagner, G. G. (2014). Does religion make you healthier and longer lived? Evidence for Germany. *Social Indicators Research, 119*(3), 1335–1361.

Hollywell, C., & Walker, J. (2009). Private prayer as a suitable intervention for hospitalised patients: A critical review of the literature. *Journal of Clinical Nursing, 18*(5), 637–651.

Hopkins, N., Reicher, S. D., Khan, S. S., Tewari, S., Srinivasan, N., & Stevenson, C. (2016). Explaining effervescence: Investigating the relationship between shared social identity and positive experience in crowds. *Cognition and Emotion, 30*(1), 20–32.

Jordan, K. D., Masters, K. S., Hooker, S. A., Ruiz, J. M., & Smith, T. W. (2014). An interpersonal approach to religiousness and spirituality: Implications for health and well-being. *Journal of Personality*, *82*(5), 418–431.

Kashdan, T. B., & Nezlek, J. B. (2012). Whether, when, and how is spirituality related to well-being? Moving beyond single occasion questionnaires to understanding daily process. *Personality and Social Psychology Bulletin*, *38*(11), 1523–1535.

Kinnvall, C. (2004). Globalization and religious nationalism: Self, identity, and the search for ontological security. *Political Psychology*, *25*(5), 741–767.

Knabb, J. J., & Pelletier, J. (2014). The relationship between problematic Internet use, God attachment, and psychological functioning among adults at a Christian university. *Mental Health, Religion and Culture*, *17*(3), 239–251.

Koohsar, A. A. H., & Bonab, B. G. (2011). Relation between quality of image of God with anxiety and depression in college students. *Procedia—Social and Behavioral Sciences*, *29*, 252–256.

Koole, S. L., McCullough, M. E., Kuhl, J., & Roelofsma, P. H. M. P. (2010). Why religion's burdens are light: From religiosity to implicit self-regulation. *Personality and Social Psychology Review*, *14*(1), 95–107.

Krause, N. (2006). Church-based social support and change in health over time. *Review of Religious Research*, *48*(2), 125–140.

Krause, N. (2010). Religious involvement, humility, and self-rated health. *Social Indicators Research*, *98*(1), 23–39.

Krause, N., Emmons, R. A., & Ironson, G. (2015). Benevolent images of God, gratitude, and physical health status. *Journal of Religion and Health*, *54*(4), 1503–1519.

Krok, D. (2015). Religiousness, spirituality, and coping with stress among late adolescents: A meaning-making perspective. *Journal of Adolescence*, *45*, 196–203.

Kugelmass, H., & Garcia, A. (2015). Mental disorder among nonreligious adolescents. *Mental Health, Religion and Culture*, *18*(5), 368–379.

Larson, D. B., & Larson, S. S. (2003). Spirituality's potential relevance to physical and emotional health: A brief review of quantitative research. *Journal of Psychology and Theology*, *31*(1), 37–51.

Lawford, H. L., & Ramey, H. L. (2015). "Now I know I can make a difference": Generativity and activity engagement as predictors of meaning making in adolescents and emerging adults. *Developmental Psychology*, *51*(10), 1395–1406.

Lawrence, R. T. (1997). Measuring the image of God: The God image inventory and the God image scales. *Journal of Psychology and Theology*, *25*(2), 214–226.

Lechner, C. M., & Leopold, T. (2015). Religious attendance buffers the impact of unemployment on life satisfaction: Longitudinal evidence from Germany. *Journal for the Scientific Study of Religion*, *54*(1), 166–174.

Lun, V. M., & Bond, M. H. (2013). Examining the relation of religion and spirituality to subjective well-being across national cultures. *Psychology of Religion and Spirituality*, *5*(4), 304–315.

Lyubomirsky, S. (2008). *The how of happiness: A new approach to getting the life you want*. New York, NY: Penguin Press.

Masters, K. S., & Hooker, S. A. (2013). Religiousness/spirituality, cardiovascular disease, and cancer: Cultural integration for health research and intervention. *Journal of Consulting and Clinical Psychology*, *81*(2), 206–216.

McCullough, M. E., & Carter, E. C. (2013). Religion, self-control, and self-regulation: How and why are they related? In K. I. Pargament, J. J. Exline, & J. W. Jones (Eds.), *APA handbook of psychology, religion, and spirituality (Vol. 1): Context, theory, and research* (pp. 123–138). Washington, DC: American Psychological Association.

Mochon, D., Norton, M. I., & Ariely, D. (2011). Who benefits from religion? *Social Indicators Research*, *101*(1), 1–15.

Myers, D. G. (2008). Religion and human flourishing. In M. Eid & R. J. Larsen (Eds.), *The science of subjective well-being* (pp. 323–343). New York, NY: Guilford Press.

Oishi, S., & Diener, E. (2014). Residents of poor nations have a greater sense of meaning in life than residents of wealthy nations. *Psychological Science*, *25*(2), 422–430.

Pargament, K. I. (1997). *The psychology of religion and coping: Theory, research, practice.* New York, NY: Guilford Press.

Pargament, K. I. (2002). The bitter and the sweet: An evaluation of the costs and benefits of religiousness. *Psychological Inquiry*, *13*(3), 168–181.

Pargament, K. I., Falb, M. D., Ano, G. G., & Wachholtz, A. B. (2013). The religious dimension of coping: Advances in theory, research, and practice. In R. F. Paloutzian & C. L. Park (Eds.), *Handbook of the psychology of religion and spirituality* (2nd ed., pp. 560–579). New York, NY: Guilford Press.

Pargament, K. I., Murray-Swank, N., Magyar, G. M., & Ano, G. G. (2005). Spiritual struggle: A phenomenon of interest to psychology and religion. In W. R. Miller & H. D. Delaney (Eds.), *Judeo-Christian perspectives on psychology: Human nature, motivation, and change* (pp. 245–268). Washington, DC: American Psychological Association.

Park, C. L., Edmondson, D., & Hale-Smith, A. (2013). Why religion? Meaning as motivation. In K. I. Pargament, J. J. Exline, & J. W. Jones (Eds.), *APA handbook of psychology, religion, and spirituality (Vol 1.): Context, theory, and research* (pp. 157–171). Washington, DC: American Psychological Association.

Paul, G. (2009). The chronic dependence of popular religiosity upon dysfunctional psychological conditions. *Evolutionary Psychology*, *7*, 398–441.

Paul, G. S. (2012). Why religion is unable to minimize lethal and nonlethal societal dysfunction within and between nations. In T. Shackelford & V. Weekes (Eds.), *The Oxford handbook of evolutionary perspectives on violence, homicide, and war* (pp. 435–470). New York, NY: Oxford University Press.

Pirutinsky, S., Rosmarin, D. H., Holt, C. L., Feldman, R. H., Caplan, L. S., Midlarsky, E., & Pargament, K. I. (2011). Does social support mediate the moderating effect of intrinsic religiosity on the relationship between physical health and depressive symptoms among Jews? *Journal of Behavioral Medicine*, *34*(6), 489–496.

Powell, L. H., Shahabi, L., & Thoresen, C. E. (2003). Religion and spirituality: Linkages to physical health. *American Psychologist*, *58*(1), 36–52.

Ritter, R. S., Preston, J. L., & Hernandez, I. (2014). Happy tweets: Christians are happier, more socially connected, and less analytical than atheists on Twitter. *Social Psychological and Personality Science*, *5*(2), 243–249.

Rosenblatt, A., Greenberg, J., Solomon, S., Pyszczynski, T., & Lyon, D. (1989). Evidence for terror management theory: I. The effects of mortality salience on reactions to those who violate or uphold cultural values. *Journal of Personality and Social Psychology*, *57*(4), 681–690.

Ryan, R. M., Rigby, S., & King, K. (1993). Two types of religious internalization and their relations to religious orientations and mental health. *Journal of Personality and Social Psychology*, *65*(3), 586–596.

Salsman, J. M., Brown, T. L., Brechting, E. H., & Carlson, C. R. (2005). The link between religion and spirituality and psychological adjustment: The mediating role of optimism and social support. *Personality and Social Psychology Bulletin*, *31*(4), 522–535.

Schreiber, J. A., & Brockopp, D. Y. (2012). Twenty-five years later—What do we know about religion/spirituality and psychological well-being among breast cancer survivors? A systematic review. *Journal of Cancer Survivorship*, *6*(1), 82–94.

Sethi, S., & Seligman, M. E. (1993). Optimism and fundamentalism. *Psychological Science*, *4*(4), 256–259.

Seybold, K. S., & Hill, P. C. (2001). The role of religion and spirituality in mental and physical health. *Current Directions in Psychological Science*, *10*(1), 21–24.

Sillick, W. J., & Cathcart, S. (2014). The relationship between religious orientation and happiness: The mediating role of purpose in life. *Mental Health, Religion and Culture*, *17*(5), 494–507.

Silton, N. R., Flannelly, K. J., Galek, K., & Ellison, C. G. (2014). Beliefs about God and mental health among American adults. *Journal of Religion and Health*, *53*(5), 1285–1296.

Snyder, C. R. (2002). Hope theory: Rainbows in the mind. *Psychological Inquiry*, *13*(4), 249–275.

Stavrova, O. (2015). Religion, self-rated health, and mortality: Whether religiosity delays death depends on the cultural context. *Social Psychological and Personality Science*, *6*(8), 911–922.

Stavrova, O., Fetchenhauer, D., & Schlösser, T. (2013). Why are religious people happy? The effect of the social norm of religiosity across countries. *Social Science Research*, *42*(1), 90–105.

Streib, H., & Klein, C. (2013). Atheists, agnostics, and apostates. In K. I. Pargament, J. J. Exline, & J. W. Jones (Eds.), *APA handbook of psychology, religion, and spirituality (Vol. 1): Context, theory, and research* (pp. 713–728). Washington, DC: American Psychological Association.

Stroope, S., Draper, S., & Whitehead, A. L. (2013). Images of a loving God and sense of meaning in life. *Social Indicators Research*, *111*(1), 25–44.

Sumner, R., Burrow, A. L., & Hill, P. L. (2015). Identity and purpose as predictors of subjective well-being in emerging adulthood. *Emerging Adulthood*, *3*(1), 46–54.

Tajfel, H., & Turner, J. C. (1986). The social identity theory of inter-group behavior. In S. Worchel & L. W. Austin (Eds.), *Psychology of intergroup relations* (pp. 7–24). Chicago, IL: Nelson-Hall.

Tay, L., Li, M., Myers, D., & Diener, E. (2014). Religiosity and subjective well-being: An international perspective. In C. Kim-Prieto (Ed.), *Religion and spirituality across cultures* (pp. 163–175). Dordrecht, Netherlands: Springer Science.

Thoresen, C. E., & Harris, A. H. S. (2002). Spirituality and health: What's the evidence and what's needed? *Annals of Behavioral Medicine*, *24*(1), 3–13.

van Tongeren, D. R., Hook, J. N., & Davis, D. E. (2013). Defensive religion as a source of meaning in life: A dual mediational model. *Psychology of Religion and Spirituality*, *5*(3), 227–232.

Vishkin, A., Bigman, Y., & Tamir, M. (2014). Religion, emotion regulation, and well-being. In C. Kim-Prieto (Ed.), *Religion and spirituality across cultures* (pp. 247–269). New York, NY: Springer Science + Business Media.

Weber, S. R., & Pargament, K. I. (2014). The role of religion and spirituality in mental health. *Current Opinion in Psychiatry*, *27*(5), 358–363.

Weber, S. R., Pargament, K. I., Kunik, M. E., Lomax, J. W., II, & Stanley, M. A. (2012). Psychological distress among religious nonbelievers: A systematic review. *Journal of Religion and Health*, *51*(1), 72–86.

Wilmoth, J. D., Adams-Price, C., Turner, J. J., Blaney, A. D., & Downey, L. (2014). Examining social connections as a link between religious participation and well-being among older adults. *Journal of Religion, Spirituality and Aging, 26*(2–3), 259–278.

Ysseldyk, R., Matheson, K., & Anisman, H. (2010). Religiosity as identity: Toward an understanding of religion from a social identity perspective. *Personality and Social Psychology Review, 14*(1), 60–71.

CHAPTER 10

Health

A cheerful heart is good medicine, But a crushed spirit dries up the bones.
—Proverbs, Chapter 17, Verse 22

In this chapter we find that happy people tend to live longer and healthier lives. This seems to be particularly true for individuals with high levels of positive affect (as opposed to life satisfaction) who are initially healthy (Pressman & Bowlin, 2014). But we also see this trend among individuals with low levels of negative affect, and among those who are high in life satisfaction and/or are high in eudaimonic well-being, in which they feel a strong sense of meaning and purpose in their lives.

These observations lead to other issues, including how and why happiness is associated with health, and whether happiness is one cause of health. These critically important questions have implications for public policy that we discuss at the end of the chapter. We first investigate how well-being might affect health, including behavioral and physiological pathways that might link these two variables. Then we examine relationships between various aspects of well-being and health.

PHYSIOLOGICAL AND BEHAVIORAL PATHWAYS BETWEEN HAPPINESS AND HEALTH

It makes sense to consider the relationship between happiness and physical health only if we are certain that there is a plausible pathway connecting these variables. Demonstrating this pathway increases our confidence that any correlation between happiness and health is not accidental. Fortunately, there are plausible pathways. Some of these are relatively direct, in which feelings of well-being impact physiological functioning, which then has a direct impact on physical health. Other potential pathways are less direct. In these, well-being is hypothesized to affect health-related behaviors such as exercise and diet, and these behavioral factors affect our physiology and health (DeSteno, Gross, & Kubzansky, 2013).

Direct Physiological Pathways

Positive Affect

Several links between well-being and physiological systems have implications for health. For instance, positive well-being, particularly positive affect, seems to have protective and restorative effects on bodily systems that improve physical health (Mathew & Paulose, 2011). Positive affect is associated with lower blood pressure, healthier heart rates, and, among men, improved cardiovascular functioning and quicker cardiovascular recovery from stress (Dockray & Steptoe, 2010). All of these have positive implications for cardiovascular disease (Boehm & Kubzansky, 2012; Diener & Chan, 2011; Mathew & Paulose, 2011). Positive affect is also related to better sleep, which is an important contributor to good health.

In addition, laughter lowers stress hormone levels (Dockray & Steptoe, 2010) and helps to protect the immune system from stress (Mathew & Paulose, 2011; Pressman & Cohen, 2005). Positive affect is also associated with the number of immune cells, including helper T cells, and with regulation of cytokines (Dockray & Steptoe, 2010). It is important that cytokines be regulated properly because they attract immune cells that can destroy infections toward foreign objects in the body (Pinel, 2011). Cytokines can also cause beneficial inflammation as part of an immune response. However, if poorly regulated, this inflammation can cause health problems (Denson, Spanovic, & Miller, 2009).

Furthermore, positive affect is associated with increased secretion of serotonin, a neurotransmitter that can protect against both negative moods and ill health (Mathew & Paulose, 2011). Positive affect also influences dopamine, which is both a hormone and a neurotransmitter and which affects the brain's "pleasure centers." Brain networks that respond to serotonin and dopamine interact to affect tendencies to approach rewards and withdraw from stressors (Mathew & Paulose, 2011). The extent to which positive affect can regulate overstimulation of the stress–withdrawal response has important implications for protection against chronic and inappropriate overactivation of bodily systems, which can lead to poor health.

Negative Affect

Negative affect is associated with adverse bodily activation that can lead to poor health outcomes through deteriorative processes (Boehm & Kubzansky, 2012; Mathew & Paulose, 2011). For instance, negative affect can contribute to vascular inflammation and can have important implications for cardiovascular health (Boehm & Kubzansky, 2012; Diener & Chan, 2011; Mathew & Paulose, 2011). There is also evidence that negative emotions are associated with inflammatory processes that contribute to other diseases such as some cancers, Alzheimer's, and arthritis (Diener & Chan, 2011).

Negative affect also facilitates the release of the "stress hormone" cortisol, which then influences adverse bodily activation. Specifically, stress, and the resulting negative emotion, can prompt the adrenal and pituitary glands within the hypothalamus to release cortisol into the bloodstream. Cortisol causes the liver to produce additional sugars that can be used for long-term energy in order to deal with a stress-inducing threat. Repeated releases of cortisol are associated with metabolic disorders and poor immune system functioning (Denson et al., 2009[1]; Diener & Chan, 2011).

Well-being is also related to critical functioning of our genes. Negative well-being such as depression appears to erode the length of *telomeres* (Diener & Chan, 2011), which are protective caps at the end of chromosomes. These caps help ensure that DNA replicates itself accurately (Blackburn, 2001). Premature shortening of telomeres is associated with a number of health problems including premature aging (Boccardi & Paolisso, 2014; Diener & Chan, 2011).

Happiness is also connected to physical health through the process of emotional regulation (Appleton, Buka, Loucks, Gilman, & Kubzansky, 2013; DeSteno et al., 2013; McRae, Jacobs, Ray, John, & Gross, 2012). Individuals must control their reactions to external events in order to respond appropriately to threats and opportunities. This includes refraining from overreacting to minor or illusory threats. Such overreactions lower well-being by producing anxiety and depression. But overreactions can also negatively affect physical health by unnecessarily increasing bodily activation that stresses bodily systems (Mathew & Paulose, 2011; Rickard & Vella-Brodrick, 2014).

For example, emotion regulation is associated with the level of C-reactive protein, a biomarker found in blood that indicates inflammation that can lead to heart disease. Appleton et al. (2013) examine the relationship between this biomarker and emotional regulation in a large sample of American adults. Results indicate that proper emotional regulation (i.e., appropriate emotional reactions to events) predicts lower levels of this biomarker. Importantly, happy individuals are better emotional regulators. They recover from negative events more quickly, and presumably experience less physiological stress that might make them vulnerable to disease (Rickard & Vella-Brodrick, 2014).

In summary, affective responses are linked to physiological systems that have clear implications for our health. Positive affect is associated with better cardiovascular and immune functioning, as well as better emotional regulation of stress/withdrawal responses. Negative affect is associated with adverse inflammatory processes, poor immune functioning, and premature aging. This clear path between positive and negative affect and physiological systems that affect human health makes it more plausible that well-being might cause specific health conditions.

Behavioral Pathways

Well-being also affects behavior that has implications for health. For instance, well-being is associated with social connectedness and social support, and with healthier diet and avoidance of harmful substances such as nicotine. Well-being is also associated with more "self-care activities such as exercise and use of sunscreen (DeSteno et al., 2013; Diener & Chan, 2011; Pressman & Cohen, 2005; Wilson, 2015).

Depression predicts a host of behaviors associated with poor health. Paxton, Valois, Watkins, Huebner, and Drane (2007) find that depressed individuals are more than four times more likely to drink heavily and almost 10 times more likely to use illegal drugs and take sexual risks than are the nondepressed. These results come from a nationally representative sample of American adolescents and remain significant after controlling for sociodemographic variables. The relationship between depression and health risk behaviors tends to be stronger among African American adolescents and other minority groups. The authors speculate that these results reflect adolescents' attempts to deal with feelings of unhappiness.

In addition, feelings of psychological competency and vulnerability are linked to use of the health care system, a behavior with important health implications, among older African Americans. O'Neal et al. (2014, p. 494) find that competency (e.g., "How often have you felt confident about your ability to handle your personal problems?"; "How often have you felt things were going your way?") and vulnerability ("How often have you felt nervous and stressed?"; "How often have you found that you could not cope with all the things that you had to do?") predict health care system utilization behaviors such as seeking cholesterol screening, even after taking sociodemographic variables and health insurance status into account.

Other research indicates that life satisfaction is positively related to health-inducing or health-maintaining behaviors. For instance, Grant, Wardle, and Steptoe (2009) examined a sample of more than 17,000 university students from 21 countries. Respondents with higher levels of life satisfaction were less likely to smoke, and were more likely to limit fat intake, exercise, eat fruit, and use sun protection. These results remain significant after controlling for age, sex, and nationality. Similarly, Shahab and West (2012) found that ex-smokers who had abstained for at least 1 year and individuals who had never smoked reported higher life satisfaction and life enjoyment levels than did current smokers, even after controlling for sociodemographic variables. These results were obtained from a representative sample of almost 7,000 adults in England.

You have probably noticed that these results are all correlational. While consistent with the hypothesis that happiness causes behaviors that then reduce health risks, these findings are also consistent with several alternative hypotheses, chief among them a question about the direction of any causality between happiness and health-related behavior. Could it be that these behaviors cause happiness, rather than vice versa? In truth, researchers note that the relationship is probably bidirectional (e.g., Shahab & West, 2012).

However, the researchers make logical arguments that at least part of the causal flow goes from happiness to health-related behaviors. For example, Grant et al. (2009), who conducted the study of university students from 21 countries discussed earlier, argue that it is unlikely that failure to use sun protection and to eat fruit would cause lower life satisfaction. Thus, they imply that the most parsimonious explanation for the causal direction of their results goes from life satisfaction to behavior. Similarly, another study (Lipovčan, Brkljačić, & Tadić, 2013), using a sample from Croatia, finds that smoking was negatively associated with overall happiness, but also with other satisfaction measures such as life achievements. These results favor the "happiness causes health-related behaviors" hypothesis because it is unlikely that smoking could cause life achievement satisfaction. This is particularly true given that smoking is socially acceptable in Croatia (Lipovčan et al., 2013), so smoking should not lower achievements. If smoking is unlikely to cause one type of satisfaction measure (life achievement satisfaction), it seems unlikely to cause others measuring happiness.

Other research has tried to identify the direction of causality methodologically. For instance, Koivumaa-Honkanen et al. (2012) conducted a longitudinal study of Finnish twins and found that life satisfaction and unhealthy alcohol use reciprocally predicted each other over time. In other words, there was evidence of bidirectional causality, with each variable causing the other.

In conclusion, well-being is related to a number of health-relevant behaviors including exercise, diet, smoking, and alcohol consumption. Although the causal nature of these relationships is unclear, evidence suggests that well-being contributes to health, in part, by encouraging healthy behaviors. The direction of causation problem is vexing, and the relations are probably bidirectional. However, several authors have made impressive logical arguments that well-being causes health-related behaviors.

In reviewing how direct and indirect pathways link well-being to physiological processes, we have mapped out a plausible way in which well-being might affect physical health. There are direct physiological paths between happiness and health. There are also behavioral paths such as alcohol consumption, diet, and smoking, which all have implications for our physiology and health. Although the causal nature of these relationships is unclear, evidence suggests that well-being contributes to health, in part, by encouraging healthy behaviors. The direction of the causation problem is vexing, and the relationships are probably bidirectional. However, several authors have made impressive logical arguments that well-being causes health-related behaviors. Now, having established the plausible pathways, we investigate the relationship between well-being and health in more detail.

What We Need to Study Further About the Elements of Well-Being

In most of this chapter, well-being is defined in terms of positive and negative affect and life satisfaction. However, we still do not know a lot about the relative importance of these three elements of well-being (Diener & Chan, 2011). For instance, is life satisfaction as important to health as either positive or negative affect? Does the relative importance of type of well-being depend on specific health problems?

This current lack of understanding is reflected in the rest of this chapter. I present evidence showing that all three elements of well-being are related to various measures of health in order to describe the diverse literature and give an idea of the range of research findings. But only a few studies make any attempt to directly compare the relative impact of these well-being measures.

However, we know something about how positive and negative affect influence health. Positive affect seems to have a physiologically protective function that reduces unnecessary and potentially harmful bodily activation. However, negative affect can set a pattern of chronic and harmful arousal in motion that has negative implications for our health (Boehm & Kubzansky, 2012).

Thus, negative and positive affect have independent effects on health (DeSteno et al., 2013; Diener & Chan, 2011; Howell, Kern, & Lyubomirsky, 2007; Larsen & McGraw, 2011). Functionally, these affective measures do not operate as if on a continuum in which the presence of positive affect means the absence of negative affect, and vice versa. Instead, individuals are capable of experiencing both types of affect at the same time. In addition, positive affect often predicts health outcomes even after controlling for negative affect, indicating the independence of these measures. Thus, it is often the *presence* of positive affect, for example, that promotes health, and not the mere *absence* of negative affect. This is another reason why we discuss positive and negative affect separately throughout the chapter.

Finally, we do not have a good understanding of how life satisfaction relates to health. Some of the research suggests that life satisfaction might stimulate healthy behaviors such as exercise and good diet, but more systematic research is needed on this topic.

HAPPINESS AND HEALTH

A Sampling of Findings

Life Satisfaction

Happier people are generally physically healthier (Diener & Chan, 2011). For example, *hedonic* well-being (i.e., life satisfaction, positive and negative affect) and optimism predict cardiovascular disease particularly well. *Eudaimonic* well-being (i.e., purpose in life, personal growth, social relations, self-acceptance, environmental mastery, and autonomy) is also linked to cardiovascular health. These measures of well-being predict a variety of cardiovascular health measures including clinical diagnoses and biomarkers of disease. These findings remain significant even after controlling for sociodemographic factors and other risk factors.

Life satisfaction is linked to a variety of better health outcomes. For instance, among a sample of Israeli citizens, those with higher levels of life satisfaction were 21% less likely to be diagnosed with diabetes 20 months later, even after controlling for body mass and smoking, among other factors (Shirom, Toker, Melamed, Berliner, & Shapira, 2012). Similarly, results from an Italian sample indicated that life satisfaction predicts perceived health status, a measure that closely tracks objective measures of physical health (Sabatini, 2014). This latter result holds even after controlling for the degree to which participants were socially integrated, and several sociodemographic factors. In addition, Kim, Park, Sun, Smith, and Peterson (2014) found that life satisfaction was associated with fewer doctor visits among a sample of Americans older than 50. These authors suggested that part of the reason for this association is that individuals with high life satisfaction are healthier.

Furthermore, some research suggests that women might especially benefit from high life satisfaction. Feller, Teucher, Kaaks, Boeing, and Vigl (2013) conducted an 8-year longitudinal study of more than 50,000 people in Germany and found that women with low life satisfaction were 1.45 times more likely to contract cancer, 1.69 times more likely to experience a stroke, and somewhat more likely to be diagnosed as diabetic than were women with high life satisfaction. Men with low life satisfaction were somewhat more likely to experience a stroke. All these analyses remain statistically significant after controlling for health behaviors such as smoking and several sociodemographic variables.

However, causality is always uncertain in this kind of research because of its correlational nature. One alternative explanation is that life satisfaction simply reflects and results *from* physical health rather than *causing* health. Another possibility is that there might be a bidirectional relation, such that life satisfaction and health cause each other in a reciprocating fashion over time. Studies that follow participants over time can be a powerful tool that helps sort out these kinds of causality questions.

Gana et al. (2013) conducted such a longitudinal study among French retirees (average age = 73). These authors collected data on life satisfaction and health, along with numerous control variables, every 2 years for 8 years. Because they obtained multiple observations of all the variables over time, they were able to use statistical techniques that offered strong inferences about the direction of causation between life satisfaction and health. Results indicated that good health contributed to more life satisfaction each time data were collected. However, they found no evidence that life satisfaction contributed to health at any of the measurement periods.

Thus, these findings suggest that life satisfaction is caused by good health, and not the other way around, at least in this sample of French retirees. It will be interesting to see whether these results replicate and whether they apply to younger populations. It is possible that life satisfaction may still offer some health protection to younger people whose health problems are not as severe as those likely encountered by retirees in their seventies.

In fact, at least one study indicates that life satisfaction and health are bidirectionally related among younger respondents. Garrido, Méndez, and Abellán (2013) examined a representative sample of Spanish adults (average age = 44) with statistical techniques that allowed estimates of bidirectional relationships. They assessed both life satisfaction and self-reported health, in addition to standard sociodemographic control variables. The relationship between life satisfaction and health is indeed bidirectional. A 1% increase in life satisfaction was associated with a 0.3% increase in self-reported health, while a 1% increase in self-reported health was associated with a 0.32% increase in life satisfaction.

Positive Affect

Positive affect can protect individuals from some diseases (Pressman & Bowlin, 2014). For example, Kubzansky and Thurston (2007) found that vitality, measured as having a sense of energy, feeling happy, and feeling sure of oneself, and so on, negatively predicted later coronary heart disease diagnosis in a sample that was originally free of heart disease. These results were obtained from a representative sample of American adults (average age at the beginning of the study was 48) who were followed for more than 20 years.

Participants with high vitality were 32% less likely to receive a coronary heart disease diagnosis, and those with medium vitality were 14% less likely to receive the diagnosis, than were low vitality participants. Stated differently, there was a 2% to 3% decrease in the likelihood of heart disease diagnosis for every one point increase on the 35-point vitality scale (Kubzansky & Thurston, 2007). These findings indicate a dose–response pattern, which gives us more confidence that the relationship is not coincidental and that low vitality is a cause of heart disease. The findings remain significant after statistically controlling for sociodemographic variables, health status, and health behaviors such as smoking.

These results demonstrate how well-being can protect individuals from disease. Kubzansky and Thurston (2007) found that health behaviors such as smoking and alcohol use explain part of the connection between vitality and heart disease: Low-vitality participants were more likely to drink excessively and to smoke, and these health relevant factors then, in turn, predicted heart disease. The authors speculate that the rest of the vitality/heart disease connection is explained by direct physiological effects. Specifically, they suggest that vitality might prevent ". . . hyperarousal by reducing activation of neuroendocrine, cardiovascular and inflammatory processes" related to disease (Kubzansky & Thurston, 2007, p. 1399).

Other research has obtained similar findings. Lundgren, Garvin, Jonasson, Andersson, and Kristenson (2015) found that a sense of mastery (i.e., "feelings of confidence and self-reliance," p. 78) and self-esteem protected a representative and longitudinal sample of Swedes from incidents of coronary heart disease. All participants were initially healthy, and the authors used similar controls as were used by Kubzansky and Thurston (2007). High mastery and high self-esteem participants were 33% and 31% less likely to experience a major event of coronary heart disease, respectively.

Positive affect is also associated with the ability to perform basic functions of daily living, an important health-related construct (Hirosaki et al., 2013). For instance, Japanese participants older than 65 who felt happy and full of energy and were satisfied with their lives were 22% more likely to be able to live independently 2 years later. Specifically, happy, satisfied, and energetic participants were more likely to be able to walk, ascend and descend stairs, feed themselves, and use the toilet independently than were other participants, even after controlling for age, sex, marital status, and smoking and drinking status (Hirosaki et al., 2013).

Negative Affect

Negative affect is also associated with health. Hilmert, Teoh, and Roy (2014) found that college students who were high in negative affect (i.e., nervous), and who worked hard when asked to perform a stressful task (e.g., making a public presentation) showed more cardiovascular reactivity than students lower in negative affect. These results are important because cardiovascular reactivity is a measure of stress and wear and tear on the heart (Hilmert et al., 2014). Thus, these results indicate that negative affect that results from stress can have implications for long-term health.

Another study makes an argument that negative affect causes health outcomes rather than merely being correlated with them. Cohen, Tyrrell, and Smith (1993) exposed British participants to receive a nasal spray that contained a respiratory virus. Participants were sequestered in apartments for 2 days before and 7 days after exposure to the nasal spray. Eighty-eight percent of the participants with high levels of negative affect developed viral infections,[2] compared with only 77% of those with low negative affect, a significant difference.

Although participants with high levels of negative affect were not more likely to develop cold symptoms, the results are consistent with the hypothesis that well-being influences an individual's susceptibility to disease. The results are also consistent with the argument that affect is a causal factor, because all participants had identical exposure to the virus, making some alternative explanations highly unlikely. For example, the differences in infection rates could not be explained by arguing that low negative affect individuals practice better sanitation, and thus limit their exposure to viruses. In addition, Cohen et al. statistically controlled for age, weight, education, gender, allergy status, and whether individuals had antibodies to the virus at the beginning of the study.

First- and Third-World Comparison

The relationship between well-being and health also appears in samples from third-world populations. Pressman, Gallagher, Lopez, and Campos (2014) found that positive and negative emotions predicted self-reported health in data from the annual Gallup World Poll that included more than 150,000 participants from more than 140 countries. These data are considered a representative sample of 95% of the world's population. The authors measured positive and negative emotions, asking respondents whether they had laughed and demonstrated other positivity and experienced worry and other negative feelings during the previous day. Respondents indicated their health by stating whether they were satisfied with their health, whether they felt pain, and so forth, during the previous day.

Table 10.1 represents Pressman et al.'s (2014) major findings from a sample of countries included in the survey[3] (all the correlations in the table are statistically significant). Take a minute to look these results over. Do you notice any patterns in the relations between positive and negative emotions and health, depending on the wealth of the country?[4]

What you probably noticed first is that positive and negative emotions predict health all over the world. In addition, all the correlations within a gross domestic product (GDP) level, which is a measure of a country's wealth, are pretty similar. However, notice that correlations between positive emotions and health are stronger in the low wealth GDP countries, such as Haiti, than they are in the richer countries such as the United States. These results indicate that well-being is a health concern not only in first-world, wealthy nations in which individuals' material needs are likely well satisfied. Instead, well-being predicts health all over the world, and positive emotions might be particularly important for health in poorer countries.

In fact, Pressman and colleagues did additional analyses to account for the potential impacts of food, shelter, and safety concerns on health. Throughout the globe, after accounting for these factors, positive and negative emotions uniquely predict self-reported health, over and above the predictive ability of the availability and quality of food, shelter, and safety. And remember that positive emotions are particularly strong predictors in poorer countries, again over and above food, shelter, and safety.

These results were unexpected. Pressman et al. predicted that emotional well-being would matter *less* in poorer countries, terming emotions "almost a luxury" in lives in which basic physiological and safety needs are not met (p. 545). The authors noted that the physiology of emotions and their influence on the body are universal, regardless of

TABLE 10.1 Associations of Positive and Negative Emotions With Physical Health in Countries With High, Moderate, and Low Per Capita Gross Domestic Products (GDPs)

Country	GDP Per Capita ($)	Correlations		Partial Correlations		Average PE-Health Partial Correlation	Average NE-Health Partial Correlation
		PE-Health	NE-Health	PE-Health	NE-Health		
High-GDP countries						.153	−.277
United States	41,890	.288	−.322	.166	−.196		
Ireland	38,505	.303	−.411	.149	−.325		
Switzerland	35,633	.251	−.265	.172	−.175		
Australia	31,794	.264	−.377	.145	−.273		
Japan	31,267	.383	−.540	.133	−.416		
Moderate-GDP countries						.237	−.235
Russia	10,845	.426	−.351	.320	−.192		
Brazil	8,402	.245	−.352	.101	−.254		
Ukraine	6,848	.480	−.399	.374	−.244		
China	6,757	.319	−.313	.176	−.161		
Peru	6,039	.347	−.418	.214	−.323		

Low-GDP countries						
Haiti	1,663	.387	−.408	.250	−.252	.287	−.263
Rwanda	1,206	.504	−.513	.295	−.266		
Nigeria	1,128	.396	−.444	.257	−.317		
Sierra Leone	806	.572	−.553	.337	−.287		
Malawi	667	.369	−.298	.295	−.194		
All countries worldwide	10,742	.406	−.396	.284	−.269	—	—

Note: Gross domestic product (GDP) was measured in U.S. dollars.
NE, negative emotion; PE, positive emotion.

wealth. Furthermore, they concluded their paper by urging medical professionals to consider the everyday emotions of their patients. They also note that GDP and other economic measures are commonly used as exclusive indices of whether human needs are being met in a society. However, these economic measures fail to reflect the importance of well-being on tangible outcomes such as health.

Culture

Differences in the Strength of Relationships

Pressman et al.'s (2014) results comparing first- and third-world countries were criticized because they did not seem to fit with other research showing cross-cultural differences in the way emotions relate to physical health. Curhan et al. (2014) pointed to decades of research showing that people of different cultures interpret negative emotions very differently, and argued that these differing interpretations have important implications for physical health.

Curhan et al. (2014) illustrated this point by examining survey data in the United States and Japan on negative emotions and health. Results indicated that while negative emotions were associated with poorer health in both countries, the relationship was stronger in the United States than in Japan. Curhan et al. suggested that these differences may occur because Americans view negative emotions as harmful and within the individual's control, while Japanese view negative emotions as natural.

But, Curhan et al. merely demonstrated cultural differences in the *strength* of the negative emotion/health relationship, and not that it does not exist cross-culturally (Pressman et al., 2014). Thus, the cultural impact demonstrated by Curhan et al. is limited. In addition, Pressman et al. responded to Curhan et al.'s critique by describing additional data showing that widely differing cultures exhibited similar positive affect/health relationships. These new data further strengthen the case that cultural differences in the emotion/health relationship are merely a matter of degree and are not qualitative differences.

Qualitative Cultural Differences

General negative emotions   However, some studies demonstrate qualitative cultural differences in the relationship between emotions and health. For instance, Miyamoto et al. (2013) found that negative emotions produced differing levels of interleukin-6 (IL-6), a biomarker of inflammatory processes, among Japanese and Americans. This is interesting and important because IL-6 is thought to provide a pathway between negative emotions and inflammatory processes that can lead to heart disease and cancer.

For American participants, higher levels of negative emotion were associated with more IL-6 in the blood. However, there was no relationship between negative emotion and IL-6 among Japanese participants. Miyamoto et al. argued that these differences occurred because of differing cultural interpretations of negative emotions. Japanese culture views negative emotions as natural and even desirable because of their potential motivational properties. However, American culture views negative emotions as undesirable and something that should be avoided or suppressed. As a result, the authors argue that Americans are more likely to have adverse physiological responses to negative emotions.

There are a couple of important points to note about Miyamoto et al.'s findings. First, the cultural differences are important in-and-of-themselves, but note also that they constitute *qualitative* differences in the way cultures respond to negative emotions. Unlike the Pressman et al. (2014) review, these results do not merely indicate that one culture produces a stronger or weaker response than the other. Instead, these results indicate that Americans react to negative emotions in a way that Japanese do not.

It is also important that Miyamoto et al. make a fairly strong argument that culture causes these differences in IL-6 production. These results held after controlling for sociodemographic characteristics, personality, positive emotions, health status, self-reported health, and health behaviors such as smoking. Although it is difficult to compare individuals from different cultures because they are so dissimilar, the authors did an admirable job of statistically controlling for many possible alternative explanations. For instance, we can be relatively sure that the cultural differences in IL-6 production were not caused by differences in how healthy the two samples were. Therefore, it does appear that negative emotion is unlikely to produce ill health via IL-6 protein synthesis in Japanese culture but may lead to ill health in the United States because of this pathway.

Anger   There are other qualitative cultural differences in response to negative emotions. Kitayama et al. (2015) noted that anger is consistently linked to physiological indicators of poor cardiovascular health. However, most of this literature comes from samples from Western countries, so the cross-cultural generality of this finding is unclear.

These authors examine representative samples of Americans and Japanese. Participants in both samples were asked how often they expressed angry feelings (e.g., "I slam doors") and about their personalities (e.g., "I have a fiery temper"; Kitayama et al., 2015, p. 213). The authors also obtained blood pressure measures and blood samples from all participants. Participants' blood was examined for biomarkers of cardiovascular disease. Finally, data regarding sociodemographic status, health behaviors (e.g., smoking), health status, and the experience of negative emotions other than anger were also gathered for control purposes.

As shown by Figure 10.1, results indicate that the Japanese and American samples showed qualitatively different health responses to anger. Note that the asterisks along the lines in the figure indicate that both lines have a significant slope. Thus, anger expression increases health risk in the American sample, but decreases it in the Japanese sample. These results are interesting for several reasons that we discuss in more detail, but first note that, unlike Pressman et al.'s (2014) findings, these results demonstrate that different cultures have qualitatively different health responses to a negative emotion.

There are a couple other specifics worth noting about Kitayama et al.'s results. First, these results are remarkable because they show the relationship between a negative emotion in a real-world context (not manipulated in a laboratory) and objective physiological indicators of health risk. Second, the results also show that anger is a uniquely important negative emotion, because the authors statistically controlled for other negative emotions.

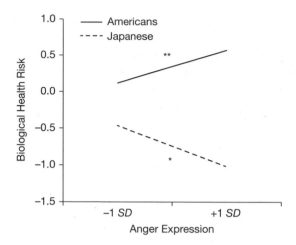

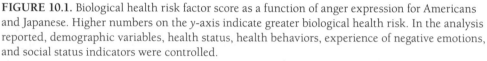

FIGURE 10.1. Biological health risk factor score as a function of anger expression for Americans and Japanese. Higher numbers on the y-axis indicate greater biological health risk. In the analysis reported, demographic variables, health status, health behaviors, experience of negative emotions, and social status indicators were controlled.

*p < .05; **p < .01.

Source: Kitayama et al. (2015).

What caused these divergent cultural effects? Similarly to the argument made by Miyamoto et al. (2013), Kitayama et al. (2015) argue that anger reflects different experiences in Japan and the United States. In the United States, anger is a universal response to negative events that is common to all social classes. However, because of the hierarchical nature of Japanese society, only socially powerful individuals are free to express anger. As a result, anger expression in Japan reflects the "degree to which individuals feel empowered and entitled" (Kitayama et al., 2015, p. 218). Therefore, the same negative emotion can be experienced very differently depending on one's culture. And this cultural difference produces categorically different effects on health.

Each of the three primary components of well-being, life satisfaction, and positive and negative affect predicts health. These relationships are fairly consistent across cultures, even when considering cultures that differ markedly in terms of wealth. However, as indicated by Miyamoto et al.'s (2013) and Kitayama et al.'s (2015) results, the well-being/health relationship is not completely culturally uniform. For instance, the relationship between anger and health is qualitatively different in Japan as compared to the United States. Future research is likely to uncover other examples of cultural differences in this relationship.

HAPPINESS AND RECOVERY FROM ILLNESS

Research Sampling

Conclusions about whether happiness can aid recovery from illness and injury have been tentative and cautious until very recently (e.g., Diener & Chan, 2011). However, researchers have recently begun to make bolder statements. In fact, recent research suggests that happier individuals who are ill tend to recover more quickly and completely, and also tend to survive longer, than less happy individuals, as long as the illness is not so far advanced that medical prognoses are poor (Pressman & Bowlin, 2014). A meta-analysis by Lamers, Bolier, Westerhof, Smit, and Bohlmeijer (2012) found that positive affect and life satisfaction increased the likelihood of recovery or survival from disease by 14% among patients suffering from a variety of maladies including cancer, heart disease, hip fracture, and diabetes. Similarly, Boehm and Kubzansky (2012) found evidence in their review of the literature that positive affect and optimism can help patients recover from heart disease. Other research indicates that positive affect promotes biological functioning that is likely to aid illness recovery (Mathew & Paulose, 2011).

It may help to see some examples of the well-being/recovery relationship. Seale, Berges, Ottenbacher, and Ostir (2010) found that stroke patients with positive emotions had greater functional recovery (for example, self-care, sphincter control, and communication). These results remained significant after controlling for sociodemographic variables, length of hospital stay, whether patients had received therapy, medical problems associated with stroke, initial level of positive emotions, and functional status when discharged from the hospital. Similarly, Gale, Cooper, Deary, and Sayer (2014) found that individuals with high well-being in a sample of elderly (older than 60) were less likely to become frail, after controlling for similar variables.

Recovery following hip fractures provides another example. Fredman, Hawkes, Black, Bertrand, and Magaziner (2006) followed a sample of hip fracture patients, all at least 65 years old, for 2 years. Participants with high levels of positive affect performed better on tests of functioning (e.g., speed rising out of a chair, normal and fast walking speeds) than did depressive participants, after statistically controlling for sociodemographic characteristics, along with cognitive impairment history and health problems that often accompany hip fractures. More recently, Langer, Weisman, Rodebaugh, Binder, and Lenze (2015) performed a similar study and found that increases in positive affect following surgery for hip fracture were associated with better physical recovery 1 year later. These results were significant after controlling for patients' initial level of positive affect and their recovery state following surgery.

Finally, other evidence links negative affect with poor recovery. Spaderna et al. (2014) examined German and Austrian patients on a heart transplant waiting list and found that depressed individuals were 64% more likely to experience a significant heart-related medical event before a transplant could be conducted. These events included death and negative change in their health status. These results were significant after controlling for age, gender, body mass, and initial estimates of disease severity.

Causality?

Thus, well-being is associated with better recovery from various illnesses. You may be skeptical about these findings, though. Is it possible that positive affect simply *follows* recovery from a hip fracture, rather than *causing* recovery? It would not be surprising to find that patients got happier as their hip felt better. How do we know the *direction* of causality?

This is a great question, and, because of the correlational nature of the results, the researchers cannot be certain which direction, if either, is correct. However, evidence points to the conclusion that positive affect aids recovery. One key piece of evidence is that the Langer et al. study controlled for baseline positive affect and level of functioning and recovery 2 to 7 days following surgery. This means that all patients were statistically equated in terms of the severity of their injury, making it unlikely that the degree of injury could cause positive affect. Recall that the research on recovery from strokes controlled for similar variables.

There is evidence that well-being aids in the recovery from illness and injury, particularly in older populations. Although the direction of causality in this relationship is not completely clear, the weight of the evidence points toward the conclusion that well-being causes recovery.

HAPPINESS AND MORTALITY

Positive Affect and Longevity

Young Adults

The evidence that happiness predicts longevity is compelling (Diener & Chan, 2011; Mathew & Paulose, 2011; Pressman & Bowlin, 2014). For example, Danner, Snowdon, and Friesen (2001) found that young adulthood happiness level predicted longevity among a sample of 180 Catholic nuns in the United States. Beginning in 1930, nuns entering this particular order were asked to write a short autobiography (200 to 300 words). The researchers obtained the nuns' consent to examine these statements and trained coders to record their positive, neutral, and negative emotional content. All coders were unaware of the nuns' health status.

Results indicated that positive emotions were strongly and significantly related to longevity, as demonstrated by Figure 10.2. The y-axis indicates the probability that an individual was still alive at a given age. Happiness levels (positive emotions) are depicted in four quartiles. Quartile 1 included the least happy 25% of individuals, and quartile 4 included the happiest 25%.

As you can see, the happiest nuns were more likely to still be living at older ages. This relationship was quite strong. In fact, the survival rate of nuns in the top 25% of happiness was 2.5 times higher than that for nuns in the bottom 25% of happiness, and 2.4 times higher than that for nuns who ranked in the 25th to 50th percentiles of happiness. There were no significant differences in the survival rates of individuals in the 50th to 75th percentiles and those in the top 25% of happiness. Another way to consider the results is that the median age of death was 86.6 for the least happy 25% of nuns, and was 93.5 for the happiest 25% of nuns, an almost 7-year difference in longevity.

All the results were found after statistically controlling for education, writing ability, and occupation (many of the nuns were teachers). These results are also particularly

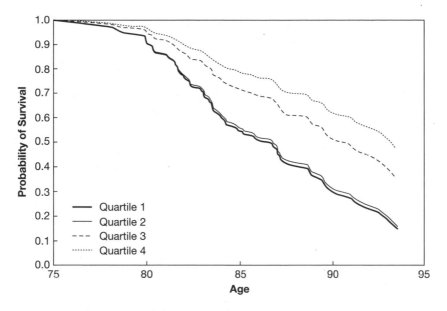

FIGURE 10.2. Quartile rankings of the number of positive emotion sentences in autobiographies written in early life and the probability of survival in late life for 180 participants in the nun study.

Note: The survival curves for quartiles 1 and 2 are virtually overlaid on each other.

Source: Danner et al. (2001).

strong because of the homogeneous lifestyles (and, presumably, personalities) of the participants. Because all the participants were nuns and belonged to the same order, it is unlikely that differences in diet, exercise, substance use, medical care, and so on, could have accounted for these differing survival rates.

Finally, there was no relationship between negative emotions and longevity. This result may have happened in this study because participants were reluctant to express negative emotions in writing as they entered the order.

Other interesting studies found similar results. Abel and Kruger (2010) found that major league baseball players who smiled most intensely lived the longest. These authors coded players' pictures from the 1952 Baseball Register as containing either no smile, partial smile, or full smile. After controlling for numerous factors related to longevity (e.g., year of birth, body mass index [BMI], and marital status), they found that players who did not smile lived to an average age of 72.9, while partial smilers lived to 75, and full smilers lived to 79.9 years. Furthermore, players showing full smiles were only half as likely to die in any given year as players who did not smile.

Remember that these results were found after statistically controlling for numerous factors. To gain even more confidence in the results, the authors recoded the pictures for attractiveness. Results indicated that attractiveness did not predict mortality. Thus, it seems that the crucial agent in these results is the positive emotion displayed by the players, and not that willingness to smile intensely made the players more attractive, or any of the other factors that were statistically controlled.

Findings are inconsistent regarding the positive emotions/longevity link among children and young adults. Pressman and Bowlin (2014) argue that these inconsistent results may occur because these studies have often used teacher and parent ratings of positive emotion, rather than self-reports by the children themselves. In addition, positive emotions in children and among college students may be linked to risk taking, which might be associated with increased probability of accidental death in adolescence and young adulthood.

However, the nun study by Danner et al. suggests that positive emotions among young adults can predict longevity in a population that is less susceptible to risk taking. In addition, other research indicates that happiness is universally associated with decreased mortality at all ages after age 25 (e.g., Keyes & Simoes, 2012) or 30 (e.g., Yang & Waliji, 2010), ages after which risk taking probably diminishes. It therefore appears that Pressman and Bowlin (2014) are likely correct in their interpretation of these inconsistent findings for children and young adults. Positive emotions can increase life expectancy, but this boost can also be offset in some populations because of an associated increase in propensity to take risks.

The Elderly

There is an interesting study regarding the longevity of famous psychologists that mimics the nun study by Danner et al. Pressman and Cohen (2012) found that the number of positive words used in autobiographical statements by 88 influential psychological scientists born between 1843 and 1926 positively predicted the length of their lives. Psychologists who used such words lived 5 years longer than those who did not.

But the most consistent associations between positive emotions and longevity are from populations of nonmedically institutionalized (not living in a nursing home) elderly individuals. In fact, about 30 studies have confirmed this association in this population (Pressman & Bowlin, 2014; Pressman & Cohen, 2005). Westerhof and Wurm (2015) concluded from a review of literature that well-being among the aged predicts survival rates. In addition, a meta-analysis by Lamers et al. (2012) indicates that well-being in general, and positive affect in particular, is associated with higher survival rates among ill patients.

For instance, Koopmans, Geleijnse, Zitman, and Giltay (2010) found a happiness/longevity association in a large sample of noninstitutionalized elderly Dutch men and women (65 to 85 years old). As shown in Figure 10.3, higher percentages of initially happy individuals were still living throughout the 15 years of the study than were individuals who were less happy at the beginning of the study. These mortality differences were significant even after statistically controlling for sex, age, marital status, education, and socioeconomic status, thus buttressing the argument that happiness causes increased longevity.

In addition, Newall, Chipperfield, Bailis, and Stewart (2013) found that elderly individuals with positive emotion were 36% less likely to die within 7 years than were unhappy elderly participants. These results held even after controlling for age, gender, marital status, and initial health and loneliness levels. Furthermore, happiness also acted as a protective factor against loneliness, which was a strong predictor of longevity.

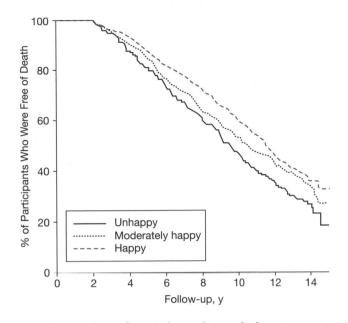

FIGURE 10.3. Kaplan–Meier analysis of survival according to the happiness categories for 861 participants. The categories range from "unhappy" to "happy" subjects—those reporting to be "happy" showed an increased survival rate ($p = .006$ by log-rank test).
Source: Koopmans et al. (2010).

These findings that positive emotions lengthen life among healthy elderly individuals makes theoretical sense. Wiest, Schüz, Webster, and Wurm (2011) argue from their reading of the literature that positive emotions may serve an especially important protective function among the elderly because of their age-related weakened immune systems. Wiest et al. also argue that the elderly may be better at regulating their emotions and are better at focusing on emotionally rewarding goals than are younger individuals. As a result, positive emotions may be particularly beneficial among the elderly.

However, the positive emotions/longevity link is less clear among the medically institutionalized elderly. Pressman and Bowlin (2014) reviewed this literature and found mixed results for this hypothesis among this population. These authors speculate that positive emotions might have a smaller impact on longevity among individuals who are less healthy (as suggested by their residential care status).

Positive affect decreases mortality in both younger and elderly populations, although the relationship is most consistent among noninstitutionalized elderly. This finding for noninstitutionalized elderly makes sense, given that they are likely healthy, but may need extra protection from disease given age-related physiological vulnerabilities. The evidence that these effects are large and that positive affect causes lower mortality rates is significant. For instance, positive affect is associated with a substantially lower probability of mortality in several of the studies cited earlier. Also, the statistical controls used in several studies, along with other factors, increase our confidence that positive affect is a causal factor for longevity.

Negative Affect and Longevity

Loneliness and Social Isolation

Research indicates that individuals with negative affect live shorter lives (Diener & Chan, 2011). Loneliness predicted mortality in studies of the nonmedically institutionalized elderly in Western Canada (Newall et al., 2013) and in Finland (Tilvis, Laitala, Routasalo, Strandberg, & Pitkala, 2012). The lonely elderly were 15% to 20% more likely to die in any given year than the nonlonely elderly, even after controlling for age, gender, and other sociodemographic factors.

Furthermore, Tay, Tan, Diener, and Gonzalez (2013) reviewed the literature and found a relationship between weak social relationships, an approximate measure of loneliness, and mortality in general populations. Eichstaedt et al. (2015) found that negative social relationships expressed in Twitter messages across the United States predicted heart disease mortality after controlling for socioeconomic status.

Eichstaedt et al. examined a data set containing more than 10 million tweets and used software to code them on several dimensions, including negative social relationships. Tweets containing words such as *hate*, *alone*, *jealous*, *blame*, *evil*, and *rude* were considered indicative of negative social relations. They then linked the tweeted words to heart disease mortality by identifying the tweet's county of origin and consulting mortality data for that county from the Centers for Disease Control and Prevention (CDC). Although the authors could not determine whether the *issuers* of the tweets were more likely to die of heart disease, the results are consistent with the hypothesis that negative emotions produced by poor social relationships predict mortality. Counties with more negative social relationship tweets had higher heart disease mortality levels.

Depression Among Nonpatient Samples

Depressed individuals die earlier than the nondepressed, even among groups of people from the general population who presumably have few if any preexisting illnesses (Charlson et al., 2013; Doherty & Gaughran, 2014; Moustgaard, Joutsenniemi, Sihvo, & Martikainen, 2013). Numerous studies have found that depression significantly increases the risk of early death in the general population, with increased mortality risk factors ranging from 37% to 100% (e.g., Hannah, Batty, & Benzeval, 2013; Markkula et al., 2012; Tilvis et al., 2012).

In addition, Charlson et al. (2013) estimated that more than 3.5 million "life years" were lost worldwide in 2010 due to the effects of major depression on heart disease fatalities. In other words, when the authors estimated how much depression shortened individuals' lives in 2010, the total for all individuals who died prematurely summed to more than 3.5 million years. This estimate was derived from a meta-analysis of studies that sampled from the general, nonhospitalized population. Thus, these findings indicate the effect of major depression on mortality among otherwise relatively healthy individuals.

Table 10.2 is from Charlson et al.'s (2013) publication and indicates estimates for each region of the globe. "Disability-Adjusted Life Years" refers to the number of years that individuals live with a disability, plus the number of years of life they lose because of premature death. Thus, note that "Years of Life Lost" and "Years Lived With a Disability" sum within each row to equal disability-adjusted life years. The numbers in the parentheses indicated the 95% confidence interval around each estimate. Thus, the authors are 95% confident that the true value global years of life lost (estimated as 3,572,770) is between 1,791,433 and 5,411,987.

Pathways that connect depression to mortality in the general population are becoming clearer. Depression seems to decrease social activities, which might, in turn, increase mortality rates (Finlay, Oliva, Timko, Moos, & Cronkite, 2014). Unhealthy behaviors such as smoking (Fortes et al., 2012) and excessive alcohol use (Markkula et al., 2012; Moustgaard et al., 2013) may also link depression and mortality. Furthermore, depression probably has direct negative physiological consequences, in addition to promoting unhealthy behaviors. These behavioral and physiological effects are likely cumulative and probably emerge in complicated patterns over long periods of time (Thomson, 2011).

TABLE 10.2 Attributable Ischemic Heart Disease (IHD) Cases and Burden Estimates by Region, 2010 (95% CI)

Region	Disability-Adjusted Life Years	Years of Life Lost	Years Lived With a Disability
Asia Pacific, High Income	39,982 (19,701–66,462)	33,769 (16,218–56,464)	6,212 (2,413–12,936)
Asia, Central	112,925 (57,161–177,173)	108,331 (54,721–170,514)	4,593 (1,983–8,725)
Asia, East	386,610 (186,346–616,455)	347,277 (164,890–550,414)	39,332 (17,416–70,703)
Asia, South	863,351 (429,292–1,375,835)	829,281 (411,750–1,325,451)	34,069 (15,321–60,095)
Asia, Southeast	263,285 (135,382–421,193)	245,258 (125,893–395,411)	18,026 (7,955–32,258)
Australasia	9,622 (4,870–15,408)	8,541 (4,344–13,721)	1,081 (421–2,028)
Caribbean	29,484 (14,661–46,004)	27,773 (13,791–43,647)	1,710 (728–3,224)
Europe, Central	137,495 (69,706–214,634)	129,873 (65,902–202,094)	7,621 (3,384–14,119)
Europe, Eastern	664,145 (321,237–1,063,148)	639,605 (308,328–1,023,931)	24,540 (10,754–43,824)

(*continued*)

TABLE 10.2 Attributable Ischemic Heart Disease (IHD) Cases and Burden Estimates by Region, 2010 (95% CI) *(continued)*

Region	Disability-Adjusted Life Years	Years of Life Lost	Years Lived With a Disability
Europe, Western	284,320 (144,755–435,735)	252,487 (127,659–387,169)	31,833 (13,996–56,870)
Latin America, Andean	12,761 (6,305–20,517)	11,495 (5,747–18,348)	1,266 (529–2,470)
Latin America, Central	84,115 (43,308–132,587)	77,860 (39,465–122,414)	6,255 (2,652–12,031)
Latin America, Southern	31,373 (15,066–53,307)	28,547 (13,876–47,362)	2,825 (1,140–5,412)
Latin America, Tropical	127,581 (65,215–208,633)	115,548 (58,951–191,580)	12,032 (5,224–21,858)
North Africa/ Middle East	363,828 (183,937–571,914)	342,820 (171,720–533,404)	21,008 (9,630–37,854)
North America, High Income	244,716 (125,676–394,058)	223,728 (114,409–358,292)	20,987 (9,588–38,059)
Oceania	3,628 (1,751–6,339)	3,355 (1,623–5,891)	272 (107–507)
Sub-Saharan Africa, Central	28,336 (13,710–47,204)	26,682 (12,849–44,673)	1,653 (667–3,421)
Sub-Saharan Africa, East	62,438 (31,898–99,496)	55,098 (28,007–88,043)	7,340 (3,205–13,455)
Sub-Saharan Africa, Southern	18,385 (9,071–30,166)	16,567 (8,175–27,355)	1,817 (771–3,341)
Sub-Saharan Africa, West	54,615 (27,511–86,304)	48,864 (24,879–76,381)	5,750 (2,483–11,008)
Global	3,823,004 (1,942,771–5,778,350)	3,572,770 (1,791,433–5,411,987)	250,233 (114,845–444,063)

Source: Charlson et al. (2013).

Some evidence also suggests that women suffer more of a mortality risk from depression than do men (Thomson, 2011).

Depression Among Cardiac Patients

Depression is strongly linked to mortality among cardiac patients. An earlier review of this literature showed that negative affect was related to disease-related mortality, perhaps because of a giving up syndrome in which individuals become hopeless and helpless (Buerki & Adler, 2005, p. 184). Diener and Chan (2011) described two studies in their review that focused on depression and mortality among cardiac patients. Both found that depressed patients died sooner. Most subsequent reviews have confirmed these findings. A meta-analysis by Fan et al. (2014) found that among patients diagnosed with heart failure,[5] depressed individuals were more than twice as likely to die in the following years than were nondepressed patients. Several other literature reviews reached similar conclusions (e.g., Celano & Huffman, 2011; Doherty & Gaughran, 2014; Freedland, Carney, & Rich, 2011; Huffman, Celano, Beach, Motiwala, & Januzzi, 2013; Whooley & Wong, 2013).

It also appears that major depression is a much stronger predictor of mortality among cardiac patients than is minor depression (Fan et al., 2014; Freedland et al., 2011). This association is so strong and consistent that several authors suggest routine depression screening among cardiac patients (e.g., Celano & Huffman, 2011; Scott, 2014; Whooley & Wong, 2013). However, while it is clear that depression *predicts* mortality among cardiac patients, there is debate about whether it is a *cause* of mortality in this population.

A principal concern about causality is that psychological interventions designed to treat depression have often failed to lower mortality rates among cardiac patients (Meijer, Zuidersma, & de Jonge, 2013; Reid, Ski, & Thompson, 2013; Whalley, Thompson, & Taylor, 2014). Although well-being interventions have been linked to physiological processes that influence depression (Rickard & Vella-Brodrick, 2014), the fact that these interventions have not yet been shown to lower mortality is an important concern. Obviously, if depression causes mortality, then lowering depression should lower the death rate. Meijer et al. (2013) did not find any studies in which treatments of depression lowered mortality rates in clinical samples.

It is also unclear whether depression is a cause or a result of heart disease. Meijer et al. (2013) recognize that longitudinal studies indicate that depression in early adulthood predicts heart disease later in life, which is consistent with the argument that depression is causal. However, Meijer et al. also point out that heart disease also causes depression in clinical patients. Thus, it is not clear which happens first, heart disease or depression. Obviously, there must be clear evidence depression precedes heart disease before we can be confident that it is a casual factor.

However, an argument can be made that depression causes earlier death among cardiac patients. Meijer et al. (2013) note that the intervention studies that attempted to lower patients' depression were only "moderately" successful in doing so (p. 3). Therefore, it is possible that depression was not lowered enough to have a meaningful effect on mortality. Some authors who have reviewed the literature (e.g., Celano & Huffman,

2011) are somewhat more optimistic about the effectiveness of depression-lowering interventions, particularly those that involve medications.

There are also logical reasons to expect that depression could cause mortality among heart disease patients. For instance, depression could increase mortality by first causing decreases in physical activity or poor dietary habits (Bonnet et al., 2005). Depression could also overactivate the autonomic nervous system and/or cause systemic inflammation, both of which are linked to heart disease (Celano & Huffman, 2011; Whooley & Wong, 2013). The existence of these potential pathways between depression and mortality among cardiac patients makes it more likely that the depression/mortality association is a causal one.

Unfortunately, research has not yet progressed to the point of knowing whether depression causes mortality among cardiac patients, although it is certainly associated with mortality in this population. This is a challenging question to answer. Depression cannot be randomly assigned in a controlled experiment. There are also potential ethical problems with implementing untested depression interventions among patients with an illness as serious as heart disease.

However, researchers have already made tremendous progress by recognizing and validating the association between these two variables and beginning to test possible causal pathways. Researchers have also seemed to recognize that identifying causality is an important next step and have begun suggesting how to do this. For instance, both Fan et al. (2014) and Celano and Huffman (2011) suggest that future research should investigate the ability of antidepressant medications to lower both depression and mortality rates. These authors also suggest careful testing of each step in potential causal pathways (e.g., depression to systemic inflammation to heart disease mortality) as another method of answering this causality question. The researchers now know what the important question is and have a good idea of who is likely to get an answer. It is likely only a matter of time until the answer surfaces.

Life Satisfaction and Longevity

Life Satisfaction Without Comparisons to Affect

Some research indicates that life satisfaction predicts mortality, although there are some inconsistencies regarding gender and culture. For example, Kimm, Sull, Gombojav, Yi, and Ohrr (2012) found that unsatisfied men were 42% more likely to die and unsatisfied women were 51% more likely to die than their satisfied counterparts during the 12-year course of the study. Participants lived in a rural agricultural area of South Korea, and results were significant after controlling for age, disease history, smoking and alcohol use, education, body mass, and disability status.

Other research has found gender differences. Guven and Saloumidis (2014) found that life satisfaction predicts mortality among the married and among men in general (whether or not they were married), but not among women in general. These results, from a representative sample of German adults (average age at the beginning of the study was 42), remain significant after controlling for socioeconomic and subjective and objective indicators of health. Guven and Saloumidis (2014) do not offer an explanation for the gender differences in their findings, although they do note that women generally live longer than men. Perhaps their study did not follow participants long enough to allow life satisfaction to predict mortality among German women. It is also possible that differences in measures of life satisfaction from study to study can account for differences in gender effects.

As we have seen throughout this chapter, causality is a concern for much of this research. Some longitudinal studies demonstrate that initial measures of life satisfaction predict future mortality. This is consistent with causal hypotheses, because of the temporal order of the variables, with the potential cause (life satisfaction) preceding the potential effect (mortality). These studies also statistically control for a number of factors such as age, income, and education, helping to increase our confidence that the relationships might be causal.

Even more importantly, initial health is also held statistically constant in this research. This is important because it argues against the alternative hypothesis that life satisfaction is merely a function of initial health. For instance, it could be that poor health at the beginning of a study lowers initial life satisfaction (at the beginning of the study) and also leads to premature death later, indicating that life satisfaction is not a causal factor in this relationship. However, by controlling for initial health, the data argue against this alternative explanation. For example, in the Guven and Saloumidis (2014) study, the relationship between initial life satisfaction (at the beginning of the study) and mortality is not changed when initial health is controlled.

It is important to remember that all these data are correlational, so we cannot be sure whether any of the relationships are causal. But a good argument can be made that it appears that there is a causal relation.

Life Satisfaction With Comparisons to Affect

This area is unique because it is one of the few in which researchers have directly paired differing measures of well-being against each other in order to gauge the relative impact of each on predicting a health outcome. Specifically, several researchers have measured life satisfaction and affect, especially positive affect, in studies investigating mortality. Results generally indicate that positive affect has predictive power over and beyond that of life satisfaction.

For example, Wiest et al. (2011) examined a longitudinal sample in Germany and found that older adults with high life satisfaction were 11% less likely to die in any given year than were equivalent individuals with lower life satisfaction after controlling for the standard socioeconomic and health variables used in most studies. In addition, respondents with high positive affect were 19% less likely to die in a given year. There was no relationship for negative affect.

However, when positive affect and lifestyle were examined, controlling for each other, those with high levels of positive affect were still 18% less likely to die in a given year, while life satisfaction no longer predicted mortality. Pitkala, Laakkonen, Strandberg, and Tilvis (2004) and Tilvis et al. (2012) found similar results among Finnish older adults. Thus, while life satisfaction is associated with mortality, it may not predict any better or differently than does positive affect.

EUDAIMONIC WELL-BEING

Eudaimonia is another conceptualization of well-being that emphasizes human flourishing and is distinct from affect and life satisfaction (Kimiecik, 2011). Eudaimonic well-being is largely derived from Ryan and Deci's (2000) Self-Determination Theory (SDT), and Ryff and Singer's (1998) concept of self-realization and involves engaging in the process of meeting basic psychological needs and realizing one's true potential. Ryff (1989) developed a commonly used measure of eudaimonia that assesses self-realization on six dimensions: self-acceptance, purpose in life, personal growth, positive relations with others, environmental mastery, and autonomy. Thus, eudaimonia is different from the hedonic measures of happiness. Instead of reflecting simple pleasure or satisfaction, eudaimonia reflects a well-being made up of personal fulfillment and growth (Ryan & Deci, 2001).

Eudaimonic well-being has been linked to health, and research has even suggested pathways by which it might predict health. For instance, in a review of the literature Ryff (2013) and Ryff and Singer (2000) connected flourishing relationships with better cardiovascular, neuroendocrine, and immune functioning (see also Ng et al., 2012 for a self-determination perspective). Miquelon and Vallerand (2006, 2008) reported that eudaimonic well-being predicts better self-reported health because it facilitates healthier coping responses to stress. These authors also found that hedonic well-being did not predict self-reported health after controlling for eudaimonic well-being.

Miquelon and Vallerand (2006) asked French-Canadian college students to state three academic goals they had at the beginning of a semester and to indicate why they were pursuing these goals on four dimensions. Two of these dimensions indicated the extent to which the goals were "autonomous" (because it is important, because it is fun) and two indicated the extent to which the goals were "controlled" (because you would feel ashamed not to, because someone else wants you to). Participants also indicated their happiness, in terms of positive and negative affect, and their level of eudaimonia (self-realization levels on three dimensions: self-acceptance, purpose in life, and personal growth).

Then, 2 weeks before the end of the semester, participants indicated their coping style as either vigilant (active, accepting) or avoidant (based on denial), and also reported their stress levels through the semester in addition to their current physical symptoms and self-rated health. The results are shown in Figure 10.4. The numbers between the arrows are path coefficients, which indicate relationships between variables when they are associated with an asterisk. Be sure to pay attention to the sign (plus or minus) of each coefficient.

See whether you can make sense out of Figure 10.4. What relationships do autonomous and controlled goals have with self-rated health and physical symptoms at the end of the semester, and why? Remember that Time 1 symptoms, self-rated health, and neuroticism are control variables, so you can ignore them, except to remember that these control variables are unlikely to explain why, for instance, autonomous and controlled goals have different relations to health.

These results are interesting for several reasons, but one is that there is no significant path between happiness and either physical symptoms or self-rated health. In other

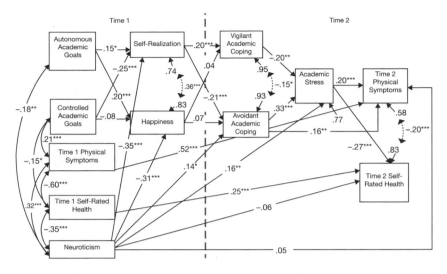

FIGURE 10.4. Study of the relationships between eudaimonic well-being, coping, stress, and self-reported health.

*p < .05; **p < .01, ***p < .001.

Source: Miquelon and Vallerand (2006).

words, happiness did not predict health after controlling for initial health, eudaimonia (self-realization), and neuroticism. But eudaimonia did predict health because it reduced stress by promoting healthy (vigilant) and decreasing unhealthy (avoidant) coping. Furthermore, note that autonomous academic goals were also associated with fewer physical symptoms and better self-rated health because these goals were also associated with eudaimonia. The opposite was true for controlled goals.

Thus, several take-aways here are important. One is the finding that autonomous goals, goals that we engage with because they are fun or are important in themselves, are associated with better eudaimonic well-being and happiness. Second, it is eudaimonia, not happiness, that is associated with better health, because eudaimonia seems to promote more effective coping that reduces stress. This second point is also interesting because it fits with our earlier discussion of the long-term negative effect of bodily activation and stress on health. Although there are some obvious shortcomings of this data set (e.g., college student sample and self-report measures of health), these results are exciting because they offer a direct comparison between hedonic and eudaimonic well-being, and they also suggest a path by which eudaimonic well-being might affect health.

Other research has found health benefits of eudaimonia using different outcome measures. Zaslavsky et al. (2014) found that elderly American women who were low in feelings of personal growth and purpose in life were more likely to die during the course of the study. The authors controlled for sociodemographic variables, in addition to body mass, alcohol use, depression, smoking, exercise, and whether the participant lived alone. The authors concluded by arguing for the importance of encouraging "flourishing" among elderly populations.

Other research has echoed this emphasis on encouraging flourishing for health and other reasons. Schwartz et al. (2011) found that American college students with high levels of eudaimonia used illegal drugs, practiced unsafe sex, and drove while impaired less frequently than did low eudaimonic students. Schwartz et al. (2011, p. 32) concluded that students who "perceive themselves as 'doing well' in life—feeling in control over their lives and enjoying satisfying relationships with others—are least likely to engage in risky behaviors." Thus, according to Schwartz and colleagues, eudaimonia offers some protection against the temptation of risky behaviors. These authors also suggest intervention programs designed to increase eudaimonia.

SUMMARY

It is clear that well-being, including positive and negative affect, life satisfaction, and eudaimonia, is associated with better health, recovery from illnesses, and lower mortality rates and that these relationships are large enough to be meaningful, as noted by the risk percentages described throughout the chapter. There is also some evidence that these associations are largely cross-culturally consistent and apply in both wealthy and poor nations. However, evidence also suggests that individuals in Asian cultures interpret negative emotions, particularly anger, differently than do Westerners. These differences can produce different relationships between negative affect and health.

Causality

The most important question about these associations is whether they are causal. Evidence suggests that they often are. Although the research is necessarily correlational, longitudinal studies and statistical controls strengthen our confidence that well-being can cause health.

Furthermore, the longitudinal data sets demonstrate that well-being at an earlier time predicts health at a later time, thus supporting the crucial causal assumption that cause precedes effect. Although it is still possible that health at the beginning of the longitudinal study caused initial well-being, the fact that many researchers have statistically controlled for initial health in these studies undermines this hypothesis.

Another argument in favor of causality comes from Diener and Chan's (2011) review of the literature. These authors identify seven different types of evidence linking well-being to health and conclude that the general relationship is causal. These authors argue that these diffuse kinds of evidence tend to correct each other's shortcomings and conclude that evidence for causality is "compelling" (Diener & Chan, 2011, p. 1).

We are also uncertain about the relative impact on health of the various components of well-being. With few exceptions, we know little about whether one specific type of well-being (e.g., positive affect versus life satisfaction) is particularly advantageous. Nor do we know whether particular combinations of well-being (e.g., high positive and low negative affect) might be especially helpful. So there is much more work to be done.

Public Policy

But enough is known that some researchers have begun making public policy suggestions. For instance, researchers have noted the probable causal association between well-being and health, and have suggested that policy makers could therefore track and seek to increase well-being in order to promote health. In fact, the U.S. CDC notes that positive emotions should be encouraged because of their contribution to good health. The CDC has integrated well-being, which it minimally defines as the presence of positive affect and life satisfaction, and the absence of negative affect, into its health promotion activities since 2007.

Others have suggested that well-being research can identify public spending priorities. For instance, Dolan and White (2007) suggested that money should be directed toward health care because of research indicating it has a relatively large impact on life satisfaction compared to other social issues. Dolan and White (2007) and Diener, Lucas, Schimmack, and Helliwell (2009) suggested that well-being research be used to identify health problems that have the greatest impact on life satisfaction so that more resources can be directed toward those specific issues. Lee et al. (2013) suggested that well-being be used as a measure of the quality of health care, rather than traditional measures such as staffing levels and infection rates. In summary, there are many ways that well-being research can be used to inform policy decisions regarding health care.

NOTES

1. Denson et al. (2009) found that the role of negative emotion in this process is complicated by cognitive appraisal. But negative emotion is part of the process, and the role of appraisal highlights the importance of the brain.

2. Infections were defined as the virus multiplying inside the body.

3. The numbers in the table are correlation coefficients, and represent the relationship between either positive or negative affect and self-reported health. Recall that correlations close to zero indicate no relationship, and those close to an absolute value of one indicate a one-to-one correspondence between the variables. Negative values indicate that the variables are inversely related.

4. The "partial" correlations indicate the relationship between both positive and negative emotions and health, after controlling for the other type of emotion (for instance, the relationship between positive emotion and health, after controlling for negative emotion). Because all the partial correlations are significant, they indicate that the relationships between positive and negative emotion and health are *independent* of each other.

5. "[Heart failure] is a clinical condition in which the heart has lost its ability to supply enough blood and oxygen to the body's tissues" (Whooley & Wong, 2013, p. 331).

REFERENCES

Abel, E. L., & Kruger, M. L. (2010). Smile intensity in photographs predicts longevity. *Psychological Science, 21*(4), 542–544.

Appleton, A. A., Buka, S. L., Loucks, E. B., Gilman, S. E., & Kubzansky, L. D. (2013). Divergent associations of adaptive and maladaptive emotion regulation strategies with inflammation. *Health Psychology, 32*(7), 748–756.

Blackburn, E. H. (2001). Switching and signaling at the telomere. *Cell, 106*(6), 661–673.

Boccardi, V., & Paolisso, G. (2014). Telomerase activation: A potential key modulator for human health span and longevity. *Ageing Research Reviews, 15*, 1–5.

Boehm, J. K., & Kubzansky, L. D. (2012). The heart's content: The association between positive psychological well-being and cardiovascular health. *Psychological Bulletin, 138*(4), 655–691.

Bonnet, F., Irving, K., Terra, J. L., Nony, P., Berthezène, F., & Moulin, P. (2005). Depressive symptoms are associated with unhealthy lifestyles in hypertensive patients with the metabolic syndrome. *Journal of Hypertension, 23*(3), 611–617.

Buerki, S., & Adler, R. H. (2005). Negative affect states and cardiovascular disorders: A review and the proposal of a unifying biopsychosocial concept. *General Hospital Psychiatry, 27*(3), 180–188.

Celano, C. M., & Huffman, J. C. (2011). Depression and cardiac disease: A review. *Cardiology in Review, 19*(3), 130–142.

Charlson, F. J., Moran, A. E., Freedman, G., Norman, R. E., Stapelberg, N. J. C., Baxter, A. J., . . . Whiteford, H. A. (2013). The contribution of major depression to the global burden of ischemic heart disease: A comparative risk assessment. *BMC Medicine, 11*(1). doi:10.1186/1741-7015-11-250

Cohen, S., Tyrrell, D. A., & Smith, A. P. (1993). Negative life events, perceived stress, negative affect, and susceptibility to the common cold. *Journal of Personality and Social Psychology, 64*(1), 131–140.

Curhan, K. B., Sims, T., Markus, H. R., Kitayama, S., Karasawa, M., Kawakami, N., . . . Ryff, C. D. (2014). Just how bad negative affect is for your health depends on culture. *Psychological Science, 25*(12), 2277–2280.

Danner, D. D., Snowdon, D. A., & Friesen, W. V. (2001). Positive emotions in early life and longevity: Findings from the nun study. *Journal of Personality and Social Psychology, 80*(5), 804–813.

Denson, T. F., Spanovic, M., & Miller, N. (2009). Cognitive appraisals and emotions predict cortisol and immune responses: A meta-analysis of acute laboratory social stressors and emotion inductions. *Psychological Bulletin, 135*(6), 823–853.

DeSteno, D., Gross, J. J., & Kubzansky, L. (2013). Affective science and health: The importance of emotion and emotion regulation. *Health Psychology, 32*(5), 474–486.

Diener, E., & Chan, M. Y. (2011). Happy people live longer: Subjective well-being contributes to health and longevity. *Applied Psychology: Health and Well-Being, 3*(1), 1–43.

Diener, E., Lucas, R., Schimmack, U., & Helliwell, J. (2009). *Well-being for public policy.* New York, NY: Oxford University Press.

Dockray, S., & Steptoe, A. (2010). Positive affect and psychobiological processes. *Neuroscience and Biobehavioral Reviews, 35*(1), 69–75.

Doherty, A. M., & Gaughran, F. (2014). The interface of physical and mental health. *Social Psychiatry and Psychiatric Epidemiology, 49*(5), 673–682.

Dolan, P., & White, M. P. (2007). How can measures of subjective well-being be used to inform public policy? *Perspectives on Psychological Science, 2*(1), 71–85.

Eichstaedt, J. C., Schwartz, H. A., Kern, M. L., Park, G., Labarthe, D. R., Merchant, R. M., . . . Seligman, M. E. P. (2015). Psychological language on Twitter predicts county-level heart disease mortality. *Psychological Science, 26*(2), 159–169.

Fan, H., Yu, W., Zhang, Q., Cao, H., Li, J., Wang, J., . . . Hu, X. (2014). Depression after heart failure and risk of cardiovascular and all-cause mortality: A meta-analysis. *Preventive Medicine, 63*, 36–42.

Feller, S., Teucher, B., Kaaks, R., Boeing, H., & Vigl, M. (2013). Life satisfaction and risk of chronic diseases in the European prospective investigation into cancer and nutrition (EPIC)-Germany study. *PLOS ONE, 8*(8). doi: 10.1371/journal.pone.0073462

Finlay, A. K., Oliva, E. M., Timko, C., Moos, R. H., & Cronkite, R. (2014). Predictors of 30-year mortality in depressed and comparison samples. *Journal of Affective Disorders, 165,* 114–119.

Fortes, C., Mastroeni, S., Alessandra, S., Lindau, J., Farchi, S., Franco, F., . . . Borgia, P. (2012). The combination of depressive symptoms and smoking shorten life expectancy among the aged. *International Psychogeriatrics, 24*(4), 624–630.

Fredman, L., Hawkes, W. G., Black, S., Bertrand, R. M., & Magaziner, J. (2006). Elderly patients with hip fracture with positive affect have better functional recovery over 2 years. *Journal of the American Geriatrics Society, 54*(7), 1074–1081.

Freedland, K. E., Carney, R. M., & Rich, M. W. (2011). Effect of depression on prognosis in heart failure. *Heart Failure Clinics, 7*(1), 11–21.

Gale, C. R., Cooper, C., Deary, I. J., & Sayer, A. A. (2014). Psychological well-being and incident frailty in men and women: The English longitudinal study of ageing. *Psychological Medicine, 44*(4), 697–706.

Gana, K., Bailly, N., Saada, Y., Joulain, M., Trouillet, R., Hervé, C., & Alaphilippe, D. (2013). Relationship between life satisfaction and physical health in older adults: A longitudinal test of cross-lagged and simultaneous effects. *Health Psychology, 32*(8), 896–904.

Garrido, S., Méndez, I., & Abellán, J. (2013). Analysing the simultaneous relationship between life satisfaction and health-related quality of life. *Journal of Happiness Studies, 14*(6), 1813–1838.

Grant, N., Wardle, J., & Steptoe, A. (2009). The relationship between life satisfaction and health behavior: A cross-cultural analysis of young adults. *International Journal of Behavioral Medicine, 16*(3), 259–268.

Guven, C., & Saloumidis, R. (2014). Life satisfaction and longevity: Longitudinal evidence from the German Socio-Economic Panel. *German Economic Review, 15,* 453–472.

Hannah, M. K., Batty, G. D., & Benzeval, M. (2013). Common mental disorders and mortality in the west of Scotland twenty-07 study: Comparing the general health questionnaire and the hospital anxiety and depression scale. *Journal of Epidemiology and Community Health, 67*(7), 558–563.

Hilmert, C. J., Teoh, A. N., & Roy, M. M. (2014). Effort and negative affect interact to predict cardiovascular responses to stress. *Psychology and Health, 29*(1), 64–80.

Hirosaki, M., Ishimoto, Y., Kasahara, Y., Konno, A., Kimura, Y., Fukutomi, E., . . . Matsubayashi, K. (2013). Positive affect as a predictor of lower risk of functional decline in community-dwelling elderly in Japan. *Geriatrics and Gerontology International, 13*(4), 1051–1058.

Howell, R. T., Kern, M. L., & Lyubomirsky, S. (2007). Health benefits: Meta-analytically determining the impact of well-being on objective health outcomes. *Health Psychology Review, 1*(1), 83–136.

Huffman, J. C., Celano, C. M., Beach, S. R., Motiwala, S. R., & Januzzi, J. L. (2013). Depression and cardiac disease: Epidemiology, mechanisms, and diagnosis. *Cardiovascular Psychiatry and Neurology,* 2013. doi:10.1155/2013/695925

Keyes, C. L. M., & Simoes, E. J. (2012). To flourish or not: Positive mental health and all-cause mortality. *American Journal of Public Health, 102*(11), 2164–2172.

Kim, E. S., Park, N., Sun, J. K., Smith, J., & Peterson, C. (2014). Life satisfaction and frequency of doctor visits. *Psychosomatic Medicine, 76*(1), 86–93.

Kimiecik, J. (2011). Exploring the promise of eudaimonic well-being within the practice of health promotion: The "how" is as important as the "what." *Journal of Happiness Studies, 12*(5), 769–792.

Kimm, H., Sull, J. W., Gombojav, B., Yi, S.-W., & Ohrr, H. (2012). Life satisfaction and mortality in elderly people: The Kangwha cohort study. *BMC Public Health*, *12*(1), 54.

Kitayama, S., Park, J., Boylan, J. M., Miyamoto, Y., Levine, C. S., Markus, H. R., . . . Ryff, C. D. (2015). Expression of anger and ill health in two cultures: An examination of inflammation and cardiovascular risk. *Psychological Science*, *26*(2), 211–220.

Koivumaa-Honkanen, H., Kaprio, J., Korhonen, T., Honkanen, R. J., Heikkilä, K., & Koskenvuo, M. (2012). Self-reported life satisfaction and alcohol use: A 15-year follow-up of healthy adult twins. *Alcohol and Alcoholism*, *47*(2), 160–168.

Koopmans, T. A., Geleijnse, J. M., Zitman, F. G., & Giltay, E. J. (2010). Effects of happiness on all-cause mortality during 15 years of follow-up: The Arnhem elderly study. *Journal of Happiness Studies*, *11*(1), 113–124.

Kubzansky, L. D., & Thurston, R. C. (2007). Emotional vitality and incident coronary heart disease: Benefits of healthy psychological functioning. *Archives of General Psychiatry*, *64*(12), 1393–1401.

Lamers, S. M. A., Bolier, L., Westerhof, G. J., Smit, F., & Bohlmeijer, E. T. (2012). The impact of emotional well-being on long-term recovery and survival in physical illness: A meta-analysis. *Journal of Behavioral Medicine*, *35*(5), 538–547.

Langer, J. K., Weisman, J. S., Rodebaugh, T. L., Binder, E. F., & Lenze, E. J. (2015). Short-term affective recovery from hip fracture prospectively predicts depression and physical functioning. *Health Psychology*, *34*(1), 30–39.

Larsen, J. T., & McGraw, A. P. (2011). Further evidence for mixed emotions. *Journal of Personality and Social Psychology*, *100*(6), 1095–1110.

Lee, H., Vlaev, I., King, D., Mayer, E., Darzi, A., & Dolan, P. (2013). Subjective well-being and the measurement of quality in healthcare. *Social Science and Medicine*, *99*, 27–34.

Lipovčan, L. K., Brkljačić, T., & Tadić, M. (2013). Tobacco consumption, alcohol intake frequency and quality of life: Results from a Nationally Representative Croatian Sample Study. *Drustvena Istrazivanja*, *22*(4), 627–649.

Lundgren, O., Garvin, P., Jonasson, L., Andersson, G., & Kristenson, M. (2015). Psychological resources are associated with reduced incidence of coronary heart disease: An 8-year follow-up of a community-based Swedish sample. *International Journal of Behavioral Medicine*, *22*(1), 77–84.

Markkula, N., Härkänen, T., Perälä, J., Partti, K., Peña, S., Koskinen, S., . . . Saarni, S. I. (2012). Mortality in people with depressive, anxiety and alcohol use disorders in Finland. *British Journal of Psychiatry*, *200*(2), 143–149.

Mathew, J., & Paulose, C. S. (2011). The healing power of well-being. *Acta Neuropsychiatrica*, *23*(4), 145–155.

McRae, K., Jacobs, S. E., Ray, R. D., John, O. P., & Gross, J. J. (2012). Individual differences in reappraisal ability: Links to reappraisal frequency, well-being, and cognitive control. *Journal of Research in Personality*, *46*(1), 2–7.

Meijer, A., Zuidersma, M., & de Jonge, P. (2013). Depression as a non-causal variable risk marker in coronary heart disease. *BMC Medicine*, *11*(1). doi:10.1186/1741-7015-11-130

Miquelon, P., & Vallerand, R. J. (2006). Goal motives, well-being, and physical health: Happiness and self-realization as psychological resources under challenge. *Motivation and Emotion*, *30*(4), 259–272.

Miquelon, P., & Vallerand, R. J. (2008). Goal motives, well-being, and physical health: An integrative model. *Canadian Psychology/Psychologie Canadienne*, *49*(3), 241–249.

Miyamoto, Y., Boylan, J. M., Coe, C. L., Curhan, K. B., Levine, C. S., Markus, H. R., . . . Ryff, C. D. (2013). Negative emotions predict elevated interleukin-6 in the United States but not in Japan. *Brain, Behavior, and Immunity, 34*, 79–85.

Moustgaard, H., Joutsenniemi, K., Sihvo, S., & Martikainen, P. (2013). Alcohol-related deaths and social factors in depression mortality: A register-based follow-up of depressed in-patients and antidepressant users in Finland. *Journal of Affective Disorders, 148*(2–3), 278–285.

Newall, N. E. G., Chipperfield, J. G., Bailis, D. S., & Stewart, T. L. (2013). Consequences of loneliness on physical activity and mortality in older adults and the power of positive emotions. *Health Psychology, 32*(8), 921–924.

Ng, J. Y. Y., Ntoumanis, N., Thøgersen-Ntoumani, C., Deci, E. L., Ryan, R. M., Duda, J. L., & Williams, G. C. (2012). Self-determination theory applied to health contexts: A meta-analysis. *Perspectives on Psychological Science, 7*(4), 325–340.

O'Neal, C. W., Wickrama, K. A. S., Ralston, P. A., Ilich, J. Z., Harris, C. M., Coccia, C., . . . Lemacks, J. (2014). Health insurance status, psychological processes, and older African Americans' use of preventive care. *Journal of Health Psychology, 19*(4), 491–502.

Paxton, R. J., Valois, R. F., Watkins, K. W., Huebner, E. S., & Drane, J. W. (2007). Associations between depressed mood and clusters of health risk behaviors. *American Journal of Health Behavior, 31*(3), 272–283.

Pinel, J. P. J. (2011). *Biopsychology* (8th ed.). Boston, MA: Pearson Education.

Pitkala, K. H., Laakkonen, M. L., Strandberg, T. E., & Tilvis, R. S. (2004). Positive life orientation as a predictor of 10-year outcome in an aged population. *Journal of Clinical Epidemiology, 57*(4), 409–414.

Pressman, S. D., & Bowlin, S. L. (2014). Positive affect: A pathway to better physical health. In J. Gruber & J. T. Moskowitz (Eds.), *Positive emotion: Integrating the light sides and dark sides* (pp. 183–205). New York, NY: Oxford University Press.

Pressman, S. D., & Cohen, S. (2005). Does positive affect influence health? *Psychological Bulletin, 131*(6), 925–971.

Pressman, S. D., & Cohen, S. (2012). Positive emotion word use and longevity in famous deceased psychologists. *Health Psychology, 31*(3), 297–305.

Pressman, S. D., Gallagher, M. W., Lopez, S. J., & Campos, B. (2014). Incorporating culture into the study of affect and health. *Psychological Science, 25*(12), 2281–2283.

Reid, J., Ski, C. F., & Thompson, D. R. (2013). Psychological interventions for patients with coronary heart disease and their partners: A systematic review. *PLOS ONE, 8*(9). doi:10.1371/journal.prone .0073459

Rickard, N. S., & Vella-Brodrick, D. (2014). Changes in well-being: Complementing a psychosocial approach with neurobiological insights. *Social Indicators Research, 117*(2), 437–457.

Ryan, R. M., & Deci, E. L. (2000). Self-determination theory and the facilitation of intrinsic motivation, social development, and well-being. *American Psychologist, 55*, 68–78.

Ryan, R. M., & Deci, E. L. (2001). On happiness and human potentials: A review of research on hedonic and eudaimonic well-being. *Annual Review of Psychology, 52*, 141–166.

Ryff, C. D. (1989). Happiness is everything, or is it? Explorations on the meaning of psychological well-being. *Journal of Personality and Social Psychology, 57*(6), 1069–1081.

Ryff, C. D. (2013). Eudaimonic well-being and health: Mapping consequences of self-realization. In A. S. Waterman (Ed.), *The best within us: Positive psychology perspectives on eudaimonia* (pp. 77–98). Washington, DC: American Psychological Association.

Ryff, C. D., & Singer, B. (1998). The role of purpose in life and personal growth in positive human health. In P. T. P. Wong & P. S. Fry (Eds.), *The human quest for meaning: A handbook of psychological research and clinical applications* (pp. 213–235). Mahwah, NJ: Lawrence Erlbaum.

Ryff, C. D., & Singer, B. (2000). Interpersonal flourishing: A positive health agenda for the new millennium. *Personality and Social Psychology Review, 4*(1), 30–44.

Sabatini, F. (2014). The relationship between happiness and health: Evidence from Italy. *Social Science and Medicine, 114,* 178–187.

Schwartz, S. J., Waterman, A. S., Vazsonyi, A. T., Zamboanga, B. L., Whitbourne, S. K., Weisskirch, R. S., . . . Ham, L. S. (2011). The association of well-being with health risk behaviors in college-attending young adults. *Applied Developmental Science, 15*(1), 20–36.

Scott, K. M. (2014). Depression, anxiety and incident cardiometabolic diseases. *Current Opinion in Psychiatry, 27*(4), 289–293.

Seale, G. S., Berges, I., Ottenbacher, K. J., & Ostir, G. V. (2010). Change in positive emotion and recovery of functional status following stroke. *Rehabilitation Psychology, 55*(1), 33–39.

Shahab, L., & West, R. (2012). Differences in happiness between smokers, ex-smokers and never smokers: Cross-sectional findings from a national household survey. *Drug and Alcohol Dependence, 121*(1–2), 38–44.

Shirom, A., Toker, S., Melamed, S., Berliner, S., & Shapira, I. (2012). Life and job satisfaction as predictors of the incidence of diabetes. *Applied Psychology: Health and Well-Being, 4*(1), 31–48.

Spaderna, H., Vögele, C., Barten, M. J., Smits, J. M. A., Bunyamin, V., & Weidner, G. (2014). Physical activity and depression predict event-free survival in heart transplant candidates. *Health Psychology, 33*(11), 1328–1336.

Tay, L., Tan, K., Diener, E., & Gonzalez, E. (2013). Social relations, health behaviors, and health outcomes: A survey and synthesis. *Applied Psychology: Health and Well-Being, 5*(1), 28–78.

Thomson, W. (2011). Lifting the shroud on depression and premature mortality: A 49-year follow-up study. *Journal of Affective Disorders, 130*(1–2), 60–65.

Tilvis, R. S., Laitala, V., Routasalo, P., Strandberg, T. E., & Pitkala, K. H. (2012). Positive life orientation predicts good survival prognosis in old age. *Archives of Gerontology and Geriatrics, 55*(1), 133–137.

Westerhof, G. J., & Wurm, S. (2015). Longitudinal research on subjective aging, health, and longevity: Current evidence and new directions for research. *Annual Review of Gerontology and Geriatrics, 35*(1), 145–165. doi:10.1891/0198-8794.35.145

Whalley, B., Thompson, D. R., & Taylor, R. S. (2014). Psychological interventions for coronary heart disease: Cochrane systematic review and meta-analysis. *International Journal of Behavioral Medicine, 21*(1), 109–121.

Whooley, M. A., & Wong, J. M. (2013). Depression and cardiovascular disorders. *Annual Review of Clinical Psychology, 9,* 327–354.

Wiest, M., Schüz, B., Webster, N., & Wurm, S. (2011). Subjective well-being and mortality revisited: Differential effects of cognitive and emotional facets of well-being on mortality. *Health Psychology, 30*(6), 728–735.

Wilson, D. K. (2015). Behavior matters: The relevance, impact, and reach of behavioral medicine. *Annals of Behavioral Medicine, 49*(1), 40–48.

Yang, Y., & Waliji, M. (2010). Increment-decrement life table estimates of happy life expectancy for the U.S. population. *Population Research and Policy Review, 29*(6), 775–795.

Zaslavsky, O., Rillamas-Sun, E., Woods, N. F., Cochrane, B. B., Stefanick, M. L., Tindle, H., . . . LaCroix, A. Z. (2014). Association of the selected dimensions of eudaimonic well-being with healthy survival to 85 years of age in older women. *International Psychogeriatrics, 26*(12), 2081–2091.

CHAPTER 11

Enhancing Happiness

This world is but a canvas to our imagination.
—Henry David Thoreau, *A Week on the Concord and Merrimack Rivers* (1849)

Now we bring together topics discussed throughout the book to examine ways we might be able to increase happiness. The chapter is divided into two sections. The first discusses the effectiveness of using positive psychology to increase individual happiness. Sonja Lyubomirsky (2008, 2013), a leading researcher in the area, has written two books for popular audiences encouraging individuals to practice positive psychological interventions in their own lives. We also examine some positive psychology interventions (PPIs) directed toward institutions such as schools or workplaces.

The second section examines socio-structural approaches that drive toward the intersection of economics, government, public policy, psychology, and other social sciences. This section explores institutional-level approaches to increasing happiness by changing institutions with the hope that these changes will have widespread effects for individuals. For instance, are there changes we could make in our tax and social welfare policies that might work?

Note the difference in these two approaches. PPIs rely on increasing happiness by changing the behavior of individuals. The socio-structural approaches direct their efforts at institutions. Both approaches are empirically supported.

POSITIVE PSYCHOLOGY INTERVENTIONS (PPIs)

PPIs Are Effective

Positive psychology researchers have developed and tested interventions that improve individuals' happiness. For instance, Emmons and McCullough (2003) randomly assigned college students to think about things to feel grateful for or about daily hassles or to a control group in which they recalled recent events. The study continued for 9 weeks, and results showed that the intervention was effective. Participants in the grateful condition were more positive about their lives as a whole and more optimistic about the upcoming week than were participants assigned to hassles or events.

Several literature reviews examining this and similar studies confirm that PPIs increase happiness. Perhaps the first, and certainly one of the most widely cited, is a meta-analysis by Sin and Lyubomirsky (2009). They reviewed 49 studies that examined a total of 4,266 participants. These studies tested a variety of PPIs, including ones designed to increase feelings of hope, gratitude, kindness, forgiveness, and mindfulness. Other studies promoted positive writing exercises, goals training, and other types of interventions. The results showed that PPIs significantly increased well-being. Furthermore, these interventions increased the well-being of both (mildly) depressed and nondepressed individuals.

Although the effect size of these PPIs was small or moderate, it was still meaningful. Imagine a group of 200 individuals, half of whom experienced a PPI and half of whom did not. The meta-analytic results predicted that 65 of the 100 participants who experienced the intervention would have greater well-being afterward, compared to only 35 of the 100 participants who did not experience the intervention (Sin & Lyubomirsky, 2009).

This and other reviews found that the effects of PPIs depend on characteristics of the individual, how the intervention is delivered, and other factors. We review the factors that moderate the effect in a later section. However, the effect was consistent enough for Sin and Lyubomirsky (2009) to recommend that therapists consider incorporating these interventions into their practice.

Subsequent reviews reached similar conclusions. Bolier et al. (2013) followed up Sin and Lyubomirsky's (2009) meta-analysis with their own that featured several improvements. These included a focus on experimental studies, weighting studies for methodological quality, including more recent studies, and considering longer term effects of PPIs.

Although Bolier et al.'s meta-analysis found somewhat smaller effect sizes, their results confirmed Sin and Lyubormirksy's findings that PPIs increase subjective well-being. Furthermore, the effects of PPIs remained significant 3 to 6 months after treatment was discontinued. Another important finding is that although the effects of self-administered PPIs were not as strong as those produced through face-to-face meetings with a therapist, self-administration still produced significant improvements in subjective well-being. A later meta-analysis conducted by Weiss, Westerhof, and Bohlmeijer (2016) also showed PPIs are effective.

Bolier et al. concluded that PPIs offer a potentially cost-effective way of improving public mental health. Self-administered PPIs may be less stigmatizing than visits with a therapist. They also have the potential to reach large segments of the population and can be distributed cheaply. For instance, information about PPIs could be distributed free of charge in public places. Although the effects of self-administered PPIs might be relatively small, they could have a large impact if delivered to many individuals.

Specific PPI Approaches

Other reviews have focused on specific types of PPIs. Wood, Froh, and Geraghty (2010) reviewed research on gratitude and well-being and reached more cautious conclusions than some other reviewers. Nevertheless, they found that gratitude interventions increase well-being.

Another positive psychology approach is to promote character strengths. Although there have been several different attempts to define and classify character strengths (see Quinlan, Swain, & Vella-Brodrick, 2012 for a brief review), Peterson and Seligman's (2004) classification is probably the most well-known and widely used. These authors developed a classification of culturally universal human virtues and strengths based on an examination of ancient and enduring cultures that produced written records and that have most strongly influenced human thought. They closely studied the foundational texts of Confucianism, Taoism, Buddhism, Hinduism, the ancient Greeks, Judeo-Christianity, and Islam. These character strengths were sorted into six categories: wisdom, courage, humanity, transcendence, justice, and moderation. Each category includes specific character strengths. For instance, wisdom includes the character strengths of creativity and curiosity, and transcendence includes gratitude and hope (Peterson & Seligman, 2004).

Quinlan et al. (2012) conducted a traditional literature review and found small but statistically significant effects of character strength interventions on well-being. Similar to Bolier et al.'s conclusions about the potential society-wide impact of even small increases of well-being, Quinlan et al. (2012) argue that these small effects could be important when exercised by many people and that strength interventions are potentially inexpensive and easy to administer. The take-away message is that the strengths approach is another example of a PPI that offers promise in increasing happiness. Taken as a whole, there is good evidence that positive psychology can increase individuals' well-being.

Applications of PPIs

Clinical and Counseling Psychology and Psychiatry

The accumulated evidence in favor of PPIs is strong enough that clinical and counseling psychologists, and even some psychiatrists, have begun to integrate these methods into their practices. Wood and Tarrier (2010) suggested the development of positive clinical psychology as a subdiscipline within the larger field. They argue that doing so would help clinicians better recognize the importance of positive behaviors and emotions. It would also more thoroughly integrate the study of both the positive and the negative. Currently, therapists and researchers view these as separate entities rather than as separate poles on a continuum. Furthermore, researchers seem to be stuck studying one or the other and not both, and Wood and Tarrier (2010) argue that this limits the effectiveness of both research and therapy. Jeste, Palmer, Rettew, and Boardman (2015) make a similar argument in calling for a Positive Psychiatry.

Similarly, Georges and Tomlinson-Clarke (2015) advocate for the integration of positive psychology into doctoral training programs for counseling psychologists. They argue that there is a natural connection between counseling and positive psychology in that both are oriented toward promoting strengths and optimal functioning. They also argued that positive psychology is sufficiently advanced scientifically that integrating its concepts into counseling psychology would add rigor to the field.

PPIs in Workplaces and Schools

Researchers have applied the principles of positive psychology in a number of domains, including the workplace and schools. The application of positive psychology to the workplace is in its infancy, and more research is needed before firm conclusions can be drawn. However, positive psychology has been used in the workplace in several ways, including attempts to improve employee resilience through increasing social support, teaching management the skills of positive leadership, and increasing teamwork among colleagues. These and other applications show promise in making businesses more financially successful (Mills, Fleck, & Kozikowski, 2013). Research also indicates that PPIs can help increase workers' well-being and performance (Meyers, van Woerkom, & Bakker, 2013).

Several reviews indicate that PPIs can increase the well-being and perhaps the academic achievement for middle and high school students (e.g., Shankland & Rosset, 2016; Waters, 2011; Waters, Barsky, Ridd, & Allen, 2015; but see also Dawood, 2014 for a somewhat less positive perspective). For example, Shoshani and Steinmetz (2014) conducted a 2-year longitudinal study of a program using positive psychological principles, including gratitude, optimism, and goal setting, in an Israeli middle school. Teachers learned positive psychology principles in 15 2-hour training sessions during the school year. The teachers then delivered these techniques to their students in 15 classroom sessions throughout the school year. The intervention improved student well-being (e.g., self-esteem and optimism) compared to a control group of students who received the intervention later.

However, Shankland and Rosset (2016) noted that PPIs may be difficult to implement in school settings because they take so much time and energy to put in place. The Shoshani and Steinmetz (2014) study is perhaps a good example of this problem. It might be difficult for many teachers and administers to devote that much training and classroom time in today's high stakes testing environment. Therefore, Shankland and Rosset identified brief PPIs. These PPIs have several defining characteristics, including that they can be implemented by a single teacher and that they do not require intensive teacher training. Furthermore, they can be integrated into the school's existing curriculum. For instance, teachers might introduce mindfulness by asking students to train their attention toward the sound of a bell. This might help students increase their attentional capacities and become more present-moment oriented. We wait for more thorough evaluations of the effectiveness of these programs, but they offer a promising way to increase students' well-being.

PPIs Addressing Specific Disorders

Positive psychology has traditionally been oriented toward studying positive characteristics and primarily helping "normal" people live happier and more fulfilled lives. However, researchers and therapists have also used positive psychology principles to relieve suffering among individuals with various kinds of psychopathology. One example is the treatment of depression, and evidence indicates that PPIs are an effective treatment strategy. In a review of the literature, Santos et al. (2013) concluded that PPIs reduce both symptoms of depression and the potential for relapse into subsequent periods of depression (see also Waugh & Koster, 2015). PPIs may also help individuals cope with other emotional disorders such as anxiety (Carl, Soskin, Kerns, & Barlow, 2013).

PPIs may also benefit individuals with a range of other disorders. For instance, Huffman, DuBois, Millstein, Celano, and Wexler (2015) noted that PPIs increase a variety of healthy behaviors such as exercise, and therefore suggested that they may help diabetic individuals lead healthier lives. Unfortunately, many diabetics fail to stick to important recommendations for diet and level of exercise or to take their medications regularly, so Huffman et al. (2015) speculate that PPIs such as optimism training may be particularly helpful in improving compliance with medical doctors' recommendations.

Similarly, DuBois et al. (2012) suggested that PPIs might help individuals with poor heart health to engage in healthier behaviors. Tweed et al. (2011) suggested that PPIs might reduce youth violence. They specifically hypothesized that character strengths such as gratitude and forgiveness, along with an increased sense of life meaning, might be particularly helpful.

However, we should note that there is little to no direct evidence linking PPIs to compliance with medical recommendations for specific patient groups or to decreases in youth violence. Although there are theoretical reasons to expect that PPIs can be effective in these domains, we will have to wait for the data to come in to know for sure. Regardless, it is clear that positive psychology potentially has wide-ranging applications and much promise for lessening human suffering.

PURSUING HAPPINESS IN THE RIGHT WAY

Chapter 4 noted that individuals can pursue happiness effectively. That is, one can successfully increase one's own happiness by consciously deciding to act in certain ways. However, this is a tricky endeavor. Remember that the direct, conscious pursuit of happiness can backfire and make us less happy.

Therefore, it is important that we go about trying to increase our happiness in the right way. Recall that Ford and Mauss (2014) suggest that we be careful not to set our happiness expectations too high, that we involve ourselves in the appropriate happiness-increasing activities, and that we avoid monitoring our minute-to-minute happiness levels. Lyubomirsky and Layous (2013, introduced in Chapter 3) developed a complementary but more detailed approach with their Positive Activity Model. They concluded that careful attention must be given to features of the person, the activity, and the combination of person and activity in order for a PPI to increase happiness.

Features of the Activity

The dosage, variety, timing, and available social support for the activity must be considered. For instance, Lyubomirsky and Layous (2013) reported after reviewing the literature that performing multiple kind acts all in one day more effectively boosted happiness than did spreading the same number of kind acts out across an entire week. There is a similar pattern for counting one's blessings. Counting blessings once a week is more effective than engaging in this activity three times per week. Both of these findings are examples of how the timing of the positive activity matters. Once-a-week practice of positive activities seems to be the optimal timing, perhaps because it mirrors cultural practices such as once-a-week church attendance or even weekly television programs (Lyubomirsky & Layous, 2013; Lyubomirsky, Sheldon, & Schkade, 2005).

Dosage also matters. Spreading out acts of kindness across an entire week may dilute the impact of this activity. However, compressing the same number of kind acts into a single day each week may make them more noticeable and impactful. On the other hand, counting blessings three times a week may be too high a dose. Doing this activity once a week, for one third the total amount of time each week, works much better (Lyubomirsky & Layous, 2013; Lyubomirsky et al., 2005).

Variety is also important. For example, Lyubomirsky and Layous's (2013) review also reports that doing different acts of kindness each week was more effective than continuously performing the same act. They also report that performing multiple positive activities, such as kindness and gratitude, is more effective than sticking with only one positive activity.

Features of the Person

Some individuals are more likely than others to benefit from PPIs. Motivation and optimism seem particularly important. Individuals who are motivated and willing to work hard at becoming happier and who are optimistic about their chances of becoming happier benefit the most from PPIs (Layous, Chancellor, & Lyubomirsky, 2014; Lyubomirsky & Layous, 2013).

There are other individual difference factors that matter as well, including personality characteristics, demographic factors, and culture. Extraverts and individuals who are open to experience (i.e., curious, imaginative people who prefer variety; Costa & McCrae, 1992) are most likely to benefit. Age is significant, with older individuals benefitting more from positive activities. In addition, individuals from Western cultures experience more benefit than do those from Eastern cultures. Social support is also influential. Those who feel that others support their happiness quest do better in response to PPIs (Lyubomirsky & Layous, 2013).

Person by Activity Matches

In her books for popular audiences, Lyubomirsky (2008, 2013) stresses the importance of finding positive activities that match or fit our personalities and needs. Positive activities are most likely to elevate our happiness if they fit our lifestyle, the sources of our existing unhappiness, and our existing strengths. For instance, the positive activity one chooses might differ if one is having trouble finding pleasure in daily life, as opposed to being too shy to seek out social relationships. Furthermore, someone with a very busy lifestyle can choose activities that take less time to perform (Lyubomirsky, 2008).

But Lyubomirsky (2008, 2013) strongly emphasizes that no one activity is likely to work for everyone. In addition to matching activities to lifestyle, problem source, and strengths, we must also match them to our personality, demographic background, attitudes, and other factors. This matching is particularly important because we are much more likely to get a happiness benefit from positive psychological interventions if we enjoy the positive activity (Lyubomirsky & Layous, 2013).

Furthermore, particular activities may be more effective with individuals facing specific challenges. For instance, those who have lots of negative emotion, or who dwell on their problems rather than letting go and thinking about something else, may benefit from loving kindness meditation (LKM). This positive activity might help such individuals in particular because it can shift attention away from problems and toward more beneficial thoughts. In addition, pessimists may benefit from practicing optimism, while individuals with low self-esteem should try practicing acts of kindness because it could improve self-confidence and direct attention away from the self (Layous et al., 2014).

Coping With Hedonic Adaptation

People can adapt to—or, in other words, get used to—both positive and negative events in their lives. For instance, we see that we even adapt to positive events like marriage, and, to a more limited extent, to extremely negative events like severe disability. Of course, being able to adapt to negative events can be a blessing, but adaptation to positive events is one of the most important dragons we have to slay if we are serious about enhancing happiness.

Coping with adaptation is not easy. Humans seem built to adapt to negative events relatively slowly and to positive ones very quickly (Lyubomirsky, 2011). This is exactly opposite to the sequence of events we would hope for. Lyubomirsky (2011) suggests that this tendency raises a formidable challenge to increasing happiness and borrows the saying "bad is stronger than good" from Baumeister, Bratslavsky, Finkenauer, and Vohs (2001) to describe this phenomenon.

Evolution seems to have set us up this way. Positive emotions simply signal to us that things are going well, while negative emotions signal that something is wrong, possibly very wrong. Thus, it would not be adaptive to quickly shrug off the negative emotions that result when bad things happen to us. On the other hand, evolution may have prompted us to seek out fresh new positive emotions in order to ensure that we are striving to continuously better our adaptive position (Lyubomirsky, 2011).

The HAP Model

Luckily, there is a reason to hope that we can effectively cope with hedonic adaptation. Sheldon and Lyubomirsky (2012; see also Lyubomirsky, 2011; Sheldon, Boehm, & Lyubomirsky, 2013) developed a Hedonic Adaptation Prevention (HAP) Model. The HAP describes two ways that hedonic adaptation occurs and hypothesizes how it can be prevented. According to the model, individuals experience hedonic adaptation because their aspirations for positive experiences change and because repeated positive experiences lose their power to produce positive emotions over time. Figure 11.1 (Sheldon & Lyubomirsky, 2012) shows how the model works in response to positive events.

A positive life change (shown in the bottom left corner of Figure 11.1; a new car, for example, or the practice of a PPI) initially sets in motion two sequences of events. The

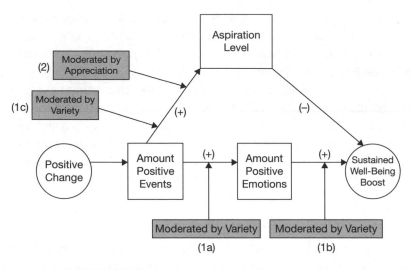

FIGURE 11.1. The Hedonic Adaptation Prevention Model.
Source: Sheldon and Lyubomirsky (2012).

positive event leads to positive emotions (bottom row of the figure), which then increases well-being, at least initially. The positive change unfortunately also increases our aspirations for more positive events (top of the figure), and this increase in aspirations lowers our well-being. This change in aspirations is part of the process of hedonic adaptation (Sheldon & Lyubomirsky, 2012).

So initially, one sequence of events increases well-being (the bottom row of the figure), while the other reduces it through part of the process of hedonic adaptation (the top of the triangle in the figure). But hedonic adaptation also eventually kicks in along the bottom row of the figure. We stop feeling strong positive emotions about the initial positive change and quickly lose the well-being boost we initially experienced. Thus, our well-being often ends up back where we started (Sheldon & Lyubomirsky, 2012).

But there is hope. Sheldon and Lyubomirsky (2012) hypothesize that variety and appreciation, coupled with happiness-boosting interventions (Lyubomirsky, 2011), can stop or reduce hedonic adaptation. As shown in the figure, individual efforts to create variety in positive events and positive emotions are predicted to forestall hedonic adaptation along the bottom row. An event that can be experienced in a variety of different ways or that produces a variety of new and unexpected opportunities is also helpful. For example, a new car that one experiences only as providing a more comfortable ride does not offer much variety. On the other hand, the car provides much more variety if it also offers the opportunity to go to new and unexpected places. Furthermore, individuals who both appreciate and seek variety in positive events are predicted to be less likely to increase their aspirations for future positive events (the top of the triangle in the figure). A similar process is hypothesized to *increase* adaptation of negative events (Lyubomirsky, 2011).[1]

Confirmation of the HAP Model

Sheldon and Lyubomirsky (2012; see also Lyubomirsky, 2011; Sheldon et al., 2013) reviewed indirect evidence that supported HAP. They also conducted a direct test of the model's predictions about adaptation to positive events. Participants were tracked for 3 months. During the first part of the study they indicated positive events that had occurred in their lives. They also indicated positive emotions they experienced, the variety of emotions and experiences that occurred in response to the initial positive event they identified, and how much they appreciated this event. The results largely confirm the HAP model. Variety and appreciation were associated with less hedonic adaptation (Sheldon & Lyubomirsky, 2012).

Other research at least partially confirms these findings. Quoidbach and Dunn (2013) randomly assigned participants to either not eat any chocolate for a week or to receive an ample supply of chocolate and encouraged them to eat as much as they comfortably could or to receive no chocolate eating instructions. The next week, all participants tasted a piece of chocolate. Consistent with the model, students who were asked not to eat any chocolate the previous week savored the chocolate given at the end of the study more, and expressed more positive emotion in response to the chocolate than participants in either of the other two groups.

What do these results suggest? It looks like the participants who ate an unlimited supply of chocolate became hedonically adapted to it and lost at least some of their ability to enjoy chocolate. However, those who did not eat chocolate did not hedonically adapt. They savored the end of the week piece of chocolate more and were therefore more appreciative, and they also had a stronger positive emotional response to the chocolate, indicating that they had not lost any enjoyment of chocolate. Thus, denial, or at least moderation of pleasures, may be a way to avoid hedonic adaptation (Quoidbach & Dunn, 2013). Most importantly, these results help to confirm the role of appreciation in thwarting hedonic adaptation.

These results are important because they demonstrate that we can resist the natural tendency to adapt to positive events. Consistent with the conclusions of the studies in this section, if we practice PPIs in the right way, we can increase our happiness. In terms of short circuiting hedonic adaptation to positive events, such as practicing mindfulness or kindness, we must remember to seek variety in how we experience these events and the positive emotions they produce. We must also make sure we appreciate positive events and resulting emotions to avoid having our aspirations for positivity rise too much (Sheldon & Lyubomirsky, 2012).

SOCIAL POLICY AND ECONOMICS

Do Economists Have a Clue?

The British economist Richard Layard asked this provocative question about economists, who traditionally see economic growth as a solution to human problems, in his book, *Happiness: Lessons From a New Science* (Layard, 2005). Layard meant the question as a critique of economists' ability to explain well-being. Many social scientists doubt that promoting economic growth can meaningfully raise well-being in relatively wealthy industrialized countries, although these same scientists agree that it can in poorer countries.

They arrive at this conclusion because any happiness-increasing effects of growth in wealthy countries can be offset by happiness-decreasing effects of adaptation (Easterlin, 2013; Layard, 2005), the effects of relative income (Bartolini, 2007; Layard, 2005), environmental degradation (Bartolini, 2007; Diener, Oishi, & Lucas, 2015; Diener & Tay, 2015), income inequality (Abbott & Wallace, 2014; Hajdu & Hajdu, 2014), loss of social cohesion (Abbott & Wallace, 2014; Diener & Tay, 2015), and social isolation (Bartolini, 2007; Layard, 2005) that often accompany economic growth. Many of these researchers (e.g., Diener & Tay, 2015) do not dismiss the possibility that economic growth might potentially boost happiness under certain circumstances. And none advocate abandoning economic growth completely. However, few see it as a panacea for increasing the happiness of wealthy countries.

This realization has led to a major reconsideration of economists' assumptions about human happiness. Specifically, standard theory in economics postulates that monetary wealth, usually operationalized as gross domestic product (GDP) on a national level and average household income on an individual level, is the primary indicator of well-being (Diener, Lucas, Schimmack, & Helliwell, 2009). The logic here is that wealth allows individuals to purchase experiences and materials that provide well-being. An embedded assumption is that individuals are rational and that they make wise choices with their purchases so that their well-being is maximized (Diener et al., 2009). This view of human nature is often summed up as *homo-economicus*, or humans as rational economic actors (Hertwig & Herzog, 2009; O'Boyle, 2005; Schneider, Gräf, & Peter, 2010).

The failure of GDP and income to closely track well-being in relatively wealthy societies is a major blow to the homo-economicus model. There are several nonmutually exclusive reasons why economic measures do not predict well-being among citizens of prosperous nations, all of which are incompatible with the standard model of economics. It is important to go through these because they point to money-related policy suggestions that may foster increased well-being.

Problems With Homo-Economicus

One set of reasons involve humans' insistence on less-than-rational behavior from time to time. The effects of relative income and hedonic adaptation are two examples of nonrationality. If one is completely rational, it should not matter to that person how much money others have, nor should it matter how long one has experienced his or her present state of wealth. But it does matter to people a great deal. Any potentially fruitful discussion of happiness-boosting social policy has to account for these effects, even though homo-economicus is supposedly oblivious to them.

A second reason why money poorly predicts well-being is that people do not always make wise, happiness-increasing choices with money, thus indicating a lack of rationality (Diener et al., 2009). For instance, individuals often make foolish investments and buy fatty foods and tobacco products that lower their long-run well-being. Indeed, a wealth of psychological research shows that humans often lack rationality (Hertwig & Herzog, 2009), which has helped give rise to a new and overlapping field called *behavioral economics* that marries the field of economics with psychology.

Third, wealth can have unintended negative consequences that detract from well-being. One is the possible development of materialistic values that lead to treasuring material wealth over social relationships (Kasser & Ryan, 1993). This can corrode happiness because social relationships are so important for well-being, as seen by Baumeister and Leary's (1995) Need to Belong Theory.

Fourth, economic measures do not naturally reflect well-being. Many of the most important sources of happiness cannot be bought. For example, economic measures cannot capture the value of spirituality, friendships, love, and many other factors of life that have important consequences for happiness (Diener et al., 2009). We saw in Chapter 6 that the happiness-inducing effects of money are often matched or even overshadowed by nonmonetary factors. Similarly, economic growth does not necessarily reflect happiness because it can increase in response to objectively negative events. For example, Superstorm Sandy in October 2012 caused all sorts of misery and very little happiness. Yet, it increased economic growth because it provided a huge market for building supplies.

These negative consequences are summed up by the term *externality*, a word economists use to describe consequences of a market exchange that are not directly experienced by the buyer and seller. Imagine that you want to buy a warehouse load of bobby pins, and I happen to have a factory that makes them. We agree on a price, I ship them to you, and we are both happy.

This seems like the end of the story, but it is not. Our agreement has produced positive and negative externalities (i.e., consequences) for many other people. On the positive side, our agreement provided work to many people, including my employees, those of the shipping company, and those who mined and manufactured the materials used to make the bobby pins. However, there are also negative externalities, including the consumption of irreplaceable raw materials and the pollution generated by manufacturing and shipping bobby pins. The costs of these negative externalities are not fully borne by the buyer and seller, and instead are socialized across many people who suffer negative effects of this pollution.

Economic growth can produce income inequality, stress, and social disruption. While homo-economicus may not be bothered by these events, you and I are. Layard refers to these negative externalities as *pollution*. Economic growth and individuals can produce *psychological pollution* that lowers happiness (Bartolini, 2007; Diener et al., 2015; Diener & Tay, 2015). Similarly, if one works too hard to increase personal income, one reduces the time spent with friends and family, potentially reducing one's own happiness. The extra income also potentially pollutes our environment by pushing others farther down the relative income scale.

A deeper understanding of human behavior has developed from the emerging field of behavioral economics that has begun to replace the homo-economicus model of human behavior. This newer model recognizes that humans compare their circumstances to others, that we adapt to our circumstances, that we are emotionally affected by many factors that are not easily measured by dollars, that we are deeply social creatures, and that economic growth has both positive and negative consequences.

POTENTIAL SOCIAL POLICIES

Measure Subjective Well-Being

One straightforward but very important policy suggestion is to simply measure subjective well-being with something approaching the effort and enthusiasm now invested in collecting economic data. This is a logical starting point for several reasons. First, as Diener and Seligman (2004, p. 1) explain:

> Policy decisions at the organizational, corporate, and governmental levels should be more heavily influenced by issues related to well-being. . . . We show that economic indicators have many shortcomings, and that measures of well-being point to important conclusions that are not apparent from economic indicators alone. For example, although economic output has risen steeply over the past decades, there has been no rise in life satisfaction during this period, and there has been a substantial increase in depression and distrust. We argue that economic indicators were extremely important in the early stages of economic development, when the fulfillment of basic needs was the main issue. As societies grow wealthy, however, differences in well-being are less frequently due to income. . . .

Diener and colleagues (e.g., Diener et al., 2015) are careful to explain that they do not advocate abandoning economic measures, but well-being measures can offer important complementary information that has not been available in the past.

A second reason well-being measures are needed is that they can identify areas in need of intervention and assess potential progress. These measures can be useful in broad, money-related areas of social policy (Diener et al., 2015; Seaford, 2013). For instance, we could use well-being measures to assess which form of taxation maximizes well-being. Well-being measures could also be useful in more individual contexts, for instance, as a way to objectively measure suffering or loss in court cases. An individual who suffered sexual harassment might receive compensation based on the degree to which her happiness was reduced from the experience (Diener et al., 2015).

Third, the mere act of assessing well-being signals that it is valued and can make it easier to build political and social support for well-being enhancement (Seaford, 2013). Diener et al. (2015, p. 237) make the argument very clearly:

> It is often said that what is measured is what receives attention, and that measurement is a key to effective intervention programs. For instance, public interest in school performance in the United States results in part from the publicity surrounding measures that show that students in many other nations score higher on standardized tests of school learning. Similarly,

unemployment receives widespread attention in the press because societies track it and publish statistics about it. Thus, national accounts of well-being will help focus attention on psychological variables that are important to quality of life.

Finally, measures of subjective well-being are valuable because of their connection to happiness, a widely shared value. But well-being measures also predict more tangible realities such as health, productivity, and the general quality of life. These quality of life variables include topics such as crime rates, educational attainment, and the availability of fine arts (Diener et al., 2015; Diener & Tay, 2015).

Progress in Measurement

Governments and international institutions around the world seem to recognize the potential benefits of assessing well-being. More than 40 countries, including the United States, have begun to measure well-being in at least some form (Diener et al., 2015). The "Stiglitz Report" (Stiglitz, Sen, & Fitoussi, 2010), commissioned by French president Nicolas Sarkozy in 2008 and coauthored by Nobel-Prize winning economists Joseph Stiglitz and Amartya Sen, along with fellow economist Jean-Paul Fitoussi, is another indication that subjective well-being measures are becoming more accepted among policy makers. President Sarkozy was dissatisfied with the ability of economic indicators as measures of social progress. He asked the commission to investigate the limitations of these economic measures and report on potential improvements.

The report is not a refutation of economic measures, but it does recognize their limitations and it also calls for the inclusion of well-being measures. For instance, it includes an example of how a traffic jam could increase GDP because of additional fuel consumption, but that this should not be seen as an increase in well-being. The report also calls for additional awareness and monitoring of income inequality and for the recognition that nonmarket activities have substantial impacts on well-being. Finally, and most importantly for our purposes, it calls for regular and systematic surveys of individual level subjective well-being, along with traditional economic data.

The report is a remarkable example of a major wealthy Western industrial democracy placing measures of subjective well-being in such a central role. It is also remarkable that the prominent economists who coauthored the report, not just psychologists and other social scientists, recognize the importance of well-being measures. Well-being measures are apparently gaining wide acceptance.

Measurement and Democracy

Measures of subjective well-being can also be an important component of democracy. Seaford (2013) notes that economic indicators have not accomplished the primary goal of public policy, increasing life satisfaction, particularly since the financial collapse in 2008. He also argues that well-being measures are better suited for maximizing life satisfaction and that they can help the public participate more fully in policy debates.

Seaford (2013) maintains that framing these debates around which well-being indicators we wish to maximize makes assumptions and goals more explicit and easily identifiable by the public, thereby supporting the democratic engagement of the public in informed debate about policy issues. For instance, the consequences and assumptions behind the goal to maximize economic output (GDP) are less clear to the public than goals such as maximizing general life satisfaction or housing satisfaction. Because the primary goal of public policy is to maximize the public's well-being, it makes sense, according to Seaford, to directly measure happiness instead of using proxy measures such as GDP.

Added emphasis on well-being measures would make it easier for the public to evaluate the success or failure of social programs. For example, it is not clear to the public whether an increase in GDP benefited the general public unless well-being data are also available. Seaford uses the example that reduction of working hours (without an accompanying decrease in wages) often benefits well-being. The business argument that such a policy would necessarily be accompanied by economic damage that would lower overall well-being is often taken at face value in the absence of well-being data that might counter this position. The ability to more fully evaluate the arguments would facilitate democratic debate because it would lead to a more informed electorate.

Well-being measures might also benefit democracy by drawing attention to the concerns of less powerful groups. Findings that significant numbers of poor or otherwise disadvantaged individuals are less happy than the wealthy may give them a more proportionate share of political power. Such a finding might at least help draw more resources in their direction.

Are Well-Being Measures Politically Neutral?

This is an important question. Some might be concerned that well-being measures favor a politically liberal perspective, perhaps because they might suggest more government intervention in social policy (Diener & Seligman, 2004). However, the goal should be to provide objective, relevant, and scientific information that can better inform policy debates, not to give a political advantage to a particular interest group. Diener and Seligman (2004, p. 24) conclude that well-being measures are politically neutral.

> . . . measures of well-being are—and must be—exactly as neutral politically as are economic indicators. The indicators are descriptive, not prescriptive, and must remain so. They simply yield facts that can be used either by the left or by the right, and therefore they provide an added way to better assess the claims of various political viewpoints by revealing how policies actually influence well-being.

Note that well-being measures do not typically have strong value components. For instance, respondents are asked a variety of questions about how satisfied they are with their life as a whole, not politically loaded questions about "freedom" or "oppression." The questions are quite politically neutral.

Furthermore, well-being measures must be as politically neutral as economic measures. If we insist on concern about the potential political nature of well-being measures, we should also consider possible bias of economic measures. The argument might be that focusing attention on GDP places an undue emphasis on the needs of business owners rather than those of workers.

Another important point embedded in the Diener and Seligman quotation is that well-being measures simply provide additional data that might be helpful. The democratic process should decide how to use these data (if at all). If the goal of public policy is truly to maximize well-being, why would we choose not to measure well-being?

Diener and Seligman acknowledge and respond to other specific concerns about the potential political nature of well-being measures. For instance, they argue that well-being measures should not lead to an "interventionist" or "paternalistic" central government any more than economic measures would. They also argue that noninterventionists, who believe that an activist central government reduces happiness by eroding individual liberty, should be pleased to have well-being data available, which might support their beliefs.

There is also the argument that happiness is more personal than is economics. Diener and Seligman characterize this argument as claiming that the economy affects and connects everyone, but happiness is an individual entity. Therefore, happiness-based governmental interventions are more threatening to individual liberty. Diener and Seligman respond that individual happiness does not exist in isolation either and instead is affected by other people, including those in our wider community and nation. For example, the stability of a national government also influences well-being.

Diener and Seligman also note that the results of well-being surveys could conceivably give advantage to both conservatives and liberals. For instance, it is true that some happiness data (e.g., income inequality) seem to confirm liberal positions. However, other data indicate that citizens of free-market democracies are happier than those in less democratic countries, and that religious individuals are happier than the nonreligious, results that should please conservatives.

It is also worth noting that at least some prominent conservatives, including conservative French former president Nicolas Sarkozy, who commissioned the Stiglitz report, and David Cameron, the conservative former prime minister of the United Kingdom, have embraced using subjective well-being measures for public policy (Diener et al., 2015).

Policy Modeled After Countries With High Well-Being

One sensible approach is to examine the countries with the highest levels of well-being and then identify their common characteristics. Social policies designed to promote happiness could then be modeled after these countries. Diener et al. (2015) list 10 characteristics of high well-being countries. Notably, they state that these characteristics are not a simple function of wealth but instead predict well-being even after wealth is controlled. Following is a summary of the common characteristics of the happiest economically developed countries:

- ▶ Individuals' basic needs and wants are satisfied
- ▶ Respect for the rule of law and human rights
- ▶ Low levels of corruption
- ▶ High-quality and efficient government services
- ▶ Progressive tax rates in which the wealthy pay a higher proportion of their income in taxes

- ▶ Adequate income security programs such as pensions and unemployment benefits
- ▶ Political freedom, protection of property rights, and stable currency
- ▶ Low levels of unemployment, and generous employment benefits
- ▶ Healthy, disease-free populations with generous health care systems
- ▶ Healthy natural environments

Government, business, and social organizations can influence many of these characteristics (Diener et al., 2015). Thus, happy societies can be crafted by social policies and other intentional actions taken by social leaders and demanded by an aware citizenry. Diener et al. use these data to suggest a number of potential policies. These include many non–income-related policies such as increasing green space in cities; reducing commute times, air pollution, and corruption; and using zoning laws and other planning tools to engineer safer, friendlier neighborhoods.

Their recommendations also include a number of income-related policies. They recommend examining income security programs, unemployment and health insurance, social welfare policies, and consumer protections as ways to boost societal well-being. These recommendations are tentative predicated on additional confirming research, and expanding upon existing findings. But they cite research indicating that requirements that businesses give severance pay—and give specific reasons for firing employees, for example—are associated with higher well-being. They also note that businesses, as well as governments, can and should be interested in boosting well-being because it is linked to better productivity. Businesses can boost well-being in a number of ways including cultivating a positive social atmosphere and providing job autonomy and variety to workers.

It is also worthwhile to reiterate Diener et al.'s point that national well-being is not simply a function of wealth or income. The list of characteristics generated by these authors and their specific suggestions described do not require tremendous levels of national wealth. Although the suggestions do require that nations be able to meet their citizens' basic needs, policies such as increasing urban green space and providing basic employment protections are probably within reach of many nations.

To further illustrate the point that great wealth is not essential for promoting societal happiness, it is interesting to note that the world's wealthiest nation, the United States, ranks as the 15th happiest nation (out of 158 countries) in data collected by the 2015 World Happiness Report (Helliwell, Layard, & Sachs, 2015). We are sandwiched between Mexico, which ranks 14th, and Brazil, which ranks 16th. The countries that made the top 10 are listed as follows:

1. Switzerland
2. Iceland
3. Denmark
4. Norway

5. Canada

6. Finland

7. Netherlands

8. Sweden

9. New Zealand

10. Australia

So great wealth does not necessarily place a country at the top of the world happiness rankings. The 10 happiest nations, though wealthy, are not as wealthy as the United States. In many ways, their objective standard of living is lower than that in the United States. For example, the average new home built in Denmark had 137 square meters (1,474 square feet) of floor space compared to 214 square meters (2,303 square feet) for the average U.S. new home, according to a 2009 story by the British Broadcasting Company (http://news.bbc.co.uk/2/hi/uk_news/magazine/8201900.stm).

Most of the happiest countries have relatively small and seemingly homogeneous populations. Could it be that these characteristics, and not something about their social welfare policies, drive their happiness? It is certainly possible. Perhaps small and homogeneous countries have higher levels of trust and less social discord, both of which contribute to well-being.

This is an important question because we ultimately want to know what causes well-being. And these are not experimental data. No one randomly assigned countries to social welfare policies, so we cannot assume that just because the happiest countries have generous social welfare policies that these policies cause their happiness. Other factors, such as population size and homogeneity, may be the driving factor.

However, these alternative explanations seem unlikely when we examine the data closely. Helliwell et al. (2015), who authored the World Happiness Report in 2013, point out that there is no systematic association between national population size and well-being. Both large- and small-population countries claim spots throughout the distribution of happiness.

Furthermore, the happy Scandinavian countries are more ethnically diverse than we might think. For instance, data from Denmark's official government statistical site (www.statistikbanken.dk/statbank5a/default.asp?w=1280) indicate that there were 5.63 million Danish residents in 2015 who were born in non-Western countries, constituting 7.5% of the total population. In comparison, 8% of the residents of the United Kingdom (a fellow European country with a weaker social welfare system and an appreciably lower happiness ranking) were born outside the European Union in 2012, according to a 2013 Bulletin by the British Office of National Statistics.

In addition, although 10.2% of Danish residents were born abroad or had a parent born abroad, compared to 20% in England and Wales, the numbers for foreign-born citizens are not very different: 6.3% in Denmark as compared to 8% in England and Wales. And perhaps surprisingly, Sweden, another country with a strong social safety net that ranks high in happiness, has a higher percentage of foreign-born residents than do England and Wales (21.7% versus 20%; www.migrationobservatory.ox.ac.uk/briefings

/immigration-population-and-ethnicity-uk-international-perspective). Thus, it is not at all clear that ethnic homogeneity can explain the international happiness rankings.

Easterlin's Policy Suggestions

Social Safety Net and Full Employment

Recall that Easterlin (1974) is the researcher who discovered the paradox that wealth predicts well-being within nations but not between nations. He also found that economic growth does not affect well-being over long periods of time. Easterlin (2013) repeated many of the arguments showing that economic growth does not substantially increase well-being in the long term. But he also makes explicit suggestions for social policy based on these arguments. His suggestion is to promote the social welfare programs that Northern European countries are noted for.

> If society's goal is to increase people's feelings of well-being, economic growth in itself will not do the job. Full employment and a generous and comprehensive social safety net do increase happiness (Easterlin, 2013, p. 1).

Easterlin (2013, p. 13) explicitly states that economic growth should not necessarily be abandoned, but he further notes:

> In principle, economic growth should contribute to greater employment and make safety net policies easier to implement, although this has not been demonstrated here. Clearly, there is much more research to be done, but it is evident that the sole promotion of economic growth as a cure-all is not a valid policy solution to raising happiness.

Thus, Easterlin (2013) advises policies that encourage full employment and that offer a secure social safety net. Growth may be helpful in producing these conditions, but it is not a happiness-increasing goal in itself. Furthermore, Easterlin, who is an economist, argues that generous social welfare programs are affordable, even in many relatively poor countries, if spending priorities are recognized.

Easterlin (2013) does not describe policies that might lead to full employment. This is a muddy and politically tangled concept. But the basic idea is clear. He notes the data we discussed in Chapter 6 and concludes that societies should do what they can to ensure that individuals do not suffer long-term unemployment. Denmark, perennially one of the happiest nations on Earth, for example, has an explicit employment policy called "flexicurity." According to the national government website (www.denmark.dk/en/society/welfare), it is relatively easy for businesses to fire unneeded workers, but the national government also has an "active labour market policy" that offers assistance, education, or a job to all the unemployed. The unemployed also have the responsibility for actively looking for work and for accepting a job when offered. Empirical reviews of these active labor market policies are positive, finding that they reduce the psychological distress of unemployment (Coutts, Stuckler, & Cann, 2014).

A secure social safety net is also an important component of Easterlin's (2013) advice for happiness-increasing social policy. Let us look at Denmark again to see what this might mean. The term *welfare* is rather prominently displayed on the country's official website (www.denmark.dk). Click the "society" button on the homepage, and welfare is listed along with buttons for the monarchy, Danish history and religion, and so on. Perhaps this suggests the Danish commitment to their social welfare programs. They describe their system as follows:

> The basic principle of the Danish welfare system, often referred to as the Scandinavian welfare model, is that all citizens have equal rights to social security. Within the Danish welfare system, a number of services are available to citizens, free of charge. This means that for instance the Danish health and educational systems are free. The Danish welfare model is subsidised by the state, and as a result Denmark has one of the highest taxation levels in the world. (Description of welfare by Denmark Government. Retrieved from http://denmark.dk/en/society/welfare)

It is particularly interesting that the Danes advertise having high tax rates, particularly in the context of describing their welfare system. Indeed, taxes on personal income amount to 26.4% of GDP in Denmark, as compared to 9.8% in the United States (https://data.oecd.org). Denmark's commitment to social welfare is evidenced by its spending priorities. For instance, in 2011 Denmark spent the equivalent of 2.2% of its GDP on unemployment benefits, which dwarfs the 0.4% of GDP spent by the United Kingdom, another European country with a less secure social safety net, that year (https://data.oecd.org/socialexp/public-unemployment-spending.htm#indicator-chart). Similarly, Denmark spent the equivalent of 4.7% of its GDP on disability benefits in 2011, compared to the United Kingdom, which spent 2.5% of its GDP on disability benefits (https://data.oecd.org/socialexp/public-spending-on-incapacity.htm#indicator-chart). Consider Denmark was the happiest nation in the world in the latest World Happiness Report, while the United Kingdom ranked 22nd.

Evidence

In support of this advice, Easterlin (2013) identified three "ultra-welfare states"—Denmark, Sweden, and Finland—and compared their well-being to four "semi-welfare states"—Germany, Austria, France, and the United Kingdom. The ultra-welfare states were considerably more generous with pensions, unemployment, and sickness benefits than were the semi-welfare states. The two groups of countries had almost identical GDPs and inflation rates. Consistent with expectations, citizens of the ultra-welfare states were happier than those of the less generous states. They were also more satisfied with their work and family lives, their health, and public services. Citizens in the ultra-welfare states were apparently aware of the generous public services they received and were appreciative of them. They gave higher ratings to public services for health, education, child care, and public pensions and expressed more trust in the political system.

Studies of progressive taxation also support Easterlin's (2013) suggestion that we should build stronger social safety nets.[2] Progressive taxes are those in which wealthy individuals are taxed at higher rates than are poorer individuals. Progressive taxes are considered *redistributive* because they channel money away from the wealthy that can then be used by governments to help the poor. Progressive taxes are also associated with effective antipoverty programs (Gatzia & Woods, 2014). Oishi, Schimmack, and Diener (2012) found that progressive taxation is associated with higher well-being even after controlling for national wealth and income inequality. Consistent with Easterlin's (2013) support for social welfare systems, Oishi et al. also found that progressive taxes are associated with high well-being because they generate more satisfaction with public infrastructure systems such as education, health care, housing, and transportation. Thus, progressive taxation seems to promote happiness because it is also associated with social welfare projects.

Other evidence also shows that citizens of welfare states are more satisfied with their lives. Flavin and Radcliff (2009) found that social safety nets predicted lower suicide rates within the United States. The strength of the social safety net was measured in several ways including family assistance (traditionally known as "welfare"), medical benefits, and overall transfer payments (money paid by the government to individuals for disability insurance, educational assistance, veterans' benefits, retirement, and so on). Findings were significant even after statistically controlling for social capital (levels of trust, volunteerism, engagement in community life, and so forth), divorce rates, residential mobility, and unemployment rates. And, the relationship between social spending and suicide rates was large enough to be meaningful. The authors estimate that if each state raised social welfare spending by about $45 per year/per person, there would be about 3,000 fewer deaths by suicide each year (a 10% reduction in overall suicide rates).

In addition, Flavin, Pacek, and Radcliff (2011) examined life satisfaction in 15 industrially developed democracies[3] with differing investments in their social safety nets. Consistent with Easterlin's (2013) suggestion that social safety nets promote well-being, results indicate that citizens were more satisfied if they lived in countries with higher levels of government spending directed toward social programs. Specifically, tax revenue, the government spending as a share of GDP, unemployment benefits, and government social welfare expenditures were all positively related to life satisfaction, even after controlling for demographic, cultural, and economic variables. And these relationships were not just statistically significant; they were also large enough to be practically important. The effects of social welfare spending were roughly equivalent to the individual effects of getting married or of personal income. Flavin et al. (2011) later replicated these findings with different measures.

Interestingly, life satisfaction was positively related to these government social spending variables almost regardless of personal income (Flavin et al., 2011). The wealthiest citizens were *less* satisfied as tax revenues and the government spending as a percentage of GDP increased. However, these decreases in satisfaction were not large. Flavin et al. conclude that these macroeconomic variables should be added to the traditional personality, cultural, and microeconomic variables (e.g., personal income) that researchers use to predict well-being.

Flavin et al. (2011, p. 264) draw the following conclusion:

> Our results thus do not indict the market as it affects satisfaction with life, but suggest instead that the quality of human life is best when the inequalities and uncertainties of the market are mitigated by state intervention acting in the interests of workers and citizens. Our results might thus be most easily summarized by suggesting that . . . "compassionate capitalism". . . seems most consistent with well-being.

These are the same social welfare state policies that Easterlin favors.

One final caution about social spending is necessary. Cullis, Hudson, and Jones (2011) examine the effects of redistributing income via tax policy, both within and between countries within the European Union. They find that a redistribution of wealth from rich to poor countries would likely increase overall happiness. However, redistributing wealth within any particular country appeared to have only minimal effects on happiness. The key might be how redistributed money is spent, because social welfare spending itself may not always increase happiness. Instead, the way social welfare programs are administered and the particular programs emphasized are important. Jakubow (2014) found that state spending on social welfare programs is effective when citizens perceive the government as fair and efficient, and when it emphasizes unemployment protections and aid directed toward families struggling with work–life balance problems, particularly in regard to child rearing. This concern should be incorporated into any social policy discussion about welfare spending.

In summary, Easterlin (2013) suggests building strong social safety nets that are publicly financed and modeled after those of Northern European countries. He advises that unemployment protections receive particular emphasis. Although he advises against abandoning economic growth, he does not see growth by itself as a solution to lagging happiness.

Value judgments are always intermingled with policy suggestions, so it is difficult to state objectively that the data support any particular policy. At base, policy is about promoting what is "good" and discouraging what is "bad," and people might disagree about these. Is happiness itself "good" or "bad?" This is not a question we can answer with data.

However, the data indicate that residents of countries with strong social welfare programs have higher well-being than residents of comparison countries. The data also suggest that economic growth by itself does not strongly increase well-being. Of course, we must always be receptive to more data that address these questions in different ways and with different controls. But if our sole objective is to promote well-being, a good argument can be made that strong social welfare programs are an effective strategy.

Layard's Utilitarian Perspective

British economist Richard Layard (2005, 2006) takes a pragmatic, utilitarian approach that emphasizes maximizing happiness for the greatest number of people. Layard's policy suggestions weave together the results of modern psychological research with the language and thought processes of traditional economics.

Layard's (2005) starting point is that economic growth by itself is unlikely to increase the happiness in relatively wealthy countries. He calls on much of the same data already presented to argue that we are happier when we have political freedom and are free from poverty, but also when we have trust in others and feel economically and socially secure. Thus, unemployment and disruption of family and other social bonds can create a tremendous drag on our happiness.

Layard (2006) identifies three primary problems that lower happiness in Western industrialized countries. One is that our "tastes," which is economics-speak for our preferences and desires, are culturally constructed. In other words, culture influences what we think is desirable. This is not surprising to any psychology student, but it is a bit of a revelation in economics, which has long assumed that tastes are natural (Layard, 2005, 2006).

Social comparisons are a second problem. The media and advertising are tremendously influential in shaping preferences in industrialized cultures such as ours. The media expose us to examples of fabulous wealth, which stokes the fires of social comparisons. Therefore, we are strongly influenced by *relative income*, or how our income compares to those around us. Income inequality also contributes to these comparison effects (Layard, 2005).

A third problem is that exposure to these models of wealth also sparks us to higher levels of acquisitiveness as we try to keep up in the wealth arms race (Layard, 2006). But we also naturally experience hedonic adaptation to new levels of income and material possessions, receiving less pleasure from them over time. The balance between our work and family lives is also upset by this acquisitiveness because we work too many hours, particularly those of us in the United States. As a result of these long work hours, our family and social lives are less satisfying.

Layard (2005, 2006) refers to "a race for status" and argues that by participating in this race we not only lower our own happiness but also lower the happiness of those around us. In fact, by joining the race for status by seeking more income, for example, a person creates a negative externality (a form of pollution) that lowers another's well-being. Here Layard is borrowing ideas and terminology from economics, and the idea of homo-economicus. Of course, the rationale is that because relative income is so important, when someone raises his or her own income, that person lowers the satisfaction of others with their own incomes. This creates a losing game for everyone.

Policy Suggestions

Taxes   Layard's policy suggestion is to adjust tax rates such that income (and work) beyond a certain level is discouraged. Layard (2005, 2006) specifically proposes that we discourage "excessive" or "unnecessary" work that is designed not just to acquire the basic necessities for a given society, but instead to acquire higher status. Tax rates would be fixed such that one would lose the incentive to work for more than a certain amount of money, because everything earned above that amount would be heavily taxed.

Another related suggestion from Layard is to eliminate or heavily tax performance-based pay. The rationale here is that there is no objective way to measure performance in most professions, so performance-based pay is based on comparisons between workers. How many bobby pins should a factory worker make? Because there is no objective answer, the common solution is to give Susan the merit raise because she made more bobby pins than did Stan. But this just makes Stan, and the other workers, envious and unhappy. Susan has *polluted* the happiness in the factory, according to Layard. And it does not make Susan happy in the long run because she quickly adapts to her new income level. Susan is also not likely to remain happy with her new income because she must work even harder now to keep the other workers from overtaking her (Layard, 2005, 2006).

Layard's views on taxes are based on the relative income effect, social comparisons, the hedonic treadmill, and other, nonmonetary factors that make us happy. Any effort one makes to raise one's own income, either through extra work or by seeking merit raises, is ultimately self-defeating (Layard, 2005, 2006). For one thing, the extra effort at work (long hours, emotional energy expended, and so on) may interfere with family life and other social relationships, which also have strong positive effects on well-being. Layard (2005) sees this point about work interfering with social relationships, particularly involving family, as extremely important. Note that it is consistent with the data we reviewed earlier in this chapter. Income and wealth are only one set of factors that influence well-being, and their effects are usually relatively small. Family and social relationships (Baumeister & Leary, 1995) have important impacts on well-being, so anything that interferes with them is likely to have strong negative effects

It is also self-defeating because one is likely to adapt to the extra income (assuming one is already above the breadline). It is also likely to prompt others to increase their own incomes, because they are influenced by social comparisons. Once others catch up with the first person to increase his or her income, the benefits from those extra dollars diminish quickly. And, just as importantly, the extra income pollutes the happiness of others because they now feel the need to catch up.

Improving family relationships   Layard (2005) emphasizes the importance of social relationships, particularly our relationship with our families, in building and maintaining happiness. He sees "overwork" as significantly interfering with family time. We see in Chapter 7 that "time affluence" was related to more happiness and time scarcity to less happiness. We also see that heavy time demands at work predict lower happiness. Both of these findings are consistent with Layard's argument. In response to this research, several theorists suggest that we should at least consider shortening the work week (Coote, Franklin, & Simms, 2010; Hansen, 2015; Reisch, 2001; Schor, 2010).

In addition, Kasser and Sheldon (2009) endorse three proposals offered by "Take Back Your Time" (TBYT; www.timeday.org), an activist group committed to reducing time stress. Specifically, Kasser and Sheldon (2009) agree with TBYT that businesses should offer paid family leave (to care for newborns or sick or aging family members) and a minimum of 3 weeks of paid vacation. In addition, businesses should not demand that their employees work overtime (Kasser & Sheldon, 2009).

Other suggestions   Layard (2005, 2006) also suggests restricting advertising, particularly toward children, in order to lower acquisitiveness. This acquisitiveness serves only to strengthen the self-defeating status race, according to Layard. We should also recognize that humans are *loss averse*. This means that losses lower happiness more than an equivalent gain raises happiness. One is unhappier when losing a dollar than happy when gaining a dollar. As a result, Layard (2005, 2006) suggests that we should find ways to bring stability to our economy to protect individuals from losses such as unemployment. Part of this means having a strong economic safety net for workers, similar to Easterlin's (2013) suggestion. Layard takes the data regarding the happiness-reducing effects of unemployment very seriously.

He also suggests that we should do more to help the poor around the world who are struggling to provide for their own basic necessities (Layard, 2005). Income does matter for them. Finally, he suggests that we should look for ways to reduce competition between individuals (Layard, 2005, 2006) and find alternative ways for individuals to earn respect. Layard (2005) suggests encouraging greater respect for those who help others as opposed to those who are temporarily ahead in the material status race.

Note Layard's full-throated pragmatism and utilitarianism here. It is clear that his intent is to follow the data to find what will work for the most people, no matter how unconventional the approach. And his suggestions about taxes and performance-based pay are very unconventional for capitalist societies. But no matter how unconventional the approach, we should take a close look at this logic before making an evaluation.

For instance, his suggestions are based on sound science surrounding adaptation and social comparison effects. This leads him to refer to the taxes he advocates as *corrective*. The logic of economics dictates that various social practices can *distort* markets if they tilt behavior away from efficient use of resources and money. Thus, sometimes corrective measures are necessary. Layard (2005, 2006) argues that if our goal is to maximize the happiness of everyone, then we should eliminate distortions in our economy that interfere with the efficient maximization of this goal.

Potential Objections

One potential objection to Layard's (2005, 2006) policy suggestions is that they are a radical departure from convention. Perhaps we would want to move slowly to implement his policies to make sure they work in real-world conditions. Another likely objection is that Layard's plan might create a *moral hazard* in which we encourage envy. Libertarians, who believe in maximizing individual liberty, might be particularly offended by Layard's suggestions. Might it be better to instruct individuals to "just grow up and get over" their unhappiness when they recognize that someone else has more income than they do? Layard (2005, p. 153) responds sharply to this objection, calling it "extraordinarily weak." For one thing, many existing social policies encourage greed, but no one seems to object to this moral hazard. But more importantly, Layard argues that envy and the desire for status are part of human nature, and that efforts to reduce income disparities are necessary to maximize human happiness.

We might also think that taxing work might reduce productivity and economic advancement. It might also slow the rate of development of technological achievements such as new medicines and electronic conveniences. One of Layard's (2005) major theses is that economic advancement over the last several decades has not increased happiness in industrialized economies. We have seen this in the data reviewed throughout the book. Therefore, if the goal is to increase happiness, why should we worry about slowing the growth of material luxuries? They do not seem to have made us happier in the past. Furthermore, it is unlikely that the lack of new material conveniences would make us less happy (Gilbert, 2006). Were people in the 1950s less happy because they did not have color TV?

In addition, strong external rewards, such as performance-based pay, are likely to reduce rather than increase motivation. Layard (2005) cites several findings from Self-Determination Theory (SDT; Deci & Ryan, 1985) to support this point. Research from this area indicates that external rewards reduce intrinsic motivation to do a good job for its own sake. Workers instead pursue the reward and lose a sense of professional pride that is essential to doing good work. Research shows that focus on the external financial reward also reduces happiness. Layard describes the problems that can occur when there is too much focus on financial rewards. Layard (2005), who remember is an economist himself, argues that economists place too much emphasis on external rewards such as money, and that this reduces both job satisfaction and happiness.

Would slowing economic growth lead to job losses and other happiness-decreasing effects? Layard (2005, 2006) does not think so. For one thing, he does not advocate ending economic growth, so there should not be too much pressure on employment. Instead, he merely states that growth is not a panacea, and that other factors are as or more important for happiness. Layard (2003, Lecture 2), in a series of lectures published on the web as part of the Lionel Robbins Memorial Lecture Series sponsored by the London School of Economics and Political Science (http://cep.lse.ac.uk/_new/events/robbins.asp), acknowledges that his tax proposals will slow GDP growth, but he does not see this as a concern. His interest is in happiness, not economic growth. The data convince him that the two are not the same thing.

> We should be clear that such taxation is almost certainly reducing our measured GDP, by reducing work effort. But we should be equally clear that this does not matter, because GDP is a faulty measure of well-being. (Layard, 2003, Lecture 2, p. 11)

Let us entertain one other potential objection. Is there something "unnatural" about what Layard is proposing? We learned in Chapter 2 that status seeking has been selected for in our species. Layard (2005, 2006) suggests that we discourage unnecessary or excessive work that seeks to raise status. Does this suggestion ignore a biological imperative? Again, Layard (2005, 2006) does not think so. First, he recognizes the importance of culture, and that biological imperatives are probably rare. Second, his suggestion is not to ignore or suppress impulses for status, but instead to channel them away from work and income by using corrective taxes. He hopes that impulses for status will then manifest in more productive ways, such as efforts to help others.

In summary, Layard is as direct as he is unconventional. *If* our goal is to maximize the happiness of as many people as possible (and everyone's happiness counts equally), this is what he thinks we should do: use taxes to discourage "overworking," place restrictions on advertising (particularly ads directed toward children), do what we can to strengthen families and communities, and focus our economic attention on helping poor people around the world. And his advice about what we should do, particularly regarding discouraging "excessive work" with taxation, is indeed unconventional. But his logic is very clear. Excessive work, performance-based pay, and the monetarily based race for status are all sources of "pollution" that lower everyone's happiness, including those who win what Layard (2005) calls the *rat race*. This logic is based on a solid base of research on relative income, the hedonic treadmill, and other aspects of human motivation (e.g., SDT, loss aversion).

SUMMARY

This is an exciting chapter and a fitting way to end the book because it shows that we can be happier, both as individuals and as a society. The PPIs offer effective ways we can improve our own happiness by changing the way we think about events and the goals we choose to pursue. Rethinking social policies regarding taxes, social welfare systems, family and work balance, and so on, offers the opportunity to improve the happiness of our society as a whole. Perhaps most exciting, these suggestions for improving both individual and society-wide happiness are based on sound scientific evidence. We have every reason to be optimistic that they will work.

Embedded in all these suggestions are consistent themes we have discovered throughout the book. Once we have the financial resources to meet our basic physical and psychological needs, there is little use in pursuing wealth or fame if happiness is our goal. Similarly, if happiness is our goal, we should be particularly careful to avoid becoming entangled in consumer and materialistic culture. Instead, we should focus on things that are most likely to bring us happiness.

Much of this involves how we construe or think about the world. Happiness comes from seeing the world in ways that value meaningful relationships, encourage gratitude, avoid social comparisons, and savor positive experiences. We should also seek out environments that improve our happiness. Meaningful work and other environments that help us find meaning and purpose are important. Likewise, living in trustful, relatively egalitarian societies with stable and efficient governments that provide effective social safety nets and that allow workers sufficient time with their families significantly increases happiness.

The magic of empiricism has identified paths to greater happiness. I hope we can find these paths.

NOTES

1. Again, there are two processes, but in both the goal is to *decrease* the variety of events and emotions associated with the negative event. We want to draw our attention away from the negative

event so that it does not keep producing negative emotions. This will reduce or eliminate the number and severity of the negative emotions produced by the event (the bottom row of the figure) and allow adaptation to occur. It will also increase our aspirations for positive emotions (the top of the triangle in the figure). Unlike the desired response to positive events, we should try to increase aspirations for positive emotions after a negative event, because this will help distract us from the negative event (Lyubomirsky, 2011).

2. However, see Cullis et al. (2011) for a partially dissenting view.

3. Australia, Canada, Finland, France, Germany, Great Britain, Italy, Japan, the Netherlands, Norway, South Korea, Spain, Sweden, Switzerland, and the United States.

REFERENCES

Abbott, P., & Wallace, C. (2014). Rising economic prosperity and social quality. The case of new member states of the European Union. *Social Indicators Research*, 115(1), 419–439.

Bartolini, S. (2007). Why are people so unhappy? Why do they strive so hard for money? Competing explanations of the broken promises of economic growth. In L. Bruni & P. L. Porta (Eds.), *Handbook on the economics of happiness* (pp. 337–364). Cheltenham, UK: Edward Elgar.

Baumeister, R. F., Bratslavsky, E., Finkenauer, C., & Vohs, K. D. (2001). Bad is stronger than good. *Review of General Psychology*, 5(4), 323–370.

Baumeister, R. F., & Leary, M. R. (1995). The need to belong: Desire for interpersonal attachments as a fundamental human motivation. *Psychological Bulletin*, 117(3), 497–529.

Bolier, L., Haverman, M., Westerhof, G. J., Riper, H., Smit, F., & Bohlmeijer, E. (2013). Positive psychology interventions: A meta-analysis of randomized controlled studies. *BMC Public Health*, 13(1). doi:10.1186/1471-2458-13-119

Carl, J. R., Soskin, D. P., Kerns, C., & Barlow, D. H. (2013). Positive emotion regulation in emotional disorders: A theoretical review. *Clinical Psychology Review*, 33(3), 343–360.

Coote, A., Franklin, J., & Simms, A. (2010). *21 Hours: Why working shorter hours can help us all to flourish in the 21st century*. London, UK: New Economics Foundation. Retrieved from https://b.3cdn.net/nefoundation/f49406d81b9cd9c977_p1m6ibgje.pdf

Costa, P. T., & McCrae, R. R. (1992). The five-factor model of personality and its relevance to personality disorders. *Journal of Personality Disorders*, 6(4), 343–359.

Coutts, A. P., Stuckler, D., & Cann, D. J. (2014). The health and well-being effects of active labor market programs. In F. A. Huppert & C. L. Cooper (Eds.), *Wellbeing: Interventions and Policies to Enhance Wellbeing* (Volume 6, Part 2, Chapter 13). Hoboken, NJ: John Wiley.

Cullis, J., Hudson, J., & Jones, P. (2011). A different rationale for redistribution: Pursuit of happiness in the European Union. *Journal of Happiness Studies*, 12(2), 323–341.

Dawood, R. (2014). Positive psychology and child mental health; a premature application in school-based psychological intervention? *Procedia - Social and Behavioral Sciences*, 113, 44–53.

Deci, E. L., & Ryan, R. M. (1985). The general causality orientations scale: Self-determination in personality. *Journal of Research in Personality*, 19(2), 109–134.

Diener, E., Lucas, R., Schimmack, U., & Helliwell, J. (2009). *Well-being for public policy*. New York, NY: Oxford University Press.

Diener, E., Oishi, S., & Lucas, R. E. (2015). National accounts of subjective well-being. *American Psychologist*, 70(3), 234–242.

Diener, E., & Seligman, M. E. P. (2004). Beyond money: Toward an economy of well-being. *Psychological Science in the Public Interest, 5*(1), 1–31.

Diener, E., & Tay, L. (2015). Subjective well-being and human welfare around the world as reflected in the Gallup World Poll. *International Journal of Psychology, 50*(2), 135–149.

DuBois, C. M., Beach, S. R., Kashdan, T. B., Nyer, M. B., Park, E. R., Celano, C. M., & Huffman, J. C. (2012). Positive psychological attributes and cardiac outcomes: Associations, mechanisms, and interventions. *Psychosomatics, 53*(4), 303–318.

Easterlin, R. A. (1974). Does economic growth improve the human lot? Some empirical evidence. In P. A. David & M. W. Reder (Eds.), *Nations and households in economic growth: Essays in honour of Moses Abramovitz* (pp. 89–126). New York, NY: Academic Press.

Easterlin, R. A. (2013). Happiness, growth, and public policy. *Economic Inquiry, 51*, 1–15. doi:10.1111 /j.1465-7295.2012.00505.x

Emmons, R. A., & McCullough, M. E. (2003). Counting blessings versus burdens: An experimental investigation of gratitude and subjective well-being in daily life. *Journal of Personality and Social Psychology, 84*(2), 377–389.

Flavin, P., Pacek, A. C., & Radcliff, B. (2011). State intervention and subjective well-being in advanced industrial democracies. *Politics and Policy, 39*(2), 251–269.

Flavin, P., & Radcliff, B. (2009). Public policies and suicide rates in the American states. *Social Indicators Research, 90*(2), 195–209.

Ford, B. Q., & Mauss, I. B. (2014). The paradoxical effects of pursuing positive emotion: When and why wanting to feel happy backfires. In J. Gruber & J. T. Moskowitz (Eds.), *Positive emotion: Integrating the light sides and dark sides* (pp. 363–381). New York, NY: Oxford University Press.

Gatzia, D., & Woods, E. (2014). Progressive taxation as a means to equality of condition and poverty alleviation (co-authored with Douglas Woods). *Economics, Management, and Financial Markets, 9*(4), 29–43.

Georges, C. M., & Tomlinson-Clarke, S. M. (2015). Integrating positive psychology into counseling psychology doctoral education. *Counseling Psychologist, 43*(5), 752–788.

Gilbert, D. T. (2006). *Stumbling on happiness.* New York, NY: A. A. Knopf.

Hajdu, T., & Hajdu, G. (2014). Reduction of income inequality and subjective well-being in Europe. *Economics, 8.* doi:10.5018/economics-ejournal.ja.2014-35

Hansen, K. B. (2015). Exploring compatibility between "subjective well-being" and "sustainable living" in Scandinavia. *Social Indicators Research, 122*(1), 175–187.

Helliwell, J. F., Layard, R., & Sachs, J. (Eds.). (2015). *World Happiness Report 2015.* New York, NY: Sustainable Development Solutions Network. Retrieved from http://worldhappiness.report/wp-content/ uploads/sites/2/2015/04/WHR15.pdf

Hertwig, R., & Herzog, S. M. (2009). Fast and frugal heuristics: Tools of social rationality. *Social Cognition, 27*, 661–698.

Huffman, J. C., DuBois, C. M., Millstein, R. A., Celano, C. M., & Wexler, D. (2015). Positive psychological interventions for patients with type 2 diabetes: Rationale, theoretical model, and intervention development. *Journal of Diabetes Research, 2015.* doi:10.1155/2015/428349

Jakubow, A. (2014). State intervention and life satisfaction reconsidered: The role of governance quality and resource misallocation. *Politics and Policy, 42*(1), 3–36.

Jeste, D. V., Palmer, B. W., Rettew, D. C., & Boardman, S. (2015). Positive psychiatry: Its time has come. *Journal of Clinical Psychiatry, 76*(6), 675–683.

Kasser, T., & Ryan, R. M. (1993). A dark side of the American dream: Correlates of financial success as a central life aspiration. *Journal of Personality and Social Psychology, 65*(2), 410–422.

Kasser, T., & Sheldon, K. M. (2009). Time affluence as a path toward personal happiness and ethical business practice: Empirical evidence from four studies. *Journal of Business Ethics, 84*, 243–255.

Layard, R. (2003). *Happiness: Has social science a clue? (Lecture Two): The Lionel Robbins Memorial Lecture Series.* London, UK: London School of Economics and Political Science. Retrieved from http://cep.lse.ac.uk/_new/events/robbins.asp

Layard, R. (2005). *Happiness: Lessons from a new science.* London, UK: Allen Lane.

Layard, R. (2006). Happiness and public policy: A challenge to the profession. *Economic Journal, 116*(510), C24–C33.

Layous, K., Chancellor, J., & Lyubomirsky, S. (2014). Positive activities as protective factors against mental health conditions. *Journal of Abnormal Psychology, 123*(1), 3–12.

Lyubomirsky, S. (2008). *The how of happiness: A new approach to getting the life you want.* New York, NY: Penguin Press.

Lyubomirsky, S. (2011). *Hedonic adaptation to positive and negative experiences.* New York, NY: Oxford University Press.

Lyubomirsky, S. (2013). *The myths of happiness: What should make you happy, but doesn't, what shouldn't make you happy, but does.* New York, NY: Penguin Press.

Lyubomirsky, S., & Layous, K. (2013). How do simple positive activities increase well-being? *Current Directions in Psychological Science, 22*(1), 57–62.

Lyubomirsky, S., Sheldon, K. M., & Schkade, D. (2005). Pursuing happiness: The architecture of sustainable change. *Review of General Psychology, 9*(2), 111–131.

Meyers, M. C., van Woerkom, M., & Bakker, A. B. (2013). The added value of the positive: A literature review of positive psychology interventions in organizations. *European Journal of Work and Organizational Psychology, 22*(5), 618–632.

Mills, M. J., Fleck, C. R., & Kozikowski, A. (2013). Positive psychology at work: A conceptual review, state-of-practice assessment, and a look ahead. *Journal of Positive Psychology, 8*(2), 153–164.

O'Boyle, E. (2005). "Homo Socio-Economicus": Foundational to social economics and the social economy. *Review of Social Economy, 63*(3), 483–507.

Oishi, S., Schimmack, U., & Diener, E. (2012). Progressive taxation and the subjective well-being of nations. *Psychological Science, 23*(1), 86–92.

Peterson, C., & Seligman, M. E. P. (2004). Introduction to a "manual of the sanities." In C. Peterson & M. E. P. Seligman (Eds.), *Character strengths and virtues: A handbook and classification* (pp. 3–32). New York, NY: Oxford University Press and Washington, DC: American Psychological Association.

Quinlan, D., Swain, N., & Vella-Brodrick, D. (2012). Character strengths interventions: Building on what we know for improved outcomes. *Journal of Happiness Studies, 13*(6), 1145–1163.

Quoidbach, J., & Dunn, E. W. (2013). Give it up: A strategy for combating hedonic adaptation. *Social Psychological and Personality Science, 4*(5), 563–568.

Reisch, L. A. (2001). Time and wealth: The role of time and temporalities for sustainable patterns of consumption. *Time and Society, 10*(2–3), 367–385.

Santos, V., Paes, F., Pereira, V., Arias-Carrion, O., Silva, A. C., Carta, M. G.,. . . Machado, S. (2013). The role of positive emotion and contributions of positive psychology in depression treatment: Systematic review. *Clinical Practice and Epidemiology in Mental Health*, 9, 221–237.

Schneider, S., Gräf, B., & Peter, M. (2010). Homo economicus—or more like Homer Simpson? *Deutsche Bank Research*. Retrieved from https://www.dbresearch.com/PROD/DBR_INTERNET_EN-PROD/PROD0000000000259291.pdf

Schor, J. (2010). *Plenitude: The new economics of true wealth*. New York, NY: Penguin Press.

Seaford, C. (2013). The multiple uses of subjective well-being indicators. *Social Indicators Research*, *114*(1), 29–43.

Shankland, R., & Rosset, E. (2016). Review of brief school-based positive psychological interventions: A taster for teachers and educators. *Educational Psychology Review*, 2016. doi:10.1007/s10648-016-9357-3

Sheldon, K. M., Boehm, J., & Lyubomirsky, S. (2013). Variety is the spice of happiness: The hedonic adaptation prevention model. In S. A. David, I. Boniwell, & A. Conley Ayers (Eds.), *The Oxford handbook of happiness* (pp. 901–914). New York, NY: Oxford University Press.

Sheldon, K. M., & Lyubomirsky, S. (2012). The challenge of staying happier: Testing the hedonic adaptation prevention model. *Personality and Social Psychology Bulletin*, *38*(5), 670–680.

Shoshani, A., & Steinmetz, S. (2014). Positive psychology at school: A school-based intervention to promote adolescents' mental health and well-being. *Journal of Happiness Studies*, *15*(6), 1289–1311.

Sin, N. L., & Lyubomirsky, S. (2009). Enhancing well-being and alleviating depressive symptoms with positive psychology interventions: A practice-friendly meta-analysis. *Journal of Clinical Psychology*, *65*(5), 467–487.

Stiglitz, J., Sen, A., & Fitoussi, J. P. (2010, August). Report by the Commission on the Measurement of Economic Performance and Social Progress. Retrieved from https://www.insee.fr/fr/publications-et-services/dossiers_web/stiglitz/doc-commission/RAPPORT_anglais.pdf

Tweed, R. G., Bhatt, G., Dooley, S., Spindler, A., Douglas, K. S., & Viljoen, J. L. (2011). Youth violence and positive psychology: Research potential through integration. *Canadian Psychology*, *52*(2), 111–121.

Waters, L. (2011). A review of school-based positive psychology interventions. *Australian Educational and Developmental Psychologist*, *28*(2), 75–90.

Waters, L., Barsky, A., Ridd, A., & Allen, K. (2015). Contemplative education: A systematic, evidence-based review of the effect of meditation interventions in schools. *Educational Psychology Review*, 27, 103–134.

Waugh, C. E., & Koster, E. H. W. (2015). A resilience framework for promoting stable remission from depression. *Clinical Psychology Review*, *41*, 49–60.

Weiss, L. A., Westerhof, G. J., & Bohlmeijer, E. T. (2016). Can we increase psychological well-being? The effects of interventions on psychological well-being: A meta-analysis of randomized controlled trials. *PLOS ONE*, *11*(6). doi:10.1371/journal.pone.0158092

Wood, A. M., Froh, J. J., & Geraghty, A. W. A. (2010). Gratitude and well-being: A review and theoretical integration. *Clinical Psychology Review*, *30*(7), 890–905.

Wood, A. M., & Tarrier, N. (2010). Positive clinical psychology: A new vision and strategy for integrated research and practice. *Clinical Psychology Review*, *30*(7), 819–829.

INDEX